fP

INTERPRETATIONS OF
AMERICAN HISTORY

PATTERNS AND PERSPECTIVES

Seventh Edition

Volume II: From Reconstruction

EDITED BY

FRANCIS G. COUVARES

MARTHA SAXTON

GERALD N. GROB

GEORGE ATHAN BILLIAS

THE FREE PRESS   *New York London Toronto Sydney Singapore* *f*P

THE FREE PRESS
A Division of Simon & Schuster Inc.
1230 Avenue of the Americas
New York, NY 10020

THE FREE PRESS and colophon are trademarks
of Simon & Schuster Inc.

Manufactured in the United States of America

10 9 8 7 6 5 4 3 2 1

Library of Congress Cataloging-in-Publication Data

Interpretations of American history : patterns and perspectives / edited by Francis G.
Couvares . . . [et al.].—7th ed.
p.   cm.
Includes bibliographical references and index.
Contents: v. 1. Through Reconstruction— v. 2. From Reconstruction.
1. United States—History.   2. United States—Historiography.   I. Couvares, Francis G.,
1948–
E178.6.I53   2000
973—dc21   00-024709

ISBN 0-684-87118-1

To Gerald F. Linderman and Alexander Saxton,
teachers and historians

ACKNOWLEDGMENTS

For all their generous help we would like to thank David Blight, Kevin Boyle, Rhea Cabin, Betty Couvares, Enrico Ferorelli, Eric Foner, Dan Freedberg, Naana Frimpong, Hugh Hawkins, Chris Kuipers, Bruce Laurie, Gordie Levin, Douglas Little, Kim Palmer, Lisa Raskin, Mary Renda, Kevin Sweeney, Lauren Winner, and Nancy Woloch.

CONTENTS

INTRODUCTION

These volumes, as their title suggests, reflect our understanding that history is an act of interpretation. They also reflect the dramatic changes in the practice of history over the last thirty years. Thirty years ago the subjects historians most often interpreted were politics, diplomacy, and war. Those privileged to do the interpreting were mostly white and male. Since then, civil rights, antiwar, and women's movements have reshaped dramatically what historians and readers consider suitable topics of study and have brought into the profession women, African Americans, Hispanics, and Native Americans. Contemporary American historians write about nearly everything that has affected nearly everybody—from agriculture to housework, illness to leisure, banking systems to sewer systems. Their expansive new history touches nearly every American and invites each to make a personal interpretation of history.

But the influx of a wide variety of new historians has, in a way, only linked the past more strongly to the present. Over a hundred years ago, the Italian philosopher Benedetto Croce observed that "Every true history is contemporary history."[1] He was trying to cast doubt on arguments of late-nineteenth-century historians (called "historicists" or "positivists") that history was a science and could recover objective truths if properly practiced. Croce insisted that the past "in itself" is unknowable. History rather reflects the need of historians (and readers) to make sense out of their own worlds. Opening up the practice of history to groups previously excluded from the profession has demonstrated the validity of Croce's view in new ways. Views of the past vary not only with generations but also because of divergent experiences stemming from the historian's sex, ethnicity, class, and race. This does not mean that we cannot find out anything solid about

---

[1]Benedetto Croce, in *History: Its Theory and Practice* (New York, 1921), develops ideas he first articulated in 1893. For a sampling of the work of Croce and other philosophers of history in the first half of the twentieth century, see Hans Meyerhoff, ed., *The Philosophy of History in Our Time* (New York, 1959), and Patrick Gardiner, ed., *Theories of History* (Glencoe, Ill., 1959). See also Fritz Stern, ed., *Varieties of History: From Voltaire to the Present* (Cleveland and New York, 1956). An excellent guide through these philosophical thickets, designed especially for students, is Michael Stanford, *A Companion to the Study of History* (Oxford, 1994).

the past. But it does mean that no account of the past is free of the per-spectives, prejudices, and priorities of its author.

When we read history we are reading a particular historian's en-counter with the world. The historian is devoted to the "facts," spends hours, indeed years of his or her life combing through the archives, and believes that the story she or he comes away with represents reality. But in writing, the historian renders this material into a story. The de-signing of this narrative reflects the authors' social circumstances and views of the good, the true, and the beautiful. Thus, historians can be characterized by nationality, or school of thought, or theoretical and methodological preference. One historian is, we say, a Jeffersonian lib-eral, another a nationalist, another a Progressive, still another a femi-nist or postmodernist. Perry Miller's account of the Puritans, for example, seems to reflect his sense of alienation from twentieth-century American liberalism; Kenneth Stampp's account of Recon-struction is shaped by his engagement with the civil rights movement; Oscar Handlin's saga of immigration reflects his own ethnic experi-ence; Kathryn Sklar's ideas about Progressivism are informed by her feminism.

If history is partly craft and partly polemic, however, it is also partly science. An error as common as thinking history is "just the facts" is thinking it is "just your story." Whereas the nineteenth-cen-tury positivists thought that scientific method could guarantee objec-tive truth in history just as in physics, some present-day postmodern literary theorists maintain that history is entirely opinion. Postmodern criticism has encouraged historians to be more attentive to the possible layers of meaning in their documents, and also to their own use of lan-guage in writing history. But those postmodernists who assert that his-torians cannot arrive at truth, or that history is no different from fiction, err as much as the positivists in the opposite direction. How-ever parallel some of the techniques of ideologue, novelist, and histo-rian, the historian is constrained by the record in a way the other two are not. As one literary critic has recently written, the historian's "alle-giance is to fact."[2] Historians willingly acknowledge that no account is absolutely true, and certainly no account is ever final, but they also in-sist that some histories are better than others. Something other than the historian's political, moral, or esthetic preferences comes into play in judging one history better than another, something, for want of a bet-ter term, objective. While committed to a particular interpretation, the historian remains faithful to the evidence and determined to test the accuracy, the reliability, and the adequacy of every historical account.

---

[2]Sue Halpern, "The Awful Truth," *New York Review of Books* (September 25, 1997): 13.

History succeeds when it tells us how things really were, yet at the same time reminds us that the only access we have to that past is through the imagination of a finite and very contemporary human being. History reveals the contours of a landscape from a distinct perspective, but it does not invent the landscape.[3]

One important check on possible imaginative excess is that historians constantly criticize, correct, and supplement each other's views. That is, historians get closer to the truth by arguing with one another. The shape and dimensions of a selected landscape come more clearly into view the more historians bring different perspectives and common skills to the tasks of documentation, description, and narration. So history is historiography, the study of history and its changing interpretations.[4] Every historian begins work by immersing himself or herself in the subject and remains in dialogue with others interested in similar matters. Most books by serious historians include historiographical essays that locate the work within the context of related works.

Historiography reminds us that history is not a closed book, not a collection of inarguable facts or a seamless story. Historiography is a reminder that there is always something to argue about in history, something that makes us think about the conduct of our contemporary lives. Thus, in a world of liberation movements and resurgent nationalism, it matters how we tell the story of the American Revolution or the growth of America's overseas empire. In a society riven by conflicts over racial justice, sexual exploitation, and growing disparities between

---

[3]The most recent denial of history's truth claims is Peter Novick, *That Noble Dream: The "Objectivity Question" and the American Historical Profession* (Cambridge, 1988). Dorothy Ross, "Grand Narrative in American Historical Writing: From Romance to Uncertainty," *American Historical Review* 100 (June 1995): 651–677, offers brilliant critiques of historians' narrative strategies and somewhat elusive postmodernist suggestions about alternatives. Arguments for a middle ground between "objectivism" and Novick's "relativism" can be found in James T. Kloppenberg, "Objectivity and Historicism: A Century of American Historical Writing," *American Historical Review* 94 (October 1989): 1011–1030; Thomas L. Haskell, "Objectivity Is Not Neutrality: Rhetoric vs. Practice in Peter Novick's *That Noble Dream*," *History & Theory* 29 (1990): 129–157; David Hollinger, *In the American Province: Studies in the History and Historiography of Science* (Bloomington, Ind., 1985); and the "*AHR* Forum: Peter Novick's *That Noble Dream:* The Objectivity Question and the Future of the Historical Profession," *American Historical Review* 96 (June 1991): 675–708, with contributions from Hollinger and others, and with a reply from Novick. See also Joyce Appleby, Lynn Hunt, and Margaret Jacoby, *Telling the Truth About History* (New York, 1994); Alan B. Spitzer, *Historical Truth and Lies about the Past: Reflections on Dewey, Dreyfus, de Man, and Reagan* (Chapel Hill, N.C., 1996); and Richard J. Evans, *In Defense of History* (New York, 1999). A more conservative and alarmist defense of objectivity is Keith Windschuttle, *The Killing of History: How Literary Critics and Social Theorists are Murdering Our Past* (New York, 1997).

[4]J. H. Hexter defines it as "the craft of writing history" or the "rhetoric of history," in "The Rhetoric of History," originally published in the *International Encyclopedia of the Social Sciences*, Vol. 6 (New York, 1968), pp. 368–394, and republished in revised form in his *Doing History* (Bloomington, Ind., 1971), pp. 15–76.

rich and poor, it matters how we narrate the history of labor, or the New Deal, or the rights movements of the 1960s and 1970s. Knowing that black state governments in the Reconstruction era were no more or less corrupt than those that preceded or succeeded them makes it impossible to justify the black disfranchisement of the 1880s and 1890s. It may also affect the way we think about the politics of race in our own day. Knowing that great numbers of turn-of-the-century migrants to America returned to their homelands may require us to revise how we explain the motivation of immigrants or the timing and completeness of their assimilation. It may also change the way we think of the dual loyalties of contemporary migrants.

Historical scholarship is thus in continual flux. Even in fields of study where new evidence scarcely ever comes to light, consensus is always elusive. But for careful students of historiography, disagreement is more interesting than agreement could ever be, for the conflict holds the secret to understanding not just the past but, just possibly, the present and future as well.

With these comments in mind, what follows is a sketch of the evolution of American history as a discipline over the course of the last two centuries.[5] As with all attempts to fit diverse strands of thought and experience into a single story, ambiguities haunt this narration or are suppressed in the interest of a continuous story line. As much as possible, the following tries to balance human complexity with narrative simplicity.

Broadly speaking, the writing of American history has passed through four stages: the providential, the rationalist, the nationalist, and the professional. The ministers and magistrates of the seventeenth and eighteenth centuries, and all the women who wrote history through the Civil War, wrote a form of providential history. The Puritan practitioners who originated this form had no doubt about what they were doing and why. They wished to justify the ways of God to man, and vice-versa. Their history was a holy chronicle, revealing His Providence toward His Chosen People and their efforts to build a New Canaan in the wilderness. The preeminent work in this tradition was William Bradford's *Of Plimouth Plantation.* Written over the course of the 1630s and 1640s when Bradford was governor of the colony, the book recounts the fate of a tiny band of Pilgrims who fled England for Holland and then for the New World. They rested in the certainty that God's hand led them forward, that their disasters were His rebukes, their successes His merciful rewards. Governor John Winthrop of Massachusetts wrote such a history, as did Cotton Mather in the next

---

[5]On the development of the historical profession in America, see John Higham, *History: Professional Scholarship in America* (New York, 1973). See also works cited in footnote 3.

century. Mary Rowlandson's eyewitness account of her own captivity employed the same providential themes. Well into the nineteenth century, male and female historians, including Mercy Otis Warren, Elizabeth Peabody, and Hannah Adams, viewed the story of America as an extension of the history of the Protestant Reformation. The Revolution became for them a triumph of reformed Christianity over paganism and Catholicism. And the United States as a whole took the place of New England as the model of Christian virtue for the corrupt Old World to emulate.[6]

In the late eighteenth century, as the European Enlightenment came to America, history took on a secular and naturalistic cast. A new class of intellectuals, profoundly influenced by Newton, Locke, and the French philosophes, had come to see history, like the physical universe, as subject to natural law. These rationalist historians flourished alongside and sometimes superseded the clerics who had once dominated the educated class in the colonies. The new story they told was of progress and reason—and, indeed, "the progress of reason"—in human affairs. Although some Protestant ministers responded vibrantly to the new intellectual currents,[7] most historians in the late eighteenth century were lawyer-politicians, planter-aristocrats, merchants, or professionals—one, Judith Sargent Murray, was the daughter and wife of ministers. Among the most prominent were Thomas Hutchinson, leading merchant and royal governor of Massachusetts; William Smith, physician, landowner, and lieutenant governor of New York; and Robert Beverly and William Byrd of Virginia, both planter-aristocrats and office-holders. These men possessed classical educations, fine private libraries, and the leisure time to use both. Their writing was more refined and allusive than the studiously plain prose of their Puritan predecessors. They wrote history for their own satisfaction, but also to explain to the enlightened world the success of men like themselves: free, bold, intelligent, and ambitious—men who built fortunes and governed provinces that embodied a perfect balance between liberty and order.

Thomas Jefferson's *Notes on the State of Virginia* (written in the midst of revolutionary turmoil and finally published in 1785) is a highly evolved product of this rationalist tradition. America is for Jefferson, as it was for the Puritans, a model for the world, but natural law takes the place of divine providence in directing its affairs. Self-interest, not piety, motivates men; reason, not faith, allows them to discover and pursue their destiny. The fruits of liberty include not only astonishing material prosperity and advances in knowledge but moral

---

[6]Nina Baym, *American Women Writers and the Work of History* (New Brunswick, N.J., 1995), particularly "History from a Divine Point of View," pp. 46–66.

[7]See Edmund S. Morgan, *The Gentle Puritan: A Life of Ezra Stiles, 1727–1795* (New Haven, Conn., 1962).

progress as well. The new nation is destined to open the way toward a new era in human history not only because its natural resources are vast but because free people are virtuous and possessed of the moral energy to change the world. Some evangelical Protestants called Jefferson a "confirmed infidel" and a "howling atheist" for his emphasis on human as opposed to divine agency. But Jefferson's most potent enemies were political: in the 1790s he led the Republican opposition to the Federalist party of Washington and Adams. During the brutal presidential election campaigns of 1800 and 1804, both of which Jefferson won, Federalist writers combed the *Notes* to find ammunition against Jefferson the infidel, the apologist for slavery, the lover of French revolutionary excess. Their charges reveal, among other things, that history had already become politicized. History was a story about how wealth, power, rights, and wrongs came to be in this world—how causes produced effects, and how human actions could change those effects. But the story for the rationalists was no more open-ended than it was for the providentialists: it still pointed upward. Through most of the nineteenth century and into the early twentieth, American history was the story of the progress of the "Empire of Liberty."

As the nineteenth century wore on, historians began to temper their Enlightenment assurance about human beings' capacity for rational improvement. They came increasingly to view races as having different capacities, and to see America as the triumph of Anglo-Saxon people over inferior races. Similar strains of thinking in Europe helped to justify colonization. George Bancroft, the most distinguished American historian of the mid-nineteenth century, organized the history of America around three themes: progress, liberty, and Anglo-Saxon destiny. Bancroft deviated from his own rationalist background after studying in Germany, where he absorbed the romantic emphasis on the inborn virtues of the "folk." The idea that Teutonic peoples (which included Anglo-Saxons) were racially destined to spread freedom across the globe was central to this romantic nationalism. According to Bancroft, the Anglo-Saxons developed the most distinctive tradition of free institutions, and American democracy produced the most advanced forms. In twelve volumes published between 1834 and 1882, Bancroft chronicled the march of history, which corresponded to the spread of American democratic institutions throughout the world and culminated at home in Jacksonian democracy.[8]

Even women historians such as Hannah Adams, Susanna Rowson, Elizabeth Peabody, and Emma Willard, whose evangelical commitments made them political enemies of the Jacksonian Democratic

---

[8]On Bancroft and other romantic historians see David Levin, *History as Romantic Art* (New York, 1963).

party, manifested romantic nationalist thinking not unlike Bancroft's. In her *Pioneer Women of the West* (1852), Elizabeth Ellet focused on conflict between white settlers and indigenous people. As Nina Baym put it in 1995, Ellet "is as close to a genocidal writer as one is likely to find."[9] Some women, however, did break the barriers of gender and nationalist history. Helen Hunt Jackson explored white-Indian relations in both fiction and history. Her *Century of Dishonor* (1881)—which she sent to every member of Congress—documented the American nation's shameful dealings with Indians. Intent on reaching a wider popular audience she then published a novel, *Ramona*, which dramatized white appropriation of Indian lands and other cruelties. At the same time, white and Indian anthropologists began studying native cultures, some because they thought Indians were disappearing, others because they wished to counteract racist myths by displaying the vigor and richness of Indian cultures.[10] Unfortunately, neither criticism nor ethnographic knowledge seriously affected the trajectory of mainstream history. Not until the arrival of the inclusionary politics of the late twentieth century would the work of anthropologists and ethnographers find its way into the pages of mainstream history.

By the 1870s, Bancroft's self-congratulatory epic history had become second nature to most Americans who thought about the past. But changes were afoot in the discipline. The first change was in leadership: amateur writers increasingly gave way to professional historians. As college education became more common among middle-class Americans, and as industrialization reinforced the value of technical and scientific knowledge, historians increasingly concerned themselves with specialized training, research methodology, and educational credentials. History was now a profession like any other—that is, it was practiced by the only sort of people who had access to advanced education: white men. Many of them were trained in Germany, but in 1876 Johns Hopkins University became the first exclusively graduate research institution in the United States. Soon thereafter, graduate study spread to the midwestern land-grant universities and the Ivy League. These newly minted historians usually planned careers in the same university system that had trained them. They prided themselves on rigorous research and a capacity to distinguish scientifically verified truth from romantic notion. Reflecting on these developments in 1894, Henry Adams imagined this new professional historian "dreaming of the immortality that would be achieved

---

[9]Baym, *The Work of History*, pp. 219, 238. Other enemies of Jackson, such as historians Francis Parkman and W. H. Prescott, wrote a similar kind of romantic-racial epic: see Levin, *History as Romantic Art.*

[10]See Robert F. Berkhofer, Jr., *The White Man's Indian: Images of the American Indian from Columbus to the Present* (New York, 1968).

by the man who should successfully apply Darwin's method to the facts of human history."[11]

Along with Frederick Jackson Turner, Adams exemplified the first generation of professional historians, which held sway from about 1870 to 1910. A scion of the great family that had produced presidents and statesmen, Adams might appear at first to be a throwback to the era of patrician amateurs. Politics was the career he had hoped for, while history seemed an avocation. But as his political hopes dimmed, his professional ambitions ignited. In 1870 he was invited to Harvard to teach the first seminar ever devoted to historical research at that institution. Adams taught the meticulous methods of German scholarship and insisted that history's goal was to develop knowledge every bit as sound as that in physics. His exhaustively researched, nine-volume history of the Jefferson and Madison administrations represented the fruit of his own commitment to that scientific method and has remained a classic. Although he left Harvard after a few years, his career symbolized the passing of the guard from patrician amateurs to professionals, which would permanently transform the discipline from his time forward.

If Turner inherited Adams's mantle, he could not have been more different from him in background and personal circumstances. Born of modest means in a rural town in Wisconsin, he attended the University of Wisconsin, received a Ph.D. in history at Johns Hopkins, and went on to teach at Wisconsin and Harvard. Different from Adams in so many ways, Turner shared his belief that history should be a science. He fulfilled Adams's prophecy in using Darwin's evolutionary theory to reveal the contours of American history. Just as one species surpassed another, he argued in his famous "The Significance of the Frontier in American History," so one frontier environment succeeded another in the course of American expansion. As successive frontiers grew more remote from European antecedents, they increasingly nurtured the distinctive American virtues—self-reliance, egalitarianism, tolerance, practicality, realism.[12] Although he embodied the new scientific history, Turner's sweeping generalizations and his assumptions about the "progress of the race" linked him to his nationalist predecessors. Like them he conflated America with capitalism, democracy, and the heroic deeds of the pioneers. Turner's epic was, like that of his predecessors, a hymn to America's glory.

---

[11]Henry Adams, "The Tendency of History," *Annual Report of the American Historical Association for the Year 1894* (Washington, D.C., 1895), p. 19.

[12]Turner's essay, originally delivered as his presidential address to the American Historical Association in 1893, can be found in *The Frontier in American History* (New York, 1920). For more on Turner, see John Higham, *Writing American History: Essays on Modern Scholarship* (Bloomington, Ind., 1970), pp. 118–129; see also the discussion in Volume I, Chapter 7.

Between 1910 and 1945 a second generation of professional scholars—the Progressive historians—rose to prominence. As their name
implies, they were identified with the Progressive movement in politics, which took aim at corporate arrogance and political corruption in
early-twentieth-century America.[13] They observed that modernity—
industrialization, urbanization, and class conflict—had fundamentally
transformed the society. If democracy was to survive, people needed a
history of changing institutions and economic interests, not fables
about liberty and justice. Progressives saw history as politics, not science (or art). To be sure, science was needed to produce usable facts,
and art to persuade people to act on them, but it was political action
that Progressive historians wanted their history to provoke. Neither
genteel amateurs nor morally neutral scientists, Progressives were
muscular intellectuals—or, as they would have gladly called themselves, reformers.

In 1913, the most famous Progressive historian, Charles A. Beard,
published *An Economic Interpretation of the Constitution*, quite possibly the most influential book ever written in American history. It argued that the Constitution was the product not of wise men intent on
balancing liberty and order, but of a clique of wealthy merchants and
landowners who wanted a central government strong enough to defend their privileges against the unruly masses. A series of books culminating in *The Rise of American Civilization* (1927), which Beard
wrote with his wife Mary Ritter Beard, elaborated the thesis that
American history was a succession of conflicts between economic interest groups. Although critics found flaws in his economic determinism and faith in Progressive reform, Beard managed to inspire a
generation to seek in history answers to the questions that pressed
most insistently upon the democratic citizenry.

With a literary flair that exceeded that of either Turner or Beard,
Vernon L. Parrington brought the Progressive interpretation to intellectual history in *Main Currents in American Thought*. His story was
arrestingly simple: all of American history was shaped by the contest
between Jeffersonian and Hamiltonian ways of thinking. Jefferson,
champion of the people, represented decentralized agrarian democracy; Hamilton, tribune of the privileged, stood for centralized commercial aristocracy. From the moment the Revolution ended, these
two ideas fought for control of American minds. In whatever guise—
Federalist versus Republican, Whig versus Jacksonian, Progressive versus Conservative—all these conflicts reflected a continuous economic
dynamic that animated American history. The function of history was
to uncover the economic basis of political ideas and thereby to educate
the citizenry. Like the patricians and the nationalists, Parrington

---

[13]See Volume II, Chapter 6.

wanted his fellow citizens to see that, despite periods of reaction, the direction of their history was upward, but determined in the end by the forces of reform.

Progressive history challenged the profession in another way: it insisted that historical knowledge is relative. In an essay published in 1935 entitled "That Noble Dream," Charles Beard observed that one bar to objectivity is that the historian's documentation is always partial. More important, like Croce he insisted that the historian is never neutral and therefore must write an interpretation, not a scientific re-creation, of the past. The noble but illusory dream of objectivity must be discarded by any serious and honest historian. Acknowledging one's politics and prejudices does not weaken the value of the historian's work, Beard insisted, but rather strengthens it. An interpretation—which he defined as an "overarching hypothesis or conception employed to give coherence and structure to past events"—should be measured not by whether it is correct or incorrect but by whether it is useful to people who are trying to improve their world.[14] Carl L. Becker, a Progressive historian of early America, made the promotion of relativism one of the central purposes of his career. In his famous 1931 presidential address to the American Historical Association, "Everyman His Own Historian," and in other essays, Becker repeated that, however indispensable the scientific pursuit of facts, history meant nothing unless it were yoked to the political necessities of real people. History's obligation is not to the dead but to the living; its account of the past is "perhaps neither true nor false, but only the most convenient form of error."[15]

Female and African American scholars challenged the profession in still other ways, though historians were not yet ready to respond. For example, Mary Ritter Beard, who published many works with her husband and many books about women on her own, culminating in *Woman as a Force in History* in 1946, achieved little or no recognition from the profession. After having a baby, she entered Columbia graduate school with her husband in 1902, but dropped out two years later and subsequently nurtured a hostility for academics and for college education for women. Women with careers, she wrote scornfully, were "capitalist entrepreneurs or retainers of the bourgeoisie." She chose to wear her amateur status like a crown in the face of a profession that re-

---

[14]Charles A. Beard, "That Noble Dream," *American Historical Review* 41 (October 1935): 74–87.

[15]This and related essays may be found in *Everyman His Own Historian* (New York, 1935). See also Phil L. Snyder, ed., *Detachment and the Writing of History: Essays and Letters of Carl L. Becker* (Ithaca, N.Y., 1958). For more on historical relativism, see Higham, *History*. A neorelativist argument can be found in Peter Novick, *That Noble Dream*, and other works cited in note 3, above. Still very useful as a philosophical guide is Jack W. Mieland, *Scepticism and Historical Knowledge* (New York, 1965).

fused to welcome her.[16] Other women in the Progressive era who chose to write women's history similarly saw their work ignored by their male colleagues.[17]

African American historians fared little better. At the American Historical Association meeting in 1909, W.E.B. Du Bois, having earned a Ph.D. from Harvard, offered a startling reinterpretation of Reconstruction that focused on the lives of poor blacks and whites. In the face of a daunting tradition condemning Reconstruction, he argued that it had briefly provided the South with democratic government, public schools, and other needed social legislation. Like other Progressives, Du Bois found economic causes underlying political events; unlike them, however, he included black people as legitimate historical subjects. This simple act of inclusion irrevocably altered his assessment of Reconstruction. Published in 1935, his book attracted many favorable reviews but was ignored by most historians. Du Bois's views did not enter the mainstream of the profession until John Hope Franklin's and Kenneth Stampp's revisionist interpretations appeared in the 1960s.[18]

The Progressives' economic determinism and their relativism both had an enormous impact on the history profession, but neither Beard nor Becker held the center stage exclusively or for long. At the very moment of their triumph—each elevated to the presidency of the American Historical Association, each hailed as a great mind and, more important, a sound political guide amidst the darkness and confusion of the Great Depression years—critics of both Progressive and relativist assertions began to multiply. In part the critics were responding to the rise of totalitarianism, which made faith in progress seem naive and relativism seem cowardly. That Charles Beard quite conspicuously continued to oppose American involvement in the Second World War, at a time when most left-wing intellectuals were rapidly shifting from pacifist to interventionist positions, seemed to many intellectuals to emphasize the narrowmindedness of the Progressive point of view. In the face of Hitler and Stalin, and especially after the horrors of Auschwitz, Dresden, and Hiroshima, American historians asked themselves if Progressive history had ill-prepared them and their fellow citizens for the harrowing obligations of the twentieth century. But it was not just the weight of tragic events that shifted the historiographical terrain.

---

[16]Ann J. Lane, *Mary Ritter Beard, A Sourcebook* (New York, 1977), pp. 33, 53–54.

[17]Helen Sumner's *Women and Industry in the U.S.* and Edith Abbott's *Women in Industry*, both published in 1910, were barely noticed by the male profession.

[18]W.E.B. Du Bois, *Black Reconstruction in America, 1860–1880* (New York, 1992), pp. vii–viii, xvi. For more on the historiography of Reconstruction, see Chapter 2 in this volume.

In the 1930s and 1940s younger historians increasingly found the Progressive historians' psychology shallow, their social analysis predictable, and their moral judgments superficial. Like the philosophers and theologians who were criticizing liberalism for its facile optimism and obtuseness in the face of human tragedy, they criticized Progressive historians for underestimating humankind's propensity for evil, overestimating its capacity for good, and turning history into a simple morality play. More important, they found the Progressive insistence on explaining most events as the product of conflict between rich and poor, East and West, reactionaries and reformers, and so forth to be more hindrance than help in making sense of specific historical problems. More and more historians were insisting that, for better *and* worse, consensus rather than conflict marked American political history; that the absence of European-style class conflict had indelibly shaped American institutions and ideas. In Europe the crises of depression and war led many historians in radical directions; here, under the influence of the Cold War, they led toward what came to be called "consensus history."

The caricature of consensus historians is that they asserted the unity and homogeneity of America's past, the stability of basic institutions, and the existence of a homogeneous national character. When they did acknowledge that conflict occurred between sections, classes, and groups, the consensus historians insisted that such struggles were fought within a common liberal framework and that the protagonists were never really in disagreement over fundamentals. Moreover, this caricature continues, consensus historians doubted the value of social change and, having observed a world brutalized by fascism and communism, feared mass movements of any kind. In this reading, consensus historians were neoconservatives who trimmed the sails of history to the anticommunist winds of the McCarthy era. In fact, so-called consensus historians were remarkably diverse, and many were liberals. Some were, indeed, "Cold War liberals" who believed that a defense of American values and institutions was more important than social criticism at a moment when totalitarianism threatened to take over the world. However, there was no simple correlation between Cold War attitudes and consensus historiography. Arthur M. Schlesinger, Jr., who never departed from the Progressive camp, was the leading "Cold War liberal" in the history profession. On the other hand, the distinguished Columbia University historian Richard Hofstadter, who was called a consensus historian and was definitely a critic of Progressive historiography, was equally if not more critical of the consensus he found in American history.

Some consensus historians did tell a comforting tale for Cold War America. In his influential *The Liberal Tradition in America*, Louis Hartz argued that because America lacked a feudal tradition it escaped the struggles between reactionaries, liberals, and socialists that characterized the history of most European countries. The United States instead had a three-century-long tradition of liberal consensus, wherein all Americans subscribed to the Lockean tenets of individualism, private property, natural rights, and popular sovereignty. The differences among Americans, Hartz maintained, were over means rather than ends. And thus America had very little class conflict and little ground for the breeding of class-based ideologies. Socialism could mean little in America because nearly everyone had access to a middle-class way of life. Conservatism too could mean little because the only thing to conserve—the only continuous tradition—was liberalism.[19]

Another consensus historian whose work was labeled "neoconservative" was Daniel Boorstin. In his three-volume epic story of settlement, westward migration, and community-building, Boorstin echoed the Progressive Turner in many ways. But in contrast to Turner, Boorstin described characters who were largely uninterested in politics and ideology. Most of them were pragmatic, energetic, healthy-minded "Versatiles," ready to conquer a continent, invent the balloon-frame house, experiment with popular democracy, and in the process develop the freest and most prosperous society on earth. Boorstin's approach was social-historical. Like the more radical social historians who would soon transform the discipline, Boorstin insisted that American society and culture were decisively shaped by millions of ordinary folk, not by elites. But for Boorstin, those anonymous masses were middle-class at heart and yearned for nothing so much as a house with a picket fence and a little room to breathe. Distinct from most of the other consensus historians, Boorstin preached a political message that might be called conservative populism.

If Hartz's insistence on ideological homogeneity and Boorstin's populist social history seemed conservative, it was not so easy to gauge the political tonality of Richard Hofstadter's work. Beginning in 1948 with the publication of *The American Political Tradition and the Men Who Made It*, Hofstadter argued that the liberal tradition had failed because it could not escape the acquisitive and individualistic assumptions that had originally shaped it. Supposed reformers such as the Populists and Progressives looked back with nostalgia to an era of self-made men; neither faced up to the fundamental problems of an industrialized and corporate America. Even Franklin Delano Roosevelt, who did not share the nostalgia common to the Progressive tradition, was primarily a pragmatist whose attraction lay in the force of his personality rather than in any consistent ideology or philosophy. In *The Age of Reform: From Bryan to F.D.R.* Hofstadter exposed what he saw as the curious blend of racism, nativism, and provincialism that shaped the Populists and would later manifest itself in national paranoid scares such as McCarthyism in the 1950s. All such movements meant "to restore the

[19]Louis Hartz, *The Liberal Tradition in America: An Interpretation of American Political Thought Since the Revolution* (New York, 1955).

conditions prevailing before the development of industrialism and the commercialization of agriculture."[20] Hofstadter maintained that American political conflicts mostly reflected not the clash of economic interests but the search by different ethnic and religious groups for a secure status in society. By the latter third of the nineteenth century, Hofstadter asserted, professional scions of Anglo-Saxon Protestant families were finding themselves displaced from traditional positions of leadership by a nouveau-riche plutocracy, on the one hand, and urban immigrant political machines, on the other. Responding to this displacement, the elite launched a moral crusade to resuscitate older Protestant and individualistic values—the Progressive movement. In this campaign "to maintain a homogeneous Yankee civilization," Hofstadter wrote, "I have found much that was retrograde and delusive, a little that was vicious, and a good deal that was comic."[21]

Hofstadter emerged from within the Progressive historiographical tradition, briefly flirted with Marxism in the 1930s, and thereafter considered himself a liberal partisan. In a sense, his entire career can be seen as a lover's quarrel with liberalism, in the course of which he relentlessly exposed its inadequacies, delusions, and failures. The implication of Hofstadter's interpretation was indeed striking: the United States had never had a viable or effective progressive tradition. Those who professed liberalism—Populists, Progressives, and even New Dealers—were mostly well-to-do, middle-to-upper-class reformers, alienated from their society by technological and industrial changes and resentful of those who had succeeded in the scramble for money and status. While Hofstadter himself wrote from the left of the political spectrum, he resisted completely the temptation to find heroic victories for the people in what he saw as a depressing chronicle of consensus based on common cupidity. America was more illiberal than either the Progressive historians or he himself would prefer; they wrote history that fostered the illusion of liberal reform, but he would not.

Hofstadter's powerful critique of American liberalism was shaped not only by his evolving political views, but also by his reading of twentieth-century social science research. Based on that reading he began to address in new ways a familiar set of questions about American society. Who were American reformers and what did they want? Hofstadter used the findings of social scientists to explain the significance of status in shaping social behavior. If abolitionists, Populists, and Progressives had not in fact democratized America, just what had they accomplished? Hofstadter looked to the sociology of bureaucracy and complex organizations, as well as research into the modernization of

---

[20]Richard Hofstadter, *The Age of Reform: From Bryan to F.D.R.* (New York, 1955), p. 62.

[21]Ibid., p. 11.

societies in the European and non-European world, to illuminate an era in which Americans were moving from small towns to big cities, from simple and homogeneous to complex and pluralistic social structures. To explain the reformers' passions he employed social-psychological concepts such as projection, displacement, scapegoating, and the authoritarian personality.

If Hofstadter derived critical insights from social science, another consensus historian, Edmund S. Morgan, looked elsewhere. A student of Perry Miller, the distinguished Harvard historian of early American religion and culture, Morgan echoed his mentor's distrust of Progressive history and of liberalism generally. Liberalism, Miller had believed, possessed few intellectual resources with which to criticize the modern pursuit of individualism, self-expression, and material success. In the premodern and therefore preliberal Puritan world, Morgan (like Miller) found depths of wisdom that seemed lacking in the twentieth century. Wary of those who applied present-day assumptions to the task of understanding the past, Morgan refused to see Puritans as cartoon bluenoses, sexually repressed and obsessed with sin. And he refused to see colonial dissidents as anticipators or forerunners of latter-day democratic liberalism. Thus, in his earliest works he portrayed Anne Hutchinson and Roger Williams not as progressive critics of Puritan oligarchy, but as self-righteous zealots, nihilists even. In contrast, Governor John Winthrop was not a repressive Puritan oligarch but a man striving to live responsibly in a deeply imperfect world, a world that required order more than individual freedom for visionaries.[22]

If Progressives and Marxists insisted that economic interests and material forces shaped history, Morgan would follow his mentor Perry Miller in insisting that ideas mattered. Winthrop and his adversaries were obsessed with ideas, led by them, willing to suffer and even die for them. In 1967, in a striking demonstration of this belief, Morgan admitted that he had been wrong about Roger Williams. *Roger Williams: The Church and the State* argued that Williams's ideas were momentous. He had understood that conscience was not a mask for anarchy but a vehicle of reason, that conscientious protest was an act "not so much of defiance as of discovery." What Roger Williams discovered—what John Winthrop could not—was that separation of church and state was absolutely necessary, first and foremost, to preserve religion from being corrupted by the state, and second, to protect the state from becoming the engine of religious intolerance. Thus, the historian who had begun his career by rebuking modern liberals for misrepresenting the strange world of seventeenth-century Puritanism found himself in the 1960s affirming the connection between Puri-

[22]See especially Edmund S. Morgan, *The Puritan Dilemma: The Story of John Winthrop* (Boston, 1958).

tanism and the tradition of civil-libertarian protest that became a hall-mark of the later democratic republic.[23] Perhaps the America he and his students encountered in the 1960s forced this most scrupulous of historians to reflect on what Croce called the contemporaneous character of history.

Morgan's work spanned a great variety of subjects, from Puritan thought, to the Revolution, to slavery. Although he never abandoned his faith in the power of ideas, by the late 1960s his research into the origins of slavery had plunged him deeply into social history, that is, into the realm of group experience and collective fate that seemed very far away from the world of intellectuals and political leaders that had once so occupied him. Executing a dazzling intellectual pirouette, Morgan came to insist that there was nothing incompatible between asserting that consensus dominated mainstream American political and intellectual history and insisting that the most egregious form of oppression—slavery—lay at the heart of the American social experience. Indeed, he claimed, it was precisely because white America relied on slavery to keep the lowest of the low under control, thereby minimizing class conflict among the free, that liberal democracy was able to flower in the late-eighteenth and nineteenth centuries.

Morgan's *American Slavery, American Freedom* is the book named "most admired" more frequently than any other in a recent poll of American historians.[24] Morgan's complex argument cannot be summarized here, but its power can be attributed to its capacity to span the "historiography wars" that marked the history profession in the 1960s and for several decades thereafter. What historian John Higham called the "Cult of American Consensus" had made American history tame and predictable.[25] Within that perspective, eighteenth-century America appeared to be the spawning ground for middle-class democracy; the Revolution was a uniquely intellectual movement; radical abolitionists, Reconstructionists, socialists, and so forth, were maladjusted sufferers from status anxiety; and the Cold War was a noble (if reluctant) effort to save the world from totalitarianism. In the face of this antiseptic treatment of the past, dissenters predictably arose. A new generation of neo-Progressives began to insist that conflict not consensus marked the American past.

The assault on consensus history reflected the erosion of political consensus in 1960s America. Already in the late 1950s, the emergence of the civil rights movement signaled the beginning of a new aware-

---

[23]Edmund S. Morgan, *Roger Williams: The Church and the State* (New York, 1967).

[24]Edmund S. Morgan, *American Slavery, American Freedom: The Ordeal of Colonial Virginia* (New York, 1975). The historians' poll and commentary on it can be found in the *Journal of American History* 81 (December 1994).

[25]John Higham, "The Cult of 'American Consensus': Homogenizing Our History," *Commentary* 27 (February 1959): 93–100.

ness of inequality and division in American society. For a time, the movement could be subsumed under the rubric of liberal reform, welcomed as a perfection of liberal democracy rather than a fundamental challenge to it. But by the mid-1960s, the racial animosity and poverty that had once been invisible, and for a time appeared readily curable, came to seem more endemic and intractable. Radical inequality would require radical measures—at least, some insisted, measures more radical than integration or the war on poverty. When New Left critics of American society looked back for radical antecedents in contemporary historical accounts, they found chronicles of consensus. But not for long. Increasingly, younger historians found in older Progressive historical works and in neo-Marxist scholarship from Europe the inspiration to rewrite American history as a chronicle of struggle—for working-class power, for racial equality, for women's rights, for ethnic identity, and for all forms of social justice. The Vietnam War added immense energy to this endeavor. As college campuses became centers of protest against the war, historians absorbed the growing suspicion that the U.S. foreign policy establishment served interests quite distinct from "the national interest." They focused their scholarly sights on all forms of concentrated power—corporations, political parties, government bureaucracies, professional organizations, and the like—that seemed to profit from inequality and promote injustice not only in America but around the world.

External pressures only reinforced internal tendencies toward radical critique already under way in the history profession. Some of these were methodological, involving the increased interaction of history with social science, the increased interest in comparative history, and the new use of quantitative methods. While some consensus historians, such as Hofstadter and Hartz, had already begun to pay attention to social science research and comparative approaches, the move to quantification was new. With the exception of economic historians, most historians had no acquaintance with the use of scientifically measurable historical data. One of the attractions of quantitative techniques was quite old-fashioned: like the positivists of the late-nineteenth and early-twentieth centuries, modern-day quantifiers sought the authority of science. They also wanted to strengthen their claim to the growing pools of research money available in the postwar United States from both government and private funders of social science research. At the same time, the urge to quantify was related to a democratic urge to capture the reality of ordinary lives through social history. Peasants, workers, slaves, migrants—whole categories of human beings were invisible because they had been "inarticulate," that is, illiterate and ignored by those who left written documents. Quantitative history suggested a way to make them speak: through records that traced collective behavior and from which ideas, values, intentions, and beliefs might be inferred. Thus John Demos could bring surprisingly to view the interior lives of the earliest settlers of Plymouth colony through the analysis of wills, deeds, contracts, and probate records.[26] On a much broader canvas, Paul Kleppner's quantitative analysis of voting records revealed the ethnic motives of voters in the nineteenth-century Midwest, and Stephen Thernstrom discovered as a result of computer analysis of manuscript censuses and other data the astounding geographical (and limited social) mobility of working-class New Englanders in the industrial era.[27]

Quantitative historians drew inspiration not only from the social and behavioral sciences but also from the work of historians associated with the French journal *Annales*. Led by Lucien Febvre and Marc Bloch, who had begun using quantitative techniques in the 1930s and 1940s, these French historians strove for "total history": a history that recorded the myriad experiences of masses of people, not just the dramatic events that featured prominent actors. In the hands of a leading figure in the *Annales* school, Fernand Braudel, history became a slow, majestic procession of material change—change in population, agricultural production, prices, trade, and so forth—that created, unbeknownst to any individual, the true conditions of life in medieval and early modern Europe. This version of social history was "history with the politics left out," indeed, history with all of the usual markers of individual consciousness left out.[28]

Others trying to write a new social history took a very different tack. For them social history meant history from the bottom up. Though sometimes inspired by the quantifiers' capacity to occupy a distant perch and from there comprehend a vast historical terrain, these new social historians were more interested in small-bore institutional change and group action. They refused to believe that the masses were inaccessible to creative historical research. In fact, social historians began to find copious evidence of conscious thought and action among the lower orders. Slave narratives, diaries of farm wives and artisan workers, letters and articles in obscure newspapers, broadsides and pamphlets, court and police records, institutional memoranda and reports—these and many other sources, having been uncovered or used in new ways, began to give up their secrets. Inspired by the civil rights and antiwar movements, new social historians rewrote American history as a history of struggle. Neo-Progressives, in

---

[26]John Demos, *A Little Commonwealth: Family Life in Plymouth Colony* (New York, 1970).

[27]Paul Kleppner, *The Third Electoral System: 1853–1892: Parties, Voters, and Political Cultures* (Chapel Hill, N.C., 1979); Stephen Thernstrom, *Poverty and Progress: Social Mobility in a Nineteenth-Century City* (Cambridge, Mass., 1964) and *The Other Bostonians: Poverty and Progress in an American Metropolis* (Cambridge, Mass., 1973).

[28]Of Braudel's many works, perhaps the most accessible is *Capitalism and Material Life, 1400–1800* (New York, 1967).

a way, they were far more radical than Beard and Becker. Piecemeal political reform would not easily remake a society hideously distorted by
racism and sexism, dominated by immense corporations, regulated by
"therapeutic" bureaucracies, and dedicated to the systematic exploitation of the Third World. Not Progressive reform, but militant, even
revolutionary activism—like that of artisan revolutionaries in the
1770s, the abolitionists and radical Reconstructionists in the nineteenth century, and the most militant unionists in the 1930s—were
the models for latter-day radicals in the 1960s and 1970s.[29]

As Chapter 3 in this volume makes clear, among the first subjects
to respond to this approach was labor history or, as it came increasingly to be called, working-class history. Inspired especially by the
English neo-Marxist E. P. Thompson, new labor historians rewrote the
history of unions and unionization, but more important, of working-
class families and communities, working-class politics and culture.
The people whom they studied, far from seeming to be either aspirants
to middle-class status or alien radicals, came to seem at once both
more militantly class-conscious and more deeply rooted in American
society and culture. Other fields, such as immigration history, African
American history, and women's history, similarly experienced a dramatic renaissance. Both white and black scholars helped to turn the
history of slavery into one of the most exciting and fruitful fields of
history. Recovering the seminal scholarship of African American historians such as W.E.B. Du Bois and Eric Williams,[30] and plunging into
previously ignored archival sources, the historians of the 1960s found
not passivity but agency among slaves, not absorption of their descendants into white culture but cultural resistance and the endurance of
African traditions and practices. They insisted that the Civil War had
been fought to abolish slavery, that African Americans played a crucial
part in its conduct and success, and that only force and betrayal—not
the alleged cultural deprivation or political immaturity of blacks—had
led to the failure of Reconstruction.

Women's historians began to effect a similarly profound change in
the standard narrative of American history. If women had been excluded from electoral politics, diplomacy, corporate management, the
academy, the clergy, and other public and therefore conventionally
male realms of power and respectability, they had no less been excluded from the pages of American history. Inspired by the women's
liberation movement and by the simultaneous and notable arrival of

---

[29]A sweeping narrative (and celebration) of the rise of radical history can be found
in Jonathan M. Wiener, "Radical Historians and the Crisis in American History, 1959–
1980," *Journal of American History* 76 (September 1989): 399–434, part of a "Round
Table" that includes criticism and commentary from a variety of historians and a response from Wiener.

[30]See these and other works cited in Volume I, Chapters 4 and 9.

history from the bottom up in the 1960s and 1970s, male and especially female historians began to hear the voices of women and transfer them to the pages of history.[31] In the suffrage movement and the labor movement; in the records of settlement houses and women's academies and colleges; in the records of births and marriages, of prostitution arrests and temperance campaigns; in the copious records of literary and moral reform publications, in which women argued both for equality and for recognition of their distinctive feminine gifts; and in many other sources, historians of women rewrote the story of America from its very beginnings up to the recent past. They did not merely give women a place in the existing narratives; rather, they reconceived whole fields of history. Thus, for example, the culture of slavery appears to be a realm not simply of *either* accommodation *or* resistance, but—when women are brought centrally into its historical reconstruction—a realm of endurance and cultural creativity.[32] Likewise, the history of Progressive reform becomes the story of women, denied direct access to political office, asserting their right to set the public agenda and to demand maternalist state action in the interest of reforming the social household.[33]

In these and many other ways, historians of women and of African Americans joined a broader wave of socially critical scholarship that had moved very far away from even the history of the most progressive men of earlier generations. The findings of these scholars were so diverse that by the 1980s interpretive coherence vanished from the profession. Many historians feared that fragmentation threatened to consign scholars to increasingly microscopic and specialized enclaves, making it impossible to communicate with one another, let alone a broader public. To others this lack of coherence seemed a healthy state of ferment and pluralistic openness: "Maybe drift and uncertainty," one such historian remarked, ". . . are preconditions for creativity."[34] It is probably true that coherence and fragmentation, harmony and polytonality, the pursuit of the microscopic and the synthetic, are parallel rather than alternative practices within the history profession.

Today it seems that every man and woman has become his or her own historian in a way even Carl Becker would have found surprising

---

[31]See Volume II, Chapter 10.

[32]See Volume I, Chapter 9.

[33]See Volume II, Chapter 6, and also Volume I, Chapter 8.

[34]On the perils of fragmentation, see Thomas Bender, "Wholes and Parts: The Need for Synthesis in American History," *Journal of American History* 73 (June 1986): 120–136. See the ensuing debate on Bender's essay in "A Round Table: Synthesis in American History," *Journal of American History* 74 (June 1987): 107–130. See also John Higham, "The Future of American History," *Journal of American History* 80 (March 1994): 1289–1309. The quotation is from Jackson Lears, "Mastery and Drift," *Journal of American History* 84 (December 1997): 979–988.

(and cheering). A real measure of success in democratizing the academy in the wake of civil rights and women's rights movements has unseated dominant perspectives and opened the way for diverse schools of interpretation in history and other disciplines. But a diversity of perspectives does not rule out a broadly synthetic multicultural history. The ambition to make sense of a complex past—to narrate a big story—should not be conflated with an urge to drown difference in a wave of false or oppressive homogeneity. To the contrary, if men and women desire "to chart their lives by what they believe to be true," then in that task history "offers a variety of tools for effecting liberation from intrusive authority, outworn creeds, and counsels of despair."[35]

A final note about the way in which each chapter in this collection presents competing interpretations of a common historical phenomenon: while it is certainly true that interpretive argument is among the most common and necessary of practices in the discipline, it is equally true that the "either-or" format can distort the true nature of historians' arguments. Indeed, burlesquing this format is a happy pastime common in graduate student lounges all over the country ("Fat-Free Mozzarella: Noble Experiment or Tragic Error?"). We have, in fact, tried wherever possible in this edition to offer differences in interpretation that are not polar or mutually exclusive, but rather partially overlapping and complementary. Sharp differences there are, and sometimes hot debate produces light. But historians usually do not differ by excluding each other's evidence or utterly demolishing each other's arguments. More often they try to incorporate as much of the former and recast as much of the latter as possible in their efforts to better explain a historical phenomenon. Thus, for example, whereas once Progressive historians might have portrayed the New Deal as a radical advance in liberal reform, and New Left historians as a triumph of corporate hegemony, both William Leuchtenberg and Alan Dawley in their essays in Volume II acknowledge a good deal of common ground, even while clearly disagreeing over important points. Whether the New Deal was "radical within limits" or "conservative with radical implications" remains truly a matter of opinion, but the common ground shared by these two historians makes clear the cumulative and "objective" quality of scholarship on the subject. In coming to a judgment on this and other questions posed in the chapters below, we hope that students will find in the debates, and the historiographical essays that precede them, a pathway to understanding the world they live in and an encouragement to change that world for the better.

---

[35]Appleby et al., *Telling the Truth About History*, pp. 301, 308.

2

RECONSTRUCTION

Change or Stasis?

To students of American history the Civil War years stand in sharp contrast to those of the Reconstruction era. The war years represented a period of heroism and idealism; out of the travail of conflict there emerged a new American nationality that replaced the older sectional and state loyalties. Although the cost in lives and money was frightful, the divisions that had plagued Americans for over half a century were eliminated in the ordeal of fire. Henceforth America would stand as a united country, destined to take its rightful place as one of the leading nations in the world.

Reconstruction, on the other hand, had to address the problems of putting the nation back together again. The federal government had to bring the South back into the union on terms that permitted reconciliation, protect newly freed slaves from the wrath of angry whites, and construct a biracial society of free people. The era was marked by conflict, brutality, and corruption, and historians still do not agree on evaluating the results. To date there have been three schools of thought about Reconstruction: the Dunning school, the revisionists, and the neorevisionists.

The first dominant view of Reconstruction, called the Dunning school, after its founder, was forged in the widespread racism of both North and South in the years after the Civil War. It was reinforced by the worldwide European imperialism of the late nineteenth century and the racist ideology that intensified to justify it. Social Darwinism bolstered notions of white supremacy.

By the 1920s American historiography had come under the influence of the Progressive, or new history, school. Growing out of the dissatisfaction with the older scientific school of historians that emphasized the collection of impartial empirical data and eschewed "subjective" interpretations, this school borrowed heavily from the new social sciences. The new history sought to explain historical change by isolating underlying economic and social forces that transformed institutions and structures. In place of tradition and stability it emphasized change and conflict. Liberal and democratic in their orientation, Progressive historians attempted to explain the present in terms of the dynamic and impersonal forces that had transformed American society.

Economic issues, they maintained, were basic in shaping this era. The real conflict was not between North and South, white and black; it was between industrial capitalism and agrarianism, with the former ultimately emerging victorious. The question of the status of black people in American society was simply a facade for the more basic conflicts that lay hidden beneath the surface. Reconstruction, they concluded, was the first phase in the emergence of the United States as a leading industrial and capitalist nation.

The neorevisionist school, although owing much to the revisionists, was influenced by the egalitarianism of the period following World War II and the idealism and optimism of the civil rights movement. Equal rights for blacks, neorevisionists maintained, was complicated by economic and other factors but was, nevertheless, a potent issue in its own right. In a real sense the fundamental problem of Reconstruction was whether white Americans were prepared to accept the freedmen as equal partners. Even though the Radicals ultimately failed in achieving the egalitarian goals, they left an enduring legacy in the forms of the Fourteenth and Fifteenth amendments. That America did not honor these promises to political participation and equal protection under the law in the decades after Reconstruction in no way detracted from the idealism of those responsible for these amendments. Indeed, these amendments took on a new meaning as they gave legal sanction to civil rights after 1945. This is a broad school and today includes social historians whose work has been to broaden history to include the poor, blacks, other minorities, and women.

Led in the 1890s by Professor William A. Dunning of Columbia University—who literally founded the school of Reconstruction historiography that still bears his name—the historical profession set out to prove that the years following the Civil War were marked by tragedy and pathos because men of good will were momentarily thrust out of power by the forces of evil. This period, in the words of one historian, "were years of revolutionary turmoil. . . . The prevailing note was one of tragedy. . . . Never have American public men in responsible positions, directing the destiny of the Nation, been so brutal, hypocritical, and corrupt. . . . The Southern people literally were put to the torture."[1]

Underlying the interpretation of the Dunning school were two important assumptions. The first was that the South should have been restored to the Union quickly and without being exposed to Northern vengeance. Most Southerners, it was argued, had accepted their military defeat gracefully and were prepared to pledge their good faith and loyalty

---

[1]Claude G. Bowers, *The Tragic Era: The Revolution After Lincoln* (Cambridge, Mass., 1929), pp. v–vi.

to the Union. Second, responsibility for the freedmen should have been entrusted to white Southerners. Blacks, these historians believed, could never be integrated into American society on an equal plane with whites because of their former slave status and inferior racial characteristics.

Historians in the Dunning school tradition studied Reconstruction as a struggle between elements of good and evil. The forces of good—Northern and Southern Democrats and Republicans like Andrew Johnson—recognizing the necessity for compassion and leniency, were willing to forget the agonies of war and to forgive the South. Scalawags, carpetbaggers, and, above all, a group of radical and vindictive Republicans intent upon punishing the South by depriving the native aristocracy of their power and status constituted the forces of evil whose aim was to insure the dominance of the Republican party. The Radical Republicans, who had little or no real concern for the welfare of the freedman once he had left the ballot box, manipulated the helpless and ignorant blacks. According to the Dunning school, the Radical carpetbag state governments that came into power were totally incompetent—in part because they included illiterate blacks who were unprepared for the responsibilities of self-government. Still worse, these governments were extraordinarily expensive because they were corrupt. Most of them, indeed, left nothing but a legacy of huge debts.[2]

The decent whites in the South, the Dunning argument continued, united out of sheer desperation to force the carpetbaggers, scalawags, and blacks from power. In one state after another, Radical rule was eventually overthrown and good government restored. By the time of the presidential campaign of 1876 only three states remained under Radical control. When the dispute over the contested election was resolved, Hayes withdrew the remaining federal troops from the South, and the three last Radical regimes fell from power. Thus the tragic era of Reconstruction came to an end.

For nearly three decades after the turn of the century the Dunning point of view was dominant among most American historians. As late as 1942 Albert B. Moore, in his presidential address at the Southern Historical Association, argued that Reconstruction had the effect of converting the South into a colonial appendage of the North. The political enfranchisement of blacks, which laid the basis for carpetbag government, was to Moore perhaps the most incredible event of an incredible era. The South, he concluded, was still paying for the dark legacy of Reconstruction in the twentieth century.[3]

---

[2]E. Merton Coulter, *The South During Reconstruction 1865–1877* (Baton Rouge, La., 1947), p. 148.

[3]Albert B. Moore, "One Hundred Years of Reconstruction in the South," *Journal of Southern History* 9 (May 1943): 153–165.

In the late 1920s, however, historians began to look at the events between 1865 and 1877 from a new and different perspective. These revisionists, influenced by Progressive thinking, particularly its emphasis on the importance of economic considerations, changed the interpretive framework of the Reconstruction era.

Generally speaking, the revisionists accepted most, if not all, of the findings of the Dunning school. The disagreement between the two groups arose because the revisionists did not view events between 1865 and 1877 in terms of a morality play that depicted Reconstruction as a struggle between good Democrats and evil Radical Republicans. Nor were the revisionists willing to accept the view that responsibility for the freedmen should have been entrusted to native white Southerners.

In 1939 Francis B. Simkins, a distinguished Southern historian who published with Robert Woody in 1932 one of the first revisionist studies, summed up some of the findings of the revisionist school. He emphasized many of the constructive achievements of this era. Simkins denied that the Radical program was radical; indeed, the Radicals failed because they did not provide freedmen with a secure economic base. Past historians, he concluded, had given a distorted picture of Reconstruction because they had assumed that blacks were racially inferior. The result was an approach to Reconstruction that was based on ignorance and prejudice. Only by abandoning their biases could historians contribute to a more accurate understanding of the past.[4]

While the revisionists often disagreed among themselves, there were common areas of agreement. For example, most viewed the problem of corruption in American society during these years as national rather than sectional in scope. To single out the South in this regard was patently unfair and ahistorical.[5] Revisionists also denied that the Radical governments in the South were always dishonest, incompetent, and inefficient. On the contrary, they claimed, such governments accomplished much of enduring value. The new constitutions written during Reconstruction represented a vast improvement over the older ones and often survived the overthrow of the men who had written them. Radical governments brought about many long-needed social reforms, including state-supported school systems for both blacks and whites, a revision of the judicial system, and improvements in local administration. Above all, these governments operated—at least in

---

[4]Francis B. Simkins, "New Viewpoints of Southern Reconstruction," *Journal of Southern History* 5 (February 1939): 49–61.

[5]For a revisionist synthesis see J. G. Randall and David Donald, *The Civil War and Reconstruction*, 2d ed. (Boston, 1961). The first edition, written by Randall in 1937, was in the Dunning school tradition.

theory—on the premise that all men, white and black alike, were entitled to equal political and civil liberties.

Second, the revisionists drew a sharply different portrait of blacks during Reconstruction. They denied that developments in the postwar South resulted from black participation in government or that the freedmen were illiterate, naive, and inexperienced. In no Southern state, they pointed out, did blacks control both houses of the legislature. Moreover, there were no black governors and only one black state supreme court justice. Only two blacks were elected to the United States Senate and fifteen to the House of Representatives. Such statistics hardly supported the charge that the supposed excesses of Reconstruction were due to political activities of black Americans.

Indeed, the revisionists maintained that blacks, as a group, were quite capable of understanding where their own interests lay without disregarding the legitimate interests of others. The freedmen were able to participate at least as intelligently as other groups in the American political process. As Vernon L. Wharton concluded in his pioneering revisionist study of the Negro in Mississippi after the Civil War, there was "little difference . . . in the administration of . . . counties [having blacks on boards of supervisors] and that of counties under Democratic control. . . . Altogether, as governments go, that supplied by the Negro and white Republicans in Mississippi between 1870 and 1876 was not a bad government. . . . With their white Republican colleagues, they gave to the state a government of greatly expanded functions at a cost that was low in comparison with that of almost any other state."[6]

Revisionists refuted the Dunning school contention that state governments were controlled by evil, power-hungry, profit-seeking carpetbaggers and renegade scalawags who used black votes to maintain themselves in power. The stereotype of the carpetbagger and scalawag, according to revisionists, was highly inaccurate. Carpetbaggers, for example, migrated to the South for a variety of reasons—including the lure of economic opportunities as well as a desire to serve the former slaves in some humanitarian capacity. Among them were former Southern unionists and Whigs, lower-class whites who sought to use the Republican party as the vehicle for confiscating the property of the planter aristocrats, and businessmen attracted by the promise of industrialization. The Radical governments, then, had a wide base of indigenous support in most Southern states.[7]

---

    [6]Vernon L. Wharton, *The Negro in Mississippi 1865–1890* (Chapel Hill, N.C., 1947), pp. 172, 179–180. See also Willie Lee Rose, *Rehearsal for Reconstruction: The Port Royal Experiment* (New York, 1964), and Joel Williamson, *After Slavery: The Negro in South Carolina During Reconstruction 1861–1877* (Chapel Hill, N.C., 1965).

    [7]See Otto H. Olsen, "Reconsidering the Scalawags," *Civil War History* 12 (December 1966): 304–320, and Allen W. Trelease, "Who Were the Scalawags?," *Journal of Southern History* 29 (November 1963): 445–468.

Finally, the revisionists rejected the charge that the Radical governments were extraordinarily expensive and corrupt, or that they had saddled the South with a large public debt. State expenditures did rise sharply after the war, but for good reasons. The war's destruction required an infusion of public funds. Deferring regular appropriations during the war years also meant that a backlog of legitimate projects had accumulated. Most important of all, the South for the first time had to build schools and provide other facilities and services for blacks, which did not exist before the 1860s and for which public funds had never been expended.

The revisionists also found that the rise in state debts, in some instances, was more apparent than real. Grants to railroad promoters, which in certain states accounted for a large proportion of the increase in the debt, were secured by a mortgage on the railroad property. Thus the rise in the debt was backed by sound collateral. The amount of the debt chargeable to theft, the revisionists maintained, was negligible. Indeed, the restoration governments, which were dominated by supposedly honest Southerners, proved to be far more corrupt than those governments controlled by the Radicals.

One idea on which the revisionists were united was their conviction that economic forces, which were related to the growth of an urban and industrialized nation, somehow played a major role during this period. Beneath the political and racial antagonisms of this era, some revisionists argued, lay opposing economic rivalries. Anxious to gain an advantage over their competitors, many business interests used politics as the vehicle to further their economic ambitions—especially since the South, like the North and West, was ardently courting businessmen. The result was that economic rivalries were translated into political struggles.[8]

Revisionists also emphasized the crucial issue of race. During Reconstruction many former Whigs joined the Republican party because of its probusiness economic policies. These well-to-do conservatives, at first, were willing to promise blacks civil and political rights in return for their support at the polls. Within the Democratic party, however, revisionists argued that lower-class whites, fearful of possible encroachments by blacks upon their social status and economic position, raised the banner of race. Conservatives found their affiliation with the Republican party increasingly uncomfortable, and they slowly began to drift back into the Democratic party. The fact that

---

[8]Recent historians have once again begun to study the importance of economic factors and rivalries in Reconstruction. See Mark W. Summers, *Railroads, Reconstruction, and the Gospel of Prosperity: Aid Under the Radical Republicans, 1867–77* (Princeton, N.J., 1984), and Terry L. Seip, *The South Returns to Congress: Men, Economic Measures, and International Relationships* (Baton Rouge, La., 1983).

both parties were under the control of conservatives made it easier for former Republicans to shift their political allegiance. This changed alignment left Southern blacks politically without white allies, which later made it easy to eliminate them from political life. This move came at a time when Northerners, tired of conflict and turmoil, became reconciled to the idea of letting the South work out its own destiny—even if it meant sacrificing black people. Northern businessmen likewise became convinced that only Southern conservatives could restore order and stability and thus create a favorable environment for investment.

The result polarized Southern politics along racial rather than economic lines and defined the Democratic party as the white man's party. Lower-class whites' primary goal was to maintain the South as a white man's country. And upper-class whites acquired the uncontested power to determine the future economic development of their section.

The end of Reconstruction, according to the revisionists, accompanied the triumph of business values and industrial capitalism. When the contested presidential election of 1876 resulted in an apparent deadlock between Rutherford B. Hayes, the Republican candidate, and Samuel J. Tilden, his Democratic opponent, some prominent Republicans saw an opportunity to rebuild their party in the South upon a new basis. Instead of basing their party upon propertyless former slaves, they hoped to attract well-to-do former Whigs who had been forced into the Democratic party to fight against Reconstruction governments. To accomplish this goal a group of powerful Republican leaders began to work secretly to bring about a political realignment. If Southern Democratic congressmen would not stand in the way of Hayes's election and would also provide enough votes to permit the Republicans to organize the House of Representatives, these leaders were willing to promise the South federal subsidies—primarily for railroads—and also to name a Southerner as postmaster general. The Compromise of 1877, as this political deal was called, was not fully carried out, but its larger implications survived unscathed.

Perhaps the most important, and certainly the most overlooked revisionist was W.E.B. Du Bois, who published *Black Reconstruction, 1860–1880,* in 1935. Du Bois, like the other revisionists, claimed that economics, not race, shaped Reconstruction and black-white relations. In his passionately argued volume he insisted that Reconstruction involved an effort to unite Northern workers with Southern blacks. The attempt failed because Southern conservatives employed racial animosity to fragment working-class unity and thus maintain their own class hegemony. Racism, in this view, was a tool that upper-class whites used to their advantage, not an inherent, unchanging characteristic of poor whites, as most historians portrayed it. For Du Bois, Reconstruction was a valiant but shortlived attempt to establish true democracy in the South, an opportunity quickly foreclosed. But, at least in public education, black voters made a powerful contribution to the region.

The *Journal of American History* ignored the book and most professional historians disparaged it. One complaint was that W.E.B. Du Bois had based his work on secondary sources, not archival materials. This was true, but it was also true that during Du Bois's research most Southern archives were closed to blacks. Or, if they were allowed in, they would have to hide themselves from view of the white scholars. C. Vann Woodward was one of the few professional historians who recognized the value of Du Bois's work at the time. He wrote Du Bois in 1938 of his "indebtedness for the insight which your admirable book, *Black Reconstruction,* has provided me."[9]

Woodward, the historian who propounded the thesis of the Compromise of 1877, concluded, the bargain "did not restore the old order in the South, nor did it restore the South to parity with other sections. It did assure the dominant whites political autonomy and nonintervention in matters of race policy and promised them a share in the blessings of the new economic order. In return the South became, in effect, a satellite of the dominant region. So long as the Conservative Redeemers held control they scotched any tendency of the South to combine forces with the internal enemies of the new economy—laborites, Western agrarians, reformers. Under the regime of the Redeemers the South became a bulwark instead of a menace to the new order."[10]

After the early 1950s a new school of Reconstruction historiography called "the neorevisionists" emerged. Many of these historians had been affected by the racial injustice that the civil rights movement demonstrated. They emphasized the moral rather than the economic basis of Reconstruction. Generally speaking, while the neorevisionists accepted many findings of the revisionists, they rejected the idea of interpreting Reconstruction in strictly economic terms. The Republican party, the neorevisionists maintained, was not united on a probusiness economic program; it included individuals and groups holding quite different social and economic views.[11]

The neorevisionists stressed the critical factor of race as a moral is-

---

[9]W.E.B. Du Bois, *Black Reconstruction, 1860–1880* (New York, 1992), pp. x, xvi.

[10]C. Vann Woodward, *Reunion and Reaction: The Compromise of 1877 and the End of Reconstruction* (Boston, 1951), p. 246.

[11]Robert Sharkey, *Money, Class, and Party: An Economic Study of the Civil War and Reconstruction* (Baltimore, 1959), and Irwin Ungar, *The Greenback Era: A Social and Political History of American Finance, 1865–1879* (Princeton, N.J., 1964).

sue. One of the unresolved dilemmas after the Civil War, they claimed, was the exact role that blacks were to play in American society. Within the Republican party a number of factions each offered their own solution to this question. Andrew Johnson, who had been nominated as Lincoln's running mate in 1864 on a Union party ticket despite his Democratic party affiliations, spoke for one segment of the party. To Johnson blacks were incapable of self-government. Consequently he favored the state governments in the South that came back into the Union shortly after the end of the war under his own plan of reconstruction and went along with the Black Codes that denied black Americans many of their civil rights.

Although Johnson was president as well as titular head of Lincoln's party, Radical Republicans fiercely opposed him. The Dunning school painted the Radicals as vindictive, power-hungry politicians; they were merely interested in blacks for their votes. To revisionists the Radicals represented, at least in part, the interests of the industrial Northeast—men who wanted to use black votes to prevent the formation of a strong, oppositional coalition of western and Southern agrarian interests.[12]

To the neorevisionists, on the other hand, the Radicals were a much more complex group. Many of the Radicals, they claimed, joined the Republican party in the 1850s for antislavery rather than economic motives. These men, before and after the war, demanded that blacks be given the same rights as white Americans. Their beliefs brought them to a confrontation with President Johnson in the postwar period. In the ensuing struggle the inept president soon found himself isolated. Taking advantage of the situation, the Radicals set out to remake Southern society by transferring political power from the planter class to the freedmen. The program of the Radicals was motivated in large measure by idealism and a sincere humanitarian concern.[13]

In 1965 Kenneth M. Stampp published an important synthesis that emphasized the moral dimension of the Reconstruction years. Stampp argued that the central question of the postwar period was the place of the freedmen in American society. President Johnson and his followers believed in the innate inferiority of blacks, rejecting any program based upon egalitarian assumptions. The Radicals, many of whom had been abolitionists, on the other hand, took seriously the ideals of equality, natural rights, and democracy. Stampp did not deny that the

---

[12]This point of view was best expressed by Howard K. Beale, one of the fathers of the revisionist school, in *The Critical Year: A Study of Andrew Johnson and Reconstruction* (New York, 1930).

[13]See James H. McPherson, *The Struggle for Equality: Abolitionists and the Negro in the Civil War and Reconstruction* (Princeton, N.J., 1964), and Hans L. Trefousse, *The Radical Republicans: Lincoln's Vanguard for Social Justice* (New York, 1969).

Radicals saw black Americans as valuable additions to the Republican party. But most politicians, he insisted, identify the welfare of the nation with the welfare of their party. To argue that the Radicals had invidious and selfish motives, Stampp concluded, does them a severe injustice and results in a distorted picture of the Reconstruction era.

The Radicals, according to the neorevisionists, ultimately failed in their objectives. Most Americans, harboring conscious and unconscious racial antipathies, were not willing to accept blacks as equals. By the 1870s the North was prepared to abandon blacks to the white South for three reasons: a wish to return to the amicable prewar relations between the sections; a desire to promote industrial investment in the South; and a growing conviction that the cause of black Americans was not worth further strife. The tragedy of Reconstruction, the neorevisionists maintained, was not that it occurred, but that it had ended short of achieving the major goal sought by the Radicals.

The struggle over Reconstruction, nevertheless, had not been in vain. In addition to the many achievements of the Radical governments, the Radicals had succeeded in securing the adoption of the Fourteenth and Fifteenth amendments. These amendments, in Stampp's words, "which could have been adopted only under the conditions of radical reconstruction, make the blunders of that era, tragic though they were, dwindle into insignificance. For if it was worth four years of civil war to save the Union, it was worth a few years of radical reconstruction to give the American Negro the ultimate promise of equal civil and political rights."[14]

During and after the 1970s neorevisionist scholarship began to take a more pessimistic turn even while interest in Reconstruction remained strong. The pervasiveness of inequality and racial friction after the civil rights movement seemed to highlight the failure of post–Civil War Americans to insure that blacks would be integrated into the social and political framework of the Union. Neorevisionist scholars continued to debate the same issues and problems as their predecessors. To what degree were Americans committed to an equal-rights ideology? Why were black Americans left in such a vulnerable position? What was the nature of such political events as the impeachment of Andrew Johnson? Why did Reconstruction come to an end far short of achieving its goals?[15]

To these and other questions neorevisionist historians gave varied answers that demonstrated that few differences had been conclusively resolved. In his study of the Ku Klux Klan, Allen W. Trelease argued

[14]Kenneth M. Stampp, *The Era of Reconstruction* (New York, 1965), p. 215.

[15]For a descriptive analysis of black Americans after slavery that does not deal with Reconstruction as a political event, see Leon F. Litwack's important *Been in the Storm So Long: The Aftermath of Slavery* (New York, 1979).

that Radical Reconstruction failed because the seeds of biracial democracy fell on barren soil in the South, and the federal government's
artificial nurture was ephemeral and quickly discontinued. George C.
Rable emphasized the counterrevolutionary guerilla warfare employed
by white Southerners concerned with the destruction of the Republican party in the South. Michael Perman insisted that in the context of
the political tensions that prevailed in the immediate postwar era, the
very moderation that marked presidential and congressional Reconstruction was doomed to fail; only a coercive policy could have succeeded. In a subsequent work Perman emphasized the ways in which
the center in both Republican and Democratic parties proved unable
to hold together, thus permitting color to become the political line.
And in a broad study of national politics, William Gillette observed
that Reconstruction was so easily reversed because it had always been
"fragmentary and fragile."[16]

Nor has interest in the role of Andrew Johnson flagged. Michael
Les Benedict, for example, insisted that Johnson was impeached because he seemed to be violating the principle of the separation of powers and because he failed to carry out some key provisions in
legislation pertaining to Reconstruction. Hans Trefousse emphasized
the degree to which Johnson thwarted Radical policies and strengthened conservative forces, thereby facilitating the latter's eventual triumph in the 1870s. Of three other studies of Johnson, two (by Patrick
W. Riddleberger and James E. Sefton) emphasized his commitment to
sometimes incompatible principles, which rendered him impotent,
and one (by Albert Castel) accentuated the degree to which his inordinate ambition and desire for power helped to destroy him.[17]

Robert J. Kaczorowski synthesized many themes that have res-

[16]Allen W. Trelease, *White Terror: The Ku Klux Klan Conspiracy and Southern Reconstruction* (New York, 1971); George C. Rable, *But There Was No Peace: The Role of
Violence in the Politics of Reconstruction* (Athens, Ga., 1984); Michael Perman, *Reunion Without Compromise: The South and Reconstruction, 1865–1868* (Cambridge,
1973), and *The Road to Redemption: Southern Politics, 1869–1879* (Chapel Hill, N.C.,
1984); William Gillette, *Retreat from Reconstruction 1869–1879* (Baton Rouge, La.,
1979), p. 380.

[17]Michael Les Benedict, *The Impeachment and Trial of Andrew Johnson* (New York,
1973); Hans L. Trefousse, *Impeachment of a President: Andrew Johnson, the Blacks, and
Reconstruction* (Knoxville, Tenn., 1975); Patrick W. Riddleberger, *1866: The Critical Year
Revisited* (Carbondale, Ill., 1979); James E. Sefton, *Andrew Johnson and the Uses of Con-
stitutional Power* (Boston, 1980); Albert Castel, *The Presidency of Andrew Johnson*
(Lawrence, Kans., 1979). See also the following works: Michael Les Benedict's *A Compro-
mise of Principle: Congressional Republicans and Reconstruction, 1863–1869* (New
York, 1974) and *The Fruits of Victory: Alternatives in Restoring the Union, 1865–1877*
(Philadelphia, 1975); Dan T. Carter, *When the War Was Over: The Failure of Self-Recon-
struction in the South, 1865–1867* (Baton Rouge, La., 1985); and Richard N. Current,
Those Terrible Carpetbaggers: A Reinterpretation (New York, 1988).

onated throughout Reconstruction historiography through the 1980s. The Thirteenth and Fourteenth amendments represented a revolutionary change in American federalism, for citizenship was no longer within state jurisdiction. Consequently, Congress had authority to protect all citizens in their enjoyment of rights. This radical congressional Republican theory of constitutionalism, however, Kaczorowski argued, was altered during the 1870s by a Supreme Court bent on permitting partisans of states' rights in the South to reestablish their domination over former slaves.[18]

Using comparative history better to evaluate the American experience, George M. Fredrickson compared Reconstruction with the experiences of Jamaica and South Africa. He concluded that white Southerners—for a number of reasons—were less able than Jamaicans or South Africans to make even a limited adjustment to the concept of equality. The result was the development of a racist order in the United States that was not exceeded until the formal adoption of apartheid in South Africa after 1948. Although comparative history has yet to find a broad following, it clearly has the ability to transform in fundamental ways the manner in which Americans perceive themselves and their past.[19]

At the same time that interest in national politics remained high, monographs dealing with individual states continued to appear. Here too the traditional dichotomy was evident; some emphasized the degree to which Reconstruction succeeded while others pointed to its failures. Jon Wiener's study of postwar Alabama, excerpted below, argued that Reconstruction might never have happened for all the difference it made in the lives of black people. White elites retained control of the land and forced blacks into a form of tenant serfdom in which they were little better off than in slavery. In a novel study of black political leadership in South Carolina that used quantitative techniques, Thomas Holt argued that black leaders were divided among themselves by education and prewar status; their divisions contributed to the fall of the Republican party in the state. Holt's profile of black leadership demonstrated that most owned property and were literate, and 10 percent were professionally or college trained. And Barbara Fields, focusing on the changing economy in her study of Maryland, argued for eventual changes as the market slowly transformed the border

---

[18]Robert J. Kaczorowski, "To Begin the Nation Anew: Congress, Citizenship, and Civil Rights after the Civil War," *American Historical Review* 92 (February 1987): 45–68.

[19]George M. Frederickson, "After Emancipation: A Comparative Study of White Responses to the New Order of Race Relations in the American South, Jamaica & the Cape Colony of South Africa," in *What Was Freedom's Price?* David G. Sansing., ed. (Jackson, Miss., 1978).

state. But the racist fallout from slavery persisted with such intensity that change came painfully slowly when it came.[20]

The 1988 publication of Eric Foner's massive *Reconstruction: America's Unfinished Revolution, 1863–1877*, excerpted below, was a milestone. The work represented an effort to restore cohesion to a field long fragmented by disputation. Foner's work in many ways hearkened back to W.E.B. Du Bois's *Black Reconstruction*. Like him, Foner centered his analysis on class and the political initiatives of newly freed black people. Unlike Du Bois and other earlier black scholars, Foner could and did make use of enormous archival material providing his political and economic history a deep base in vivid social history. Initially, he argued, Reconstruction was a radical attempt to destroy the South's antebellum social structure. But by the 1870s fear of class conflict in the North led that section's industrial leaders to evince greater sympathy for the South. The result was a resurgence of white domination below the Mason-Dixon line. Looking at the political and economic experience of blacks, Foner charted the demise by the 1870s of the free labor ideology that had brought the Republican party into existence. White fear of social conflict and concern to restrict the conditions of work for blacks led to a virtual abandonment of the equal rights and free labor ideology. Foner saw Reconstruction as a failure, but an immensely important one, and while it left much unfinished, it had made a beginning that would remain in such institutions as schools and in the memories of freed people.

After the publication of Foner's epic, the historian Michael Perman asked, "What is left to be done?,"[21] a question that women historians, at least, had no problem answering. Nina Silber published *The Romance of Reunion* in 1992, a study of sex and the way the South, while losing the war itself, managed to win the interpretation of it. In her analysis, in the face of rapid postwar industrialization and immigration, Northerners and Southerners looked to antebellum Southern myths of manliness and femininity to give order to a fragmenting society. Romantic myths of prewar chivalry, delicate femininity, and interracial harmony blossomed in the stress of labor agitation, the violent retaliation of industrialists, the arrivals of millions of foreign poor and militant suffragists.[22] In 1995, LeeAnn Whites interpreted the Civil War and Reconstruction eras as a sexual crisis. In her study of Au-

---

[20]Thomas Holt, *Black over White: Negro Political Leadership in South Carolina during Reconstruction* (Urbana, Ill., 1977); Barbara Fields, *Slavery and Freedom on the Middle Ground, Maryland, 1860–?* (New Haven, Conn., 1985): See also Jerrell H. Shofner, *Nor Is It Over Yet: Florida in the Era of Reconstruction, 1863–1877* (Gainesville, Fla., 1974); Joe Gray Taylor, *Louisiana Reconstructed, 1863–1877* (Baton Rouge, La., 1974); William C. Harris, *The Day of the Carpetbagger: Republican Reconstruction in Mississippi* (Baton Rouge, La., 1979); Ted Tunnell, *Crucible of Reconstruction: War, Radicalism and Race in Louisiana, 1862–1877* (Baton Rouge, La., 1984).

[21]Brooks D. Simpson, *The Reconstruction Presidents* (Lawrence, Kans., 1998).

gusta, Georgia, Whites studied the conflicts for Confederate women as the war took their men away and called upon them to increase their domestic activities to help supply the troops. Moving women's traditional activities into the public sphere empowered them in a way that created tension when their defeated men came home. Emancipation exacerbated this because in its aftermath, white males could now legitimately dominate only their wives. Women's associational life after the war to memorialize it continued to give them public clout, but, with Reconstruction and redemption, men assumed these tasks and forced women back into the private sphere.[23]

Tera Hunter's *To 'Joy My Freedom* in 1997 was a rich and fascinating study of black women's lives in the South after the war, particularly in Atlanta. Combining social, urban, political, economic, and sexual history, Hunter portrayed labor conditions for freed women in postwar Atlanta, discovering widespread postwar labor agitation, particularly among militant African American laundresses. She also showed how real estate developers and city officials planned the city's neighborhoods and amenities to be sure blacks in Atlanta would get as few benefits, such as running water, as possible. In the same year Laura Edwards published *Gendered Strife and Confusion*, a subtle study of sex in Granville County in North Carolina. She argued that domestic institutions, particularly marriage, and social ideas of masculinity and femininity served new political and social functions in Reconstruction because of the demise of slavery as a method of control. Arguing that appealing to constructions of maleness, femaleness, and family sanctity provided freed people and poor whites with some new options for themselves, Edwards also describes how conservative Democrats could and did use the tool of sexual construction to bring about the expulsion of blacks from political life.[24]

Foner's inquiries into the ideology of free labor and ideas of contract prompted various studies of those topics. Foner himself addressed the issue in "The Meaning of Freedom in the Age of Emancipation" as well as in the book that grew out of that article.[25] He wrote: "Reconstruction emerges as a decisive moment in fixing the dominant understanding of freedom as self-ownership and the right to compete in the

---

[22]Nina Silber, *The Romance of Reunion, Northerners and the South, 1865–1900* (Chapel Hill, N.C., 1993).

[23]LeeAnn Whites, *The Civil War as a Crisis in Gender, 1860–1890* (Athens, Ga., 1995).

[24]Tera Hunter, *To 'Joy My Freedom, Southern Black Women's Lives and Labors after the Civil War* (Cambridge, Mass., 1997); Laura Edwards, *Gendered Strife and Confusion, The Political Culture of Reconstruction* (Urbana, Ill., 1997). See also Elsa Barkley Brown's "Negotiating and Transforming the Public Sphere: African American Political Life in the Transition from Slavery to Freedom," *Public Culture*, Vol. 7 (1994): 107–146.

[25]Eric Foner, "The Meaning of Freedom in the Age of Emancipation," *Journal of American History* 81, no. 2: 435–460. See also Eric Foner, *The Story of American Freedom* (New York, 1998).

labor market, rather than propertied independence." Subsequently, Foner expanded on the transformation during Reconstruction of the meaning of the Fourteenth Amendment. In his view, it came to mean the freedom to contract, not equality before the law.

Legal scholar Peggy Cooper Davis came at the disappointment blacks experienced with postwar interpretations of the Fourteenth Amendment from a different tack. In *Neglected Stories, The Constitution and Family Values*, she recreated through stories from slavery and Reconstruction the problems the Fourteenth Amendment was attempting to address, particularly the complete absence of white respect for the rights of blacks to make and protect their families. The failure of the Supreme Court to interpret the Fourteenth Amendment in light of its framers' intent has had the effect of protecting industrialists' right to make and enforce unjust contracts with poor laborers, while not protecting the rights of black men and women to a secure family life.[26]

Pursuing the sometimes paradoxical links between contract and freedom, Amy Dru Stanley's 1998 study, *From Bondage to Contract*, explored the tension implicit in the understanding that the Civil War and Reconstruction emancipated slaves to participate in freedom defined by the buying and selling of everything but people. In Stanley's view, prostitution remained the most flagrant violation of the postwar notion of freedom as self-possession.[27]

Julia Saville contributed another study of these themes. In her monograph on South Carolina from 1860 to 1870, she interpreted the activism of free people as rejecting the domination of their fomer owners, while at the same time contesting the notion of freedom as subjection to landowners in particular and to market values in general.[28]

While there have been a few hardy souls publishing traditional political studies in the wake of Foner's volume, perhaps the most original exploration of a Reconstruction theme is Mark Summers's *The Era of Good Stealing*.[29] The Dunning school claimed that Reconstruction governments cried out to be overthrown because of their massive corruption. Revisionists and the neorevisionists claimed there was corruption in both the North and South, so the issue was a red herring. Summers, instead, argued that while there was serious but not para-

---

[26]Peggy Cooper Davis, *Neglected Stories, The Constitution and Family Values* (New York, 1997).

[27]Amy Dru Stanley, *From Bondage to Contract, Wage Labor, Marriage and the Market in the Age of Slave Emancipation* (New York, 1998).

[28]Julia Saville, *The Work of Reconstruction, from Slave to Wage Laborer in South Carolina, 1860–1870* (New York, 1994).

[29]Recent political studies include William C. Harris, *With Charity for All, Lincoln and the Restoration of the Union* (Lexington, Ky., 1997); Brooks D. Simpson, *The Reconstruction Presidents* (Lawrence, Kans., 1998); Mark Wahlgren Summers, *The Era of Good Stealing* (New York, 1993).

lyzing corruption nationwide, the question was not the amount but its significance in the minds of Americans. And there, he argued, it was sufficient to undermine the faith citizens had in government. Hence, the issue was not a red herring because citizen cynicism about government needs remedy even if the level of corruption is not crippling government's ability to function.

Although it is possible to demonstrate that particular interpretations grew out of and reflected their own milieu, historians must still face the larger and more important problem of evaluating interpretations.[30] Were the revisionists correct in emphasizing the fundamental economic factors? Were the neorevisionists justified in insisting that the major issue during Reconstruction was indeed moral in nature? Or were the two intertwined? Did the particular structural form of state and national politics preclude effective governmental action in dealing with the problems growing out of emancipation? What should have been the proper policy for both the federal and state governments to follow with regard to black Americans, and how were the voices of blacks to be heard during policy formation and implementation?

Was the American experience dissimilar from or similar to that of other nations that also experienced the transition from a slave to a free society? Was Reconstruction a meaningless experiment after which the Southern elite resumed business as usual complete with white supremacy? Or was Reconstruction a brave but shortlived attempt to fashion real democracy in the South—one that would lay the groundwork for the civil rights movement one hundred years later? How did the juggernaut of postwar capitalism affect the terrain on which Reconstruction was being attempted?

Although that period is more than a century from our own, many of the basic conflicts common to both remain unresolved and are as pressing as ever. Perhaps most fundamental of all is the question Reconstruction raised and did not answer. How can Americans give meaning to freedom in a market-driven society when those in power keep the market's rewards from blacks and other poor people?

---

[30]For a discussion of schools of Reconstruction historiography see Gerald N. Grob, "Reconstruction: An American Morality Play," in *American History: Retrospect and Prospect*, George A. Billias and Gerald N. Grob, eds. (New York, 1971), pp. 191–231; Richard O. Curry, "The Civil War and Reconstruction, 1861–1877: A Critical Overview of Recent Trends and Interpretations," *Civil War History* 20 (September 1974): 215–238; Michael Les Benedict, "Equality and Expediency in the Reconstruction Era: A Review Essay," ibid., 23 (December 1977): 322–335.

JONATHAN M. WIENER

JONATHAN M. WIENER (1944–   ) is professor of history at the University of California, Irvine. He is the author of Social Origins of the New South *(1978),* Come Together: John Lennon and His Time *(1984), and* Professors, Politics and Pop *(1994).*

The postwar planters were a new class because they were in new social relations of production. But they were a new class made up of families which to a significant extent had been part of the antebellum elite. The old families persisted in a quantitative sense; in a qualitative sense, their relationship to production had been transformed. Yet they were not a fully modern bourgeoisie.

The development of the postwar southern economy can be understood first of all in terms of the relations between this planter class and the freedmen. After the war, the planters sought to preserve the plantation as a centralized productive unit, worked by laborers in gangs. The freedmen, however, wanted to own their own farms. These differences were resolved, not by the workings of the invisible hand of the free market, but rather by a process that can only be called class conflict. The planters used three tactics in particular: they sought informally to enlist the Freedmen's Bureau in preserving the gang labor plantation; they developed formal legal institutions to limit the free market in labor; and some turned from legalistic to illegal methods, from repressive law to terror, from the Black Codes to the Ku Klux Klan. The freedmen fought back in the only ways they could: they withdrew their labor, and they organized politically to demand the confiscation and distribution of plantations owned by rebels.

The outcome of this conflict gave the South its distinctive character, and indicates that the economic and political development of the South differed from that of the North not just in degree, but in kind. Postwar southern development was not following the same path as the North, in an evolutionary manner, because the landlord-tenant relation was of a different type than the capitalist-proletarian relation prevailing in the North. The key difference was the coercive mode of labor control the planters developed in their conflict with the freedmen. . . .

The Gang Labor Plantation

At the direction of the occupying Union army, slave labor was re-placed by the "contract system"; the freedmen were to sign contracts with planters specifying their duties and their pay. The contracts with planters for 1865 and 1866 provided for gang labor for wages rather than family tenancy. Because of the shortage of currency, wage laborers were usually paid with a share of the crop rather than in cash; this has led some to confuse the gang system of the immediate postwar period with its successor, sharecropping. But it is the organi-zation of production, rather than the form of payment, that is crucial: wage laborers worked in a gang under an overseer, as they had under slavery; their hours and tasks were clearly specified in their contract, and carefully supervised; infractions, such as not showing up on time or taking extra days off, were punished. . . . It must be clearly distin-guished from the system of family tenancy where the rent was paid with a share of the crop—"sharecropping." . . . The crucial difference was the greater power of the planters over the daily lives of gang la-borers, and the sharecroppers' greater independence from supervision and control.

The Freedmen's Bureau reports on the reorganization of agricul-ture and labor in 1865 and 1866 described a system based on gang la-borers receiving wages. . . .

While wage labor was ostensibly the basis of plantation agriculture in 1865 and 1866, many planters avoided paying any wages at all to their former slaves. One Alabama Freedmen's Bureau agent reported incidents in which "the negro promises to work for an indefinite time for nothing but his board and clothes," and Peter Kolchin has con-cluded that, in numerous places in Alabama, blacks were "working without pay." The contracts were supposed to specify the tasks for which the freedmen were to be paid, but many planters apparently avoided this provision. . . . Indeed there is evidence that some planters went so far as to try to sell their laborers as if they were still slaves. . . .

The planters not only tried to maintain many of the repressive as-pects of slavery in the postwar wage system; they also tried to keep their own former slaves as laborers. Colonel George H. Hanks, super-intendent of Negro labor in the army's Department of the Gulf, told the War Department's Freedmen's Inquiry Commission early in 1864 that the planters "make great endeavors to recover what they call their own negroes." An extreme case was that of one of the "richest and most extensive" planters, who refused to work his own plantation at all "unless he could have his own negroes returned to him." . . .

The assumption behind this view could only have been that planters would have more control over wage laborers who had been their own slaves and then "stayed on." And the evidence is overwhelming that the freedmen were determined to avoid staying on for precisely this reason. Carl Schurz was one of the first to argue that leaving the old slave plantation was the most fundamental definition of "freedom" among the former slaves; "that they could so leave their former masters was for them the first test of the reality of their freedom," he told a Senate committee. . . .

The planters in these immediate postwar years formed organizations to protect their interests, class conscious efforts to place plantation agriculture on a firmly repressive basis. . . .

In Sumter County . . . a "meeting of citizens" discussing the "labor system" unanimously resolved that "concert of action is indispensable among those hiring laborers." They agreed that all planters should offer the same terms: one-fourth of the crop for the laborer when the planter supplied the provisions, or one-half the crop when the tenants paid half the expenses as well as their own provisions. "Tenants who don't comply with terms will be discharged," the meeting declared, and concluded "we pledge ourselves not to employ any laborer discharged for violation of contracts." . . .

A statewide "Planters Convention" met in the Alabama House of Representatives in February, 1871. Those who called for the convention announced that their purpose was for planters to "put their heads, and if need be, their means, together for mutual benefit and protection." . . . The convention, widely reported in the planter press, seemed to echo the sentiments of an Alabama planter who summed up his view of the labor situation for John Trowbridge in 1866: "The nigger is going to be made a serf, sure as you live. It won't need any law for that. Planters will have an understanding among themselves: 'You won't hire my niggers, and I won't hire yours;' then what's left for them? They're attached to the soil, and we're as much their masters as ever."

The planters' attempt to preserve the plantation as a centralized labor unit, using supervised gang labor, was a logical effort to preserve a mode of production that had evolved and developed over sixty years. The planters' desire to incorporate wage labor into the organizational structure of the antebellum plantation was not only an effort to preserve planter domination of the freedmen, but also to continue production along the lines of established agricultural methods and procedures. This effort, comprehensible as it was in economic terms, confronted an insurmountable obstacle: the freedmen's refusal to agree to it. Their widespread resistance to working in gangs for wages appears in the historical record as a "shortage of labor," and it played a crucial role in the reorganization of plantation agriculture after the war.

The Labor Shortage

... The most important cause of the labor shortage in 1865 and 1866 seems to have been the freedmen's refusal to work for wages, which was in turn based on their hope of becoming landowners. The Joint Congressional Committee on Reconstruction reported the freedmen had a "strong desire, amounting almost to a passion . . . to obtain land." In the words of the Montgomery *Advertiser*, "the negro is ravenous for land." . . . A Union officer wrote that "all concurred in the opposition to the contract system."

A convention of black leaders met in Montgomery in May, 1867, and issued an "address . . . to the People of Alabama," which expressed the blacks' desire to own land. They explained that blacks supported the Republican party, among other reasons, because "it passed new homestead laws, enabling the poor to obtain land." The convention said of their planter-antagonists that "the property which they hold was nearly all earned by the sweat of our brows—not theirs. It has been forfeited to the government by the treason of its owners, and is liable to be confiscated whenever the Republican Party demands it."

This expectation of land distribution was no idle fantasy in the black community, but one firmly based on political facts. General Nathaniel P. Banks, head of the military occupation of Louisiana, had provided small plots for freedmen in 1863 and 1864. John Eaton, who had jurisdiction over freedmen flocking to Grant's army, had 2,000 blacks on government-financed farms, and in January, 1865, Sherman provided for the establishment of homesteads for freedmen in the Sea Islands of South Carolina; this he did in direct response to requests from black leaders. The Freedmen's Bureau Bill, passed in March, 1865, provided that forty acres of abandoned and confiscated lands should be assigned to "every male citizen, whether refugee or freedman," to be rented for three years, and then purchased from the United States. Commissioner Howard of the Freedmen's Bureau had originally intended to turn over abandoned and confiscated land to freedmen, and it was only President Johnson's veto of this policy in the fall of 1865 that forced the bureau to begin returning confiscated land to its original owners. The following year, Congress passed the Southern Homestead Act, allowing blacks to file applications for homesteads in 1866, while most whites had to wait until 1867. . . .

Freedmen hesitated to work for wages in the immediate postwar period for additional reasons. The increasing refusal to work for wages corresponded to a decrease in the wages planters offered. According to Department of Agriculture statistics, the annual wages offered black men in Alabama fell from $117 in 1867 to $87 in 1868, a decline of 26 percent in one year.

The chief complaint of the freedmen working for wages, according to the Freedmen's Bureau, was "fraudulent division of the crops." Apparently planters were not only reducing wages, but also cheating on the shares paid to laborers—or at least the freedmen accused them of doing so. One authority reports that the number of such complaints rose "steadily.". . . .

A final cause of the labor shortage was the withdrawal of women and children from the labor force. As slaveowners, the planters had commanded the labor of black women and children; as employers of free labor, they found black women and children unwilling to work as they had under slavery. *DeBow's Review* reported in 1866 that, in contrast to slave times, "most of the field labor is now performed by men, the women regarding it as the duty of their husbands to support them in idleness," and that "there is a settled opposition on the part of the women to go into the fields again."

The Planters and the Freedmen's Bureau

The planters' bitter opposition to the presence first of the Union army and later of the Freedmen's Bureau in their own counties did not stop them from seeking to enlist the bureau in keeping the black labor force on the plantation. Their efforts tended to be successful; while the bureau opposed some of the more extreme proposals made on behalf of the planters, many bureau officials worked to perpetuate the planters' domination, and the bureau in some crucial respects became part of the repressive apparatus of the new agricultural system. . . .

Brigadier General C. C. Andrews, commander of Union forces in Selma, observed that the freedmen were filled with "restlessness and disquiet" over the persistence of the plantation system; this led him to issue a proclamation to the freedmen of the west Alabama black belt in May, 1865, in which he supported the planters' claims. "Quite a number of freedmen have complained to me," he told the blacks, but "planters have represented to me that the loss they have suffered . . . and the depreciation of their currency . . . have cramped their means . . . so that they cannot promise you much compensation." Andrews found that what the planters said was "true to a considerable extent," and told the dissatisfied freedmen, "you . . . appear misinformed of your real interests. [Therefore] I now offer you my advice: I do not believe you hazard your liberty by remaining where you are and working for such compensation as your employers are able to give." This was not a confidential memo to a superior; it was a public proclamation by the commander of U.S. forces in the area. . . .

Military authority over the freedmen gave way to the Freedmen's Bureau in Alabama officially in July, 1865. The assistant commissioner in charge of Alabama was Brigadier General Wager Swayne. Swayne's view of the labor situation in Alabama was classically laissez-faire capitalist: "The system of annual contracts was regarded as a make-shift," he wrote in his 1866 report, "which it was hoped would disappear as confidence should grow out of experience on both sides, and leave to each the benefit of an appeal at any time to competition. The demand for labor promised a comfortable future for the freedmen on this basis." Swayne thought that legal regulation of labor was undesirable, that the free market in labor should be established, and that the high demand for black labor would assure the prosperity of the freedmen. In spite of these declarations of a laissez-faire policy, Swayne in practice intervened repeatedly on the side of the planters and against the freedmen. . . .

Upon his arrival in Alabama, Swayne took on the task of "removing" from the freedmen the "belief . . . that they could live without labor." He candidly identified his task as "compelling the able-bodied to labor." And he commented that he was pleased by the "reasonable temper of the planters," a temper which was not surprising, given the bureau's declared purpose of compelling the freedmen to labor for wages on the plantations. . . .

Of course not all bureau agents worked closely with local planters. One Alabama agent, shocked at the bureau's pro-planter policy, wrote that his predecessor "worked with a view to please the white citizens, at the expense of, and injustice to, the Freedmen." The previous officials "have invariably given permission to inflict punishment for insolence or idleness, and have detailed soldiers to tie up and otherwise punish the laborers who have, in the opinion of the employers, been 'refractory.'". . .

Why were the planters so successful in influencing the bureau? First of all, it was Swayne's policy to appoint "native whites" as bureau agents whenever possible, and to ignore the "tales of outrage" reported by agents who were northerners. Fleming suggests that the appointment of agents from the locality contributed to the closeness of the bureau to the local planter elite. . . .

Those bureau agents in Alabama who were neither local whites nor army officers met intense and calculated social pressure from the planter-dominated communities to which they were assigned. . . . The Montgomery *Weekly Mail* explained in 1866, "Union officers . . . who are gentlemen, are received into the best families in our city. It is true that they are taken in on probation. . . . Some [who] keep company with Negroes . . . could not get into society. . . . But all who are kind and considered gentlemen . . . will always be met by kind and considerate southern people." . . .

The bureau's free labor ideology made it thoroughly antagonistic to slavery. Nevertheless it supported planter interests in some crucial respects. The profoundly bourgeois conception on which bureau policy was based regarded the lash of slavery to be both inhumane and inefficient as a form of labor discipline. The discipline of the market economy itself, however, was not only necessary, but a desirable way of shaping a free laboring class. Freedom the bureau understood to be in large part freedom to enter into a wage contract with a planter; and the free man has an obligation to fulfill his terms of the contract. As for the planters, the bureau insisted that they too needed to fulfill their contracts, and to learn to use the market rather than the lash to discipline labor. The bureau and the planters, whatever their other differences, agreed that free labor was still labor, on the plantations and under the planter class.

Legal Repression: The Black Codes

The passage of the Black Codes was the planters' attempt to end the "labor shortage" by legal means—parallel to their informal effort to enlist the aid of the Freedmen's Bureau in achieving the same goal. The Black Code of Alabama included two key laws intended to assure the planters a reliable supply of labor—a vagrancy law, and a law against the "enticement" of laborers. The "Vagrant Law" defined vagrants to include "stubborn servants . . . a laborer or servant who loiters away his time, or refuses to comply with any contract . . . without just cause." It provided as punishment for such hideous crimes a fine of $50 plus court costs, and allowed judges to "hire out" vagrants until their fines were paid, with a six-month limit. . . .

The second law, passed explicitly "for the purpose of regulating labor," made it a crime to "hire, entice away, or induce to leave the service of another" any laborer who had already contracted to work for another. The penalty for those who "induce laborers . . . to abandon their contracts, or employ such without the consent of their original employer," was a fine of $50 to $500. If a laborer was found working for "another," "that fact shall be *prima facie* evidence that such person is guilty of violating this act," unless the new employer "shall upon being notified of such antecedent contract, forthwith discharge said laborer." . . .

The law prohibiting enticement of labor was aimed not at the blacks, but at the planters; it was intended to reduce conflict within the planter class. It was also intended to stop agents from Mississippi seeking to recruit Alabama blacks. Mississippi planters during the late sixties were opening up new plantation areas in the western delta regions of the state, and had a severe shortage of black laborers there. They needed blacks not only to raise cotton, but also to drain swamps, build levees, clear cropland, and construct roads. Not only did private agents of Mississippi planters recruit in Alabama, but Mississippi established an official state bureau of immigration which sent agents into Alabama. . . .

The planters' attempt to control black labor by legal means seems to have backfired. Even Fleming found the Black Code provisions for the regulation of labor to have been "carelessly drawn" and "technically unconstitutional." . . . The planters had proposed labor regulations whose repressive character was undeniable; the freedmen, however, refused to end the "labor shortage," and some planters, increasingly desperate to preserve the large-scale plantation organization based on wage labor, turned to terror, to the Ku Klux Klan.

The Social Base of the Klan

The extent to which the black belt Klan was an instrument of the planter class, rather than of poor whites, is often overlooked. The two white groups had conflicting interests, and the Klan in the black belt worked in pursuit of the goals of the planters. The congressional investigation of the Klan focused on its political use of terror against Republicans; subsequent interpretations have tended to emphasize this evidence. In so doing, they have underemphasized the role Klan terror played in creating and perpetuating the South's repressive plantation labor system.

The Ku Klux Klan was "more widespread and virulent" in the black belt of western Alabama in 1869 and 1870 than in any other part of the South, except perhaps for northern Alabama. . . .

The hill country whites used Klan terror to drive blacks off the land, opening it to white small farmers. But the social base and strategy of the Klan in the black belt was "exactly the opposite," Fleming wrote; there, "the planters preferred Negro labor, and never drove out the blacks."

Planters used Klan terror to keep blacks from leaving the plantation regions, to get them to work, and keep them at work, in the cotton fields. Other sources support Fleming's interpretation that "the best men" were members of the black belt Klan. John L. Hunnicutt claims to have organized the Klan in the black belt of western Alabama; he wrote in his memoirs that he did so at the request of "some of the best citizens." Richard Busteed, a U.S. district judge for Alabama, told the congressional investigating committee that "gentlemen of education and intelligence . . . compose the class called Ku-Klux." . . .

Fleming, with typical directness, listed among the "causes of the ku klux movement" the fact that "people in the Black Belt felt that labor must be regulated in some way." The Klan was necessary, Marengo planter F. S. Lyon told the congressional committee, to counter the fact that blacks "are told by some . . . that planters do not pay sufficient wages for their labor." . . . As early as 1866, masked bands in the black belt "punished Negroes whose landlords had complained of them." . . .

The ever-respectable Montgomery *Advertiser* often printed articles like the one which argued that "the negro's inherent sloth seems to communicate itself to domestic animals that live with him. His pigs are too lazy to root, his sneaking dogs won't bark, . . . his cabin looks more like a deserted dog kennel than a human dwelling." The Eutaw *Whig*, noting that northern white women were coming south to teach, wrote, "When they come the buck niggers will welcome them with ebony arms, to African couches, and then the next generation of Radicals in the South . . . will smell only half as bad as the present generation." It was cultured discourse of this kind, appearing in the most respected journals of the planter class, that was intended to justify Klan terror.

From Gang Labor to Sharecropping

In spite of the momentous political events taking place in 1867 and 1868—the attempted impeachment of the president and the beginning of Radical Reconstruction—Alabama planters were preoccupied first of all with their attempts to revive the plantation system. . . . The discussions increasingly came to one conclusion: the attempt had failed to preserve the plantation as a single, large-scale unit, cultivated by labor gangs paid in wages. The planters in increasing numbers were dividing their plantations into small plots, and assigning each to a single family, which was paid with a share of the crop; the old slave quarters were broken up and replaced with cabins scattered across the plantation. . . .

The "labor shortage" was a leading cause of this momentous decision by the planters, but it was not the only one. A series of bad cotton crops in 1865, 1866, and 1867 contributed to the planters' doubts that the plantations could be reorganized profitably on the basis of gang labor. The Radical constitutional convention met in December, 1867, and the Radical state constitution was ratified in February, 1868. The first Radical legislature gave agricultural laborers a lien on the crop in 1868. This could only have discouraged the planters further; giving the laborer the first lien meant that, in case of a dispute over wages, the laborer's claim had precedence over that of the planter. And the freedmen's most common complaint, it should be recalled, was fraudulent division of the crop.

Once the planters accepted the breakup of the antebellum plantation into small units, why did they not simply rent them? The key issue was the planter's control over his tenants. . . . The Selma *Southern*

Argus agreed, observing that if the black was permitted to rent, "the power to control him is gone." The wage system gave the planters a maximum of control over the daily activities of the freedmen, and it was precisely to this extensive control that the freedmen objected. . . .

The planters' argument was that black laborers required supervision because they were lazy and incompetent workers. Sharecropping contracts gave the planter specified rights to supervise the labor of his tenants, since he was "investing" his own capital in the crop as well as renting his land. The planters' claim that blacks were incapable of labor without supervision was an ideological justification of their own existence as a class and of their right to the surplus they acquired.

Although the move to sharecropping represented a substantial defeat for the planters, it was not without benefit for them. The *Advertiser* pointed to the benefits of the labor repressive aspects of the system. . . . Sharecropping offered the additional advantage of increasing the labor force considerably in comparison with the gang system; by making the family the unit of labor rather than the wage hand, it brought women and children back into the fields. . . .

Sharecropping and Economic Development

. . . For the dominant class in the immediate postwar South, there were two possible responses to a shortage of labor. One was to develop capital-intensive methods of production. The alternative to this classic capitalist road was to rely on the coercion of labor, to extract a larger surplus not by increasing productivity through improved technology, but by squeezing more out of the laborers. Because this intensification was likely to provoke resistance and flight, this second route required formal restrictions on labor mobility, laws that tied the workers to the land and restricted their access to alternative employment. This second route is not necessarily economically stagnant; it is capable of bringing economic development, but in a manner distinct from the classic capitalist method. Barrington Moore, mindful of European developments, has called it the "Prussian Road" to modern society: economic development that preserves and intensifies the authoritarian and repressive elements of traditional social relations.

The possibility that the South could take the classic capitalist road was not ignored in the immediate postwar period. Some of the most astute southerners pushed for precisely such a solution to the problems of postwar agricultural adjustment. The Selma *Southern Argus*, for one, argued tirelessly during the late 1860s that the planters should end their reliance on labor-intensive methods of producing cotton, and instead diversify crops, introduce stock raising, and substitute labor-saving machinery for black tenant labor.

The planter class, rooted as it was in the antebellum elite, chose the other solution, the Prussian Road. The Black Codes passed in 1865–1867 expressed that choice; temporarily abolished by the Radicals, many were resurrected by the planter regimes that regained power in the seventies. And once the institutions of a labor-repressive system of agriculture had been established, the planters had little incentive to mechanize or introduce more rational techniques to increase efficiency and productivity. Thus while wheat-growing capitalist farmers in the North were transforming their productive techniques with a technological revolution, southern sharecroppers in 1900 relied on hand tools and mule power; the result was southern economic stagnation, as crop outputs, yields per acre, and agricultural technology changed little from year to year.

Too much of the recent debate has treated southern economic and political development as separate questions. The South's characteristic poverty and political oppression arose out of the same social relations: the Prussian Road, with its dominant planter class and its labor-repressive system of agricultural production, which posed a major obstacle not only to economic development, but also to democracy, to the political freedoms present in the North and so glaringly absent from the South.

ERIC FONER

ERIC FONER (1943–   ) is the DeWitt Clinton Professor of History at Columbia University. He is the author of Free Soil, Free Labor, Free Men *(1970),* Tom Paine and Revolutionary America *(1976),* Reconstruction: America's Unfinished Revolution, *winner of the Bancroft Prize and Francis Parkman Prize (1988), and* The Story of American Freedom *(1998).*

Thus, in the words of W.E.B. Du Bois, "the slave went free; stood a brief moment in the sun; then moved back again toward slavery." The magnitude of the Redeemer counterrevolution underscored both the scope of the transformation Reconstruction had assayed and the consequences of its failure. To be sure, the era of emancipation and Republican rule did not lack enduring accomplishments. The tide of change rose and then receded, but it left behind an altered landscape. The freedmen's political and civil equality proved transitory, but the autonomous black family and a network of religious and social institutions survived the end of Reconstruction. Nor could the seeds of educational progress planted then be entirely uprooted. While wholly inadequate for pupils of both races, schooling under the Redeemers represented a distinct advance over the days when blacks were excluded altogether from a share in public services.

If blacks failed to achieve the economic independence envisioned in the aftermath of the Civil War, Reconstruction closed off even more oppressive alternatives than the Redeemers' New South. The post-Reconstruction labor system embodied neither a return to the closely supervised gang labor of antebellum days, nor the complete dispossession and immobilization of the black labor force and coercive apprenticeship systems envisioned by white Southerners in 1865 and 1866. Nor were blacks, as in twentieth-century South Africa, barred from citizenship, herded into labor reserves, or prohibited by law from moving from one part of the country to another. As illustrated by the small but growing number of black landowners, businessmen, and professionals, the doors of economic opportunity that had opened could never be completely closed. Without Reconstruction, moreover, it is difficult to imagine the establishment of a framework of legal rights enshrined in the Constitution that, while flagrantly violated after 1877, created a vehicle for future federal intervention in Southern affairs. As a result of this unprecedented redefinition of the American body politic, the South's racial system remained regional rather than national, an outcome of great importance when economic opportunities at last opened in the North.

Nonetheless, whether measured by the dreams inspired by emancipation or the more limited goals of securing blacks' rights as citizens and free laborers, and establishing an enduring Republican presence in the South, Reconstruction can only be judged a failure. Among the host of explanations for this outcome, a few seem especially significant. Events far beyond the control of Southern Republicans—the nature of the national credit and banking systems, the depression of the 1870s, the stagnation of world demand for cotton—severely limited the prospects for far-reaching economic change. The early rejection of federally sponsored land reform left in place a planter class far weaker and less affluent than before the war, but still able to bring its prestige and experience to bear against Reconstruction. Factionalism and corruption, although hardly confined to Southern Republicans, undermined their claim to legitimacy and made it difficult for them to respond effectively to attacks by resolute opponents. The failure to develop an effective long-term appeal to white voters made it increasingly difficult for Republicans to combat the racial politics of the Redeemers. None of these factors, however, would have proved decisive without the campaign of violence that turned the electoral tide in many parts of the South, and the weakening of Northern resolve, itself a consequence of social and political changes that undermined the free labor and egalitarian precepts at the heart of Reconstruction policy.

For historians, hindsight can be a treacherous ally. Enabling us to trace the hidden patterns of past events, it beguiles us with the mirage of inevitability, the assumption that different outcomes lay beyond the limits of the possible. Certainly, the history of other plantation societies offers little reason for optimism that emancipation could have given rise to a prosperous, egalitarian South, or even one that escaped a pattern of colonial underdevelopment. Nor do the prospects for the expansion of scalawag support—essential for Southern Republicanism's long-term survival—appear in retrospect to have been anything but bleak. Outside the mountains and other enclaves of wartime Unionism, the Civil War generation of white Southerners was always likely to view the Republican party as an alien embodiment of wartime defeat and black equality. And the nation lacked not simply the will but the modern bureaucratic machinery to oversee Southern affairs in any permanent way. Perhaps the remarkable thing about Reconstruction was not that it failed, but that it was attempted at all and survived as long as it did. Yet one can, I think, imagine alternative scenarios and modest successes: the Republican party establishing itself as a permanent fixture on the Southern landscape, the North summoning the resolve to insist that the Constitution must be respected. As the experiences of Readjuster Virginia and Populist-Republican North Carolina suggest, even Redemption did not entirely foreclose the possibility of biracial politics, thus raising the question of how Southern life might have been affected had Deep South blacks enjoyed genuine political freedoms when the Populist movement swept the white counties in the 1890s.

Here, however, we enter the realm of the purely speculative. What remains certain is that Reconstruction failed, and that for blacks its failure was a disaster whose magnitude cannot be obscured by the genuine accomplishments that did endure. For the nation as a whole, the collapse of Reconstruction was a tragedy that deeply affected the course of its future development. If racism contributed to the undoing of Reconstruction, by the same token Reconstruction's demise and the emergence of blacks as a disenfranchised class of dependent laborers greatly facilitated racism's further spread, until by the early twentieth century it had become more deeply embedded in the nation's culture and politics than at any time since the beginning of the antislavery crusade and perhaps in our entire history. The removal of a significant portion of the nation's laboring population from public life shifted the center of gravity of American politics to the right, complicating the tasks of reformers for generations to come. Long into the twentieth century, the South remained a one-party region under the control of a reactionary ruling elite who used the same violence and fraud that had helped defeat Reconstruction to stifle internal dissent. An enduring consequence of Reconstruction's failure, the Solid South helped define the contours of American politics and weaken the prospects not simply of change in racial matters but of progressive legislation in many other realms.

The men and women who had spearheaded the effort to remake Southern society scattered down innumerable byways after the end of Reconstruction. Some relied on federal patronage to earn a livelihood. The unfortunate Marshall Twitchell, armless after his near-murder in 1876, was appointed U.S. consul at Kingston, Ontario, where he died in 1905. Some fifty relatives and friends of the Louisiana Returning Board that had helped make Hayes President received positions at the New Orleans Custom House, and Stephen Packard was awarded the consulship at Liverpool—compensation for surrendering his claim to the governorship. John Eaton, who coordinated freedmen's affairs for General Grant during the war and subsequently took an active role in Tennessee Reconstruction, served as federal commissioner of education from 1870 to 1886, and organized a public school system in Puerto Rico after the island's conquest in the Spanish-American War. Most carpetbaggers returned to the North, often finding there the financial success that had eluded them in the South. Davis Tillson, head of Georgia's Freedman's Bureau immediately after the war, earned a fortune in the Maine granite business. Former South Carolina Gov. Robert K. Scott returned to Napoleon, Ohio, where he became a successful real estate agent—"a most fitting occupation" in view of his involvement in land commission speculations. Less happy was the fate of his scalawag successor, Franklin J. Moses, Jr., who drifted north, served prison terms for petty crimes, and died in a Massachusetts rooming house in 1906.

Republican governors who had won reputations as moderates by courting white Democratic support and seeking to limit blacks' political influence found the Redeemer South remarkably forgiving. Henry C. Warmoth became a successful sugar planter and remained in Louisiana until his death in 1931. James L. Alcorn retired to his Mississippi plantation, "presiding over a Delta domain in a style befitting a prince" and holding various local offices. He remained a Republican, but told one Northern visitor that Democratic rule had produced "good fellowship" between the races. Even Rufus Bullock, who fled Georgia accused of every kind of venality, soon reentered Atlanta society, serving, among other things, as president of the city's chamber of commerce. Daniel H. Chamberlain left South Carolina in 1877 to launch a successful New York City law practice, but was well received on his numerous visits to the state. In retrospect, Chamberlain altered his opinion of Reconstruction: a "frightful experiment" that sought to "lift a backward or inferior race" to political equality, it had inevitably produced "shocking and unbearable misgovernment." "Governor Chamberlain," commented a Charleston newspaper, "has lived and learned."

Not all white Republicans, however, abandoned Reconstruction ideals. In 1890, a group of reformers, philanthropists, and religious leaders gathered at the Lake Mohonk Conference on the Negro Question, chaired by former President Hayes. Amid a chorus of advice that blacks eschew political involvement and concentrate on educational and economic progress and remedying their own character deficiencies, former North Carolina Judge Albion W. Tourgée, again living in the North, voiced the one discordant note. There was no "Negro problem," Tourgee observed, but rather a "white" one, since "the hate, the oppression, the injustice, are all on our side." The following year, Tourgée established the National Citizens' Rights Association, a short-lived forerunner of the National Association for the Advancement of Colored People, devoted to challenging the numerous injustices afflicting Southern blacks. Adelbert Ames, who left Mississippi in 1875 to join his father's Minnesota flour-milling business and who later settled in Massachusetts, continued to defend his Reconstruction record. In 1894 he chided Brown University President E. Benjamin Andrews for writing that Mississippi during his governorship had incurred a debt of $20 million. The actual figure, Ames pointed out, was less than 3 percent of that amount, and he found it difficult to understand how Andrews had made "a $19,500,000 error in a $20,000,000 statement." Ames lived to his ninety-eighth year, never abandoning the conviction that "caste is the curse of the world." Another Mississippi carpetbagger, Massachusetts-born teacher and legislator Henry Warren, published his autobiography in 1914, still hoping that one day, "possibly in the present century," America would live up to the ideal of "equal political rights for all without regard to race."

For some, the Reconstruction experience became a springboard to lifetimes of social reform. The white voters of Winn Parish in Louisiana's hill country expressed their enduring radicalism by supporting the Populists in the 1890s, Socialism in 1912, and later their native son Huey Long. Among the female veterans of freedmen's education, Cornelia Hancock founded Philadelphia's Children's Aid Society, Abby May became prominent in the Massachusetts women's suffrage movement, Ellen Collins turned her attention to New York City housing reform, and Josephine Shaw Lowell became a supporter of the labor movement and principal founder of New York's Consumer League. Louis F. Post, a New Jersey-born carpetbagger who took stenographic notes for South Carolina's legislature in the early 1870s, became a follower of Henry George, attended the founding meeting of the NAACP, and as Woodrow Wilson's Assistant Secretary of Labor, sought to mitigate the 1919 Red Scare and prevent the deportation of foreign-born radicals. And Texas scalawag editor Albert Parsons became a nationally known Chicago labor reformer and anarchist, whose speeches drew comparisons between the plight of Southern blacks and Northern industrial workers, and between the aristocracy resting on slavery the Civil War had destroyed and the new oligarchy based on the exploitation of industrial labor it had helped to create. Having survived the perils of Texas Reconstruction, Parsons met his death on the Illinois gallows after being wrongfully convicted of complicity in the Haymarket bombing of 1886.

Like their white counterparts, many black veterans of Reconstruction survived on federal patronage after the coming of "home rule." P. B. S. Pinchback and Blanche K. Bruce held a series of such posts and later moved to Washington, D.C., where they entered the city's privileged black society. Richard T. Greener, during Reconstruction a professor at the University of South Carolina, combined a career in law, journalism, and education with various government appointments, including a stint as American commercial agent at Vladivostok. Long after the destruction of his low-country political machine by disenfranchisement, Robert Smalls served as customs collector for the port of Beaufort, dying there in 1915. Mifflin Gibbs held positions ranging from register of Little Rock's land office to American consul at Madagascar. Other black leaders left the political arena entirely to devote themselves to religious and educational work, emigration projects, or personal advancement. Robert G. Fitzgerald continued to teach in North Carolina until his death in 1919; Edward Shaw of Memphis concentrated on activities among black Masons and the AME Church; Richard H. Cain served as president of a black college in Waco, Texas; and Francis L. Cardozo went on to become principal of a Washington, D.C., high school. Aaron A. Bradley, the militant spokesman for Georgia's low-country freedmen, helped publicize the Kansas Exodus and died in St. Louis in 1881, while Henry M. Turner, ordained an AME bishop in 1880, emerged as the late nineteenth century's most prominent advocate of black emigration to Africa. Former Atlanta councilman William Finch prospered as a tailor. Alabama Congressman Jeremiah Haralson engaged in coal mining in Colorado, where he was reported "killed by wild beasts."

Other Reconstruction leaders found, in the words of a black lawyer, that "the tallest tree . . . suffers most in a storm." Former South Carolina Congressman and Lieut. Gov. Alonzo J. Ransier died in poverty in 1882, having been employed during his last years as a night watchman at the Charleston Custom House and as a city street sweeper. Robert B. Elliott, the state's most brilliant political organizer, found himself "utterly unable to earn a living owing to the severe ostracism and mean prejudice of my political opponents." He died in 1884 after moving to New Orleans and struggling to survive as a lawyer. James T. Rapier died penniless in 1883, having dispersed his considerable wealth among black schools, churches, and emigration organizations. Most local leaders sank into obscurity, disappearing entirely from the historical record. Although some of their children achieved distinction, none of Reconstruction's black officials created a family political dynasty—one indication of how Redemption aborted the development of the South's black political leadership. If their descendants moved ahead, it was through business, the arts, or the professions. T. Thomas Fortune, editor of the New York *Age*, was the son of Florida officeholder Emanuel Fortune; Harlem Renaissance writer Jean Toomer, the grandson of Pinchback; renowned jazz pianist Fletcher Henderson, the grandson of an official who had served in South Carolina's constitutional convention and legislature.

By the turn of the century, as soldiers from North and South joined to take up the "white man's burden" in the Spanish-American War, Reconstruction was widely viewed as little more than a regrettable detour on the road to reunion. To the bulk of the white South, it had become axiomatic that Reconstruction had been a time of "savage tyranny" that "accomplished not one useful result, and left behind it, not one pleasant recollection." Black suffrage, wrote Joseph Le Conte, who had fled South Carolina for a professorship at the University of California to avoid teaching black students, was now seen by "all thoughtful men" as "the greatest political crime ever perpetrated by any people." In more sober language, many Northerners, including surviving architects of Congressional policy, concurred in these judgments. "Years of thinking and observation" had convinced O. O. Howard "that the restoration of their lands to the planters provided for [a] future better for the negroes." John Sherman's recollections recorded a similar change of heart: "After this long lapse of time I am convinced that Mr. Johnson's scheme of reorganization was wise and judicious. . . . It is unfortunate that it had not the sanction of Congress."

This rewriting of Reconstruction's history was accorded scholarly legitimacy—to its everlasting shame—by the nation's fraternity of professional historians. Early in the twentieth century a group of young Southern scholars gathered at Columbia University to study the Reconstruction era under the guidance of Professors John W. Burgess and William A. Dunning. Blacks, their mentors taught, were "children" utterly incapable of appreciating the freedom that had been thrust upon them. The North did "a monstrous thing" in granting them suffrage, for "a black skin means membership in a race of men which has never of itself succeeded in subjecting passion to reason, has never, therefore, created any civilization of any kind." No political order could survive in the South unless founded on the principle of racial inequality. The students' works on individual Southern states echoed these sentiments. Reconstruction, concluded the study of North Carolina, was an attempt by "selfish politicians, backed by the federal government . . . to Africanize the State and deprive the people through misrule and oppression of most that life held dear." The views of the Dunning School shaped historical writing for generations, and achieved wide popularity through D. W. Griffith's film *Birth of a Nation* (which glorified the Ku Klux Klan and had its premiere at the White House during Woodrow Wilson's Presidency), James Ford Rhodes's popular multivolume chronicle of the Civil War era, and the national best-seller *The Tragic Era* by Claude G. Bowers. Southern whites, wrote Bowers, "literally were put to the torture" by "emissaries of hate" who inflamed "the negroes' egotism" and even inspired "lustful assaults" by blacks upon white womanhood.

Few interpretations of history have had such far-reaching consequences as this image of Reconstruction. As Francis B. Simkins, a South Carolina-born historian, noted during the 1930s, "the alleged horrors of Reconstruction" did much to freeze the mind of the white South in unalterable opposition to outside pressures for social change and to any thought of breaching Democratic ascendancy, eliminating segregation, or restoring suffrage to disenfranchised blacks. They also justified Northern indifference to the nullification of the Fourteenth and Fifteenth Amendments. Apart from a few white dissenters like Simkins, it was left to black writers to challenge the prevailing orthodoxy. In the early years of this century, none did so more tirelessly than former Mississippi Congressman John R. Lynch, then living in Chicago, who published a series of devastating critiques of the racial biases and historical errors of Rhodes and Bowers. "I do not hesitate to assert," he wrote, "that the Southern Reconstruction Governments were the best governments those States ever had." In 1917, Lynch voiced the hope that "a fair, just, and impartial historian will, some day, write a history covering the Reconstruction period, [giving] the actual facts of what took place."

Only in the family traditions and collective folk memories of the black community did a different version of Reconstruction survive. Growing up in the 1920s, Pauli Murray was "never allowed to forget" that she walked in "proud shoes" because her grandfather, Robert G. Fitzgerald, had "fought for freedom" in the Union Army and then enlisted as a teacher in the "second war" against the powerlessness and ignorance inherited from slavery. When the Works Progress Administration sent agents into the black belt during the Great Depression to interview former slaves, they found Reconstruction remembered for its disappointments and betrayals, but also as a time of hope, possibility, and accomplishment. Bitterness still lingered over the federal government's failure to distribute land or protect blacks' civil and political rights. "The Yankees helped free us, so they say," declared eighty-one-year-old former slave Thomas Hall, "but they let us be put back in slavery again." Yet coupled with this disillusionment were proud, vivid recollections of a time when "the colored used to hold office." Some pulled from their shelves dusty scrapbooks of clippings from Reconstruction newspapers; others could still recount the names of local black leaders. "They made pretty fair officers," remarked one elderly freedman; "I thought them was good times in the country," said another. Younger blacks spoke of being taught by their parents "about the old times, mostly about the Reconstruction, and the Ku Klux." "I know folks think the books tell the truth, but they shore don't," one eighty-eight-year-old former slave told the WPA.

For some blacks, such memories helped to keep alive the aspirations of the Reconstruction era. "This here used to be a good county," said Arkansas freedman Boston Blackwell, "but I tell you it sure is tough now. I think it's wrong—exactly wrong that we can't vote now." "I does believe that the negro ought to be given more privileges in voting," echoed Taby Jones, born a slave in South Carolina in 1850, "because they went through the reconstruction period with banners flying." For others, Reconstruction inspired optimism that better times lay ahead. "The Bible says, 'What has been will be again'," said Alabama sharecropper Ned Cobb. Born in 1885, Cobb never cast a vote in his entire life, yet he never forgot that outsiders had once taken up the black cause—an indispensable source of hope for one conscious of his own weakness in the face of overwhelming and hostile local power. When radical Northerners ventured South in the 1930s to help organize black agricultural workers, Cobb seemed almost to have been waiting for them: "The whites came down to bring emancipation, and left before it was over. . . . Now they've come to finish the job." The legacy of Reconstruction affected the 1930s revival of black militancy in other ways as well. Two leaders of the Alabama Share Croppers Union, Ralph and Thomas Gray, claimed to be descended from a Reconstruction legislator. (Like many nineteenth-century predecessors, Ralph Gray paid with his life for challenging the South's social order—he was killed in a shootout with a posse while guarding a union meeting.)

Twenty more years elapsed before another generation of black Southerners launched the final challenge to the racial system of the New South. A few participants in the civil rights movement thought of themselves as following a path blazed after the Civil War. Discussing the reasons for his involvement, one black Mississippian spoke of the time when "a few Negroes was admitted into the government of the State of Mississippi and to the United States." Reconstruction's legacy was also evident in the actions of federal judge Frank Johnson, who fought a twelve-year battle for racial justice with Alabama Gov. George Wallace. Johnson hailed from Winston County, a center of Civil War Unionism, and his great-grandfather had served as a Republican sheriff during Reconstruction. By this time, however, the Reconstruction generation had passed from the scene and even within the black community, memories of the period had all but disappeared. Yet the institutions created or consolidated after the Civil War—the black family, school, and church—provided the base from which the modern civil rights revolution sprang. And for its legal strategy, the movement returned to the laws and amendments of Reconstruction.

"The river has its bend, and the longest road must terminate." Rev. Peter Randolph, a former slave, wrote these words as the dark night of injustice settled over the South. Nearly a century elapsed before the nation again attempted to come to terms with the implications of emancipation and the political and social agenda of Reconstruction. In many ways, it has yet to do so.

3

THE TRIUMPH OF CAPITALISM

Efficiency or Class War?

"The old nations of the earth," Andrew Carnegie observed in 1886, "creep on at a snail's pace; the Republic thunders past with the rush of the express. The United States, [in] the growth of a single century, has already reached the foremost rank among nations, and is destined soon to outdistance all others in the race. In population, in wealth, in annual savings, and in public credit; in freedom from debt, in agriculture, and in manufactures, America already leads the civilized world."[1] This is the true voice of American triumphalism; having long congratulated itself on being the freest place in the world, America at the turn of the century looked around and noticed it had (or was about to) become the most powerful industrial economy on the face of the earth.

Though Carnegie evoked the dominant note of public self-congratulation, other Americans detested the greed and ugliness that accompanied the industrial transformation. Walt Whitman, in "Democratic Vistas," summed up their sort of criticism: "The depravity of the business classes of our country is not less than has been supposed but infinitely greater. The official services of America, national, state, and municipal . . . are saturated in corruption, bribery, falsehood, maladministration; . . . The great cities reek with respectable as much as nonrespectable robbery and scoundrelism. . . . I say that our New World democracy, however great a success in uplifting the masses out of their sloughs, in materialistic development . . . is, so far, an almost complete failure in its social aspects, and in really grand religious, moral, literary, and esthetic results."[2]

Most prominent critics of capitalism came from the ranks of the literate middle and upper classes. But even at their most pessimistic or radical, such critics could never capture the quality of pain, bewilderment, and outrage that inflected the voices of workers, farmers, and other lower-class Americans who felt themselves to be victims of tri-

---

[1] Andrew Carnegie, *Triumphant Democracy* (New York, 1886), p. 1.

[2] Walt Whitman, "Democratic Vistas," in *Prose Works 1892*, Floyd Stovall, ed., 2 vols. (New York, 1963–1964), 2: 370.

umphant capitalism. A skilled iron molder, one of the supposed "aristocrats of labor," wrote the following in his diary during a serious depression in 1876: "No money, rent due . . . Coal nearly out. Little food in the house. And, worst of all, no prospects ahead either to pay what is due or to replace what is nearly out. Even if I got a job, it would be a month before I could have any money. God only knows what I will or can do under such circumstances."[3] In addition to plain misery, hard times inflicted on ordinary folk a crushing sense of humiliation. Thus a midwestern farmer wrote to a Populist editor in 1891: ". . . I am one of those Poor and unprotected . . . I settled on this Land in good Faith Built House and Barn Broken up Part of the Land. Spent years of hard labor in grubing fencing and Improving are they going to drive us out like trespassers wife and children . . . and give us away to the Corporations. . . . [W]e are robbed of our means . . . We are Loyal Citicens . . . We love our wife and children just as Dearly as any of you But how can we protect them give them education as they should wen we are driven from sea to sea. . . ."[4]

The promise of freedom and prosperity seemed to have been revoked for those who labored, as opposed to those who owned and managed the nation's resources and industrial enterprises. Fundamental decisions about their lives—from whether they worked and for how much, to whose influence would shape politics and government on the local level and beyond—were no longer in their control. Pain and bewilderment led to outrage and action. Unionizing workers called for "industrial democracy"; Populist farmers for a "cooperative commonwealth." Thus, while corporate capitalists saw themselves as champions of one version of American democracy, organized labor and other advocates for the poor and dispossessed saw themselves as vindicating an egalitarian version of that democracy.

Americans have continued to debate the merits of industrialization since its onset. They have argued about facts: How was wealth produced? How evenly was it distributed? How much social mobility took place between classes? And they argued about interpretations: Was the impoverishment of certain groups of laborers exceptional or endemic to industrial capitalism? Did labor unions and regulatory legislation represent a democratic restraint on capital, or a way to buy off radical protest? Was class conflict an aberration produced by greed and bad policy, or a permanent feature of industrial capitalism? Was corpo-

---

[3]Neil L. Shumsky, "Frank Roney's San Francisco—His Diary: April, 1875–March, 1876," *Labor History* 17 (Spring 1976): 258. A survey of the history of unemployment in one state is Alexander Keyssar, *Out of Work: The First Century of Unemployment in Massachusetts* (Cambridge, 1986).

[4]Quoted in Norman Pollack, ed., *The Populist Mind* (Indianapolis, 1967), pp. 33–34. Variant spelling and punctuation in the original. On Populism, see Chapter 6 in this volume.

rate capitalism an achievement or a betrayal of American democracy (or, most painful to contemplate, perhaps both)? On these questions, historians of industrialization have been no less divided than journalists, politicians, and other citizens. Not all of their differences can be explored here, but it is possible to focus on two prominent areas of scholarly attention and debate: the character of the modern American corporation, and the character of the American labor movement.

The first attempts to evaluate critically the achievements of the "captains of industry" who built the great corporations occurred at the beginning of the twentieth century. Against the prevailing triumphalism, Washington Gladden, Henry George, Henry Demarest Lloyd, and others agitated against those they saw as robber barons. For Gladden, a Protestant minister who preached the Social Gospel, capitalist competition was warfare, and its antidote a social welfare policy based on Christian brotherhood. For George, author of *Progress and Poverty* (1879), all the inequities of capitalist society derived from the monopolization of the land and its resources by a handful of lucky speculators; a "single tax" on their entirely unearned landed wealth thus represented the crucial antidote to inequality. A journalist and a scholar, Lloyd, until his death in 1903, insisted that the American people were confronted with a choice between reform or revolution. In *Wealth Against Commonwealth* (1894), a book that anticipated the writings of later muckrakers and Progressive reformers, Lloyd insisted that public ownership of monopolies and government regulation of the economy were absolutely necessary if the American people were to avoid the fratricidal class struggles—the "misery, plagues, hatreds, [and] national enervation"—that had wracked other nations in the industrialized world.[5] Within a general critique of industrial capitalist society, Lloyd focused specifically on John D. Rockefeller's attempt to gain a virtual monopoly over the petroleum industry. Businessmen like Rockefeller, wrote Lloyd, paid lip service to the ideal of competition but their true purpose was to achieve a form of monopolistic power that harkened back to the age of feudalism. Like Lloyd, other critics of capitalism at the turn of the century tended to personalize their critiques. Focusing on the unbridled selfishness of the captains of industry permitted critics to mobilize a language of moral and religious condemnation that resonated with a great majority of Protestant Americans. And focusing on the robber baron's lust for power allowed the critics to mobilize an even more resonant language of democratic equality.

While critics etched the negative image of robber barons in the public's imagination, and the Progressive reform movement sought to restrain the power of the corporation, historians began to inquire into

---

[5]Henry Demarest Lloyd, *Wealth Against Commonwealth* (New York, 1894), p. 517.

the economic realities of capitalism. Among the greatest of these Progressive historians were Charles and Mary Beard and Vernon L. Parrington. The Beards compared the industrial barons to the feudal barons of the medieval past,[6] but Parrington, in his monumental *Main Currents in American Thought,* issued the severest judgment. Placing himself squarely within the tradition of Jeffersonian liberalism, Parrington portrayed the industrialists as predatory and materialistic, their bloated corporations as threats to those humane and democratic values that had made America great. Business tycoons had turned modern America, with "its standardized life, its machine culture, its mass-psychology," into a place in which "Jefferson and Jackson and Lincoln would be strangers." The giants of industry, Parrington thundered, "were primitive souls, ruthless, predatory, capable; single-minded men; rogues and rascals often, but never feeble, never hindered by petty scruple, never given to puling or whining—the raw materials of a race of capitalistic buccaneers."[7]

The 1930s provided a favorable climate for the image of the businessman as robber baron. For decades the business community had asserted that the nation's greatness rested on the achievements of ambitious and energetic entrepreneurs. They applauded President Coolidge's dictum: "The business of America is business." Having taken credit for the apparent prosperity of the 1920s, however, the business community had to accept responsibility for the catastrophic depression of the 1930s. As unemployment, bankruptcy, and even starvation afflicted millions of Americans, the businessman's time-honored cliché—that wealth was the product of ambition, talent, and moral uprightness—seemed an obscene joke. Perhaps free enterprise capitalism had come to the end of the road, many now boldly suggested; new approaches were required if the needs of a modern, complex industrial society in America were to be met.

The themes that Beard and Parrington had explored in the 1920s, and which were echoed in the fiction of the 1930s, most notably in Sinclair Lewis's *Babbitt,* developed into a full-scale historical critique in the work of Matthew Josephson. Josephson dedicated his 1934 book, *The Robber Barons: The Great American Capitalists 1861–1901,* to Charles and Mary Beard, who had interpreted American history as a struggle between haves and have-nots. "This book," he began, "attempts the history of a small class of men who arose at the time of our Civil War and suddenly swept into power. . . . Under their hands the renovation of our economic life proceeded relentlessly: large-scale pro-

---

[6]Charles and Mary Beard, *The Rise of American Civilization,* 2 vols. (New York, 1927), 2: 177.

[7]Vernon L. Parrington, *Main Currents in American Thought,* 3 vols. (New York, 1927–1930), 3: 12 and 26.

duction replaced the scattered, decentralized mode of production, industrial enterprises became more concentrated, more 'efficient' technically, . . . But all this revolutionizing effort is branded with the
motive of private gain on the part of the new captains of industry. To
organize and exploit the resources of a nation upon a gigantic scale, to
regiment its farmers and workers into harmonious corps of producers,
and to do this only in the name of an uncontrolled appetite for private
profit—here surely is the great inherent contradiction whence so
much disaster, outrage, and misery has flowed."[8]

Just as the robber baron concept was reaching maturity, another
school of thought was emerging: "business history." The foundations
of business history were laid in the 1930s by scholars at the Harvard
Graduate School of Business Administration, as well as by sympathetic biographers of individual business leaders, all of whom rejected
the robber baron view of industrial history. Business history represented a distinctively new approach to the study of American economic history. Indeed, business historians by the 1950s had created
their own professional organization, developed a new vocabulary and
research techniques, published their own journal, and in some cases
even founded new departments within universities.

Business historians insisted that industrial leaders were far more
complex figures than earlier scholars had realized. Historian Allan
Nevins, who published major revisionist biographies of John D. Rockefeller in 1940 and 1953, argued that much of the blame heaped on this
captain of industry was unwarranted. While conceding that Rockefeller
used methods that were ethically dubious, Nevins insisted that the
kind of monopoly control attained by Rockefeller's Standard Oil Company was a natural response to the cutthroat competition of the period
and reflected the trend toward business consolidation in all industrial
nations. No robber baron, Rockefeller was instead an "innovator,
thinker, planner, bold entrepreneur," who imposed upon American industry "a more rational and efficient pattern." Although motivated by
urges toward "competitive achievement, self-expression, and the imposition of [his will] on a given environment," he also created a model of
philanthropy for all to follow. Had it not been for men like him—men
who created great industrial units in steel, oil, textiles, chemicals, electricity, and automotive vehicles—"the free world might have lost the
First World War and most certainly would have lost the Second."[9]

---

[8]Matthew Josephson, *The Robber Barons: The Great American Capitalists
1861–1901* (New York, 1934), pp. vii–viii. See also Hal Bridges, "The Robber Baron Concept in American History," *Business History Review* 32 (Spring 1958): 1–13.

[9]Allan Nevins, *John D. Rockefeller: The Heroic Age of American Enterprise*, 2 vols.
(New York, 1940), 2:707–714; and *Study in Power: John D. Rockefeller, Industrialist and
Philanthropist*, 2 vols. (New York, 1953), 1: viii–ix; 2: 436. For a direct confrontation of
views, "Should American History Be Rewritten? A Debate Between Allan Nevins and
Matthew Josephson," *Saturday Review* 37 (February 6, 1954): 7–10 and 44–49.

Like scholars in the robber baron tradition, business historians began with assumptions that influenced their approach to the subject. Relatively conservative politically, they believed that, in an era of war and Cold War, American economic and political institutions deserved to be admired, emulated, and defended. The business historians insisted that the costs of industrialization were far lower, less degrading to the mass of Americans, and less threatening to liberal democracy than anti-business reformers and writers asserted. They criticized Progressive historians for exaggerating the tension between democracy and corporate power, and charged them with employing historical analysis as an ideological weapon against capitalism. That they themselves were occupying an ideological position seemed not to occur to them. In any event, the Cold War certainly reinforced the tendency of business historians (and others) to find consensus, not conflict, over values and institutions in American society.

A more sophisticated development in business history emerged in the 1960s in the work of Alfred D. Chandler, Jr. Unlike Nevins, Chandler had no interest in vindicating or otherwise morally assessing the career of any individual or group of individuals. He was instead absorbed in analyzing the impersonal processes whereby new business forms, methods, and structures came into being in the late-nineteenth and twentieth centuries. Borrowing from social science theories and methods, Chandler identified four stages in the development of large industrial enterprises. First came a period of expansion and accumulation of resources, and then a period in which these resources were "rationalized." In the third phase the organization expanded its operations to include new products. In the fourth and final phase the organization created new structures to promote effective use of resources and to manage long-term adaptation to market conditions. "Strategic growth," he noted, "resulted from an awareness of the opportunities and needs—created by changing population, income, and technology— to employ existing or expanding resources more profitably."[10]

Eschewing individual biography, Chandler had in essence written the collective biography of a social institution: the large, decentralized, multidivisional corporation. In a subsequent Pulitzer Prize–winning book, *The Visible Hand*, Chandler analyzed the manner in which the development of large-scale corporations altered the American economy between the Civil War and the depression of the 1930s.[11] Here he emphasized the crucial role of management and business executives in

[10]Alfred D. Chandler, Jr., *Strategy and Structure: Chapters in the History of the Industrial Enterprise* (Cambridge, Mass., 1962), p. 15. A revised edition of this work appeared in 1990.

[11]Alfred D. Chandler, Jr., *The Visible Hand: The Managerial Revolution in American Business* (Cambridge, Mass., 1977). For a summary of the findings of business historians see Glenn Porter, *The Rise of Big Business, 1860–1910* (New York, 1973).

guiding these changes (especially in adopting new technology), and rejected forcefully laissez-faire notions of a self-realizing and self-correcting market. The first selection in this chapter is an article by Chandler
on the role of business and businessmen in American society.[12]

Not all business or economic historians were content to analyze
the corporation in structural and functional terms. In the late 1950s
and 1960s, a younger cohort of scholars revived the Progressive insight
that huge economic conglomerations were a threat to democratic institutions and egalitarian social relations. Typical of these was Carl
Kaysen, an economist who noted that large corporations accumulated
not just economic but political and social power as well. American society possessed three alternative ways of controlling that business
power: the promotion of competitive markets, regulation by agencies
external to business, and self-regulation by the socially responsible
corporation. Traditionally the United States relied on the first in the
form of antitrust legislation, although far more could have been done
along this line. As to government regulation and corporate self-regulation, the American experience was minimalist; effective control of
business power remained an unfinished task, Kaysen concluded.[13]
Scholars like Kaysen, consciously drawing inspiration from Progressive-era antitrust crusaders, sought to eliminate imperfections in
American society by breaking up anti-competitive distortions in the
economy. By the early 1960s, however, a small but growing number of
scholars in a variety of disciplines were concluding that American society was fundamentally malformed and required radical change.

New Left historians in the 1960s argued that war, poverty, and
racism were direct outgrowths of American capitalism and that only
the abolition of capitalism could usher in a just and peaceful society.
They rejected scholarship that defended business as well as that which
proposed to reform and regulate it. One of the first such monographs
was Gabriel Kolko's *The Triumph of Conservatism*, which appeared in
1963. Kolko argued that the most distinctive feature of modern American society—which he designated political capitalism—dated only
from the first two decades of the twentieth century. Rejecting the belief that large-scale business enterprise was inevitable, Kolko maintained that competition was actually increasing at the turn of the
century. Even the merger movement and the creation of new combina-

<hr/>

[12]Other historians have emphasized the personal efficacy of businessmen in shaping
business history: Harold C. Livesay, "Entrepreneurial Persistence through the Bureaucratic Age," *Business History Review* 51 (Winter 1977): 415–443; see also his fine short
biography, *Andrew Carnegie and the Rise of Big Business* (Boston, 1975). Most recently
see H. W. Brands, *Masters of Enterprise: Giants of American Business from John Jacob
Astor and J. P. Morgan to Bill Gates and Oprah Winfrey* (New York, 1999), and Jean
Strouse, *Morgan: American Financier* (New York, 1999).

[13]Carl Kaysen, "The Corporation: How Much Power? What Scope?" in *The Corporation in Modern Society*, Edward S. Mason, ed. (Cambridge, Mass., 1959), Chapter 5.

tions on an unprecedented scale failed to stem the tide of competitive growth. However vast their ambition and long their reach, that is, men like Rockefeller and J. P. Morgan could not squeeze the competitive unpredictability out of the American economy, or turn gigantic corporations into models of efficiency. In contrast to Chandler, Kolko believed that large-scale units turned to government regulation precisely because of their inefficiency and inability to control boom-and-bust swings in the economy.

Failure to control market swings not only meant economic losses for investors; Kolko showed that it also raised the specter of outraged masses using their democratic franchise to impose their own political solutions on business. In an era of labor radicalism, Populism, and a growing socialist movement, therefore, big business turned to government to control competition and to prevent the possibility that democratic politics might lead to a redistribution of wealth. The result was a synthesis of business and government, with the former emerging as the dominant element. Unlike Populism or socialism, Kolko finally argued, Progressivism was a business-led movement that equated the general welfare with the well-being of corporations. In his view, all those reformers who thought that state and federal regulation of business constituted democratic control over consolidated economic power were duped. The people who wrote the legislation and staffed the regulatory commissions were the very people who wanted to rationalize the economy by confirming the rule of finance capitalists.[14]

Many scholars rejected Kolko's ideological assumptions and questioned his conclusions. Edward A. Purcell, Jr., who examined the attitudes of businessmen during the passage of the Interstate Commerce Act of 1887, found that entrepreneurs and managers adhered to no coherent body of thought. In trying to develop a political strategy, they were rather interested in solving particular problems at the level of the firm or the sector of industry. Some favored regulation but fought over alternative models of regulation; others opposed it altogether. In general, Purcell concluded, diverse economic groups who felt threatened by the new national economy turned to the federal government without a general political strategy but rather in the hope of simply protecting their own interests.[15] However powerful Kolko's insights into the ideological and strategic ambitions of a small class of finance capitalists, his top-down assumptions about how businessmen pursued poli-

---

[14]In addition to Gabriel Kolko, *The Triumph of Conservation: A Reinterpretation of American History, 1900–1916* (New York, 1963), see Kolko's *Railroads and Regulation 1877–1916* (Princeton, 1965) for a case study of his interpretation.

[15]Edward A. Purcell, Jr., "Ideas and Interests: Businessmen and the Interstate Commerce Act," *Journal of American History* 54 (December 1967): 561–578. See also Albro Martin, *Enterprise Denied: Origins of the Decline of American Railroads 1897–1917* (New York, 1971); and Thomas K. McGraw, ed., *Regulation in Perspective: Historical Essays* (Cambridge, Mass., 1981).

tics and how politics actually worked could not explicate the social
and economic complexity of turn-of-the-century America.

Another new turn in the history of American capitalism has come
in the last several decades as a result of the intersection of economic
history with the history of technology. That intersection generated difficult questions: How and when does technological innovation occur?
What are the economic, as well as social and political, consequences of
technological innovation? Does technology shape or respond to the social and economic organization of modern society? Chandler gave
technology an increasingly important place in his interpretation of the
origins and development of big business. Some businessmen, in this
view, used new machinery in creative ways to promote efficiency and
business success; others failed to understand the inevitable force of
new technology and consequently fell behind in the race for strategic
advantage.[16] The disruptive consequences of technological change are,
in this view, unfortunate but inevitable, and in the long run consumers (and even workers) profit from increased productivity.

Other historians have come to very different conclusions. The economic historian Hugh G. J. Aitken's remarkable *Taylorism at Watertown Arsenal: Scientific Management in Action, 1908–1915* went well
beyond available business history models of scholarship. One of the
founding studies in the history of technology as a subfield, *Taylorism
at Watertown Arsenal* was informed by the author's reading in social
history and his sympathetic understanding of the men who labored in,
not just those who managed, the business enterprise. Insisting that
"the historian must have not one point of view but many," Aitken
demonstrated that the "technological innovation" of scientific management was also "a highly complex social change" that revealed "all
the stresses of an industrial society exposed to constant revolution in
technology and organization." This perspective revealed that technical
managerial strategies were not the only (or sometimes even the most
important) element in the evolution of the industrial corporation.[17]

The radical historian David F. Noble went much further than
Aitken in turning business history into a sort of anti-business history.
In *America by Design* he argued that machines and technology are
never by themselves "the decisive forces of production." At every
point technology was controlled by managers who sought unchallenged power over their enterprises and workers, and whose "institutional fantasies of progress" allowed them to believe they were the
driving force in modern history. Noble further argued that when engi-

---

[16]See Louis Galambos, "Technology, Political Economy, and Professionalization:
Central Themes of the Organizational Synthesis," *Business History Review* 57 (Winter
1983): 472–478.

[17]Hugh G. J. Aitken, *Taylorism at Watertown Arsenal: Scientific Management in Action, 1908–1915* (Cambridge, Mass., 1960), p. 12.

neers failed to develop professional independence they ceased being agents of efficiency, becoming instead the uncritical servants of capitalists' thirst for control. Implicit in Noble's work was a political point: that social relations, rather than technological change, determined the rise of corporate power, and that only a movement from below could shift the balance of power to liberate the mass of workers from an economic system that subjected them to machines.[18]

Historian James Livingston has also emphasized the flaws in business historians' interpretations of the triumph of corporate capitalism. Livingston suggested that neither structural nor technological forces were decisive. Like Noble, employing neo-Marxist categories and borrowing from the new social and economic histories, he insisted that the victory of corporate capitalism was neither inevitable nor easy. The working class, for example, was capable of well-conceived collective action that had often succeeded in winning concessions from big business in the decades before 1900; its members were neither powerless nor irrational. During these same years, as prices declined, managers tried to restore profits by cutting wages, but this led to strikes and other workplace disturbances. When their efforts to regulate output and market shares led to bitter and acrimonious conflict among businessmen, they found themselves unable to impose hegemony either through banker-led consolidation or through "political capitalism." In the end, businessmen employed different tactics at different times (and sometimes simultaneously): consolidation designed to weed out weak enterprises and thereby restrain "ruinous competition"; reorganization of the workplace to cut labor costs and, even more importantly, to shift control of the labor process from workers to employers; and creation of a new class of professionalized corporate managers. The rise of corporate capitalism, then, represented an improvised economic solution to a complex and unstable social stalemate.[19]

The evolution of business history—from the highly personalized tales of "industrial statesmen" or "robber barons" (depending on one's point of view), to the highly impersonal account of structural responses to market forces and technology, and finally to more complex narratives that connect the rise of corporations to broad social and political contexts—intersected with another kind of history that was evolving at the same time but in very different ways: labor history. Like business history, labor history after World War II developed its own professional organization and journal. Inspired and supported by

---

[18]David F. Noble, *America by Design: Science, Technology, and the Rise of Corporate Capitalism* (New York, 1977); see also his *Forces of Production: A Social History of Industrial Automation* (New York, 1984).

[19]James Livingston, "The Social Analysis of Economic History and Theory: Conjectures on Late Nineteenth-Century American Development," *American Historical Review* 92 (February 1987): 69–97.

the New Deal and the great mobilization of industrial workers by the C.I.O. in the 1930s, labor history became an important subfield in most major history departments by the 1960s. Like business historians, labor historians' political leanings were quite evident—situating them usually on the left wing of American politics. Likely to think of businessmen as robber barons, labor historians portrayed labor leaders as democratic heroes. But labor history intrinsically tended toward social history and tales of collective, rather than individual, struggle.

Well before the Second World War, John R. Commons and his Wisconsin School of labor economics had laid the groundwork for the emergence of labor history. With his colleagues at the University of Wisconsin, Commons published a massive four-volume *History of Labor in the United States* (New York, 1918–1935) that set the terms of scholarly research for several generations. Distilled in the work of Selig Perlman,[20] Commons's most acute student and later his collaborator, the narrative of American labor history was shaped by several key elements. First, it was institutional: the unit of study was the labor union and the central question was how and why the modern "pure-and-simple" (or "bread-and-butter") trade union emerged, as opposed to a broad socialist movement for the fundamental reform of capitalism. Second, it was workplace-oriented: the subject of study was the evolution of wages and working conditions. Except for labor's piecemeal efforts to influence politics, little of the world outside the workplace mattered to Commons and his followers. Third, it was progressive in two senses. It was politically progressive in that it was pro-labor, endorsing the right of workers to collective bargaining and the responsibility of government to regulate economic relations. And it was historiographically Progressive[21] in that it saw labor history as a maturation from confused nineteenth-century attempts at utopian reform to sensible trade unionism in the early twentieth century. The latter trait made Wisconsin school labor history sometimes predictable. Historians who adopted this approach saw American "realities" overcoming ideology: the grand socialist strategies that some immigrants brought with them from Europe, like the Jacksonian and Populist fantasies harbored by some American-born workers, were no match for the promise of middle-class prosperity and the likelihood of cumulative piecemeal gains at the bargaining table and the ballot box.[22]

---

[20]Selig Perlman, *Theory of the Labor Movement* (New York, 1928).

[21]See Chapter 1.

[22]The Marxist historian Philip S. Foner produced an even more massive survey of labor history in six volumes, *History of the Labor Movement in the United States* (New York, 1947–83). Ironically, it is no less institutional or progressive than that of Commons, merely reversing the latter's interpretive judgments: early "utopians" are here judged to be proto-revolutionary; narrowly job-conscious workers with middle-class aspirations appear deluded, not sensible; the truly progressive adaptation to modern industrial conditions is socialism not reformist capitalism, etc.

Whatever its limitations, the Wisconsin School approach to labor history yielded a host of carefully wrought studies of labor relations and unionization in a wide variety of industries.[23] By the 1960s, these institutional studies had reached a very high level of professional polish and intellectual richness.[24] They showed how changes in technology and the national economy, along with workforce recruitment and composition, determined the evolution of union structure and leadership.[25] However, the pathbreaking book that took the study of unions beyond the workplace was David Brody's *Steelworkers in America: The Nonunion Era* (Cambridge, Mass., 1960). With admirable economy and graceful prose, Brody told the story of the organizational achievements and failures of the iron and steel workers, but his narrative encompassed much more: the immigrant experience, the cultural world of the skilled industrial artisan, the allure of new technology to managers and its threat to workers, and the meaning of politics (from local to national) for workers in company towns and big cities—in eras of depression, expansion, and world war. It was a remarkable achievement, but it was not the only one.

The most influential of a growing number of new labor historians were David Montgomery and Herbert Gutman. With the work of these two scholars, clearly, a "New Labor History" had arrived, but it did so by an indirect route that is worth briefly tracing. Even in the heyday of the institutional approach to labor history, a few American historians had been telling a different story. Among the most noteworthy was Norman Ware, whose work departed significantly from the Commons-Perlman narrative. For Ware, industrialization was a revolution not just in production and worker-management relations but in society and culture. Workers were not just wage-earners, Ware insisted, but citizens who valued their "status and independence." The industrial revolution was a "social revolution in which sovereignty in economic affairs passed from the community as a whole into the keeping of a

---

[23]For a fine overview of the historiography of the Commons School and the "New Labor History," see David Brody, "The Old Labor History and the New: In Search of an American Working Class," *Labor History* 20 (Winter, 1979): 511–526; David Montgomery, "To Study the People: The American Working Class," Ibid., 21 (Fall, 1980): 485–512. See also Melvyn Dubofsky, *Industrialism and the American Worker, 1860–1925,* 2/e (Arlington Heights, Ill. 1985).

[24]See, for example, Robert A. Christie, *Empire in Wood: A History of the United Brotherhood of Carpenters and Joiners of America* (Ithaca, N.Y., 1956), and Robert Ozanne, *A Century of Labor-Management Relations at McCormick and International Harvester* (Madison, Wis., 1967).

[25]An unusual work in the Wisconsin tradition is Gerald Grob, *Workers and Utopia: A Study of Ideological Conflict in the American Labor Movement, 1865–1900* (Evanston, Ill., 1961). Although Grob adhered to the Commons thesis, his attention to the intellectual history of the labor movement proved fruitful in connecting institutional history to the wider currents of politics and culture in nineteenth-century America.

special class."[26] Ware's work vivified Marx's original contribution to history: his explanation of the significance of class conflict in shaping the entire range of human experience, particularly during the era of industrial capitalism. It was precisely this insight which came rushing into American labor history from across the Atlantic in the 1960s.

The development of British neo-Marxist social history may be one of the signal events in modern historiography. In the work of historians Eric Hobsbawm, George Rude, Brian Harrison, and Gareth Stedman-Jones (and the literary historian Raymond Williams), but most momentously in E. P. Thompson's *The Making of the English Working Class* (London, 1963), Marxist analysis of history was transformed to encompass the lives of human beings imbedded in webs of culture and society. This history was therefore never static, impenetrable, or finished. The story Thompson told was of the "making" and "remaking" of class experience and class consciousness in the face of changing economic compulsions, political opportunities, cultural traditions, local developments, even individual imagination and heroism. From such a perspective, the building of labor unions is only one important feature of the lives of working-class people caught up in the industrial revolution. It was precisely in changing the subject from the history of unions to the history of the industrial working class that the historiographical equivalent of "the British invasion" had its greatest impact in the United States.

Inspired by the English neo-Marxists and a few native scholars, American labor history took off in the 1960s. The New Labor History also drew energy from the contemporaneous New Left critique of American inequality and from a wave of labor militancy that sprang up in American factories, fueled in part by the rebellious energies of the baby boom generation of workers. Works of labor history became studies of urban development, ethnic conflict, political culture, family organization, and popular culture as much as studies of labor organization and workplace struggle. Thus, in David Montgomery's seminal *Beyond Equality*, working-class radicals appear on the page of history already deeply engaged in the struggle for equality. Inheritors of the American republican tradition of self-government, they were born political. Workers who fought politically against the ascendance of capitalism were not romantic and immature utopians. They were perfectly capable of acting like pure-and-simple craft unionists, fighting for better wages and benefits, but at the same time they could assume the mantle of utopian reformers, opposing the National Bank, campaigning in favor of the Homestead Act, or organizing to build a cooperative

---

[26]Norman Ware, *The Industrial Worker, 1840–1860* (Boston, 1924), pp. x–xi; see also *The Labor Movement in the United States, 1860–1895* (New York, 1929). Another historian who departed somewhat from the Commons-Perlman approach to create an original interpretation of the earliest years of American labor was Richard B. Morris, in *Government and Labor in Early America* (New York, 1946).

commonwealth. Such reform-minded unionists were fully engaged citizens, "attempting to impart to the emerging industrial order some values other than purely commercial ones, to impose moral order on the market economy."[27] Montgomery's book connected the early history of the trade union movement to the legacy of Revolutionary republicanism and to the "new birth of freedom" that was the deepest meaning of the Civil War. In so doing, *Beyond Equality* planted labor history squarely in the center of the historical map.

In a different way, Herbert Gutman opened broad new avenues of study for labor history, or the "history of the working class," as it was coming to be called.[28] Gutman's findings appeared in bits and pieces, but cumulatively they were an impressive achievement.[29] In his most important early essay, "The Workers' Search for Power,"[30] he insisted that workers had never thought of themselves simply as wage-earners but also as "locals" who sustained ties of kinship and community with neighbors who were mostly farmers, shopkeepers, professionals, or small businessmen. Thus, workers' broad and fuzzy conception of class was not, as Commons thought, a sign of immaturity or delusion, but a useful way to understand a world in which bonds of interest and fellowship were not forged exclusively (or primarily) in the workplace. In the early industrial era, indeed, the fight against monopoly was often a community affair, with non-workers supporting strikes and joining political movements to curb corporate power. Of course, at other times and in other places, the bonds of community were insidious. Local workers and their neighbors sometimes united against foreigners or blacks brought in to work (often to break strikes) in mines and factories, using vigilante tactics to temporarily restore the aggrieved community's sense of economic justice.[31]

In his most synthetic essay, "Work, Culture, and Society in Industrializing America," published in 1973, Gutman made a bid to turn the history of the working class into the history of America.[32] In both its

---

[27]David Montgomery, *Beyond Equality: Labor and the Radical Republicans, 1862–1872* (New York, 1967), p. 445.

[28]The appearance in the mid-1970s of a new journal, *International Labor and Working-Class History*, confirmed this new ambition.

[29]Some of these are collected in *Work, Culture, and Society in Industrializing America* (New York, 1977).

[30]Herbert G. Gutman, "The Workers' Search for Power," originally published in 1970, can be found in his *Power and Culture: Essays on the American Working Class* (New York, 1987).

[31]This tendency erupted into virulent racism in California, as documented in Alexander Saxton's *The Indispensable Enemy: Labor and the Anti-Chinese Movement in California* (Berkeley, 1971).

[32]Herbert G. Gutman, "Work, Culture, and Society in Industrializing America, 1815–1919," *American Historical Review* 78 (June 1973): 531–588; reprinted in *Work, Culture, and Society in Industrializing America: Essays in American Working-Class and Social History* (New York, 1977).

success and its failures, that essay marked a turning point in the evolution of labor history. In Gutman's story, modern history is a chronicle of the transformation of preindustrial people into industrial men and women and of their cultures into industrial cultures. Preindustrial people lived in a world, as E. P. Thompson had shown, marked by flexible notions of time and personal relationships within small communal boundaries. Industrialization imposed clock-time and repetitive routines on workers, who now sustained connections to their work and to one another that were impersonal, functional, and governed by the cash nexus. People were also ripped from their traditional settings and sent careening across the countryside or even the globe. While Thompson described industrialization in England as complex but of limited duration, Gutman portrayed the process in America as a rolling and overlapping series of encounters, conflicts, and transformations, from the early-nineteenth to the twentieth century, involving one ethnic group after another.

Dozens of young historians from the 1960s onward exhibited the powerful influence of Gutman's and Montgomery's work. Bruce Laurie showed how class, ethnicity, and religion intersected to shape the possibilities of labor power in Jacksonian-era Philadelphia. Alan Dawley and Paul Faler studied the fate of artisan shoe workers and their community in Lynn, Massachusetts, under the assault of mechanization and industrial consolidation. Roy Rosenzweig and Francis G. Couvares explored the ways in which an evolving mass culture interacted with ethnic or workplace conflicts to shape class consciousness and class relations in Worcester, Massachusetts, and Pittsburgh, Pennsylvania, respectively. Thomas Dublin on Lowell, Massachusetts, and Christine Stansell on New York, made clear not only that female labor was central to the history of industrialization and unionization, but also that women's history, no less than the history of race, ethnicity, politics, and popular culture, was indispensable to a proper understanding of class formation and class conflict in the United States.[33]

These and a host of other works usually focused on single communities over a fairly limited span of years. But approaches that highlighted

---

[33]Bruce Laurie, *Working People of Philadelphia, 1800–1850* (Philadelphia, 1980); Alan Dawley, *Class and Community: The Industrial Revolution in Lynn* (Cambridge, Mass., 1976); Paul G. Faler, *Mechanics and Manufacturers in the Early Industrial Revolution: Lynn, Massachusetts, 1780–1860* (Albany, 1981); Roy Rosenzweig, *Eight Hours for What We Will: Workers and Leisure in an Industrial City, 1870–1920* (New York, 1983); Francis G. Couvares, *The Remaking of Pittsburgh: Class and Culture in an Industrializing City, 1877–1919* (Albany, 1984); Thomas Dublin, *Women and Work: The Transformation of Work and Community in Lowell, Massachusetts, 1826–1860* (New York, 1979); Christine Stansell, *City of Women: Sex and Class in New York, 1789–1860* (New York, 1986). See also Michael H. Frisch and Daniel J. Walkowitz, eds., *Working-Class America: Essays on Labor, Community, and American Society* (Urbana, Ill., 1983); Daniel J. Leab, ed., *The Labor History Reader* (Urbana, Ill., 1985); and Herbert G. Gutman and Donald H. Bell, *The New England Working Class and the New Labor History* (Urbana, Ill., 1987).

the local and particular made generalization across cases difficult. While many labor and social historians eschewed calls for "synthesis," increasing numbers of them acknowledged the need to develop connections both among their numerous findings and between them and the works of political, intellectual, and other historians.[34] Some historians began to question the only rubric available for synthesis: the Thompson-Gutman narrative of transformation from preindustrial to industrial culture. In an incisive critique, Daniel T. Rodgers suggested that this narrative oversimplified both the nature of capitalism and the complexity of culture.[35] When stripped of its Marxist touches, Rodgers argued, "the hypothesis of initial shock and gradual acculturation" that is at the heart of Gutman's story looks very much like the "modernization" thesis that liberal and conservative social scientists have employed for decades, and not unlike the progressive tale of the Wisconsin School. Rodgers reminded readers that "all men in all cultures are born premodern," and that "working-class cultures are not made once and set in motion but must be refashioned with each generation." In the end, therefore, "traditional-to-modern," "preindustrial-to-industrial," however attractive a rubric, overgeneralizes the past and cannot in itself become the basis of a new synthesis of American history.

A number of historians in the 1980s and 1990s found other ways to connect local studies with broad themes in American history. In *Chants Democratic*, Sean Wilentz turned the history of labor in New York City from 1788 to 1850 into an interpretation of the fate of the republican heritage in the Jacksonian era. Exploring similar themes, Leon Fink showed that the Knights of Labor struggled to adapt the republican heritage to the class realities of post–Civil War America.[36] For the twentieth century, Ronald Edsforth and Lizabeth Cohen showed that working-class Americans in Flint, Michigan, and Chicago, Illinois, respectively, could be both militant unionists *and* job-conscious employees, both advocates of the reform of unbridled capitalism *and* ardent consumers, both "ethnics" *and* "Americans."[37]

---

[34]One attempt to write a popular (and populist) narrative based on the new labor history is Bruce Levine et al., eds., *Who Built America? Working People and the Nation's Economy, Politics, Culture, and Society* (New York, 1989), published under the auspices of the American Social History Project, which was directed by Gutman until his death in 1985.

[35]Daniel T. Rodgers, "Tradition, Modernity, and the American Industrial Workers: Reflections and a Critique," *Journal of Interdisciplinary History* 7 (1977): 655–681.

[36]Sean Wilentz, *Chants Democratic: New York City and the Rise of the American Working Class, 1788–1850* (New York, 1984); Leon Fink, *Workingmen's Democracy: The Knights of Labor and American Politics* (Urbana, Ill., 1983).

[37]Ronald Edsforth, *Class Conflict and Cultural Consensus: The Making of a Mass Consumer Society in Flint, Michigan* (New Brunswick, N.J., 1987); Lizabeth Cohen, *Making a New Deal: Industrial Workers in Chicago, 1919–1939* (Cambridge, Mass., 1990).

Biography also bloomed as a way to make particular stories speak to larger themes in American history. Nick Salvatore brilliantly narrated the life of Eugene V. Debs, showing that indisputably middle-American roots gave issue to a class-conscious "Citizen and Socialist." Nelson Lichtenstein made the life of Walter Reuther, perhaps the greatest labor leader of the period from the late 1930s through the 1960s, speak to every important issue that faced the United States through the Depression, World War II, and the Cold War.[38]

In works published in the 1990s, Bruce Laurie and Walter Licht took up the challenge of writing historical syntheses that spanned the whole nineteenth century experience of industrialization. Among its other virtues, Laurie's book offered a convincing explanation of the emergence of what he dubbed "prudential unionism."[39] Not quite the Progressive achievement that Commons would have considered it, but neither the sell-out that radical historians of the 1960s sometimes made it seem, Sam Gompers' trade union movement was limited by many factors, internal and external; among the most important was the repressive power of American corporations and business-oriented state and federal governments. These powers never hesitated to use coercive force to keep unions from becoming anything other than "pure-and-simple" collective bargaining institutions, i.e., from evolving into broader class-based or populist uprisings. Licht's work, from which the second reading in this unit is drawn, similarly makes clear that the tremendous power wielded by capital, including the power of violence, significantly shaped the labor union (and working-class life generally) throughout the nineteenth century.

The intersection of women's history and labor history has provided another opportunity for historians to reconceive the narrative of industrial history. Monographic studies of women workers in particular industries have proliferated in the last several decades,[40] but in 1982 Alice Kessler-Harris encompassed the entire span of American

---

[38]Nick Salvatore, *Eugene V. Debs: Citizen and Socialist* (Urbana, Ill., 1972); Nelson Lichtenstein, *The Most Dangerous Man in Detroit: Walter Reuther and the Fate of American Labor* (New York, 1995); see also Melvin Dubofsky and Warren Van Tine, *John L. Lewis: A Biography* (Ann Arbor, Mich., 1969).

[39]Bruce Laurie, *Artisans into Workers: Labor in Nineteenth-Century America* (New York, 1989).

[40]Excellent case studies include Susan Porter Benson, *Counter Cultures: Saleswomen, Managers, and Customers in American Department Stores, 1890–1940* (Urbana, Ill., 1986); Nancy Schrom Dye, *As Equals and as Sisters: Feminism, the Labor Movement, and the Women's Trade Union League of New York* (New York, 1980); and Vicki L. Ruiz, *Cannery Women, Cannery Lives: Mexican Women, Unionization, and the California Food Processing Industry, 1930–1950* (Albuquerque, 1987). See also Ruth Milkman, ed., *Women, Work, and Protest: A Century of U.S. Women's Labor History* (Boston, 1985). On gender analysis in labor history, see Ava Baron, "Gender and Labor History: Learning from the Past, Looking to the Future," in her *Work Engendered: Toward a New History of American Labor* (Ithaca, N.Y., 1991).

history in *Out to Work*. She took as her theme the process whereby "wage work simultaneously sustained the patriarchal family and set in motion the tensions that seem now to be breaking it down."[41] In a recent collection of essays and documents in "the history of American workers," Eileen Boris and Nelson Lichtenstein argue that the history of women and the history of labor (as, also, the history of race and ethnicity) are inextricably intertwined and indispensable to an understanding of the major problems in American history.[42]

To some young historians in the 1990s, labor history seemed to position class as the most important unit of analysis, and white male workers as the most important subject of study. Some of these looked to an approach that bid to become a new synthesis of labor and race history, under the rubric of "whiteness studies." In *The Wages of Whiteness*, David Roediger argued that the American labor movement was fundamentally shaped by racism.[43] The trade union was one among many institutions designed to award limited benefits to white Americans in return for their collaboration in reinforcing the racial dividing line. The trade union's most time-honored values and practices—e.g., seniority and solidarity—were designed to reinforce the privileges of whites (and of men). Thus, "first hired, last fired" clauses in contracts protected white, male jobs and sacrificed black and female ones; and defending the union against strikebreakers became a way to keep white men employed and blacks and females unemployed. Even the hallowed heritage of republicanism, which many historians had sought to claim as labor's own, was basically a legacy of white men's democracy.

In the 1990s, labor history has increasingly merged with the history of women, of immigrants, of African Americans, and of urban politics, to name only a few subjects. That fewer young historians identify themselves as labor historians, as opposed to social historians, historians of industrialization, or historians of race and gender, may in fact be a tribute to a field that has always insisted that the history of the industrial revolution and its human consequences is the central story of the modern world. In similar, though possibly less dramatic

---

[41]Alice Kessler-Harris, *Out to Work: A History of Wage-Earning Women in the United States* (New York, 1982), p. ix. See Elizabeth H. Pleck, "Two Worlds in One: Work and Family," *Journal of Social History* 10 (Winter 1976): 178–189, on the cross-fertilization of labor history and family history; also Tamara K. Hareven, *Family Time and Industrial Time: The Relationship between Family and Work in a New England Industrial Community* (Cambridge, 1982); Jacqueline Jones, *Labor of Love, Labor of Sorrow: Black Women, Work, and the Family from Slavery to the Present* (New York, 1985); and Jacqueline Dowd Hall et al., *Like a Family: The Making of a Southern Cotton Mill World* (Chapel Hill, N.C., 1987).

[42]Eileen Boris and Nelson Lichtenstein, eds., *Main Problems in the History of American Workers* (Lexington, Mass., 1991).

[43]See Chapter 5, p. 148n.

ways, business history has stretched to include the history of technology, managerial and workplace cultures, and the rise of corporate capitalism. Both business history and labor history have broadened to address some of the most challenging questions about the nature of modern industrial society. What are the sources of innovation and prosperity? Is pursuit of efficiency and profit a good in itself, or should the engine of capitalist growth be harnessed by government to more egalitarian ends? Have the purposes of labor unions been limited to collective bargaining for bread-and-butter issues, or implicated inevitably in broader political movements for social justice and equality? Does capitalist society fundamentally create and depend upon class inequality? How is class inequality intertwined with racial, ethnic, and gender inequalities, and what kinds of strategies have succeeded or failed in reducing those inequalities? These and similar questions will continue to be asked by scholars who call themselves business historians and labor historians, as well as by those who have been influenced by these historians' best work over the last several decades.

ALFRED D. CHANDLER, JR.

ALFRED D. CHANDLER, JR. (1918–   ) is Straus Professor of Business History at the Harvard Graduate School of Business Administration. He is the author of a number of books in American business history, including Henry Varnum Poor *(1956),* Strategy and Structure *(1969), and the Pulitzer Prize–winning* The Visible Hand *(1977).*

For a paper on the historical role of business in America to provide a solid foundation for discussions of the present and future, it must examine a number of questions: Who were the American businessmen? How did they come to go into business? How were they trained? How broad was their outlook? And, of even more importance, what did they do? How did they carry out the basic economic functions of production, distribution, transportation, and finance? How was the work of these businessmen coordinated so that the American economic system operated as an integrated whole? Finally, how did these men and the system within which they worked adapt to fundamental changes in population, to the opening of new lands, resources, and markets, and to technological developments that transformed markets, sources of supply, and means of production and distribution? The answers to these questions, as limited as they may be, should help to make more understandable the present activities and future capabilities of American business.

The Colonial Merchant

The merchant dominated the simple rural economy of the colonial period. By the eighteenth century he considered himself and was considered by others to be a businessman. His economic functions differentiated him from the farmers who produced crops and the artisans who made goods. Although the farmers and artisans occasionally carried on business transactions, they spent most of their time working on the land or in the shop. The merchant, on the other hand, spent nearly all his time in handling transactions involved in carrying goods through the process of production and distribution, including their transportation and finance.

The colonial merchant was an all-purpose, non-specialized man of

Alfred D. Chandler, Jr., "The Role of Business in the United States: A Historical Survey," *Daedalus* 98 (Winter 1969): 23–40. Reprinted by permission of *Daedalus,* Journal of the American Academy of Arts and Science, Boston, Mass.

business. He was a wholesaler and a retailer, an importer and an ex-porter. In association with other merchants he built and owned the ships that carried goods to and from his town. He financed and insured the transportation and distribution of these goods. At the same time, he provided the funds needed by the planter and the artisan to finance the production of crops and goods. The merchant, operating on local, inter-regional, and international levels, adapted the economy to the relatively small population and technological changes of the day and to shifts in supply and demand resulting from international tensions.

These men of business tended to recruit their successors from their own family and kinship group. Family loyalties were important, indeed essential, in carrying on business in distant areas during a pe-riod when communication between ports was so slow and uncertain. Able young clerks or sea captains might be brought into the family firm, but sons and sons-in-law were preferred. Trading internationally as well as locally, the merchants acquired broader horizons than the farmer, artisan, and day laborer. Only a few of the great landowners and leading lawyers knew the larger world. It was the colonial mer-chants who, allied with lawyers from the seaport towns and with the Virginia planters, encouraged the Revolution, brought about the ratifi-cation of the Constitution, and then set up the new government in the last decade of the eighteenth century.

The Rise of the Wholesaler, 1800–1850

During the first half of the nineteenth century, although the American economy remained primarily agrarian and commercial, it grew vigor-ously. The scope of the economy expanded as the nation moved west-ward into the rich Mississippi Valley, and as increasing migration from Europe still further enlarged its population. Even more important to American economic expansion were the technological innovations that occurred in manufacturing in Great Britain. Without the new ma-chines of the Industrial Revolution, the westward movement in the United States and the migration to its shores would have been slower. These innovations reshaped the British textile industry, creating a new demand for cotton from the United States. Before the invention of the water frame, the spinning jenny, the mule, and then the power loom, cotton had never been grown commercially in the United States, but by 1800 it had become the country's major export. The new planta-tions in turn provided markets for food grown on the smaller farms in both the Northwest and Southwest. The growth of eastern commer-cial cities and the development of the textile industry in New England and the middle states enlarged that market still further. The titanic struggle between Great Britain and Napoleon obscured the significance of these economic developments, but shortly after 1815 the economy's new orientation became clear.

The merchants who continued to act as economic integrators had the largest hand in building this new high-volume, regionally specialized, agrarian-commercial system. The merchants of Philadelphia, Baltimore, and New York took over the task of exporting cotton, lumber, and foodstuffs and of importing textiles, hardware, drugs, and other goods from Great Britain and the Continent. Those in the southern coastal and river ports played the same role in exporting cotton and importing finished goods to and from the eastern entrepôts; those in the growing western towns sent out local crops and brought in manufactured goods in a similar way. At first the western trade went via rivers of the Mississippi Valley and New Orleans. Later it began to be transported east and west through the Erie Canal and along the Great Lakes. To meet the needs of the expanding trade, the merchants, particularly those of the larger eastern cities, developed new forms of commercial banking to finance the movement of crops, set up packet lines on "the Atlantic Shuttle" between New York and Liverpool to speed the movement of news and imports, founded specialized insurance companies, and helped to organize and finance the new canals and turnpikes that improved transportation between them and their customers.

These innovations enabled the merchants to handle still more business, and the high-volume trade in turn forced the merchants to alter their functions and, indeed, their whole way of life. They began to specialize, becoming primarily wholesalers or retailers, importers or exporters. They came to concentrate on a single line of goods—dry goods, wet goods, hardware, iron, drugs, groceries or cotton, wheat or produce. Some became specialists in banking and insurance and spent their time acting as managers for these new financial corporations.

Of the new specialists, the wholesalers played the most influential role, taking the place of the colonial merchants as the primary integrators and adaptors of the economy. More than the farmers or the retailers, the wholesalers were responsible for directing the flow of cotton, corn, wheat, and lumber from the West to the East and to Europe. More than the manufacturers, they handled the marketing of finished goods that went from eastern and European industrial centers to the southern and western states.

Moreover, the wholesalers financed the long-term growth of the economy. Enthusiastic promoters of canals, turnpikes, and then railroads, they provided most of the local capital for these undertakings. They pressured the state and municipal legislatures and councils (on which they or their legally trained associates often sat) to issue bonds or to guarantee bonds of private corporations building transportation enterprises. At times they even persuaded the state to build and operate transport facilities.

The wholesalers also encouraged the adoption of the new technology in manufacturing. In Boston, the Appletons, the Jacksons, and the Cabots financed the new textile mills of Lowell and Lawrence. In New York, the Phelps and the Dodges started the brass industry in the Connecticut Valley, while in Philadelphia and Baltimore wholesalers like Nathan Trotter and Enoch Pratt financed the growing Pennsylvania iron industry. They not only raised the funds for plants and machinery, but also supplied a large amount of the cash and credit that the new manufacturers needed as working capital to pay for supplies and labor.

Although the wholesalers made important contributions to early-nineteenth-century economic life, they played a less dominant role in the economy than had the colonial merchant of the eighteenth century. The economic system had become too complex—involving too many units of production, distribution, transportation, and finance—for one group to supervise local, inter-regional, and international flows. Nonetheless, the wholesalers had more influence in setting prices, managing the flow of goods, and determining the amount and direction of investment than had other groups—the farmers, manufacturers, retailers, and bankers.

As the economy expanded, the recruitment of businessmen became more open than it had been in the colonial period. At the same time, the outlook of even the most broad-gauged businessmen grew narrower. Family and family ties became less essential, although they could still be a useful source of capital. Businessmen began to place more value on personal qualities, such as aggressiveness, drive, and self-reliance. Nor did one need any lengthy training or education to set up a shop as a wholesaler. Because of their increasing functional specialization, this new breed of wholesalers rarely had the international outlook of the colonial merchants. Not surprisingly, they and the lawyers and politicians who represented them saw their needs in sectional rather than national terms—as did so many Americans in the years immediately prior to the Civil War.

The Rise of the Manufacturer Before 1900

By mid-century the American agrarian and commercial economy had begun to be transformed into the most productive industrial system in the world. The migration of Americans into cities became more significant in this transformation than the final settling of the western frontier. Immigration from Europe reached new heights, with most of the new arrivals staying in the cities of the East and the old Northwest. By 1900, therefore, the rate of growth of the rural areas had leveled off. From then on, the nation's population growth would come almost wholly in its cities.

The second half of the nineteenth century was a time of great technological change—the age of steam and iron, the factory and the rail-road. The steam railroad and the steamship came quickly to dominate transportation. In 1849 the United States had only six thousand miles of railroad and even fewer miles of canals, but by 1884 its railroad cor-porations operated 202,000 miles of track, or 43 per cent of the total mileage in the world. In 1850 the factory—with its power-driven ma-chinery and its permanent working force—was a rarity outside the tex-tile and iron industries, but by 1880 the Bureau of the Census reported that 80 per cent of the three million workers in mechanized industry labored in factories. And nearly all these new plants were powered by steam rather than by water.

America's factories made a vital contribution to the nation's eco-nomic growth. By 1894 the value of the output of American industry equalled that of the combined output of the United Kingdom, France, and Germany. In the next twenty years American production tripled, and by the outbreak of World War I the United States was producing more than a third of the world's industrial goods.

As manufacturing expanded, the wholesaler continued for many years to play a significant role in the economy. The period up to 1873 was one of increasing demand and rising prices. The manufacturers, concentrating on building or expanding their new factories, were more than happy to have the wholesalers supply them with their raw and semifinished materials and to market their finished goods. In addition, wholesalers continued to provide manufacturers with capital for build-ing plants, purchasing equipment and supplies, and paying wages.

After the recession of 1873, however, the manufacturers began to replace the wholesaler as the man who had the most to say about coor-dinating the flow of goods through the economy and about adapting the economy to population and technological changes. The shift came for three reasons. First, the existing wholesale network of hundreds of thousands of small firms had difficulty in handling efficiently the growing output of the factories. Secondly, the manufacturer no longer needed the wholesaler as a source of capital. After a generation of pro-duction, he was able to finance plant and equipment out of retained profits. Moreover, until 1850 the commercial banking system had been almost wholly involved in financing the movement of agricultural products, but about mid-century it began to provide working capital for the industrialist. Commercial banks also began to provide funds for plant and equipment, particularly to new manufacturing enterprises.

The third and most pervasive reason why the manufacturer came to a position of dominance resulted from the nature of factory produc-tion itself. This much more efficient form of manufacturing so swiftly increased the output of goods that supply soon outran demand. From the mid-1870's to the mid-1890's, prices fell sharply. Moreover, the large investment required to build a factory made it costly to shut down and even more expensive to move into other forms of business activity. As prices fell, the manufacturers organized to control prices and the flow of goods within their industries. If the wholesalers would and could help them in achieving such control, the manufacturers welcomed their cooperation. If not, they did it themselves. In most cases, the industrialist came to play a larger role than the wholesalers in integrating the economy.

The wholesaler was pushed aside in transportation before he was in manufacturing. Railroad construction costs were high, and after 1849 when railroad expansion began on a large scale, the local merchants simply could not supply the necessary capital. Modern Wall Street came into being during the 1850's to meet the need for funds. By 1860 the investment banker had replaced the wholesaler as the primary supplier of funds to American railroads.

In the 1850's and 1860's the railroads also captured many of the merchant's functions. They took over freight forwarding in large towns and eliminated the merchant by handling through traffic in many commercial centers along the main routes west and south. Indeed, during the 1860's the railroads had absorbed most of the fast freight and express companies developed earlier by the wholesalers in order to use the new rail transportation. By the 1870's the coordination of the flow of most inter-regional transportation in the United States had come under the direction of the traffic departments of a few large railroads.

The first manufacturers to move into the wholesalers' domain were those who found that the wholesaler could not meet their special needs. These were of two types. The makers of new technologically complex and relatively expensive durable products quickly realized that wholesalers were unable to handle the initial demonstration to the consumer, provide consumer credit, or ensure the repair and servicing of the products sold. Thus manufacturers of agricultural implements, sewing machines, typewriters, cash registers, carriages, bicycles, or, most important of all, electrical machinery and equipment created national and even international marketing organizations well before the turn of the century. So did the second type, the processors of perishable goods requiring refrigeration, quick transportation, and careful storage for their distribution—fresh meat, beer, bananas, and cigarettes.

Once the pioneers of both types of enterprises—the McCormicks, the Remingtons, George Westinghouse and Charles Coffin, the Swifts and Armours, the Pabsts and Schlitzes, Andrew Preston and James B. Duke—had created their widespread distribution networks, they began again to eliminate the wholesaler by doing their own purchasing. They could not run the risk of stopping complex fabricating or assembling processes because they lacked critical parts or materials. Some integrated backwards even further, doing their own purchasing by building or buying factories to manufacture parts, controlling their own iron, steel, or lumber, or obtaining their own refrigerated cars and ships.

The manufacturers who produced standard commodities that might be distributed easily through the existing wholesaler network were slower to move into wholesaling. Even though the pioneering firms were demonstrating the economies resulting from a combination of mass production and mass distribution, most manufacturers had to be pushed rather than enticed into a strategy of vertical integration. They did so only after they failed to meet the oppressive pressure of falling prices by the more obvious methods of price control through trade associations, cartels, and other loose combinations.

The railroads pioneered in developing ways to control prices in the face of excess capacity and heavy fixed costs. During the 1870's, the railroads formed regional associations, of which the Eastern Trunk Line Association was the most powerful. By the 1880's, however, the railroad presidents and traffic managers admitted defeat. The associations could only be effective if their rulings were enforced in courts of law, but their pleas for legalized pooling went unheard. Indeed, the Interstate Commerce Act of 1887 specifically declared pooling illegal. As a result, the American railroad network became consolidated into large "self-sustaining," centrally managed regional systems. By 1900 most of American land transportation was handled by about twenty-five great systems informally allied in six groupings.

Where the railroads had hoped for legalized pooling, the manufacturers sought other ways of obtaining firmer legal control over the factories in their industries. They began personally to purchase stock in one another's companies. After 1882 when the Standard Oil Company devised the trust as a way of acquiring legal control of an industry, companies began to adopt that device. The holding company quickly superseded the trust as a more effective and inexpensive way of controlling price and production after 1889, when New Jersey passed a general incorporation law that permitted one company to hold stock in many others. The Supreme Court's interpretations of the Sherman Antitrust Act (1890) encouraged further consolidation in manufacturing. Court decisions discouraged loose combinations of manufacturers (or railroads) in any form, but (at least until 1911) appeared to permit consolidation of competing firms through a holding company if that company came to administer its activities under a single centralized management.

In many cases these new consolidations embarked on a strategy of vertical integration. Where the railroads formed "self-sustaining" systems to assure control of traffic over primary commercial routes, the manufacturers attempted to assure the uninterrupted flow of goods into and out of their production and processing plants. John D. Rockefeller and his associates at Standard Oil were the first of the combinations to adopt this strategy. The Standard Oil Trust had been formed after associations in the petroleum industry had proven to be, in Rockefeller's words, "ropes of sand." Legal control of the industry was followed by administrative consolidation of its refineries under a single centralized management. In the mid-1880's, the trust began to build its own distribution network of tank farms and wholesaling offices. Finally, after enlarging its buying organization, it moved in the late-1880's into the taking of crude oil out of the ground.

The examples of Standard Oil, the Swifts, the McCormicks, and others who had by-passed the wholesaler, the rulings of the Supreme Court, the memories of twenty years of declining prices resulted between 1898 and 1902 in the greatest merger movement in American history. Combinations, usually in the form of holding companies, occurred in nearly all major American industries. Holding companies then were often transformed into operating companies. After manufacturing facilities were centralized under a single management, the new consolidated enterprise integrated forwards and backwards.

At the same time, retailers who began to appreciate the potential of mass markets and economies of scale also moved to eliminate the wholesalers—although they did so in a more restricted way than the manufacturers. The mail order houses (Sears, Roebuck and Montgomery Ward), which turned to the rural markets, and the department and chain stores, which looked to the growing cities, began to buy directly from the manufacturers. By the turn of the century, some large retailers had even bought into manufacturing firms. As a result, wholesalers' decisions were of less significance to the operation of the economy than they had been fifty years earlier. Far more important were the decisions of the manufacturers who had combined, consolidated, and integrated their operations and the few giant retailers who had adopted somewhat the same strategy.

As manufacturers replaced wholesalers as key coordinators in the national economy, they became the popular symbol of American business enterprise. The industrialists and the railroad leaders were indeed the reality as well as the symbol of business power in the Gilded Age. The recruitment of this new dominant business group remained open, at least for a generation. As had been true earlier for the wholesaler, aggressiveness, drive, and access to capital or credit were prerequisites for success. Lineage or specialized learning were less important, but some technological knowledge was an advantage. Although the manufacturers' horizons were more national and less regional than the wholesalers', they came to view the national scene from the perspective of their particular industry. They and their representatives in Washington tended to take positions on the major issues of the day— tariff, currency, immigration, and the regulation of business—from an industrial rather than a sectional or regional viewpoint.

It was not long, however, before the needs of the manufacturers and their response to these needs altered the recruitment and training of the nation's most powerful businessmen. The increasingly high investment required for large-scale production made the entry of new men and firms more difficult. The emergence of the vertically integrated enterprise limited opportunities still further. By 1900 it was becoming easier to rise to positions of business influence by moving through the new centralized managements than by starting a business enterprise of one's own. This pattern was already clear in the railroads, the nation's first modern business bureaucracies.

The Dominance of the Manager Since 1900

Although the twentieth century was to become the age of the manager, the growing significance of the manager's role in the operation of the American economy was not immediately apparent. Until the 1920's manufacturers and their assistants concentrated on rounding out their integrated enterprises, creating the internal structures and methods necessary to operate these business empires, and employing the managers necessary to staff them.

At first, external conditions did not seriously challenge the new enterprises. Population trends continued, and heavy migration from abroad sustained urban growth until the outbreak of World War I. During the war, migration from the rural areas to the cities increased. At the same time, impressive technological innovations, particularly those involved with the generating of power by electricity and the internal combustion engine created new industries and helped transform older ones. The continuing growth of the city, the expansion of the whole electrical sector, and the coming of the automobile and auxiliary industries made the first decades of the twentieth century ones of increasing demand and rapid economic growth.

The initial task of the men who fashioned the first integrated giants at the beginning of this century was to build internal organizational structures that would assure the efficient coordination of the flow of goods through their enterprises and permit the rational allocation of the financial, human, and technological resources at their command. First came the formation of functional departments—sales, production, purchasing, finance, engineering, and research and development. At the same time, central offices were organized, usually in the form of an executive committee consisting of the heads of the functional departments. These offices supervised, appraised, and coordinated the work of the departments and planned long-term expenditures.

By the late-1920's the pioneer organization-builders at du Pont, General Motors, General Electric, Standard Oil of New Jersey, and Sears, Roebuck had developed new and sophisticated techniques to perform the vital coordinating and adaptive activities. They based both long- and short-term coordination and planning on a forecast of market conditions. On the basis of annual forecasts, revised monthly and adjusted every ten days, the companies set production schedules, purchases of supplies and semifinished products, employment and wage rolls, working capital requirements, and prices. Prices were determined by costs, which in turn closely reflected estimated volume of output. The annual forecasts took into consideration estimates of national income, the business cycle, seasonal fluctuations, and the company's normal share of the market. Long-term allocations were based on still broader estimates of demand. After 1920, the managers of many large corporations began to include in these allocations the funds and personnel needed to develop new products and processes through technological innovation. From that time on, the integrated firm began to diversify. The Depression and World War II helped to spread these methods, so that by mid-century most of the key industries in the United States were dominated by a few giant firms administered in much the same way.

Their managers considered themselves leaders in the business community and were so considered by others. Yet they differed greatly from the older types of dominant businessmen—the merchants, the wholesalers, and the manufacturers. They were not owners; they held only a tiny portion of their company's stock; they neither founded the enterprise nor were born into it; and most of them had worked their way up the new bureaucratic ladders.

Even to get on a ladder they were expected to have attended college. Studies of business executives in large corporations show that by 1950 the large majority had been to college—an advantage that was shared by few Americans of their age group. Like most of those who did receive higher education, these managers came primarily from white Anglo-Saxon Protestant stock. Once the college man with his WASP background started up the managerial ladder, he usually remained in one industry and more often than not in a single company. That company became his career, his way of life.

As he rose up the ranks, his horizon broadened to national and international levels. Where his firm diversified, his interests and concerns spread over several industries. Indeed, in some ways his perspectives were wider in the 1950's than those of most Americans; nevertheless, because of his specialized training, he had little opportunity to become aware of the values, ideas, ambitions, and goals of other groups of Americans. He had even fewer direct contacts with farmers, workers, and other types of businessmen than had the wholesaler and the manufacturer.

The dominance of the large integrated enterprise did not, of course, mean the disappearance of the older types of businessmen. Small business remained a basic and essential part of the American economy. The small non-integrated manufacturer, the wholesaler, and retailer have all continued to be active throughout the twentieth century. The number of small businesses has continued to grow with the rapid expansion of the service industries (such as laundries and dry cleaners, service and repair shops not directly tied to the large firm); with the spread of real-estate dealers, insurance agencies, and stock brokerage firms; and with the continuing expansion of the building and construction industries. Throughout the century small businessmen have greatly outnumbered the managers of big business. The former were, therefore, often more politically powerful, particularly in the local politics, than the latter. Economically, however, the managers of the large integrated and often diversified enterprises remained the dominant decision-makers in the urban, industrial, and technologically sophisticated economy of the twentieth century. Their critically significant position has been repeatedly and properly pointed out by economists ever since Adolf A. Berle and Gardner C. Means wrote the first analysis of the role and functions of the modern corporation in 1932.

In many ways, the managers were more of an elite than the earlier businessmen had been. Even though this elite was based on performance rather than birth and played a critically constructive role in building and operating the world's most productive economy, its existence seemed to violate basic American democratic values. At the same time, its control of the central sector of the American economy challenged powerful economic concepts about the efficacy of a free market. After 1930, the managers came to share some of their economic power with others, particularly the federal government. Nevertheless, they were forced to do so *not* because of ideological reasons, but because they failed by themselves to assure the coordination and growth of the economy, the basic activities they had undertaken after 1900.

Until the Depression, the government had played a minimal part in the management of the American economy. The merchants had used the government to assist in financing internal improvements that they found too costly or risky to undertake themselves, and the manufacturers had called upon the government to protect them from foreign competition. Small businessmen—wholesalers and retailers—had joined farmers and workers to use the government to regulate the large corporation, but such regulation did not deter the growth of big business nor significantly alter the activities of the managers. Before the Depression, the government had developed few means to influence consciously the over-all performance of the American economy, the major exception being the creation of a central banking system in 1913.

The Depression clearly demonstrated that the corporation managers alone were unable to provide the coordination and adaptation necessary to sustain a complex, highly differentiated, mass-production, mass-distribution economy. The coming of the Depression itself reflected population and technological developments. Legislation in the 1920's cut immigration from abroad to a tiny flow. After World War I, migration from country to city slowed. Meanwhile, new industries, particularly the electric and automobile industries, reached the limit of demand for their output permitted by the existing size and distribution of the national income. At the same time, improved machinery as well as the more efficient management of production and distribution meant that in still other industries potential supply was becoming greater than existing demand. By the mid-1920's prices had begun to decline. Only the existence of credit helped maintain the economy's momentum until 1929.

Corporate giants, like General Motors, General Electric, and du Pont, fully realized that the demand was leveling off in the 1920's, but they could do little more than maintain production at the existing rate or even cut back a bit. When the 1929 crash dried up credit and reduced demand, they could only roll with the punch. As demand fell, they cut production, laid off men, and canceled orders for supplies and materials. Such actions further reduced purchasing power and demand and led to more cuts in production and more layoffs. The downward pressure continued relentlessly. In less than four years, the national income was slashed in half. The forecasts at General Motors and General Electric for 1932 indicated that, at best, the firms would operate at about 25 per cent capacity.

The only institution capable of stopping this economic descent appeared to be the federal government. During the 1930's it undertook this role, but with great reluctance. Until the recession of 1937, Franklin D. Roosevelt and his Secretary of the Treasury still expected to balance the budget and to bring the end to government intervention in the economy. Roosevelt and his Cabinet considered large-scale government spending and employment only temporary. When Roosevelt decided in 1936 that the Depression was over despite high unemployment, he sharply reduced government expenditures. National income, production, and demand immediately plummeted in 1937. The nation then began to understand more clearly the relationship between government spending and the level of economic activity, although acceptance of the government's role in maintaining economic growth and stability was a decade away.

World War II taught other lessons. The government spent far more than the most enthusiastic New Dealer had ever proposed. Most of the output of these expenditures was destroyed or left on the battlefields of Europe and Asia. But the resulting increased demand sent the nation into a period of prosperity the like of which had never before been seen. Moreover, the supplying of huge armies and navies fighting the most massive war of all time required a tight, centralized control of the national economy. This effort brought corporate managers to Washington to carry out one of the most complex pieces of economic planning in history. That experience lessened the ideological fears over the government's role in stabilizing the economy. This new attitude, embodied in legislation by the Employment Act of 1946, continued to be endorsed by Eisenhower's Republican Administration in the 1950's.

The federal government is now committed to ensuring the revival of investment and demand if, and only if, private enterprise is unable to maintain full employment. In 1949 and again in 1953, 1957, and 1960, the government carried out this role by adjusting its monetary and fiscal policies, building roads, and shifting defense contracts. The continuing Cold War made the task relatively easy by assuring the government ample funds. The new role has been defined so that it meets the needs of the corporate managers. The federal government takes action only if the managers are unable to maintain a high level of aggregate demand; it has not replaced the managers as the major coordinators in the economy, but acts only as a coordinator of last resort.

The Depression helped bring the federal government into the economy in another way. During the late-nineteenth and twentieth centuries, workers, farmers, and (to some extent) retailers, wholesalers, and other small businessmen had formed organizations to help them share in making the economic decisions that most intimately affected their well-being. During the 1930's, when the managers were having difficulties in maintaining economic stability, these numerically larger and more politically influential groups were able to get the federal and state governments to support their claims. Through government intervention many workers acquired a say in determining policies in wages, hours, working rules, promotions, and layoffs; farmers gained control over the prices of several basic commodities; and retailers and wholesalers increased their voice in the pricing of certain goods they sold. Nevertheless, the Wagner Act, the Agricultural Adjustment Acts, the Robinson-Patman Act, and the "fair trading" laws did not seriously infringe on the manager's ability to determine current output and to allocate resources for present and future economic activities.

The growth of organized labor during the twentieth century indicates much about the economic power of the large corporation, for this politically powerful group has been able to impress its will on the decisions of corporate managers only in a limited way. Until the Depression, labor unions had little success in organizing key industries dominated by large, managerially operated enterprises. Even during its first major period of growth at the turn of the century, the American Federation of Labor was not successful in the manufacturing industries. From the start, organized labor's strength lay in mining, transportation, and the building and construction trades. In the manufacturing sector, the Federation's gains came not in factory but small-shop industries, such as cigar, garment, hat, and stove-making and ship-building. During the first quarter of the twentieth century, organized labor acquired its members in those industries where skilled workers achieved their goals by bargaining with many small employers. (The railroads were the exception.) The geographically oriented operating structure developed by the American Federation of Labor unions was admirably suited to this purpose.

Precisely because the craft union had grown up in industries where the factory and the large integrated enterprise had never been dominant, the American Federation of Labor found itself in the 1930's unable to organize, even with strong government support, the mass-production, mass-distribution industries so basic to the operation of the modern economy. To unionize these industries required the creation of a structure to parallel the structure of the large integrated enterprise and a program that appealed to semiskilled rather than skilled workers. The AF of L failed to meet this challenge. Only after "a civil war" within the ranks of labor and the creation of a new national labor organization, the CIO, did the automobile, iron and steel, nonferrous metal, rubber, electrical machinery, and other key industries become fully unionized.

During the great organizing drives of the late-1930's and immediately after World War II, union leaders rarely, if ever, sought to gain more than a voice in the determination of wages and hours, working rules, and hiring as well as promotion and layoff policies. Even when they asked (unsuccessfully) for an opportunity "to look at the company's books," union spokesmen did so primarily with the hope of assuring themselves that they were obtaining what they considered a fair share of the income generated by the firm. The critical issue over which management and labor fought in the years immediately following World War II was whether the managers or the union would control the hiring of workers. The unions almost never asked to take part in decisions about output, pricing, or resources allocation. With the passage of the Taft-Hartley Act of 1947, the managers obtained a control over hiring which has never been seriously challenged. Nor have any further inroads into "management's prerogatives" been seriously proposed.

Since 1950, business managers have continued to make the decisions that most vitally affect the coordination of the economy and the pace of its growth. They have also continued to have a major say in how the economy adapts to external forces generated by population movements and technological change.

Population movements in the 1960's present a different challenge than they did before the 1930's. Migration from abroad has remained only a trickle and that from the country to the city has continued to drop. The move to the suburbs, the most significant post-Depression development, has expanded the urban sprawl and undermined the viability of the central city. The resulting problems are, however, more political and social than economic. Whether government officials are better trained than corporate managers to handle these new problems is open to question. If the business managers fail to meet these new challenges, the government will obviously have to do so.

Meanwhile, technological change has maintained a revolutionary pace. Through their concentration on research and development of new products and new methods of production and distribution, corporate managers have been trained to handle the processes and procedures of technological innovation. The large corporation had so "internalized" the process of innovation that this type of change is no longer simply an outside force to which businessmen and others in the economy adjust. Here the expertise of the business manager covers a broader field than that of governmental or military managers. In most of the costly government programs involving a complex technology, the development and production of new products have been turned over to the large corporations through the contracting process. The federal government does, however, supply the largest share of funds for research and development. Thus, even though the business manager continues to play a critical part in adapting the economy to technological change, government officials are in a position to determine the direction and the areas in which research and development will be concentrated.

This brief history of the role of business in the operation of the American economy suggests several tentative conclusions. From the beginning, it seems, businessmen have run the American economy. They can take the credit and the blame for many of its achievements and failures. They, more than [any] other group in the economy, have managed the production, transportation, and distribution of goods and services. No other group—farmers, blue-collar workers, or white-collar workers—has ever had much to do with the over-all coordination of the economic system or its adaptation to basic changes in population and technology.

Over the two centuries, however, the businessman who ran the economy has changed radically. Dominance has passed from the merchant to the wholesaler, from the wholesaler to the manufacturer, and from the manufacturer to the manager. In the last generation, businessmen have had to share their authority with others, largely with the federal government. Even so, the government's peace-time role still remains essentially a supplementary one, as coordinator of last resort and as a supplier of funds for technological innovation.

In the past, businessmen have devoted their energies to economic affairs, giving far less attention to cultural, social, or even political matters. Precisely because they have created an enormously productive economy and the most affluent society in the world, the noneconomic challenges are now becoming more critical than the economic ones. There is little in the recruitment, training, and experience of the present business leaders—the corporate managers—to prepare them for handling the difficult new problems, but unless they do learn to cope with this new situation, they may lose their dominant position in the economy. As was not true of the merchant, wholesaler, or manufacturer, the corporate managers could be replaced by men who are not businessmen. To suggest how and in what way the managers will respond to the current challenges is, fortunately, not the task of the historian. Such analyses are properly left to social scientists and businessmen.

WALTER LICHT

WALTER LICHT (1946–   ) is professor of history at the University of Pennsylvania. He is the author of several works including Working for the Railroad: The Organization of Work in the Nineteenth Century *(1983) and* Getting Work: Philadelphia, 1840–1950 *(1992).*

MONDAY, JULY 16, 1877. Martinsburg, West Virginia. A date and place emblazoned neither in history books nor in the historical consciousness of the American people. Yet, on that day and in that location, the people of the United States stepped precipitously into the future.

On July 16, 1877, railway workers in Martinsburg, employees of the Baltimore & Ohio Railroad, refused to handle rail traffic or let trains pass through the town. They were protesting the implementation of a 10 percent cut in wages that had been announced simultaneously a few weeks earlier by railway executives of the major rail lines in the country. The concerted nature of the announcement would be an important element in the story to unfold. In response to the job action, the president of the B&O persuaded the governor of West Virginia to send regiments of the state militia to Martinsburg to see to the safe movement of trains. The easy access of corporate leaders to the levers of government power would be an additional ingredient in the saga. To the dismay of B&O officials, however, the troops who arrived on the sixteenth initially fraternized with townspeople. Later that day a melee did erupt, and in the ensuing fracas a striking railwayman guarding a track switch was shot and killed. That proved to be the spark that ignited a nationwide conflagration.

Word soon spread along the tracks of the B&O, and work and traffic on the entire line ground to a halt. On Wednesday evening, angry

Walter Licht, *Industrializing America*, pp. 166–168, 174–181. Copyright © 1995 The Johns Hopkins University Press.

railwaymen and their supporters gathered in Baltimore to protest directly to B&O officials. Protest turned to riot; and by night's end, 10 people were dead, 16 injured, and 250 arrested through confrontations between demonstrators and city police. Shocked by the insurrection, the governor of Maryland prevailed on the president of the United States, Rutherford B. Hayes, to send federal troops to Baltimore to quell the disturbance—the first time in American history that federal forces were employed to suppress labor unrest.

The fire then spread to other communities in the country. Following the example of B&O workers in refusing to accept wage cuts, railwaymen from other lines walked off their jobs and were joined by fellow townspeople in demonstrations. Protests soon emerged in such places as Hornelsville and Buffalo, New York, and Reading, Harrisburg, and Altoona, Pennsylvania. The greatest explosion, however, was to occur in Pittsburgh. On Thursday, July 19, railwaymen from the Pennsylvania Railroad stopped rail traffic in the city. On Friday, state militia from the area were called in at the request and insistence of Thomas Scott, influential president of the road, with the aim of restoring train service. The local guardsmen, however, refused to take up their posts. Troops then had to be sent in from other parts of the state—a move that residents of Pittsburgh perceived as an invasion— and this set the stage for a brutal confrontation on Saturday. Pennsylvania Railroad executives were determined to renew freight traffic, and they arranged for troops to be stationed on the trains. As the first guarded train moved through the city, crowds gathered to block its progress. Troops then fired into the crowd of demonstrators, killing an estimated twenty people and wounding more than seventy more. Word of the massacre quickly spread, and the people of Pittsburgh took to the streets, attacking militiamen, looting stores, and setting fires to the property of the Pennsylvania Railroad. By late evening of Saturday, July 21, 1877, a red glow lit up the city; and daybreak revealed the stations and shops of the Pennsylvania reduced to embers.

Sunday did not prove to be a day of rest. Crowds continued to roam the streets, and a semblance of order would not be restored in the city until Tuesday. Over the weekend, more than two score lives had been lost, 104 locomotives and 2,153 railcars had been destroyed, and few buildings of the Pennsylvania Railroad remained standing.

Chicago was next. Three days of serious disturbances began in that city on Monday, the twenty-third, and confrontations between protestors and police would lead to eighteen dead. The railroad strikes in Chicago evolved into a general strike as workers across trades in the city walked off their jobs in sympathy. Order was restored only with the arrival of Illinois guardsmen from other parts of the state and a contingent of federal troops just fresh from fighting Native Americans on the Plains. After Chicago, the contagion spread further west to St.

Louis, Kansas City, Galveston, and even San Francisco. Only two weeks after its onset did the fever run its course. Trains first rolled again on a normal basis through Martinsburg on July 27, through Pittsburgh on July 29, and through Chicago on August 3.

The events of July 1877 shocked the nation, and the toll was enormous. The nation's commerce had been effectively stilled; railroad companies lost more than $30 million in lost property and business; railwaymen went without pay during the strikes, and many returned to work only to be discharged for their protests and blackballed from further employment in the trade; thousands had also been jailed, hundreds wounded, and at least fifty killed.

From the last two decades of the nineteenth century through World War II, ongoing and vexing conflict between capital and labor marked the American experience. The great railroad strikes of July 1877 represent the formal and abrupt beginning to this history. In the immediate years following the unrest of that month and until the turn of the new century, industrial strife was particularly intense and violent. The severity of the unrest can only be understood as a twofold response: while economic insecurity, not hardship per se, definitely spurred revolt, Americans from different walks of life also took to the streets to support striking workers in the period to challenge the growing, encroaching political and economic power of concentrated capital and the threat the corporation posed to cherished democratic republican values and practices.

During the last two decades of the nineteenth century, the country was also rocked by other kinds of explosions. Most notably, the period witnessed evolving and escalating protest by American farmers. Various social critics and reformers also came to the fore to question contemporary developments, galvanize public opinion, and suggest changes in economic and political practices. The economic instabilities of the times and the sway of the new corporations figured significantly in the complaints of farmers and intellectuals as well.

Unrest during the last decades of the nineteenth century would lead to a restructuring of American institutions and the creation of a new American political economic order. This remaking, however, occurred slowly over a fifty-year period, in stages and unsystematically, and would involve no single set of actors. Various groups would emerge and, often with cross-purposes and differing motives, contribute to the same building of a new United States. What is of interest is the *convergence* of efforts. What was sought in common was greater security and a more administered economy and polity. . . .

Despite the clear advantages held by business managers in countering the job actions of workers—access to the policing powers of government, the ability to hire strikebreakers in great numbers, especially with immigrants and African Americans in desperate search of work—

the deck obviously was not completely stacked against the strikers. One important weapon they had at their disposal was community support. An interesting statistic compiled by labor bureau officials speaks to this point. Strikes were recorded as ordered or not ordered by established unions. In the early 1880s, more than 50 percent of all strikes did not involve a formal trade union organization. The proportion of work stoppages orchestrated by unions rose over the next two decades, but by 1900, one-third of all strikes were still waged without union intervention.

The absolute grassroots insurgent nature of many late-nineteenth-century strikes has to be appreciated. State and federal investigative commissions established to determine the causes of the unrest of the period often searched in vain to find leaders or organizations to which responsibility could be assigned. The strikes also appeared to be as much community uprisings as work stoppages. Investigators found and local newspapers reported ample evidence of widespread support for strikers. Workers from trades not directly involved walked off their jobs in sympathy; local shopkeepers offered food and extended credit to families of strikers; editors of community newspapers blasted company officials for not dealing fairly with their employees; townsmen called up for service in state militia fraternized with their neighbors who were on strike and failed to take up positions in guarding business properties. Community members also took to the streets in protest with strikers. Arrest records for the period reveal people from all walks of life incarcerated for rioting, arson, and attacks on police forces during labor upheavals. Women participated in demonstrations as visibly as men. During railroad strikes, brigades of women greased and soaped tracks to impede the passage of trains.

Why did people who were not directly involved in labor disputes join in protest with striking workers in large numbers? Economic bad times is a contributing factor. Community uprisings accompanying strikes generally occurred during years of economic depression. Yet, material grievance alone cannot explain local insurgencies. The target of community aggression was corporate enterprise. During disputes, corporate property was attacked, not the businesses of local entrepreneurs. Tension exploded to riot when troops sent at the behest of corporate leaders entered the local scene. Reporters covering the disturbances discovered local shopkeepers sympathizing with striking workers and joining protest because the national based corporations threatened their existence; in the case of the railroads, proprietors were angered both at the physical incursions of the carriers and the seemingly unjust rates charged them for shipping goods. The very livelihoods and the autonomy of members of communities appeared challenged by the impersonal decisions made by executives in remote and unapproachable corporate headquarters.

The distrust of the first generation of Americans to be faced with the corporation is explicable; less easy to fathom is the violence. Protestors picked up bricks and rifles to defend their communities and republican ideals. The common ownership of guns in a nation where the right to bear arms was constitutionally protected is part of the explanation for the dramatic loss of life and limb in labor uprisings. The frontier also played somewhat of a role. Not every American community witnessed death and destruction during the labor upheavals. However, historians have been unable to discern patterns of insurgency; labor insurrection occurred in both metropolitan areas and small towns. Unrest unfolded in medium-sized cities as well, but notably in newly developed industrial communities—common to the Midwest—without established elites or ways. Finally, and crucially, the determination of American corporate executives to suppress strikes and unions at all cost and to employ public and private police forces to silence protest was also a key ingredient in the remarkably fierce battles that transpired. Fire was fought with fire.

Spontaneity and community support notably marked labor protest, but over the course of the last decades of the century, trade unions assumed a greater presence and importance in strikes. A trade union revival had first occurred in the 1850s. With economic recovery after the depression of the late 1830s and early 1840s, skilled workers on the local level reestablished their antebellum craft societies and then joined with workers from other localities to found national organizations. The arrival of skilled German and British workers, who were highly politicized and had trade union experience, fueled the rebirth; and vast improvements in transportation and communications during the 1850s allowed for (and demanded) greater cooperation across geographical boundaries.

The revival of trade unionism in the 1850s was followed by increased labor organization and strikes during the Civil War, especially as workers attempted to keep their wages in line with rising wartime prices. In another kind of labor protest, white workers in the North during the war took to the streets to protest the inequities of the military draft system, taking their wrath out on recruitment officers and, tragically, often on African Americans as well.

An expansion of trade union activity and membership during the Civil War led to the formation of the National Labor Union in 1866, the nation's first national federation of unions. Under the leadership of William Sylvis, an articulate iron molder, the NLU convened yearly conventions where trade unionists and various labor sympathizers discussed issues of the day. Delegates supported motions in favor of the eight-hour day, government monetary policies that favored debtors, federal land distribution programs for working people, increased efforts at labor organizing, and most notably, the building of so-called producers' cooperatives (if yeoman producership was increasingly untenable with rapid industrialization, then republican principles could be sustained with yeoman cooperatives). The NLU maintained a visible presence for five years, with some strike and legislative success, but the movement then dissipated and passed from the scene. The organization failed to survive the depression of 1873 and was further incapacitated by internal divisions over economic policy, political activism, and gender and racial issues. From the ashes of the NLU, however, rose another trade union federation, drawing upon and extending many of its predecessor's ideals, but having a much greater impact. This organization was the Knights of Labor.

Uriah Stephens and James Wright, skilled garment cutters, founded the Noble and Holy Order of the Knights of Labor in Philadelphia in 1869 as a secret organization. Little is known about the society in its early years, though it did survive the depression of 1873 and included some 500 lodges and 6,000 members by 1877. In 1878, the order went public (although a good many of the rituals of the original clandestine organization were maintained), and under the leadership of Terrence Powderly, a machinist by trade, members of the "producing classes," regardless of occupation, nationality, race, religion, or sex, were encouraged to join a movement bent on achieving better working conditions and a new social order based on equality and cooperation. Explicitly barred from membership were bankers, stockbrokers, lawyers, liquor dealers (temperance remained a guiding principle of the organization), and gamblers.

In the early 1880s, the society grew and spread throughout the country; recent analyses of the organization's surviving documents reveal lodges established in every state and county of the nation. In 1885, striking Knights railwaymen in the West won their spectacular victory over the powerful Jay Gould, boosting the organization's fortunes and membership to 750,000. The year 1886 saw the order at its peak of prominence as Knights of Labor members rushed into political activity, launching successful independent party ventures throughout the United States. From this zenith of visibility and impact, however, the Knights of Labor declined precipitously under the force of increased employer resistance to Knights-led strikes, internal divisions, and the defection of craft unionists from the cause. By the mid-1890s, few traces of the order remained.

An overview of the history of the Knights can thus be rendered, but understanding the Knights phenomenon has always provided difficulties for historians. For one thing, the activities of the federation varied from year to year and place to place. The organization itself was a crazy quilt of local assemblies of individuals, neighborhood groups, reform associations, existing craft unions, and workers variously organized by factory, trade, and geographical locale, and wider city, district, and state assemblies. The order stood for the enrollment of all workers—upholding the principle of so-called industrial unionism—yet craft unions joined the federation and maintained their autonomy and identities. The order made unprecedented strides in organizing women and African American workers though gender and racial divisions still marked its history. Knights activists moved into independent political party activity with a vengeance in 1886, yet an ambivalence toward politics, politicians, and the role of government—stemming from the republican and antistatist sentiments and ideals of those drawn into the movement—blunted the Knights' political initiatives once Knights candidates found themselves actually elected to office. Temperance and chivalric behavior were hallmarks of the order, yet a number of Knights officials were involved in swindles and intrigues that rivaled the worst corruptions of the age. The organization stood officially for the abandonment of the wage labor system, but with the exception of support for public ownership of financial and transportation institutions, Knights leaders openly repudiated socialism. Knights officials upheld the building of producers' cooperatives as a principal goal and ideal, yet their actual record on establishing cooperative ventures was poor. Finally, and most notably, while the organization's leadership formally renounced strikes and espoused harmonious relations with fair-minded, hard-working employers and arbitration in the case of disputes, its members nonetheless participated fervently in hundreds of strikes under the Knights banner.

The Knights of Labor thus defies simple characterization. Can it be deemed a backward-looking movement aimed at recreating a mythical yeoman producer past, as some historians have suggested? Not really. Knights leaders and followers harked back to a more harmonious time, yet they were permanent wage laborers, decidedly immersed in modern issues like arbitration proceedings, challenging traditional mainstream politics, and struggling to find new forms of relationships. Was the organization instead a typical reform movement merely bent on extending the benefits of capitalism to the yet unbenefitted? Not really, again. The Knights were ambivalent about the capitalist system, definitely antagonistic to corporate or monopoly capitalism, and certainly not boosters of capitalism in general.

Was the organization an alternative movement looking forward to the building of a "cooperative commonwealth" (a frequently invoked phrase) to replace the bureaucratic and corporate future that loomed ahead? There is evidence to substantiate this interpretation, but how widely this vision was held by those enrolled is unclear. Was it, as other historians have suggested, a democratic movement at heart, an attempt to significantly widen political participation? Ample proof exists for this contention as well, though the notion hardly provides a comprehensive understanding. Was it simply a trade union effort? Certainly not.

Perhaps the only solution is to term the Knights of Labor an amorphous social movement of laboring people; the extent to which hundreds of thousands of American working men and women were enlisted, educated, and politicized in the 1870s and 1880s is what is to be ultimately appreciated. Recognition of the mobilization is apparent from studies of local Knights' activity and the countless meetings, lectures, parades, and picnics attended by those moved to join. If historians have to remain unsure in their estimations of the Knights, the Knights of Labor moment in American history nonetheless continues to fascinate.

Some trade unionists of the era, however, viewed the Knights venture as just pure folly. Leaders of the so-called brotherhoods of railway workers, for example, expressly forbade their members from joining the Knights; the brotherhoods, in fact, avoided participation in all of the great uprisings of the day. Leaders of most craft unions similarly viewed the Knights with a jaundiced eye. Among detractors of the Knights, the key and historically critical figure was Samuel Gompers.

Samuel Gompers was born in England in 1850 and immigrated to New York City at the age of thirteen. Entering the cigar-making trade, he found himself immersed in a community of skilled English and German immigrant workers who ate, drank, and breathed Marxism and socialism. Gompers thus received lessons about the seeming hard truths of capitalism: a permanent proletariat had been formed; capital was concentrating and gaining overwhelming economic and political power; realism was in order; focused and well-organized trade unions had to be established to achieve gains for workers.

Despite this sober perspective, Gompers and his fellow craft trade unionists were swept into the Knights crusade. Having risen to the leadership of the Cigar Makers' International Union, he joined with other skilled men in 1881 in founding the Federation of Organized Trades and Labor Unions, which allied with the Knights. Over the next five years, however, Gompers and his associates became increasingly disenchanted with the movement. They resented Terrence Powderly's attempt to dictate policy, found themselves engaged in various jurisdictional disputes (what constituted a local or an assembly of the Knights organization remained a fuzzy and disputed matter), deemed most Knights pronouncements as naive and Knights-sponsored strikes as quixotic, and saw the sudden move of Knights members into independent party politics as misguided and wasteful of valuable time and energy. In 1886, Gompers thus led numerous craft unions out of the Knights of Labor and into his newly formed American Federation of Labor. The absolute loss in membership and the defection of the best-organized of the Knights' members contributed greatly to that order's subsequent demise.

Under Samuel Gompers' leadership, both the constituent unions of the AFL and the offices of the federation grew in strength and permanence. Gompers himself became the most important labor leader in the country, listened to by politicians, businessmen, and the press. Until his death in 1924, he was arguably the chief spokesman for the working people of the United States. This all occurred, however, because Gompers forged a limited agenda.

Gompers' strategy for the AFL included the following:

1. Organize the organizable—that is, skilled workers who possessed leverage in the workplace and who could win victories.

2. Do not pour energies into enrolling less skilled, easily replaced workers. In practice, this meant ignoring women, blacks, and most immigrants.

3. Build strong organizations with high dues, well-paid officers, and strike funds and other benefits that would engender the great loyalty of members.

4. Fight for what can be gained—"bread and butter" issues—meaning higher wages within reason, shorter hours, and work rules that curtailed the arbitrary decision making of firm managers.

5. Do not become involved and waste time and money in independent political action, much less radical political activity. Work within the system, in other words.

6. Support mainstream politicians of any party who favor prolabor legislation.

Gompers' strategy proved successful—in many ways it was programmed to be—and with each victory for AFL men, Gompers could upbraid his many detractors in the labor movement and point to the wisdom of his stance.

The history of Samuel Gompers and the AFL in the late nineteenth century, like that of the Knights of Labor, is not without its inconsistencies. Gompers developed his strategy over time and with experience, not presciently or at once. He fashioned his approach to trade unionism after his experiences with the Knights, through watching corporate capital become entrenched and powerful, after disastrous defeats for labor at Homestead and Pullman, in light of increasing judicial assaults on trade union activity and conservative court rulings against the government regulation of working conditions, after turning back significant challenges to his leadership by militants from within the AFL, and after seeing the efficacy of ingratiating himself to business leaders (as he warned, if they did not deal with him and the skilled workers he represented, they would have to deal with more radical groups within the laboring community). Gompers also asserted himself as a visible spokesman, but he insisted that the AFL be as decentralized as possible and that constituent unions be afforded maximum autonomy (the example of Powderly glared in his mind). Gompers also upheld the principle of craft unionism, yet the AFL included so-called federal unions, such as the United Mine Workers, which organized workers across skill levels. While in practice the AFL rendered little assistance to women and African American workers who struggled to form unions, Gompers himself spoke against racial and sexual prejudice, opposed segregated unions, and warned that without outreach, strikes would be lost through the employment of strikebreakers who remained antagonistic to the exclusive craft unions. Gompers similarly argued for labor to be nonpartisan and nonreliant on politicians (he espoused "voluntarism"), yet he would ultimately hitch the fortunes of the AFL to the Democratic Party. Finally, Gompers placed a definite conservative stamp on the American trade union movement, yet as noted, he constantly faced challenges from groups within the AFL who mobilized to see the federation adopt a much more militant, socialistic, and inclusive posture.

There are a number of great ironies in the story of the Knights of Labor, the American Federation of Labor, and other labor campaigns in the last decades of the nineteenth century. Samuel Gompers, schooled in Marxism, became a force for moderation and acceptance of the powers that be. Eugene Victor Debs, on the other hand, born in small-town America, steeped in American republican traditions, would emerge a socialist after defeat at the hands of the powerful Pullman Company and the U.S. government. In launching effective strikes Gompers and his associates challenged capital head on, but not the capitalist system. The Knights, conversely, in raising on high the notion of a cooperative commonwealth and in their spontaneous protests, challenged the capitalist order but not, effectively, capital.

Egging on labor revolt during the late nineteenth century were also a host of socialists, anarchists, and other radicals, operating in such organizations as the Socialist Labor Party. During the great railroad strikes of July 1877, for example, leaders of the socialist Workingmen's Party assumed a key role in mobilizing protest in the city of St. Louis, one of the only instances during the nationwide stoppage where there is clear evidence of leadership and organization. Individuals and groups—whether craft unionists, Knights, or radicals—thus contributed to the labor upheavals of the period. Ultimately, however, a lesser role has to be assigned to all of them, for the unrest is only partially explicable in terms of formal organization and agitation. General resentment among working people and often among their middle-class neighbors against the emerging power of the corporation played a larger role. So, too, did anger about economic hard times.

4

AMERICAN IMPERIALISM

Economic Expansion or Ideological Crusade?

Around the turn of the twentieth century, the United States emerged as a great power. Having won the Spanish-American war in 1899, it acquired the Hawaiian Islands, Puerto Rico, the Philippines, and part of the Samoan archipelago, thereby coming to dominate the Caribbean and exert enormous influence in the Pacific. This acquisition of an overseas empire seemed sudden to many, but the United States had been tending toward such an outcome for many years. Even before this time, its continental expanse, industrial and agricultural productivity, extensive trade, and growing population had made it a rising economic power. The construction of a modern navy was the final element required for the United States to set its course toward empire.

Many Americans were ambivalent about their country's new role. Some feared that America's democratic institutions were incompatible with an overseas empire and the large military establishment that would be required to sustain it. Others rejected empire because it implied bringing under the American flag groups they regarded as racial or social inferiors. Some Americans, on the other hand, favored the entry of the United States into world affairs, either because of a crusading zeal to spread American institutions and values or a desire to find new economic markets. These divisions over foreign policy had their counterparts in the works of diplomatic historians. Just as Americans debated the wisdom of particular policies, so historians disagreed about interpretations of past events. The historical debate, in reality, was not confined simply to an analysis of the past; implicit in each interpretation of diplomatic history was a vision of what America ought to be. Those who argued that the United States had traditionally been a champion of democracy were likely to take an interventionist position in debates about current-day policies toward "emerging nations." Similarly, those who recounted the imposition of American economic and military power on other countries tended to criticize the imperialist character of contemporary foreign policy.

The historical literature dealing with the decade of the 1890s, which culminated in the Spanish-American War, is a central case in point. Charles and Mary Beard, whose *Rise of American Civilization* was a landmark in the Progressive school of American historiography,[1] argued that the pursuit of economic interests led President William McKinley to seek war with Spain. Neither sympathy for Cubans, nor anticolonial impulse, nor any other democratic ideal led to war fever. The Spanish government had practically acceded to most of McKinley's demands. McKinley, the Beards insisted, revised Cleveland's policy of neutrality because American businessmen made him understand that Spanish policy threatened their investments in and trade with Cuba. The ensuing acquisition of overseas territory provided further proof of the Beards' charge that the business community played an important role in determining the country's foreign policy. Although the Beardian thesis was presented in somewhat qualified form, it clearly implied the primacy of economic forces in shaping foreign policy.[2]

Relatively few scholars, however, followed the Beards' interpretation. To Samuel Flagg Bemis, whose synthesis of American diplomatic history appeared in 1936, the acquisition of an overseas empire represented a "great aberration." Before the war, Bemis noted, "there had not been the slightest demand for the acquisition of the Philippine Islands." Military victory, however, fanned a jingoist tide that McKinley proved unable to resist. In demanding the Philippine Islands in the course of peace negotiations, the president demonstrated "adolescent irresponsibility." McKinley's decision, concluded Bemis, was unplanned and an indication of his weakness and folly. It was definitely not in accord with the traditional American aversion to colonial empire.[3]

Another anti-Beardian interpretation of the causes of war appeared at almost the same moment as Bemis's influential textbook. In *Expansionists of 1898* Julius W. Pratt suggested that intellectual and emotional factors were responsible for the new expansionism. The emergence of social Darwinism provided some people with an intellectual justification for expanding America's sphere of influence. In this view, nations, like individuals, were engaged in a remorseless test of their fitness to survive. The criterion of success was dominion over others; failure to expand meant stagnation and decline. Other expansionist-minded individuals recruited religious and humanitarian zeal to the task of bringing American civilization to less advanced peoples. A small group of strategic thinkers adopted the doctrines of Captain Alfred Thayer Mahan, who declared sea power to be the key to a nation's greatness and overseas naval bases the key to sea power. These ideological factors, not economic interest, drove expansionist policies, Pratt in-

---

[1]On the Progressive school of history, see Chapter 1.

[2]Charles A. Beard and Mary R. Beard, *The Rise of American Civilization*, 2 vols. (New York, 1927), 2: 369–382.

[3]Samuel Flagg Bemis, *A Diplomatic History of the United States*, 4th ed. (New York, 1955), pp. 463–475.

sisted. Indeed, he noted that the business community, which was still recovering from the depression that began in 1893, opposed intervention in Cuba for fear that it might block the road to economic recovery. It was only after Admiral Dewey's dramatic victory in the Philippines that American businessmen were converted to the expansionist cause by the alluring prospect of the potentially enormous Chinese market. Businessmen eventually found it just as easy to apply the same rationale to the Caribbean. The reasons that the United States went to war, therefore, were quite different from the reasons it acquired an overseas empire. American imperialism, Pratt concluded, was born in ideological impulse but matured in economic ambition.[4]

After the publication of Pratt's work in 1936, scholarly interest in the early years of American imperialism waned. Between the 1930s and the 1950s diplomatic historians focused primarily on the causes and consequences of the First and Second World Wars. But in 1959 William Appleman Williams published one of the most influential books ever written about American foreign policy, *The Tragedy of American Diplomacy.*[5] Called by one historian America's "preeminent critic of empire,"[6] Williams could never easily be categorized as New Left. Nevertheless, his writings were seized upon and extended by New Left and revisionist historians of all kinds. What Williams offered was a provocative set of hypotheses to explain the entire historical record of American diplomacy. First of all, he insisted, foreign policies were never just "reactions" to external events; they were always intimately related to domestic concerns. Conflicts over interests among different sectors of the economy, different regions, different classes, different political coalitions—these were the motivators of foreign policy.

Given this primary assumption, Williams continued, U.S. foreign policy revealed itself to have been expansionist from its very beginnings. Even before gaining independence, Americans had striven to achieve economic self-sufficiency within the British Empire. Only independent control over their own economy could guarantee colonial elites continued dominance over contentious masses, who demanded land and other resources needed to realize their "American dream." Once independence had been won, the United States determined to

---

[4]Julius W. Pratt, *Expansionists of 1898* (Baltimore, 1936) and *America's Colonial Experiment: How the United States Gained, Governed, and in Part Gave Away a Colonial Empire* (New York, 1950).

[5]William Appleman Williams (hereafter Williams), *The Tragedy of American Diplomacy,* 2nd ed. (New York, 1972); this was followed by *The Contours of American History* (Cleveland, 1961) and *The Roots of the Modern American Empire* (New York, 1969).

[6]Paul Buhle, "William Appleman Williams: Grassroots against Empire," in *Rethinking the Cold War,* Allen Hunter, ed., (Philadelphia, 1998), pp. 289–306.

meet such demands by developing ever-expanding markets for its products, i.e, by pursuing an American empire. Until the 1890s that empire lay mostly in the western regions of the American continent, but once the frontier was gone the search for markets continued overseas. During the depressions of the 1880s and 1890s, Williams specifically argues, the American business community concluded that, since economic depression resulted from America's tendency to produce more goods than its people could consume, it needed foreign markets to absorb growing productive capacity.

Despite the controversy between imperialists and anti-imperialists around the turn of the twentieth century, both groups agreed that economic expansion overseas was vital to the nation's prosperity and stability. The debate was over means rather than ends. Imperialists believed that formal acquisition of colonies was necessary to insure strategic security and market control; anti-imperialists, on the other hand, believed that security and economic expansion could be achieved without the material expense of maintaining a colonial empire or the ideological expense of betraying the nation's anti-colonial heritage. The Open Door policy, according to Williams, resolved the dilemma and ultimately became the basis for America's future foreign policy. It sought to achieve all the advantages of economic expansion without the disadvantages of maintaining a colonial empire. It demanded that each nation maintain an open door for trade with all other countries on a most-favored-nation basis. By requiring all other nations to compete with the exuberant American economy, Open Door strategists believed, the United States would come out ahead in the scramble for trade advantages. Although formulated originally to apply to China, the policy was expanded to cover the entire globe and to include American investments as well as trade.[7] The Open Door, "through which America's preponderant economic strength would enter and dominate all underdeveloped areas of the world," Williams insisted, was designed to assure the nation's economic supremacy on a global scale.

Williams proclaimed the consequences of this continuous imperial policy to be disastrous. First of all, it was a betrayal and corruption of American democracy. Even worse were the consequences for people outside the United States. Armored with the "posture of moral and ideological superiority," American policy-makers over the twentieth

---

[7]For a revisionist account of the role of the mythic "China trade" in shaping U.S. foreign policy, see Thomas J. McCormick, *The China Market: America's Quest for Informal Empire, 1893–1901* (Chicago, 1967), and "Insular Imperialism and the Open Door: The China Market and the Spanish American War," *Pacific Historical Review* 32 (1963): 155–169.

century proceeded to penetrate and dominate one underdeveloped nation after another, proclaiming their good intentions while reaping immense material rewards. They hoped to control markets and raw materials without having to resort to direct political or military intervention, but economic hegemony almost always required political hegemony. Cuba, the first case in point, set the pattern for others. The United States "dominated the economic life of the island by controlling, directly or indirectly, the sugar industry, and by overtly and covertly preventing any dynamic modification of the island's one-crop economy. It defined clear and narrow limits on the island's political system. It tolerated the use of torture and terror, of fraud and farce, by Cuba's rulers. But it intervened with economic and diplomatic pressure and with force of arms when Cubans threatened to transgress the economic and political restrictions established by American leaders."[8]

In 1963 Walter LaFeber published a prize-winning volume on American expansionism from 1860 to 1898 that lent strong support to the Williams thesis. The Civil War, LaFeber noted, marked an important dividing line in America's expansionist policies. Before 1860 expansionism was confined to the American continent; it reflected the desire of an agrarian society to find new and fertile lands. Post–Civil War expansionism, on the other hand, was motivated by the belief that foreign markets were vital to America's well-being. By the 1890s the American business community had concluded that additional foreign markets "would solve the economic, social, and political problems created by the industrial revolution." They found a coterie of new strategic thinkers, centered about Theodore Roosevelt, to lead the imperialist charge. Given Europe's imperialist penetration into many regions of the world, this line of strategic thought concluded, the United States needed strategic bases if it were to compete successfully. The diplomacy of the 1890s and the Spanish-American War grew out of these concerns. Debate between the imperialists and anti-imperialists during this decade was over the tactical means needed to attain common objectives. Whether they believed that the Open Door could operate entirely free of traditional colonialism, or that some formal colonization was necessary, Americans had come to accept the larger reality. "By 1899," concluded LaFeber, "the United States had forged a new empire."[9] LaFeber's classic expression of this argument is the first reading in this unit.

The Williams-LaFeber interpretation of the origins of modern American foreign policy was extremely influential within the history

---

[8]Williams, *Tragedy of American Diplomacy*, pp. 2 and 59.

[9]Walter LaFeber, *The New Empire: An Interpretation of American Expansionism 1860–1898* (Ithaca, 1963).

profession.[10] It also had a wider appeal during the 1960s and 1970s as disillusionment with American policy grew during the Vietnam conflict. The argument that the nation's diplomacy was based less on democratic idealism and more on a desire to safeguard an international order that made America's economic supremacy possible seemed to resonate among scholars and citizens. The Cold War, for example, rather than resting on a moral foundation that pitted freedom against communism, was seen as a product of America's continued insistence on structuring a world order along lines that preserved its liberal capitalist hegemony. Thus American foreign policy, which grew out of domestic institutions and developments, was allegedly responsible in large measure for initiating and perpetuating the Cold War and causing the Vietnam conflict.[11]

The Williams thesis, however, did not gain universal acceptance in historical circles. Even scholars who shared its leftist tone and its assumptions about the domestic sources of foreign policy found a much more complex range of motives for American expansionism. Reflecting the surge of interest in social and cultural history, for example, John Higham and Christopher Lasch located motivation for imperialism in developments within the inner life of the American middle and upper classes. As professionalism and bureaucracy transformed the meaning of success in modernizing America, and as immigration and urbanization created a more polyglot and complex social order, white men found a way to reassert their individualism—and their masculine and racial supremacy—through the "strenuous life." What this meant was the way of life embodied by America's first politician-celebrity, Theodore Roosevelt, a life of continual exertion: challenging nature, playing organized sports, cleaning up urban corruption, busting the trusts, waving the imperial "big stick."[12]

Other scholars departed altogether from the Williams school,

---

[10]See Thomas J. McCormick's attempt to develop a general strategy for diplomatic history based on the Williams thesis: "Drift or Mastery? A Corporate Synthesis for American Diplomatic History," *Reviews in American History* 4 (December 1982): 318–330. See also Lloyd C. Gardner, "American Foreign Policy 1900–1921: A Second Look at the Realist Critique of American Diplomacy," in *Towards a New Past: Dissenting Essays in American History*, Barton J. Bernstein, ed. (New York, 1968), pp. 202–231; David Healy, *U.S. Expansionism: The Imperialist Urge in the 1890s* (Madison, Wis., 1970); Milton Plesur, *America's Outward Thrust: Approaches to Foreign Affairs, 1865–1890* (DeKalb, Ill., 1971); Ernest N. Paolino, *The Foundations of American Empire: William Henry Seward and U.S. Foreign Policy* (Ithaca, 1973); Charles S. Campbell, *The Transformation of American Foreign Relations 1865–1900* (New York, 1976).

[11]On Cold War historiography see Chapter 8.

[12]John Higham, "The Reorientation of American Culture in the 1890s," in *Writing American History: Essays on Modern Scholarship* (Bloomington, Ind., 1970), pp. 73–102; and Christopher Lasch, "The Moral and Intellectual Rehabilitation of the Ruling Class," in *The World of Nations: Reflections on American History, Politics, and Culture* (New York, 1974), pp. 80–99.

denying its fundamental assumptions. They disputed its assessment of the relative importance of domestic factors in the determination of foreign policy. They denied in particular that one domestic factor—the expansive needs of capitalism—played the preponderant role in determining the character and direction of American society and therefore of its foreign policy. Some of these especially accused Williams and his followers of ignoring or trivializing the efficacy of other nations in shaping international relations. A more balanced approach, they argued, called not only for an understanding of the behavior of other governments, but for a recognition of the inherently multinational character of all diplomacy. For the historian this implied a multi-archival approach to research and a multi-perspectival approach to narration. A more critical examination of a wider range of sources and a renewed attention to non-economic influences on policy-making, these critics of the Williams thesis argued, led to a rejection of the idea that the United States was omnipotent in world affairs.

Typical of this approach was Ernest R. May's *Imperial Democracy*, published in 1961. May argued that in the 1890s the United States had not sought to play a new role in world affairs. On the contrary, diplomatic problems concerning Hawaii, China, Venezuela, and Cuba had intruded upon the consciousness of political leaders who were preoccupied with domestic issues. "Some nations," May observed, "achieve greatness; the United States had greatness thrust upon it." President McKinley was not the harbinger of imperialism but rather a leader trying to keep his nation out of war in the face of a fractious Congress and a public inflamed by press accounts of Spanish atrocities in Cuba. Only after presidential initiatives designed to grant Cuba autonomy under Spain failed did McKinley issue an ultimatum: Spain would come to an agreement with the Cubans or the United States would mediate the conflict in such a way as to produce a form of Cuban independence. When the Spanish government rejected the ultimatum, McKinley faced a crucial choice. He could embark upon a war that he did not want or he could defy public opinion and thereby risk unseating Republican majorities in both houses of Congress. "When public opinion reached the point of hysteria, he succumbed," said May. "Neither the President nor the public had any aim beyond war itself." Coming as it did at a moment when depression, labor unrest, huge new inflows of immigration, and corruption scandals were shaking the political equanimity of many Americans, the Cuban crisis became a sort of psychic obsession. "In some irrational way, all these influences and anxieties translated themselves into concern for suffering Cuba. For the people as for the government, war with monarchical Catholic, Latin Spain had no purpose except to relieve emotion."[13]

---

[13]Ernest R. May, *Imperial Democracy: The Emergence of America as a Great Power* (New York, 1961), pp. 268–270.

May's thesis had been anticipated a decade earlier by Richard Hofstadter. Hofstadter's work in the 1940s and 1950s contributed to the emerging rejection of the basic tenets of the Progressive school of American historiography. In 1952 he published an article that rejected an economic explanation of American diplomacy in the 1890s.[14] In Hofstadter's eyes modern American liberalism reflected less a concern for the welfare of the masses and more hysteria and jingoism spurred by the inner feelings of Protestant, middle-class Americans who, buffeted by economic and technological change, feared a decline in their social status. May's diplomatic history borrowed some of Hofstadter's insights into these irrational and non-economic influences, as well as his use of social science theory and his interest in comparative history. Regarding the last, May's scholarship was especially suggestive. The forging of a new imperialist consensus at the turn of the century, May argued, owed much to European, and especially British, influence on American elites. Moreover, the eventual shift in opinion away from imperialism reflected not only a resurgence of traditional anticolonial sentiment but an awareness (especially in an era of vastly expanded newspaper readership) of the difficulties faced by the British during the Boer War in South Africa and the growth of an anti-imperialist movement in Britain. May concluded by insisting that the American debate between imperialist and anti-imperialist could be understood only in the context of a much broader Atlantic civilization.[15]

One of the most interesting interpretations of the origins of the war with Spain and the rise of imperialism came from Gerald F. Linderman, who authored the second reading in this unit. Agreeing fully with Williams and his followers that foreign policy emerged out of domestic concerns, Linderman nonetheless described a society caught up in the drama of the Cuban struggle. Like Hofstadter, and even more like Robert Wiebe, whose *Search for Order* described the transformation of late-nineteenth-century America from a nation of island communities into a complex modern society, Linderman saw the war less

---

[14]Richard Hofstadter, "Manifest Destiny and the Philippines," in *America in Crisis: Fourteen Crucial Episodes in American History*, Daniel Aaron, ed. (New York, 1952), pp. 173–200; republished in Hofstadter's *The Paranoid Style in American Politics and Other Essays* (New York, 1965), pp. 145–187. Hofstadter proposed a comparable explanation of the roots of the 1950s anticommmunist hysteria known as McCarthyism; for more on Hofstadter's career and influence, see Chapter 1 and Chapter 11.

[15]Ernest R. May, "American Imperialism: A Reinterpretation," *Perspectives in American History* 1 (New York, 1967): 123–283; also published as *American Imperialism: A Speculative Essay* (New York, 1968). On the anti-imperialists see Robert L. Beisner, *Twelve Against Empire* (New York, 1968; rev. ed. 1985); and Christopher Lasch, "The Anti-Imperialists, the Philippines, and the Inequality of Man," in *The World of Nations: Reflections on American History, Politics, and Culture* (New York, 1974), pp. 70–79. For international perspectives see Philip Darby, *Three Faces of Imperialism: British and American Approaches to Asia and Africa, 1870–1970* (New Haven, 1987), and Paul Kennedy, *The Rise and Fall of the Great Powers* (New York, 1987).

as a proclamation of capitalist expansionism than as a "twilight expression" of a perishing nineteenth-century way of life. People of small towns and limited vision, Americans read the conflict through the lens of their traditional prejudices—at first seeing perfidious Spaniards vs. Cuban freedom-fighters; later seeing white Europeans against black primitives. The new yellow press played an enormous role in deploying and manipulating these changing "images of enemy and ally," even as the president struggled to forge a modern executive office capable of managing foreign crises. The nation that went to war with Spain and became a great power did so in the process of grappling with the turbulence and uncertainty of modernization. The United States moved without clear purpose into the age of empire.

A more vehement attack on the Williams-LaFeber thesis came from James A. Field, Jr. He argued that nearly all accounts of American foreign policy in the 1890s suffered from serious faults: the adoption of a strictly rational explanation of events and a rejection of chance; the use of overly broad terms to describe complex situations; an American-centered, ethnocentric treatment of diplomacy; and inattention to factors crucial in determining foreign policy, including "time, distance, costs, [and] technological feasibility." Rather than grapple with such difficulties, Field charged, the Williams school preferred to begin with perceptions of American immorality in the twentieth century and then read them back into the past with "false continuities and imputations of sin." Field rejected such explanations of American imperialism, as well as those based on the influence of Darwinian theory (à la May), the psychic or cultural crisis of the 1890s (à la Hofstadter and Linderman), the rise of grand strategic theory (à la LaFeber), and the importance of the China market (à la McCormick). In their place Field proposed his own set of hypotheses. The new American navy that came into existence in the late nineteenth century was a defensive answer to European developments. The search for bases was a response to the strategic problems of the proposed canal linking the Atlantic and Pacific oceans. The rapid deployment of the American navy headed by Admiral Dewey in the Pacific was largely a result of the rapidity of communication made possible by new cables linking nations and continents. Democratic sympathy for the Cubans may have aroused Americans to confront Spain, but it was Dewey's victory in Manila Bay that focused public attention on the Far East; only then did an avalanche of publicity for the advantages of empire descend upon the American people. "Imperialism," according to Field, "was the product of Dewey's victory."[16]

[16]James A. Field, Jr., "American Imperialism: The Worst Chapter in Almost Any Book," *American Historical Review* 83 (June 1978): 644–683, which includes rejoinders from Walter LaFeber and Robert L. Beisner. For a somewhat different rejection of the Williams school, see Richard E. Welch, Jr., *Response to Imperialism: The United States and the Philippine-American War, 1899–1902* (Chapel Hill, 1979).

Other critics of the Williams-LaFeber interpretation of the origins of American imperialism added to these arguments. Paul A. Varg, for example, determined that China was not of major importance to the American policy officials whom he studied. Even Caribbean policy, which did occupy the attention of these officials, was never pursued solely for economic considerations. Moreover, whatever interests—economic, strategic, ideological—drove policy, most policy-makers were, like most Americans, fairly insular; few ever believed that the nation's welfare hinged on developments in other parts of the world. And finally, every American intervention, actual or proposed, elicited strong opposition from other elites in business, politics, and the press, and even occasionally from the broader public. Although the United States did become a world power, this was not because of any master plan designed to control the destinies of other nations.[17]

Some historians challenged the very idea that imperialism necessarily inflicted harm. Stanley Lebergott, after noting the relative insignificance of American foreign investment in Latin America from 1890 to 1929, denied that it worked to the detriment of either workers or landowners in the nations that were affected. Indeed, American foreign investments increased the income of workers and peasants by expanding the need for labor, and improved land values by opening American markets to native products. Lebergott conceded that American business enterprise sometimes threatened the vested interests of native businesses, and sometimes created rivalries among entrepreneurial groups. But this sort of conflict was not a struggle between U.S. imperialists and Latin American freedom-fighters. It was rather between two capitalist groups, one native and the other foreign, each fighting over the spoils of progress.[18]

Legerbott's effort to acquit imperialism of the most grievous charges against it runs into great difficulty. While critics of the Williams-LaFeber thesis mounted strong arguments for the salience of non-economic influences on the shaping of foreign policy, those who denied the baneful consequences of imperial interventions strained credibility. By the 1980s, some scholars managed to endorse arguments for broad socio-cultural causes of the war with Spain, such as

---

[17]Paul A. Varg, "The United States as a World Power, 1900–1917: Myth or Reality?" in *Twentieth-Century American Foreign Policy,* John Braeman, Robert H. Bremner, and David Brody, eds. (Columbus, Ohio, 1971), and *The Making of a Myth: The United States and China, 1897–1912* (East Lansing, Mich., 1968). For other examples of work in this line see Howard K. Beale, *Theodore Roosevelt and the Rise of America to World Power* (Baltimore, 1956), and Raymond A. Esthus, *Theodore Roosevelt and the International Rivalries* (Waltham, Mass., 1970).

[18]Stanley Lebergott, "The Returns to U.S. Imperialism, 1890–1929," *Journal of Economic History* 40 (June 1980): 229–249; a level-headed review of some of these issues is David M. Pletcher, "Rhetoric and Results: A Pragmatic View of Economic Expansionism, 1865–1898," *Diplomatic History* 5 (Spring 1981): 93–104.

that of Linderman, with a sharp acknowledgment of the horrors of imperial domination. Thus Stuart Creighton Miller carefully narrated the
entry of U.S. forces into the Philippines and their awful transformation into an army of occupation and conquest. Although cautious
about exaggerating the "tragic parallels" between the Philippine and
Vietnam wars, Miller insisted that a fateful line of descent connects
Cuba and the Philippines in the 1890s to Vietnam in the 1960s.[19] Similarly, Walter LaFeber assembled much evidence to support the argument that the foreign policy forged in the 1890s continued throughout
the twentieth century to shape American actions in Central America
and the Caribbean. Although he tells a complex story, by the end few
readers can doubt that over the course of the century the United States
wreaked great havoc among its neighbors to the south.[20]

In the 1980s and 1990s historians have placed new emphasis on
ideological and cultural—especially racial—determinants of foreign
policy. Recalling Linderman's discussion of "images of enemy and
ally," Michael Hunt argues that racial supremacy has been a "core
idea," inextricably intertwined with the idea of "national greatness,"
and strongly determinative of American foreign policy since the nineteenth century.[21] Focusing on the cultural components of imperial
domination, Emily S. Rosenberg has argued that the ideology of "liberal-developmentalism" underlay a century of efforts to spread the
"American dream of high technology and mass consumption." However rationalized in terms of "open doors" and "free markets," the policy that grew out of this ideology was really about privately
owned—and distinctly American owned—markets.[22]

These historians depart in significant ways from Williams's original thesis, but they reinforce the more general conclusion of his work
that the United States was—and is—an expansive power, seeking advantage and even hegemony in the world of great powers. Although
they have learned from Williams's critics, they in no way portray the
United States as a reluctant crusader for liberal democracy in a violent
and alien world. Especially those who approach the history of American expansion from the perspective of foreign nations tell a tale of aggression, domination, and exploitation. That tale appears, for example,

---

[19]Stuart Creighton Miller, *"Benevolent Assimilation": The American Conquest of the Philippines, 1899–1903* (New Haven, 1982).

[20]Walter LaFeber, *Inevitable Revolutions: The United States in Central America* (New York, 1983).

[21]Michael H. Hunt, *Ideology and U.S. Foreign Policy* (New Haven, 1987).

[22]Emily S. Rosenberg, *Spreading the American Dream: American Economic and Cultural Expansion 1890–1945* (New York, 1982); see also Daniel F. Headrick, *The Tentacles of Progress: Technology Transfer in the Age of Imperialism* (New York, 1988), and Robert W. Rydell, *All the World's a Fair: Visions of Empire at American International Expositions, 1876–1916* (Chicago, 1984).

in the work of Louis A. Perez, Jr., not so much as a history of U.S. policy but as a history of Cuba and the Caribbean trying to live within the orbit of U.S. hegemony. Thus, in Perez's provocative interpretation, the United States intervened in 1898 not to support the Cuban independence movement but to defeat it. Having accomplished that, the United States turned Cuba into a compliant plantation (and later vacation) colony.[23]

As long as Americans continue to debate the proper role of their nation in world affairs, the events of the 1890s and the early years of the twentieth century will continue to interest historians. In studying the origins and consequences of the Spanish-American War scholars will probably continue to raise many of the same questions asked by their predecessors for over three quarters of a century. Did the United States go to war to resolve basic contradictions within its economic and social systems? Was the acquisition of an overseas empire a cause or a consequence of war? To what degree did moral, religious, and humanitarian sentiments play a role in the diplomacy of the 1890s and thereafter? To what extent was American foreign policy a response to the diplomacy of other nations and events beyond its control? Did the United States create a new form of "open door" imperialism through the use of its economic power? Did business and strategic thinkers direct the U.S. thrust toward world power status or did the nation stumble into its new status without plan or conscious purpose? Even if American intentions were benign, mixed, or confused, to what extent were the consequences of American policy harmful to those who experienced it as intrusion? Americans will struggle with these and other questions as long as they continue to debate the role America has played and should play as a world power.

---

[23]Louis A. Perez, Jr., *Cuba Between Empires* (Pittsburgh, 1982); *Cuba Under the Platt Amendment, 1902–1934* (Pittsburgh, 1986); *Cuba and the United States: Ties of Singular Intimacy* (Athens, Ga., 1990); *The War of 1898: The United States and Cuba in History and Historiography* (Chapel Hill, N.C., 1998). See also his "Intervention, Hegemony, and Dependency: The United States in the Circum-Caribbean, 1898–1980," *Pacific Historical Review* 51 (May 1982): 165–194.

WALTER LAFEBER

WALTER LAFEBER (1933–   ) is professor of diplomatic history at Cornell University. He is the author of The New Empire: An Interpretation of American Expansionism 1860–1898 *(1963),* America, Russia, and the Cold War 1945–1966 *(8th ed., 1997),* Inevitable Revolutions: The United States in Central America *(2nd ed., 1993), and* The Clash: A History of U.S.–Japan Relations *(1997).*

The "Splendid Little War" of 1898, as Secretary of State John Hay termed it at the time, is rapidly losing its splendor for those concerned with American foreign policy. . . . Over the past decade few issues in the country's diplomatic history have aroused academics more than the causes of the Spanish-American War, and in the last several years the argument has become not merely academic, but a starting point in the debate over how the United States evolved into a great power, and more particularly how Americans got involved in the maelstrom of Asian nationalism. The line from the conquest of the Philippines in 1898 to the attempted pacification of Vietnam in 1968 is not straight, but it is quite traceable, and if Frederick Jackson Turner was correct when he observed in the 1890s that "The aim of history, then, is to know the elements of the present by understanding what came into the present from the past," the causes of the war in 1898 demand analysis from our present viewpoint.

Historians have offered four general interpretations to explain these causes. First, the war has been traced to a general impulse for war on the part of American public opinion. This interpretation has been illustrated in a famous cartoon showing President William McKinley, in the bonnet and dress of a little old lady, trying to sweep back huge waves marked "Congress" and "public opinion," with a very small broom. The "yellow journalism" generated by the Hearst-Pulitzer rivalry supposedly both created and reflected this sentiment for war. A sophisticated and useful version of this interpretation has been advanced by Richard Hofstadter. Granting the importance of the Hearst-Pulitzer struggle, he has asked why these newspaper titans were able to exploit public opinion. Hofstadter has concluded that psychological dilemmas arising out of the depression of the 1890s made Americans react somewhat irrationally because they were uncertain, frightened, and consequently open to exploitation by men who would show them how to cure their frustrations through overseas adventures. In other words, the giddy minds of the 1890s could be quieted by foreign quarrels.

From "That 'Splendid Little War' in Historical Perspective," *Texas Quarterly* 11 (1968): 89–98. Copyright © Walter LaFeber.

A second interpretation argues that the United States went to war for humanitarian reasons, that is, to free the Cubans from the horrors of Spanish policies and to give the Cubans democratic institutions. That this initial impulse resulted within ten months in an American protectorate over Cuba and Puerto Rico, annexation of the Philippines, and American participation in quarrels on the mainland of Asia itself, is explained as accidental, or, more familiarly, as done in a moment of "aberration" on the part of American policy-makers.

A third interpretation emphasizes the role of several Washington officials who advocated a "Large Policy" of conquering a vast colonial empire in the Caribbean and Western Pacific. By shrewd maneuvering, these few imperialists pushed the vacillating McKinley and a confused nation into war. Senator Henry Cabot Lodge, of Massachusetts, Captain Alfred Thayer Mahan, of the U.S. Navy, and Theodore Roosevelt, assistant Secretary of the Navy in 1897–1898, are usually named as the leaders of the "Large Policy" contingent.

A fourth interpretation believes the economic drive carried the nation into war. This drive emanated from the rapid industrialization which characterized American society after the 1840s. The immediate link between this industrialization and the war of 1898 was the economic depression which afflicted the nation in the quarter-century after 1873. Particularly important were the 1893–1897 years when Americans endured the worst of the plunge. Government and business leaders, who were both intelligent and rational, believed an oversupply of goods created the depression. They finally accepted war as a means of opening overseas markets in order to alleviate domestic distress caused by the overproduction. For thirty years the economic interpretation dominated historians' views of the war, but in 1936 Professor Julius Pratt conclusively demonstrated that business journals did not want war in the early months of 1898. He argued instead the "Large Policy" explanation, and from that time to the present, Professor Pratt's interpretation has been pre-eminent in explaining the causes of the conflict.

As I shall argue in a moment, the absence of economic factors in causing the war has been considerably exaggerated. At this point, however, a common theme which unites the first three interpretations should be emphasized. Each of the three deals with a superficial aspect of American life; each is peculiar to 1898, and none is rooted in the structure, the bed-rock, of the nation's history. This theme is important, for it means that if the results of the war were distasteful and disadvantageous (and on this historians do largely agree because of the divisive problems which soon arose in the Philippines and Cuba), those misfortunes were endemic to episodes unique to 1898. The peculiarities of public sentiment or the Hearst-Pulitzer rivalry, for example, have not reoccurred; the wide-spread humanitarian desire to help Cubans has been confined to 1898; and the banding together of Lodge, Mahan, and Roosevelt to fight for "Large Policies" of the late 1890s was never repeated by the three men. Conspiracy theories, moreover, seldom explain history satisfactorily.

The fourth interpretation has different implications. It argues that if the economic was the primary drive toward war, criticism of that war must begin not with irrational factors or flights of humanitarianism or a few stereotyped figures, but with the basic structure of the American system.

United States foreign policy, after all, is concerned primarily with the nation's domestic system and only secondarily with the systems of other nations. American diplomatic history might be defined as the study of how United States relations with other nations are used to insure the survival and increasing prosperity of the American system. . . .

When viewed within this matrix, the diplomatic events of the 1890s are no longer aberrations or the results of conspiracies and drift; American policymakers indeed grabbed greatness with both hands. As for accident or chance, they certainly exist in history, but become more meaningful when one begins with J. B. Bury's definition of "chance": "The valuable collision of two or more independent chains of causes." The most fruitful approach to the war of 1898 might be from the inside out (from the domestic to the foreign), and by remembering that chance is "the valuable collision of two or more independent chains of causes."

Three of these "chains" can be identified: the economic crisis of the 1890s which caused extensive and dangerous maladjustments in American society; the opportunities which suddenly opened in Asia after 1895 and in the Caribbean and the Pacific in 1898, opportunities which officials began to view as poultices, if not cure-alls, for the illnesses at home; and a growing partnership between business and government which reached its nineteenth-century culmination in the person of William McKinley. In April 1898, these "chains" had a "valuable collision" and war resulted.

The formation of the first chain is the great success story of American history. Between 1850 and 1910 the average manufacturing plant in the country multiplied its capital thirty-nine times, its number of wage-earners nearly seven times, and the value of its output by more than nineteen times. . . . The United States traded more in international markets than any nation except Great Britain.

But the most accelerated period of this development, 1873–1898, was actually twenty-five years of boom hidden in twenty-five years of bust. That quarter-century endured the longest and worst depression in the nation's history. After brief and unsatisfactory recoveries in the mid-1880s and early 1890s, the economy reached bottom in 1893. Unparalleled social and economic disasters struck. One out of every six laborers was unemployed, with most of the remainder existing on substandard wages; not only weak firms but many companies with the best credit ratings were forced to close their doors; the unemployed slept in the streets; riots erupted in Brooklyn, California, and points in between, as in the calamitous Pullman Strike in Chicago; Coxey's Army of broken farmers and unemployed laborers made their famous march on Washington; and the Secretary of State, Walter Quentin Gresham, remarked privately in 1894 that he saw "symptoms of revolution" appearing. Federal troops were dispatched to Chicago and other urban areas, including a cordon which guarded the Federal Treasury building in New York City.

Faced with the prospect of revolution and confronted with an economy that had almost ground to a stop, American businessmen and political officials faced alternative policies: they could attempt to re-examine and reorient the economic system, making radical modifications in the means of distribution and particularly the distribution of wealth; or they could look for new physical frontiers, following the historic tendency to increase production and then ferreting out new markets so the surplus, which the nation supposedly was unable to consume, could be sold elsewhere and Americans then put back to work on the production lines. . . .

Some business firms tried to find such security by squashing competitors. Extremely few, however, searched for such policies as a federal income tax. Although such a tax narrowly passed through Congress in 1894, the Supreme Court declared it unconstitutional within a year and the issue would not be resurrected for another seventeen years. As a result, business and political leaders accepted the solution which was traditional, least threatening to their own power, and (apparently) required the least risk: new markets. . . .

This consensus included farmers and the labor movement among others, for these interests were no more ingenious in discovering new solutions than were businessmen. . . . The agrarians acted out of a long and successful tradition, for they had sought overseas customers since the first tobacco surplus in Virginia three hundred and fifty years before. Farmers initially framed the expansionist arguments and over three centuries created the context for the growing consensus on the desirability of foreign markets, a consensus which businessmen and others would utilize in the 1890s. . . .

Industrialists observed that export charts demonstrated the American economy to be depending more upon industrial than agrarian exports. To allow industrial goods to be fully competitive in the world market, however, labor costs would have to be minimal, and cheap bread meant sacrificing the farmers. Fully comprehending this argument, agrarians reacted bitterly. They nevertheless continued searching for their own overseas markets, agreeing with the industrialist that the traditional method of discovering new outlets provided the key to prosperity, individualism, and status. . . .

The political conflict which shattered the 1890s revolved less around the question of whether conservatives could carry out a class solution than the question of which class would succeed in carrying out a conservative solution. This generalization remains valid even when the American labor movement is examined for its response to the alternatives posed. This movement, primarily comprised of the newly-formed American Federation of Labor, employed less than 3 per cent of the total number of employed workers in nonfarm occupations. In its own small sphere of influence, its membership largely consisted of skilled workers living in the East. The AFL was not important in the West or South, where the major discontent seethed. Although Samuel Gompers was known by some of the more faint-hearted as a "social-ist," the AFL's founder never dramatized any radical solutions for the restructuring of the economy. He was concerned with obtaining more money, better hours, and improved working conditions for the Federa-tion's members. Gompers refused, moreover, to use direct political ac-tion to obtain these benefits, content to negotiate within the corporate structure which the businessman had created. The AFL simply wanted more, and when overseas markets seemed to be a primary source of benefits, Gompers did not complain. . . .

The first "chain of causes" was marked by a consensus on the need to find markets overseas. Fortunately for the advocates of this policy, another "chain," quite complementary to the first, began to form be-yond American borders. By the mid-1890s, American merchants, mis-sionaries, and ship captains had been profiting from Asian markets for more than a century. Between 1895 and 1900, however, the United States for the first time became a mover-and-pusher in Asian affairs.

In 1895 Japan defeated China in a brief struggle that now appears to be one of the most momentous episodes in the nineteenth century. The Japanese emerged as the major Asian power, the Chinese suddenly seemed to be incapable of defending their honor or existence, Chinese nationalism began its peculiar path to the 1960s, and European powers which had long lusted after Asian markets now seized a golden opportu-nity. Russia, Germany, France, and ultimately Great Britain initiated policies designed to carve China and Manchuria into spheres of influ-ence. Within a period of months, the Asian mainland suddenly became the scene of international power politics at its worst and most explosive.

The American reaction to these events has been summarized re-cently by Professor Thomas McCormick: "The conclusion of the Sino-Japanese War left Pandora's box wide open, but many Americans mistook it for the Horn of Plenty." . . . Now, just at the moment when key interest groups agreed that overseas markets could be the salva-tion of the 1890s crisis, China was almost miraculously opening its doors to the glutted American factories and farms. United States trade with China jumped significantly after 1895, particularly in the critical area of manufactures; by 1899 manufactured products accounted for more than 90 per cent of the nation's exports to the Chinese, a quadrupling of the amount sent in 1895. In their moment of need, Americans had apparently discovered a Horn of Plenty.

But, of course, it was Pandora's box. The ills which escaped from the box were threefold. Least important for the 1890s, a nascent Chinese nationalism appeared. During the next quarter-century, the United States attempted to minimize the effects of this nationalism either by cooperating with Japan or European powers to isolate and weaken the Chinese, or by siding with the most conservative groups within the nationalist movement. Americans also faced the competition of European and Japanese products, but they were nevertheless confident in the power of their newly-tooled industrial powerhouse. Given a "fair field and no favor," as the Secretary of State phrased the wish in 1900, Americans would undersell and defeat any competitors. But could fair fields and no favors be guaranteed? Within their recently-created spheres of influence European powers began to grant themselves trade preferences, thus effectively shutting out American competition. In 1897, the American business community and the newly-installed administration of William McKinley began to counter these threats.

The partnership between businessmen and politicians, in this case the McKinley administration, deserves emphasis, for if the businessman hoped to exploit Asian markets he required the aid of the politician. Americans could compete against British or Russian manufacturers in Asia, but they could not compete against, say, a Russian manufacturer who could turn to his government and through pressure exerted by that government on Chinese officials receive a prize railroad contract or banking concession. United States businessmen could only compete against such business-government coalitions if Washington officials helped. Only then would the field be fair and the favors equalized. To talk of utilizing American "rugged individualism" and a free enterprise philosophy in the race for the China market in the 1890s was silly. There consequently emerged in American policy-making a classic example of the business community and the government grasping hands and, marching shoulder to shoulder, leading the United States to its destiny of being a major power on a far-Eastern frontier. As one high Republican official remarked in the mid-1890s: "diplomacy is the management of international business."

William McKinley fully understood the need for such a partnership. He had grown to political maturity during the 1870s when, as one Congressman remarked, "The House of Representatives was like an auction room where more valuable considerations were disposed of under the speaker's hammer than in any other place on earth." . . . The new Chief Executive believed there was nothing necessarily manifest about Manifest Destiny in American history, and his administration was the first in modern American history which so systematically and completely committed itself to helping businessmen, farmers, laborers, and missionaries in solving their problems in an industrializing, supposedly frontierless America. . . .

Often characterized as a creature of his campaign manager Mark Hanna, or as having, in the famous but severely unjust words of Theodore Roosevelt, the backbone of a chocolate eclair, McKinley was, as Henry Adams and others fully understood, a master of men. McKinley was never pushed into a policy he did not want to accept. Elihu Root, probably the best mind and most acute observer who served in the McKinley cabinets, commented that on most important matters the President had his ideas fixed, but would convene the Cabinet, direct the members toward his own conclusions, and thereby allow the Cabinet to think it had formulated the policy. In responding to the problems and opportunities in China, however, McKinley's power to exploit that situation was limited by events in the Caribbean.

In 1895 revolution had broken out in Cuba. By 1897 Americans were becoming increasingly belligerent on this issue for several reasons: more than $50,000,000 of United States investments on the island were endangered; Spaniards were treating some Cubans inhumanely; the best traditions of the Monroe Doctrine had long dictated that a European in the Caribbean was a sty in the eye of any red-blooded American; and, finally, a number of Americans, not only Lodge, Roosevelt, and Mahan, understood the strategic and political relationship of Cuba to a proposed isthmian canal. Such a canal would provide a short-cut to the west coast of Latin America as well as to the promised markets of Asia. Within six months after assuming office, McKinley demanded that the island be pacified or the United States would take a "course of action which the time and the transcendent emergency may demand." Some Spanish reforms followed, but in January 1898, new revolts wracked Havana and a month later the "Maine" dramatically sank to the bottom of Havana harbor.

McKinley confronted the prospect of immediate war. Only two restraints appeared. First, a war might lead to the annexation of Cuba, and the multitude of problems (including racial) which had destroyed Spanish authority would be dumped on the United States. Neither the President nor his close advisers wanted to leap into the quicksands of noncontiguous, colonial empire. The business community comprised a second restraining influence. By mid-1897 increased exports, which removed part of the agricultural and industrial glut, began to extricate the country from its quarter-century of turmoil. Finally seeing light at the end of a long and treacherous tunnel, businessmen did not want the requirements of a war economy to jeopardize the growing prosperity.

These two restraints explain why the United States did not go to war in 1897, and the removal of these restraints indicates why war occurred in April 1898. The first problem disappeared because McKinley and his advisers entertained no ideas of warring for colonial empire in the Caribbean. After the war Cuba would be freed from Spain and then ostensibly returned to the Cubans to govern. The United States would retain a veto power over the more important policy decisions made on the island. McKinley discovered a classic solution in which the United States enjoyed the power over, but supposedly little of the responsibility for, the Cubans.

The second restraint disappeared in late March 1898, exactly at the time of McKinley's decision to send the final ultimatum to Madrid. The timing is crucial. Professor Pratt observed in 1936 that the business periodicals began to change their antiwar views in mid-March 1898, but he did not elaborate upon this point. The change is significant and confirms the advice McKinley received from a trusted political adviser in New York City who cabled on March 23 that the larger corporations would welcome war. The business journal and their readers were beginning to realize that the bloody struggle in Cuba and the resulting inability of the United States to operate at full-speed in Asian affairs more greatly endangered economic recovery than would a war.

McKinley's policies in late March manifested these changes. This does not mean that the business community manipulated the President, or that he was repaying those businessmen who had played vital roles in his election in 1896. Nor does it mean that McKinley thought the business community was forcing his hand or circumscribing his policies in late March. The opinions and policies of the President and the business community had been hammered out in the furnace of a terrible depression and the ominous changes in Asia. McKinley and pivotal businessmen emerged from these unforgettable experiences sharing a common conclusion: the nation's economy increasingly depended upon overseas markets, including the whole of China; that to develop these markets not only a business-government partnership but also tranquillity was required; and, finally, however paradoxical it might seem, tranquillity could be insured only through war against Spain. Not for the first or last time, Americans believed that to have peace they would have to wage war. Some, including McKinley, moved on to a final point. War, if properly conducted, could result in a few select strategic bases in the Pacific (such as Hawaii, Guam, and Manila) which would provide the United States with potent starting-blocks in the race for Asian markets. McKinley sharply distinguished between controlling such bases and trying to rule formally over an extensive territorial empire. In the development of the "chains of causes" the dominant theme was the economic, although not economic in the narrow sense. As discussed in the 1890s, business recovery carried most critical political and social implications.

Some historians argue that McKinley entered the war in confusion and annexed the Philippines in a moment of aberration. They delight in quoting the President's announcement to a group of Methodist missionaries that he decided to annex the Philippines one night when after praying he heard a mysterious voice. Most interesting, however, is not that the President heard a reassuring voice, but how the voice phrased its advice. The voice evidently outlined the points to be considered; in any case, McKinley numbered them in order, demonstrating, perhaps, that either he, the voice, or both had given some thought to putting the policy factors in neat and logical order. The second point is of particular importance: "that we could not turn them [the Philippines] over to France or Germany—our commercial rivals in the Orient—that would be bad business and discreditable. . . . "Apparently everyone who had been through the 1890s knew the dangers of "bad business." Even voices.

Interpretations which depend upon mass opinion, humanitarianism, and "Large Policy" advocates do not satisfactorily explain the causes of the war. Neither, however, does Mr. Dooley's famous one-sentence definition of American imperialism in 1898: "Hands acrost th' sea an' into somewan's pocket." The problem of American expansion is more complicated and historically rooted than that flippancy indicates. George Eliot once observed, "The happiest nations, like the happiest women, have no history." The United States, however, endured in the nineteenth century a history of growing industrialism, supposedly closing physical frontiers, rapid urbanization, unequal distribution of wealth, and an overdependence upon export trade. These historical currents clashed in the 1890s. The result was chaos and fear, then war and empire.

In 1898 McKinley and the business community wanted peace, but they also sought benefits which only a war could provide. Viewed from the perspective of the 1960s, the Spanish-American conflict can no longer be viewed as only a "splendid little war." It was a war to preserve the American system.

GERALD F. LINDERMAN

GERALD F. LINDERMAN (1934–   ) is professor of history emeritus at the University of Michigan. He is the author of Mirror of War: American Society and the Spanish-American War *(1974),* Embattled Courage: The Experience of Combat in the American Civil War *(1987), and* The World Within War: America's Combat Experience in World War II *(1997).*

From "The Image of Enemy and Ally" in *The Mirror of War: American Society and the Spanish American War,* Ann Arbor: University of Michigan Press, 1974. Copyright © Gerald F. Linderman.

In nineteenth-century America . . . [n]o people fared worse in the schoolbooks than the Spanish. In the American view, Spanish history was a syllabus of barbarism that left both participants and their progeny morally misshapen. Such an image, moreover, did not exist only as an intellectual abstraction. With so few alternative sources of information available, it often set the lines of political debate. In the prelude to the Spanish-American War those who wished to resist American intervention in Cuba were handicapped by their inability to say anything in defense of the Spanish character. Those who urged American participation had the easier task of demonstrating that Spanish behavior was the simple extension of that Spanish history every American had memorized from his reader.

Americans at first hardly distinguished the image of the Cuban from that of the Spaniard. As anger against Spain mounted, however, it became necessary for them to differentiate, to convert to ally the enemy of their enemy. This was accomplished, but not through any objective examination of the conditions or attributes of the Cuban people. Instead, Americans of public consequence employed various and often contradictory historical analogies which, with scant reference to the Cubans themselves, had by 1898 persuaded most Americans that the Cubans were a moral, enlightened, and kindred race. The first physical contacts of American with Cuban and Spaniard would test these images of good and evil.

In mid-December 1895 President Grover Cleveland and Secretary of State Richard Olney precipitated a diplomatic crisis over a fifty-year-old boundary dispute between Venezuela and Great Britain's colony of Guiana. Angry at London's rejection of earlier Washington suggestions that the controversy be submitted to arbitration, the president announced to Congress on December 17 his decision to appoint an American commission to determine the "true divisional line" between the two territories. Once the boundary was set, Cleveland warned, "it will . . . be the duty of the United States to resist, by every means in its power, as a willful aggression upon its rights and interests, the appropriation by Great Britain of any lands or the exercise of governmental jurisdiction over any territory which . . . we have determined of right belongs to Venezuela." The United States, charging Britain with violating the Monroe Doctrine, threatened war. . . .

Of special concern here are the terms employed by Americans in debating the meaning of Britain's behavior.

Joseph Pulitzer—in 1864 an emaciated German-Hungarian immigrant without resources save for his own will to succeed, thirty years later the powerful publisher of the New York *World* whose extraordinary energies had already cracked the frail shell of his body—was one of those who led public opposition to Cleveland's policy. The president's bludgeon diplomacy, he told the *World*'s half-million readers, was "a grave blunder"; an Anglo-American war would be unpardon-

124 American Imperialism

able folly. Into his antiwar editorials Pulitzer wove three themes. There was in the Venezuelan dispute, he insisted, no possible menace to the United States. He further denied Cleveland's contention that the controversy challenged, or that its outcome could affect, the validity of the Monroe Doctrine. Finally, he cautioned against what he judged to be the nation's state: "Let the war idea once dominate the minds of the American people and war will come whether there is cause for it or not"—an interesting hypothesis that Pulitzer himself did much to verify two years later.

Laced through these arguments were the lineaments of an image of a Britain benevolently disposed to American interests, of an admirable people friend rather than foe. England was a "friendly and kindred nation," "the great naval and commercial and banking nation of the world" whose political system was "essentially . . . of the people, more quickly and completely responsible to the popular will as expressed in the elections than our government is." . . .

In short, who the English were determined what the English did. By definition, kindred peoples would not harm one another's vital interests in Venezuela or anywhere else. War was incomprehensible when Anglo-American ties meant that it must be a species of civil war.

Supporters of the Cleveland-Olney ultimatum wove into their attack on the English a very different image. Henry Cabot Lodge charged that the British government, having already hemmed in the United States with a fortified line in the Pacific, was forging another ring in the Caribbean. London had recently fortified Santa Lucia, Trinidad, and Jamaica. The South American mainland was the next, but not the final, link. "If . . . [Britain] can do it successfully in Venezuela she can do it in Mexico or Cuba; if she can do it other nations can also."

Lodge found nothing remarkable in such notions of British conspiracy. It was the thing to expect of a people no less treacherous and hostile to American interests than any other people. As he earlier told the Senate, "Since we parted from England her statesmen have never failed to recognize that in men speaking her language, and of her own race she was to find her most formidable rivals. She has always opposed, thwarted, and sought to injure us." . . .

Did England's behavior constitute a threat to the United States? One's answer had less to do with London's behavior in this particular controversy, still less with what was transpiring on the banks of the Orinoco, than on the image of England that Cleveland's message summoned to mind. The availability of alternative images set the lines of the American debate.

In a valuable study Ruth Miller Elson has suggested the influence of the stereotyped figures of foreign nationalities so prominent in the grammar-school readers one hundred years ago. The belief that specific personality traits inhere in all members of designated nationality groups is still today a part of our intellectual baggage, but several factors added to the tyranny of nineteenth-century national images. Children, spending on average far fewer years in school, were deeply stamped by the long passages they were compelled to memorize. Moreover, American small-town life offered few of the experiences that today render rigid national stereotypes vulnerable to a more complex reality. Only the rich traveled abroad. Few European tourists or cultural organizations visited this country. . . .

A people buoyed by a sense of its own uniqueness, requiring no continuous relationships with other nationalities, and lacking bridges between its own and other cultures, was likely to find authoritative the lessons of the reader, "that first and only formal presentation of other nations."

The world of the nineteenth-century schoolbook was almost static. Authors precipitated from each nation's history certain men and events on which they pronounced moral judgment and then offered the reader as the embodiment of a collective personality. The character traits thus extracted were often more censorious than complimentary, but almost every characterization combined the two categories. The English, as the rhetoric of the Venezuelan crisis made clear, could be both exemplar and oppressor, a parent solicitous, neglectful, or cruel. . . .

By contrast, schoolbooks found almost nothing to praise in the Spanish. . . . Characteristics that drew American attention (though not necessarily praise) at midcentury—Spanish dignity, honor, military prowess—were subject to slow dilution, it seemed, as Spain disintegrated. That was nothing worthy, and much that was repugnant to Americans, in a conqueror grown indolent. . . .

"No single good thing in law, or science, or art, or literature . . . has resulted to the race of men . . . from Spanish domination in America. . . . I have tried to think of one in vain," announced Charles Francis Adams in 1897. The same theme received scholarly treatment six months later when the president of the University of Wisconsin asked graduating seniors: "What has Spain ever done for civilization? What books, what inventions have come from Spain? What discoveries in the laboratory or in scientific fields?" His own answer was brief: "So few have they been that they are scarcely worth mentioning." He then returned in the climax of his address to the central American perception of Spain—changeless cruelty. "Examination of the Spanish character shows it to be the same as it was centuries ago. Wherever the Spaniard has endeavored to rule he has shown an unrivaled incapacity for government. And the incapacity was such and the cruelty was such that all their colonies and provinces have slipped away." . . .

The image's ability to distort reality, to obscure the logic of particular situations, was most pronounced at the time of the *Maine*'s destruction. Today, though neither proven nor disproven, official Spanish culpability seems unlikely: Spain had nothing to gain, and much to lose, by sinking the vessel. Today the American rush to condemn

Spain appears a psychic aberration, a lapse into irrationality. At the
time, however, the image of the Spaniard made any *other* explanation
appear illogical. A sneak bombing against a background of treacherous
assurances of Spanish goodwill; sleeping men plunged to watery
graves—it was Spanish history come alive, this time with young
Americans as its victims. Rough-shaped pieces of fact could be made
to fit. When the Havana command offered the American survivors expressions of regret and every appropriate aid, Henry Watterson concluded that, while Cuban sadness was genuine, Spanish sympathy, so
"ostentatious," must conceal an inward festiveness. . . .

If there was near unanimity on the nature of the enemy, there remained considerable uncertainty regarding his capacity. The Spaniard
was malevolent, all agreed, but what danger did he pose for Americans? On this point the image was ambiguous. Henry Cabot Lodge had
spoken of Spain as "mediaeval, cruel, dying." How rapid was her decline? How much harm was she still capable of inflicting on others?

These questions produced speculation and considerable anxiety.
Since there could be no definitive answers short of a test of arms,
Americans anticipated war with ambivalent emotions. Those who often voiced the fear that the Spanish would not stand and fight could
not always suppress the fear that they would. When Henry Watterson
complained that Spanish courage was not the courage of "cool tenacity
and hope," but that of desperation, others sensed the unspoken corol-
lary: desperate men could exact a high toll from their enemies.

No one caught better than Sherwood Anderson the American vac-
illation in definitions of Spanish prowess. At one moment he was confident war would be "a kind of glorious national picnic." He could
even indulge in a thin guilt that the job would be so easy, "like robbing
an old gypsy woman in a vacant lot at night after a fair." In other moments, however, the Spaniard as cyclonic evil seemed very near:
"Dark cruel eyes, dark swaggering men in one's fancy." Anderson
dreamed of grappling with a Spanish commandant who, half drunk and
surrounded by his concubines, plunged his sword into a serving-boy
who had spilled the wine. Americans like Sherwood Anderson, con-
ceiving of themselves as moral vindicators, were given pause: was the
Spaniard a still vigorous and thus dangerous evil-doer or only an unre-
pentant invalid?

This uncertainty may have had some bearing on the undulation of
public emotion before and during the Spanish-American War. So often the
objective situation seemed insufficient explanation for those roller
coaster spurts up and down emotional inclines and through the curves. . . .

Public tension before battles, public jubilation afterward, seems
inordinate. The unprecedented celebration of Dewey's victory at
Manila Bay suggests relief from the fear of disaster, disaster overtaking
Americans in distant islands so exotic and unfamiliar. Dewey was dei-
fied. In the Caribbean campaign too there were wide swings of emo-

tion. General Shafter, vacillating between the enemy as destroyer and as invalid, was never able to gauge clearly the danger that the Spanish Army posed for his own forces. Indecisive, he tried in the aftermath of the battle of San Juan to act so as to encompass both images. At the same moment that he telegraphed Washington that his Army was in such extreme danger that he was preparing to retreat, he sent an ultimatum to his opponent demanding the immediate surrender of Santiago. Americans certain of Spanish malevolence but unsure of Spanish power swung rapidly back and forth between an almost swaggering confidence and a deep-seated dread, between excessive celebration and excessive fear.

The image of the Cuban had at first none of the compelling emotional quality of the Spaniard. Indeed, since few Americans prior to 1895 counted the Cubans a distinct people, the image of the ally required simultaneously both separation from the image of the enemy and a delineation of its own.

The crafting of distinctions between Cuban and Spaniard did not begin with the arrival of the news of the Cuban revolt. Americans convinced of Spanish immorality assumed, correctly, that there had been considerable racial mixture in Cuba; Cubans must have thereby inherited every unlovely Spanish trait. Learning of the Cuban insurrection, Americans did not rush to embrace Cubans as kindred. There was no automatic assumption of Cuban virtue as there was of Spanish wrongdoing. Initial statements reveal both denunciation of the Spaniards *and* a deprecation of the *insurrectos* that hewed to Madrid's line. The Cubans were insignificant black rioters or bandits who would be easily dispersed. Richard Franklin Pettigrew, a South Dakota senator who wished war because he thought it would remonetize silver, cared nothing for Spaniard or Cuban: the best idea was to sink the island for twenty-four hours "to get rid of its present population." A prominent Methodist clergyman thought the Cubans "indolent, seditious, ignorant, superstitious and greatly useless." Somewhat less genteel was William Allen White: the Cubans were "Mongrels with no capacity for self government . . . a yellow-legged, knife-sticking, treacherous outfit." Speaker of the House Reed called them "yellow-bellies."

No evidence suggests that Reed, with McKinley a last-ditch opponent of the war, ever changed his mind about Cuban deficiencies. There is, however, ample evidence for the assertion that in the period 1895–97 the majority of Americans began to view Cubans in a favorable, or at least a different, way. It became increasingly difficult to deny sympathy to an enemy of *the* enemy. How could the Spaniards so richly deserve chastisement if the Cubans were undeserving of freedom? How could American strength secure justice for the weak if the weak were themselves malicious? . . .

To some Americans the Cuban rising became a latter-day American Revolution. Richard Harding Davis, watching a Spanish firing

squad execute an "erect and soldierly" Cuban youth named Ro-
driquez, invoked for his many readers the death of Nathan Hale. Governor John P. Altgeld of Illinois declared in public address that the
Cubans' struggle was their American Revolution, and Senator George
G. Vest of Missouri drew out the moral: the insurrectionists deserved
American support because they were emulating the American experience. Senator William E. Mason of Illinois claimed a more substantial
connection. Cuban boys had come to our colleges, learned about
George Washington and returned home to tell their compatriots. Revolution was an inevitable result. These judgments were based on a
widespread but erroneous assumption that the Cubans had revolted to
secure, not their own government, but good government on the American model.

Another prominent analogy was that of the Cuban as Southerner.
Many former Confederates discovered in Spanish oppression echoes of
the North's military occupation of the South during Reconstruction.
Joseph Bailey's biographer assigns nine-tenths of the Texan's sympathy
to empathy with those whom he thought resisting the same sort of
military despotism he had opposed three decades before. . . . Racist and
racial liberal thus moved from opposite poles to join hands in support
of the Cuban.

Other groups looked to European history for images to unlock the
meaning of events in the Caribbean. To staunch Protestants, especially
the clergy, the Cubans were another in a series of peoples who had
risen against Catholic oppression. (Anti-clericalism was an insignificant factor in the revolt of the Cubans. It was prominent in the Philippines, but few Americans had heard that there was a simultaneous
Filipino uprising.) American Catholic publications, unable to support
either "brigands" or a revolt advertised by Protestants as anti-
Catholic, found a quite different analogy: Cuba was suffering Spanish
tyranny as Ireland endured English tyranny. Its persuasiveness lay in
the suggestion that the Cubans, like the Irish, were oppressed *because*
of their religion, the faithful persecuted for their beliefs. Its weakness
lay in the necessity to overlook the Catholicism of the Spaniards. . . .

However confusing and contradictory, the various roles which
Americans imposed on the Cuban had one element in common: support
for American intervention on behalf of the Cuban. However divided at
home on political, economic, or religious grounds, Americans found an
appropriate interventionist argument in the grab bag of history. . . .

White Americans of the 1890s were all but unanimous in their belief in black inferiority and the necessity of the social separation of the
races. For prominent Americans to champion the aspirations of a
mixed people—for a Joseph Wheeler, for example, to wage a viciously
negrophobic campaign for the House of Representatives and then refer
to Cubans as "our brethren"—required reappraisal of Cuban color and
temperament. One avenue . . . involved the bleaching of the Cuban.

In his influential Senate speech of March 17, 1898, Vermont's Red-field Proctor assured his countrymen that better than three of four Cubans were "like the Spaniards, dark in complexion, but oftener light or blond." The figure whom Americans came to accept as the proto-typical victim of Spanish inhumanity, William Randolph Heart's most successful promotion, the rescued maiden Evangelina Cisneros, was described as possessing "a white face, young, pure and beautiful." The Kansas soldier of fortune Frederick Funston, a volunteer smuggled to the island along underground routes maintained by the Cuban Junta's New York headquarters, wrote that "fully nine-tenths [of the insurrec-tionists] were white men." General Gomez was himself "of pure Span-ish descent." Most Cuban officers were former planters, stockmen, farmers, professionals, and businessmen—"the best men." Later, when Gomez ordered General Garcia to join forces, Funston noted an important difference: rebel units from eastern Cuba contained a much higher proportion of Negroes. Few other Americans were aware of the distinction. Correspondents, almost all of them strongly intervention-ist, made their way into rebel territory by working east from Havana. Few penetrated easternmost Santiago Province where black Cubans were most numerous. Their reports, like Funston's first letters, con-veyed the impression that the Cuban Army was almost entirely white. This misconception would be corrected with abrupt and calamitous results when the Fifth Corps landed only thirty miles from the city of Santiago.

Another theme, Americanization, accompanied the stress on Cuban whiteness. This enlarged the basis of Cuban-American coopera-tion beyond bonds of color to include temperamental similarities. Af-ter a visit to rebel territory, Grover Flint wrote in *McClure's Magazine* that Gomez had shown an "Anglo-Saxon tenacity of purpose." The general's staff was "businesslike." When Flint and others then praised the Cuban Army for its self-respect, determination, discipline, and concern for its wounded, the insurrectionary forces seemed an organi-zation very similar to the United States Army. A plausible extension would suggest comparable fighting capacities. Here again Americans built unrealistic expectations. In fact they understood neither the Cuban Army nor the nature of the war it was fighting. . . .

Images of ally and enemy reversed rapidly, though not simultane-ously. Members of the Fifth Corps reappraised the Cuban almost as they touched the beaches. The Cuban *insurrectos* who greeted them did not *look* like soldiers. Their clothes were in tatters, their weapons a strange assortment, their equipment woefully incomplete—"a crew," thought Theodore Roosevelt, "as utter tatterdemalions as human eyes ever looked on." . . .

Personal contact converted admiration to disgust. The English cor-respondent John Black Atkins, noting that the insurgents looked "in-credibly tattered and peaked and forlorn," thought "by far the most notable thing" about the American volunteers' reaction "was their sudden, open disavowel of friendliness toward the Cubans." Unaware of the true nature of the Cubans' war, Americans were quick to generalize from appearance to fighting ability. Roosevelt immediately concluded that the Cubans would be useless in "serious fighting." Captain John Bigelow's professional eye caught little more: "Bands of Cubans in ragged and dirty white linen, barefooted, and variously armed, marched past us, carrying Cuban and American flags. . . . The Cubans were evidently undisciplined. I thought from their appearance that they would probably prove useful as guides and scouts, but that we would have to do practically all the fighting." George Kennan of the Red Cross, perhaps the most judicious observer of events in Cuba, found himself struggling to reconcile his preconception of Cuban military prowess with an appearance that seemed to preclude fighting qualities. The *insurrectos* "may have been brave men and good soldiers," but "if their rifles and cartridge belts had been taken away . . . they would have looked like a horde of dirty Cuban beggars and ragamuffins on the tramp."

If before white Americans had imagined Cuban complexions as pale as their own, now the darker shades seemed ubiquitous. Roosevelt thought Cuban soldiers "almost all blacks and mulattoes." In a later letter to Secretary of War Alger, Leonard Wood elaborated the significance of color: the Cuban Army "is made up very considerably of black people, only partially civilized, in whom the old spirit of savagery has been more or less aroused by years of warfare, during which time they have reverted more or less to the condition of men taking what they need and living by plunder.". . .

Cuban behavior soon joined appearance as the next item in a lengthening indictment of the ally. American soldiers had accepted earnestly public declarations of their country's unselfishness in entering the war; they did, nevertheless, expect a return. Implicit in the dominant concept of the war—the disinterested relief of suffering Cubans—was the confidence that Cubans would view themselves as victims delivered from oppression and would be grateful. In reality, there was little Cuban gratitude. No cheering greeted the American landings. The *insurrecto* accepted gifts of American rations but, thought Stephen Crane, "with the impenetrable indifference or ignorance of the greater part of the people in an ordinary slum." "We feed him and he expresses no joy." The volunteers could not miss Cuban stolidity. At first surprised, they became resentful and then angry.

Additional disillusionment was to come. Sharing his rations in what he thought an act of charity, the volunteer who went unthanked was not likely to repeat the gesture, especially when it was already obvious that the Army commissariat could not keep his own stomach full. The hungry *insurrecto*, however, contrasting the supply bonanza on the beach with his own meager resources, concluded that the Americans would hardly miss what would suffice to feed him. He returned several times to his original benefactors, who were perplexed and then indignant at the conversion of charity at lunch-time to obligation by the dinner hour. When the Cubans found that this method produced diminishing results, they began pilfering from food stocks and picking up discarded items of equipment. With each episode American contempt grew.

Other Cuban behavior antagonized the volunteers. The principal charge here, precisely that against the Spaniard, was cruelty. Atkins reported the disgust of Americans watching Cubans stab a bull to death and, later, decapitating a Spaniard caught spying out American positions. After the battle of Santiago Bay, Captain Robley Evans, USN, was shocked by Cubans shooting at Spanish sailors swimming ashore to escape their burning vessels. . . .

Angry at what Cubans did, Americans were equally perturbed by what they would not do—act as labor forces for American fighting units. The Cubans "while loitering in the rear"—half of them feigning illness or simply lazing about, it was reported—refused to aid in building roads or cutting litter poles for the American wounded. They would not act in mere logistical support of American units whose anxiety to close with the enemy would in any case have left little substantial role for the Cubans. . . .

The first trial of Cuban-American cooperation came at Guantanamo where just prior to the main landings a Cuban detachment assisted a unit of Marines under Lieutenant Colonel Robert W. Huntington. The Cubans, cabled Admiral Sampson to the president, were "of great assistance" in securing the beachhead and repulsing Spanish attacks. Stephen Crane, one of the few Americans to see the landings at both Guantanamo and Daiquiri, was less complimentary. Conceding that the Cubans were at first efficient in supporting Huntington, he insisted that they soon traded the fight for food and a nap. Americans "came down here expecting to fight side by side with an ally, but this ally has done little but stay in the rear and eat Army rations, manifesting an indifference to the cause of Cuban liberty which could not be exceeded by some one who had never heard of it." . . .

A short time later Shafter decided to exclude all *insurrectos* from the ceremony marking Santiago's surrender and to maintain largely intact the city's Spanish administration: "This war," he told Garcia, ". . . is between the United States of America and the Kingdom of Spain, and . . . the surrender . . . was made solely to the American Army." . . .

Disillusionment with America's ally reached those at home very quickly. Correspondents, often busier as participants than as observers, shared the soldiers' bitterness toward the Cuban. Confident of their objectivity and immune to appeals to higher statecraft, they filled their stories with their anger. Just as important was the informal communications network. Visitors returning home from the war zone and uncensored letters published by the hundreds in hometown newspapers spread the news of Cuban villainy. The speed of the reversal was impressive. On June 30, 1898, an editorial in the Clyde *Enterprise* referred to the Cuban Army, old style, as "a large and effective fighting force of intelligent soldiers, who have already been repeatedly complimented for bravery by the generals of the invading [American] Army. Before this war is over it will be found that the people who for three years have been opposing Spanish tyranny . . . are as brave as any who wear the blue." It was the last such reference. On July 21 the *Enterprise* announced that the Cubans were "worthless allies.". . . .

American soldiers concluded shortly after landing that Cubans were no better than Spaniards. The next revelation was equally unexpected: Spaniards were superior to Cubans. . . .

El Caney was a small crossroads hamlet of thatched huts and tileroof buildings dominated by a stone church. On the morning of July 1 Shafter sent units totaling six thousand men under the command of General Henry W. Lawton to seize the town. The resistance was much stiffer than the Americans had expected. Despite the fatalism of the Spanish high command, middle-grade officers and their men, conceding nothing, resisted stubbornly. The fighting lasted into the afternoon. When the church and a nearby fort were at last reduced, almost four hundred of the six hundred defenders were dead, wounded, or captured. The attackers suffered four hundred and forty-one casualties, including eighty-one dead.

At El Caney the stereotyped Spaniard dissolved. As soon as his men overran the final Spanish bastion, General Chaffee advanced to shake the hand of the Spanish lieutenant in charge. In turn, a Spanish officer praised the courage of the Americans who had thrown themselves at Caney's trenches. George Kennan was sure that the "moral effect of this battle was to give each of the combatants a feeling of sincere respect for the bravery of the other." A second battle that day on the San Juan ridges enlarged the volunteers' regard for Spanish valor. Americans whose commander calculated that they would sustain four hundred wounded suffered three times that number. When the crests were finally in American hands, Theodore Roosevelt felt a new esteem for a tenacious enemy. "No men of any nationality could have done better." The Spaniards were "brave foes."

There was a similar, though not identical, turn in the war at sea. When Admiral Sampson hit on a scheme to block the channel from Santiago harbor by sinking the collier *Merrimac* in its midpassage, Lieutenant Richmond Pearson Hobson accepted the assignment. Enemy fire, however, disrupted the plan. Hobson and his crew were unable to scuttle the vessel at the critical spot or make their way to rescue craft. The next day, just as Americans were beginning to despair of Hobson's fate, Admiral Cervera sent a message to his blockaders: he had captured Hobson and his men and now offered assurances of their well-being. American officers were impressed. There was, said Captain Robley Evans, "never a more courteous thing done in war."

A reconsideration of the enemy begun with Cervera's note ended with the destruction of the Spanish fleet. American naval officers who on July 4 inflicted terrible destruction on the Spaniards immediately felt a sympathy for foes crushed so decisively. Evans was sorry for Cervera, who was hauled from the water and then received with military honors and champagne. There was an even greater measure of sympathy and respect when Americans soon discovered the abominable physical condition of the vessels in which the Spaniards had tried to fight them. The ties of professional standards were cemented; with wretched resources, the Spaniards had played the game honorably. . . . For many Americans the ally of early 1898 had become enemy and the enemy, ally.

In a 1912 article entitled "The Passing of San Juan Hill," Richard Harding Davis reported that on a return visit to Cuba he had found changes "startling and confusing." The course of the San Juan River had altered and obliterated the Bloody Bend of such moment to the battle. More troubling was the Cuban view of what had happened on that terrain fourteen years earlier. The battlefield guide insisted that American forces, arriving just as the Cubans were about to conquer the Spaniards, had by luck alone received all the credit. He further reported that Cubans now ranked the fighting qualities of their Spanish foes much higher than those of their American allies.

5

THE NEW IMMIGRATION

Assimilation or Ethnic Pluralism?

"We are all immigrants." For many Americans, this statement sums up a relatively uncomplicated affirmation of inclusive nationalism. In their view, America is an idea more than a "nation" in the European sense. Rather than affiliations of blood and tradition, Americans sustain consensual ties of citizenship based on common devotion to core principles of liberty, equality, and tolerance. In the words of former New York Governor Mario M. Cuomo, ours is a "politics of inclusion"[1] and, while the struggle to realize this ideal never ends, the trajectory is clear. Unity will come from diversity, the One from the Many.

As an ideal there is much to be said for this formulation (though some would argue whether unity or diversity should be more highly valued). Aside from such ideological questions, however, historians must ask whether a stirring tale of immigrant struggle and successful inclusion adequately captures either the reality or the significance of the immigration experience over several centuries. Why did certain people at certain times leave their homelands? Why did they go to certain destinations? Were they sojourners intending to return to old worlds, or refugees intent on permanently residing in new ones? How did they settle—in large groups, in family units, as individuals? How did they build new lives—what work did they find, where did they reside, what sort of cultural institutions did they reproduce or create? To what extent did they retain old world customs, gender relations, and family values, and to what extent did they assimilate into the host culture? What sort of ethnic identity did they develop as an outcome of this process? With what degree of welcome or hostility were they treated by their American predecessors? What was the character of that host culture—was it Anglo-Saxon, or a diverse mix of subcultures, or some sort of amalgam? What impact did the immigrants have on the society they entered, on local or national politics, on gender and racial practices, on intellectual and cultural developments?

---

[1]Mario M. Cuomo, "The American Dream and the Politics of Inclusion," *Psychology Today* (July 1986): 54–56.

These and many other questions have occupied American historians since the founding of the nation. Crèvecoeur announced even before the Revolution had run its course that the new world immigrant had become a "new man," one who sloughed off his old world skin and set forth toward a new destiny: "Here individuals of all nations are melted into a new race of men, whose labours and posterity will one day cause great changes in the world."[2] With a minimum of anxiety and full confidence in the future that opened before him, this new man was a creature of his environment, imbibing entirely new ideas, principles, and habits from the salubrious air of freedom all around him. Within the context of a European world that had for several centuries witnessed state oppression of religious minorities as well as bloody religious struggles within and among states, the American social fabric appeared something of a miracle. It seemed to have harmoniously woven together English and French Catholics, Dutch Calvinists, German and Scandinavian Lutherans, Moravian Pietists, Scots Presbyterians, English Congregationalists and Anglicans, as well as Baptists, Quakers, Methodists, and a dizzying proliferation of breakaway Protestant denominations and nearly irreligious Deists and freethinkers. Although the term was not yet in use, "pluralism" was practiced in the United States to a significant and noteworthy extent.[3] But it was a pluralism that was understood as temporary—eventually the melting pot of America would assimilate these different subgroups into a common "new man" culture.

Although a few dissenting voices could be heard in the century after Crèvecoeur wrote, most American writers and orators continued to sound the confident note of transformation and assimilation that was the hallmark of the "new man" theory of Americanization. Certainly, the brief anti-alien campaign of the 1790s and the more substantial Know-Nothing movement of the 1850s marked moments in which confidence in the assimilative capacity of the American republic (as well as the assimilative intentions of the newcomers) dimmed considerably. More troubling to proponents of assimilation, white Americans

---

[2] J. Hector St. John de Crèvecoeur, *Letters of an American Farmer* (1782; New York, 1963), p. 70. Although Crèvecoeur pioneered use of the metaphor, the term "melting pot" did not come into general use until the twentieth century, especially after the publication of Israel Zangwill's play, *The Melting-Pot* (New York, 1908): see Arthur Mann, *The One and the Many: Reflections on the American Identity* (Chicago, 1979), Chapter 5. The term "pluralism," employed most assertively in 1915 by Horace Kallen, who is discussed below, came into use somewhat later: see Ibid., Chapter 6.

[3] On Pennsylvania, see Sally Schwartz, *"A Mixed Multitude": The Struggle for Toleration in Colonial Pennsylvania* (New York, 1987); J. William Frost, *A Perfect Freedom: Religious Liberty in Pennsylvania* (Cambridge, 1990); on Rhode Island, Carla Gardina Pestana, *Liberty of Conscience and the Growth of Religious Diversity in Early America, 1636–1786* (Providence, 1986).

almost never entertained the idea of equal coexistence, let alone amalgamation, with the red and black inhabitants of the continent. When forced to consider the unthinkable by abolitionists or advocates of Indian rights, most Americans declined to extend their pluralistic ideals to any but fellow descendants of Europeans. Nevertheless, it was not until the simultaneous arrival of both labor radicalism and millions of new immigrants in the late nineteenth century that large numbers of Americans came seriously to doubt the "new man" myth.

To understand the significance of immigration to American history it is useful to consider the scale of the phenomenon. According to one estimate, approximately 100 million people emigrated from a myriad of homelands between the mid-sixteenth and the mid-twentieth century.[4] At least 45 million, i.e., almost half of the total, headed for the United States or the colonies that preceded it, and most of them—around 38 million—ended up staying in America.[5] By any measure, this immense migration is a major event in the history of the modern world and especially of the United States. Even in the eighteenth and nineteenth centuries, the immigrants were diverse, including not just English but very large numbers of Scottish, Irish, and German migrants, as well as smaller numbers of other western Europeans. By the late-nineteenth and early-twentieth centuries, however, the composition of the influx changed significantly. Continuing streams of Irish and Germans were accompanied by larger streams of southern and eastern Europeans, and small but sharply increased numbers of Asian and Mexican immigrants. These new immigrants, especially the Italians, Jews, and Slavs who together sometimes became majorities in industrial towns throughout America, generated fear, anger, and perplexity among millions of older-stock Americans.

From the start, these immigrants were pushed by need and pulled by opportunity. At first, American historians focused on the latter, assuming that "the land of opportunity" was itself an irresistible argument for migration. Of course, historians found themselves referring to "religious oppression" or "economic upheaval" in Europe as a cause of foreigners' determination to come to America. But this dark background (sometimes luridly, but always briefly sketched) only served to set off the glory of America, which always shone brightly in the foreground. In whatever form, the redemptive tale of immigration achieved the status of folk legend or religious epic, and historians usually adopted some version of it in shaping their narratives of national development well into the twentieth century. The Harvard historian

---

[4]Virginia Yans-McLaughlin, ed., *Immigration Reconsidered: History, Sociology, and Politics* (New York, 1990), p. 3.

[5]Stephan Thernstrom, ed., *The Harvard Encyclopedia of American Ethnic Groups* (Cambridge, Mass. 1980), p. 476.

Albert Bushnell Hart expostulated in 1907: "O Marvellous Constitution! Magic Parchment! Transforming Word! Maker, Monitor, Guardian of Mankind! Thou hath gathered to thy impartial bosom the peoples of the earth, Columbia, and called them equal. . . ."[6] The far more restrained Frederick Jackson Turner, in his famous 1893 essay, "The Significance of the Frontier in American History," declared: "In the crucible of the frontier, the immigrants were Americanized, liberated, and fused into a mixed race, English in neither nationality nor characteristics."[7] Whatever we make of these pronouncements today, we should note that such melting pot rhetoric could serve a progressive political function at the beginning of the twentieth century. At a time when many old-stock Americans were lamenting "the passing of the great race" and the mongrelization of America, writers who idealized assimilation were suggesting that America's traditional welcome to the refugees of the world, and the new man myth that underlay it, deserved to be extended indefinitely.

In the twentieth century such views came to be supported not only by folk legend but by social science. Especially in the Chicago School of sociology, historians found a persuasive account of assimilation in stages. As described in the so-called "race relations cycle," immigrants underwent a general and straight-line development from peasants to moderns. The process began with the formation of ethnic communities within a competitive social environment; it proceeded through conflict, accommodation, and assimilation, at which point former outsiders had shed immigrant identities and emerged as fully Americanized moderns.[8] What distinguished the sociological from the mythic tale, however, was the capacity of the former to acknowledge not only the success of assimilation but its costs. In the years following World War II, a new generation of historians was ready to weigh those costs in narrating the story of immigration.

The revised story of immigration emerged after the war concurrently with the entrance into the academic profession of descendants of those new immigrants who had come to the United States in the late-nineteenth and early-twentieth centuries. Even when these social scientists and historians celebrated the transformative and redemptive power of America, they tended to linger more intently than had earlier scholars on the sufferings of immigrants striving to realize the Ameri-

---

[6]Quoted in Mann, The One and the Many, 63.

[7]Reprinted in Turner, The Frontier in American History (New York, 1920), pp. 22–23.

[8]See Robert E. Park and Ernest W. Burgess, Introduction to the Science of Sociology, 2/e (Chicago, 1924); Robert E. Park and Herbert A. Miller, Old World Traits Transplanted (New York, 1921); and William I. Thomas and Florian Znaniecki, The Polish Peasant in Europe and America: Monograph of an Immigrant Group, 5 vols. (Boston, 1918–1920).

can dream. The greatest of the new immigration historians was Oscar Handlin. His *The Uprooted,* published in 1951, took the form of an "epic," the trajectory of which—from "uprooting" to "acculturation"—was faithful to both new man legend and Chicago School theory.[9] What distinguished Handlin's account from that of all his predecessors was his determination to give a dramatic and detailed account of the high costs of the immigration experience. Clearly, Handlin saw the immigrants whose experience he traced as *his* ancestors, not some mass of anonymous foreigners ready for the melting pot.

Ten years earlier, in *Boston's Immigrants,* Handlin had already shown how sympathetic identification with the travails of the immigrants could generate convincing social history.[10] In that book, however, he tentatively suggested that ethnic identity might endure for a long time alongside the inevitable process of "adjustment" to the host society. In *The Uprooted* he downplayed suggestions of ethnic resilience, while generalizing the story of adjustment to cover the experience of millions. With characteristic grandeur, he identified the immigrant experience with the American experience: "The newcomers were on the way toward being Americans almost before they stepped off the boat, because their own experience of displacement had already introduced them to what was essential in the situation of Americans," i.e., fluidity of social role, acceptance of continuous change, reliance upon individual resources to navigate the shoals of modernity. And with equal grandeur he employed the first person plural to identify himself with the epic of his ancestors and the epic of America: "In our flight, unattached, we discovered what it was to be an individual, . . . we discovered the unexpected, invigorating effects of recurrent demands upon the imagination, upon all our human capacities."[11] Handlin drew a harrowing picture of the immigrants' plight, their alienation and suffering, and their desperate embrace of one another in the struggle to survive dislocation. In the end, however, *The Uprooted* left little doubt that those immigrants eventually departed from peasant conformism and adopted modern individualism. "America was the land of separated men," he declared, and each immigrant eventually learned to become "an individual alone."

Although Handlin's book became the standard for a whole generation of students of immigration, voices of dissent emerged before long. Many historians of immigration discerned flaws in the grand epic and the methods Handlin used to tell it. Why had he dispensed with foot-

---

[9]Oscar Handlin, *The Uprooted: The Epic Story of the Great Migrations That Made the American People* (Boston, 1951). In a second edition (Boston, 1973) Handlin responded to some of his critics.

[10]*Boston's Immigrants: A Study in Acculturation* (Cambridge, Mass., 1941).

[11]Handlin, *The Uprooted,* pp. 272–273.

notes? How could he be so sure about the thoughts, feelings, and attitudes of the people he depicted—did he actually have evidence of such states of mind and feeling? Even assuming his evidence was solid, these historians doubted the inferences Handlin drew from that evidence, and the sweeping generalizations and uni-directional narrative he imposed on it. Most particularly, they dissented from the thesis that cultural differences dissolved inevitably into a composite American identity. Handlin's critics insisted that ethnic identity was durable, that ethnic pluralism, not assimilation, has been the American norm.[12] In doing so, historians made use of the ethnic pluralist theory that the philosopher Horace Kallen had propounded earlier in the century. Reacting to anti-immigrant Americanizers, Kallen had insisted that group particularism, not assimilation, was the real story of immigrant adjustment to America. In refusing to be "melted," immigrants not only preserved the distinctive values of their heritage but enriched and strengthened America. A nation of nations, America would be the model of pluralist democracy for the twentieth-century world.

More important than a revival of Kallen's sort of pluralism, new sociological theory encouraged historians in the 1960s to revise their accounts of the assimilation process. In the years just after World War II, Ruby Jo Reeves Kennedy and Will Herberg had proposed that assimilation occurred in a "triple melting pot" based on religion, rather than in a single process of cultural conformity. Protestant, Catholic, and Jewish subcultures assimilated diverse co-religionists, but did not themselves melt into a homogeneous American identity. In the 1960s sociologists further revised the Chicago School account of ethnic assimilation, opening the door to a far more pluralistic theory of ethnicity. Milton Gordon developed a highly complex theory that distinguished cultural assimilation from structural assimilation and marital assimilation. For Gordon, structural assimilation—widespread entrance of outsiders into "cliques, clubs, and institutions" of the dominant group—was the most decisive of the three. From it proceeded marital assimilation, whereby outsiders and insiders amalgamated and dissolved lines of difference between them. However, cultural assimilation could occur without entailing any of these more substantial forms of interaction. Adopting the styles and foodways, the language and habits of the mainstream society—as most immigrants or their children had quite readily done—did not guarantee admission to the circles of influence and hierarchies of power in the society.

In fact, according to Gordon, America was a series of "subsocieties," each with its own subculture. Some of these subsocieties were based on ethnicity, others on class, and the intersections of the two

---

[12]One of the first was Rudolph J. Vecoli, "Contadini in Chicago: A Critique of *The Uprooted*," *Journal of American History* 51 (1964): 404–417.

produced what Gordon dubbed "ethclass." The core subsociety of white, Protestant, middle-class folk had elaborated a core subculture to which outsiders could gain access; the children of immigrants had indeed assimilated to that core subculture in many ways. Nevertheless, Gordon insisted, even such culturally assimilated descendants of immigrants retained vital attachment to the ethnic subculture because they continued to need the subsociety—i.e., the institutions and networks and support systems that linked Poles to Poles, Italians to Italians, Jews to Jews, etc. Boundary crossing of the "triple melting pot" sort was occurring, as well as some old-fashioned cleaving to ethnic enclaves, and resistance on the basis of race to boundary crossing. The overall picture was one of considerable and increasing cultural assimilation, alongside very slowly increasing structural assimilation. In the early 1970s, going even further than Gordon, Michael Novak proposed that ethnicity was "unmeltable," and Daniel Patrick Moynihan and Nathan Glazer argued that ethnic boundaries defined political entities whose salience was increasing rather than declining. Moynihan and Glazer saw ethnicity not as constraining but as empowering, and insisted that there was no prospect whatever of such an indispensable form of identity melting away.[13]

Historians readily picked up on this more pluralistic social science theory partly because fellow historians had already been marking the way. As early as 1940, Marcus Lee Hanson had pioneered the argument that immigrants' experiences could not be collapsed into a single, unidirectional theory of assimilation. Over time, he contended, immigrants and their descendants sometimes let go of, and at other times revived or invented versions of ethnicity as historical circumstances demanded. Frank Thistlethwaite insisted in 1960 that immigrants came from many different places, had different motives, goals, and experiences, and interacted in many different ways with transnational labor markets and a variety of host societies. No straight-line theory could comprehend the diversity of experiences within so vast and complex a phenomenon. This more complex view of immigration not only liberated historians from the "new man" myth and the unidirectional assimilation model, it also allowed scholars to study immigration to America in connection with the economic and demographic transformations in the wider Atlantic world and beyond.[14]

---

[13]Nathan Glazer and Daniel P. Moynihan, *Beyond the Melting Pot: The Negroes, Puerto Ricans, Jews, Italians, and Irish of New York City* (Cambridge, Mass., 1963). In the revised 1970 edition, the authors respond to critics. See also Michael Novak, *The Rise of the Unmeltable Ethnics* (New York, 1971).

[14]Marcus Lee Hanson, *The Atlantic Migration, 1607–1860* (Cambridge, Mass., 1940); Frank Thistlethwaite, "Migration from Europe Overseas in the Nineteenth and Twentieth Centuries," reprinted in *Population Movements in Modern European History*, Herbert Moller, ed. (New York, 1964), pp. 73–93; see also Virginia Yans-McLaughlin, ed., *Immigration Reconsidered: History, Sociology, and Politics* (New York, 1990).

Beyond the realm of scholarship, in the late 1950s and 1960s the civil rights movement made Americans more conscious of the wide gap between the nation's ideals and its racial practices. Historians responded by producing a host of new studies of slavery and racial conflict in America.[15] But they also uncovered the history of vicious prejudice against foreigners. Thus, John Higham in *Strangers in the Land* traced the cycles of nativist hostility to immigrants from the 1860s to the 1920s.[16] With subtlety and amazing thoroughness, Higham made it plain that America was not as welcoming to strangers as the myth of assimilation would have it. At least at times when national confidence waned in the face of economic downturns or other traumas, a streak of vicious ethnic bigotry was a recurrent thread in the American fabric. This new history coincided with a "new ethnicity": just as African Americans were announcing that "black is beautiful," descendants of the Italian, Jewish, and Slavic immigrants of the early twentieth century began reclaiming names like Korczenowski, Lipschutz, and Pignataro, which had been Anglicized at Ellis Island or abandoned by anxious ancestors. Rather than a fading attachment to tradition, ethnicity increasingly seemed a repository of authentic experience. American "white-bread" culture seemed not just an aesthetically featureless wasteland but a machine for homogenizing people, thereby depriving them of an essential form of personal empowerment. For many reasons, therefore, historians in the 1960s plunged into the search for diverse and persistent ethnic experiences—and inter-ethnic conflict—in America.

The first of the new pluralist historians to recast Handlin's picture of immigrant assimilation was Rudolph Vecoli. The southern Italian immigrants he studied in Chicago lived in an ethnic world that excluded not only "American" identity, but even "Italian-American" identity. In tightly bound clusters from specific villages and kinship groups, they had been impelled upon the course of migration by vast economic forces, and were inured to the requirements of the capitalist market and the rhythms of migratory gang labor. They survived the harrowing ordeal by sticking to what they knew, not by embracing the process of heroic transformation outlined by Handlin. "Amoral familism" not "ethnicity" shaped their identity; magic not religion haunted their consciousness; persistence not change characterized their behavior over time. Similarly, if less starkly, Virginia Yans-McLaughlin showed how Italian and Polish immigrants adapted quite differently to the challenges of industrial Buffalo, New York. Bringing energy from the growing women's movement and the burgeoning field of women's

---

[15]See Volume I, Chapters 4 and 9.

[16]John Higham, *Strangers in the Land: Patterns of American Nativism, 1860–1925* (New Brunswick, N.J., 1955). Higham began work on the subject as as graduate student in 1948.

history to bear on the subject, Yans-McLaughlin was especially insightful about the role of women in regulating the family, and of the family in governing the immigrants' responses to a threatening social environment. Like Caroline Golab, who studied Poles in Philadelphia, Yans-McLaughlin painted a picture of women-centered families successfully managing the transition to a new world with a minimum of change and disruption.[17]

Some historians in the 1970s found considerable assimilation, even submergence, of immigrants into the dominant Anglo-American culture, but usually their subjects were English, Scandinavians, Germans, or other northern Europeans.[18] More recently, historians have more substantially qualified the picture sketched by Vecoli and other neopluralists in the 1960s and 1970s. They contend that neither the ethnic enclave nor American society itself was ever as unitary as Handlin and his many critics all made it seem. Along with considerable ethnic resilience, considerable assimilation took place, because immigrants neither resisted nor accommodated something called "America." Rather, they came to terms with local and changing circumstances, over decades and generations, in ways that require tales with multiple trajectories. These historians also give greater credence to ordinary people's agency in shaping their lives. Many immigrants sought to assimilate into American ways not out of cultural self-abandonment or self-hatred but as the result of a reasoned accommodation to a relatively tolerant environment. When that environment proved itself hostile to their interests and sense of dignity, they resisted it, defending their traditions though not abjuring their commitment to assimilation. Thus, Eva Morawska has found considerable cultural adaptation among Slavic immigrants in Pennsylvania, some of it in the direction of ethnic identity, some of it evolving toward a highly assimilated, working-class Americanism.[19] In this view, ethnicity is not a primordial feature of the immigrants' cultural identity but a tool to help them negotiate labor

---

[17] Virginia Yans-McLaughlin, *Family and Community: Italian Immigrants in Buffalo, 1880–1930* (Ithaca, N.Y., 1977); Caroline Golab, "The Impact of the Industrial Experience on the Immigrant Family: The Huddled Masses Reconsidered," in *Immigrants in Industrial America, 1850–1920*, Richard L. Ehrlich, ed., (Charlottesville, Va., 1977). See also Rudolph J. Vecoli and Suzanne M. Sinke, eds., *A Century of European Migrations, 1830–1930* (Urbana, Ill., 1991).

[18] See, for example, Kathleen Neils Conzen, "Immigrants, Immigrant Neighborhoods, and Ethnic Identity: Historical Issues," *Journal of American History* 66 (December 1979): 603–615. See also the review of this and other questions in Russell A. Kazal, "Revisiting Assimilation: The Rise, Fall, and Reappraisal of a Concept in American Ethnic History," *American Historical Review* 100 (April 1995): 437–471.

[19] Eva Morawska, "The Internal Status Hierarchy in the Eastern European Immigrant Communities of Johnstown, Pa., 1890–1930s," *Journal of Social History* 16 (Fall 1982): 75–108; also "The Sociology and Historiography of Immigration," in *Immigration Reconsidered: History, Sociology, and Politics*, Virginia Yans-McLaughlin, ed. (New York, 1990), pp. 187–238.

markets, social networks, and political crosscurrents. Neither peasant villagers nor alienated moderns, the immigrants and their children discovered a variety of ways of "becoming American" that rejected repressive versions of Americanization while validating more inclusive forms of American identity.

In the mid-1980s, two major synthetic accounts of immigration history appeared, each in its own way striving to recast along more pluralist lines the tale of migration, settlement, and assimilation. Although embracing the findings of the neo-pluralists, both Thomas Archdeacon in *Becoming American* and John Bodnar in *The Transplanted* find ample evidence of assimilation as well as ethnic, racial, and class divisions in the United States.[20] Even in their titles, both authors announce the intention to set the narrative of immigration on a course more complex than that proposed either by new man myth, or by Chicago School sociology, or by advocates of cultural pluralism. "Becoming" emphasizes the elastic quality of identity formation, while "transplanted" suggests not alienation from the past but the re-rooting of durable stock in new environments. In both Archdeacon and Bodnar, international capitalism drives the migrants; families and larger groups and institutions, not individuals, are the key historical actors; racial division plays a part in assimilating descendants of immigrants to a white American mainstream, even as it reinforces the political assertion of ethnic "rights"; multiple melting pots appear to work effectively for some purposes, but pale in significance before the determinant power of class, race, and gender in shaping historical outcomes. The stories told with such an approach are more complex than those allowed by the simple assimilationist or pluralist models of the past, as this quote from Bodnar shows:

> Between the microscopic forces of daily life, often centering around ethnic communal and kinship ties, and the macroscopic world of economic change and urban growth stood the culture of everyday life. This was a culture not based exclusively on ethnicity, tradition, class, or progress. More precisely, it was a mediating culture which confronted all these factors. . . . Even within similar ethnic aggregations, a preoccupation with the practical and the attainable did not create identical life strategies.

Both readings in this chapter reflect this maturation of immigration history in the last decade. James R. Barrett emphasizes the significance of class in shaping both assimilation and resistance to it by immigrants and their descendants in the first half of the twentieth

---

[20]Thomas Archdeacon, *Becoming American: An Ethnic History* (New York, 1983); John Bodnar, *The Transplanted: A History of Immigrants in Urban America* (Bloomington, Ind., 1985).

century. Barrett sees ethnic identity as one among many forms of consciousness developed by people who were also men and women, workers and citizens. Most importantly, as Lizabeth Cohen has similarly argued, ethnicity is transitional, evolving by the 1930s into a trans-ethnic working-class identity.[21] What both Barrett and Cohen suggest is a working-class melting pot that, like the religious melting pots proposed by Herberg and Kennedy in the 1950s, assimilated immigrants across ethnic lines while falling short of absorbing them into an undifferentiated American mainstream.

George J. Sanchez shows in the second reading that Mexican immigrants forged a new identity that drew on all their resources, including Mexican, Anglo-American, and newly synthesized elements, all the while dealing with the hard realities of class hierarchy in America. As Sanchez sees it, the "new ethnicity" paradigm that dominated so much of the scholarship in the field of immigration history in the 1970s and 1980s treated ethnicity as "an undifferentiated cultural position." Both old-world and United States cultures were "depicted largely as static, impermeable, . . . bipolar cultural opposites" by proponents of a highly pluralist view of history. Moreover, by presenting the alternatives as either absorption by the "dominant culture" or courageous preservation of a precious "ethnic identity," pluralists made questions about class and gender divisions within an immigrant community seem almost a form of cultural betrayal.

By the 1980s, a new generation of scholars, many of them feminists and some influenced by postmodernist thought, sought to "de-essentialize" ethnicity. That is, they insisted that ethnic identity, like race, gender, and other seemingly "natural" or "essential" qualities, was actually a social construction; that it was unstable and ever-changing in response to circumstances; and that it was a part, not the whole, of anyone's identity. Thus, a lesbian Latina scholar, Gloria Anzaldua, could find in her Mexican heritage both treasure and dross. Rejecting the homophobia and "cultural tyranny," she gloried especially in the pre-Hispanic Aztec spirituality that had been a submerged element in her upbringing.[22] Aware of cultural criticism such as Anzaldua's, Sanchez argues "in favor of the possibility of multiple identities and contradictory positions" among immigrants and their descendants. Ethnicity is "a collective identity that emerged from daily experience in the United States," neither "Mexican" nor "American," but

---

[21]James R. Barrett, "Americanization from the Bottom Up: Immigration and the Remaking of the Working Class in the United States, 1880–1930," *Journal of American History* 79 (December 1992): 996–1020. See also Lizabeth Cohen, *Making a New Deal: Industrial Workers in Chicago, 1919–1939* (Cambridge, 1990); and Gary Gerstle, *Working-Class Americanism: The Politics of Labor in a Textile City, 1914–1960* (Cambridge, 1989).

[22]Gloria Anzaldua, *Borderlands/La Frontera: The New Mestiza* (San Francisco, 1987).

an evolving synthesis of elements. Finally, recalling Milton Gordon's assertion that cultural assimilation can occur without entailing structural assimilation, Sanchez argues that for Mexican Americans, "cultural adaptation occurred without substantial social mobility."[23]

In the last decade historians have even further emphasized the significance of race as a social category in American history. Some of these scholars make race the crucial factor in shaping American ethnic identity, even as they come to quite different conclusions about it. Many "multiculturalists," inspired by the huge new inflows of immigrants from Asia, Africa, and Latin America, believe that recognizing the diversity of the American population in past and present entails a radical pluralism. Thus Ronald Takaki insists that fully acknowledging the history of blacks, Latinos, Asians, and other racial outsiders will finally allow Americans to discard Anglocentric notions and construct a realistic picture of their heterogeneous society. Many commentators see the multilingualism of cities such as New York, Miami, and Los Angeles as evidence of the approach of a radically de-centered, postmodern society, which will make it impossible for any one group to dominate the national culture. Ironically, Takaki suggests that acknowledging diversity will lead Americans to an almost mystical unity. He ends his book with paeans to "wholeness" and a quote from Whitman: "Of every hue and caste am I, . . . I resist any thing better than my own diversity."[24]

Far from trying to find an affirmative note of "America singing," those scholars who associate themselves with "whiteness studies" have constructed a grim tale of racial division in America. Most European immigrants, in this viewpoint, learned quickly after arriving that America was free and full of opportunity for those who could win recognition as white. At one time or another, many of them—Irish, Italians, and Jews, among others—were denied membership, especially during the flush years of racial nationalism in the nineteenth and early twentieth centuries. Still, by virtue of skin color most of these—or at least their children—could aspire to and eventually win a place within the world of whiteness. For Asians, Latinos, and American Indians, the chances were far lower. Historians of Asian American experience have made especially clear the extent to which racial hatred and racial ideology repeatedly subverted efforts to generate class solidarity or pluralist national identity among working-class Americans in the late-nineteenth and early-twentieth centuries.[25] Whatever the fate of immi-

---

[23]George J. Sanchez, *Becoming Mexican American: Ethnicity, Culture and Identity in Chicano Los Angeles, 1900–1945* (New York, 1993), pp. 4–13.

[24]Ronald Takaki, *A Different Mirror: A History of Multicultural America* (Boston, 1993), p. 428.

[25]See, for example, Alexander Saxton, *The Rise and Fall of the White Republic: Class Politics and Mass Culture in Nineteenth-Century America* (London, 1990).

grants, for African Americans racial otherness was an indelible feature of their social identity. White Americans could not allow that crucial dividing line to be breached and still hope to retain the opportunities and privileges that kept them ahead in America's competitive economic and social system. The psychic investment that whites—including descendants of immigrants—made in their whiteness was too valuable to tamper with. Solving America's racial dilemma, then, would require not just good will but a readiness on the part of whites to disinvest themselves in whiteness and to suffer the material consequences of doing so. It also requires scholars to abandon their fixation on the narrative of inclusion and assimilation and to focus instead on America's racial divide.[26]

Some scholars of "whiteness" seem to resort to a uni-directional narrative that makes the building and maintenance of racial hegemony the master dynamic of American history. Resisting this tendency, the intellectual historian David A. Hollinger has sought to trace a middle way between the narrative of smooth assimilation and that of racial polarization. He insists that "ethnos" neither has nor should dominate American culture, that a "cosmopolitan" alternative exists and has historic roots, and that only by facing class inequalities can Americans give to ethnicity the important but limited place it deserves in their lives.[27] In somewhat different terms, Lawrence H. Fuchs insists that "Americans have gone farther than any other multiethnic nation in developing a humane and decent multiethnic society," and rejects any suggestion that immigrant assimilation depends upon reinforcement of the racial divide.[28] On the other hand, many historians argue that the rosier possibilities of cosmopolitanism are figments of the liberal imagination; that coercion, far more than voluntary embrace, has marked the process of adaptation to the American mainstream; that race is not like ethnicity, but is rather a permanent impediment to assimilation of blacks (and possibly others). Moreover, other historians, taking their cue from the post–Cold War devolution of nation states, insist that the very subject of assimilation is given ex-

---

[26]David Roediger, *The Wages of Whiteness: Race and the Making of the American Working Class* (New York, 1991), and *Toward an Abolition of Whiteness: Essays on Race, Politics, and Working Class History* (New York, 1994); see also Matthew Frye Jacobson, *Whiteness of a Different Color: European Immigrants and the Alchemy of Race* (Cambridge, Mass., 1998).

[27]David A. Hollinger, *Postethnic America: Beyond Multiculturalism* (New York, 1995). Also affirming the continuing power of cosmopolitan liberalism, see John Higham, "Multiculturalism and Universalism: A History and Critique," *American Quarterly* 45 (June 1993): 195–219, as well critical responses in the same issue. In the realm of literary analysis, see Werner Sollors, *Beyond Ethnicity: Consent and Descent in American Culture* (New York, 1986).

[28]Lawrence H. Fuchs, *The American Kaleidoscope: Race, Ethnicity, and the Civic Culture* (Hanover, N.H., 1995).

aggerated emphasis by nationalistic American historians and should be replaced by the study of "transnational" migration flows, "border-lands," "diasporas," and the like.[29]

For students of history, these recent developments in the study of immigration and ethnicity should reinforce two conclusions. First, cycles of interpretation recur; and second, even as interpretations recycle, distinctively new elements are added to historical narratives in response to new evidence, new approaches (especially ones that evolve out of the intersection of previously distinct areas of study), and new social and intellectual influences upon historians. Given the ferment that continues to unsettle the field of immigration studies, as well as the continuing flow of migrants to contemporary America, it is unlikely that the history of mass migration will recede from the foreground of historical interest. Moreover, however sharply historians focus on the failures of assimilation in the United States, the long-term incorporation of tens of millions of diverse immigrants to a fairly stable democracy will continue to win the attention of scholars, especially in a world where ethnic hatred takes its toll with frightening regularity. And finally, as long as race continues to haunt American dreams of equality, the assimilative possibilities of American society will evince doubt in those who observe—and experience—the burdens of race.

---

[29]See the lively debate, "People in Motion, Nation in Question: The Case of Twentieth-Century America," with contributions from Gary Gerstle, David Hollinger, and Donna Gabaccia, in *Journal of American History* 84 (September 1997): 524–580.

JAMES R. BARRETT

JAMES R. BARRETT (1950–   ) is professor of history at the Univer-sity of Illinois at Urbana. He is the author of Work and Community in "The Jungle": Chicago's Packing House Workers, 1894–1922 *(1981) and, with Rob Ruck, of* Steve Nelson, American Radical *(1981).*

The scene is the athletic field at the Ford Motor Company's famous Model T assembly plant at Highland Park, Michigan, on the Fourth of July in the midst of World War I. The occasion is a graduation ceremony for the Ford English School, a language and civics program for the company's immigrant workers, part of Ford's ambitious Five Dollar Day corporate welfare program. The pageant incorporates a symbol that has acquired peculiar importance in Americans' self-image. While the ritual is heavy-handed and perhaps in rather bad taste, its importance lies in the meaning it holds for both the immigrant workers and their corporate sponsors. Ford's director of Americanization describes the scene.

> All the men descend from a boat scene representing the vessel on which they came over; down the gangway representing the distance from the port at which they landed to the school, into a pot 15 feet in diameter and 7½ feet high, which represents the Ford English School. Six teachers, three on either side, stir the pot with ten foot ladles representing nine months of teaching in the school. Into the pot 52 nationalities with their foreign clothes and baggage go and out of the pot after vigorous stirring by the teachers comes one nationality, viz, American.

Lest anyone miss the point, each of the workers emerges from the pot dressed in an identical suit and carrying a miniature American flag. . . .

Between 1880 and 1924, the year immigration was severely restricted,more than twenty-five million immigrants poured into the country; they transformed the face of America's laboring population. From the late nineteenth century on, in a movement that gathered momentum after the turn of the century, teachers, settlement house workers, and professional patriots aimed to "Americanize" these immigrants, to guide and hasten the process of acculturation by which they might embrace the values and behavior of mainstream America.

James R. Barrett, "Americanization from the Bottom Up: Immigration and the Remaking of the Working Class in the United States, 1880–1930," *Journal of American History* 79 (December 1992). Reprinted with the permission of the *Journal of American History*.

During and immediately after World War I, the movement became a kind of crusade as employers, nationalist groups, and various state and federal agencies sought to remold the values and behavior of immigrant workers and their families.

But what did it mean to be Americanized and who was fittest and best placed to do the Americanizing? Typically, the term *Americanization* has had conservative connotations. It conveys a unified notion of what it meant to be American and more than a hint of nativism. It was something the native middle class did to immigrants, a coercive process by which elites pressed WASP values on immigrant workers, a form of social control. That side of Americanization was very real, particularly during the era of World War I and the Red Scare. But . . . Americanism was, in fact, a contested ideal. There were numerous understandings of what it meant to be an American, divergent values associated with the concept, and so, many ways that an immigrant might "discover" America.

Ethnic culture certainly persisted in the New World, and immigrants employed older cultural values and behavior in facing the problems of urban industrial society. . . . But if we wish to understand how working-class formation took place in the midst of great ethnic, cultural, and racial diversity and change, then we must study the widespread contacts and interaction between workers from diverse ethnic and racial backgrounds, the gradual acculturation of new immigrants, and the transformation of immigrant worker consciousness.

We need an analytical framework that acknowledges the very uneven and continual quality of American working-class formation, shaped by constant migration, and allows us to do more than simply describe instances of interethnic class cooperation, one that also enables us to explain how and why they occurred. Such an analysis would incorporate the sequential character of the process and the element of cultural continuity noted by immigration historians but would also assess the impact on the newcomers of existing working-class culture and organizations. . . .

This process undoubtedly occurred in many ways and in many settings for various age, gender, and occupational groups in immigrant communities—at the dancehall or on the street corner, at a club meeting, in a city park, in a movie theater, or in a saloon. Labor organizations were not necessarily involved. For my purposes here, however, "bottom" refers to wage-earning people, and by "Americanization from the bottom up," I mean the gradual acculturation of immigrants and their socialization in working-class environments and contexts—the shop floor, the union, the radical political party. These settings provided immigrants with alternatives to the world view and the values advocated in programs sponsored by employers and the government. . . . Conceptualizing the "remaking" of the working class in the early twentieth century as the interaction between two historical generations and class formation itself as an Americanization from the bottom up provides a new perspective on both working-class and immigration history. . . .

Two fairly distinct generations of workers lived in many American industrial communities between the end of the nineteenth century and the 1920s. The first consisted of native-born and "old" immigrant workers and their children—British, Germans, and Irish, with smaller numbers of Scandinavians, English-speaking Canadians, and others. By the late nineteenth century, these workers had not only had years of industrial and urban experience, they had also created institutions and developed and popularized ideas that they used to cope with the rigors of wage labor. They had organized and now led trade unions, Knights of Labor assemblies, co-ops, and labor parties. . . .

By the turn of the century, a new generation of workers, drawn to the United States largely from eastern and southeastern Europe, shared the cities and industrial towns with these older, more experienced groups and their American-born children. By the end of World War I, these "new immigrants" were joined by black and Mexican migrants to create a new working-class population. Few of these newcomers were ignorant peasants recently uprooted from the land and casting about in the city, disoriented and demoralized, but all of them faced major adjustments if they were to cope with life in large factories and in city neighborhoods. To some degree, they relied on the material and cultural resources of their own ethnic communities, but for good or ill, they had also to contend with the structures already in place, those created by the earlier generation of industrial workers, who played major roles in acculturating and socializing the newcomers.

Various forms of old-country radicalism and social mobilization shaped the development of labor radicalism in the United States. The precise content of such cultural and ideological continuity varied in important ways from one ethnic group to another, but we might think about such continuity as part of what might be termed either *ethnocultural* or *segmented* class formation. . . . Some immigrant workers did indeed create viable working-class cultures with distinct institutions, political ideas, forms of socialization, organizations, and strategies. But they tended to do this *within* their own ethnic communities, often developing such cultures partly on the basis of Old World experiences and then adapting them to the conditions of the New. The phrase segmented class formation suggests a different vantage point on the same process. Class formation in the United States was segmented in the sense that it took place simultaneously in various ethnic communities. . . . Especially by the early twentieth century, *American* working-class formation was of necessity interethnic, emerging from the mixture of people from diverse backgrounds and depending on contact across ethnic boundaries. . . .

These older native-born and immigrant workers often embraced a

"social republicanism" that fused notions of economic and social reform with democratic nationalist ideals. . . . The traditions with which
many of the earlier immigrants identified were those of 1848, not
those of 1776; both those traditions had more to do with nationalism
than with internationalism and class solidarity. . . . Whatever the republican consensus that may have obtained among earlier immigrants,
it had clearly fragmented by the turn of the century.

Nor was such ideology always progressive in content. The same
defensive mindset that might impart great cohesion and solidarity for
resistance against employers and state authorities could also manifest
itself in exclusionary impulses that shaped responses to new immigrant workers. A common reaction to labor's decline in status during
the late nineteenth and early twentieth centuries, for example, was
the demand for immigration restriction that enjoyed great popularity
among not only the native-born but also many Irish and British and
some German labor activists. Even as an instrumental approach to
problems of unemployment or low wages, the demand for restriction
revealed an exclusionary quality to workers' thinking, and it sometimes betrayed a narrow, nativist conception of "labor" shared not
only by American Federation of Labor (AFL) craft unionists but also by
Knights of Labor activists and even socialist militants.

In its extreme form, that perspective infused the anti-Chinese
movement that swept the West and other parts of the country in the
late nineteenth century. Here the element of race added an enduring
and explosive quality to the mixture of defensive sentiments characterizing conservative and even some radical workers. Some Socialist
party leaders, for example, held profoundly racist attitudes toward
Asian, black, and many immigrant workers and strongly supported
immigration restriction.

Immigrant socialization in working-class settings could perpetuate this negative strain of thought and feeling: Older immigrants and
natives passed their own prejudices on to the newcomers. Irish immigrants, who had been in job competition with Asians and blacks for
more than a generation before eastern European immigrants arrived
and who had themselves suffered discrimination and violence at the
hands of nativists, often developed racist attitudes and repertoires of
behavior. Inside the labor movement, the Catholic church, and the political organizations of many working-class communities, the Irish occupied vital positions as Americanizers of later groups. Racism was a
learned value, deeply ingrained in the world views of many workers by
the end of the nineteenth century; it was passed on to immigrants
along with values enhancing class solidarity.

The AFL's craft unionism was, of course, exclusionary by definition; keeping nonmembers out of the labor market through control of
hiring was its *raison d'être*. In the context of mass immigration, craft

organization reinforced any nativist tendencies derived from other sources. . . .

The earlier generation, then, sometimes reacted to new immigrants defensively, seeking to exclude them from the labor market and from the broader working-class community. Yet the older, entrenched generation often could not afford to shut out the newcomers. Relations between the two generations occurred in a context of massive technical and economic upheaval, something like a second industrial revolution. The American working-class population was transformed in the course of the early twentieth century precisely because the economy and the nature of work itself were also being transformed. In some sectors of the economy, for instance, the building trades, where skills were still required and complex work rules hung on, craft unions might retain control over the labor market. In many industries, however, such unions faced a sustained crisis throughout the late nineteenth and early twentieth centuries. The desperation of their struggle to retain some control over the work process and jobs varied considerably from one trade to another, but most skilled workers felt the pressure. . . .

The ongoing social transformation and the related technological revolution in industry presented the labor movement with an enormous challenge, one with both social and organizational dimensions. The integration of the newcomers into the labor movement called not only for new forms of organization, new organizing strategies, and new strike tactics, but also for a new means of socializing and acculturating the new people, a "remaking" of the working class between the turn of the century and the Great Depression. That involved the organized efforts of unions and other labor organizations, myriad informal contacts between workers in various settings, and a long struggle with management for the loyalty of the immigrant worker.

We know most about the impulse for immigrant acculturation that came from the native middle class in public school classrooms, settlement houses, and factories. Because most of the new immigrant's waking hours were spent at the workplace, much of his or her learning about what it meant to be an American occurred there. Certainly employers had their own lessons to teach. They experimented with English instruction and citizenship classes during the early years of this century and took a special interest in the movement during the labor shortage and unionization of the World War I era.

Henry Ford launched the most ambitious of these plans at his Highland Park Model T plant as part of the Five Dollar Day plan, which, beginning in 1914, combined assembly-line technology with a shorter work day, incentive pay, and an elaborate personnel management system. Accepting prevailing Progressive notions that environment shaped one's behavior and attitudes, Ford engineers established a Sociology Department to remake the lives of their immigrant workers and win them over to thrift, efficiency, and company loyalty. Case workers fanned out into Detroit's working-class neighborhoods, ready to fight for the hearts and minds of the immigrant auto workers. They investigated each worker's home life as well as his work record, and one could qualify for the Five Dollar Day incentive pay only after demonstrating the proper home environment and related middle-class values. Thus the company sought to show workers not only the "right way to work" but also the "right way to live." . . . By the spring of 1919, there were at least eight hundred industrial plants sponsoring their own classes or working in conjunction with the YMCA and other agencies to put on evening or plant classes.

Of course, learning also went on at work outside the structured programs. The workplace was by its nature an authoritarian environment, and foremen and other supervisors were always "teaching" immigrants—to do what they were told, to act promptly, to keep working. There was one phrase "every foreman had to learn in English, Polish, and Italian," recalled William Klann, a Ford Motor assembly foreman: "'Hurry up.'" The verbal abuse of immigrant workers for which steel mills and some other factories were notorious derived in part from the heartfelt prejudices of lower-level management, but it was also a crude effort to teach the immigrant "who was boss." . . .

But there were other teachers—older, more experienced, sometimes politicized workers, who conveyed different notions of what was right or wrong in the workshop and in the United States as a society. Immigrants learned restriction of output and other aspects of a new work culture from their workmates and, according to David Montgomery, "exchanged portions of their traditional culture, not for the values and habits welfare plans sought to inculcate, but for working-class mores." Immigrant strikers' frequent demands for humane treatment and for the discharge of abusive foremen suggest the importance of such socialization. Clearly, immigrants themselves were constructing identities and embracing values that reflected situations they faced in the workplace.

Not all workplace conversations were concerned with work itself. Nor did all one's lessons come from earlier immigrants. Some had broader implications that might be conveyed by more experienced and sophisticated workers from within one's own community. Something like the ethnocultural class formation that characterized the "old immigrant" communities in the late nineteenth century was occurring in "new immigrant" communities in the early twentieth. Here too workers developed the ideas, organization, institutions, and movements commonly associated with the phrase "working-class culture." Once again such cultures were built in part on Old World experiences and values, but they were soon tailored to American industrial settings. Sicilian peasants and artisans who created Italy's "red towns" and then carried a radical oral tradition to Tampa, Chicago, and New York are examples of this phenomenon, as are the Jewish socialists of the ghettos of eastern Europe and America or the Finnish leftists of the Mesabi Range. . . .

Stjepan Mesaroš, a twenty-year-old Croatian immigrant . . . when he arrived for his first day on the job at Berk's slaughterhouse in Philadelphia, . . . was overwhelmed by what he found there and in the streets of his neighborhood. . . . Among the many mysteries was the verbal abuse meted out to a young black man with whom Stjepan shared his duties. Noticing a Serbian laborer who seemed to spend every free moment reading Serbo-Croatian pamphlets and newspapers, Stjepan took a chance and asked him about it. Almost sixty years later, he recalled the conversation which took place amidst the blood of the slaughterhouse and changed the course of his life. "The Serb sat down next to me and explained that both bosses and workers were prejudiced against black people. 'You'll soon learn something about this country,' he said. 'Negroes never get a fair chance.'" . . .

The Serb handed him some Socialist Labor party pamphlets and soon after gave him other reading matter of the sort favored by self-educated worker radicals around the world—not just on politics but on popular science, temperance, health foods, atheism. Such literature conveyed more than a formal political ideology—socialism—it also incorporated a new world view. This too was Americanization, but not the sort that employers or most adult educators had in mind when they used the term. Stjepan had discovered America.

Stjepan Mesaroš's slaughterhouse conversation raises the important question of how other immigrant workers discovered the significance of race in American life. The black migrants arriving from the Deep South in the war years and the 1920s were part of the same generation as the new immigrants, and the two groups had a great deal in common. Yet we know very little about the relations between them or for that matter about the more general problem of the evolution of racism among white workers. It seems likely, however, that racial attitudes were part of the legacy that older, more Americanized workers passed on to newcomers. . . . The fact that newer immigrants played little part in the race riots of the World War I era suggests that it took some time for them and their children to make these prejudices their own, but their prominent presence in post–World War II racial conflicts demonstrates that many learned their lessons only too well.

The results of Stjepan's friendship with the Serb and his later career also suggest another context for Americanization—radical working-class politics. Stjepan joined a South Slav branch of the Socialist Labor party and later the Communist party. He changed his name to Steve Nelson, learned to read the party press in English, with the help of a young German-American radical, and studied public speaking, organizing methods, economics, Marxist philosophy, and labor history at party schools in New York and Moscow. He became a union organizer and later an organizer of the unemployed. He worked in Detroit, Chicago, and the anthracite coal fields of eastern Pennsylvania. During the Spanish civil war he served as commissar of the American Abraham Lincoln Battalion, fighting for his own notion of democracy. Jailed for his political activities during the McCarthy era, he left the Communist party in 1957 but remained a committed socialist.

The Communist party gave Nelson more than language and speaking skills. It brought him into contact with educated and politically committed young people from a wide range of ethnic backgrounds, provided him with a key to understanding the world around him, and gave him a vision of a new and better world. Ironically, Steve Nelson's Americanization came in the context of a revolutionary party, a path he trod with a small but important group of immigrant radicals. . . .

In each ethnic community, whether it was preponderantly new immigrants or old, small groups of radicals assumed a disproportionate significance in the acculturation of immigrant workers. Already sympathetic to the goals of the movement, perhaps a bit more articulate or cosmopolitan than their workmates, they provided labor activists with invaluable links to the immigrant communities. As newspaper editors, street-corner speakers, and organizers, they carried the socialist message into their communities in a language workers could understand, and in the process they provided a framework within which the individual immigrant could comprehend the American political and economic system and her or his place in it.

The Communist party in the 1920s was a bit different from earlier socialist organizations. In the mid-twenties, the Communists made a conscious decision to "Americanize" the party (their term). They dissolved language federations, shifted immigrant activists into neighborhood branches, shop nuclei, and other ethnically mixed mass organizations, and even asked foreign-born comrades to change their names. During the Popular Front of the late 1930s, Americanization was even more elaborate. Proclaiming that "Communism Is Twentieth Century Americanism," Earl Browder and other party leaders consciously cultivated an American image, using patriotic symbols and language to convey their message. . . .

Labor organizations striving to organize in the era of mass immigration also became contexts for acculturation. Indeed, when organizers reached out to the newcomers—and this happened rather more often than we have realized during the early twentieth century—they had little choice but to engage the immigrants in a dialogue about unionization. Too often union drives are thought of in purely institu-

tional terms—as attempts to build up organizations. Surely, this was
the goal and sometimes the end result. But each of these efforts was a
process of socialization as well, an effort to convey to the immigrants
basic values as well as the structure and function of unions and other
working-class organizations. . . .

There were several elements to labor's version of Americanism.
Not surprisingly, activists frequently emphasized basic civil liberties,
particularly free speech, and encouraged immigrants to speak up and
defend their rights. Nor were these ideals abstract. In coal company
and steel mill towns and in many other industrial communities, labor's ability to organize depended on the maintenance of such rights,
and immigrants frequently learned the values of these freedoms in the
midst of organizing activities, strikes, and demonstrations. Workers'
notions of these rights, moreover, were often much broader than the
law itself. They tended to reflect rights that were more idealized than
real. "It is time that some people learned," wrote a West Virginia
miner in the midst of the 1921 coal strike, "that working men have
some rights under the Constitution, among them the right to organize
for mutual protection, the right of collective bargaining and the right
to quit work when conditions surrounding their employment become
unbearable. And these rights we are going to maintain at any cost." . . .

Organizers frequently invested their material demands with the
power of democratic rhetoric and patriotism by speaking of an American standard of living, by which they meant higher wages, shorter
working hours, and decent working conditions. Reference to the
"American" standard could be and sometimes was used to exclude
newcomers, as in the case of the working-class agitation against Chinese immigrants. But it could also be the basis for integrating newcomers and imparting the basic values of the movement, while
establishing a legitimacy in the eyes of the public at large. During
World War I, the "American standard of living" provided the unions
with a patriotic image and immigrant workers with the prospect of an
ideal American life for themselves and their children. "We cannot
bring up our children as Americans on 15 and a half cents an hour," a
Polish stockyards worker argued, "We cannot live decently. Our
wives, our children, our homes demand better wages."

Finally, many labor activists embraced the concept of cultural pluralism, if only in the interests of labor solidarity, and tried to impart
this value to immigrants. What this might have looked like at the
level of the local union is suggested by the scene at a meeting of Local
183, which included all women working in the Chicago stockyards, regardless of race, nationality, or trade. When the young Irish chairwoman called for a discussion of grievances, a young black woman
complained that a Polish member had insulted her. The chairwoman
asked both to come forward.

"Now what did yez call each other?"
"She called me a Nigger."
"She called me a Pollock first."
"Both of yez oughta be ashamed of yourselves. You're both to blame.
But don't you know that this question in our ritual don't mean that
kind of griev-e-ances, but griev-e-ances of the whole bunch of us?"

Ethelbert Stewart, the United States commissioner of labor, observed labor's version of Americanization as it unfolded in Chicago's
slaughterhouses and meat packing plants during the early years of this
century. Here ethnic hostilities had been rife, and ethnic communities
tended to be dominated by charismatic "clan leaders" who fought the
unions for influence over the immigrants. Since the workers' worlds
were organized largely on the basis of nationality, the union "represented the first, and for a time the only, point at which [the immigrant]
touches any influence outside of his clan. . . . The Slav mixes with the
Lithuanian, the German, and the Irishman—and this is the only place
they do mix until, by virtue of this intercourse and this mixing, clan-
nishness is to a degree destroyed, and a social mixing along other lines
comes into play." . . . Immigrants themselves were the critical element
in this process. They responded better to unions than to official programs because the unions stressed issues that were vital to the welfare
of ethnic communities but simply could not be resolved without looking beyond their boundaries to class-based organization.

Besides teaching immigrants interethnic solidarity, unions did
more than any civics lesson to impart the principles and methods of
democratic government by relating them to practical matters: wages,
hours, and working conditions. For most immigrants, introduction to
the American political and economic system came not through night-
school classes but through discussion and debate at union meetings
(with interpreters), informal conversations with fellow workers, and
labor movement publications (often printed in various languages). And
the union's version of Americanism was likely to be different from the
one conveyed in employer programs, emphasizing the free expression
of one's opinions and the importance of standing up with fellow workers to demand one's rights. . . .

Americanization, whether official or labor, was also fundamentally shaped by issues of gender. Concentrated in precisely those professions—teaching, settlement house work, public health—that
brought them into close contact with immigrant families, women assumed major roles at the highest reaches of the corporate and government bureaucracies that provided the Americanization movement
with its structure, ideas, and legitimacy. Thousands of them taught
English and civics in evening school, settlement house, Young
Women's Christian Association (YWCA), and factory programs, con-

veying the Americanization message. But the message itself encoded notions of domestic orthodoxy and other gender values in English primers, loyalty parades, and citizenship plays. In its early stages, when it chiefly emphasized naturalization and the right to vote, the movement focused almost entirely on men. When Americanizers did begin to address women, it was because of their key role in child rearing and for fear of the dangers posed by the "un-Americanized mother." Long after woman suffrage, Americanizers placed far more emphasis on the immigrant mother's role in the home than on her duties as a citizen. She was urged to maintain the new American standard of living in diet, hygiene, and infant and child care and to be mindful of her crucial role in producing a second generation of "true Americans."

Working-class Americanizers made their own approaches to immigrant women. Organizing them presented special problems, some created by the changing occupational structure of women's work in the early twentieth century, others by the patriarchal values of the immigrant household and the labor movement itself. Yet the proportion of the female labor force in unions doubled during the first two decades of the twentieth century, and the Women's Trade Union League (WTUL), a coalition of working women and middle-class reformers, played a particularly important role in socializing immigrant women. In organizing garment workers, the league employed activists from the communities involved and printed leaflets in various languages. During and after the garment strikes of 1909 and 1910, Jewish and Italian organizers visited women in their homes to explain the issues involved in the strikes and the importance of unions. The Chicago WTUL set up neighborhood committees to organize social and educational events, a tactic that was later used in immigrant neighborhoods in New York. Chicago teachers' union volunteers assumed a function comparable to that of "home teachers" in the official Americanization movement, bringing English to immigrant women in their own homes. The New York league produced a labor-oriented English primer, *New World Lessons for Old World Peoples,* in Lithuanian, Italian, Yiddish, Bohemian, and English. . . . These immigrant women learned English in a way that developed important values of class solidarity and personal relationships that they relied upon in later organizing and strikes. "For the WTUL," Colette Hyman concludes, "teaching English was a point of entry into these women's lives through which lessons of unionism could be taught. It was the first step in female institution-building among immigrant women."

World War I and the years immediately following represented a watershed in the Americanization process. Labor's own notions about Americanism stood out in bold relief against the war's backdrop. The massive immigration of the preceding decade had produced a remarkably diverse population who might come to see their chances for a decent life in America embodied in labor's efforts. In this context, interethnic and often interracial organizing was vital to union efforts. The economic effects of the war—increased demand, labor shortages, and steep inflation—sharply raised the issue of living standards and mutual sacrifice for the good of the war effort. In the process the war greatly strengthened unions' bargaining position and ability to organize and raised questions of democratic ideology, providing union organizers and immigrant workers with a vocabulary with which to express their grievances and aspirations. . . .

In the interests of stimulating sacrifice and hard work on the part of immigrant workers, employers and government agencies couched their propaganda in a democratic idiom. For their part, labor activists sought to appropriate such democratic rhetoric and symbols in the name of labor. More than ever before, the plight of the immigrants, their status as workers, and their vision of the labor movement became part of a discourse on Americanism. The concept was hotly contested, and the immigrants were very much at the center of this symbolic struggle.

For their part, the unions, seizing on the war situation to launch ambitious organizing drives in non-union basic industry where most of the immigrants were employed, framed their appeals in patriotic terms. The March 17, 1918, issue of the *United Mine Workers Journal* put the issue forcefully:

> If this war is waged for the destruction of political autocracy, we demand . . . the elimination of industrial autocracy in this country. The workers demand a voice in the conditions of their service, in all sections of the country; thus shall they be assured that this is indeed their war.

. . . Ironically, it was the recent immigrant rather than the native-born worker who was most receptive to the democratic rhetoric. The committee's large red, white, and blue campaign badges were favorites in the immigrant neighborhoods. Far from being abstract, David Brody concludes, "The democratic theme made unionism comprehensible." A Polish steelworker made the connection between trade unionism and democratic war aims in rather more eloquent terms: "just like a horse and wagon, work all day. . . . For why this war? For why we buy Liberty Bonds? For the mills? No, for freedom and America—for everybody. No more horse and wagon. For eight-hour day." . . .

During World War I, the National Committee for Organizing Iron and Steel Workers launched an ambitious organizing drive and had garnered more than 100,000 workers, most of them recent immigrants, by the spring of 1919. In textiles and clothing and in many other industries, the emergence of the so-called "new unions" represented efforts on the part of an earlier generation of activists or of radicals *within* the various "new immigrant" communities to integrate the second generation of immigrant workers into the movement by creating new sorts of unions with new organizing and strike strategies. A massive strike wave, the largest in American history to that point, involving more than a million strikers per year for several years, accompanied this organizing, and many of the activists who led the strikes emerged from radical subcultures in the various ethnic communities.

Union locals, national unions, and city labor federations across the country launched educational programs for new immigrant members. These incorporated not only English and civics instruction but also courses in economics, political economy, history, and literature taught by lawyers and college professors as well as labor activists and socialist elected officials. Sam Levin, business agent of the Amalgamated Clothing Workers' Chicago Council, explained why it was essential to teach such classes from labor's perspective:

> it is not sufficient to tell the workers that they are entitled to all profit since they create all wealth. They know this, but it is important to tell them how each individual institution of our political and economic system is composed, how it works, and how it is possible to improve upon it, and whether it is possible or necessary to abolish it.

The successful wartime organizing among very recent immigrants and the related strike wave raise two crucial questions that deserve a great deal more research. The first has to do with the immigrants themselves: What do these phenomena suggest about their thinking? The second is equally vital: What happened to this impressive movement?

One might begin to think of the consciousness characterizing many of the new immigrants of the early twentieth century as a sort of transitional mentality, an amalgam of Old World traditions, values, and behaviors with new working-class ideas, forms of organization, and strategies. Whatever the content of the transition, it was neither linear nor inevitable. Perhaps it was a sort of conversation in the immigrants' own minds and between older voices and newer ones, which were still not quite clear. There was undoubtedly an infinite variation to such thinking, beginning with differences between various ethnic groups and ranging down to the personality of each individual immigrant. Each person embraced multiple identities shaped by her or his experiences as a woman or man, an Italian or Pole living in a particular type of community in the United States, working in a particular industry. But conceptualizing consciousness as transitional lends the analysis a dynamic and fluid dimension and suggests that such identities were not entirely idiosyncratic, that they were created within a specific historical context that is vital to explaining them. It also directs our attention away from particular ethnic communities and toward the relationship between ethnicity and class identity. . . .

But if there was a gradual transformation in the consciousness of unskilled recent immigrants, reflected in the changing strategies and social composition of the labor movement, then what happened to the new movement that was emerging in these years? . . . Several short-term factors in the postwar years devastated the immigrant-based movement that had provided a context for Americanization from the bottom up, fragmenting the impressive wartime movement along ethnic, racial, and political lines.

In the midst of a serious depression, which had a particularly disastrous effect on the new unions of unskilled immigrants, employers attacked in one industry after another between late 1919 and early 1922. Among the strikebreakers in many of these conflicts were the most recent migrants to join the labor force, southern blacks and Mexicans. Race emerged as the decisive division within many working-class communities, and employers clearly manipulated this development to deepen racial tensions. Race riots broke out in two dozen American cities and towns in 1919, leaving any dream of an interracial labor movement in tatters. . . .

State and local governments' own version of one-hundred-percent Americanism involved the widespread use of injunctions and mounted police to quell strikes. Workers usually lost these struggles, and the new organizations that had provided the context for integrating the new immigrants were demolished. During the Red Scare, federal and local authorities raided meeting places, closed down presses, seized organizational records, and jailed or simply deported immigrant activists, decimating the ranks of radical labor in immigrant communities. . . . The Red Scare amounted to a kind of enforced Americanization.

Again labor radicals contested the term's meaning. The Farmer-Labor party's 1920 platform demanded democratic control of industry, abolition of imperialism, public ownership and operation of railroads and mines, the legal right to collective bargaining, the eight-hour day, unemployment compensation, and government old-age pensions. . . .

But the Red Scare undeniably enhanced the more general development of nativism and other forms of intolerance that split the working class and the labor movement in the early 1920s. Already on the defensive, unions made fewer efforts to reach new immigrant and black migrant workers as nationality, race, and patriotism once again became sources of identification for many native-born and old immigrant workers. Indeed, the resulting fragmentation represented the social basis for labor's organizational decline in the course of the 1920s.

GEORGE J. SANCHEZ

GEORGE J. SANCHEZ (1959–   ) is associate professor of American studies and ethnicity at the University of Southern California.

Just south of Los Angeles' central Plaza lay the area known throughout the city as the main arena for activities of leisure in the Mexican community of the 1920s. Sundays were not only a big day for religious practice; they also were big business days for the area's movie theatres, gambling dens, and pool halls—all of which dominated the streets to the south. The constant sound of Mexican music—music that ranged from traditional Mexican ballads to newly recorded *corridos* depicting life in Los Angeles—was everywhere. A burgeoning Mexican music industry flourished in the central and eastern sections of the city during the 1920s, largely hidden from the Anglo majority.

The diminished role of organized religion in the day-to-day life of Mexican immigrants was coupled with increased participation in secular activities. In Mexico, most public events in rural villages were organized by the Catholic Church, with few other opportunities outside the family for diversion. Los Angeles, however, offered abundant entertainment of all sorts. These amusements were generally part of a rapidly growing market in leisure which targeted working-class families during the 1920s. Money spent on leisure-time activities easily outstripped donations to the Church, revealing much about the cultural changes occurring in the Mexican immigrant community. Chicano entrepreneurs responded to the emerging ethnic mass market in cultural forms, even though that market was often dominated by outside advertising and controlled primarily by non-Mexicans. Still, the presence of a growing ethnic market in Los Angeles provided room for many traditional practices to continue, some flourishing in the new environment, but most being transformed in the process. . . .

The various actors who helped shape the creation of a market aimed at providing Mexican immigrants with products, services, and activities that somehow connected with the ethnic self-identification and collective culture will be identified. The complicated nature of this exchange can best be described, however, by looking at one particular arena of cultural interaction. Music, specifically the creation of a Spanish-language music industry and market in Los Angeles, provides one of the best windows for viewing this nexus of cultural transformation in detail.

The Plaza itself continued to cater to single males, offering pool halls, dance rooms, bars, and a small red-light district. Protestant reformers, therefore, consistently viewed Plaza residents as prime targets for moral rejuvenation. In addition, many small, immigrant-owned eateries were located in the area which catered to a male clientele often unable or unwilling to cook for themselves.

A description of a dancing club frequented by single males during this period indicates the extent of the intermingling between sexes and nationalities in the Plaza, a situation which concerned reformers. Located on Main Street, the club "Latino" . . . was illuminated by red, white, and green lights, the colors of the Mexican flag. Entrance to the club cost 25 cents, and tickets were 10 cents apiece to dance with women. The female employees were mostly immigrant Mexicans or Mexican Americans, although Anglo American, Italian, Filipino, Chinese, and Japanese women also were available. The band, however, was made up of black musicians and played only American pieces. Mexican immigrant men, dressed in working-class garb, danced "Mexican style" to the American songs; a ticket was required for every dance; and the women partners earned 5 cents per dance. In one corner of the dance floor a Mexican woman sold sandwiches, tacos, pastries, and coffee.

As Los Angeles Mexicans moved away from the Plaza and the community became more familial in structure, different diversions predominated. Some customs were carried over to marriage from single life. For example, a federal survey reported that three-quarters of Mexican families in Los Angeles continued to spend an average of $14 a year for tobacco. Almost two-thirds read the newspaper on a regular basis. Increasingly Mexican families began to purchase other forms of entertainment which could be enjoyed by all ages and in the confines of one's home. Over one-third of the families in the Los Angeles study owned radios, often buying the equipment "on time" for an average of $27 a year. . . .

During the 1920s, many American manufacturers and retailers discovered a fairly lucrative market in the local Mexican immigrant community. Despite the clamor for Mexican immigration restrictions, these producers understood that Los Angeles contained a large and growing population of Spanish-speaking immigrants. By 1930, some national products were advertised in the Spanish-language press, and increasingly large distributors sponsored programs in Spanish on the radio. Among products heavily advertised in *La Opinión* during this period were cigarettes, medicinal remedies, and recordings to help immigrants learn the English language.

Even more widespread were appeals to Mexican shoppers by certain downtown department stores. In 1929, for example, the Third Street Store advertised in *La Opinión* by asking, "Why are we the store for Mexicans?" The answer stressed the appeal of special merchandise, prices, and service. Located near the Plaza, offering generous credit, the store had apparently already become a favorite in the Mexican community. . . .

Many of the mass-produced consumer goods in the 1920s were specifically marketed with an appeal to youth. This appeal had profound consequences for Mexican immigrant families. Older children who entered the work force often earned enough to become more autonomous. Adolescents and young adults were often the first to introduce a Mexican family to certain foods, clothing, or activities that were incompatible with traditional Mexican customs. For example, younger Mexican women began to use cosmetics and wear nylon stockings. Young men were more likely to seek out new leisure-time activities, such as American sports or the movie houses. . . .

Despite some initial reservations, most Mexican parents joined other Americans in the 1920s in a love affair with motion pictures. Ninety percent of all families in the Los Angeles survey spent money on the movies, averaging $22 a year per family. . . .

The movie industry in Los Angeles aided Mexicans in retaining old values, but also played a role in cultural change. On the one hand, films produced in Mexico made their way into the many theatres in the downtown area in the late 1920s catering to the Mexican immigrant population. These supplemented American- and European-made silent films which were aimed by their promoters at an often illiterate immigrant population. Sound was not introduced until 1929, so that throughout the decade of the 1920s, movies stressed visual images and presented few language barriers for the non-English speaker.

Since their inception in the nickelodeons of eastern seaboard cities, American films consistently contained storylines intentionally made for the immigrant masses. Messages tended to be largely populist and democratic in tone. Plots stressed the commonality of all Americans. The children of Mexican immigrants were especially intrigued by the open sexuality depicted on the screen. The experience of sitting alone in a darkened theatre and identifying with screen characters, as Lary May has argued, could feel quite liberating.

What made American-made films even more appealing was the appearance of actors and actresses who were Mexican by nationality. Although Ramón Navarro and Lupe Vélez were introduced to audiences in the early twenties, the arrival of Dolores del Río in 1925 brought Mexican immigrants flocking to the box office. . . . *La Opinión*, for example, the city's leading Spanish-language periodical, regularly followed the Hollywood scene, paying particular attention to the city's rising Latin stars. . . .

While the motion-picture industry displayed one aspect of the impact of consumerism on immigrant cultural adaptation, opportunities for other entrepreneurs to make an ethnic appeal emerged during this period. Ethnic marketing, usually considered a recent phenomena, in fact has long-standing roots in this era. While huge American corporations consolidated their hold on a national mass market of goods during the 1920s, much room was left for local entrepreneurs to seek sub-markets that catered to the interests and desires of particular groups. . . .

As early as 1916, small Mexican-owned businesses advertised in Spanish-language newspapers. These establishments were generally store-front operations which allegedly provided items that were "typically Mexican." El Progreso Restaurant on North Main Street, for example, claimed that it cooked food in the "truly Mexican style." Similar restaurants were frequented by the large Mexican male population around the Plaza. Other businesses attempted to bring Mexican products into the Los Angeles market directly. . . .

By 1920, large, well-financed operations dominated the Mexican retail business. Their advertisements regularly appeared in the city's Spanish-language periodicals for the next two decades. Farmacia Hidalgo, run by G. Salazar and located at 362 North Main street, declared that it was the only store "positively of the Mexican community." Farmacia Ruiz was founded by an influential Mexican expatriate and quickly gained much status in the immigrant community. Over the next ten years, it was frequented by several candidates for the Mexican presidency, most notably José Vasconcelos. Mauricio Calderón, another emigrant from Mexico, would soon dominate the Spanish-language music industry in Los Angeles. During this decade he established the Repertorio Musical Mexicana, an outlet for phonographs and Spanish-language records, which he claimed was "the only Mexican house of Mexican music for Mexicans." Finally, two theatres, the Teatro Novel and the Teatro Hidalgo, located on Spring and Main streets respectively, were already in operation in 1920, offering both silent films imported from Mexico as well as live entertainment.

A host of rival Mexican-owned firms gave these early businesses much competition. Advertisements usually stressed that their particular establishment was the most "genuinely Mexican" of the group. The Farmacia Hidalgo went so far as to place an Aztec eagle on some of its products to insure "authenticity." A new and important enterprise was the Librería Lozano, providing Spanish-language books to the literate Mexican community and owned by Ignacio Lozano, the editor of La Opinión. Not surprisingly, Lozano heavily advertised in his own paper.

In addition, the 1920s witnessed the emergence of Mexican professionals who also targeted their fellow countrymen for patronage. A small, but significant group of doctors, dentists, and lawyers from Mexico set up shop in Los Angeles, and their advertisements stressed that their training had been conducted in the finest Mexican universities.

Mexican entrepreneurs, however, were not the only individuals in Los Angeles who appealed to the Mexican consumer; non-Mexicans also tried to capitalize on the growing ethnic clientele. Leading this effort was the medical profession, particularly women doctors and physicians from other ethnic groups not likely to develop a following within a highly male-dominated, Anglo Protestant profession. Most of these physicians were located near the Plaza area, particularly along Main Street, an area which provided direct access to the immigrant population. Female physicians held special appeal as specialists for women, capitalizing on the sense of propriety among immigrant women. "Doctora" Augusta Stone, for example, advertised as a specialist for "las señoras," and was among the first to use the phrase "Habla Español" in her advertisements. Dr. Luigi Gardini, an Italian American physician, also advertised in Spanish-language newspapers in 1916. Asian American physicians, however, were the largest group of non-Mexican professionals to appeal to Mexican immigrants, largely stressing their training in herbal medicine, an area not unfamiliar to rural Mexicans. Among them was Dr. Chee, who characterized himself as "Doctor Chino" in 1920, and Dr. Y. Kim, who boasted the combination of a Yale degree and a speciality in Oriental herbal treatments.

The growth and increasing economic stability of the Mexican immigrant community in Los Angeles made these appeals profitable. While the Mexican middle class remained small and relatively insignificant, the large working-class community was quickly developing east of the Los Angeles River. Lack of capital and professional training in the Mexican community made it difficult for most Mexicans to take direct economic advantage of this growth. Yet their cumulative purchasing power did allow for the growth of certain enterprises which catered to the unique backgrounds of Mexican immigrants, while creating new modes of ethnic expression.

One of the most important of these enterprises was music. Although the musical legacies of different regions in Mexico were significant, traditions were both reinforced and transformed in the environment of Los Angeles. As a diverse collection of immigrant musicians arrived from central and northern Mexico, often via south Texas, they stimulated the growth of a recording industry and burgeoning radio network that offered fertile ground for musical innovation.

Of 1,746 Mexican immigrants who began the naturalization procedure, 110 were musicians (6.3% of the total), making them the second largest occupational group in the sample, well behind the category of "common laborer." Although 80 percent of the musicians did not complete the process, their ample presence among those who initiated the naturalization process indicates their willingness to remain in the

United States. Unlike working-class musicians of Mexican descent in Texas, it appears that many Los Angeles–based musicians were willing to consider changing their citizenship. If, as Manuel Peña has claimed, musicians do function as "organic intellectuals" for the working class, challenging American cultural hegemony while expressing the frustrations and hopes of their social group, then the experiences of Los Angeles musicians indicate a complex, if not contradictory, relationship with American cultural values.

Compared with the larger sample of Mexican immigrants, musicians were more likely to have been born in the larger cities of the central plateau in Mexico, particularly Guadalajara and Mexico City. . . .

The musical traditions brought to the United States from these locales were varied. The mobility within Mexico caused by economic upheaval and violence related to the revolution had pushed many rural residents, including folk musicians, to seek shelter in towns and cities. There, previously isolated folk music traditions from various locations were brought together, and musicians also encountered the more European musical tastes of the urban upper classes. One study of street musicians in Mexico City during the 1920s, for example, found twelve different regional styles performing simultaneously on the corners and in the marketplaces of the capital. One could hear mariachis from Jalisco, *canciones norteñas* from Chihuahua, troubadors from Yucatán, *bandas jarochas* from Veracruz, and marimba groups from Chiapas and Oaxaca.

If there was one particular musical style which stood out from the rest in popularity during this period, it was certainly the *corrido*. A prominent student of this genre has called the *corrido* "an integral part of Mexican life" and the creative period after 1910 its "most glorious epoch." During the Mexican Revolution, almost every important event, and most political leaders and rebels, became the subjects of one or more *corridos*. . . . As these *corridos* made their way into Mexico's urban centers, they were codified and transformed from folk expression to popular songs.

The *corrido*'s continued popularity during the 1920s in areas far away from its folk origins can be explained by particular characteristics of its style which made it appealing as an urban art form. First, the urban *corrido*, like the *canción ranchera*, embodied what was a traditional music style from the countryside, while adapting it to a more commercially oriented atmosphere. It reminded those who had migrated from rural areas of their provincial roots, and gave urban dwellers a connection to the agrarian ideal which was seen as typically Mexican. Second, most *corridos* appealed to a Mexican's nationalist fervor at a time when the pride of Mexican people, places, and events was flourishing. Several observers have identified the period between 1910 and 1940 as one of "national romanticism" in Mexican cultural affairs, extending beyond music to literature and mural painting. *Corridos* produced in the United States often exalted "Mexicanism" at the expense of American culture, but even those composed within Mexico paid inordinate attention to promoting Mexican cultural identity.

Finally, the *corrido* was an exceptionally flexible musical genre which encouraged adapting composition to new situations and surroundings. Melodies, for the most part, were standardized or based on traditional patterns, while text was expected to be continuously improvised. A vehicle for narration, the *corrido* always intended to tell a story to its listeners, one that would not necessarily be news but rather would "interpret, celebrate, and ultimately dignify events already thoroughly familiar to the *corrido* audience." As such, *corrido* musicians were expected to decipher the new surroundings in which Mexican immigrants found themselves while living in Los Angeles. Its relation to the working-class Mexican immigrant audience in Los Angeles was therefore critical to its continued popularity. . . . This adaptive style was particularly well suited for the rapidly expanding Los Angeles Mexican community of the 1920s and the ever-complex nature of intercultural exchange in the city.

The first commercial recording of a *corrido* in the United States was "El Lavaplatos." . . . The *corrido* describes a Mexican immigrant who dreams of making a fortune in the United States but, instead, is beset with economic misfortune. Finally, after being forced to take a job as a dishwasher, the narrator bemoans: "Goodbye dreams of my life, goodbye movie stars, I am going back to my beloved homeland, much poorer than when I came."

Most Mexican composers and musicians had firsthand knowledge of working-class life in Los Angeles; not only were they products of working-class homes, but most continued in some form of blue-collar occupation while struggling to survive as musicians. Pedro J. González, for example, worked as a longshoreman on the San Pedro docks before being "discovered," and the two musicians who played with him, Victor and Jesus Sánchez, were farmworkers. The vast majority of Mexican musicians never were able to support themselves as full-time artists. . . .

Los Angeles during the 1920s, however, presented more possibilities for earning a livelihood as a musician than any other location outside of Mexico City, or perhaps San Antonio. To begin with, the Los Angeles metropolitan area contained a huge Spanish-speaking population, second only to Mexico City itself. By 1930 the Chicano population in the city of Los Angeles was larger than any other in the United States. The potential audience for Mexican music was enormous. Since most of these residents were recent migrants from Mexico, they often longed for tunes from their homeland. Others had come from south Texas, where the Spanish-language musical tradition was strong and widespread. In fact, one writer claimed in 1932 that more Mexican music had been composed in the United States than in Mexico.

One stimulus to the Mexican music industry was the explosion of Chicano theatre in Los Angeles during the 1920s. Over thirty Chicano playwrights moved to the city during the decade, producing shows ranging from melodrama to vaudeville. The Spanish-speaking population of the region was able to support five major theatre houses from 1918 until the early 1930s. . . .

A more disparate, yet still lucrative market for Mexican musicians existed among the streets and informal gatherings of Los Angeles. During Mexican patriotic festivals and the Christmas season, musicians had larger audiences, more exposure, and greater potential for earnings. From these "auditions," Mexican groups were often recruited to play for weddings and other ethnic festivities. Moreover, a market for "traditional" Mexican music also existed among some Anglo residents of Los Angeles, often to provide a nostalgic backdrop to the distinctive "Spanish" past of the city. . . .

The emergence of Hollywood as the leading movie-making capital in the United States during the 1920s stimulated a flourishing recording industry in the city that began to rival New York's. Both these developments boded well for Mexican musicians in Los Angeles, although prejudice, union discrimination, and the lack of formal training kept many out of regular employment in the entertainment industries in the western part of town. Still, by providing the music in English-speaking theatres or working as studio musicians, some were able to break into the larger music business in Los Angeles. Even the possibility of such employment—"the dream of a life in Hollywood"— was enough to attract some performers from south of the border.

Thus musicians from Mexico flocked to Los Angeles during the 1920s, becoming a significant segment of the Mexican cultural renaissance of that decade. Unlike the Harlem Renaissance, where black writers and entertainers were often sponsored by white patrons, this Chicano/Mexicano renaissance was largely supported by Mexican immigrants themselves and existed far out of the sight of the majority of Angelinos. The presence of large numbers of Mexican musicians in the city not only preserved the sights and sounds familiar to Mexican immigrants; it also created an environment of cultural experimentation where traditional music was blended with new methods. In short, musicians often served as social interpreters who translated and reflected the cultural adaptations that were taking place among the Mexican immigrant population as a whole. In fact, one astute observer of *corridos* in Los Angeles recognized that this music often served to "sing what they cannot say":

> Mexicans are so intimidated by the government officials, even by so-
> cial workers, and so timid on account of the language difficulty that it
> is almost unheard of for a Mexican to express his opinion to an Amer-
> ican. Here, however, he is speaking to his own group and an emo-
> tional outlet is offered in the writing of *corridos* on the subject so well
> known to every Mexican. He is reasonably sure that only Mexicans
> will ever hear his *corrido.*

. . . Already, several large American recording companies such as
Vocalion, Okeh (a subsidiary of Columbia), Decca, and Bluebird (RCA)
had begun to produce "race" records, featuring black folk music. These
companies now realized the potential ethnic market among Mexicans,
and sought out Chicano musicians and singers from Texas to California. Many of the early recording sessions took place in temporary stu-
dios located in Los Angeles hotels, where a steady stream of performers
were expected to produce a finished product in one or two "takes."

To most musicians, the $15 or $20 they earned per record seemed
substantial for a few hours' work, especially when compared with the
wages they earned as laborers or the limited income from playing on
the streets. Yet these tiny sums were a pittance relative to the hundreds or thousands of dollars any single recording could earn, even
with records selling for 35 cents apiece. Musicians rarely earned sufficient income to feel secure as recording artists. Offering only "contracts" that were usually verbal agreements consisting of no royalties
or other subsidiary rights, the recording companies profited handsomely from this enterprise. . . .

Local ethnic middlemen played an important role in identifying
talented musicians and putting them in contact with recording companies. . . .

American laws prohibited the importation of records from Mexico,
a fact which greatly stimulated the recording industry in Los Angeles.
In addition, Mexican companies were not allowed to record in the
United States. These restrictions severely crippled the music industry
in Mexico, while creating a vast economic opportunity for American
companies and ethnic entrepreneurs. When Mexican recordings were
finally admitted during the 1950s, interest in immigrant and native-
born Spanish-language talent evaporated quickly, and many Chicano
musicians were left without an outlet in the recording world. In fact,
some labels which had showcased Mexican artists, such as Imperial,
began concentrating on black rhythm and blues artists, such as Fats
Domino and T-Bone Walker.

During the 1920s and 1930s, however, a vibrant environment for
Mexican music existed in Los Angeles. Another factor in creating this
cultural explosion was the advent of the radio. During the 1920s, commercial radio was still in an experimental era where corporate sponsors

and station managers tried to discover how best to make radio broadcasting profitable and enlightening. For most of the decade, the radio
was seen as a way of uplifting the masses, of bringing elite American
culture into the homes of common laborers. By the end of the decade,
however, advertising and corporate economic interests dominated the
airwaves. This transformation created a market for Spanish-language
broadcasts. Although many Anglo Americans continued to believe that
only English should be heard on the nation's airwaves, the goal of
reaching Spanish-speaking consumers silenced their opposition.

American radio programmers scheduled Spanish-language broadcasts during "dead" airtime—early morning, late night, or weekend
periods which had proven to be unprofitable for English programs.
Pedro J. González remembers first broadcasting from 4 to 6 a.m. on
Station KELW out of Burbank. He often scheduled live music, including many amateur musicians and singers from the community. While
Anglo Americans were rarely listening at this hour, many Mexican immigrants tuned into González's broadcasts while they prepared for
early morning work shifts. González's daily shows provided day laborers important information about jobs as well as cherished enjoyment
to workers who toiled all day.

Corporate radio sponsors in the mid-1920s were quick to understand the profitability of ethnic programs. Large advertisers such as
Folgers Coffee used airtime to push their product in the Spanish-
speaking market. More often, local businesses appealed to Mexican
immigrants to frequent their establishments. In Los Angeles, radio
broadcasting soon became a highly competitive industry. By selling
blocks of airtime to foreign-language brokers, marginally profitable
stations could capture a ready-made market. During the late 1920s,
the hours dedicated to Spanish-language broadcasts multiplied.
González's program was expanded until 7 a.m., and additional hours
were added at lunchtime and in the early evening. Chicano brokers
such as Mauricio Calderón profited handsomely as they negotiated
with stations, paying them a flat rate during cheap broadcasting time,
which they then sold to businesses advertisements.

Key to the success of Spanish-language broadcasting was its appeal
to the thousands of working-class Mexican immigrants within the
reach of a station's radio signal. Radio, unlike La Opinión and other
periodicals, reached Mexican immigrants whether or not they could
read. In addition, the content of radio programming focused less on the
tastes of the expatriate middle class and more on those of the masses.
A 1941 analysis of Spanish-language programming found that over 88
percent of on-air time (outside of advertisements) was dedicated to
music, with only 4 percent used for news. Programming was dominated by "traditional" music from the Mexican countryside, rather
than the orchestral, more "refined" sounds of the Mexican capital and

other large urban centers. "The corrido, the shouts, and all that stuff was popular" with working people, remembered González. Although some bemoaned the commercialization of the *corrido* tradition and its removal from its "folk tradition," most Mexican immigrants found this transformation to their liking because it fit well with their own adaptations to urban living.

The potential power generated by this mass appeal was so substantial that it not only threatened the cultural hegemony of the Mexican middle class in Los Angeles but also worried local Anglo American officials. González himself was the target of District Attorney Buron Fitts, who in 1934 had the musician arrested on trumped-up charges. Earlier, Fitts had attempted to force González off the air by getting federal authorities to rescind his broadcasting license. Along with other government authorities, Fitts believed that only English should be heard on the radio and that only American citizens should have the right to broadcast. As a result, many radio stations curtailed their Spanish-language programs during the early 1930s, often because of the continued harassment directed at ethnic broadcasters and the imposition of more strigent rules for radio licensing.

These restrictions in the United States encouraged the growth of Spanish-language broadcasting in Mexico. Although many American stations continued to reserve Spanish-language blocks, entrepreneurs based just across the border capitalized on the potential market on both sides by constructing powerful radio towers capable of reaching far-flung audiences. Increasingly, individuals unable to be heard on American-based stations moved their operations to Mexico. It proved much harder for American authorities to control the airwaves than the recording industry. . . .

The economic crisis of the 1930s curtailed much of Mexican cultural activity in Los Angeles. First, deportation and repatriation campaigns pushed almost one-third of the Mexican community back to Mexico, effectively restricting the market for Spanish-language advertising campaigns. Second, the enthusiasm of American companies for investing in "experimental" markets that did not insure a steady flow of income understandably cooled. The Mexican immigrant community itself had fewer resources to support cultural activities, given its precarious economic situation. Since expenditures on leisure-time activities were the first to be reduced during times of need, many families cut back drastically on attendance at musical events or the purchase of radios and phonographs. Many theatres in the community shut down during the Great Depression.

Movies and other forms of cheap, cross-cultural entertainment continued to thrive in Depression-era Los Angeles. Simply because of the economics of scale, Hollywood was able to continue to produce entertainment accessible to families at every economic level. In addition, the introduction of sound to motion pictures made it more difficult to sustain a steady Spanish-language audience with Mexican imports, since the Mexican film industry had difficulty throughout the transition of the 1930s. English talking-pictures, on the other hand, had a wider, and therefore more secure audience. The advent of sound coincided with the rise of the second generation of Mexicans in this country, more likely to be as fluent in English as in Spanish. Increasingly, changing demographics and limited economic resources stunted the growth of the ethnic market. A new era in Mexican/Chicano cultural activity began.

Although commercial activity was slowed during the Depression, Mexican cultural life did not die out in Los Angeles. Indeed, aspects of cultural life were altered dramatically, reflecting the changing composition and nature of the Mexican/Chicano community. Musical activity, for example, became less dependent on *corrido* story-telling (which required the ability to understand Spanish lyrics) and more concentrated in dance clubs. La Bamba night club, at Macy and Spring streets, and La Casa Olvera, adjacent to Olvera Street, were only two of many small clubs which opened during the decade. Dancing, of course, did not require a working knowledge of Spanish, and had appeal well beyond the Mexican immigrant population.

Second-generation youth, in particular, flooded the dance clubs during the 1930s. Social commentators of the period commented on the "dance craze" that had seemingly overtaken adolescents and young adults in Mexican American families. One such nineteen-yearold, known only as Alfredo to his interviewer, boastfully explained this "craze":

> I love to dance better than anything else in the world. It is something that gets in your blood. Lots of boys are that way. I go to five dances a week. I can't wait for Saturday night because all the time I am thinking of the dance. It is in my system. I could get a job playing my trumpet in an orchestra but then I couldn't dance. I quit school because I got plenty of everything they teach, but dancing.

This new "dance craze" did not often sit well with Mexican immigrant parents. Even when participation was closely chaperoned in school clubs and community centers, public dancing seemed to offend the sensibilities of decency among older Mexicans. Increasingly, however, it became difficult for parents to withstand the effect of peer pressure on their children, as evidenced by the words of one mother in the early 1930s:

> Juanita has joined a club and now she wants to learn to dance. That is what comes of these clubs. It is wrong to dance and my Juanita wants

to do it because the others do. Because everybody does it does not make it right. I know the things I was taught as a girl and right and wrong cannot change.

Although the vast majority of musicians and clientele in each of these establishments were Mexican, the music demonstrated a wide variety of American and Latin American styles. Cuban music was especially popular in the latter half of the decade, with many orchestras specializing in the mambo. The Cuban style was popular throughout Latin America, and this trend filtered into Los Angeles through traveling bands and musicians. Regular groups that played in these clubs all included Mexican songs in their repertoire. In addition, English-language music increasingly became popular among American-born youth. Many Mexican immigrants bemoaned this turn of events, as evidenced by the comments of one unnamed señora:

> The old Spanish songs are sung only be the old people. The young ones can sing the "Boop-da-oop" like you hear on the radio but they can't sing more than one verse of *La Cruz*. Do you know *La Cruz?* It is very beautiful. It is about our Lord carrying the cross. It is sad. In Mexico we would all sing for hours while someone played a guitar. But here, there are the drums and the saxophones.

Undoubtedly, a more eclectic and diverse musical life than in former decades emerged among the Mexican/Chicano community in Los Angeles. In fact, Los Angeles probably offered a richer environment for such leisure-time activity than any other city in the American Southwest.

This diversity of choice in musical styles and taste not only created a more experimental environment for musicians themselves but also reflected developments in Chicano culture as a whole. Clearly, the control of the individual over his or her own cultural choices paralleled the growth of an ethnic consumer market. In a consumer society, each Mexican immigrant alone, or in conjunction with family, embraced cultural change—consciously or unconsciously—through the purchase of material goods or by participation in certain functions. Neither the Mexican elite nor the Anglo American reformers intent on Americanization could completely determine the character of these private decisions. Instead, an unsteady relationship between American corporations, local businesses, Mexican entrepreneurs, and the largely working-class community itself influenced the range of cultural practices and consumer items available in the Spanish-language market. If appeals to Mexican nationalism could be used to sell a product, then so be it. Although barriers to the ethnic market were constructed by local officials, particularly during the Great Depression, change in economic circumstances and in cultural tastes of the population had the most important impact.

Appeal to the tastes of youth also created subtle power shifts within the Chicano community. In Mexico, few outlets were available to young people for influencing cultural practices in an individual village or even one's own family. The American metropolis, on the other hand, gave Mexican youth an opportunity to exercise more cultural prerogatives merely by purchasing certain products or going to the movies. Rebellion against family often went hand in hand with a shift toward more American habits. This pattern was stimulated by the extent to which adolescents and unmarried sons and daughters worked and retained some of their own income. As the second generation came to dominate the Chicano population by the late 1930s, their tastes redefined the community's cultural practices and future directions of cultural adaptation.

Behind the vast American commercial network lay an enterprising group of ethnic entrepreneurs who served as conduits between the Mexican immigrant population and the corporate world. These individuals were often the first to recognize cultural changes and spending patterns among the immigrant population. Individuals such as Mauricio Calderón and Pedro J. González were able to promote Mexican music in entirely new forms in Los Angeles because they had daily contact with ordinary members of the Los Angeles Mexican community. Although they found tangible financial rewards in their efforts, they also served an important role in redefining Mexican culture in an American urban environment.

6

THE PROGRESSIVE MOVEMENT

Elitist or Democratic?

In the years between the end of the Civil War and the onset of World War I, the United States underwent dramatic social change. That change was accelerated by the Civil War, but it involved a set of interconnected processes that had been in train for decades: the shift from a commercial and agricultural economy to an industrial one; the rapid growth of cities; the diversification of the American population as a result of new immigration; and the development of a more pervasive consumer culture. These economic and social innovations had far-reaching consequences, requiring Americans to reexamine cultural values and political practices that had seemed unchallengeable only a few years earlier.

Among the most central of all those values was individualism. Although the rise of industry was often rationalized as a triumph of "self-made men" of talent, drive, and probity, by the end of the nineteenth century it was becoming more difficult to conceive of industrial progress solely in terms of the achievements of individuals. The growth of a national transportation and communications system, which had led to the rise of a national market, stimulated the formation of huge industrial enterprises. This "organizational revolution," to use Kenneth Boulding's phrase,[1] raised profound questions for Americans at the turn of the twentieth century. If America's greatness was related to individual achievement, what would happen as giant corporations limited individual opportunities for self-employment and diminished individual liberty within machinelike and bureaucratic settings? If families and communities were being disrupted by urbanization and shifting demands for labor, how could healthy individuals be nurtured? Was not the growing disparity between rich and poor introducing an almost European class strife into America's open society? Could democracy survive the diminishment of the individual and the elephantine growth of new structures of domination that one historian

---

[1]Kenneth E. Boulding, *The Organizational Revolution: A Study in the Ethics of Economic Organization* (New York, 1953).

has dubbed "the incorporation of America?"[2] In trying to answer these questions many Americans turned to moral reform and ultimately to politics to restore dignity to the individual and vitality to democracy.

The forces of reform gradually gathered momentum in the last quarter of the nineteenth century, although their roots reached back to antebellum abolitionist, labor, women's rights, public education, and prison reform movements, among others. Reformers could not agree upon a specific diagnosis, let alone remedial measures, but, especially after two sharp depressions in the 1870s and 1880s, and the growing social turmoil they triggered, increasing numbers came to the conviction that the United States was in crisis. Positive action was required if the nation was to survive with its traditional values intact. Proponents of antitrust measures focused on dissolving or reducing the size of corporations, which would presumably restore market competition and thereby revive rugged individualism. Proponents of civil service reform hoped to insulate public administration from political corruption. Seeking to recreate the solidarity and authority that seemed to be vanishing with the "island community," advocates of the Social Gospel, Populism, socialism, and government regulation contributed to the swelling chorus of reform.

Some social critics imagined that new forms of voluntary collective action would suffice to effect necessary change. For example, evangelical and temperance campaigns might convince individuals to forswear sin, and thereby to find on a personal level what their society seemed unable to supply: a balance between competitive struggle and middle-class respectability. Some advocates of labor organization and collective bargaining believed that purely private arrangements could restore the dignity of work. Similarly, proponents of the corporate merger movement thought private agreements among businessmen could restore rationality to the marketplace. Other reformers looked to government, especially on the municipal and state levels, to impose the particular reforms they believed necessary to restore harmony to society. Proponents of railroad regulation, of prohibition, of Americanization of immigrants, of the single tax, of city-manager or city-commission forms of urban governance, and of many other policies came increasingly to recognize that governments would have to act in order to address social problems that neither individuals nor voluntary associations could solve.

What brought these diverse and even incompatible efforts together and added urgency to the cause of reform was the catastrophic depression that began in 1893 and lasted most of the decade. Outstripping

---

[2]Alan Trachtenberg, *The Incorporation of America: Culture and Society in the Gilded Age* (New York, 1982).

the depressions of the previous two decades in intensity and scope, the crisis of the 1890s produced a precipitous drop in the value of productive enterprises, a rash of bankruptcies, rural devastation, and mass unemployment. There seemed to be no escape from the catastrophe. Part of what fueled the Progressive movement was a sense of sheer outrage at those who had acquired so much wealth and used it so irresponsibly. Beyond outrage was a new understanding of social reality. What had happened to the American economy since the Civil War had suddenly become apparent to all: the scale of enterprise had vastly expanded; the market had become truly national, even international; the fate of the individual was now inextricably connected to the collective fate of corporations, classes, nations. Whatever the efficacy and continuing value of personal, voluntary, and local solutions to problems, few Americans could doubt any longer that the authority and force of government were needed to relieve and prevent their misery. While faith in progress remained strong, and revolutionary thoughts occupied only relatively few, there could be little doubt at the turn of the century that political change was inevitable and necessary.

Between 1900 and 1917 formerly discrete reform efforts increasingly found common cause in what came to be known as the Progressive movement. Pluralistic rather than unitary, the Progressive movement was actually a series of loose coalitions—at the local, state, and national levels—made up of quite diverse reformers who sought a variety of goals: political reforms such as the initiative, referendum, and recall, as well as the replacement of "corrupt" urban political machines with "clean" city-manager or city-commission forms of government; economic reforms such as the regulation of corporate mergers, public utilities, and banks; and social reforms such as prohibition, minimum-wage, maximum-hour, and child labor laws, building and public health codes, and other measures. Among the symbolic leaders of the movement were several women, for instance Jane Addams, the great pioneer of the settlement house and the social work profession, and Frances Willard, leader of the Women's Christian Temperance Union, which fought not only demon rum but a host of social ills, including child labor. Among other leaders were academics such as Richard Ely and John Dewey, who promoted the professionalization of social science and the application of expert knowledge to the solution of public problems; and muckraking journalists such as Lincoln Steffens, who exposed urban corruption, Ida Tarbell, who exposed the Standard Oil monopoly, and Upton Sinclair, who exposed the oppressive labor conditions and unsafe health standards of the meat-packing industry. Progressive champions included politicians: Robert M. La Follette, governor of Wisconsin (1901–1906), taxed corporate wealth and forced railroads to submit to state regulation; Tom L. Johnson, mayor of Cleveland (1901–1909), a businessman turned "municipal socialist," instituted a comprehensive system of public utility regulation. Although diverse and multifarious, Progressivism came to be associated particularly with two presidents, Theodore Roosevelt and Woodrow Wilson. These two not only revived the moral authority and expanded the role of the presidential office, but they supported the enactment of an extraordinarily large number of laws that seemed to many of their contemporaries to bring to fruition the major social reforms pursued in the previous decade and a half.

Until after World War II there was relatively little controversy among historians about the nature and character of the Progressive movement. Most American historians, influenced by Charles Beard and his Progressive school of history, interpreted these reform movements as challenges to big business and the privileged classes. The reformers' goals had been clear and simple: to restore government to the people, to abolish special privilege and ensure equal opportunity for all, and to promote social justice through legislation and sound administration. The reformers, Progressive historians emphasized, were not anticapitalist; they had not advocated the abolition of private property or sought the establishment of a socialist society. On the contrary, they had taken seriously the American dream and wanted simply to make it attainable. The enemies of that dream were greedy businessmen, dishonest politicians, and "special interests," all of whom posed a serious threat to the realization of American democracy. Vernon L. Parrington, one of the best-known Progressive historians, saw Progressivism as a "democratic renaissance"—a movement of the masses against a plutocracy that had been corrupting the very fabric of American society since the Civil War. The movement concerned itself with economic as well as political democracy. To Parrington, Progressivism was a broad-based movement of middle-class citizens whose consciences had been aroused by the "cesspools that were poisoning the national household," and who set about awakening the American people to the task of purification.[3]

Implicit in this point of view was the conviction that the course of American history had been characterized by a continuous struggle between liberalism and conservatism, democracy and aristocracy, equal opportunity and special privilege. Most historians writing in the Progressive tradition believed that reformers, regardless of their specific goals or the eras in which they appeared, invariably supported the "people" against their enemies. Such was the position of John D. Hicks, whose textbooks in American history were used by tens of thousands of high school and college students between the 1930s and

---

[3]Vernon L. Parrington, *Main Currents in American Thought*, 3 vols. (New York, 1927–1930), 3: 406.

1960s. In 1931 Hicks published *The Populist Revolt*, the first major account of Populism based on wide research in the original sources. To Hicks the Populists represented the first organized protest of the mass citizenry against the encroachments of a monopolistic plutocracy. Although the Populist movement ultimately failed, it was victorious in the long run, Hicks held, because much of its program was taken over by Progressive reformers and enacted into law during the first two decades of the twentieth century. To a large extent his thesis rested on the assumption that American reform efforts drew much of their inspiration from the Jeffersonian agrarian tradition which had survived intact among the nation's farmers and rural population.[4]

Not all historians were as friendly and well-disposed toward Populism and Progressivism as was Hicks. Those historians writing within a Marxist tradition, for example, found Progressive reform superficial because it failed to adopt radical solutions to the fundamental problem of class inequality. To John Chamberlain, a young Marxist who in 1932 published a devastating critique of American reform, the Progressive movement was an abysmal failure. Its adherents, claimed Chamberlain, were motivated by an escapist desire to return to a mythic past where honesty and virtue held sway over egoism and evil.[5] In the midst of the Great Depression, even historians who rejected Chamberlain's Marxism and identified themselves as liberals acknowledged the inadequacies of Progressive reform. Still, they insisted that what was required was not a rejection of Progressivism but a realization of its radical ambition to redeem popular democracy from the special interests and the privileged classes.

Beginning in the 1940s and continuing in the 1950s and 1960s, the mood of American historians began to change. Many scholars of the World War II generation had begun to reject the Progressive tradition of historiography. Like the philosophers and theologians who were criticizing liberalism for its facile optimism and obtuseness in the face of human tragedy, they criticized Progressive historians (and liberals, more generally) for underestimating humankind's propensity for evil, overestimating its capacity for good, and turning history into a simple morality play. The new appreciation for the tragic dimension of human affairs led contemporaneous European historians in radical directions; under the influence of the Cold War, however, it led most Americans toward what came to be called "consensus" history.

The caricature of consensus historians is that they asserted the unity and homogeneity of America's past, the stability of basic institu-

---

[4]John D. Hicks, *The Populist Revolt: A History of the Farmers' Alliance and the People's Party* (Minneapolis, 1931).

[5]John Chamberlain, *Farewell to Reform* (New York, 1932).

tions, and the existence of a homogeneous national character. They insisted that social conflict always occurred within a common liberal framework and that the protagonists were never really in disagreement over fundamentals. Moreover, this caricature continues, in a world brutalized by fascism and communism, consensus historians doubted the value of social change and feared mass movements of any kind. In this reading, they were neoconservatives who trimmed the sails of history to the anti-Communist winds of the McCarthy era. In fact, as the introduction to this volume makes clear, those called consensus historians were remarkably diverse, and most were liberals. Some were, indeed, "Cold War liberals" who believed that a defense of American values and institutions was more important than social criticism at a moment when totalitarianism threatened to take over the world. However, there was no simple correlation between Cold War defensiveness and anti-Progressive historiography. Arthur M. Schlesinger, Jr., who never departed from the Progressive historiographical camp, was the leading Cold War liberal in the history profession. On the other hand, the distinguished Columbia University historian Richard Hofstadter, who was definitely a critic of Progressive historiography, judged Progressive reform (and liberalism, more generally) insufficiently tough-minded in its critique of American social inequality. Hofstadter was more dismayed than satisfied with the excess of consensus and the absence of conflict he found in American history.

Whatever the political implications, there is no doubt that a sharp shift occurred in the way historians after World War II interpreted the Progressive movement. Perhaps most importantly, consensus historians began to ask questions about the Progressive era based on their reading of twentieth-century social science research. If turn-of-the-century reformers were not champions of the masses, who were they and what did they want? Perhaps the findings of social scientists about the significance of status in shaping social behavior might be useful in explaining Progressivism. If Progressives did not democratize America, just what did they accomplish? Findings in the sociology of bureaucracy and complex organizations, as well as research into the modernization of societies in the European and non-European world, might illuminate an era in which Americans were moving from small towns to big cities, from simple to complex and pluralistic social structures.

Hofstadter led the attack on the Progressive interpretation. His critique was a form of self-criticism: he emerged from the Progressive historiographical tradition and considered himself a liberal partisan. In a sense, Hofstadter's entire career can be seen as a lifelong lover's quarrel with liberalism, in the course of which he relentlessly exposed its inadequacies, delusions, and failures. The process began in 1948 with the publication of *The American Political Tradition and the Men Who*

Made It. This book attempted to delineate the basic characteristics of the American political tradition by studying the careers of political leaders from Andrew Jackson to Franklin Delano Roosevelt. Hofstadter argued that the liberal tradition had failed because it could not escape the acquisitive and individualistic assumptions that had originally shaped it. Both the Populists and Progressives looked back with nostalgia to an era of self-made men; neither faced up to the fundamental problems of an industrialized and corporate America. The Populists, he argued, "looked backward with longing to the lost agrarian Eden, to the republican America of the early years of the nineteenth century in which there were few millionaires and, as they saw it, no beggars, when the laborer had excellent prospects and the farmer had abundance, when statesmen still responded to the mood of the people and there was no such thing as the money power." Unable to explain why their world had changed, they blamed Easterners, Wall Street bankers, Jews, and foreigners. Their curious blend of racism, nativism, and provincialism would later manifest itself in national paranoid scares such as McCarthyism in the 1950s.

Nor were the Progressives, according to Hofstadter, much more sophisticated. By the latter third of the nineteenth century, the scions of Anglo-Saxon Protestant families were finding themselves displaced from traditional positions of leadership by a *nouveau-riche* plutocracy, on the one hand, and political machines controlled by alien elements, on the other. Responding to this displacement, these clergymen, lawyers, professors, and other bourgeois reformers launched a moral crusade to resuscitate older Protestant and individualistic values—the Progressive movement. This crusade was based on the simple idea that only men of character—the "right sort of people"—should rule. "In the attempts of the Populists and Progressives to hold on to some of the values of agrarian life, to save personal entrepreneurship and individual opportunity and the character type they engendered, and to maintain a homogeneous Yankee civilization," Hofstadter wrote, "I have found much that was retrograde and delusive, a little that was vicious, and a good deal that was comic."[6]

The implication of Hofstadter's interpretation was indeed striking: the United States had never had a viable or effective liberal tradition. Those who wore the mantle of liberalism—Populists, Progressives, and even New Dealers—were mostly well-to-do, middle- to upper-class reformers, alienated from their society by technological and industrial changes, and resentful of those who had succeeded in the scramble for status. There is no doubt that Hofstadter himself wrote from the Left of the political spectrum, but he resisted completely the

---

[6]Richard Hofstadter, *The Age of Reform: From Bryan to F.D.R.* (New York, 1955), p. 11.

tendency of some on the Left to find heroic victories for "the people" in what he saw as a mostly conservative chronicle of consensus.

Hofstadter's interpretation of Progressivism meshed with that of other post–World War II historians, particularly George E. Mowry. Author of a number of important books on Theodore Roosevelt and the Progressive movement, Mowry was one of the first historians to see Progressivism as the effort of middle-class Protestants to restore declining status and recapture a world of individualism and face-to-face community, rather than a serious attempt to tackle fundamental economic reforms.[7] The Mowry-Hofstadter thesis did not go unchallenged by a number of historians who pointed to a serious methodological flaw. To argue—as Mowry and Hofstadter did—that the Progressives were a distinct social group requires a demonstration that their political adversaries represented a quite different group. One historian found that in one state the social, economic, and ideological characteristics of anti-Progressives were almost identical to those of the Progressives.[8] However damaging to the "status anxiety" thesis, however, this criticism only reinforced Hofstadter's larger argument about the triviality of American reform. Progressives and their adversaries were drawn from the same class; whatever they argued about, it was not class equality or the redistribution of wealth and power. Most historians in the 1950s and early 1960s seemed to agree that the older interpretation of Progressivism as a struggle between the people and special interests was oversimplified, if not erroneous.

Louis Hartz, in his influential *The Liberal Tradition in America,* argued that because America lacked a feudal tradition it escaped the struggles between conservatives, reactionaries, liberals, and socialists that characterized the history of most European countries. The United States instead had a three-century-long tradition of consensus, wherein all Americans subscribed to the Lockean tenets of individualism, private property, natural rights, and popular sovereignty. The differences among Americans, Hartz maintained, have been over means rather than ends. America never had a conservative party of tradition rooted in a way of life that preceded the emergence of capitalism and the liberal state. And thus America had very little class conflict and little ground for the breeding of class-based ideologies. Socialism could mean very little in America because nearly everyone had access to a

---

[7]George E. Mowry, "The California Progressive and His Rationale: A Study in Middle Class Politics," *Mississippi Valley Historical Review* 36 (September 1949): 239–250. See also *The California Progressives* (Berkeley, 1951) and *The Era of Theodore Roosevelt and the Birth of Modern America, 1900–1912* (New York, 1958).

[8]See Richard B. Sherman, "The Status Revolution and Massachusetts Progressive Leadership," *Political Science Quarterly* 78 (March 1963): 59–65; and Jerome M. Clubb and Howard W. Allen, "Collective Biography and the Progressive Movement: The 'Status Revolution' Revisited," *Social Science History* 4 (1977): 518–534.

middle-class way of life. Conservatism could mean very little in America because the only thing to conserve—the only continuous tradition—was liberalism.[9]

After Hofstadter, Mowry, and Hartz, most historians abandoned the Progressive school's search for instances of popular struggle against vested interests, but not all fell into a uniform interpretive line. Historian John Morton Blum followed the consensus historians in seeing early-twentieth-century reform as essentially conservative, but unlike them he saw that conservatism as a sign of the progressive movement's strength, rather than weakness. For Blum, Theodore Roosevelt was a sort of American Disraeli, i.e., a pragmatic conservative who tried to force the privileged classes to recognize the need to adapt to change. Among Roosevelt's greatest ambitions was to convince his fellow Republicans and the men they represented that expanding the powers of the presidency was required to manage an increasingly complex and conflictual society.[10] Conversely, in Blum's reading, Woodrow Wilson's righteous moralism seemed too close to the simpleminded reform tradition that Hofstadter had discredited. Wilson's "New Freedom" seemed to harken back to a bygone age when all individuals had equal opportunity in the economic sphere. His foreign policies also turned out to be dismal failures because they emerged out of a moralism that could not appreciate the reality of national interests.[11]

As some historians undermined the Progressive emphasis on class and group conflict, other historians were in the process of developing a new synthesis based on organizational theory (a species of modernization theory) derived from work in the social and behavioral sciences in the 1950s and 1960s. Organizational historians pictured American society as increasingly dominated by hierarchical and bureaucratic structures, and marked by a sharp acceleration in the process of professionalization. Associated with these developments was a corresponding shift from nineteenth-century individualism to the values of order, efficiency, and systematic control.[12] Already employed by the business historian Alfred D. Chandler, Jr.,[13] to explain the emergence of large

---

[9]Louis Hartz, *The Liberal Tradition in America: An Interpretation of American Political Thought Since the Revolution* (New York, 1955).

[10]John Morton Blum, *The Republican Roosevelt* (Cambridge, Mass., 1954).

[11]John Morton Blum, *Woodrow Wilson and the Politics of Morality* (Boston, 1956). For a critical but more sympathetic interpretation see Arthur S. Link's two-decade-long engagement with Wilson: *Wilson*, 5 vols. (Princeton, 1947–1965). His *Woodrow Wilson and the Progressive Era, 1910–1917* (New York, 1954; rev. ed. 1963) focuses on Wilson's record during the Progressive years.

[12]See Louis Galambos, "The Emerging Organizational Synthesis in Modern American History," *Business History Review* 44 (Autumn 1970): 279–290, as well as his follow-up analysis, "Technology, Political Economy, and Professionalism: Central Themes of the Organizational Synthesis," ibid. 57 (Winter 1983): 471–493.

[13]See Chapter 3 in this volume.

corporations, the organizational model could also be used to advance the thesis that Progressivism was an attempt to govern society in accordance with the ideals of scientific management and efficiency.

The conservation movement, for example, was not—as historians of the Progressive school had maintained—a struggle by the people against special interests bent on hijacking natural resources and despoiling the landscape. On the contrary, according to Samuel P. Hays, conservation was promoted by scientists and corporate managers interested in "rational planning to promote efficient development and use of all natural resources." Conversely, small farmers, cattlemen, homesteaders, and other groups that Progressive historians had portrayed as democratic masses actually opposed conservation because it thwarted their hopes of economic advancement through the exploitation of cheap natural resources. "The broader significance of the conservation movement," Hays concluded, "stemmed from the role it played in the transformation of a decentralized, nontechnical, loosely organized society, where waste and inefficiency ran rampant, into a highly organized, technical, and centrally planned and directed social organization which could meet a complex world with efficiency and purpose."[14] Like other reform efforts it had little or nothing to do with the liberal/conservative categories of the Progressive school of historiography. In a similar vein Hays argued that support for reform in municipal government came from men and women of the business and professional classes. These "cosmopolitans" insisted that the welfare of the city could be served only if city governments were run in a businesslike manner. This meant essentially removing decision-making from the hands of corrupt political machines, whose aims were strictly local and political, and relocating it in "nonpolitical," centralized administrative structures staffed by people like themselves. Hays's classic articulation of this view appears as the first selection in this chapter.

Hays's survey of Progressive reform, *The Response to Industrialism*, captured the essence of the era in the phrase "Organize or Perish."[15] An even more comprehensive version of this approach, *The Search for Order*, by Robert H. Wiebe, has remained probably the leading historical synthesis of the Progressive era for the past thirty years. For much of the nineteenth century, Wiebe argues, the United States was a nation more in name than in fact. Most individuals resided in nearly autonomous "island communities" where relationships were personal, communication was face-to-face, and the knowledge needed to live successfully was accessible without much recourse to the

---

[14]Samuel P. Hays, *Conservation and the Gospel of Efficiency: The Progressive Conservation Movement, 1890–1920* (Cambridge, Mass., 1959), pp. 2 and 265. See also *American Political History as Social Analysis: Essays by Samuel P. Hays* (Knoxville, Tenn., 1980).

[15]Samuel P. Hays, *The Response to Industrialism, 1885–1914* (Chicago, 1957).

world outside. By the 1880s, however, technological and economic change had undermined the cohesiveness of such locales, leaving individuals vulnerable to "dislocation and bewilderment." The result, according to Wiebe, was a "search for order." Some of the searchers attempted to restore the local community to a position of significance; others turned to agrarian or monetary reform; still others joined moral crusades against alcohol or prostitution, hoping thereby to buttress traditional values even as traditional structures eroded.

Up to this point, Wiebe sounds much like Hofstadter. But whereas Hofstadter located the origins of Progressivism in the problems of an old and declining middle class, Wiebe identified it with the ambition and professional élan of a new middle class. Whatever anxiety might have been felt by older middle-class types such as yeomen farmers, shopkeepers, and small businessmen, their children, who were increasingly college-educated professionals or salaried employees of large institutions, believed they could master the future. In such diverse fields as law, medicine, economics, social work, architecture, business, and agriculture—to cite only a few examples—these new middle-class folk emerged with the conviction that their expertise could bring order to a fragmented society. "The heart of progressivism," Wiebe argued, "was the ambition of the new middle class to fulfill its destiny through bureaucratic means."[16] In thus fulfilling its destiny, this middle class helped to modernize the United States and prepare it for the twentieth century.

Both consensus and organizational interpretations of the Progressive movement grew in influence in the 1950s and 1960s, even after New Left historians had begun to challenge received wisdom in this and other fields of study. Ironically, in denying that Progressive reform was very "progressive" (or liberal or radical), consensus and organizational interpretations had paved the way for the New Left historians. Disillusioned by the continued existence of war, poverty, and racism, New Left scholars tended to write about the shortcomings and failures of American reform, a point of view that grew out of their own belief that only radical changes in the structure of society could establish true justice and equality in America. Consequently, New Left historians adopted their predecessors' awareness of the importance of organizations in twentieth-century America, as well as their view of Progressive reformers as essentially conservative.

Gabriel Kolko, whose work is discussed in Chapter 3, argued that both major political parties shared a common ideology—what Kolko called political capitalism. Political capitalism "redirected the radical

---

[16]Robert H. Wiebe, *The Search for Order, 1877–1920* (New York, 1967), p. 166.

potential of mass grievances and aspirations" into the promotion of government regulation of business. Regulation was invariably controlled by and served the ends of the regulated industries, because the regulatory movement was initiated by businessmen who wanted stable markets, and also because politicians and other elites shared a belief in the basic justice of private property. Progressivism, argued Kolko, was a movement founded on the assumption among elites that the welfare of the nation (and of each community and individual) was synonymous with the interests of business. Since neither the Populist nor the Socialist party developed a persuasive diagnosis of social injustice, Americans had no viable political alternative to the two business-dominated major parties. "The Progressive Era," concluded Kolko, "was characterized by a paucity of alternatives to the status quo, a vacuum that permitted political capitalism to . . . determine the ground rules for American civilization in the twentieth century, and to set the stage for what was to follow."[17]

Not all historians agreed with such disparagement of the Progressive movement. Some rejected the radical idea that reformers were either agents or dupes of corporate capitalism. Others questioned the organizational view that reform was nothing more than adjustment to modernization (or the consensus view that it was nothing more than maladjustment). While admitting that the older Progressive historians' saga of "the people versus the special interests" was untenable, and acknowledging that "the search for order" was a part of what motivated reformers, many scholars continued to see Progressive reform as a serious critique of inequality and injustice. J. Joseph Huthmacher, for example, explicitly rejected the Mowry-Hofstadter idea that Progressivism was a middle-class movement dominated by anxious, small-town Yankee Protestants. On the contrary, Huthmacher maintained that Progressivism in the city was much more broadly based, incorporating the views and drawing the active participation of workers and other urban lower-class groups. Huthmacher insisted that Progressivism addressed complex dilemmas of an urban-industrial society. Although he clearly rejected the simplisms of the old Progressive school interpretation, his was essentially an updating and elaboration of the view that the reform movement of 1900–1920 was a continuing phase in the perennial struggle between liberal have-nots and conservative haves.[18]

Nor was Huthmacher alone in reasserting a version of the old in-

---

[17]Gabriel Kolko, *The Triumph of Conservatism: A Reinterpretation of American History, 1900–1916* (New York, 1963), pp. 2–3, 285, and 303. See also James Weinstein, *The Corporate Ideal in the Liberal State, 1900–1918* (Boston, 1968).

[18]J. Joseph Huthmacher, "Urban Liberalism and the Age of Reform," *Mississippi Valley Historical Review* 44 (September 1962): 231–241.

terpretation of Progressivism. John C. Burnham, for example, took issue with the view implicit in the organizational interpretation that
Progressives were cold and passionless experts rather than passionate
volunteers in a reform crusade. In fact, he showed, Progressives strove
to merge Protestant moral fervor with the hard facts of science and
technology. Indeed, Burnham insisted, moral commitment and imme-
diacy lay at the heart of the movement and contributed to such specific achievements as child-labor legislation and public health reform.
Melvin Holli found in his study of Detroit that the reform movement
was a coalition of the "cool" and the "hot." "Structural" reformers,
who resembled Hays's technocrats, sought clean and efficient government; "social" reformers, often with a sense of class grievance and
evangelical zeal, sought justice and new municipal benefits for immigrant workers, as well as a stronger hand in restraining the power of
corporations. Sometimes the two sorts of reformers fell out over issues
such as taxes or temperance, but often enough they found common
cause and succeeded in bringing both a measure of order and a measure
of justice to the industrial city.[19]

    After Huthmacher and Holli, a number of historians developed
with great sophistication the idea of Progressivism as coalition politics. In their hands reform movements revealed themselves to be alliances not just of structural and social reformers, but of a great variety
of different groups and interests, ranging broadly across the social con-
tinuum. They insisted that Progressive politics was *real* politics, not
just a shadow-act behind which "political capitalists" or "new middle
class" technocrats pulled the strings. On the other hand, they seemed
to be saying that Progressivism was "small" politics—i.e., local politics that varied enormously from place to place, interest to interest.
This approach could lead to a highly fragmented and incoherent picture of Progressivism. If it was not a coherent movement with a unitary ideology, organizational structure, and social basis, what was it?
One historian, Peter G. Filene, decided that it was nothing at all—just
an empty label superimposed upon a gaggle of unrelated phenomena.[20]
But other historians had a better answer.

    Progressivism was a series of "shifting coalitions," to use John D.
Buenker's phrase, that enabled previously separate groups and causes to
form alliances around specific issues. If urban liberals and trade unionists made common cause with the WCTU on labor legislation, they

---

[19]Melvin G. Holli, *Reform in Detroit: Hazen S. Pingree and Urban Politics* (New
York, 1969); Martin J. Schiesl complicated the picture by showing that the two types of
reform were less contradictory and more interconnected than Holli suggested: *The Politics of Efficiency: Municipal Administration and Reform in America, 1880–1920* (Berkeley, 1977).

[20]Peter G. Filene, "An Obituary for 'The Progressive Movement,'" *American Quarterly* 22 (Spring 1970): 20–34.

parted company on Prohibition. Similarly, as David Thelen showed, if Wisconsin farmers joined the Milwaukee Chamber of Commerce in promoting railroad regulation, they diverged on tax equalization. Thus, even if Progressivism was not a movement of the people against the interests, as the old Progressive historians would have it, it was certainly neither an elite phenomenon. Though Hays had exposed the folly of taking all the Progressives' democratic rhetoric at face value, Buenker, Thelen, and others exposed the folly of reducing so complex a movement to a single explanatory rubric, especially one based on so vague a social category as "new middle class" or "cosmopolitans." Progressivism is more fruitfully seen, said Thelen, as a revolt against "corporate arrogance" that inspired working-class, middle-class, and even some upper-class Americans to rally around men like Tom Johnson, Robert La Follette, and Theodore Roosevelt, who promised to take on the bullies in the interest of the general citizenry. "When the progressive characteristically spoke of reform as a fight of 'the people' or the 'public interest' against the 'selfish interests,' he was speaking quite literally of his political coalition because the important fact about progressivism, at least in Wisconsin, was the degree of cooperation between previously discrete social groups now united under the banner of the 'public interest' . . . Both conceptually and empirically it would seem safer and more productive to view reformers first as reformers and only secondarily as men who were trying to relieve class and status anxieties."[21]

In uncovering the political astuteness and effectiveness of women reformers, some recent historians have reinforced the notion that, however diverse, Progressivism was in fact animated by a broad critique of inequality and injustice in industrial America. In the second essay in this unit, Kathryn Kish Sklar argues persuasively that women used the language of "maternalism" to suffuse Progressive reform with a passion to restrain the powerful and promote justice for all. With organized labor relatively weak and socialism branded as alien, middle-class women assumed responsibility for applying moral judgments to market relations, for bringing both Christian charity and modern hygiene to bear upon the problems of the "social household." Since women were denied the vote, they ironically made use of their "nonpolitical" status to act as nurturers, teachers, and scolds toward those men who had become morally disoriented by the competitive and unscrupulous world of business and politics.

---

[21]By John D. Buenker, see "The Progressive Era: A Search for a Synthesis," *Mid-America* 51 (July, 1969): 175–193, and *Urban Liberalism and Progressive Reform* (New York, 1973). By David P. Thelen, see "Social Tensions and the Origins of Progressivism," *Journal of American History* 56 (September, 1969): 323–341; *The New Citizenship: Origins of Progressivism in Wisconsin, 1885–1900* (Columbia, Mo., 1972); and *Robert M. La Follette and the Insurgent Spirit* (Boston, 1976). See also John D. Buenker, John C. Burnham, and Robert M. Crunden, *Progressivism* (Cambridge, Mass., 1977).

Generations of such experience in church organizations and reform causes from abolitionism to temperance had well prepared them to take on new tasks. They fought, of course, for women's suffrage, sometimes basing it on the claim that they embodied the Victorian virtues of restraint, moral sensitivity, and "passionlessness" that were increasingly needed to calm a diverse and conflictual society. Beyond "women's issues," they fought both the machine politicians who failed to provide clean water to immigrant masses, and the businessmen who polluted the water in the first place. They lobbied for minimum-wage, maximum-hour, and child-labor legislation, often infuriating the same men who were their allies in campaigns to restrict liquor licenses or to enact civil service reforms. Whatever the rationale, the activism of middle-class women in organizations such as the General Federation of Women's Clubs, the YWCA, the Women's Trade Union League, and the National Consumers' League provided the grassroots support for the emerging welfare state that was supplied in Europe by unions and socialist parties. In the United States, Sklar argues, it was women's activism that "served as a surrogate for working-class social-welfare activism."[22]

If Buenker, Thelen, Sklar, and other historians rescued Progressivism from diminishment at the hands of many consensus, organizational, and New Left interpreters, they did not inoculate it from all attacks. A few historians showed that Progressivism in some places and guises was more conservative—and more reprehensible—than even earlier detractors had made it seem. In a significant analysis of Alabama during the Progressive era, Sheldon Hackney found a few similarities with, but some disturbing differences from, the better-known movements in the Midwest. He noted, echoing the pioneering work of C. Vann Woodward, that there was little continuity between Populism and Progressivism; following the demise of their party, Alabama Populists either voted Republican or else withdrew from politics. Unlike Woodward (but not unlike Hofstadter), Hackney found Populists to be "primitive rebels." They viewed society in static terms, employed a backward-looking republican rhetoric, and preferred a minimal rather than an activist government. Progressives, by contrast, saw society in dynamic terms and insisted that economic opportunity could come only through greater economic growth stimulated by governmental action. Progressives were earnestly interested in changing southern society and bringing it into the modern indus-

---

[22]See also Linda Gordon, ed., *Women, the State, and Welfare* (Madison, Wis., 1990), and *Pitied but Not Entitled: Single Mothers and the History of Welfare, 1890–1935* (New York, 1994).

trial era. Indeed, Hackney found that Alabama Progressivism resembled more the urban, midwestern, and northeastern brand of Progressivism associated with Theodore Roosevelt than the Populist-tinged rural variety associated with William Jennings Bryan.[23]

But Progressivism, as both Woodward and Hackney observed, had sharply negative implications for the status of black Americans. During the years from 1890 to 1910 the pattern of race relations in the South was highly fluid; inconsistency was its primary characteristic. One manifestation of this uncertainty was the high frequency of lynchings. In Alabama, Hackney showed, social instability, generally—and lynching, specifically—began to decline only when the Constitutional Convention of 1901 in effect eliminated black citizens from political participation. Ironically, the movement for disfranchisement was led by proponents of reform, who equated restriction of the franchise with "purification" of the body politic. Their success helped Progressives create a new coalition from the purged (and less numerous) electorate that owed little to Populist antecedents. Progressivism in Alabama, therefore, rested on the institutionalization of legal and political inequality. Hackney's book certainly made it difficult to characterize Progressivism in the South as a broad-based coalition for "social welfare" or against "corporate arrogance." Whatever was true of Progressivism in other places, in the land of Jim Crow it was a profoundly racist and conservative movement.

Progressivism also had other negative effects. It certainly strengthened the hand of Prohibitionists and advocates of immigration restriction. The Progressive years marked a high point in the history of American racism. All non-"Nordic" people—descendants of Africa, Asia, Latin America, and southern and eastern Europe, among others—became targets of those who considered themselves descendants of "the great race." As John Higham showed, anti-foreign, anti-Catholic, anti-Semitic, and anti-radical tendencies in American politics came together in the early twentieth century and culminated in the World War I period. Those years saw hysterical assaults upon the liberty of German-Americans; the passage of the Alien and Sedition Acts, which sent hundreds of pacifists and critics of the war to jail; the Red Scare, which resulted in the jailing and deportation of hundreds of socialists and anarchists, and finally the Immigration Restriction Act of 1924.[24] Historians disagree as to whether such baneful forms of chauvinism were the fruits of Progressivism or a corruption of it. But

---

[23]Sheldon Hackney, *Populism to Progressivism in Alabama* (Princeton, 1969). See also C. Vann Woodward, *Origins of the New South, 1877–1913* (Baton Rouge, La., 1951).

[24]John Higham, *Strangers in the Land: Patterns of American Nativism 1860–1925* (New York, 1963). See also Chapter 5 in this volume.

certainly Progressivism furthered a new sense of nationalism and the urge to purify the body politic of corrupting influences. And it gave political advantage to those Protestant professionals who were best able to organize themselves into special interest groups, and who were most tempted to explain social instability as a product of alien influences upon "our country."

As political historians have recently shown, the urge to purify the electoral system produced some of the most anti-democratic results of Progressive reform. Many of the Progressives' favorite structural reforms—e.g., primaries, voter registration, city commissions—contributed to a dramatic shrinkage in the electorate. Walter Dean Burnham, a political scientist, identified the period immediately following the depression of the 1890s as a moment of major realignment in American politics. These years also witnessed a weakening of party loyalty accompanied by a massive decline in voting. The decline of party, in turn, magnified the significance of pressure groups of all kinds.[25]

In his book on New York State politics in the Progressive era, Richard L. McCormick set out to show why the pull of parties had declined. The hold of party bosses, he explained, weakened under attacks from reformers who saw themselves as nonpartisan and even antiparty, and who raised new issues incapable of being resolved by the traditional party technique of distributing favors as widely as possible. McCormick further showed that between 1904 and 1908 the regulatory authority of government increased in precisely the same period that voter turnout declined, ticket-splitting increased, and organized pressure groups gained power at the expense of party. In discovering that business corrupted politics, Progressive-era Americans created a demand for the regulatory and administrative state. But the rise of that state disempowered lower-class constituents of political machines at the same time as it empowered organizationally skilled individuals from business and the professions. Men or women, more liberal or more conservative, structural or social reformers, these middle- to upper-class Progressives achieved political efficacy at the expense of mass democracy whether they intended to or not.[26]

As Daniel Rodgers has observed, historians no longer attempt to describe the Progressive era within a unitary political or ideological

[25]Walter Dean Burnham, "The Changing Shape of the American Political Universe," *American Political Science Review* 59 (March 1965): 7–28, and *Critical Elections and the Mainsprings of American Politics* (New York, 1970).

[26]Richard L McCormick, *From Realignment to Reform: Political Change in New York State, 1893–1910* (Ithaca, 1981), and "The Discovery that Business Corrupts Politics: A Reappraisal of the Origins of Progressivism," *American Historical Review* 86 (April 1981): 247–274.

framework.[27] The roots, forms, and outcomes of Progressivism were diverse and even conflicting. But if Progressives lacked a systematic intellectual system and a coherent politics, they did share a sense—which can only be called modern—that a new scale had come to human affairs; that great enterprises, cities, and organizations, both private and public, would thenceforth shape the destinies of most people in the industrial world. Appalled by corporate arrogance and political corruption, and sometimes moved by the sufferings of less-fortunate Americans, these mostly middle- and upper-class reformers sought order or justice or both, using their new professional and bureaucratic skills. Most of them tried to preserve what they valued in the legacies of individualism, decentralized government, citizen voluntarism, and the like, even as they embraced new forms of solidarity and government intervention in social problems. America changed as a result of Progressivism, but it did not become a science-fiction version of bureaucratic dystopia. Moreover, those who rejected Progressive reform in all or large part—proponents of laissez-faire and small government, for example, not to mention champions of Anglo-Saxon supremacy and patriarchal privilege—would continue to shape American history along with their more progressive fellow citizens. In the New Deal years a generation of reformers from more diverse ethnic and class origins proposed reforms that went well beyond Progressivism. But in going beyond Progressivism they pursued the path it had cleared. For better or worse, Progressivism shaped, to some degree, every effort by twentieth-century Americans to come to terms with their diverse, unequal, and ever-changing industrial society.

---

[27]Daniel T. Rodgers, "In Search of Progressivism," *Reviews in American History* 10 (December 1982): 113–132.

SAMUEL P. HAYS

SAMUEL P. HAYS (1921–   ) is professor of history emeritus at the University of Pittsburgh. His books include The Response to Industrialism 1885–1914 (1957), Conservation and the Gospel of Efficiency (1959), and American Political History as Social Analysis (1980).

In order to achieve a more complete understanding of social change in the Progressive Era, historians must now undertake a deeper analysis of the practices of economic, political, and social groups. Political ideology alone is no longer satisfactory evidence to describe social patterns because generalizations based upon it, which tend to divide political groups into the moral and the immoral, the rational and the irrational, the efficient and the inefficient, do not square with political practice. Behind this contemporary rhetoric concerning the nature of reform lay patterns of political behavior which were at variance with it. Since an extensive gap separated ideology and practice, we can no longer take the former as an accurate description of the latter, but must reconstruct social behavior from other types of evidence.

Reform in urban government provides one of the most striking examples of this problem of analysis. The demand for change in municipal affairs, whether in terms of overall reform, such as the commission and city-manager plans, or of more piecemeal modifications, such as the development of citywide school boards, deeply involved reform ideology. Reforms loudly proclaimed a new structure of municipal government as more moral, more rational, and more efficient and, because it was so, self-evidently more desirable. But precisely because of this emphasis, there seemed to be no need to analyze the political forces behind change. Because the goals of reform were good, its causes were obvious; rather than being the product of particular people and particular ideas in particular situations, they were deeply imbedded in the universal impulses and truths of "progress." Consequently, historians have rarely tried to determine precisely who the municipal reformers were or what they did, but instead have relied on reform ideology as an accurate description of reform practice.

The reform ideology which became the basis of historical analysis is well known. It appears in classic form in Lincoln Steffens' Shame of the Cities. The urban political struggle of the Progressive Era, so the

Samuel P. Hays, "The Politics of Reform in Municipal Government in the Progressive Era," Pacific Northwest Quarterly 55 (October 1964): 157–169. Reprinted by permission of the Pacific Northwest Quarterly.

argument goes, involved a conflict between public impulses for "good government" against a corrupt alliance of "machine politicians" and "special interests."

During the rapid urbanization of the late nineteenth century, the latter had been free to aggrandize themselves, especially through franchise grants, at the expense of the public. Their power lay primarily in their ability to manipulate the political process, by bribery and corruption, for their own ends. Against such arrangements there gradually arose a public protest, a demand by the public for honest government, for officials who would act for the public rather than for themselves. To accomplish their goals, reformers sought basic modifications in the political system, both in the structure of government and in the manner of selecting public officials. These changes, successful in city after city, enabled the "public interest" to triumph.

Recently, George Mowry, Alfred Chandler, Jr., and Richard Hofstadter have modified this analysis by emphasizing the fact that the impulse for reform did not come from the working class. This might have been suspected from the rather strained efforts of National Municipal League writers in the "Era of Reform" to go out of their way to demonstrate working-class support for commission and city-manager governments. We now know that they clutched at straws, and often erroneously, in order to prove to themselves as well as to the public that municipal reform was a mass movement.

The Mowry-Chandler-Hofstadter writings have further modified older views by asserting that reform in general and municipal reform in particular sprang from a distinctively middle-class movement. This has now become the prevailing view. Its popularity is surprising not only because it is based upon faulty logic and extremely limited evidence, but also because it, too, emphasizes the analysis of ideology rather than practice and fails to contribute much to the understanding of who distinctively were involved in reform and why.

Ostensibly, the "middle-class" theory of reform is based upon a new type of behavioral evidence, the collective biography, in studies by Mowry of California Progressive party leaders, by Chandler of a nationwide group of that party's leading figures, and by Hofstadter of four professions—ministers, lawyers, teachers, editors. These studies demonstrate the middle-class nature of reform, but they fail to determine if reformers were distinctively middle-class, specifically if they differed from their opponents. One study of 300 political leaders in the state of Iowa, for example, discovered that Progressive-party, Old Guard, and Cummins Republicans were all substantially alike, the Progressive differing only in that they were slightly younger than the others and had less political experience. If its opponents were also middle-class, then one cannot describe Progressive reform as a phenomenon whose special nature can be explained in terms of middle-class characteristics. One cannot explain the distinctive behavior of people in terms of characteristics which are not distinctive to them.

Hofstadter's evidence concerning professional men fails in yet another way to determine the peculiar characteristics of reformers, for he describes ministers, lawyers, teachers, and editors without determining who within these professions became reformers and who did not. Two analytical distinctions might be made. Ministers involved in municipal reform, it appears, came not from all segments of religion, but peculiarly from upper-class churches. They enjoyed the highest prestige and salaries in the religious community and had no reason to feel a loss of "status," as Hofstadter argues. Their role in reform arose from the class character of their religious organizations rather than from the mere fact of their occupation as ministers. Professional men involved in reform (many of whom—engineers, architects, and doctors—Hofstadter did not examine at all) seem to have come especially from the more advanced segments of their professions, from those who sought to apply their specialized knowledge to a wider range of public affairs. Their role in reform is related not to their attempt to defend earlier patterns of culture, but to the working out of the inner dynamics of professionalization in modern society.

The weakness of the "middle-class" theory of reform stems from the fact that it rests primarily upon ideological evidence, not on a thorough-going description of political practice. Although the studies of Mowry, Chandler, and Hofstadter ostensibly derive from behavioral evidence, they actually derive largely from the extensive expressions of middle-ground ideological position, of the reformers' own descriptions of their contemporary society, and of their expressed fears of both the lower and the upper classes, of the fright of being ground between the millstones of labor and capital.

Such evidence, though it accurately portrays what people thought, does not accurately describe what they did. The great majority of Americans look upon themselves as "middle-class" and subscribe to a middle-ground ideology, even though in practice they belong to a great variety of distinct social classes. Such ideologies are not rationalizations or deliberate attempts to deceive. They are natural phenomena of human behavior. But the historian should be especially sensitive to their role so that he will not take evidence of political ideology as an accurate representation of political practice.

In the following account I will summarize evidence in both secondary and primary works concerning the political practices in which municipal reformers were involved. Such an analysis logically can be broken down into three parts, each one corresponding to a step in the traditional argument. First, what was the source of reform? Did it lie in the general public rather than in particular groups? Was it middle-class, working-class, or perhaps of other composition? Second, what was the reform target of attack? Were reformers primarily interested in ousting the corrupt individual, the political or business leader who made private arrangements at the expense of the public, or were they interested in something else? Third, what political innovations did reformers bring about? Did they seek to expand popular participation in the governmental process?

There is now sufficient evidence to determine the validity of these specific elements of the more general argument. Some of it has been available for several decades; some has appeared more recently; some is presented here for the first time. All of it adds up to the conclusion that reform in municipal government involved a political development far different from what we have assumed in the past.

Available evidence indicates that the source of support for reform in municipal government did not come from the lower or middle classes, but from the upper class. The leading business groups in each city and professional men closely allied with them initiated and dominated municipal movements. Leonard White, in his study of the city manager published in 1927, wrote:

> The opposition to bad government usually comes to a head in the local chamber of commerce. Business men finally acquire the conviction that the growth of their city is being seriously impaired by the failures of city officials to perform their duties efficiently. Looking about for a remedy, they are captivated by the resemblance of the city-manager plan to their corporate form of business organization.

In the 1930s White directed a number of studies of the origin of city-manager government. The resulting reports invariably begin with such statements as, "the Chamber of Commerce spearheaded the movement," or commission government in this city was a "businessmen's government." Of thirty-two cases of city-manager government in Oklahoma examined by Jewell C. Phillips, twenty-nine were initiated either by chambers of commerce or by community committees dominated by businessmen. More recently James Weinstein has presented almost irrefutable evidence that the business community, represented largely by chambers of commerce, was the overwhelming force behind both commission and city-manager movements.

Dominant elements of the business community played a prominent role in another crucial aspect of municipal reform: the Municipal Research Bureau movement. Especially in the larger cities, where they had less success in shaping the structure of government, reformers established centers to conduct research in municipal affairs as a springboard for influence.

The first such organization, the Bureau of Municipal Research of New York City, was founded in 1906; it was financed largely through the efforts of Andrew Carnegie and John D. Rockefeller. An investment banker provided the crucial support in Philadelphia, where a Bu-

reau was founded in 1908. A group of wealthy Chicagoans in 1910 established the Bureau of Public Efficiency, a research agency. John H.
Patterson of the National Cash Register Company, the leading figure
in Dayton municipal reform, financed the Dayton Bureau, founded
in 1912. And George Eastman was the driving force behind both the
Bureau of Municipal Research and city-manager government in
Rochester. In smaller cities data about city government were collected
by interested individuals in a more informal way or by chambers of
commerce, but in larger cities the task required special support, and
prominent businessmen supplied it.

The character of municipal reform is demonstrated more precisely
by a brief examination of the movements in Des Moines and Pittsburgh. The Des Moines Commercial Club inaugurated and carefully
controlled the drive for the commission form of government. In January 1906 the club held a so-called "mass meeting" of business and professional men to secure an enabling act from the state legislature. P. C.
Kenyon, president of the club, selected a Committee of 300, composed
principally of business and professional men, to draw up a specific proposal. After the legislature approved their plan, the same committee
managed the campaign which persuaded the electorate to accept the
commission form of government by a narrow margin in June 1907.

In this election the lower-income wards of the city opposed the
change, the upper-income wards supported it strongly, and the middle-
income wards were more evenly divided. In order to control the new
government, the Committee of 300, now expanded to 530, sought to determine the nomination and election of the five new commissioners,
and to this end they selected an avowedly businessman's slate. Their
plans backfired when the voters swept into office a slate of anticommission candidates who now controlled the new commission government.

Proponents of the commission form of government in Des Moines
spoke frequently in the name of "the people." But their more explicit
statements emphasized their intent that the new plan be a "business
system" of government, run by businessmen. The slate of candidates
for commissioner endorsed by advocates of the plan was known as the
"businessman's ticket." J. W. Hill, president of the committees of 300
and 530, bluntly declared: "The professional politician must be ousted
and in his place capable business men chosen to conduct the affairs of
the city." I. M. Earle, general counsel of the Bankers' Life Association
and a prominent figure in the movement, put the point more precisely:
"When the plan was adopted it was the intention to get businessmen
to run it."

Although reformers used the ideology of popular government, they
in no sense meant that all segments of society should be involved
equally in municipal decision-making. They meant that their concept
of the city's welfare would be best achieved if the business community
controlled city government. As one businessman told a labor audi-

ence, the businessman's slate represented labor "better than you do yourself."

The composition of the municipal reform movement in Pittsburgh demonstrates its upper-class and professional as well as its business sources. Here the two principal reform organizations were the Civic Club and the Voters' League. The 745 members of these two organizations came primarily from the upper class. Sixty-five percent appeared in upper-class directories which contained the names of only 2 percent of the city's families. Furthermore, many who were not listed in these directories lived in upper-class areas. These reformers, it should be stressed, comprised not an old but a new upper class. Few came from earlier industrial and mercantile families. Most of them had risen to social position from wealth created after 1870 in the iron, steel, electrical equipment, and other industries, and they lived in the newer rather than the older fashionable areas.

Almost half (48 percent) of the reformers were professional men: doctors, lawyers, ministers, directors of libraries and museums, engineers, architects, private and public school teachers, and college professors. Some of these belonged to the upper class as well, especially the lawyers, ministers, and private school teachers. But for the most part their interest in reform stemmed from the inherent dynamics of their professions rather than from their class connections. They came from the more advanced segments of their organizations, from those in the forefront of the acquisition and application of knowledge. They were not the older professional men, seeking to preserve the past against change; they were in the vanguard of professional life, actively seeking to apply expertise more widely to public affairs.

Pittsburgh reformers included a large segment of businessmen; 52 percent were bankers and corporation officials or their wives. Among them were the presidents of fourteen large banks and officials of Westinghouse, Pittsburgh Plate Glass, U.S. Steel and its component parts (such as Carnegie Steel, American Bridge, and National Tube), Jones and Laughlin, lesser steel companies (such as Crucible, Pittsburgh, Superior, Lockhart, and H. K. Porter), the H. J. Heinz Company, and the Pittsburgh Coal Company, as well as officials of the Pennsylvania Railroad and the Pittsburgh and Lake Erie. These men were not small businessmen; they directed the most powerful banking and industrial organizations of the city. They represented not the old business community, but industries which had developed and grown primarily within the past fifty years and which had come to dominate the city's economic life.

These business, professional, and upper-class groups who dominated municipal reform movements were all involved in the rationalization and systematization of modern life; they wished a form of government which would be more consistent with the objectives inherent in those developments. The most important single feature of their perspective was the rapid expansion of the geographical scope of affairs which they wished to influence and manipulate, a scope which was no longer limited and narrow, no longer within the confines of pedestrian communities, but was now broad and citywide, covering the whole range of activities of the metropolitan area.

The migration of the upper class from central to outlying areas created a geographical distance between its residential communities and its economic institutions. To protect the latter required involvement both in local ward affairs and in the larger city government as well. Moreover, upper-class cultural institutions, such as museums, libraries, and symphony orchestras, required an active interest in the larger, municipal context from which these institutions drew much of their clientele.

Professional groups, broadening the scope of affairs which they sought to study, measure, or manipulate, also sought to influence the public health, the educational system, or the physical arrangements of the entire city. Their concerns were limitless, not bounded by geography, but as expansive as the professional imagination. Finally, the new industrial community greatly broadened its perspective in governmental affairs because of its new recognition of the way in which factors throughout the city affected business growth. The increasing size and scope of industry, the greater stake in more varied and geographically dispersed facets of city life, the effect of floods on many business concerns, the need to promote traffic flows to and from work for both blue-collar and managerial employees—all contributed to this larger interest. The geographically larger private perspectives of upper-class, professional, and business groups gave rise to a geographically larger public perspective.

These reformers were dissatisfied with existing systems of municipal government. They did not oppose corruption per se—although there was plenty of that. They objected to the structure of government which enabled local and particularistic interests to dominate. Prior to the reforms of the Progressive Era, city government consisted primarily of confederations of local wards, each of which was represented on the city's legislative body. Each ward frequently had its own elementary schools and ward-elected school boards which administered them.

These particularistic interests were the focus of a decentralized political life. City councilmen were local leaders. They spoke for their local areas, the economic interests of their inhabitants, their residential concerns, their educational, recreational, and religious interests—i.e., for those aspects of community life which mattered most to those they represented. They rolled logs in the city council to provide streets, sewers, and other public works for their local areas. They defended the community's cultural practices, its distinctive languages or national customs, its liberal attitude toward liquor, and its saloons and dance halls which served as centers of community life. One observer described this process of representation in Seattle:

> The residents of the hill-tops and the suburbs may not fully appreciate the faithfulness of certain downtown ward councilmen to the interests of their constituents. . . . The people of a state would rise in arms against a senator or representative in Congress who deliberately misrepresented their wishes and imperilled their interests, though he might plead a higher regard for national good. Yet people in other parts of the city seem to forget that under the old system the ward elected councilmen with the idea of procuring service of special benefit to that ward.

In short, pre-reform officials spoke for their constituencies, inevitably their own wards which had elected them, rather than for other sections or groups of the city.

The ward system of government especially gave representation in city affairs to lower-and middle-class groups. Most elected ward officials were from these groups, and they, in turn, constituted the major opposition to reforms in municipal government. In Pittsburgh, for example, immediately prior to the changes in both the city council and the school board in 1911 in which citywide representation replaced ward representation, only 24 percent of the 387 members of those bodies represented the same managerial, professional, and banker occupations which dominated the membership of the Civic Club and the Voters' League. The great majority (67 percent) were small businessmen—grocers, saloonkeepers, livery-stable proprietors, owners of small hotels, druggists—white-collar workers such as clerks and bookkeepers, and skilled and unskilled workmen.

This decentralized system of urban growth and the institutions which arose from it reformers now opposed. Social, professional, and economic life had not only developed in the local wards in a small community context, but had also on a larger scale become highly integrated and organized, giving rise to a superstructure of social organization which lay far above that of ward life and which was sharply divorced from it in both personal contacts and perspective.

By the late nineteenth century, those involved in these larger institutions found that the decentralized system of political life limited their larger objectives. The movement for reform in municipal government, therefore, constituted an attempt by upper-class, advanced professional, and large-business groups to take formal political power from the previously dominant lower- and middle-class elements so that they might advance their own conceptions of desirable public policy. These two groups came from entirely different urban worlds, and the political system fashioned by one was no longer acceptable to the other.

Lower- and middle-class groups not only dominated the pre-reform governments but vigorously opposed reform. It is significant that none of the occupational groups among them, for example, small business-men or white-collar workers, skilled or unskilled artisans, had impor-tant representation in reform organizations thus far examined. The case studies of city-manager government undertaken in the 1930s un-der the direction of Leonard White detailed in city after city the partic-ular opposition of labor. In their analysis of Jackson, Michigan, the authors of these studies wrote:

> The *Square Deal,* oldest Labor paper in the state, has been consis-
> tently against manager government, perhaps largely because labor has
> felt that with a decentralized government elected on a ward basis it
> was more likely to have some voice to receive its share of privileges.

In Janesville, Wisconsin, the small shopkeepers and workingmen on the west and south sides, heavily Catholic and often Irish, opposed the commission plan in 1911 and in 1912 and the city-manager plan when adopted in 1923. "In Dallas there is hardly a trace of class con-sciousness in the Marxian sense," one investigator declared, "yet in city elections the division has been to a great extent along class lines." The commission and city-manager elections were no exceptions. To these authors it seemed a logical reaction, rather than an embarrassing fact that had to be swept away, that workingmen should have opposed municipal reform.

In Des Moines working-class representatives, who in previous years might have been council members, were conspicuously absent from the "businessman's slate." Workingmen acceptable to reformers could not be found. A workingman's slate of candidates, therefore, ap-peared to challenge the reform slate. Organized labor, and especially the mineworkers, took the lead; one of their number, Wesley Ash, a deputy sheriff and union member, made "an astonishing run" in the primary, coming in second among a field of more than twenty candi-dates. In fact, the strength of anticommission candidates in the primary so alarmed reformers that they frantically sought to appease labor.

The day before the final election they modified their platform to pledge both an eight-hour day and an "American standard of wages." They attempted to persuade the voters that their slate consisted of men who represented labor because they had "begun at the bottom of the ladder and made a good climb toward success by their own unaided efforts." But their tactics failed. In the election on March 30, 1908, vot-ers swept into office the entire "opposition" slate. The business and professional community had succeeded in changing the form of gov-ernment, but not in securing its control. A cartoon in the leading re-form newspaper illustrated their disappointment; John Q. Public sat dejectedly and muttered, "Aw, What's the Use?"

The most visible opposition to reform and the most readily available target of reform attack was the so-called "machine," for through the "machine" many different ward communities as well as lower- and middle-income groups joined effectively to influence the central city government. Their private occupational and social life did not naturally involve these groups in larger citywide activities in the same way as the upper class was involved; hence they lacked access to privately organized economic and social power on which they could construct political power. The "machine" filled this organizational gap.

Yet it should never be forgotten that the social and economic institutions in the wards themselves provided the "machine's" sustaining support and gave it larger significance. When reformers attacked the "machine" as the most visible institutional element of the ward system, they attacked the entire ward form of political organization and the political power of lower- and middle-income groups which lay behind it.

Reformers often gave the impression that they opposed merely the corrupt politician and his "machine." But in a more fundamental way they looked upon the deficiencies of pre-reform political leaders in terms not of their personal shortcomings, but of the limitations inherent in their occupational, institutional, and class positions. In 1911 the Voters' League of Pittsburgh wrote in its pamphlet analyzing the qualifications of candidates that "a man's occupation ought to give a strong indication of his qualifications for membership on a school board." Certain occupations inherently disqualified a man from serving:

> Employment as ordinary laborer in the lowest class of mill work would naturally lead to the conclusion that such men did not have sufficient education or business training to act as school directors. . . . Objection might also be made to small shopkeepers, clerks, workmen at many trades, who by lack of educational advantages and business training, could not, no matter how honest, be expected to administer properly the affairs of an educational system, requiring special knowledge, and where millions are spent each year.

These, of course, were precisely the groups which did dominate Pittsburgh government prior to reform. The League deplored the fact that school boards contained only a small number of "men prominent throughout the city in business life . . . in professional occupations . . . holding positions as managers, secretaries, auditors, superintendents and foremen" and exhorted these classes to participate more actively as candidates for office.

Reformers, therefore, wished not simply to replace bad men with good; they proposed to change the occupational and class origins of decision-makers. Toward this end they sought innovations in the formal machinery of government which would concentrate political power by sharply centralizing the processes of decision-making rather than distribute it through more popular participation in public affairs. Accord-

ing to the liberal view of the Progressive Era, the major political innovations of reform involved the equalization of political power through
the primary, the direct election of public officials, and the initiative,
referendum, and recall. These measures played a large role in the political ideology of the time and were frequently incorporated into new
municipal charters. But they provided at best only an occasional and
often incidental process of decision-making. Far more important in
continuous, sustained, day-to-day processes of government were those
innovations which centralized decision-making in the hands of fewer
and fewer people.

The systematization of municipal government took place on both
the executive and the legislative levels. The strong-mayor and city-
manager types became the most widely used examples of the former.
In the first decade of the twentieth century, the commission plan had
considerable appeal, but its distribution of administrative responsibility among five people gave rise to a demand for a form with more centralized executive power; consequently, the city-manager or the
commission-manager variant often replaced it.

A far more pervasive and significant change, however, lay in the
centralization of the system of representation, the shift from ward to
citywide election of councils and school boards. Governing bodies so
selected, reformers argued, would give less attention to local and particularistic matters and more to affairs of citywide scope. This shift, an
invariable feature of both commission and city-manager plans, was often adopted by itself. In Pittsburgh, for example, the new charter of
1911 provided as the major innovation that a council of twenty-seven,
each member elected from a separate ward, be replaced by a council of
nine, each elected by the city as a whole.

Cities displayed wide variations in this innovation. Some re-
grouped wards into larger units but kept the principle of areas of representation smaller than the entire city. Some combined a majority of
councilmen elected by wards with additional ones elected at large. All
such innovations, however, constituted steps toward the centralization of the system of representation.

Liberal historians have not appreciated the extent to which municipal reform in the Progressive Era involved a debate over the system of
representation. The ward form of representation was universally condemned on the grounds that it gave too much influence to the separate
units and not enough attention to the larger problems of the city.
Harry A. Toulmin, whose book *The City Manager* was published by
the National Municipal League, stated the case:

> The spirit of sectionalism had dominated the political life of every
> city. Ward pitted against ward, alderman against alderman, and legis-
> lation only effected by "log-rolling" extravagant measures into opera-
> tion, mulcting the city, but gratifying the greed of constituents, has

too long stung the conscience of decent citizenship. This constant treaty-making of factionalism has been no less than a curse. The city-manager plan proposes the commendable thing of abolishing wards. The plan is not unique in this for it has been common to many forms of commission government. . . .

Such a system should be supplanted, the argument usually went, with citywide representation in which elected officials could consider the city "as a unit." "The new officers are elected," wrote Toulmin, "each to represent all the people. Their duties are so defined that they must administer the corporate business in its entirety, not as a hodge-podge of associated localities."

Behind the debate over the method of representation, however, lay a debate over who should be represented, over whose views of public policy should prevail. Many reform leaders often explicitly, if not implicitly, expressed fear that lower- and middle-income groups had too much influence in decision-making. One Galveston leader, for example, complained about the movement for initiative, referendum, and recall:

We have in our city a very large number of negroes employed on the docks; we also have a very large number of unskilled white laborers; this city also has more barrooms, according to its population, than any other city in Texas. Under these circumstances it would be extremely difficult to maintain a satisfactory city government where all ordinances must be submitted back to the voters of the city for their ratification and approval.

At the National Municipal League convention of 1907, Rear Admiral F. E. Chadwick (USN Ret.), a leader in the Newport, Rhode Island, movement for municipal reform, spoke to this question even more directly:

Our present system has excluded in large degree the representation of those who have the city's well-being most at heart. It has brought, in municipalities . . . a government established by the least educated, the least interested class of citizens.

It stands to reason that a man paying $5,000 taxes in a town is more interested in the well-being and development of his town than the man who pays no taxes. . . . It equally stands to reason that the man of the $5,000 tax should be assured a representation in the committee which lays the tax and spends the money which he contributes. . . . Shall we be truly democratic and give the property owner a fair show or shall we develop a tyranny of ignorance which shall crush him.

Municipal reformers thus debated frequently the question of who should be represented as well as the question of what method of representation should be employed.

That these two questions were intimately connected was revealed in other reform proposals for representation, proposals which were rarely taken seriously. One suggestion was that a class system of representation be substituted for ward representation. For example, in 1908 one of the prominent candidates for commissioner in Des Moines proposed that the city council be composed of representatives of five classes: educational and ministerial organizations, manufacturers and jobbers, public utility corporations, retail merchants including liquor men, and the Des Moines Trades and Labor Assembly. Such a system would have greatly reduced the influence in the council of both middle- and lower-class groups. The proposal revealed the basic problem confronting business and professional leaders: how to reduce the influence in government of the majority of voters among middle- and lower-income groups.

A growing imbalance between population and representation sharpened the desire of reformers to change from ward to citywide elections. Despite shifts in population within most cities, neither ward district lines nor the apportionment of city council and school board seats changed frequently. Consequently, older areas of the city, with wards that were small in geographical size and held declining populations (usually lower- and middle-class in composition), continued to be overrepresented, and newer upper-class areas, where population was growing, became increasingly underrepresented. This intensified the reformers' conviction that the structure of government must be changed to give them the voice they needed to make their views on public policy prevail.

It is not insignificant that in some cities (by no means a majority) municipal reform came about outside of the urban electoral process. The original commission government in Galveston was appointed rather than elected. "The failure of previous attempts to secure an efficient city government through the local electorate made the business men of Galveston willing to put the conduct of the city's affairs in the hands of a commission dominated by state-appointed officials." Only in 1903 did the courts force Galveston to elect the members of the commission, an innovation which one writer described as "an abandonment of the commission idea," and which led to the decline of the influence of the business community in the commission government.

In 1911 Pittsburgh voters were not permitted to approve either the new city charter or the new school board plan, both of which provided for citywide representation; they were a result of state legislative enactment. The governor appointed the first members of the new city council, but thereafter they were elected. The judges of the court of common pleas, however, and not the voters, selected members of the new school board.

The composition of the new city council and new school board in

Pittsburgh, both of which were inaugurated in 1911, revealed the degree to which the shift from ward to citywide representation produced a change in group representation. Members of the upper class, the advanced professional men, and the large business groups dominated both. Of the fifteen members of the Pittsburgh Board of Education appointed in 1911 and the nine members of the new city council, none were small businessmen or white-collar workers. Each body contained only one person who could remotely be classified as a blue-collar worker; each of these men filled a position specifically but unofficially designed as reserved for a "representative of labor," and each was an official of the Amalgamated Association of Iron, Steel, and Tin Workers. Six of the nine members of the new city council were prominent businessmen, and all six were listed in upper-class directories. Two others were doctors closely associated with the upper class in both professional and social life. The fifteen members of the Board of Education included ten businessmen with citywide interests, one doctor associated with the upper class, and three women previously active in upper-class public welfare.

Lower- and middle-class elements felt that the new city governments did not represent them. The studies carried out under the direction of Leonard White contain numerous expressions of the way in which the change in the structure of government produced not only a change in the geographical scope of representation, but also in the groups represented. "It is not the policies of the manager or the council they oppose," one researcher declared, "as much as the lack of representation for their economic level and social groups." And another wrote:

> There had been nothing unapproachable about the old ward aldermen. Every voter had a neighbor on the common council who was interested in serving him. The new councilmen, however, made an unfavorable impression on the less well-to-do voters. . . . Election at large made a change that, however desirable in other ways, left the voters in the poorer wards with a feeling that they had been deprived of their share of political importance.

The success of the drive for centralization of administration and representation varied with the size of the city. In the smaller cities, business, professional, and elite groups could easily exercise a dominant influence. Their close ties readily enabled them to shape informal political power which they could transform into formal political power. After the mid-1890s the widespread organization of chambers of commerce provided a base for political action to reform municipal government, resulting in a host of small-city commission and city-manager innovations. In the larger, more heterogeneous cities, whose subcommittees were more dispersed, such communitywide action was extremely difficult. Few commission or city-manager proposals materialized here. Mayors became stronger, and steps were taken toward centralization of representation, but the ward system or some modified version usually persisted. Reformers in large cities often had to rest content with their Municipal Research Bureaus, through which they could exert political influence from outside the municipal government.

A central element in the analysis of municipal reform in the Progressive Era is governmental corruption. Should it be understood in moral or political terms? Was it a product of evil men or of particular sociopolitical circumstances? Reform historians have adopted the former view. Selfish and evil men arose to take advantage of a political arrangement whereby unsystematic government offered many opportunities for personal gain at public expense. The system thrived until the "better elements," "men of intelligence and civic responsibility," or "right-thinking people" ousted the culprits and fashioned a political force which produced decisions in the "public interest." In this scheme of things, corruption in public affairs grew out of individual personal failings and a deficient governmental structure which could not hold those predispositions in check, rather than from the peculiar nature of social forces. The contestants involved were morally defined: evil men who must be driven from power, and good men who must be activated politically to secure control of municipal affairs.

Public corruption, however, involves political even more than moral considerations. It arises more out of the particular distribution of political power than of personal morality. For corruption is a device to exercise control and influence outside the legal channels of decision-making when those channels are not readily responsive. Most generally, corruption stems from an inconsistency between control of the instruments of formal governmental power and the exercise of informal influence in the community. If powerful groups are denied access to formal power in legitimate ways, they seek access through procedures which the community considers illegitimate. Corrupt government, therefore, does not reflect the genius of evil men, but rather the lack of acceptable means for those who exercise power in the private community to wield the same influence in governmental affairs. It can be understood in the Progressive Era not simply by the preponderance of evil men over good, but by the peculiar nature of the distribution of political power.

The political corruption of the "Era of Reform" arose from the inaccessibility of municipal government to those who were rising in power and influence. Municipal government in the United States developed in the nineteenth century within a context of universal manhood suffrage which decentralized political control. Because all men, whatever their economic, social, or cultural conditions, could vote, leaders who reflected a wide variety of community interests and who represented the views of people of every circumstance arose to guide and direct municipal affairs. Since the majority of urban voters were workingmen or immigrants, the views of those groups carried great and often decisive weight in governmental affairs. Thus, as Herbert Gutman has shown, during strikes in the 1870s city officials were usually friendly to workingmen and refused to use police power to protect strikebreakers.

Ward representation on city councils was an integral part of grass-roots influence, for it enabled diverse urban communities, invariably identified with particular geographical areas of the city, to express their views more clearly through councilmen peculiarly receptive to their concerns. There was a direct, reciprocal flow of power between wards and the center of city affairs in which voters felt a relatively close connection with public matters and city leaders gave special attention to their needs.

Within this political system the community's business leaders grew in influence and power as industrialism advanced, only to find that their economic position did not readily admit them to the formal machinery of government. Thus, during strikes, they had to rely on either their own private police, Pinkertons, or the state militia to enforce their use of strikebreakers. They frequently found that city officials did not accept their views of what was best for the city and what direction municipal policies should take. They had developed a common outlook, closely related to their economic activities, that the city's economic expansion should become the prime concern of municipal government, and yet they found that this view had to compete with even more influential views of public policy. They found that political tendencies which arose from universal manhood suffrage and ward representation were not always friendly to their political conceptions and goals and had produced a political system over which they had little control, despite the fact that their economic ventures were the core of the city's prosperity and the hope for future urban growth.

Under such circumstances, businessmen sought other methods of influencing municipal affairs. They did not restrict themselves to the channels of popular election and representation, but frequently applied direct influence—if not verbal persuasion, then bribery and corruption. Thereby arose the graft which Lincoln Steffens recounted in his *Shame of the Cities*. Utilities were only the largest of those business groups and individuals who requested special favors, and the franchises they sought were only the most sensational of the prizes, which included such items as favorable tax assessments and rates, the vacating of streets wanted for factory expansion, or permission to operate amid anti-liquor and other laws regulating personal behavior. The relationships between business and formal government became a maze of accommodations, a set of political arrangements which grew up because effective power had few legitimate means of accomplishing its ends.

Steffens and subsequent liberal historians, however, misread the significance of these arrangements, emphasizing their personal rather than their more fundamental institutional elements. To them corruption involved personal arrangements between powerful business leaders and powerful "machine" politicians. Just as they did not fully appreciate the significance of the search for political influence by the rising business community as a whole, so they did not see fully the role of the "ward politician." They stressed the argument that the political leader manipulated voters to his own personal ends, that he used constituents rather than reflected their views.

A different approach is now taking root, namely, that the urban political organization was an integral part of community life, expressing its needs and its goals. As Oscar Handlin has said, for example, the "machine" not only fulfilled specific wants, but provided one of the few avenues to success and public recognition available to the immigrant. The political leader's arrangements with businessmen, therefore, were not simply personal agreements between conniving individuals; they were far-reaching accommodations between powerful sets of institutions in industrial America.

These accommodations, however, proved to be burdensome and unsatisfactory to the business community and to the upper third of socioeconomic groups in general. They were expensive; they were wasteful; they were uncertain. Toward the end of the nineteenth century, therefore, business and professional men sought more direct control over municipal government in order to exercise political influence more effectively. They realized their goals in the early twentieth century in the new commission and city-manager forms of government and in the shift from ward to citywide representation.

These innovations did not always accomplish the objectives that the business community desired because other forces could and often did adjust to the change in governmental structure and reestablish their influence. But businessmen hoped that reform would enable them to increase their political power, and most frequently it did. In most cases the innovations which were introduced between 1901, when Galveston adopted a commission form of government, and the Great Depression, and especially the city-manager form which reached a height of popularity in the mid-1920s, served as vehicles whereby business and professional leaders moved directly into the inner circles of government, brought into one political system their own power and the formal machinery of government, and dominated municipal affairs for two decades.

Municipal reform in the early twentieth century involves a paradox: the ideology of an extension of political control and the practice of its concentration. While reformers maintained that their movement rested on a wave of popular demands, called their gatherings of business and professional leaders "mass meetings," described their reforms as "part of a worldwide trend toward popular government," and proclaimed an ideology of a popular upheaval against a selfish few, they were in practice shaping the structure of municipal government so that political power would no longer be broadly distributed, but would in fact be more centralized in the hands of a relatively small segment of the population. The paradox became even sharper when new city charters included provisions for the initiative, referendum, and recall. How does the historian cope with this paradox? Does it represent deliberate deception or simply political strategy? Or does it reflect a phenomenon which should be understood rather than explained away?

The expansion of popular involvement in decision-making was frequently a political tactic, not a political system to be established permanently, but a device to secure immediate political victory. The prohibitionist advocacy of the referendum, one of the most extensive sources of support for such a measure, came from the belief that the referendum would provide the opportunity to outlaw liquor more rapidly. The Anti-Saloon League, therefore, urged local option. But the League was not consistent. Towns which were wet, when faced with a countrywide local-option decision to outlaw liquor, demanded town or township local option to reinstate it. The League objected to this as not the proper application of the referendum idea.

Again, "Progressive" reformers often espoused the direct primary when fighting for nominations for their candidates within the party, but once in control they often became cool to it because it might result in their own defeat. By the same token, many municipal reformers attached the initiative, referendum, and recall to municipal charters often as a device to appease voters who opposed the centralization of representation and executive authority. But, by requiring a high percentage of voters to sign petitions—often 25 to 30 percent—these innovations could be (and were) rendered relatively harmless.

More fundamentally, however, the distinction between ideology and practice in municipal reform arose from the different roles which each played. The ideology of democratization of decision-making was negative rather than positive; it served as an instrument of attack against the existing political system rather than as a guide to alternative action. Those who wished to destroy the "machine" and to eliminate party competition in local government widely utilized the theory that these political instruments thwarted public impulses, and thereby shaped the tone of their attack.

But there is little evidence that the ideology represented a faith in a purely democratic system of decision-making or that reformers actually wished, in practice, to substitute direct democracy as a continuing system of sustained decision-making in place of the old. It was used to destroy the political institutions of the lower and middle classes and the political power which those institutions gave rise to, rather than to provide a clear-cut guide for alternative action.

The guide to alternative action lay in the model of the business enterprise. In describing new conditions which they wished to create, reformers drew on the analogy of the "efficient business enterprise," criticizing current practices with the argument that "no business could conduct its affairs that way and remain in business," and calling upon business practices as the guides to improvement. As one student remarked:

> The folklore of the business elite came by gradual transition to be the symbols of governmental reformers. Efficiency, system, orderliness, budgets, economy, saving, were all injected into the efforts of reformers who sought to remodel municipal government in terms of the great impersonality of corporate enterprise.

Clinton Rodgers Woodruff of the National Municipal League explained that the commission form was "a simple, direct, businesslike way of administering the business affairs of the city . . . an application to city administration of that type of business organization which has been so common and so successful in the field of commerce and industry." The centralization of decision-making which developed in the business corporation was now applied in municipal reform.

The model of the efficient business enterprise, then, rather than the New England town meeting, provided the positive inspiration for the municipal reformer. In giving concrete shape to this model in the strong-mayor, commission, and city-manager plans, reformers engaged in the elaboration of the processes of rationalization and systematization inherent in modern science and technology. For in many areas of society, industrialization brought a gradual shift upward in the location of decision-making and the geographical extension of the scope of the area affected by decisions.

Experts in business, in government, and in the professions measured, studied, analyzed, and manipulated ever wider realms of human life, and devices which they used to control such affairs constituted the most fundamental and far-reaching innovations in decision-making in modern America, whether in formal government or in the informal exercise of power in private life. Reformers in the Progressive Era played a major role in shaping this new system. While they expressed an ideology of restoring a previous order, they in fact helped to bring forth a system drastically new.

The drama of reform lay in the competition for supremacy between two systems of decision-making. One system, based upon ward representation and growing out of the practices and ideas of representative government, involved wide latitude for the expression of grass-roots impulses and their involvement in the political process. The other grew out of the rationalization of life which came with science and technology, in which decisions arose from expert analysis and flowed from fewer and smaller centers outward to the rest of society. Those who espoused the former looked with fear upon the loss of influence which the latter involved, and those who espoused the latter looked only with disdain upon the wastefulness and inefficiency of the former.

The Progressive Era witnessed rapid strides toward a more centralized system and a relative decline for a more decentralized system. This development constituted an accommodation of forces outside the business community to the political trends within business and professional life rather than vice versa. It involved a tendency for the decision-making processes inherent in science and technology to prevail over those inherent in representative government.

Reformers in the Progressive Era and liberal historians since then misread the nature of the movement to change municipal government because they concentrated upon dramatic and sensational episodes and ignored the analysis of more fundamental political structure, of the persistent relationships of influence and power which grew out of the community's social, ideological, economic, and cultural activities. The reconstruction of these patterns of human relationships and of the changes in them is the historian's most crucial task, for they constitute the central context of historical development. History consists not of erratic and spasmodic fluctuations, of a series of random thoughts and actions, but of patterns of activity and change in which people hold thoughts and actions in common and in which there are close connections between sequences of events. These contexts give rise to a structure of human relationships which pervade all areas of life; for the political historians the most important of these is the structure of the distribution of power and influence.

The structure of political relationships, however, cannot be adequately understood if we concentrate on evidence concerning ideology rather than practice. For it is becoming increasingly clear that ideological evidence is no safe guide to the understanding of practice, that what people thought and said about their society is not necessarily an accurate representation of what they did. The current task of the historians of the Progressive Era is to stop taking the reformers' own description of political practice at its face value and to utilize a wide variety of new types of evidence to reconstruct political practice in its own terms. This is not to argue that ideology is either important or unimportant. It is merely to state that ideological evidence is not appropriate to the discovery of the nature of political practice.

Only by maintaining this clear distinction can the historian successfully investigate the structure of political life in the Progressive Era. And only then can he begin to cope with the most fundamental problem of all: the relationship between political ideology and political practice. For each of these facets of political life must be understood in its own terms, through its own historical record. Each involves a distinct set of historical phenomena. The relationship between them for the Progressive Era is not now clear; it has not been investigated. But it cannot be explored until the conceptual distinction is made clear and evidence tapped which is pertinent to each. Because the nature of political practice has so long been distorted by the use of ideological evidence, the most pressing task is its investigation through new types of evidence appropriate to it. The reconstruction of the movement for municipal reform can constitute a major step toward the goal.

KATHRYN KISH SKLAR

KATHRYN KISH SKLAR (1939–   ) is distinguished professor of history at the State University of New York, Binghamton. She is the author of Catharine Beecher, a Study in American Domesticity *(1973) and* Florence Kelley and the Nation's Work: The Rise of Women's Political Culture, 1830–1900 *(1995).*

One of the most exciting features of the new stream of scholarship on women and the creation of the American welfare state during what has been called the "watershed" of American history between 1880 and 1920 has been its tendency to draw large conclusions about the relationship between the political activism of white middle-class women and that of other social groups. . . .

This essay examines . . . features of American life that help us explain the power that middle-class women exercised in the white polity between 1890 and 1920 as they channeled the resources of the state in new directions. . . .

From "The Historical Foundations of Women's Power in the Creation of the American Welfare State, 1880–1920" in Seth Koven and Sonya Michel (editors), *Mothers of a New World: Maternalist Politics and the Origins of Welfare States*, New York: Routledge, 1993. Copyright © Kathryn Kish Sklar.

Women's activism was crucial because it served as a surrogate for working-class social-welfare activism. For complex historical reasons that derived partly from the political culture of middle-class women, partly from American political culture generally, women were able to provide systematic and sustained grass-roots support for social-welfare programs at a time when the working-class beneficiaries of those programs could lend only sporadic support. . . .

"Welfare" carries quite different connotations today than it did when the word first entered into common usage in the 1920s. Today "welfare" refers primarily to single mothers who receive Aid to Families with Dependent Children through the program that built "mothers' pensions" into the Social Security Act in 1935. . . .

Those who laid the foundations for the "welfare state" between 1880 and 1920 had a different perspective. For them, workers, not mothers, formed the chief focus of social legislation. Contemporary debate about how to alleviate social problems arising from industrialization revolved around wage-earning men, women, and children. "Mothers' pension" plans were one of the least-contested consequences of a larger policy debate about the regulation of the modern workplace and the intervention of the state in relation between capital and labor. Then, as now in the United States, the relatively unregulated workplace produced much higher rates of injuries and deaths than were common elsewhere. In tracing the origins of the American welfare state, feminist scholars have focused on the antecedents of AFDC or "mothers' pensions," but they have often overlooked the larger context within which mothers' pensions emerged—the large population of widows and orphans created by industrial injuries. "Make fewer widows!" one leading woman reformer declared when asked for her opinion on mothers' pensions. Her harsh but realistic reply shows us that there is more to the story of the emerging American welfare state than the "maternalism" that historians have called its chief characteristic. . . .

Opportunities for the expression of women's political activism multiplied after 1870, when traditions of limited government in the United States curbed forces that in England and Europe aided in the creation of welfare legislation. Traditions of limited government had three consequences. They undercut the development of problem-solving governmental agencies and bureaucracies; they promoted the power of professional politicians within the two major political parties; and they invested an uncommon degree of authority in the judiciary branch of government. . . .

Historians once believed that political bosses met the social-welfare needs of urban immigrant constituencies, but recent scholarship challenges that assumption. While municipal governments did dispense most nonfederal state spending before 1940, and hundreds of patronage-based jobs were distributed on the basis of party loyalty, taxes remained low and social services rudimentary. Partly due to a lack of imagination among party bosses, partly due to the restraining influence of the tax-conscious middle-class, urban political machines did not meet their constituencies' needs for positive government. They distributed food at Christmas, and mediated between members of their constituencies and social-service agencies. Sometimes they championed pure-milk campaigns, supported woman suffrage, and welcomed the construction of new schools, but most machine politicians were fiscal conservatives who, except in the business of getting votes, shunned policy innovations. Moreover, machine coalitions reinforced the power of capital by blocking pressures from below that might challenge its hegemony.

Thus policies to help the working poor survive the negative effects of industrialization went against the grain of American political structures, and crucial groups that advanced those policies elsewhere were hobbled in their attempts to do so in the United States. These circumstances created unprecedented opportunities for women reformers. When they moved into the political arena in large numbers in the 1890s, women became crucial catalysts, forming effective coalitions with men and with them constituting a new majority of politically active middle-class people in support of systematic changes in the political status quo. Men in every social group capable of advancing social legislation—lawyers, labor leaders, social scientists, industrialists, party politicians, middle-class male reformers, and even socialists—worked closely with middle-class women and their class-bridging organizations to achieve what men had not been able to accomplish separately. . . .

In the 1870s middle-class northern women propelled autonomous, mass-based women's organizations into the nation's political mainstream. This was the development stage of women's political culture. By far the most important organization, the Woman's Christian Temperance Union (WCTU), formed in 1874, carried women's pan-Protestant voluntarism into a new scale of political activism and a new depth of cultural meaning for its participants. Organizing their locals geographically to coincide with congressional districts, the WCTU endorsed woman suffrage as early as 1879. Through its "do everything" policy the Union became an umbrella organization with thirty-nine departments in 1896, twenty-five of which dealt wholly or mostly with nontemperance issues. . . .

The WCTU created new opportunities for middle-class women's social activism in a social environment that was absorbing massive numbers of recent European immigrants and a political environment where municipal, state, and national governments offered little if any assistance to needy men, women, and children. . . .

At the same time, other changes in American life democratized access to higher education and opened institutions of higher learning to women on an unprecedented scale. By 1880 more than forty thousand women were pursuing higher education, and one out of every three undergraduates was female. The feminization of the teaching profession generated these high statistics. Historically controlled by local rather than state or national governments, public schools vastly increased in number between 1800 and 1880 as the Euro-American population spread across the continent. In the competition among neighboring towns for settlers and other commercial advantages, the number or quality of village schools could define the difference between a potential county seat and a permanent backwater. The feminization of the teaching profession occurred in this context of unprecedented demand for teachers, because women were cheaper (and, many argued, better) than the traditional schoolmaster. . . . When the American welfare state began to emerge in the 1890s, a sizable second generation of college graduates was mobilized for action.

Tens of thousands of urban middle-class women put their education to use in the women's club movement. In 1890 the General Federation of Women's Clubs (GFWC) drew together a vast network of local women's organizations, which since 1869 had emerged as the secular equivalent of the WCTU. Generating an effective intermediate level of organization through state federations, and channeling women's energies into concerted political action, the GFWC became the chief voice of "organized womanhood" after 1900. By 1910 it represented 800,000 women, some of whom could vote in local elections, and most of whom had at least some influence on the male voters in their families. Even more remarkable than their formidable numbers was the impressive range of topics women's clubs explored. By 1890 these extended far beyond what might be expected to be their class-specific or gender-specific interests, or even the issues raised by the National American Woman Suffrage Association. For example, the Chicago Women's Club in the early 1880s, under its motto "Nothing Human can be Alien to Us," discussed such political questions as "Free Trade," "The Eight Hour Day," and "Bismarck and His Policy." They circulated petitions in 1886 for state legislative bills to place the treatment of women in public institutions under the supervision of women and city-council ordinances to add more women to the Board of Education. In response to Eleanor Marx's tour of the United States in 1887, members debated "Socialism and the Home." Two years later a club member spoke on "The Influence and Results of Merely Palliative Measures of Reform."

Opposed to the employment of mothers of young children, the [General] Federation [of Women's Clubs] energetically campaigned for the passage of state mothers' pensions laws. Its rhetoric critiqued industrialization from the perspective of exploited women and children.

The Federation's official history in 1912 expressed the moral outrage that regularly aroused hundreds of thousands of women to social action. "Probably the most piteous cry which has reached the ears of the mothers of the nation is that which goes up from the little children whose lives are sacrificed to the greed of manufacture," it noted in a chapter on "Federation Ideals." Although the "advent of machinery" had been a great blessing to some, it also increased "the labor of women and little children." . . .

Politically aware, willing to experiment, and eager to undertake cross-class initiatives, large numbers of middle-class women were not mirror images of their fathers, husbands, and brothers but drawing on common political traditions, structured their own forms of political action.

The gendered components of American social science made it relatively easy for college-trained women to think of themselves as policy experts. By the time Progressive women reformers encountered social science in the 1880s, it was already thoroughly gendered—in a woman-friendly way. . . . Women responded to this congeniality in social science by forming their own social-science organizations as well as by joining those led by men. In New York in the early 1870s they formed the New York City Sociology Club, the Women's Progressive Association, and the Ladies' Social Science Association. By the 1890s women reformers confidently used social-science tools in ways that permitted them to engage in reform activity on an equal basis with men without surrendering the "feminine" qualities that differentiated them from men. Moreover, leading women social scientists, like Florence Kelley and Jane Addams, who were sustained by female institutions like Hull House and undeterred by the repression experienced by their male colleagues in universities, continued throughout their lives to affiliate closely with popular social movements, particularly those dominated by women.

Just as important as education and social science in drawing middle-class women into public activism was the growth of their consciousness as consumers. This consciousness reflected the unprecedented market in consumer goods and the emergence of a consumer culture that linked producers, sellers, and buyers. Waves of immigrants who entered industrial and manufacturing jobs between 1880 and 1900 lifted most northern native-born working-class Americans into white-collar work, creating a large and relatively new group of middle-class consumers. New forms of marketing emerged, visible in the size and number of advertisements in popular magazines and the scale and diversity of department stores. Consumer culture had two striking effects on women within the older, well-established middle class. It made them more conscious of their relatively elite position within emerging middle-class consumer culture; and it highlighted the contrast between their relatively privileged lives and the lives of women who toiled to produce consumer goods. The National Consumers' League and its scores of local branches embodied the new consciousness of middle-class consumers.

Amplifying the trends that deepened and intensified the potential for political activism among middle-class women, a vanguard of talented leaders emerged within the social-settlement movement. Choosing to live in working-class, immigrant neighborhoods, this vanguard acquired potent leadership skills for cross-class cooperation with working-class women, and the ability to speak for the welfare of their entire society, not merely for the needs of women and children, or for the interests of their own class. In the United States the social-settlement movement built on and consummated social trends that had steadily enlarged women's public activism since 1830: religious or moral values that justified women's activism; the gender-specific autonomy of women's organizations and institutions; women's access to higher education; and their use of social science as a reform tool.

A product of the Social Gospel movement, settlements drew on the religious roots of women's justifications of their public power. . . . For hundreds of young women between 1890 and 1920, the question, "After college, what?" was answered with a few years of settlement work before marriage. Moreover, for dozens of talented college graduates like Jane Addams, Florence Kelley, Julia Lathrop, Alice Hamilton, Grace Abbott, and Mary Simkhovitch, settlement life sustained life-long careers in reform activism. . . .

Nevertheless, the new empowerment of women reformers through the social-settlement movement did not turn women into men. Indeed, the more women acquired power and resources, the more they did so as women. Women and men remained highly differentiated—socially, politically, and economically. Women's very prominence within the American social-settlement movement reflected that difference, since for them settlements served as a substitute for the political, professional, academic, and religious careers from which they were excluded by reason of their gender. . . .

The years between 1900 and 1920 marked the maturation of the political culture of middle-class women. Able to vote in only a few states before 1910, excluded by law from public office in most states, and perceived as outsiders by lawmakers in Congress, and in state and municipal governments, women had to find ways to overcome these gender-specific "disabilities" if they were to affect public policy. They did so by drawing on the most fundamental and enduring features of women's political culture—the strength of its grass-roots organizations, and the power of its moral vision.

Structured representationally, women's organizations, even those with strong national leaders like the National Consumers' League, gave great weight to the views of state and local affiliates. This sparked grass-roots initiative. It also fostered belief in democratic processes and the capacity of large social organizations—like state and federal governments—to respond positively to social needs. Whereas the predominant moral vision of men's political culture tended to regard the state as a potential enemy of human liberty, the moral vision of women's political culture viewed the state as a potential guarantor of social rights. . . .

To a remarkable degree the creation of the American welfare state before 1930 was due to the endorsement these predominantly middle-class women's associations gave to the expansion of governmental responsibility for the welfare of able-bodied wage earners and their families. They lobbied for legislative interventions in the relations between capital and labor to protect those they viewed as the weakest and most exploited by the forces of industrial capitalism. Shorter hours, higher wages, safer work sites would, they thought, create sounder citizens and a better society. Many of these organizations were explicitly class-bridging, such as the Women's Trade Union League, the National Consumers' League, and the YWCA. All invited the influence of the vanguard of reform leadership concentrated in the social-settlement movement. All cooperated closely with a variety of men's groups.

The distinction between white middle-class women's and men's political cultures expressed deeply rooted gender-specific social structures and cultural values. Yet while this distinction maintained firm differences between women's and men's public endeavors, it also established the preconditions for close cooperation between women and men. . . .

Women needed access to the institutional power and positions of public authority that men held, and men needed the grass-roots support that women could mobilize. Thus the National Congress of Mothers drew on the help of juvenile-court judges to launch a successful campaign for state mothers' pensions laws between 1910 and 1915. The National Consumers' League relied on prominent male attorneys to argue their cases before the U.S. Supreme Court. The General Federation of Women's Clubs worked with state superintendents of education and other state and municipal officials in designing and implementing their legislative agendas. . . .

What was it about the combination of women's grass-roots activism and small groups of male experts and leaders that accounted for their success at passing welfare legislation before 1930? What did this partnership accomplish and what does it tell us about the forces that created the American welfare state? The success of these forces was limited. For example, their effort to outlaw child labor through a constitutional amendment failed, as did their attempts to create unemployment insurance nationally—two reforms that became possible only after the devastating depression of the early 1930s—and they failed to establish state-sponsored health care for workers, an issue that continues to bedevil the American polity in the 1990s. But their efforts built a foundation on which it was possible to construct the "New Deal" of the 1930s. . . .

Women's collective action in the Progressive era certainly expressed a maternalist ideology, as historians have frequently pointed out. But it was also sparked by a moral vision of a more equitable distribution of the benefits of industrialization, and the vitality of its relatively decentralized form of organization. Within the political culture of middle-class women, gender consciousness combined with an awareness of class-based injustice, and talented leaders combined with grass-roots activism to produce an impressive force for social, political, and economic change. Issues regarding women and children wage earners captured the imagination of tens of thousands of middle-class women between 1890 and 1920, so much so that gender—women's organizations and female-specific legislation—achieved much that in other industrializing nations was done through, and in the name of, class. Women did what Florence Kelley called "the nation's work" by reaching beyond the betterment of their own class to shape a new social compact for the society as a whole. . . .

Weighing the outcome of women's efforts, the cup can appear half full or half empty, depending on one's perspective. Lacking the power to dominate the American polity, women could not themselves institute a strong welfare state. From this perspective the cup seems half empty. Some historians have viewed the American welfare state as a failure and attributed its shortcomings to the women who did so much to create it, and the gender-specific policies they pursued. Yet, seen from another perspective, the cup appears half full. Women's grass-roots organizations and their network of leaders were responsible for many pathbreaking innovations that men could not achieve. The American Association for Labor Legislation, for example, gave up on its efforts to create state-sponsored programs of workers' health insurance in 1920, but in 1921 a broad coalition of women's organizations succeeded in creating a federally sponsored program for infant and maternity health, the Sheppard-Towner Maternity and Infancy Protection Act, which many state governments sustained after federal funds ceased in 1927. Women's gender-specific and child-specific strategies aimed to aid all working people, not merely the "truly needy." Rather than isolating poor women, activists envisioned a better society in which poverty could be ended. In the 1990s the Children's Defense Fund shows that their strategy remains a necessary if not sufficient surrogate for class-specific action in a polity that remains deeply hostile to class legislation.

Today, as we near the end of the twentieth century, persisting traditions of limited government empower those who discredit social-justice programs, and the lack of class-based politics erodes the power of those who advocate such programs. Today, during the height of deindustrialization, these problems seem even more grave than they were during the height of industrialization, since the nation is losing jobs that seem unlikely to return. Moreover, welfare policies today have become inextricably combined with attitudes toward race and social justice for African Americans. One hundred years ago gender served as a surrogate for class. Today class is still less prominent than gender and race in the minds of those who design American welfare policy.

Between 1890 and 1930 middle-class women changed American public policy, but they could not and did not change the fundamental nature of the state itself, or alter the character of the male-dominated polity. Nevertheless their legacy amounts to more than the policies they embraced. Their example reveals the enduring efficacy of their methods—grass-roots organizations and class-bridging visions—for those who aspire to change American public policy.

7

THE NEW DEAL

Revolution or Restoration?

It is difficult to narrate the history of the twentieth century without placing the Great Depression and World War II at the heart of the story. And, certainly for the United States, such placement requires calling Franklin Delano Roosevelt to center stage. Roosevelt was the most popular and probably the most controversial president ever to occupy the White House. For over twelve years he led the American people through the worst depression in their history and then through a war that encompassed virtually the entire globe. To his admirers he was a leader of heroic stature, who preserved free institutions by means of democratic reform rather than by authoritarian or totalitarian methods. To his enemies he was at best misguided, at worst an immoral demagogue who pretended to save democracy by taking the American people down the road to a welfare and regulatory state—the road to socialism and the negation of individual freedom. Like few other presidents, Roosevelt had an uncanny ability to arouse strong passions. He was a person who was either loved or hated; few remained neutral toward him or reacted blandly to his personality or programs.

Why has Roosevelt aroused such strong passions? Certainly there was little in his background or his accomplishments prior to 1933 that would forecast the controversial nature of his presidential tenure. Even those friends and associates who worked closely with Roosevelt during his dozen years in the White House were not always able to grasp his many-sided personality or understand why he acted as he did. Frances Perkins, his longtime secretary of labor, described him as "the most complicated human being I ever knew," a comment echoed by others who worked closely with him. Beyond the matter of Roosevelt's imposing and complex personality, the sheer magnitude of the New Deal's innovations guaranteed that FDR would become a highly controversial figure. The heights of controversy that surrounded Roosevelt's years in the White House have almost been matched by the quantity and quality of books written about him by friends, associates, and enemies. According to Alan Brinkley, "'the age of Roosevelt' . . . has generated a larger literature than any other topic in twentieth-century American history."[1]

Although his victory in 1932 was broad-based, FDR soon alienated many businessmen and other conservatives who accused him of using centralized government to threaten private enterprise capitalism. Even a staunch Democrat such as former presidential candidate Al Smith hotly argued during the campaign of 1936 that Roosevelt was heading down the road to socialism along with Marx, Lenin, and "the rest of that bunch."[2] The attack from the Right on Roosevelt's New Deal was matched by critics on the Left. Many of these felt that Roosevelt clung to a traditional American individualism and can-do pragmatism that had been rendered obsolete by the nation's industrial and technological advances. One such critic was Rexford G. Tugwell, a professor of economics and one of the early New Deal intellectuals (called "brain trusters"). He was convinced that America's competitive economy had never worked well, certainly not in the twentieth century; to attempt to reform it with minor changes would prove hopelessly inadequate. Only thorough governmental planning for all aspects of the economic system, Tugwell argued, could prevent future depressions. Much to his disappointment, he concluded that Roosevelt was merely a tinkerer, either unwilling or unable to plan in a rational and systematic manner.[3] To the left of Tugwell stood a growing number of American socialists and communists who argued that the New Deal was nothing more than a bandage on the cancer of American capitalism. The only proper approach to the depression, they insisted, was a complete overhaul of America's social and economic system and the establishment of a socialist state.[4]

Reflecting the passions of the age in which they were living, these critics helped to establish the framework of reference with which later writers approached the New Deal. The questions raised by contemporary commentators and later historians revolved around the extent to

---

[1]Alan Brinkley, "Prosperity, Depression, and War, 1920–1945," in *The New American History*, Susan Porter Benson, Stephen Brier, and Roy Rosenzweig, eds. (Philadelphia, 1990), reprinted as an American Historical Association pamphlet; the quote is from p. 10 of the latter. For historiographical overviews from the previous two decades, see Alfred B. Rollins, Jr., "Was There Really a Man Named Roosevelt?" in *American History: Retrospect and Prospect*, George A. Billias and Gerald N. Grob, eds. (New York, 1971), pp. 232–270; and the bibliographic essay in Alonzo L. Hamby, ed., *The New Deal: Analysis and Interpretation*, 2/e (New York, 1981).

[2]Quoted in William E. Leuchtenburg, *Franklin D. Roosevelt and the New Deal, 1932–1940* (New York, 1963), p. 178.

[3]See Rexford G. Tugwell, "The New Deal in Retrospect," *Western Political Quarterly* 1 (December 1948): 373–385, and his full-length study of Roosevelt, *The Democratic Roosevelt* (New York, 1957).

[4]See Harvey Klehr, *The Heyday of American Communism: The Depression Decade* (New York, 1984); and Richard Pells, *Radical Visions, American Dreams: Culture and Social Thought in the Depression Years* (New York, 1974).

which the New Deal reshaped American society and politics. Was the New Deal simply an extension of the Progressive tradition of piece-meal reform or did it involve a radical departure from the mainstream of American political history? Did it usher in the era of big govern-ment and the "imperial presidency" or create an effective and efficient state to handle the needs of a twentieth-century society? Or did it suc-cumb to the traditional centrifugal and localistic forces of American politics? Did it save capitalism or pave the way for an American ver-sion of socialism? Did it co-opt struggles of workers and other have-nots for democracy and social equality, or did it confirm the partial triumph of those movements?

For historians reared in the tradition of the Progressive school there was little doubt about the basic nature of the New Deal.[5] View-ing America's past in terms of a conflict between liberalism and con-servatism, the people versus the interests, they saw the New Deal as a significant advance in the struggle against monopoly and privilege. To them the New Deal was related to earlier reform movements, includ-ing Jeffersonian and Jacksonian Democracy, Populism, and Progres-sivism, all of which had represented the continuing popular struggle to achieve a greater measure of political, economic, and social equality. Thus, Louis Hacker referred to the New Deal as the "Third American Revolution" in the mid-1940s. Even though his description of actual New Deal programs made them sound quite unrevolutionary and uno-riginal, Hacker insisted on the New Deal's significance in countering the individualist and laissez-faire traditions of American politics and society. Always at the center of the New Deal, he wrote, "there existed the thought that the responsibility of public authority for the welfare of the people was clear and that the intervention of the state was justi-fiable."[6] To Henry Steele Commager, the distinguished historian of the American liberal tradition, the relationship between the New Deal and earlier reform movements was obvious. What was simply a new deal of old cards appeared radical for two reasons: the rapidity with which the New Deal programs were enacted into law, and the fact that the movement contrasted so sharply with the do-nothing attitude of the Harding, Coolidge, and Hoover administrations. If the New Deal were compared with the Progressive era rather than the 1920s, Com-mager maintained, "the contrast would have been less striking than the similarities. . . . [P]recedent for the major part of New Deal legisla-tion was to be found in these earlier periods."[7]

---

[5]On Progressive historians, see Chapter 1 in this volume.

[6]Louis M. Hacker, *The Shaping of the American Tradition* (New York, 1947), pp. 1125–1126.

[7]Henry Steele Commager, "Twelve Years of Roosevelt," *American Mercury* 40 (April 1945): 391–401.

Perhaps the fullest and most eloquent argument that the New Deal was a continuation and extension of America's liberal past was advanced by Arthur M. Schlesinger, Jr., who wrote squarely within the Progressive tradition. A former professor at Harvard University, Schlesinger was also a public intellectual, a prominent liberal anticommunist in the Mc-Carthy era, later an advisor to President John Kennedy, and a shrewd commentator on current affairs. Schlesinger actively championed a modified brand of American liberalism whose roots, he believed, went far back into the nation's history. Thus his Pulitzer Prize–winning study, *The Age of Jackson* (1945), argued that Jacksonian Democracy was a liberal political movement based on a coalition of urban workers and other democratic groups which, taken together, looked very much like the New Deal coalition of the 1930s. All of American history, according to Schlesinger, was characterized by a cyclical movement which saw periods of liberal reform followed by alternate periods of conservative consolidation. Thus, Jacksonian Democracy followed the complacent "era of good feelings," the Progressive era followed the age of the robber barons, the New Deal came after the sterile conservatism of the 1920s, and the New Frontier and Great Society of the 1960s were reactions to the inaction of the Eisenhower years. The generative force behind this cycle was social conflict, which arose from a constant accumulation of discontent within American society.

Schlesinger spelled out his thesis most fully in *The Age of Roosevelt*, a three-volume study of the New Deal published between 1957 and 1960. There he argued that by the 1920s the nation had tired of the Progressive crusade of the prewar years. National disinterest in politics meant that power gravitated toward businessmen and other conservative interests. Inevitably, just as Progressivism had given way to 1920s conservatism, the forces of reform were regathering their energies. Even without a depression, Schlesinger suggested, the New Deal was bound to have happened in one form or another because workers, poor farmers, ethnic minorities, and others continued to press for political redress of their grievances, mostly on the local and state level. What the Depression did was to give the New Deal its particular force and character as an inclusive, national political movement urgently responding to the immediate problem of economic collapse. The New Deal, Schlesinger concluded, rejected the dogmatic absolutes posed in contemporary ideologies such as communism and fascism. Rather, the New Deal was a pragmatic movement based on the assumption that a "managed and modified capitalist order achieved by piecemeal experiment could combine personal freedom and economic growth."[8]

---

[8]Arthur M. Schlesinger, Jr., *The Crisis of the Old Order 1919–1933* (Boston, 1957); *The Coming of the New Deal* (Boston, 1958); and *The Politics of Upheaval* (Boston, 1960). Schlesinger revisited and refined this cyclical interpretation in *Cycles of American History* (Boston, 1986).

Frank Freidel, author of a multivolume biography of Roosevelt, belonged to the same Progressive historiographical tradition as Schlesinger but posed the discussion in slightly different terms. To him the New Deal was basically the work of people who had grown to political maturity during the Progressive era and the first World War and still shared the moral fervor of that era. Like Roosevelt they were fairly conservative men whose primary goal was to save rather than destroy the free enterprise system. What made them progressive was their willingness to use the machinery and authority of government to improve the lot of the common citizenry.[9] Commager, Schlesinger, and Freidel all identified themselves with the American liberal or Progressive tradition. Whatever their criticisms of the New Deal, they wrote approvingly of Roosevelt's pragmatism, his faith in democracy and the common man, and his obvious distaste for totalitarian methods. The alternative to the New Deal, they hinted, might very well have been a dictatorship of the Right or Left, had the nation continued to drift along as it had under Hoover. Though the New Dealers experimented with radical means, they always aimed to preserve a modified version of the existing order of things.

This relatively partisan and Roosevelt-centered approach to the history of the New Deal did not go unchallenged. A few conservative writers followed former president Hoover in accusing FDR of undermining individual freedom, imposing a bloated and expensive form of centralized government on the American people, and disrupting the "natural" self-correcting processes of the marketplace.[10] But the most important critique came from so-called consensus historians. One of these was Richard Hofstadter who, although writing within a liberal framework, was among the severest critics of America's liberal political tradition and Progressive historiographical tradition. For him, the New Deal began as a "new departure" from received political values, and this was its greatest promise. American liberalism, Hofstadter argued, had failed in the past because its moralizing tendencies made it incapable of dealing with class conflict and other fundamental social issues. Reformers had generally operated under the assumption that American society was a big version of the small towns they grew up in. The reformers' "village mind" could only conceive of social problems as aberrations from a healthy democratic norm; reform meant clearing the way for individual enterprise—smashing illegitimate privilege and monopoly and providing all Americans with an equal opportunity in

---

[9]Frank Freidel, *Franklin D. Roosevelt: The Apprenticeship* (Boston, 1952); *The Ordeal* (Boston, 1954); *The Triumph* (Boston, 1956); and *Launching the New Deal* (Boston, 1973); see also *The New Deal in Historical Perspective* 2/e (Washington, D.C., 1965).

[10]Herbert Hoover, *The Challenge to Liberty* (New York, 1934); Edgar Eugene Robinson, *The Roosevelt Leadership 1933–1945* (Philadelphia, 1955); John T. Flynn, *The Roosevelt Myth*, rev. ed. (New York, 1956).

life. Within this frame of thought the national government was considered to be inherently negative, an obstacle in the way of individual success. At best, someone like Herbert Hoover—a village mind with an engineering degree—could use government to harmonize the initiatives of free economic actors and thereby maximize the potential of the marketplace. Even the more exuberant Progressive reformers could only imagine solutions to social problems in terms of mild bureaucratic oversight of the marketplace, preferably on the local or state level, by middle-class folks like themselves.

In *The Age of Reform: From Bryan to F.D.R.*, Hofstadter insisted that the New Deal initially operated on entirely different premises. Instead of viewing America as healthy, New Deal reformers saw it as a sick society in need of therapy that could only be administered through federal action. Thus, the New Deal accepted ideas that would have been anathema to most old-fashioned Progressives: permanent federal responsibility for the relief of the unemployed, social security, the regulation of wages and hours, the construction of vast public works and public housing, and the acceptance of massive deficits to fund such programs. Many of the traditional aims of past reform movements—to restore government to the people and to destroy big business and monopolies—were simply bypassed or ignored by Roosevelt. "The New Deal, and the thinking it engendered," wrote Hofstadter, "represented the triumph of economic emergency and human needs over inherited notions and inhibitions. . . . At the core of the New Deal, then, was not a philosophy (F.D.R. could identify himself philosophically only as a Christian and democrat), but an attitude, suitable for practical politicians, administrators, and technicians, but uncongenial to the moralism that the Progressives had for the most part shared with their opponents."[11] Despite early indications, however, Hofstadter found that New Deal liberalism failed to live up to its promise. FDR and his followers shrank from comprehensive planning and remained content to respond pragmatically to economic and political exigencies; i.e., they failed to go much beyond mere Progressivism.

In the end, Hofstadter's most influential contribution to New Deal historiography may have been to detach interpretations of the era from partisan attitudes. He was deeply critical of both liberal reformers and their conservative critics. Regarding the latter, he found right-wing condemnations of the New Deal's piecemeal reforms to be "hollow and cliché-ridden," the sometimes hysterical complaints of a class increasingly cut off from reality. More important were Hofstadter's criti-

---

[11]Richard Hofstadter, *The Age of Reform: From Bryan to F.D.R.* (New York, 1955), pp. 314 and 323. In *Encore for Reform: The Old Progressives and the New Deal* (New York, 1967), Hofstadter's student, Otis L. Graham, reinforced the assertion that old Progressives and New Dealers were birds of quite different feather.

cisms of Roosevelt and his followers for their political opportunism and superficial approach to the serious problem of social inequality in America. This critique was echoed by the political scientist James MacGregor Burns. The stunning first volume of Burns' biography of FDR portrayed the president as an opportunist of "no fixed convictions," but also a leader of masterly instincts. Without his capacity for displaying supreme confidence in the midst of crisis and his willingness to experiment, the American political order might not have survived. Still, Burns wondered, given Roosevelt's failure to push the New Deal toward fundamental and systematic reform, "whether the American political system can meet the crises imposed on it by this exacting century."[12] To another political scientist, Heinz Eulau, the New Deal tendency toward pragmatic and piecemeal reform was a sign of strength, not weakness. Whatever blueprints for social reconstruction some New Dealers had in mind, they neither articulated a utopian faith nor called upon people to join a crusade to remake society. But if the New Deal was not an ideology, a faith, a crusade, a revolt, or a utopia, what was it? To Eulau the answer to this question was clear. The New Deal, he suggested, was "both a symbol and evidence of the nation's political maturity," an effort to solve problems "through politics rather than through ideology or violence." By Eulau's standard, the New Deal represented a mature politics of adjustment and compromise, rather than an imposition of preconceived general solutions to problems.[13] This was the triumph not of liberal zeal but of managerial technique.

During the 1960s the stature of Franklin D. Roosevelt and the New Deal began to alter as growing social conflict raised doubts about how effective and significant New Deal reforms were. Younger scholars, often called New Left historians, asked searching questions about deep and long-term tendencies of America's social and economic order and the possibilities and consequences of liberal reform. If the New Deal had modified and humanized American society, why did poverty and racism continue to exist? If the New Deal had truly reformed an unbridled capitalism and made it more responsive to people's needs, why were so many different groups—blacks, Puerto Ricans, Mexican Americans, blue-collar workers, and middle-class youths—alienated from their society? Even before New Left critics delivered their harsher judgments, scholars had begun to build on the work of Hofstadter in narrating a tale of FDR and the New Deal that was less personalized, less partisan, and less positive.

---

[12]James MacGregor Burns, *Roosevelt: The Lion and the Fox, 1882–1940* (New York, 1956), p. x.

[13]Heinz Eulau, "Neither Ideology Nor Utopia: The New Deal in Retrospect," *Antioch Review* 19 (Winter 1959–1960): 523–537.

The first sign of this newly critical attitude to New Deal liberalism appeared in William E. Leuchtenburg's *Franklin D. Roosevelt and the New Deal*. Although Leuchtenburg left no doubt about his positive valuation of both the president and his programs, he also made clear the limitations of both. Although the New Deal brought relief to millions who suffered under the Depression, it could not achieve prosperity in peacetime. Although it empowered industrial workers, small farmers, and others who could organize themselves into interest groups, it ignored less organized and less powerful Americans, especially African Americans, who could not "ante up" for the New Deal. Roosevelt failed to break the hold of southern conservatives on the Democratic Party and thus failed to build a broad-based social democracy that could fight Jim Crow or survive the inevitable backlash of business interests and defenders of traditional values and local prerogatives.

Still, Leuchtenburg insisted, "however conservative it was," the New Deal was "a radically new departure" for American society and politics.[14] No matter how limited, the New Deal and the man who made it retain immense stature in Leuchtenburg's account. As he argues in the essay reproduced here, the achievements of the New Deal were myriad and enduring. They include reconstructing the federal government as an instrument for managing social change and cushioning the weak against the worst consequences of such change; certifying the legitimacy of labor unions and other newly-organized interests; building new respect for the public sector; preparing a diverse people for vast collective endeavors without weakening their respect for cultural differences, civil liberties, and democratic processes. In these ways, Roosevelt and his minions performed as well, and almost certainly better, than any similar political cadre in American history. America was transformed under their guidance, and mostly for the better.

In a similar though somewhat more critical interpretation, Paul K. Conkin's 1967 reassessment of the New Deal expressed considerable admiration for Roosevelt's political astuteness and charismatic qualities, but found Roosevelt's thought too shallow and unfocused even to be called pragmatic. In this the nation's leader merely reflected its people. "For the historian," noted Conkin in his thoughtful summation, "every judgment, every evaluation of the past has to be tinged with a pinch of compassion, a sense of the beauty and nobility present when honest hopes and humane ideals are frustrated. He sees that the thirties could have brought so much more, but also so much worse, than the New Deal. The limiting context has to be understood—the safeguards and impediments of our political system, Roosevelt's intellectual limitations, and most of all the appalling economic ignorance and

---

[14]William E. Leuchtenburg, *Franklin D. Roosevelt and the New Deal* (New York, 1963), p. 336.

philosophic immaturity of the American electorate. . . . The New Deal solved a few problems, ameliorated a few more, obscured many, and created new ones. This is about all our political system can generate, even in crisis."[15]

Even relatively conservative historians showed a similar dispassion in their work. In a major study of New Deal economic policy, for example, Ellis W. Hawley echoed Conkin's belief that the New Deal reflected the ambivalences and contradictions within the American people themselves. Those Americans, Hawley noted, shared a commitment to two value systems that were not wholly compatible. On the one hand they cherished liberty, which implied a competitive economic and social order and broad freedom of personal choice. On the other hand they valued progress, which implied order, rationality, and the imposing economic organizations needed to guarantee abundance and a rising standard of living. The latter value posed a potential threat to the former: monopoly negated competition; order threatened, at least in theory, liberty. Much of twentieth-century American history, Hawley observed, revolved around the search for a solution "that would preserve the industrial order, necessarily based upon a high degree of collective organization, and yet would preserve America's democratic heritage at the same time." New Deal economic policy mirrored this basic ambivalence, vacillating between rational planning and antimonopoly measures. Hawley's conclusion offered little support for any of the competing ideologies that underlay many previous historical interpretations of Roosevelt and the New Deal. "If the experiences of the nineteen thirties have any relevance at all," he wrote, "it is in illustrating the limitations of logical analysis, the pitfalls inherent in broad theoretical approaches, the difficulty of agreeing on policy goals, and the necessity of making due allowances for the intellectual heritage, current trends of opinion, and the realities of pressure-group politics."[16]

A focus on the limiting context within which Roosevelt and the New Dealers operated also shaped the work of Albert U. Romasco, who argued that Roosevelt needed to cooperate with the business community in order to stimulate investment and recovery. If Roosevelt was hostile to the "economic royalists," he nevertheless was forced to confront them with a little stick and a big carrot.[17] Looking at a very different limit on New Deal activism, Nancy Weiss made per-

---

[15]Paul K. Conkin, *FDR and the Origins of the Welfare State* (New York, 1967), p. 106; also published in paperback under the title *The New Deal* (Arlington Heights, Ill., 1967).

[16]Ellis W. Hawley, *The New Deal and the Problem of Monopoly: A Study in Economic Ambivalence* (Princeton, 1966), p. 493.

[17]Albert U. Romasco, *The Politics of Recovery: Roosevelt's New Deal* (New York, 1983). See also Michael A. Bernstein, *The Great Depression: Delayed Recovery and Economic Change in America, 1929–1939* (New York, 1987).

fectly clear that Roosevelt largely ignored the plight of black Americans during the Great Depression. Roosevelt was reluctant to support anti-lynching legislation for fear of alienating southern Democrats whom he needed to pass crucial New Deal (and, later, war preparedness) legislation. Insofar as economic issues were concerned, blacks benefited only because they were not excluded from those broad New Deal programs designed to assist the poor and the unemployed as a whole. Consequently, blacks embraced the Democratic Party and abandoned the Republican, even though Roosevelt did not directly woo their support.[18]

The sharpest critique of Roosevelt and the New Deal came from the pens of those younger historians who more fully identified with the New Left. Many of these scholars were committed to radical changes in the structure of American society, some of them active in the labor organizing or the Civil Rights movement. They believed that a searching examination of the past could illuminate the present and discover a radical path for the future. We have "sought explicitly," wrote the editor of a book of essays representing New Left scholarship, "to make the past speak to the present, to ask questions that have a deep-rooted moral and political relevance. In moving occasionally beyond description and causal analysis to judge significance, we have, by necessity, moved beyond objective history in the realm of values."[19] In his essay in that volume, historian Barton J. Bernstein argued that the liberal reforms of the 1930s had not transformed or tamed corporate capitalism or significantly redistributed power in any way. Even its bolder programs had neither extended the beneficence of government beyond affluent groups nor used the wealth of the few for the needs of the many. The New Deal followed essentially conservative goals, for it was intended to maintain the American system intact. "The New Deal," Bernstein concluded, "failed to solve the problem of depression, it failed to raise the impoverished, it failed to redistribute income, it failed to extend equality and generally countenanced racial discrimination and segregation. It failed generally to make business more responsible to the social welfare or to threaten business's pre-eminent political power. . . . In acting to protect the institution of private property and in advancing the interests of corporate capitalism, the New Deal assisted the middle and upper sectors of society. It protected them, sometimes, even at the cost of injuring the lower sectors."[20]

---

[18]Nancy J. Weiss, *Farewell to the Party of Lincoln: Black Politics in the Age of FDR* (Princeton, 1983).

[19]Barton J. Bernstein, ed., *Towards a New Past: Dissenting Essays in American History* (New York, 1968), p. xiii.

[20]Barton J. Bernstein, "The New Deal: The Conservative Achievements of Liberal Reform," in ibid., pp. 264 and 281–282.

Among labor and economic historians, in particular, the radical critique of the New Deal reached a high pitch. Thomas Ferguson defined the New Deal essentially as the political project of advanced sectors of American industrial and finance capitalism, with support from associated labor interests. Their aim was to generate expansion in the capital-intensive, high-consumption, "multinational" sector of the economy, in place of the failed labor-intensive and nationally oriented regime of steel, rail, textiles and other older industries. For Ferguson, the needs of the "multinational bloc," not the demands of grassroots protest or the pressures of electoral politics, explain the political evolution of the New Deal.[21] Similarly, Christopher L. Tomlins narrated the history of New Deal labor legislation as a triumph of bureaucratic management over grassroots labor insurgency. New Deal labor policy represented the commitment of giant corporations and the state to "stability," not justice.[22]

In a more nuanced way, labor historians Steve Fraser and Nelson Lichtenstein traced the decline of shop-floor radicals in major C.I.O. unions to the rise of bureaucratic labor managers closely tied to corporate and government elites and to the Democratic Party.[23] Although this transformation, presided over by the brilliant labor leaders Sidney Hillman and Walter Reuther, consolidated and expanded many of the gains made by industrial workers in the 1930s and 1940s, it also decisively disarmed them as a force for radical change in the future. It certainly confirmed the line between managerial elites who make policy, and workers who bargain for better wages and working conditions but not for power to determine the larger contours of their economic world. In related but quite distinctive ways, labor historians David Brody and David Montgomery also described the "New Deal Order" as a triumph as much for corporate, labor, and political elites as for the men and women who staged sit-ins at General Motors and fought the company goons in the coal towns of West Virginia.[24] And finally, historians of race have found the least to admire in the New Deal. Robin D. G. Kelley has recently shown that in rural Alabama the friends of

---

[21]In Steve Fraser and Gary Gerstle, eds., *The Rise and Fall of the New Deal Order, 1930–1980* (Princeton, 1989), pp. 3–31.

[22]Christopher L. Tomlins, *The State and the Unions: Labor Relations, Law, and the Organized Labor Movement in America, 1880–1960* (Cambridge, 1985).

[23]Steve Fraser, *Labor Will Rule: Sidney Hillman and the Rise of American Labor* (New York, 1991); Nelson Lichtenstein, *The Most Dangerous Man in Detroit: Walter Reuther and the Fate of American Labor* (New York, 1995), and also his *Labor's War at Home: The CIO and World War II* (Cambridge, 1982).

[24]David Brody, *Workers in Industrial America: Essays on the 20th Century Struggle* (New York 1980; 2/e 1993); David Montgomery, "American Workers and the New Deal Formula," in *Workers' Control in America: Studies in the History of Work, Technology, and Labor Struggles* (Cambridge, 1979).

poor blacks were more likely found in the Communist than the Democratic party; indeed Alabama's Democratic party was the agent of
white supremacy and the implacable enemy of justice for African
Americans.[25]

One of the pitfalls of some New Left interpretations lay in their
tendency to see the New Deal (and, indeed, the entire realm of politics
and the state) as a kind of shadow-act behind which the hegemonic
force of corporate capitalism worked its will. Against this tendency a
powerful new body of scholarship on state formation, some of it with
an explicitly feminist bent, brought new insights to New Deal history.
The political scientist Theda Skocpol and her collaborators have argued forcefully that the state is a semi-autonomous actor in the great
dramas of modern history—in social policy, as much as in war and revolution. Political parties and administrative elites do indeed serve the
interests of the most powerful; but they must also demonstrate a capacity to promote stability for a wide range of interests in the society.
More importantly, they also respond to their interest in reproducing
and expanding their own power. They exercise, in particular, the significant power to define the very issues of political concern that all actors, even the biggest, must attend to. This perspective allows scholars
to acknowledge the political limits of New Deal liberalism in a way
that is highly critical—"frustration," "failure," and "loss," are words
that spring from the pages of their work—and yet realistic.[26]

The historian Linda Gordon has most effectively employed the insights of state formation theory in studying the rise of social welfare
policy in the twentieth century. Seeing a range of provisions for single
mothers, families, and children as genuine achievements, Gordon
notes that the very legitimacy of the welfare state depended on the efforts of the women's movement.[27] At least until the 1930s, recipients
of such benefits were still more "pitied" than regarded as "entitled."
Though the New Deal changed things for the better, Gordon argues
from a socialist-feminist viewpoint, the welfare state has proven incapable of fundamentally correcting gender and class inequality. The
erosion of welfare benefits in recent years and the exhaustion of liberal
ideas about how to address poverty prove the shallowness of New Deal
formulas. Still, Gordon believes that the New Deal years offer a partial
model for a feminist-labor coalition that can expand to include the in-

[25]Robin D. G. Kelley, *Hammer and Hoe: Alabama Communists During the Great
Depression* (Chapel Hill, N.C., 1990).

[26]Margaret Weir, Ann Shola Orloff, and Theda Skocpol, eds., *The Politics of Social
Policy in the United States* (Princeton, 1988); Kenneth Finegold and Theda Skocpol,
State and Party in America's New Deal (Madison, Wis., 1995).

[27]On this point see Kathryn Kish Sklar's essay in Chapter 6.

terests of racial minorities and other less-powerful Americans and thereby exercise new political leverage over the state.[28]

As the above suggests, recent historians (whether their political views tend toward Right or Left) have abandoned those battle lines from which some historians presented the New Deal as either a front for socialism or a front for corporate hegemony. In part, this reflects their turn from questions of electoral politics to ones about deeper social and economic forces and the long-term (and comparative) evolution of the state and the political system. Even historians influenced only marginally by new approaches increasingly broadly contextualize the New Deal and emphasize both its limits and achievements. John A. Garraty emphasized the importance of a comparative dimension in evaluating the New Deal. In an analysis of the early years of both Roosevelt's and Adolf Hitler's regimes, he suggested that the New Deal was by no means unique. To be sure, the New Deal functioned within and maintained a commitment to democratic and representative institutions. The Nazis, in great contrast, deliberately destroyed democratic institutions, and imprisoned or murdered millions. Yet the economic policies adopted in the United States and Germany were not fundamentally dissimilar. Both combined direct relief for the indigent with public-works programs to create jobs; both created semi-military programs for the young; both were receptive to corporatist solutions that sought to enlist capitalists and workers in an effort to eliminate competition and restore social order; both adopted similar agricultural policies; and both rested in part upon the charismatic personalities of their leaders.[29] Garraty's formulation did not go unchallenged, but it possessed the great virtue of reminding American historians that the tasks before the New Dealers were not unique. Their ends reflected broad economic forces affecting a large part of the world and their means were shaped by fairly similar experiences of industrialization, state-making, social dislocation, and the rise of mass culture.

Other historians have taken the insights of the New Left historians of the 1960s and reworked them in productive and sometimes startling new ways. Thus, Ronald Edsforth showed how the transformation of shop-floor radicalism among the autoworkers of Flint, Michigan into the managed labor peace of the 1950s was not simply a product of defeat or co-optation by the forces of capital, but a reflection of the social

[28]See Linda Gordon, ed., *Women, the State, and Welfare* (Madison, Wis., 1990), and her *Pitied but Not Entitled: Single Mothers and the History of Welfare, 1890–1935* (New York, 1994).

[29]John A. Garraty, "The New Deal, National Socialism, and the Great Depression," *American Historical Review* 78 (October 1973): 907–944; see also Garraty's book, *The Great Depression* (New York, 1986).

and intellectual world of those workers. However militant they were, he argues, what labor activists wanted was restoration of the high-consumption promises of the 1920s, not the radical remaking of their world.[30] In a different way, Lizabeth Cohen traced the complex making of a new working class in Chicago in the twentieth century. From this long-term but sharply focused view, with its close attention to workplace, family, neighborhood, and cultural life, Cohen discerned a grand mobilization of poor and ethnically diverse people into a momentous political and social force. History would expose the limitations of that achievement, Cohen acknowledged: "The racial conflicts, the ideological divisions, and the centralization of authority that would come to characterize C.I.O. unions [and the New Deal state] . . . have led many postwar labor analysts to minimize the achievements of ordinary workers in the 1930s." But Cohen insists, "without romanticizing who they were or denying the imperfections in what they achieved," that those citizens changed the world they lived in for the better.[31]

Other post-1960s treatments of the era, while not fundamentally overturning received interpretations, have qualified and sharpened our understanding of how the Great Depression and New Deal affected ordinary lives. For example, in a study of Boston during the 1930s, Charles H. Trout observed that the "New Deal's manifestations were treated piecemeal and were perceived by individuals and groups according to their particular needs." Many federal programs involving social and economic change were resisted by Bostonians because of the weight of local and ethnic tradition and the power of a political machine that could make or break New Deal initiatives. The concept "of a national or even a municipal commonality of interest was seldom grasped."[32] From a local perspective, therefore, the accomplishments of the New Deal often seemed limited and remote.

Alan Brinkley's study of the careers of Huey Long and Father Charles Coughlin similarly revises historians' understanding of the limiting context within which FDR and the New Deal operated. Insisting that radicals such as Long and Coughlin were neither proto-fascists nor madmen, Brinkley described them as representatives of an "alternative political vision" which he dubbed "localism." With links to the long tradition of American republicanism, and equipped with a moral critique of the ruthless marketplace and the overbearing state, these radicals and their followers were trying to restore to ordinary

---

[30]Ronald Edsforth, *Class Conflict and Cultural Consensus: The Making of A Mass Consumer Society in Flint, Michigan* (New Brunswick, N.J., 1987).

[31]Lizabeth Cohen, *Making a New Deal: Industrial Workers in Chicago, 1919–1939* (Cambridge, 1990), p. 368.

[32]Charles H. Trout, *Boston, The Great Depression, and the New Deal* (New York, 1977), pp. 321–322.

people a measure of control over their own lives. At the very least, they were symptoms of a very widespread "ambivalence . . . about the costs of modernization."[33] Looking at working-class politics, Gary Gerstle discerned greater continuity between the 1920s and the 1950s than historians had previously understood. FDR's regime cemented the working-class descendants of immigrants and rural migrants to the New Deal state, but only by generating a new patriotism that had conservative as well as liberal potential. Besides opposition from localistic conservatives and big business, therefore, another limit to the radicalism of the New Deal came from within its most basic constituency, the industrial working class. Thus working-class anticommunism in the 1950s and electoral support for George Wallace in the 1960s and Ronald Reagan in the 1980s seem less anomalous.[34]

Alan Brinkley's new overview of the era, *The End of Reform*, displays a sense of the social, political, and ideological limits of the New Deal that is the legacy of the last several decades of scholarship. In this story, political experimentation comes up against structural limitations; liberal, even radical possibilities are partly thwarted by localistic conservatism, especially in the one-party South; proponents of egalitarian policies sometimes impressively overcome but never eliminate countervailing forces.[35] Similarly, in an attempt to construct a grand synthesis of twentieth-century reform from the standpoint of the New Left, historian Alan Dawley assesses the New Deal in a way far more balanced than those of radical historians a few decades earlier. Dawley's New Deal is a conservative effort to save capitalism from itself, but his story is not about elites co-opting populist masses. Rather, his New Deal derived energy from and helped advance the grassroots struggles for justice launched by workers and other less powerful people. In the process it "altered the organic relation between the state and society," took a "quantum leap into the business of regulating the market," and "enshrined a new set of ruling values keyed to security, so that the mass of the population . . . felt as if the government cared about their welfare."[36] Nuanced and qualified in its judgments, Dawley's assessment, reproduced in this chapter, represents a maturing of historical treatment of the New Deal. If Leuchtenburg moderated the "heroic liberal" interpretation of FDR and the New Deal, then Dawley moderated the "debunking radical" interpre-

---

[33]Alan Brinkley, *Voices of Protest: Huey Long, Father Coughlin, and the Great Depression* (New York, 1982), p. 7.

[34]Gary Gerstle, *Working-Class Americanism* (New York, 1989).

[35]Alan Brinkley, *The End of Reform: New Deal Liberalism in Recession and War* (New York, 1995).

[36]Alan Dawley, *Struggles for Justice: Social Responsibility and the Liberal State* (Cambridge, 1991).

tation. Each, like Brinkley, sees achievements and failures, though in different places and different degrees.[37]

Assessments of the achievements of the New Deal and its place in American history will largely be shaped by a series of prior assumptions about the nature of the American past and the nation's ideals in both the present and future. To scholars of a *laissez-faire* inclination, the New Deal will always appear as a movement hostile to traditional values of individualism and competition. By contrast, to those scholars (whether on the political left or right) who value communal or collective obligations above individual rights, the New Deal may appear to be a signal moment in the maturing of American politics. Historians of a liberal inclination will probably see the New Deal as a major advance in American efforts to improve social equality. But to those who maintain that only a radical restructuring of American society can establish genuine equality, the New Deal appears as a palliative designed to gloss over fundamental defects in the social and economic order. Finally, from a comparative vantage point, the New Deal suggests that the American experience is not as exceptional as many believe.

Finally, the problem of judging the nature and accomplishments of the New Deal requires the scholar to develop a view of the entire fabric of the American past. Was the New Deal a continuation of America's liberal tradition or was it a repudiation of that tradition in the face of the relentless forces of modernization? Did the New Deal reflect an attempt by corporate capitalism to maintain its power intact by forging a partnership with the federal government, with the latter in a subordinate position? Or did the New Deal represent a significant shift in power to classes and groups that in the past had been powerless? Did the New Deal possess any ideological coherence or was it simply a collection of improvised and pragmatic responses to crises? Rather than political or ideological failings, might the New Dealers' inconsistencies have been reflections of the ambivalent commitments of Americans to order and progress on the one hand, and localism and liberty on the other? These are only some of the broad questions that must be answered in order to assess the nature and significance of the New Deal. And the works cited here are only a small selection of the immense and continually growing literature on not only the Great Depression and the New Deal, but on the society and culture that was their context.

---

[37]Another fine general study is by an Englishman, Anthony J. Badger, *The New Deal: The Depression Years, 1933–1940* (New York, 1989).

WILLIAM E. LEUCHTENBURG (1922–   ) is professor of history emeritus at the University of North Carolina, at Chapel Hill. His books include Franklin D. Roosevelt and the New Deal, 1932–1940 *(1963),* In the Shadow of FDR: From Harry Truman to Ronald Reagan *(1989), and* The FDR Years: On Roosevelt and His Legacy *(1995).*

The fiftieth anniversary of the New Deal, launched on March 4, 1933, comes at a time when it has been going altogether out of fashion. Writers on the left, convinced that the Roosevelt experiment was either worthless or pernicious, have assigned it to the dustbin of history. Commentators on the right, though far less conspicuous, see in the New Deal the origins of the centralized state they seek to dismantle. Indeed, the half-century of the age of Roosevelt is being commemorated in the presidency of Ronald Reagan, who, while never tiring of quoting FDR, insists that the New Deal derived from Italian fascism.

To be sure, the New Deal has always had its critics. In Roosevelt's own day Marxists said that the New Deal had not done anything for agriculture that an earthquake could not have done better at the same time that conservatives were saying that FDR was unprincipled. Hoover even called him "a chameleon on plaid." Most historians have long since accepted the fact that New Deal policies were sometimes inconsistent, that Roosevelt failed to grasp countercyclical fiscal theory, that recovery did not come until armaments orders fueled the economy, that the President was credited with certain reforms like insurance of bank deposits that he, in fact, opposed, that a number of New Deal programs, notably aid for the marginal farmer, were inadequately financed, and that some New Deal agencies discriminated against blacks.

During the 1960s historians not only dressed up these objections as though they were new revelations but carried their disappointment with contemporary liberalism to the point of arguing either that the New Deal was not just inadequate but actually malign or that the New Deal was so negligible as to constitute a meaningless episode. . . . An "antirevolutionary response to a situation that had revolutionary potentialities," the New Deal, it was said, missed opportunities to nationalize the banks and restructure the social order. Even "providing assistance to the needy and . . . rescuing them from starvation" served conservative ends, historians complained, for these efforts "sapped or-

ganized radicalism of its waning strength and of its potential constituency among the unorganized and discontented." The Roosevelt
Administration, it has been asserted, failed to achieve more than it did
not as a result of the strength of conservative opposition but because of
the intellectual deficiencies of the New Dealers and because Roosevelt
deliberately sought to save "large-scale corporate capitalism." . . .

This emphasis has so permeated writing on the New Deal in the
past generation that an instructor who wishes to assign the latest
thought on the age of Roosevelt has a wide choice of articles and anthologies that document the errors of the New Deal but no assessment
of recent vintage that explores its accomplishments.

The fiftieth anniversary of the New Deal provides the occasion for
a modest proposal—that we reintroduce some tension into the argument over the interpretation of the Roosevelt years. If historians are to
develop a credible synthesis, it is important to regain a sense of the
achievement of the New Deal. As it now stands, we have a dialectic
that is all antithesis with no thesis. . . .

As a first step toward a more considered evaluation, one has to remind one's self not only of what the New Deal did not do, but of what
it achieved.

Above all, one needs to recognize how markedly the New Deal altered the character of the State in America. Indeed, though for decades
past European theorists had been talking about *der Staat,* there can
hardly be said to have been a State in America in the full meaning of
the term before the New Deal. If you had walked into an American
town in 1932, you would have had a hard time detecting any sign of a
federal presence, save perhaps for the post office and even many of today's post offices date from the 1930s. Washington rarely affected people's lives directly. There was no national old-age pension system, no
federal unemployment compensation, no aid to dependent children,
no federal housing, no regulation of the stock market, no withholding
tax, no federal school lunch, no farm subsidy, no national minimum
wage law, no welfare state. . . . From 1933 to 1938, the government intervened in a myriad of ways from energizing the economy to fostering
unionization. . . .

This vast expansion of government led inevitably to the concentration of much greater power in the presidency, whose authority was
greatly augmented under FDR. Rexford Tugwell has written of Roosevelt: "No monarch, . . . unless it may have been Elizabeth or her
magnificent Tudor father, or maybe Alexander or Augustus Caesar,
can have given quite that sense of serene presiding, of gathering up
into himself, of really representing, a whole people." The President became, in Sidney Hyman's words, "the chief economic engineer," to
whom Congress naturally turned for the setting of economic policy.
Roosevelt stimulated interest in public affairs by his fireside chats and

freewheeling press conferences, shifted the balance between the White House and Capitol Hill by assuming the role of Chief Legislator, and eluded the routinized traditional departments by creating emergency agencies. In 1939 he established the Executive Office of the President, giving the Chief Executive a central staff office for the first time. "The verdict of history," wrote Clinton Rossiter, "will surely be that he left the Presidency a more splendid instrument of democracy than he found it."

To staff the national agencies, Roosevelt turned to a new class of people: the university-trained experts. . . . During the First Hundred Days, large numbers of professors, encouraged by FDR's reliance on the Brain Trust, flocked to Washington to draft New Deal legislation and to administer New Deal agencies. The radical literary critic Edmund Wilson wrote, "Everywhere in the streets and offices you run into old acquaintances: the editors and writers of the liberal press, the 'progressive' young instructors from the colleges, the intelligent foundation workers, the practical idealists of settlement houses." He added: "The bright boys of the Eastern universities, instead of being obliged to choose, as they were twenty years ago, between business, the bond-selling game and the field or foreign missions, can come on and get jobs in Washington." . . .

Some may doubt today whether it is always an unmitigated good to have "the best and the brightest" in seats of power, but in the 1930s this infusion of talent gave an élan to the national government that had been sorely missing in the past. The *New Republic* commented: "We have in Washington not a soggy and insensitive mass of dough, as in some previous administrations, but a nervous, alert and hard-working group who are doing their level best to effectuate a program." . . .

This corps of administrators made it possible for Roosevelt to carry out a major change in the role of the federal government. Although the New Deal always operated within a capitalist matrix and the government sought to enhance profitmaking, Roosevelt and his lieutenants rejected the traditional view that government was the handmaiden of business or that government and business were co-equal sovereigns. As a consequence, they adopted measures to discipline corporations, to require a sharing of authority with government and unions, and to hold businessmen accountable. In the early days of the National Recovery Administration, the novelist Sherwood Anderson wrote:

> I went to several code hearings. No one has quite got their significance. Here for the first time you see these men of business, little ones and big ones, . . . coming up on the platform to give an accounting. It does seem the death knell of the old idea that a man owning a factory, office or store has a right to run it in his own way.

There is at least an effort to relate it now to the whole thing, man's relations with his fellow men etc. Of course it is crude and there will be no end to crookedness, objections, etc. but I do think an entire new principle in American life is being established.

Through a series of edicts and statutes, the administration invaded the realm of the banker by establishing control over the nation's money supply. The government clamped an embargo on gold, took the United States off the gold standard, and nullified the requirement for the payment of gold in private contracts. In 1935 a resentful Supreme Court sustained this authority, although a dissenting justice said that this was Nero at his worst. The Glass-Steagall Banking Act (1933) stripped commercial banks of the privilege of engaging in investment banking, and established federal insurance of bank deposits, an innovation which the leading monetary historians have called "the structural change most conducive to monetary stability since bank notes were taxed out of existence immediately after the Civil War." The Banking Act of 1935 gave the United States what other industrial nations had long had, but America lacked—central banking. . . .

A number of other enactments helped transfer authority from Wall Street to Washington. The Securities Act of 1933 established government supervision of the issue of securities, and made company directors civilly and criminally liable for misinformation on the statements they were required to file with each new issue. The Securities and Exchange Act of 1934 initiated federal supervision of the stock exchanges, which to this day operate under the lens of the Securities and Exchange Commission (SEC). The Holding Company Act of 1935 levelled some of the utility pyramids, dissolving all utility holding companies that were more than twice removed from their operating companies, and increased the regulatory powers of the SEC over public utilities. . . . To be sure, financiers continued to make important policy choices, but they never again operated in the uninhibited universe of the Great Bull Market. . . .

The age of Roosevelt focused attention on Washington, too, by initiatives in fields that had been regarded as exclusively within the private orbit, notably in housing. The Home Owners' Loan Corporation, created in 1933, saved tens of thousands of homes from foreclosure by refinancing mortgages. In 1934 the Federal Housing Administration (FHA) began its program of insuring loans for the construction and renovation of private homes, and over the next generation more than 10 million FHA-financed units were built. Before the New Deal, the national government had never engaged in public housing, except for the World War I emergency, but agencies like the Public Works Administration now broke precedent. The Tennessee Valley Authority laid out the model town of Norris, the Federal Emergency Relief Administration (FERA) experimented with subsistence homesteads, and the Resettlement Administration created greenbelt communities, entirely new towns girdled by green countryside. When in 1937 the Wagner-Steagall Act created the U.S. Housing Authority, it assured public housing a permanent place in American life.

The New Deal profoundly altered industrial relations by throwing the weight of government behind efforts to unionize workers. At the outset of the Great Depression, the American labor movement was "an anachronism in the world," for only a tiny minority of factory workers were unionized. Employers hired and fired and imposed punishments at will, used thugs as strikebreakers and private police, stockpiled industrial munitions, and ran company towns as feudal fiefs. In an astonishingly short period in the Roosevelt years a very different pattern emerged. Under the umbrella of Section 7(a) of the National Industrial Recovery Act of 1933 and of the far-reaching Wagner Act of 1935, union organizers gained millions of recruits in such open-shop strongholds as steel, automobiles, and textiles. Employees won wage rises, reductions in hours, greater job security, freedom from the tyranny of company guards, and protection against arbitrary punishment. Thanks to the National Recovery Administration and the Guffey acts, coal miners achieved the outlawing of compulsory company houses and stores. Steel workers, who in 1920 labored twelve-hour shifts seven days a week at the blast furnaces, were to become so powerful that in the postwar era they would win not merely paid vacations but sabbatical leaves. . . .

Years later, when David E. Lilienthal, the director of the Tennessee Valley Authority, was being driven to the airport to fly to Roosevelt's funeral, the TVA driver said to him:

> I won't forget what he did for me. . . . I spent the best years of my life working at the Appalachian Mills . . . and they didn't even treat us like humans. If you didn't do like they said, they always told you there was someone else to take your job. I had my mother and my sister to take care of. Sixteen cents an hour was what we got; a fellow can't live on that. . . . If you asked to get off on a Sunday, the foreman would say, "All right you stay away Sunday, but when you come back Monday someone else will have your job." No, sir, I won't forget what he done for us.

. . . The NRA wiped out sweatshops, and removed some 150,000 child laborers from factories. The Walsh-Healey Act of 1936 and the Fair Labor Standards Act of 1938 established the principle of a federally imposed minimal level of working conditions, and added further sanctions against child labor. If the New Deal did not do enough for the "one-third of a nation" to whom Roosevelt called attention, it at least made a beginning, through agencies like the Farm Security Administration, toward helping sharecroppers, tenant farmers, and migrants like John Steinbeck's Joads. Most important, it originated a new system of social rights to replace the dependence on private charity. The Social Security Act of 1935 created America's first national system of old-age pensions and initiated a federal-state program of unemployment insurance. It also authorized grants for the blind, for the incapacitated, and for dependent children, a feature that would have unimaginable long-range consequences. . . .

Roosevelt himself affirmed the newly assumed attitudes in Washington in his annual message to Congress in 1938 when he declared: "Government has a final responsibility for the well-being of its citizenship. If private co-operative endeavor fails to provide work for willing hands and relief for the unfortunate, those suffering hardship from no fault of their own have a right to call upon the Government for aid; and a government worthy of its name must make fitting response."

Nothing revealed this approach so well as the New Deal's attention to the plight of the millions of unemployed. During the ten years between 1929 and 1939, one scholar has written, "more progress was made in public welfare and relief than in the three hundred years after this country was first settled." A series of alphabet agencies—the FERA, the CWA, the WPA—provided government work for the jobless, while the National Youth Administration (NYA) employed college students in museums, libraries, and laboratories, enabled high school students to remain in school, and set up a program of apprentice training. In Texas, the twenty-seven-year-old NYA director Lyndon Johnson put penniless young men like John Connally to work building roadside parks, and in North Carolina, the NYA employed, at 35 cents an hour, a Duke University law student, Richard Nixon.

In an address in Los Angeles in 1936, the head of FDR's relief operations, Harry Hopkins, conveyed the attitude of the New Deal toward those who were down and out:

> I am getting sick and tired of these people on the W.P.A. and local relief rolls being called chiselers and cheats. . . . These people . . . are just like the rest of us. They don't drink any more than us, they don't lie any more, they're no lazier than the rest of us—they're pretty much a cross section of the American people. . . . I have never believed that with our capitalistic system people have to be poor. I think it is an outrage that we should permit hundreds and hundreds of thousands of people to be ill clad, to live in miserable homes, not to have enough to eat; not to be able to send their children to school for the only reason that they are poor. I don't believe ever again in America we are going to permit the things to happen that have happened in the past to people.

Under the leadership of men like Hopkins, "Santa Claus incomparable and privy-builder without peer," projects of relief agencies and of the Public Works Administration (PWA) changed the face of the land.

The PWA built thoroughfares like the Skyline Drive in Virginia and the Overseas Highway from Miami to Key West, constructed the Medical Center in Jersey City, burrowed Chicago's new subway, and gave Natchez, Mississippi, a new bridge, and Denver a modern water-supply system. Few New Yorkers today realize the long reach of the New Deal. If they cross the Triborough Bridge, they are driving on a bridge the PWA built. If they fly into La Guardia Airport, they are landing at an airfield laid out by the WPA. If they get caught in a traffic jam on the FDR Drive, they are using yet another artery built by the WPA. . . . In New York City alone the WPA employed more people than the entire War Department. . . .

The New Deal showed unusual sensitivity toward jobless white-collar workers, notably those in aesthetic fields. The Public Works of Art Project gave an opportunity to muralists eager for a chance to work in the style of Rivera, Orozco, and Siqueiros. The Federal Art Project fostered the careers of painters like Stuart Davis, Raphael Soyer, Yasuo Kuniyoshi, and Jackson Pollock. Out of the same project came a network of community art centers and the notable *Index of American Design*. . . .

The Federal Writers' Project provided support for scores of talented novelists and poets, editors and literary critics, men like Ralph Ellison and Nelson Algren, John Cheever and Saul Bellow. These writers turned out an exceptional set of state guides, with such features as Conrad Aiken's carefully delineated portrayal of Deerfield, Massachusetts, and special volumes like *These Are Our Lives*, a graphic portfolio of life histories in North Carolina, and *Panorama*, in which Vincent McHugh depicts "the infinite pueblo of the Bronx." Project workers transcribed chain-gang blues songs, recovered folklore that would otherwise have been lost, and collected the narratives of elderly former slaves, an invaluable archive later published in *Lay My Burden Down*. When the magazine *Story* conducted a contest for the best contribution by a Project employee, the prize was won by an unpublished 29-year-old black who had been working on the essay on the Negro for the Illinois guide. With the prize money for his stories, subsequently published as *Uncle Tom's Children*, Richard Wright gained the time to complete his remarkable first novel, *Native Son*.

Some thought it an ill omen that the Federal Theatre Project's first production was Shakespeare's *Comedy of Errors*, but that agency not only gave employment to actors and stage technicians but offered many communities their first glimpse of live drama. . . . If the creation of America's first state theatre was an unusual departure, the New Deal's ventures in documentary films seemed no less surprising. With Resettlement Administration funds, Pare Lorentz produced *The Plow That Broke the Plains* in 1936 and the classic *The River* in 1937. He engaged cameramen like Paul Strand, who had won acclaim for his movie on a fisherman's strike in Mexico; invited the young composer

Virgil Thomson, who had just scored Gertrude Stein's *Four Saints in Three Acts*, to compose the background music; and employed Thomas Chalmers, who had sung at the Metropolitan Opera in the era of Caruso, to read the narration. Lorentz's films were eyeopeners. American government documentaries before the New Deal had been limited to short subjects on topics like the love life of the honeybee. *The River,* which won first prize in Venice at the International Exposition of Cinematographic Art in 1938, proved that there was an audience in the United States for well-wrought documentaries. By 1940 it had drawn more than 10 million people, while *The Plow That Broke the Plains,* said one critic, made "the rape of millions of acres . . . more moving than the downfall of a Hollywood blonde."

Lorentz's films suggest the concern of the New Deal for the American land. . . . The Tennessee Valley Authority, which drew admirers from all over the world, put the national government in the business of generating electric power, controlled floods, terraced hillsides, and gave new hope to the people of the valley. In the Pacific Northwest the PWA constructed mammoth dams, Grand Coulee and Bonneville. Roosevelt's "tree army," the Civilian Conservation Corps, planted millions of trees, cleared forest trails, laid out picnic sites and campgrounds, and aided the Forest Service in the vast undertaking of establishing a shelterbelt—a windbreak of trees and shrubs: green ash and Chinese elm, apricot and blackberry, buffalo berry and Osage orange from the Canadian border to the Texas panhandle. Government agencies came to the aid of drought-stricken farmers in the Dust Bowl, and the Soil Conservation Service, another New Deal creation, instructed growers in methods of cultivation to save the land. . . .

These services to farmers represented only a small part of the government's program, for in the New Deal years, the business of agriculture was revolutionized. Roosevelt came to power at a time of mounting desperation for American farmers. Each month in 1932 another 20,000 farmers had lost their land because of inability to meet their debts in a period of collapsing prices. On a single day in May 1932, one-fourth of the state of Mississippi went under the sheriff's hammer. The Farm Credit Administration of 1933 came to the aid of the beleaguered farmer, and within eighteen months, it had refinanced one-fifth of all farm mortgages in the United States. In the Roosevelt years, too, the Rural Electrification Administration literally brought rural America out of darkness. At the beginning of the Roosevelt era, only one farm in nine had electricity; at the end, only one in nine did not have it. But more important than any of these developments was the progression of enactments starting with the first AAA (the Agricultural Adjustment Act) of 1933, which began the process of granting large-scale subsidies to growers. As William Faulkner later said, "Our economy is not agricultural any longer. Our economy is the federal government. We no longer farm in Mississippi cotton fields. We farm now in Washington corridors and Congressional committee rooms."

At the same time that its realm was being expanded under the New Deal, the national government changed the composition of its personnel and of its beneficiaries. Before 1933, the government had paid heed primarily to a single group—white Anglo-Saxon Protestant males. The Roosevelt Administration, however, recruited from a more ethnically diverse group, and the prominence of Catholics and Jews among the President's advisers is suggested by the scintillating team of the Second Hundred Days, Corcoran and Cohen. The Federal Writers' Project turned out books on Italians and Albanians, and the Federal Theatre staged productions in Yiddish and wrote a history of the Chinese stage in Los Angeles. In the 1930s women played a more prominent role in government than they ever had before, as the result of such appointments as that of Frances Perkins as the first female cabinet member, while the influence of Eleanor Roosevelt was pervasive. . . .

Although in some respects the New Deal's performance with regard to blacks added to the sorry record of racial discrimination in America, important gains were also registered in the 1930s. Blacks, who had often been excluded from relief in the past, now received a share of WPA jobs considerably greater than their proportion of the population. Blacks moved into federal housing projects; federal funds went to schools and hospitals in black neighborhoods; and New Deal agencies like the Farm Security Administration (FSA) enabled 50,000 Negro tenant farmers and sharecroppers to become proprietors. "Indeed," one historian has written, "there is a high correlation between the location of extensive FSA operations in the 1930s and the rapidity of political modernization in black communities in the South in the 1960s." Roosevelt appointed a number of blacks, including William Hastie, Mary McLeod Bethune, and Robert Weaver, to high posts in the government. . . . The reign of Jim Crow in Washington offices, which had begun under Roosevelt's Democratic predecessor, Woodrow Wilson, was terminated by Secretary of the Interior Harold Ickes who desegregated cafeterias in his department. Ickes also had a role in the most dramatic episode of the times, for when the Daughters of the American Revolution (DAR) denied the use of their concert hall to the black contralto Marian Anderson, he made it possible for her to sing before thousands from the steps of Lincoln Memorial; and Mrs. Roosevelt joined in the rebuke to the DAR. Anderson's concert on Easter Sunday 1939 was heard by thousands at the Memorial, and three networks carried her voice to millions more. Blacks delivered their own verdict on the New Deal at the polling places. Committed to the party of Lincoln as late as 1932, when they voted overwhelmingly for Hoover, they shifted in large numbers to the party of FDR during Roosevelt's first term. This was a change of allegiance that many whites were also making in those years.

The Great Depression and the New Deal brought about a significant political realignment of the sort that occurs only rarely in America. The Depression wrenched many lifelong Republican voters from their moorings. In 1928, one couple christened their newborn son "Herbert Hoover Jones." Four years later they petitioned the court, "desiring to relieve the young man from the chagrin and mortification which he is suffering and will suffer," and asked that his name be changed to Franklin D. Roosevelt Jones. In 1932 FDR became the first Democrat to enter the White House with as much as 50 percent of the popular vote in eighty years—since Franklin K. Pierce in 1852. Roosevelt took advantage of this opportunity to mold "the FDR coalition," an alliance centered in the low-income districts of the great cities and, as recently as the 1980 election, the contours of the New Deal coalition could still be discerned. Indeed, over the past half-century, the once overpowering Republicans have won control of Congress only twice, for a total of four years. . . .

Furthermore, the New Deal drastically altered the agenda of American politics. When Arthur Krock of the *New York Times* listed the main programmatic questions before the 1932 Democratic convention, he wrote: "What would be said about the repeal of prohibition that had split the Republicans? What would be said about tariffs?" By 1936, these concerns seemed altogether old fashioned, as campaigners discussed the Tennessee Valley Authority and industrial relations, slum clearance and aid to the jobless. That year, a Little Rock newspaper commented: "Such matters as tax and tariff laws have given way to universally human things, the living problems and opportunities of the average man and the average family."

The Roosevelt years changed the conception of the role of government not just in Washington but in the states, where a series of "Little New Deals"—under governors like Herbert Lehman in New York—added a thick sheaf of social legislation, and in the cities. In Boston, Charles Trout has observed, city council members in 1929 "devoted endless hours to street paving." After the coming of the New Deal, they were absorbed with NRA campaigns, public housing, and WPA allotments. "A year after the crash the council thought 5,000 dollars an excessive appropriation for the municipal employment bureau," but during the 1930s "the unemployed drained Boston's treasury of not less than 100,000,000 dollars in direct benefits, and the federal government spent even more."

In a cluster of pathbreaking decisions in 1937, the Supreme Court legitimized this vast exercise of authority by government at all levels. As late as 1936, the Supreme Court still denied the power of the United States government to regulate agriculture, even though crops were sold in a world market, or coal mining, a vital component of a national economy, and struck down a minimum wage law as beyond the authority of the state of New York. Roosevelt responded with a plan to "pack" the Court with as many as six additional Justices, and in short order the Court, in what has been called "the Constitutional Revolution of 1937," sounded retreat. Before 1937 the Supreme Court stood as a formidable barrier to social reform. Since 1937 not one piece of significant social legislation has been invalidated, and the Court has shifted its docket instead to civil rights and civil liberties.

What then did the New Deal do? It gave far greater amplitude to the national state, expanded the authority of the presidency, recruited university-trained administrators, won control of the money supply, established central banking, imposed regulation on Wall Street, rescued the debt-ridden farmer and homeowner, built model communities, financed the Federal Housing Administration, made federal housing a permanent feature, fostered unionization of the factories, reduced child labor, ended the tyranny of company towns, wiped out many sweatshops, mandated minimal working standards, enabled tenants to buy their own farms, built camps for migrants, introduced the welfare state with old-age pensions, unemployment insurance, and aid for dependent children, provided jobs for millions of unemployed, created a special program for the jobless young and for students, covered the American landscape with new edifices, subsidized painters and novelists, composers and ballet dancers, founded America's first state theater, created documentary films, gave birth to the impressive Tennessee Valley Authority, generated electrical power, sent the Civilian Conservation Corps boys into the forests, initiated the Soil Conservation Service, transformed the economy of agriculture, lighted up rural America, gave women greater recognition, made a start toward breaking the pattern of racial discrimination and segregation, put together a liberal party coalition, changed the agenda of American politics, and brought about a Constitutional Revolution.

But even this summary does not account for the full range of its activities. The New Deal offered the American Indian new opportunities for self-government and established the Indian Arts and Crafts Board, sponsored vaudeville troupes and circuses, taught counterpoint and *solfeggio,* was responsible for the founding of the Buffalo Philharmonic, the Oklahoma Symphony, and the Utah State Symphony, served hot lunches to school children and set up hundreds of nursery schools, sent bookmobiles into isolated communities, and where there were no roads, had books carried in by packhorses. And only a truly merciful and farsighted government would have taken such special pains to find jobs for unemployed historians.

The New Deal accomplished all of this at a critical time, when many were insisting that fascism was the wave of the future and denying that democracy could be effective. For those throughout the world who heard such jeremiads with foreboding, the American experience was enormously inspiriting. A decade after the end of the age of Roosevelt, Sir Isaiah Berlin wrote:

> When I say that some men occupy one's imagination for many years, this is literally true of Mr. Roosevelt and the young men of my own generation in England, and probably in many parts of Europe, and indeed the entire world. If one was young in the thirties, and lived in a democracy, then, whatever one's politics, if one had human feelings at all, the faintest spark of social idealism, or any love of life whatever, one must have felt very much as young men in Continental Europe probably felt after the defeat of Napoleon during the years of the Restoration: that all was dark and quiet, a great reaction was abroad, and little stirred, and nothing resisted.

In these "dark and leaden thirties," Professor Berlin continued, "the only light in the darkness that was left was the administration of Mr. Roosevelt and the New Deal in the United States. At a time of weakness and mounting despair in the democratic world Mr. Roosevelt radiated confidence and strength. . . . Even to-day, upon him alone, of all the statesmen of the thirties, no cloud rested neither on him nor on the New Deal, which to European eyes still looks a bright chapter in the history of mankind."

For the past generation, America has lived off the legacy of the New Deal. Successive administrations extended the provisions of statutes like the Social Security Act, adopted New Deal attitudes toward intervention in the economy to cope with recessions, and put New Deal ideas to modern purposes, as when the Civilian Conservation Corps served as the basis for both the Peace Corps and the VISTA program of the War on Poverty. Harry Truman performed under the shadow of FDR, Lyndon Johnson consciously patterned his administration on Roosevelt's, Jimmy Carter launched his first presidential campaign at Warm Springs, and Ronald Reagan has manifested an almost obsessive need to summon FDR to his side. Carl Degler has observed:

> Conventionally the end of the New Deal is dated with the enactment of the Wages and Hours Act of 1938. But in a fundamental sense the New Deal did not end then at all. Americans still live in the era of the New Deal, for its achievements are now the base mark below which no conservative government may go and from which all new reform now starts. . . . The reform efforts of the Democratic Truman, Kennedy, and Johnson administrations have been little more than fulfillments of the New Deal.

The British historian David K. Adams has pointed out that the philosophy of the New Frontier has "conscious overtones of the New Deal" and indeed that John Kennedy's "New Frontier" address of 1960 was "almost a paraphrase" of an FDR speech of 1935. Theodore White has commented that both John and Robert Kennedy shared sentences from a Roosevelt address that reporters called the "Dante sequence." When at a loss for words, each was wont to quote a favorite passage from Franklin Roosevelt: "Governments can err, Presidents do make mistakes, but the immortal Dante tells us that Divine Justice weighs the sins of the cold-blooded and the sins of the warm-hearted on a different scale. Better the occasional faults of a government living in the spirit of charity, than the consistent omissions of a government frozen in the ice of its own indifference."

By restoring to the debate over the significance of the New Deal acknowledgment of its achievements, we may hope to produce a more judicious estimate of where it succeeded and where it failed. For it unquestionably did fail in a number of respects. There were experiments of the 1930s which miscarried, opportunities that were fumbled, groups who were neglected, and power that was arrogantly used. Over the whole performance lies the dark cloud of the persistence of hard times. The shortcomings of the New Deal are formidable, and they must be recognized. But I am not persuaded that the New Deal experience was negligible. Indeed, it is hard to think of another period in the whole history of the republic that was so fruitful or of a crisis that was met with as much imagination.

ALAN DAWLEY

ALAN DAWLEY (1943–   ) is professor of history at Trenton State College. He is the author of Class and Community: The Industrial Revolution in Lynn *(1976), which won a Bancroft prize, and* Struggles for Justice: Social Responsibility and the Liberal State *(1991).*

The ink was hardly dry on Roosevelt's recovery program before the New Deal was overtaken by an unexpected development: social movements awakened from their long slumber. From the grimy coal regions of Pennsylvania to the sultry bayous of Louisiana, the sleeping giants of labor, social justice, and populism snapped the cords that had tied them down in the early stages of the depression. As the earth began to shake with the tramp of strikes and rallies, there was a revitalization of radicalism and a resurgence of faith in the common people: Why not? Everything else seemed to have failed. Carl Sandburg captured the new mood in the title of his epic poem, *The People, Yes* (1936).

Ironically, the rebirth of social movements at the grass roots was in part the consequence of elite activities in Washington. The corporate planners and Brain Trusters of the early New Deal had found it necessary to penetrate ever deeper into the daily lives of ordinary Americans. As reported in a summer 1933 issue of the *Literary Digest,* "This central government of ours has now become the almoner to 12,000,000 unemployed and distressed people. It has become the guardian of middle-class investors, of the mortgaged-farm owner, of the mortgaged-home owner, of the bank depositor, and of the railway employee. It has become the partner of industry and of agriculture. And it has even become the friend of the beer maker and the beer drinker."

The last thing New Dealers wanted was to have "distressed people" taking things into their own hands, but that is exactly what happened next. For the more the Roosevelt administration rationalized banking, industry, and agriculture, the more it raised expectations for government aid among workers, retirees, and the unemployed. Roosevelt had stumbled upon the law of unintended consequences, but anyone with a sense of the cunning of history could have seen it coming. Having cultivated the analogy between the depression "emergency" and the war "emergency," Roosevelt should not have been surprised when the people demanded delivery on the government promise of recovery, just as people had demanded that Wilson live up to his promise to "make the world safe for democracy."

Nothing better illustrated the unwritten law of unintended consequences than the way New Deal labor policy inadvertently mobilized workers. None of Roosevelt's inner circle could be accused of harboring a passion for organized labor, not even Secretary of Labor Frances Perkins, who was more of a progressive reformer than a trade unionist. The president betrayed his own indifference to the labor movement in remarking that he didn't care whether workers paid allegiance to a trade union, the Ahkoond of Swat, or the Royal Geographic Society. The fact that section 7a of the 1933 National Recovery Act piously declared that workers had the right to organize and bargain collectively "through representatives of their own choosing" did not mask any secret desire to rally workers to the union cause. It was simply a political bone thrown to the AFL in hopes of ending its support of a bill mandating a thirty-hour week, which the entire Roosevelt administration opposed.

It took a canny opportunist such as John L. Lewis to ignore all this. The flamboyant autocrat of the United Mine Workers launched a membership drive under the slogan "The President wants you to organize." As tens of thousands of mine workers signed union cards, the spirit soon spread to workers in mass production. Together with the garment workers and a few other industrial unions, Lewis prepared to commit the greatest sin known to the labor movement—dual unionism—by breaking away from the AFL in 1935 to form the Committee (later Congress) of Industrial Organizations. It may have been all a misunderstanding, but by seeming to remove government objections to labor unions, section 7a contributed to the most significant mobilization of wage earners since the war.

A dozen years of labor peace ended with a bang in 1934. From one end of the country to the other, industrial workers rediscovered a long-lost militancy. The textile industry was convulsed by the first nationwide general strike in its history, punctuated by company violence. In San Francisco a longshoremen's strike against the indignities of the "shape-up" (in which foremen hired favorites from men herded together like cattle) escalated into a citywide general strike when police killed strikers. Similarly, teamsters brought truck transport to a halt in the vital entrepôt of Minneapolis, and, again, company thugs killed strikers. Communists and Trotskyists, respectively, played vital leadership roles in these strikes. Returning from a sojourn in the Soviet Union, Walter Reuther, future president of the United Auto Workers, was amazed at what he saw: "the NRA and the series of strikes and struggles of labor that followed ushered in a new epoch in America."

Violence accompanied all the major strikes, and the reason was the same as always—business' hatred for unions. Although a handful of companies were prepared to recognize genuine unions, most fought as if there was no tomorrow. Turning section 7a to their own advantage, they set up company unions, or employee representation plans, which successfully forestalled independent trade unions in a host of places. At the same time, they brought in labor spies, hired thugs, private detectives, and "citizen" vigilantes, whose massive violations of civil liberties would soon be amply documented by a Senate investigating committee under Robert La Follette. A handful of so-called brass hats such as Tom Girdler of Republic Steel vowed never to accept collective bargaining. Girdler's intransigence led to the infamous Memorial Day Massacre of 1937, when ten members of a crowd of peaceful demonstrators were shot in the back by police. Although the number of strikes and the level of violence never reached that of the end of the First World War, industrial warfare was back.

The difference was that this time unionism often came out on the winning side. Whereas the 1919 Seattle general strike had been crushed, the strikers of San Francisco and Minneapolis could justly claim victory. Whereas mass production and heavy industry had emerged union free from the postwar battles, organizing drives were now under way that would soon bring strong unions to the auto, meat-packing, electrical and steel industries; in short, to the entire heart-land of modern capitalism. Whereas the craft unions of the AFL had lapsed into a lethargic "business unionism" during the 1920s, now the emerging industrial unions of the CIO rekindled a crusading spirit that brought in almost 3 million members and sparked an equivalent ex-pansion in the ranks of the revitalized AFL.

What explains this remarkable mobilization of "labor's new mil-lions"? Once the trigger effect of the New Deal has been duly ac-knowledged, the upsurge should be understood in the context of the evolution of modern capitalism. Class relations were being reshaped by the impersonal structures of mass society. In the realm of produc-tion, two decades of technical rationalization and bureaucratic man-agement had homogenized the labor process so that workers in widely different settings had the sense that they were all parts of a single whole. By the same token, in the realm of reproduction, the homoge-nizing impact of mass culture—from advertising and chain stores to major league baseball and public schools—had lifted people out of their parochialism and given them a common basis of communication across ethnic and religious boundaries. Everybody could root for the home team, and who didn't love Charlie Chaplin?

Taking these structural conditions as a given, real, flesh-and-blood human beings brought about the rebirth of labor. Because the working class spanned so many different cultures, the labor movement could not count on a common set of values, and in almost every struggle against the boss, there was a concurrent struggle for leadership within the movement. In the case of New England textile workers, secular radicals in the tradition of the French Revolution vied with devout Catholic French-Canadians; and in the case of the electrical workers, Communist fellow travelers competed with Catholic corporatists. The divisions had always been there. The difference was that now the com-mon struggle against the boss took precedence and drew these warring factions together. In one of the most bizarre cases, an alliance arose among New York transit workers between closet Communists and Irish nationalists in the secret Clan Na Gael.

That atheist lions could lie down with churchgoing lambs reflected the change in climate in working-class communities. After years of eclipse, visions of a just society were returning to the forefront. To judge from the many testaments they left behind, labor organizers were motivated as much by a desire to change society as by a desire for power. Certainly, that was the case for Jewish garment workers, who combined socialist ideals, *Yiddishkeit* (the transplanted culture of east-ern European Jews), and a sophisticated pursuit of political power that eventually installed Sidney Hillman of the Amalgamated Clothing Workers as one of President Roosevelt's many righthand men. And in general, the advance of social consciousness helped revitalize the labor movement and thrust it to the center of the historical stage. . . .

The change was registered as populists and progressives became major players in the midterm elections of 1934. Upton Sinclair ran a creditable campaign for governor of California on watered-down socialism and the slogan "End poverty in California." Midwestern voters elected members of the Minnesota Farmer-Labor party, sent progressive Robert La Follette, Jr., to the Senate from Wisconsin, and revived the prairie populist ideas of the Non-Partisan League. Southern populism spoke through Huey Long's Share Our Wealth campaign, and southern progressives such as Hugo Black put aside states' rights and worry about race relations to support federal assistance to the poor. Contrary to the traditional pattern in midterm elections, voters further reduced the Republican contingent in Congress, and many of the new Democrats stood to the left of Roosevelt. For the first time in a decade of reversals, the labor movement actually gained friends in high office. Once the New Deal broke the logjam in American politics, a host of reformers came flooding through.

In some respects, the new dynamic was comparable to the aftermath of the First World War. Then, the largest strike wave in American history, the onrushing women's movement, and the emergence of the New Negro confronted elites with a choice between progressive "reconstruction" that would co-opt these popular forces into a new governing system and top-down repression that would freeze things as they were. Although the Women's Suffrage Amendment was an example of cooptation, for the most part the Wilson and Harding administrations had chosen the path of repression. Nervous about Bolshevik revolution in Europe, they chose to crack down on strikers, incite the Red Scare, and abandon social reform in favor of laissez faire and immigration restriction.

Now, a decade and a half later, as the political initiative shifted from elites to masses, the Roosevelt administration faced a similar choice between repressing popular forces or co-opting them into some yet-undiscovered consensus. In the frame of international comparison, that choice translated into an ominous question of whether liberalism would be sacrificed to save capitalism. The question was posed most cruelly in Germany, where the Nazi seizure of power in 1933 had destroyed all semblance of civil liberties. If Germany could descend into fascism, was it possible that the United States would find its own road to repression?

Given all that was at stake, the choice facing the country in the mid-1930s was full of historical significance. For if the Roosevelt administration continued to take its cues from managerial liberals, and if, as seemed likely, its half-baked experiments in state planning failed to end the depression, then the inevitable protests would be met with troops and anticommunist hysteria. And if the lights of free expression were snuffed out in the land of liberty, how long could they remain lit elsewhere? If, on the other hand, the administration chose to reach out to the grass-roots movements, it would have to chart a new course for American politics. Since there were precious few precedents for incorporating wage earners in state policies, and since the interests of wage earners and capitalists were fundamentally at odds, it would not be easy to find the way.

In the event, the choice was for a new round of experiments in 1935 that became known as the Second New Deal. In what was the truly new part of the New Deal, the Roosevelt administration enacted a set of enduring reforms, including the National Labor Relations Act and the Social Security Act, that somehow reconciled capitalism and social reform, altered forever the relation between state and society in the United States, and stood as a beacon of liberal renewal to the entire world.

The original impetus for reform came not from corporate planners but from the popular movements for social justice and their allies in the administration and Congress. That fact was crystal clear in the more radical pieces of legislation, such as the Works Progress Administration (WPA). Responding to unemployed workers and social reformers, Harry Hopkins, a Chicago social worker in the Jane Addams tradition, devised a vast federal jobs program that spent over $2 billion at its peak in 1939 and had more than 3 million people on payroll doing everything from digging ditches to writing plays. Though ridiculed as "We Poke Along," it made lasting contributions in public works and even in public art through the heroic murals of people's struggle painted by the likes of Diego Rivera. To its supporters, WPA represented a rational system of production-for-use as against the chaos of production-for-profit. Verily, it prefigured the cooperative commonwealth.

No doubt the most annoying burr in the saddle of privilege was the wealth tax. Roosevelt backed the "soak the rich" tax on capital stock, estates, gifts, and excess profits to recapture political ground lost to Long's Share Our Wealth campaign. Once enacted in 1935, the tax did not, in fact, soak the rich; econometric studies attribute most of whatever downward distribution of income occurred after 1929 to market forces or the impact of the Second World War. But nothing did more to provoke fear and loathing of the New Deal and "that man in the White House," and it marked the apogee of Roosevelt's swing toward redistributive ideas. Radicalism was also evident in TVA-style planned economy, WPA production-for-use, and the presence of agrarian reformers in Henry Wallace's Department of Agriculture. Thus for the first time since the border between progressivism and socialism had closed in 1917, Washington was open to influences from the left.

The turn toward reform split the business community into pro- and anti-New Deal factions. A minority of corporate leaders such as Thomas Watson, head of International Business Machines, recognized the desirability, or at least the inevitability, of some social legislation. Rockefeller interests supported public pensions and unemployment assistance and sponsored a national tour by William Beveridge, who became the father of the British welfare state. When Secretary Perkins picked people associated with the well-connected American Association for Labor Legislation to work with the newly appointed Committee on Economic Security, the corporate-liberal wing of the business community knew it could count on Roosevelt to come up with a "sober" social insurance plan for the unemployed and the elderly. Managerial liberalism was not totally dead.

Most businessmen, however, attacked public welfare as if it flew the red flag of socialism. At the first sign that social-democratic ideas were making headway in Washington, conservatives in the U.S. Chamber of Commerce deposed its pro-New Deal leader. Although the National Association of Manufacturers raised no serious objection to unemployment aid along the lines of the "Wisconsin Plan" (privately controlled employer reserves), it opposed anything that smacked of public control. In the face of 12 million unemployed, NAM commended individual "thrift and self-denial" as the answer to unemployment. NAM's Ohio affiliate denounced the "Ohio Plan" (compulsory group insurance) as "the greatest menace that has ever faced Ohio industry," and the Ohio Chamber of Commerce thundered against this "Bolshevik" proposal. . . .

Beset by these political cross-pressures, Roosevelt was galvanized into launching the Second Hundred Days when the Supreme Court declared the National Recovery Act unconstitutional in the *Schechter* decision of May 1935. Shattering the centerpiece of Roosevelt's recovery program at a time of growing popular discontent, the Court's bombshell threatened to wreck the fragile public confidence that had returned in the preceding two years. Eager to experiment with ideas that might win votes, Roosevelt quickly shifted his labor policy. Having steadfastly ignored Senator Robert Wagner's bill for regulating labor relations, he now thrust it forward as a piece of essential legislation.

With ties to both enlightened corporate leaders and labor progressives in his home state of New York, Senator Wagner espoused an "underconsumption" theory of the Depression and argued that collective bargaining was the route to recovery because it would raise "the purchasing power of wage earners." Wagner's aim was not to redistribute wealth from capital to labor but to rationalize the chaos of competition by smoothing out the peaks and valleys between boom and bust, large and small employers, and high- and low-wage industries. In an attempt to avoid running afoul of the Supreme Court, Wagner's bill employed a bit of legalistic legerdemain in making *individual* rights the legal basis for *collective* bargaining. In fact, the words *trade union* never appeared. All the same, the Wagner Act gave the new National Labor Relations Board power to halt "unfair labor practices," supervise representation elections, and certify duly chosen bargaining agents. Hoping to reap the advantage, the AFL put aside its traditional objections to state intervention and supported the bill, a move AFL leaders regretted when it turned out the CIO would be competing for the same harvest of union members.

For all its labor sympathies, the Wagner Act did not fail to protect elite interests. Using their clout as committee chairmen, southern conservatives weakened the bill by excluding agricultural and casual laborers, thus leaving most of the Afro-American and Hispanic work force unprotected. The largely female occupations of domestic servants and retail clerks were also excluded. The friends of business, for their part, saw to it that the act confined "responsible" unions to a narrow range of bargaining issues, and, most important, it carefully avoided trenching upon the inner sanctum of managerial control over investment, product, and labor process. Freighted with such enfeeblements and exclusions, the bill passed overwhelmingly, with support from a majority of southern Democrats. Even the Supreme Court upheld the Wagner Act, granting its first approval to a major piece of New Deal legislation in the *Jones and Laughlin* decision (1937).

All in all, it was a historic turnabout. The Wagner Act constituted labor as a great estate of the realm, not the peer of business or even agriculture, but in some sense a collective entity with legitimate interests deserving state protection. Although the intent of the framers was to promote recovery, the effect was to install the government as the patron of unionism and, in some measure, to redress the balance of power toward workers. But the beauty of the Second New Deal's expansion of interest-group liberalism was its exquisite compromise between mass interests and elite privileges. . . .

Having already gone into the business of emergency relief, New Dealers were determined to create a permanent and more rational welfare system. From one side, they were buffeted by a host of modern-day Robin Hoods who pushed a cartload of reforms—the Lundeen Bill on unemployment, Townsend's revolving pensions, and Long's Share Our Wealth—all of which quite openly aimed at the redistribution of wealth through confiscatory taxes on the rich. From the other side, New Dealers were pummeled by a shrill campaign financed by business against any system of government subsidies to the poor. . . .

Artfully crafted to minimize conservative opposition, the Social

Security Act exempted many of the groups that needed help the most. To placate southern planters, agribusinessmen, and economic conservatives in general, it denied protection to farm workers, domestics, and casual laborers, the very people whose low wages and irregular employment made them among the poorest in the land. Likewise, instead of setting a minimum national unemployment benefit, the system bowed to low-wage regions and allowed state officials to set the dollar level of unemployment checks. Thus with the same enfeeblements and exclusions found in the Wagner Act, Social Security easily passed through a Congress eager to show a humane face to the public that had lived through six grinding years of depression. . . .

Sexual inequality was built into every part of the welfare state. Constructed around the nuclear family ideal, the system favored lifelong homemakers over working wives and single women. Large groups of the lowest-paid female workers who needed protection the most were systematically excluded, including 3 million domestic servants; almost a third of all working women were thus deprived of unemployment and old-age benefits. In a compounding of women's predicament, divorced women were initially denied survivor's benefits, and young widows had to wait until retirement to collect. No one can say how a vital feminist movement would have changed all this, but it is clear that the absence of the kind of agitation that characterized the 1910s allowed these gender subordinations to go unchallenged.

When it came to labor and capital, the architects of Social Security were quite explicit about their intention to buttress the ladder of wage inequality. Chief Administrator Arthur Altmeyer laid down the "fundamental principle" that benefits were not to exceed 80 percent of former wages. According to Edwin Witte, the main architect of the bill, "Only to a very minor degree does it modify the distribution of wealth and it does not alter at all the fundamentals of our capitalistic and individualistic economy. Nor does it relieve the individual of primary responsibility for his own support and that of his dependents." . . .

Contrary to common mythology, the poor and the working classes were not the only ones to receive welfare. The middle classes were also beneficiaries of massive state aid. For one thing, in the absence of a means test for old-age insurance, salaried white-collar workers were entitled to a federal pension. Although the old middle class of self-employed persons was initially exempt from the system, the fact that the new salaried middle class participated helped guarantee the political survival of Social Security through the thick and thin of successive liberal and conservative administrations in Washington. For another, small property owners also received the largesse of federal insurance on savings deposits and home loans. Tapping a deep vein of American folklore, Franklin Roosevelt proclaimed that "a nation of homeowners, of people who own a real share in their own land, is unconquerable." To stem the tide of mortgage foreclosures, in 1933 and 1934 the Roosevelt administration created the Home Owners Loan Corporation to refinance shaky mortgages, the Federal Savings and Loan Insurance Corporation to prop up wobbly financial institutions, and the Federal Housing Administration (FHA) to underwrite private loans for housing construction. Before long, the federal government held mortgages on fully one-tenth of all owner-occupied nonfarm residences in the United States. Working through Hoover's Home Loan Bank Board, the New Deal largely succeeded in repairing the bonds between middle-class families and capitalist institutions that had been ruptured by the Depression.

The middle-class bias was evident in guidelines for home loans. The Home Owners Loan Corporation devised an invidious, four-tier, color-coded system for ranking neighborhoods in which, predictably, the top-ranked were composed of "American business and professional men" (that is, no Jews, blacks, or recent immigrants), while the bottom—coded red—were crowded slums or any neighborhood with a "rapidly increasing Negro population." This was the beginning of official federal sponsorship of redlining, or disinvestment in poorer urban neighborhoods, which did so much to devastate inner cities in the middle decades of the twentieth century. To its credit, the New Deal also subsidized low-income tenants through public housing, and it was the market, not the federal government, that created the slums. But in smoothing the transition from the productive farms and workshops of the old middle classes to the consumer homes of the new, Washington became the biggest single player in the housing market, and, as such, it did much to preserve the gap between "good" neighborhoods and "bad."

The fact that New Deal reforms preserved social hierarchy does not mean the Wagner Act and Social Security were the result of a conspiracy of the rich or were devoid of humanitarian intent. Certainly, the New Deal had more than its share of humanitarian moments, including the abolition of child labor in the NRA codes and subsequently in the Fair Labor Standards Act of 1938. But even as the New Deal responded to popular demands for social justice, it was careful not to infringe too much upon the privileges of wealth. By the end of the Second New Deal, the Roosevelt administration had crafted a compromise between privileged elites and subordinate groups that restrained liberty in the name of security without upending the social order. . . .

For all its limitations, the fact remains that by the time the New Deal was checkmated at the end of the 1930s, it had already altered the organic relation between the state and society. Responding to the resurgence of popular protest, the New Deal pushed through a social compromise between corporate elites and laboring masses that forever changed the dynamics of American civilization. In institutional terms, the state took a quantum leap into the business of regulating the market, so that virtually everyone from the Wall Street investor dealing with the Securities and Exchange Commission to the Pittsburgh steelworker voting in a union election supervised by the National Labor Relations Board, felt the power of some arm of the federal bureaucracy. In terms of legitimacy, the New Deal enshrined a new set of ruling values keyed to security, so that the mass of the population, from the small savings depositor trusting in the Federal Deposit Insurance Corporation to the retired couple relying on a pension from Social Security, felt as if the government cared about their welfare.

Although Roosevelt popularized his program with populist rhetoric, the new governing system did not redress the balance of class power or redistribute wealth so much as mediate social antagonisms by creating a new set of bureaucratic institutions. Building on Hoover's initiatives, Roosevelt's New Deal expanded state intervention in the market and launched a welfare state. None of these experiments in Keynesian economics ended the Depression; prosperity would not return until war orders started coming in. But the New Deal did succeed in restoring political balance to a system all out of kilter. The "fourth branch" of government, the New Deal coalition, and the ruling myths of security and pluralism renewed popular faith in the state and narrowed the gap between the state and modern society. Thus did the modern governing system take its place alongside the consumer family and corporate property as the third leg of the stool of political stability. . . .

Taken as a whole, Nazism was the product of a historical conjuncture triggered by humiliating defeat in the First World War and economic anxiety in the Great Depression. The door to fascism was opened by traditional elites who eviscerated liberal democracy but who were themselves incapable of governing modern, capitalist societies. That created the opportunity for counterrevolutionaries to come storming through on the strength of a mass movement whose taproot lay in the lower middle class and whose appeal was built around a set of negations—anticommunism, anticonservatism, antiliberalism, anti-feminism, and anti-Semitism. Invited into power by military and industrial elites who hoped to use the Nazi party as a mass base, the Nazis gave elites more than they had bargained for. Once in power, the Nazis imposed a brutal regime whose leading traits were capitalism by violence, racial nationalism, hypermasculinism, and imperial expansion. Having already conquered Italy under Mussolini, fascism now swept Germany and Austria, gained strength in eastern Europe, and found a close cousin in imperial Japan. Whereas in 1919 and 1920 the question of social revolution had hung over world affairs, the pertinent question after 1932 was whether counterrevolution might spread throughout the globe.

Did that possibility include the United States? That some type of authoritarian regime would emerge in the land of liberty did not seem out of the question at the time. Few could match John Dewey's credentials as an astute observer of the American scene, and in 1932 he was worried: "We have permitted business and financial autocracy to reach such a point that its logical political counterpart is a Mussolini, unless a violent revolution brings forth a Lenin." In fact, there were ominous signs of a corporatist regime in the state capitalism of Hoover and of Roosevelt in his first administration. Pointing to the fusion of capitalist titans and government bureaucrats in the RFC and NRA, Walter Lippmann warned of "the dictatorship of casual oligarchs," while the *New Republic* described the early New Deal as an American-style "corporative state."

In addition, many contemporaries saw militarist glimmerings in General Hugh Johnson's Blue Eagle and the Civilian Conservation Corps. Certainly, state repression was by no means foreign to America, as the labor movement, the Bonus Army, and generations of African Americans could attest. No wonder some imaginations ran wild. Under the ironic title *It Can't Happen Here* (1935), Sinclair Lewis described the fictional seizure of power by an authoritarian regime backed by Wall Street, the Wasp establishment, and the military on the heels of a presidential victory by a bombastic demagogue bearing a strong resemblance to Huey Long.

If a repressive regime was going to develop in the United States, conservative elites would have to link up with a potent, right-wing mass movement. The fact that such a movement failed to emerge does not mean that the ingredients were altogether missing. America was no stranger to the class resentments and ethnic hatreds that fueled the revolt of the little guy in Germany. If anything could have become the basis for an American *Volksgemeinschaft*, it was white racism, and, in fact, the entire repertoire of unreason—racial bigotry, Christian anti-Semitism, nativist paranoia, anticommunism, and antifeminism—was tapped by hate groups such as the Ku Klux Klan and even by the more respectable Rotarians, American Legionnaires, and women's clubbers.

The closest thing to a counterrevolutionary movement in the United States gathered around the figure of Father Charles Coughlin. A magnetic speaker who outdid FDR in the mastery of mass communications, the Detroit "Radio Priest" reached as many as 40 million listeners, and at its peak his National Union for Social Justice attracted perhaps 5 million members. Wrapping patriarchal and corporatist views in a quasi-populist cover, he portrayed an unholy conspiracy of bankers, Communists, and Jews. With the characteristic logic-chopping of the demagogue, he could pronounce that "the most dangerous communist is the wolf in the sheep's clothing of conservatism," and in ever more putrid rhetoric he excoriated "money changers" such as Andrew Mellon and Treasury Secretary Henry Morgenthau with their "Jewish cohorts."

There was nothing unique in Coughlin's anticommunism, anticonservatism, and anti-Semitism, common elements in the underworld of American politics. Likewise, when he warned that birth control and premarital sex led to prostitution and socialism, his antifeminism was in keeping with the sentiments of a long line of purity crusaders. What was peculiar about Coughlin—and what linked him to European fascism—was his antiliberalism. Unlike most American rightists, he called for greater state control of the economy, including nationalization of the banks. Strongly influenced by the corporatist philosophy of social relations in Pope Pius XI's *Quadregesimo Anno* (1931), he urged a national welfare system. Just as the National Socialist party impersonated socialism, so his National Union for Social Justice impersonated social justice reform.

If there was a threat of tyranny, it lay in the possibility that big business would join forces with the kind of mass bigotry represented by Coughlin. Given America's liberal inheritance, there was little likelihood of an all-powerful leviathan state, but there was a good deal of experience with the undemocratic power of business and the tyranny of the majority. In the frenzy of 100 percent Americanism after the First World War, the country got a taste of what a repressive regime might look like in a set of harsh measures ranging from the open shop to immigration restriction. In many ways, the choices confronting the country in the mid-1930s were quite similar. Would the response to popular discontent be social reform or the repression of another Red Scare? With the memory of postwar violations of civil liberties still fresh, the question was not whether fascism would spread to America, but whether the United States would pick up where it had left off in the early 1920s and develop a homegrown, repressive regime of its own.

Comparison with Germany illuminates the reasons why no such regime emerged. Perhaps the starkest contrast between the two countries lay in foreign policy. From the day the Versailles Treaty was signed, Germany was a revisionist power, and the fact that the United States was not goes a long way toward explaining why there was nothing to compare with the German impulse toward militarism. While the Nazis turned resentment over defeat in the First World War into a militarist crusade for *Lebensraum*, the United States was content to reap the harvest of economic exports and corporate diplomacy in the 1920s. Then in the 1930s the United States retreated into its shell. Signs of rising economic nationalism included the Smoot-Hawley Tariff of 1930, Roosevelt's "torpedo" of the 1933 London Economic Conference, and the Neutrality Acts (1935–1937), by which Congress pretended that the United States had no vital interests outside its borders. On the positive side, Roosevelt's Good Neighbor Policy toward Latin America foreswore armed intervention. But on the negative, the United States buried its head in the sand while fascist powers conquered Ethiopia, Spain, and Manchuria, only making the inevitable reckoning that much more devastating when it finally came in September 1939. Be that as it may, the spirit of neutrality allowed little room for the sort of bellicose nationalism that would have fostered a militarist regime in the United States.

On the domestic side, it is necessary, first of all, to credit popular social movements for revitalizing democratic traditions. Undoubtedly, the most important event in this regard was the resurgence of the labor movement as embodied in the newborn Congress of Industrial Organizations. Not only did the CIO seek to give workers a say in industry— that is, to make the Bill of Rights apply inside the factory gate—but CIO organizers were forced to combat ethnic hatred in order to unite the immigrant nationalities among the rank and file. The same pluralist imperative was imposed on political parties. Capitalizing on the popularity of the repeal of Prohibition, the Democrats brought urban ethnics into the New Deal coalition and prepared the way for general acceptance of the idea that the United States was a "nation of nations."

What was especially distinctive about democracy in the 1930s was that it came with a social twist. When social movements spilled over into electoral politics behind southern populists, midwestern progressives, and the occasional leftist, it became advantageous for politicians all the way up to the president to support social-democratic reforms such as the Wagner Act and Social Security. Roosevelt may have saved liberalism; he may have saved capitalism; but grass-roots social movements were the saviors of democracy.

8

AMERICA AND THE COLD WAR

Containment or Hegemony?

With the collapse of Soviet communism and the dissolution of the U.S.S.R. in the 1980s, the Cold War, which had preoccupied American leaders and millions of ordinary Americans for almost half a century, suddenly ended. Whatever tension remained in relations between the United States and Russia, the future was not likely to be shaped by the same kind of nuclear standoff that had for decades dissuaded the great powers from direct military confrontation with one another and terrorized humankind with the prospect of nuclear Armageddon. Nor would the demands of the national security state, however unceasing, ever again seem so irresistible or unarguable, whether those demands were for the allocation of material resources or the subordination of civil liberties.

Questions of long-term consequences aside, in the United States the *end of* the Cold War was almost universally interpreted as *triumph in* the Cold War. Among contemporary historians, debate is now underway as to how wise or useful it is to let this sort of triumphalism or vindicationism shape historical accounts of the Cold War. However, one unarguable benefit is new access to Soviet archives, which is already beginning to reshape interpretations. Finally, all historians now have the opportunity to view the Cold War as a whole, a historical phenomenon—like the Progressive era or the Jacksonian era—with beginning, middle, and end. Even in this regard, however, some historians insist that the strategic, economic, and political roots of the Cold War preceded the World War II era and will continue to generate problems and conflicts into the next millennium. At the very least, the end of the Cold War has spurred historians to rethink and perhaps refresh their accounts of the origins and development of the East-West rivalry that so profoundly shaped America and the world in the second half of the twentieth century.

Most accounts of the Cold War begin with the end of World War II. Two consequences of that war established the context within which the Cold War would be waged. One was the toppling of five major nations from the ranks of first-rate powers. America's enemies—Germany, Japan, and Italy—were defeated. Its allies—Britain and France—spent

too much blood and treasure to regain their prewar military and economic power. This situation left only two superpowers, the United
States and the Soviet Union. The second development was the technological revolution in warfare. With the exploding of the atomic bomb in
1945, diplomacy entered a new age. From that moment forward every
confrontation between great powers threatened the destruction of humankind. For Americans the "age of free security" had come to an end:
neither great oceans to the east and west, nor unthreatening neighbors
to the north and south, any longer guaranteed immunity from attack.[1]
In the post-1945 world, long-range bombers, intercontinental ballistic
missiles, and atomic and nuclear bombs exposed the United States for
the first time in its history to the possibility of enormous, even total, destruction. In a sense, the United States had joined the rest of the world,
particularly Europe, and even more particularly the Soviet Union,
which not only feared but had actually experienced in two world wars
levels of destruction that were almost unimaginable. That casualties in
the tens of millions and the vaporization of millions of acres of productive terrain might have to be suffered again in the U.S.S.R.—or for the
first time in the United States—drove both superpowers toward obsessive concern with national security, and a spiral of confrontation and
arms buildup that fell just short of war. One historian likened the U.S.-
U.S.S.R. relationship to that of a scorpion and tarantula together in a
bottle, each trying to sting the other.[2]

Since 1945 scholars have disagreed about the causes of the Cold
War and the assignment of responsibility for its origination and continuation. American historians have divided into three schools: the orthodox, the revisionist, and the realist. The first to appear was the
orthodox school, which came into being during the immediate postwar years. Most Americans, including the vast majority of scholars,
were inclined to accept the official explanation of events set forth by
the Allies in justifying postwar foreign policy. According to the orthodox interpretation, Soviet aggression and expansionist desires were
primarily responsible for the coming of the Cold War. Winston
Churchill, speaking at Fulton, Missouri in the spring of 1946, set forth
the basic outline of this interpretation. An "iron curtain," said
Churchill, had been lowered across eastern Europe by the Soviets. No
one knew for sure what secret plans for expansion were being hatched
behind the iron curtain. Communist ideology, Communist parties,
and "fifth column" activities within noncommunist countries were a
growing peril to what he called "Christian civilization." President

---

[1]This term was coined by historian C. Vann Woodward in "The Age of Reinterpretation," *American Historical Review* 66 (October 1960): 1–19.

[2]Louis Halle, *The Cold War as History* (New York, 1967), p. xiii.

Truman echoed these sentiments in 1947 when announcing his now-famous Truman Doctrine. Although the United States had made every effort to bring about a peaceful world, he said, the Soviet Union had used "indirect aggression" in eastern Europe, "extreme pressure" in the Middle East, and intervention by "Communist parties directed from Moscow" in the internal affairs of many other countries. Orthodox scholars traced the start of the Cold War to the announcement of the Truman Doctrine in 1947, which they saw as a necessary response to Soviet aggression.

The orthodox interpretation was presented in scholarly books and journals in the late 1940s and early 1950s. Scholars sometimes disagreed about the Soviet motivation: they emphasized the role of Marxist-Leninist ideology in promoting Soviet expansionism, but some also focused on traditional Russian imperialism. All tended to agree that some combination of these motives led the Soviet Union to adopt an expansionist policy. Orthodox scholars also argued that it was because the Soviet Union's expansionist urges overrode its other commitments that the U.S.S.R. violated all its agreements with the Western powers, including the Yalta agreement on the political future of eastern Europe and its informal accords on the role of China in the postwar world. American foreign policy, according to the orthodox interpretation, was markedly different from that of the Soviet Union. Emerging from World War II with hopes for continued Allied cooperation and guided by the principles of collective security, American leaders looked to the newborn United Nations for the resolution of future international conflicts. Faced with Soviet intransigence and aggression, however, the United States reluctantly changed its views and its foreign policy. To prevent the spread of Soviet influence, which was the prelude to Soviet worldwide domination, the United States committed itself to "containment." Without this commitment, the orthodox argue, the Soviet Union would have become the master of all Europe, instead of only eastern Europe. The orthodox position was set forth in an influential article published by American diplomat George F. Kennan under a pseudonym, "Mr. X," in 1947. In this historic essay Kennan set the terms for the theory of containment, which would undergird the diplomatic and military policy of the Truman administration and, indeed, of the western world, for years to come.[3]

The orthodox version, despite challenges, remains the dominant

---

[3]Mr. X [George F. Kennan], "The Sources of Soviet Conduct," *Foreign Affairs* 25 (July 1947): 566–582. Subsequently, Kennan regretted exaggerating the power of ideology in shaping Soviet behavior; he also lamented that his article had been misread in a number of ways; in particular, he claimed, Truman had implemented containment in a far more militarily confrontational way than he had intended: George F. Kennan, *Memoirs, 1925–1950* (Boston, 1967).

school of thought on the origins of the Cold War. Although its proponents differ on many matters, they all conclude that responsibility for the Cold War rested to a preponderant degree with the Soviet Union.[4] Some of the earliest orthodox scholars, such as Kennan and historian Herbert Feis, have modified, though not abandoned, their views with the passage of time, emphasizing somewhat less the perfidy of the Soviets and the earnest good will of the Americans. By the early 1970s, a younger historian, John Lewis Gaddis, was striving to be as even-handed as possible while adhering to the orthodox interpretation. His important first book argued that neither the Soviet Union nor the United States was solely responsible for the Cold War, even while insisting that Stalin was more responsible than any western leader for the onset and development of hostile relations. Gaddis's masterpiece, *Strategies of Containment*, published in the early 1980s, went even further in criticizing American policy-makers. In succumbing to anti-communist hysteria, Gaddis charged, they confused essential interests (e.g., in central Europe) with peripheral interests (e.g., in southeast Asia), prolonging and worsening the Cold War. Despite this emphatic acknowledgment of American failings, Gaddis reiterated the central orthodox claim that the Cold War would never have taken place in the absence of Stalinist aggression.[5]

Although orthodox scholars were in no sense merely parroting an official U.S. line in their historical works, it is certainly true that because their views were compatible with those of governmental and private sources of research funds, not to mention mainstream politicians and the press, they achieved broader credibility and a greater degree of professional success than those who bucked the orthodox position. Nonetheless, almost from the outset of the Cold War the prevailing explanation of events provoked challenges. Henry Wallace, former vice president, sharply questioned the soundness of President Truman's analysis of Soviet intentions and policies during the immediate postwar years. Running as a presidential candidate of the minority Progressive party in 1948, Wallace made his case for a less confrontational

---

[4]For a few examples of the orthodox interpretation see Herbert Feis's three books, *The Road to Pearl Harbor* (Princeton, 1950), *The China Tangle* (Princeton, 1953), and especially *Roosevelt-Churchill-Stalin* (Princeton, 1957); see also William H. McNeill, *America. Britain. and Russia: Their Cooperation and Conflict, 1941–1946* (London, 1953); Norman Graebner, *Cold War Diplomacy: American Foreign Policy 1945–1960* (Princeton, 1962); and Andre Fontaine, *History of the Cold War from the October Revolution to the Korean War, 1917–1950*, 2 vols. (New York, 1968).

[5]John Lewis Gaddis, *The United States and the Origins of the Cold War, 1941–1947* (New York, 1972); *Strategies of Containment* (New York, 1982). See also George G. Herring, Jr., *Aid to Russia, 1941–1946: Strategy, Diplomacy, and the Origins of the Cold War* (New York, 1973); and Bruce R. Kuniholm, *The Origins of the Cold War in the Near East: Great Power Conflict and Diplomacy in Iran, Turkey, and Greece* (Princeton, 1980).

policy toward the Russians, but his poor showing marked the end of serious political challenge to the policy of containment until the 1960s.
Walter Lippmann, one of the nation's leading journalists, likewise refused to place the blame for postwar tensions exclusively on the Soviet
Union. It was Lippmann who popularized the term "Cold War," using
it in the title of a book he published in 1947.[6] He argued that America's
statesmen were assaulting Russia's vital interests in eastern Europe and
thereby furnishing the Soviet Union with a reason for seeking iron rule
over countries on its borders. These threatening U.S. policies also gave
Russians grounds to believe what Leninist ideologues had been teaching for years: that a capitalist coalition was being organized to surround
and destroy them. Lippmann's high standing as a writer and thinker
gave his views a measure of credibility, especially among revisionist-
minded historians who were skeptical about the claim that the Soviet
Union was primarily or solely responsible for precipitating the Cold
War. Over the years such revisionists proposed, in a variety of ways and
with a variety of voices, that the causes of the Cold War could be located in the interests, ideology, and policies of the United States, at
least as much as those of the Soviet Union. They suggested, to put it
bluntly, that the Cold War was "our" fault as much as—maybe more
than—"theirs."

Although the revisionist historians held diverse views, most
agreed that in 1945, having been ravaged by war, the U.S.S.R. was weak.
From this premise they argued that a weak Soviet Union was neither
willing nor able to pursue an aggressive foreign policy. Indeed, some
revisionists maintained that, although the Russians recoiled from
America's technological superiority and military power, they also
viewed the United States as the only potential source of monetary assistance and trade concessions, both of which they desperately needed
to recover from the disastrous effects of the war. Most revisionists further argued that the Soviet Union, despite its rhetoric of ideological
bravado, consistently pursued only cautious, defensive, and limited
foreign policy goals. Thus the worldwide policy of aggression which
the orthodox claimed to detect in the Soviet Union's behavior seemed
to the revisionists to be entirely out of character and beyond its means.

Revisionist-minded historians likewise offered explanations of
America's motivation that differed significantly from the orthodox
view. Some claimed that the Western powers in general, and the Truman administration in particular, tried to deny the Soviet Union the
rightful gains it had been granted in the Yalta agreement. What Roosevelt and Churchill had been compelled by circumstances to concede

---

[6]Walter Lippmann, *The Cold War* (New York, 1947). This was a collection of newspaper articles written to counter Kennan's interpretation of the motivation behind Soviet
policy.

at Yalta—i.e., a Soviet sphere of influence in eastern Europe—Truman and his advisors refused to recognize. Other historians argued that the United States, with a missionary zeal at least as fervid as that of the Soviets, intended to reshape the world to suit what it believed were universal democratic principles. Still other scholars saw economic rather than ideological expansionism as the keynote of American policy, postulating that Cold War foreign policy was meant to pave the way for a drive to capture world markets. The United States, in this reading, used its early monopoly of nuclear weapons and its economic strength to browbeat its allies and other nation-states into submitting to Washington's leadership. As proof of this position, revisionists pointed out that the Marshall Plan had been designed to preclude Soviet participation in it. And finally, some revisionists saw the demonization of the Soviet Union as a product of American domestic politics. In particular they discerned a drive by Republicans and their business allies to regain their traditional control over government and the public agenda by branding the New Deal, the unions, and the left-leaning Democrats as dupes (even agents) of the "international Communist conspiracy."[7]

The most significant challenge to the orthodox position came, ironically, from a historian whose primary interest was not the Cold War era, but who exerted an immense influence on the entire field of U.S. diplomatic history. William Appleman Williams, whose career was discussed at length in Chapter 4, was dubbed America's "preeminent critic of empire."[8] As such, he insisted that U.S. Cold War policies were not just "reactions" to Soviet aggression; they were part of a continuous American Open Door policy that was expansionist from its very beginnings. Determined to develop ever-expanding markets for its products, the United States first pursued its imperial ambitions in the western regions of the American continent. By the 1890s, however, with the frontier gone, the search for markets continued overseas. Given this general perspective, Williams saw U.S. policy after World War II as nothing more than an extension of the Open Door. Seeking market penetration into the nations of eastern Europe and the

---

[7]On the relationship between foreign and domestic policy, still indispensable is Richard M. Freeland, *The Truman Doctrine and the Origins of McCarthyism, 1946–1948* (New York, 1972). On McCarthyism, the literature is vast; especially useful are Robert Griffith, *The Politics of Fear: Joseph R. McCarthy and the Senate* (Amherst, Mass., 1970); Stanley I. Kutler, *American Inquisition: Justice and Injustice in the Cold War* (New York, 1982). A recent update with useful documents is Ellen Schrecker, *The Age of McCarthyism: A Brief History with Documents* (Boston, 1994). An insightful if idiosyncratic interpretation of the impact of the Cold War on American culture is Tom Engelhardt, *The End of Victory Culture: Cold War America and the Disillusioning of a Generation* (New York, 1995); more conventional but no less insightful is Stephen J. Whitfield, *The Culture of the Cold War* (Baltimore, 1991). See also Chapter 11.

[8]Paul Buhle, "William Appleman Williams: Grassroots against Empire," in *Rethinking the Cold War*, Allen Hunter, ed. (Philadelphia, 1998), pp. 289–306.

third world, America sought to impose on them governments that would do business with the United States. Counterrevolution to make the world safe for American capitalism, not containment of communist aggression was therefore the major motive behind the postwar policies of the United States, and the major cause of the Cold War.[9]

Williams exerted enormous (though not exclusive) influence over all those who in the 1960s began to revise prevailing interpretations of the Cold War. Still, revisionists came in many varieties, from moderate to radical, differing over the precise degree to which the United States should be held accountable for the onset of the Cold War. One of the earliest moderate revisionists was Denna F. Fleming, whose 1961 book focused on President Truman as the crucial precipitator of the Cold War. While Roosevelt had been dedicated to "Wilsonian internationalism," Truman adopted a belligerent policy toward the Russians as soon as he assumed the presidency. In April 1945 he ordered the Soviets to loosen their grip on Poland or else forfeit certain economic aid that America had promised to deliver. Contrary to the orthodox account, which generally dates the beginning of the Cold War in 1947 with the Truman Doctrine, Fleming believed it began at this moment in 1945.[10]

A somewhat more radical revisionist, Gar Alperovitz, agreed that Truman started the Cold War in 1945, but he focused on "atomic diplomacy" as the key to explaining the breakdown of wartime cooperation. The U.S. monopoly of atomic weapons permitted Truman to adopt a hard line toward the Soviets, forcing them either to acquiesce in America's postwar hegemony or go it alone. Like most of the moderate revisionists, however, Alperovitz did not heap all the blame for beginning the Cold War on the United States. The Russians' actions also helped to poison the postwar atmosphere, he said. "The cold war cannot be understood simply as an American response to a Soviet challenge" (or vice-versa), he wrote, "but rather as an insidious interaction of mutual suspicions, blame for which must be shared by all." Nevertheless the thrust of Alperovitz's work clearly placed a heavier share of responsibility for the beginnings of the Cold War on the shoulders of those American policy-makers who not only brandished, but had twice used, atomic weapons.[11]

---

[9]Williams, *The Tragedy of American Diplomacy* (New York, 1959) and *The Contours of American History* (Cleveland, 1961). On fears of economic depression as a major motive of U.S. expansionist foreign policy see the Williams student Lloyd C. Gardner, *Architects of Illusion: Men and Ideas in American Foreign Policy, 1941–1949* (Chicago, 1970).

[10]Denna F. Fleming, *The Cold War and Its Origins, 1917–1960*, 2 vols. (New York, 1961). See also Athan Theoharis, "Roosevelt and Truman on Yalta: The Origins of the Cold War," *Political Science Quarterly* 87 (June 1972): 210–241.

[11]Gar Alperovitz, *Atomic Diplomacy: Hiroshima and Potsdam* (New York, 1965).

One of Williams's most accomplished followers, Walter LaFeber, an astute scholar of American expansionism in the late nineteenth century,[12] developed and expanded this revisionist view of the Cold War. LaFeber was critical of both the United States and the Soviet Union for failing to maintain peace. Focusing upon the internal reasons behind the formulation of U.S. foreign policy, he concluded that domestic events—not just the long-term pursuit of empire, but short-term events such as presidential campaigns, economic recessions, the hysteria of McCarthyism, and factional power struggles within the government—contributed as much to the making of America's foreign policy as did external events. Within Russia the same was true: power struggles within Stalin's and later Khrushchev's Communist party, regional tensions, and problems of economic recovery, along with traditional Russian imperial ambitions, shaped most foreign policy actions. In terms of economic penetration LaFeber found that the United States and the Soviet Union showed equal interest in exploiting foreign markets wherever possible. Both nations, he concluded, created their postwar policies with an eye to maintaining freedom of action in those spheres they considered vital to their economic and strategic interests.

However even-handed, LaFeber concentrated primarily on what had gone wrong with U.S. policy. During the first phase of the Cold War, 1945 to 1953, he argued, U.S. policy was Europe-oriented; its goals were to preserve a trans-Atlantic capitalist trading sphere, to thwart the leftward drift of European politics, and to convince European powers to line up behind the U.S. policy of containing the Soviet Union.[13] Even the Korean War,[14] LaFeber insisted, was fought to preserve America's credibility among the European allies as the bulwark against Communism. After the mid-1950s both America and Russia shifted their focus from Europe to the newly emerging nations of the world, and the Cold War entered its second phase. The Vietnam War, according to LaFeber, represented an American foreign policy failure because it sought a military solution to the economic, social, and political problems of an emerging post-colonial nation. Stubbornly applying the Truman Doctrine, which imagined aggression or subversion

---

[12]See Chapter 4 in this volume.

[13]See also Michael Hogan, *The Marshall Plan: America, Britain, and the Reconstruction of Western Europe, 1947–1952* (New York, 1987), and *The Cross of Iron: Harry S. Truman and the Origins of the National Security State* (New York, 1998); and Thomas G. Paterson, *Soviet-American Confrontation: Postwar Reconstruction and the Origins of the Cold War* (Baltimore, 1973).

[14]On Korea, see also Bruce Cummings, *Origins of the Korean War: Liberation and the Emergence of Separate Regimes* (Princeton, 1981).

as the source of disorder, to an anti-colonial revolution, U.S. policy makers produced a tragedy of immense proportions.[15]

The work of Williams and these revisionists served as a point of departure for a large number of radical scholars. In 1968 Gabriel Kolko, whose earlier study of the origins of "political capitalism" from 1900 to 1917 had heralded the advent of the New Left school of historical interpretation,[16] made a detailed case for locating the origins of the Cold War in the narrow period from 1943 to 1945. The United States had acted not only to win the war in these two years, Kolko argued, but to gain the political and economic leverage needed to extend America's influence throughout the postwar world. Thus Kolko, like Williams, viewed the United States as a counterrevolutionary force bent on making the world safe for American hegemony.[17] Kolko's assumptions regarding America's postwar policies were typical of many New Left scholars. They, like he, assumed first that the United States, not Russia, was mainly responsible for bringing on the Cold War and for continuing threats to international peace and stability. Second, they assumed that, because American capitalism was dependent upon ever-expanding foreign markets for survival, the United States was dedicated to worldwide counterrevolution. And third, because of these two assumptions, they located the origins of the Cold War in the years preceding the Truman Doctrine: the World War II years, or back to World War I, or even as early as the beginnings of U.S. continental and overseas empire in the nineteenth century.

The revisionist view of the Cold War—in both moderate and radical forms—could not have emerged with any vigor had it not been for the broader emergence of the New Left in the 1960s. This decade witnessed the development of sharply critical views among American intellectuals about the nation's race relations, its economic inequalities, and, increasingly, its foreign interventions. The escalating war in Vietnam especially led many scholars to critically survey America's record of "free world leadership." They uncovered the record of U.S. support for right-wing dictatorships and subversion of popularly elected governments in Latin America. They questioned similar policies toward revolutionary, post-colonial states in Africa and Asia. Moreover, they feared

---

[15]Walter LaFeber, *America, Russia, and the Cold War, 1945–1966* (New York, 1967). See also Christopher Lasch, "The Cold War, Revisited and Re-Visioned," *New York Times*, January 14, 1968. On Vietnam, the place to start is George C. Herring, *America's Longest War: The United States and Vietnam, 1950–1975*, 3/e (New York, 1996); and see most recently Robert McMahon, *The Limits of Empire: The United States and Southeast Asia since World War II* (New York, 1999).

[16]See Chapter 3 in this volume.

[17]Gabriel Kolko, *The Politics of War: The World and United States Foreign Policy, 1943–1945* (New York, 1968). See also Joyce and Gabriel Kolko, *The Limits of Power: The World and United States Foreign Policy, 1945–1954* (New York, 1972).

that American leaders were so conditioned to fighting the "Communist menace" that they tended to see enemies where none existed. In places as different as Guatemala, the Dominican Republic, the Congo, Indonesia, and, most horrifically, Vietnam, the United States had committed itself to endless intervention, low-level and indirect to begin with, but readily escalating into direct and bloody combat if circumstances or calculations went awry.[18] Moreover, the United States had locked itself into a nuclear arms race that seemed only too well captured in the acronym MAD—mutual assured destruction. That race not only drained immense resources from American taxpayers, but also terrorized every inhabitant of the globe with the prospect that some "brush-fire war" might spiral out of control and provoke a nuclear confrontation between the superpowers. The 1962 Cuban missile crisis proved that such a possibility was not so remote.[19]

Some orthodox scholars reacted with undisguised anger and even contempt toward the revisionist challenge. Robert J. Maddox, for example, accused seven leading revisionist historians of distorting facts to prove their thesis. "Stated briefly," he charged, "the most striking characteristic of revisionist historiography has been the extent to which New Left authors have revised the evidence itself."[20]

As orthodox and revisionist scholars faced off in their own little cold war in the 1960s, others followed a distinct alternative line of interpretation that styled itself "realist." The realist school represented, in some ways, a middle-of-the-road position on the origins of the Cold War. Whereas orthodox historians saw the United States reluctantly committing itself to the containment of Soviet aggression, and revisionists saw the United States relentlessly expanding its hegemony, realists saw rival empires doing what empires normally do: defending and, wherever possible, expanding their spheres of influence. Unlike the revisionists, the realists were disinclined to condemn containment, which in their eyes represented a necessary response to Russian expansionism. On the other hand, they also refused to condemn the Soviet Union's pursuit of a legitimate sphere of influence. They criticized orthodox scholarship because of its moralistic rendering of U.S. benevolence and Soviet perfidy, and its tendency to view conflicts of interests through a distorting lens of anticommunist ideology.

---

[18]See, for example, Walter LaFeber, *Inevitable Revolutions: The United States in Central America* (New York, 1983; 2/e, 1993); Richard Barnet, *Intervention and Revolution: The United States in the Third World*, rev. ed. (New York, 1972); and *Roots of War: The Men and Institutions Behind U.S. Foreign Policy* (New York, 1972).

[19]James G. Blight and David A. Welch, *On the Brink: Americans and Soviets Reexamine the Cuban Missile Crisis* (New York, 1989). For a view of the missile crisis from the Soviet perspective, see Timothy Naftali and Alexandr Fursenko, *One Hell of a Gamble: Khrushchev, Castro, and Kennedy, 1958–1964* (New York, 1997).

[20]Robert J. Maddox, *The New Left and the Origins of the Cold War* (Princeton, 1973), pp. 10–11.

The realists, as their name implies, interpreted foreign relations in terms of the requirements of *realpolitik*—the play of long-term national interests and the power politics deployed to defend and promote them. They tended therefore to view the Cold War as a traditional power conflict, comparable to previous struggles to prevent a single nation from dominating Europe's east-central regions, or more generally to preserve the European (and eventually Asian) balance of power. Predictably, historians of the realist school declined to assign to leaders of the United States or U.S.S.R. moral responsibility for bringing on the Cold War. They preferred to attempt dispassionate identification of long-term national interests and pragmatic policy options. What they abhorred most was the prospect of irrational swings between ideological crusade and isolationist disgust, between missionary fervor and morbid national self-criticism. The policy-makers they lauded were (perhaps like themselves) wise men: cool-headed, far-seeing, not easily distracted, and capable of decisiveness under pressure.

Like the other two schools of Cold War historiography, the realists could trace their origins back to the late 1940s and early 1950s. Their writings sprang at first from a desire to counter strong right-wing criticisms of Roosevelt's foreign policy. These criticisms held that Roosevelt's misunderstanding or weakness regarding the Soviets led directly to the communist subjugation of eastern Europe. But the realists argued that Roosevelt had been faced with a *fait accompli;* his diplomatic options were severely limited by the fact that powerful Russian armies occupied every nation that was to become part of the eastern bloc. The realists held that blame for the Cold War belonged either to both sides or, more accurately, to neither. Indeed, neither the United States nor the Soviet Union had wanted to precipitate a conflict. Both had hoped that cooperation among the allies would continue—but, as much as possible, on their own terms. Each country had sought limited objectives and expected the other to accept them as such. However, whenever one side made a move in pursuit of its limited objectives, the other side misread the act as a threat and, in reacting accordingly, triggered a countermeasure which led to increasing escalation. Thus, Russia's determination to stabilize its border by creating satellite states in an unstable eastern Europe provoked western European fantasies of Russian tanks peering (like German ones a few years earlier) across the English Channel. And American efforts to secure long-term interests in the Pacific seemed to Russians just another demonstration of the capitalist determination to encircle and strangle the Soviet Union. As a result of these misperceptions, small and otherwise manageable crises led inevitably to a widening, global conflict: the Cold War.

No scholar articulated the realist interpretation more fully or eloquently than the political scientist Hans J. Morgenthau. His many published works amounted to a sustained critique of what he called the "legalistic-moralistic" tradition of foreign policy. His *In Defense of the National Interest: A Critical Examination of American Foreign Policy,* published in 1951, surveyed the whole span of America's foreign policies since 1776, condemning as utopian almost all that it surveyed. Only in the years since World War II, he suggested, had Americans become more realistic and formulated their policy on the basis of power politics and national interest. Yet even then, irrational anticommunism and the widespread fantasy that U.S. omnipotence would lead to a conflict-free world distorted American policy. In the postwar era, Morgenthau explained, American policymakers failed to see the essential continuity in the expansionist objectives long sought by czars and commissars. They therefore mistook the security goals of a continental empire for the ideological goals of a revolutionary movement. Morgenthau criticized orthodox scholars for reflecting rather than correcting these provincial American misreadings of reality.[21]

Though the realist school had emerged to counter an overly conspiratorial right-wing view of the origins of U.S.-Soviet tensions, it turned its energies against the left-wing revisionists in the 1960s. Realists agreed with revisionists like Alperovitz, who claimed that the United States had used its monopoly of atomic weapons to force other nation-states into submission. They acknowledged that the United States had dropped two atom bombs not just to defeat Japan, but to do so before the Soviet Union could enter the Pacific theater of war. Unlike the revisionists, however, realists did not scold American leaders for having made these decisions. America, they wrote, had reason to fear that Moscow might attempt to do in the Far East what it appeared to be doing in eastern Europe. Even if they partly misread Soviet motives, the Americans' new concern for balance of power in Asia was a mark of growing maturity in thinking about international relations.

The realists reacted with even greater disquiet to the more radical New Left revisionists. In his review of Kolko's *The Politics of War,* Morgenthau charged that the radical revisionist interpretation reflected the mood of a generation that, having discovered the simplistic error of those elders who blamed the Soviets for the Cold War, now seemed determined to commit an equally simplistic error, locating blame for the Cold War entirely with the United States. That mood, Morgenthau noted,

> . . . reacts negatively to the simple and simplistic equation, obligatory
> during the War and postwar periods, of American interests and poli-

---

[21]Hans J. Morgenthau, *Politics Among Nations: The Struggle for Power and Peace* (New York, 1948), and *In Defense of the National Interest: A Critical Examination of American Foreign Policy* (New York, 1951). It should be noted that George Kennan's rethinking of his earlier views brought him effectively into the realist school: see footnote 2 in this chapter.

cies with democratic virtue and wisdom, and those of their enemies with totalitarian folly and vice. As the orthodox historiography of the Second World War and the Cold War expressed and justified that ideological juxtaposition, so the revisionism of Professor Kolko expresses and justifies the new mood of ideological sobriety. However, given the moralism behind American political thinking regardless of its content, revisionism tends to be as moralistic in its critique of American foreign policy as orthodoxy is in defending it. While the moralistic approach remains, the moral labels have been reversed: what once was right is now wrong, and vice versa.[22]

One of the most important realist attacks was upon the question of what motivated U.S. and Soviet policy. The political scientist Joseph R. Starobin, a former Communist who broke with the American Communist Party in the 1950s, insisted that most American historians—the revisionists in particular—were blind to the true nature of Soviet calculations. During and after World War II, Starobin argued, the Soviet Union determined to overcome the ideological diversity within the Communist parties around the world, and to do so with whatever ruthlessness was necessary. All Communists had to set their rudders on the course determined by Stalin; all interests would be submerged in the interests of the Soviet state.[23] Viewed in this light, the struggle between the Soviet Union and the United States was the product of an internal crisis within the former. Starobin's realism was really a kind of counter-revisionism. As Williams and other revisionists found the origins of the Cold War in internal American political and economic pressures, so Starobin found it in internal Soviet pressures.

Another realist attack on the revisionists came from Robert W. Tucker, who insisted that New Left revisionism was based on a simple-minded explanatory mechanism that related all policy decisions to the imperatives of a capitalist economy.[24] Turning the tables on the revisionists, Tucker argued that if the Williams school was right about the domestic sources of foreign policy, they would have to explore cultural, social, and political motives, not just economic ones, in explaining the making of Cold War policy.

Like Tucker, most realists strove for an almost Olympian dispas-

---

[22]Hans J. Morgenthau, "Historical Justice and the Cold War," *New York Review of Books*, July 10, 1969. See also Lloyd C. Gardner, Arthur M. Schlesinger, Jr., and Hans J. Morgenthau, *The Origins of the Cold War* (Waltham, Mass., 1970), for a fascinating debate among the authors, who represent respectively revisionist, orthodox, and realist positions.

[23]Joseph R. Starobin, "Origins of the Cold War: The Communist Dimension," *Foreign Affairs* 47 (July 1969): 681–696.

[24]Robert W. Tucker, *The Radical Left and American Foreign Policy* (Baltimore, 1971).

sion and even-handedness. In *The Cold War as History*, Louis Halle described the mutual mystifications that handicapped Americans and Russians both, stressing the essentially tragic nature of the conflict. He suggested that neither side was really to blame for the Cold War. Misconceptions on both sides had led to the rise of ideological myths, which usually had little relation to social realities. The West, led by the United States, was governed by the myth of a monolithic Communist conspiracy dedicated to Soviet global domination. The Communists, from Lenin to Mao, were under the spell of another myth, that of a world divided between capitalist-imperialists and peasant-proletarians, the latter on the verge of revolution. Such ideological renderings of a world in crisis helped to promote the confrontational thinking that was the hallmark of the Cold War—and Cold War histories—on both sides.[25]

The realist Charles S. Maier likewise criticized the ideological tendentiousness of scholars on both sides of the orthodox/revisionist debate on the origins of the Cold War. "Spokesmen for each side," he noted in 1970, "present the reader with a total explanatory system that accounts for all phenomena, eliminates the possibility of disproof, and thus transcends the usual process of historical reasoning. . . . As a result much Cold War historiography has become a confrontation manqué—debatable philosophy taught by dismaying example."[26] The tendency of some historians to avoid extremes and thereby blur the lines between different interpretations is exemplified in Martin Sherwin's study of the decision to use the atomic bomb. Sherwin rejects Gar Alperovitz's contention that Truman used the bomb primarily to intimidate the Soviets. Instead, he insists, the decision to use the bomb was essentially made by Roosevelt early in the war. Truman used the bomb (as Roosevelt would have) to win the war against Japan, not to stop the Soviet Union from entering the war in the Far East. If Truman hoped that Stalin would recognize America's atomic monopoly and adopt a more conciliatory policy as a result, this would be a by-product, not a goal, of wartime nuclear strategy.[27]

The effect that evenhanded realism has had on revisionist scholars is similarly evident in the work of Daniel Yergin. Although conceding the brutality of Stalin's regime (an orthodox point), Yergin nevertheless insisted that the "U.S.S.R. behaved as a traditional Great Power"

---

[25]Halle, *The Cold War as History*.

[26]Charles A. Maier, "Revisionism and the Interpretation of Cold War Origins," *Perspectives in American History* 4 (1970): 311–347.

[27]Martin J. Sherwin, *A World Destroyed: The Atomic Bomb and the Grand Alliance* (New York, 1975). See also Robert L. Messer, *The End of an Alliance: James F. Byrnes, Roosevelt, Truman, and the Origins of the Cold War* (Chapel Hill, N.C., 1982); and Gregg F. Herken, *The Winning Weapon: The Atomic Bomb in the Cold War* (New York, 1981).

(a realist point), and that American leaders "downplayed the possibilities for diplomacy and accommodation" (a revisionist point).[28]

Events of the last decade have only added energy to the already apparent tendency within the scholarly world to find points of convergence among rival interpretations and to rethink the history of the last half-century. The collapse of the Soviet empire and the overthrow of Communism there and in eastern Europe have brought the Cold War effectively to an end. As the contours of the international order have changed radically, the need to justify (or condemn) containment or to fix blame for the advent of the Cold War has diminished, opening the way to a fundamental re-evaluation of American diplomacy. Moreover, the opening of Soviet archives to scholars has been the first opportunity to test interpretations based solely on American (or western European) sources, and to uncover a range of Soviet motives and strategic calculations that were simply unknowable for 50 years. In a paper published in 1983, the orthodox scholar John Lewis Gaddis signaled this new era by suggesting "post-revisionism" as the most accurate description of the new historiographical situation.

For Gaddis, post-revisionism meant the rejection of both the classic revisionist and orthodox interpretive systems, but the salvaging of important insights from both. Nevertheless, this new interpretation showed strong traces of his orthodox pedigree. While he credited revisionists with introducing to scholarship a healthy acknowledgment of the United States' imperial ambitions, he emphasized even more the essentially defensive and sometimes uncertain character of U.S. foreign policy. He also argued that the negative perceptions of the Soviet Union that guided containment diplomacy were clearly correct, as preliminary investigation of Soviet archives proves; moreover, these perceptions were hardly a uniquely American obsession, as shown by the fact that most Europeans, as well as inhabitants of emerging nations, shared them.[29] Gaddis's tentative call for détente with his historiographical adversaries proved less durable than real-world reconciliation among former Cold War enemies. In the essay that follows, indeed, Gaddis embodies that vindicationist tendency that has emerged very strongly among American and western scholars in the last several years.[30] Even the title of the book from which this essay is

---

[28]Daniel Yergin, *Shattered Peace: The Origins of the Cold War and the National Security State* (Boston, 1977), pp. 11–12.

[29]John Lewis Gaddis, "The Emerging Post-Revisionist Synthesis on the Origins of the Cold War," *Diplomatic History* 7 (Summer 1983): 171–191; and responses by a number of prominent historians in this same issue, pp. 191–204. See also Gaddis, *The United States and the End of the Cold War: Implications, Reconsiderations, Provocations* (New York, 1992).

[30]See Arthur Schlesinger, Jr., "Some Lessons from the Cold War," *Diplomatic History* 16 (Winter 1992): 47–53.

drawn, *We Now Know*, strikes a clear note of triumph: not only did "we" win the Cold War, but we won because we are better. As one opinion writer for the *New York Times* put it, the Cold War ended because "freedom" conquered "slavery."[31] And even Russian scholars have joined the chorus of condemnation directed at the entire Soviet experiment which Lenin conceived and Stalin brought to monstrous fruition.[32] At the very least, it has become clearer than ever that, had Hitler's Holocaust not claimed the ghastly privilege of embodying evil in the modern world, Stalin's Soviet nightmare would have done so.

Despite the strong appeal of this essentially neo-orthodox vindicationism, the revisionist critique of the Cold War, and of American foreign policy more generally, have not disappeared. In a sweeping 1990 review of the historical literature on U.S. Cold War diplomacy, Edward Pessen charged that America's postwar call to arms against the Soviet threat "was either groundless, absurd, false, or known by those making the charges to be false." Questions that should have been asked about America's Cold War policy "went largely unasked." Indeed, Pessen, a historian of nineteenth-century American history who never identified with the New Left, went beyond even the most extreme revisionist condemnations of American diplomacy. "The most rigid relativism," he concluded, "cannot deny that our government's flagrant lies, plans to incinerate much of the world, secret wars, and arbitrary assassinations are unworthy actions."[33]

More informed and measured defenses of revisionist views can be found in the work of such historians as Melvyn P. Leffler and H. W. Brands. Leffler's subtly argued and deeply researched account of the origins of the national security state clearly retains the revisionist insistence that American imperial ambitions, heavily influenced by the interests of major economic and political elites, caused the Cold War every bit as much as the Soviets did. And he shows persuasively how

---

[31]Quoted in Allen Hunter, ed., *Rethinking the Cold War* (Philadelphia, 1998), p. 4. For a thorough neo-orthodox or "vindicationist" review of the current historiography see Douglas J. MacDonald, "Communist Bloc Expansion in the Early Cold War," *International Security* (Winter 1995–96): 152–188. The Cold War International History Project, based at the Woodrow Wilson Center in Washington, publishes a *Bulletin* containing documents from Soviet (and Chinese) archives, which support a range of realist and post-revisionist interpretations.

[32]See for example Dmitri Volkogonov, *Lenin: A New Biography* (New York, 1994); Vojtech Mastny, *Cold War and Soviet Insecurity: The Stalin Years* (New York, 1996); Vladimir Zubok and Constantine Pleshakov, *The Kremlin's Cold War: From Stalin to Khrushchev* (Cambridge, Mass., 1996).

[33]Edward Pessen, "Appraising American Cold War Policy by Its Means of Implementation," *Reviews in American History* 18 (December 1990): 453–465; and also his *Losing Our Souls: The American Experience in the Cold War* (Chicago, 1993). Informed critiques of "vindicationism," as well as bibliographic references to a broad range of recent scholarship, can be found in Hunter, *Rethinking the Cold War*.

much damage the Cold War did to American society and political culture in the postwar decades.[34] In the essay following, Brands acknowledges the realist insight that the Cold War was a real "strategic
struggle"; it was not, as some revisionists had made it seem, just "the
latest episode in an ongoing search for enemies" by elites intent on
browbeating Americans into patriotic unity. Nevertheless, Brands insists on reasserting the revisionist insight that American elites and
broader publics did use the devil of Soviet communism to resolve their
own internal contradictions and rationalize their own worldly ambitions, thus helping to precipitate and sustain the Cold War. In numerous ways, as Hunter's collection of essays reveals, revisionist
historians continue to challenge complacent assumptions about the
efficacy of nuclear deterrence, the morality of both American and Soviet intentions, the bi-polarity of Cold War international relations, and
the "peacefulness" of an era that avoided nuclear holocaust but sacrificed millions of lives in "brush-fire wars" in Latin America, Asia, and
Africa.

The end of the Cold War has made possible a convergence of views
on a number of important questions, but has not settled all questions
about its causes and consequences. Did the Cold War commence at the
end of or during World War II, or did its roots stretch back to World
War I or even earlier? Was the Soviet occupation of eastern Europe the
realization of a centuries-old Russian dream of a sphere of influence, a
reaction to the more recent devastation sustained during the Nazi invasion, or an advance in the revolutionary strategy of an international
communist movement? Has the course of American diplomacy since
the Spanish-American War been committed to the defense of a global
status quo or the aggressive pursuit of hegemony? To what extent were
ever-expanding foreign markets necessary for the survival of American
capitalism, and what effect did belief in such a necessity have on the
actual making of foreign policy? Was America's containment policy
aimed at checking a Soviet plan to spread communism throughout the
world or at subjugating weaker nations to the purposes of American
capitalism? Was the Cold War "our" fault, "theirs," or a combination?
The end of the Cold War has altered the way historians address these
questions—but not the need to ask them.

---

[34]Melvyn P. Leffler, The Specter of Communism: The United States and the Origins
of the Cold War, 1917–1953 (New York, 1994). See also his A Preponderance of Power:
National Security, The Truman Administration, and the Cold War (Stanford, 1992); his
thoughtful reconsideration of one of the most debated questions in this field, "Truman's
Decision to Drop the Atomic Bomb," IHJ Bulletin 15 (Summer 1995): 1–7; and his recent
masterly overview of the historiography, "The Cold War: What Do 'We Now Know'?"
American Historical Review (April 1999): 501–524, which takes direct aim at Gaddis's
vindicationism.

JOHN LEWIS GADDIS (1941–　　) is professor of history at Yale University. He is the author of The United States and the Origins of the Cold War, 1941–1947 *(1972),* Strategies of Containment *(1982), and* The Long Peace *(1987).*

The idea of containment proceeded from the proposition that if there was not to be one world, then there must not be another world war either. It would be necessary to keep the peace while preserving the balance of power: the gap that had developed during the 1930s between the perceived requirements of peace and power was not to happen again. If geopolitical stability could be restored in Europe, time would work against the Soviet Union and in favor of the Western democracies. Authoritarianism need not be the "wave of the future"; sooner or later even Kremlin authoritarians would realize this fact and change their policies. "[T]he Soviet leaders are prepared to recognize *situations,* if not arguments," George F. Kennan wrote in 1948. "If, therefore, situations can be created in which it is clearly not to the advantage of their power to emphasize the elements of conflict in their relations with the outside world, then their actions, and even the tenor of their propaganda to their own people, *can* be modified."

This idea of time being on the side of the West came—at least as far as Kennan was concerned—from studying the history of empires. Edward Gibbon had written in *The Decline and Fall of the Roman Empire* that "there is nothing more contrary to nature than the attempt to hold in obedience distant provinces," and few things Kennan ever read made a greater or more lasting impression on him. He had concluded during the early days of World War II that Hitler's empire could not last, and in the months after the war, he applied similar logic to the empire Stalin was setting out to construct in Eastern Europe. The territorial acquisitions and spheres of influence the Soviet Union had obtained would ultimately become a source of *insecurity* for it, both because of the resistance to Moscow's control that was sure to grow within those regions and because of the outrage the nature of that control was certain to provoke in the rest of the world. "Soviet power, like the capitalist world of its own conception, bears within it the seeds of its own decay," Kennan insisted in the most famous of all Cold War texts, his anonymously published 1947 article on "The Sources of Soviet Conduct." He added, "the sprouting of those seeds is well advanced."

All of this would do the Europeans little good, though, if the new and immediate Soviet presence in their midst should so intimidate them that their own morale collapsed. The danger here came not from the prospect that the Red Army would invade and occupy the rest of the continent, as Hitler had tried to do; rather, its demoralized and exhausted inhabitants might simply vote in communist parties who would then do Moscow's bidding. The initial steps in the strategy of containment—stopgap military and economic aid to Greece and Turkey, the more carefully designed and ambitious Marshall Plan—took place within this context: the idea was to produce instant intangible reassurance as well as eventual tangible reinforcement. Two things had to happen in order for intimidation to occur, Kennan liked to argue: the intimidator had to make the effort, but, equally important, the target of those efforts had to agree to be intimidated. The initiatives of 1947 sought to generate sufficient self-confidence to prevent such acquiescence in intimidation from taking place.

Some historians have asserted that these fears of collapse were exaggerated: that economic recovery on the continent was already underway, and that the Europeans themselves were never as psychologically demoralized as the Americans made them out to be. Others have added that the real crisis at the time was within an American economy that could hardly expect to function hegemonically if Europeans lacked the dollars to purchase its products. Still others have suggested that the Marshall Plan was the means by which American officials sought to project overseas the mutually-beneficial relationship between business, labor, and government they had worked out at home: the point was not to make Wilsonian values a model for the rest of the world, but rather the politics of productivity that had grown out of American corporate capitalism. All of these arguments have merit: at a minimum they have forced historians to place the Marshall Plan in a wider economic, social, and historical context; more broadly they suggest that the American empire had its own distinctive internal roots, and was not solely and simply a response to the Soviet external challenge.

At the same time, though, it is difficult to see how a strategy of containment could have developed—with the Marshall Plan as its centerpiece—had there been nothing to contain. One need only recall the early 1920s, when similar conditions of European demoralization, Anglo-French exhaustion, and American economic predominance had existed; yet no American empire arose as after World War II. The critical difference, of course, was national security: Pearl Harbor created an atmosphere of vulnerability Americans had not known since the earliest days of the republic, and the Soviet Union by 1947 had become the most plausible source of threat. The American empire arose *primarily*, therefore, not from internal causes, as had the Soviet empire, but from a perceived external danger powerful enough to overcome American isolationism.

Washington's wartime vision of a postwar international order had
been premised on the concepts of political self-determination and economic integration. It was intended to work by assuming a set of *common* interests that would cause other countries to *want* to be affiliated
with it rather than to resist it. The Marshall Plan, to a considerable extent, met those criteria: although it operated on a regional rather than
a global scale, it did seek to promote democracy through an economic
recovery that would proceed along international and not nationalist
lines. Its purpose was to create an American sphere of influence, to be
sure, but one that would allow those within it considerable freedom.
The principles of democracy and open markets required nothing less,
but there were two additional and more practical reasons for encouraging such autonomy. First, the United States itself lacked the capability
to administer a large empire; the difficulties of running occupied Germany and Japan were proving daunting enough. Second, the idea of autonomy was implicit in the task of restoring European self-confidence;
for who, if not Europeans themselves, was to say when the self-confidence of Europeans had been restored?

Finally, it is worth noting that even though Kennan and the other
early architects of containment made use of imperial analogies, they
did not see themselves as creating an empire, but rather a restored balance of power. Painfully—perhaps excessively—aware of limited
American resources, fearful that the domestic political consensus in
favor of internationalism might not hold, they set out to reconstitute
independent centers of power in Europe and Asia. These would be integrated into the world capitalist system, and as a result they would
certainly fall under the influence of its new hegemonic manager, the
United States. But there was no intention here of creating satellites in
anything like the sense that Stalin understood that term; rather, the
idea was that "third forces" would resist Soviet expansionism while
preserving as much as possible of the multilateralist agenda American
officials had framed during World War II. What the United States really
wanted, State Department official John D. Hickerson commented in
1948, was "not merely an extension of US influence but a real European organization strong enough to say 'no' both to the Soviet Union
and to the United States, if our actions should seem so to require."

The American empire, therefore, reflected little imperial consciousness or design. An anti-imperial tradition dating back to the
American Revolution partially accounted for this: departures from
that tradition, as in the Spanish-American War of 1898 and the Philippine insurrection that followed, had only reinforced its relevance—
outside the Western hemisphere. So too did a constitutional structure
that forced even imperially minded leaders like Wilson and the two
Roosevelts to accommodate domestic attitudes that discouraged imperial behavior long after national capabilities had made it possible. And

even as those internal constraints diminished dramatically in World War II—they never entirely dropped away—Americans still found it difficult to think of themselves as an imperial power. The idea of remaking the international system in such a way as to transcend empires altogether still lingered, but so too did doubts as to whether the United States was up to the task. In the end it was again external circumstances—the manner in which Stalin managed his own empire and the way in which this pushed Europeans into preferring its American alternative—that brought the self-confidence necessary to administer imperial responsibilities into line with Washington's awareness of their existence. . . .

It is apparent now, even if it was not always at the time, that the Soviet Union did not manage its empire particularly well. Because of his personality and the structure of government he built around it, Stalin was—shall we say—less than receptive to the wishes of those nations that fell within the Soviet sphere. He viewed departures from his instructions with deep suspicion, but he also objected to manifestations of independent behavior where instructions had not yet been given. As a result, he put his European followers in an impossible position: they could satisfy him only by seeking his approval for whatever he had decided they should do—even, at times, before he had decided that they should do it. . . .

The Americans' unexpected offer of Marshall Plan aid to the Soviet Union and Eastern Europe in June 1947, caused even greater difficulties for Stalin's management of empire—which is precisely what Kennan hoped for when he recommended making it. In one of the stranger illusions arising from their ideology, Soviet leaders had always anticipated United States economic assistance in some form. Lenin himself expected American capitalists, ever in search of foreign markets, to invest eagerly in the newly formed USSR, despite its official antipathy toward them. Stalin hoped for a massive American reconstruction loan after World War II, and even authorized Molotov early in 1945 to offer acceptance of such assistance in order to help the United States stave off the economic crisis that Marxist analysis showed must be approaching. When the Marshall Plan was announced Stalin's first reaction was that the capitalists must be desperate. He concluded, therefore, that the Soviet Union and its East European allies should indeed participate in the plan, and quickly dispatched Molotov and a large delegation of economic experts to Paris to take part in the conference that was to determine the nature and extent of European needs.

But then Stalin began to reconsider. His ambassador in Washington, Nikolai Novikov, warned that the American offer to the Soviet Union could not be sincere: "A careful analysis of the Marshall Plan shows that ultimately it comes down to forming a West European bloc as a tool of US policy. All the good wishes accompanying the plan are

demagogic official propaganda serving as a smokescreen." Soviet intelligence picked up reports—accurate enough—that American Under-
Secretary of State William Clayton had been conspiring with British
officials on using the Marshall Plan to reintegrate Germany into the
West European economy and to deny further reparations shipments to
the Soviet Union. This information, together with indications at Paris
that the Americans would require a coordinated European response,
caused Stalin to change his mind and order his own representatives to
walk out. "The Soviet delegation saw those claims as a bid to interfere
in the internal affairs of European countries," Molotov explained
lamely, "thus making the economies of these countries dependent on
US interests." . . .

Unfortunately, the Czechs and the Poles, following the earlier instructions, had already announced their intention to attend. The Poles
quickly changed their mind but the Czechs procrastinated, more because of confusion than determined resistance. . . .

. . . Stalin's intentions were now clear to all including himself:
there would be no East European participation in the Marshall Plan, or
in any other American scheme for the rehabilitation of Europe. "I
went to Moscow as the Foreign Minister of an independent sovereign
state," Czech Foreign Minister Jan Masaryk commented bitterly. "I returned as a lackey of the Soviet government."

But the Kremlin boss too had shed some illusions. Marxist-Leninist
analyses had long predicted, not just a postwar economic collapse in the
West, but eventual conflict between the British and the Americans. In a
September 1946 report from Washington which Molotov had carefully
annotated, Ambassador Novikov had insisted that "the United States
regards England as its greatest potential competitor." The Anglo-American relationship, "despite the temporary attainment of agreements on
very important questions, [is] plagued with great internal contradictions
and cannot be lasting." By early 1947, Stalin was even offering the
British a military alliance: as one report to Molotov put it, "Soviet diplomacy has in England practically unlimited possibilities." What the Marshall Plan showed was how wrong these assessments were. Capitalists,
it now appeared, could indeed reconcile their differences; they considered the Soviet Union a greater threat to all than each posed to the other;
time was not on Moscow's side. Ideology again had led Stalin into romanticism and away from reality. Once he realized this—in Europe at
least—he never quite recovered from the shock. . . .

The United States, in contrast, proved surprisingly adept at managing an empire. Having attained their authority through democratic
processes, its leaders were experienced—as their counterparts in
Moscow were not—in the arts of persuasion, negotiation and compromise. . . .

. . . Americans so often deferred to the wishes of allies during the early Cold War that some historians have seen the Europeans—especially the British—as having managed *them*. . . .

But one can easily make too much of this argument. Truman and his advisers were not babes in the woods. They knew what they were doing at each stage, and did it only because they were convinced their actions would advance American interests. They never left initiatives entirely up to the Europeans: they insisted on an integrated plan for economic recovery and quite forcefully reined in prospective recipients when it appeared that their requests would exceed what Congress would approve. "[I]n the end we would not *ask* them," Kennan noted, "we would just *tell* them, what they would get." The Americans were flexible enough, though, to accept and build upon ideas that came from allies; they also frequently let allies determine the timing of actions taken. As a consequence, the British, French, and other West Europeans came to feel that they had a stake in what Washington was doing, despite the fact that it amounted to their own incorporation within an American sphere of influence.

One might argue, to be sure, that European elites agreed to all of this for their own self-interested reasons; that the European "masses" were never consulted. It is worth remembering, however, that free elections ultimately ratified alignment with the United States in every country where that took place. The newly-formed Central Intelligence Agency, not always confident of such outcomes, did take it upon itself at times to manipulate democratic processes, most conspicuously in the Italian elections of April 1948. But these covert efforts—together with clandestine CIA support for anti-communist labor unions and intellectual organizations—could hardly have succeeded had there not already existed in Europe a widespread predisposition to see the Americans as the lesser of two evils, and perhaps even as a force for good. "I am entirely convinced," the French political theorist Raymond Aron insisted, "that for an anti-Stalinist there is no escape from the acceptance of American leadership." French peasants did not see it all that differently.

The habits of democracy were no less significant when it came to defeated adversaries. . . .

The United States could of course hold out the prospect of economic recovery and the Soviet Union could not: this certainly made the advantages of democracy more evident than they might otherwise have been. But democratization . . . was well under way before there was any assurance that Germans would receive Marshall Plan aid or anything comparable. Authoritarianism, which was all Moscow would or could provide, was by far the less attractive alternative. "Soviet officers bolshevized their zone," Naimark has concluded, "not because there was a plan to do so, but because that was the only way they knew to organize society. . . . By their own actions, the Soviet authorities created enemies out of potential friends." Or, as General Clay recalled years afterwards: "We began to look like angels, not because we were angels, but we looked [like] that in comparison to what was going on in Eastern Europe."

The Americans simply did not find it necessary, in building a sphere of influence, to impose unrepresentative governments or brutal treatment upon the peoples that fell within it. Where repressive regimes already existed, as in Greece, Turkey, and Spain, serious doubts arose in Washington as to whether the United States should be supporting them at all, however useful they might be in containing Soviet expansionism. Nor, having constructed their empire, did Americans follow the ancient imperial practice of "divide and rule." Rather, they used economic leverage to overcome nationalist tendencies, thereby encouraging the Europeans' emergence as a "third force" whose obedience could not always be assumed. It was as if the Americans were projecting abroad a tradition they had long taken for granted at home: that civility made sense; that spontaneity, within a framework of minimal constraint, was the path to political and economic robustness; that to intimidate or to overmanage was to stifle. The contrast to Stalin's methods of imperial administration could hardly have been sharper.

Stalin saw the need, after learning of the Marshall Plan, to improve his methods of imperial management. He therefore called a meeting of the Soviet and East European communist parties, as well as the French and the Italian communists, to be held in Poland in September 1947, ostensibly for the purpose of exchanging ideas on fraternal cooperation. Only after the delegations had assembled did he reveal his real objective, which was to organize a new coordinating agency for the international communist movement. Stalin had abolished the old Comintern as a wartime gesture of reassurance to the Soviet Union's allies in 1943, and the International Department of the Soviet Communist Party, headed by the veteran Comintern leader, the Bulgarian Georgii Dimitrov, had taken over its functions. What had happened during the spring and summer of 1947 make it clear, though, that these arrangements provided insufficient coordination from Stalin's point of view. . . .

The French communist leader Jacques Duclos summed up the new procedures succinctly: "Paris and Rome will be able to submit their proposals, but they shall have to be content with the decisions to be adopted in Belgrade."

Even with the Cominform in place, the momentary independence Czechoslovakia demonstrated must have continued to weigh on Stalin's mind. That country, more than any other in Eastern Europe, had sought to accommodate itself to Soviet hegemony. Embittered by how easily the British and French had betrayed Czech interests at the Munich conference in 1938, President Eduard Benes welcomed the expansion of Soviet influence while reassuring Marxist-Leninists that they had nothing to fear from the democratic system the Czechs hoped to rebuild after the war. "If you play it well," he told Czech Communist Party leaders in Moscow in 1943, "you'll win."

But Benes meant "win" by democratic means. Although the Communists had indeed done well in the May 1946 parliamentary elections, their popularity began to drop sharply after Stalin forbade Czech participation in the Marshall Plan the following year. Convinced by intelligence reports that the West would not intervene, they therefore took advantage of a February 1948 government crisis to stage a *coup d'état*—presumably with Stalin's approval—that left them in complete control, with no further need to resort to the unpredictabilities of the ballot box. This development came as no surprise in Washington: Kennan had predicted that the Soviet Union would sooner or later crack down on those East European states where communists did not fully dominate the government. Czechoslovakia had figured most prominently on that list. But to an unprepared American and Western European public, the Prague takeover was the most appalling event yet in the emerging Cold War, occurring as it did in the country whose abandonment by the West only ten years earlier had led directly to World War II. There followed shortly thereafter the suicide, or murder, of Masaryk, son of the founder of the country and himself a symbol—now a martyr—to the fragility of Czech liberties.

Because of its dramatic impact, the Czech coup had consequences Stalin could hardly have anticipated. It set off a momentary—and partially manufactured—war scare in Washington. It removed the last Congressional objections to the Marshall Plan, resulting in the final approval of that initiative in April 1948. It accelerated plans by the Americans, the British, and the French to consolidate their occupation zones in Germany and to proceed toward the formation of an independent West German state. And it caused American officials to begin to consider, much more seriously than they had until this point, two ideas Bevin had begun to advance several months earlier: that economic assistance alone would not restore European self-confidence, and that the United States would have to take on direct military responsibilities for defending that portion of the Continent that remained outside Soviet control.

Stalin then chose the late spring of 1948 to attempt a yet further consolidation of the Soviet empire, with even more disastrous results. Reacting to the proposed establishment of a separate West German state, as well as to growing evidence that the East German regime had failed to attract popular support, and to the introduction of a new currency in the American, British, and French sectors of Berlin over which the Russians would have no control, he ordered a progressively tightening blockade around that city, which lay within the Soviet zone. "Let's make a joint effort," he told the East German leaders in March. "Perhaps we can kick them out." Initial indications were that the scheme was working. . . .

But the Soviet leader's plans, by this time, had already begun to backfire. There was now a quite genuine war scare in the West, one that intensified pressures for an American-West European military alliance, accelerated planning for an independent West Germany, further diminished what little support the communists still had outside the Soviet zone, and significantly boosted President Truman's re-election prospects in a contest few at the time thought he could win. Nor did the blockade turn out to be effective. "Clay's attempts to create 'an airlift' connecting Berlin with the western zones have proved futile," Soviet officials in that city prematurely reported to Moscow in April. "The Americans have admitted that the idea would be too expensive." In fact, though, the United States and its allies astonished themselves as well as the Russians by improvising so successful a supply of Berlin by air that there was no need to make concessions. Stalin was left with the choice he had hoped to avoid—capitulation or war—and in May 1949, in one of the most humiliating of all setbacks for Soviet foreign policy, he selected the first alternative by lifting the blockade.

The Berlin crisis demonstrated that Soviet expansionism in Europe had generated sufficient resistance from the United States and its allies to bring that process to a halt. Stalin had never been prepared to risk a military confrontation—at least not in the foreseeable future—and the West's response to the blockade, which included the deployment to British bases of apparently atomic-capable bombers, made it clear that further advances might indeed produce this result. The Soviet leadership, a Red Army general recalled many years later, had not been prepared to commit suicide over Berlin.

There remained, though, the task of consolidating Soviet control over those territories where communists already ruled, and here too 1948 proved to be a turning point, because for the first time this process provoked open resistance. Despite appearances of solidarity, Soviet-Yugoslav relations had become increasingly strained following earlier disagreements over the Red Army's abuse of Yugoslav civilians, plans for a Balkan federation, and support for the Greek communists. The fiercely independent Yugoslavs were finding it difficult to defer to the Soviet Union, whose interests seemed increasingly at odds with those of international communism. Stalin himself alternated between cajoling and bullying their leaders, sometimes including them in lengthy late-night eating and drinking sessions at his dacha, at other times upbraiding them rudely for excessive ideological militance and insufficient attention to Moscow's wishes. Tensions came to a head early in 1948 when the Yugoslavs and the Albanians began considering the possibility of unification. Stalin let it be known that he would not object to Yugoslavia "swallowing" Albania, but this only aroused suspicions among the Yugoslavs, who remembered how the Soviet Union had "swallowed" the Baltic States in 1940 and feared that the precedent might someday apply to them. Their concerns grew when Stalin then reversed course and condemned Belgrade bitterly for sending troops into Albania without consulting Moscow. By June of 1948, these disagreements had become public, and the communist world would never be the same again. . . .

Stalin responded to this insult in a wholly characteristic way: if he could not get at the Yugoslavs themselves, he would get at all other possible Yugoslav sympathizers elsewhere. There followed the East European purge trials, precise replicas of what Stalin had ordered within the Soviet Union a decade earlier when he detected heresy or the prospect of it. By 1949–50, there were few overt Titoists left outside Yugoslavia. But there were also few people left—apart from the party and official bureaucracies who ran it—who believed that they had anything to gain from living within a Soviet sphere of influence: vast numbers of them now became closet Titoists, with results that would make themselves evident periodically over the years in places like East Berlin in 1953, Budapest and Warsaw in 1956, Prague in 1968, and everywhere all at once in 1989.

West Europeans were meanwhile convincing themselves that they had little to lose from living within an American sphere of influence. . . .

. . . Why were allies of the United States willing to give up so much autonomy in order to enhance their own safety? How did the ideas of sovereignty and security, which historically have been difficult to separate, come to be so widely seen as divisible in this situation?

The answer would appear to be that despite a postwar polarization of authority quite at odds, in its stark bilateralism, from what wartime planners had expected, Americans managed to retain the multilateral conception of security they had developed during World War II. They were able to do this because Truman's foreign policy—like Roosevelt's military strategy—reflected the habits of domestic democratic politics. Negotiation, compromise, and consensus-building abroad came naturally to statesmen steeped in the uses of such practices at home: in this sense, the American political tradition served the country better than its realist critics—Kennan definitely among them—believed it did.

Bargains of one kind or another were struck at every step along the way in constructing the American sphere of influence in Western Europe. The Truman administration extended a postwar loan to Great Britain to replace Lend-Lease, but only on the condition that the Labour government dismantle barriers to foreign trade and investment. When the effect proved to be disastrous for the British economy, the Americans moved quickly to relieve the strain by assuming responsibility for economic and military assistance to Greece and Turkey; but at the same time they took advantage of that situation, by way of the Truman Doctrine, to issue a far more sweeping call for containing Soviet expansionism than either Bevin or Attlee had expected. The United States then extended its offer of reconstruction aid to all of Europe under the Marshall Plan, but only on the condition that recipients submerge their old national rivalries and move toward economic and political integration, including Germany in this process.

The West Europeans, unlike the Soviet Union, agreed to this, but soon found a condition of their own to impose upon the Americans. This was the requirement of a formal military alliance with the United States, to which Washington acquiesced—but with the understanding that the British, the French, and their immediate neighbors would in turn agree to the formation of an independent West German state. Confronted with this unpalatable prospect, the French made the best of it by justifying NATO to themselves as an instrument of "double containment," directed against *both* the Soviet Union and the Germans. This made it possible for them to shift from an emphasis on punishing Germany to one directed toward economic cooperation with that country in the form of the Schuman Plan to create a European Coal and Steel Community, an initiative that surprised but gratified the Americans, who had been seeking the resolution of Franco-German rivalries by pushing integration in the first place.

Meanwhile, a less obvious series of social compromises was going on within Western Europe. The Americans worried about the "tilt" toward the Left that had taken place as a result of the war; at the same time, though, they were cautious about pressuring the Europeans to move toward more centrist politics. A few officials in Washington understood that what they called the "non-communist Left" could itself become a center of resistance against the Soviet Union; there was also a more widespread fear that excessively overt pressure might backfire. The West Europeans, though, also made compromises. The United States did not *have* to pressure the French and the Italians very much to move toward the center because the leftward "tilt" in those countries had never extended so far as a rejection of capitalism in the first place. Their people could easily see that the American assistance and protection they wanted would be more likely if they themselves took the initiative in building centrist political coalitions.

What is significant, then, is not simply that the West Europeans invited the United States to construct a sphere of influence and include them within it; it is also that the Americans encouraged the Europeans to share the responsibility for determining how it would function, and that the Europeans were eager to do this. Washington officials were themselves often genuinely uncertain about what to do, and that provides part of the explanation for this pattern of mutual accommodation. But it also developed because the American vision of national security had become international in character: Franklin D. Roosevelt's most important foreign policy legacy may well have been to convince the nation that its security depended upon that of others elsewhere, not simply on whatever measures it might take on its own. Habits of compromise growing out of domestic politics made it easier than one might have thought for a formerly isolationist nation to adapt itself to this new situation; and those compromises, in turn, allowed West Europeans to define their interests in such a way as to find *common* ground with those of the United States.

It would become fashionable to argue, in the wake of American military intervention in Vietnam, the Soviet invasions of Czechoslovakia and Afghanistan, and growing fears of nuclear confrontation that developed during the early 1980s, that there were no significant differences in the spheres of influence Washington and Moscow had constructed in Europe after World War II: these had been, it was claimed, "morally equivalent," denying autonomy quite impartially to all who lived under them. Students of history must make their own judgments about morality, but even a cursory examination of the historical record will show that these imperial structures could hardly have been more different in their origins, their composition, their tolerance of diversity, and as it turned out their durability. It is important to specify just what these differences were.

First, and most important, the Soviet empire reflected the priorities and the practices of a single individual—a latter-day tsar, in every sense of the word. Just as it would have been impossible to separate the Soviet Union's internal structure from the influence of the man who ran it, so too the Soviet sphere of influence in Eastern Europe took on the characteristics of Stalin himself. The process was not immediate: Stalin did allow a certain amount of spontaneity in the political, economic, and intellectual life of that region for a time after the war, just as he had done inside the Soviet Union itself after he had consolidated his position as Lenin's successor in 1929. But when confronted with even the prospect of dissent, to say nothing of challenges to his authority, Stalin's instinct was to smother spontaneity with a thoroughness unprecedented in the modern age. This is what the purges had accomplished inside the USSR during the mid-1930s, and Eastern Europe underwent a similar process after 1947. There was thus a direct linkage from Stalin's earliest thinking on the nationalities question prior to the Bolshevik Revolution through to his management of empire after World War II: the right of self-determination was fine as long as no one sought to practice it.

The American empire was very different: one would have expected this from a country with no tradition of authoritarian leadership whose constitutional structure had long ago enshrined the practices of negotiation, compromise, and the balancing of interests. What is striking about the sphere of influence the United States established in Europe is that its existence and fundamental design reflected as frequently pressures that came *from those incorporated within it* as from the Americans themselves. Washington officials were not at all convinced, at the end of World War II, that their interests would require protecting half the European continent: instead they looked toward a revival of a balance among the Europeans themselves to provide postwar geopolitical stability. Even the Marshall Plan, an unprecedented extension of American assistance, had been conceived with this "third force" principle in mind. It was the Europeans themselves who demanded more: who insisted that their security required a military shield as well as an economic jump-start.

One empire arose, therefore, by invitation, the other by imposition. *Europeans* made this distinction, very much as they had done during the war when they welcomed armies liberating them from the west but feared those that came from the east. They did so because they saw clearly at the time—even if a subsequent generation would not always see—how different American and Soviet empires were likely to be. It is true that the *extent* of the American empire quickly exceeded that of its Soviet counterpart, but this was because *resistance* to expanding American influence was never as great. The American empire may well have become larger, paradoxically, because the American *appetite* for empire was less that of the USSR. The United States had shown, throughout most of its history, that it could survive and even prosper without extending its domination as far as the eye could see. The logic of Lenin's ideological internationalism, as modified by Stalin's Great Russian nationalism and personal paranoia, was that the Soviet Union could not.

The early Cold War in Europe, therefore, cannot be understood by looking at the policies of either the United States or the Soviet Union in isolation. What evolved on the continent was an interactive system in which the actions of each side affected not only the other but also the Europeans; their responses, in turn, shaped further decisions in Washington and Moscow. It quickly became clear—largely because of differences in the domestic institutions of each superpower—that an American empire would accommodate far greater diversity than would one run by the Soviet Union: as a consequence most Europeans accepted and even invited American hegemony, fearing deeply what that of the Russians might entail.

Two paths diverged at the end of World War II. And that, to paraphrase an American poet, really did make all the difference.

H. W. BRANDS (1953–) is professor of history at Texas A&M University. He is the author of Bound to Empire: The United States and the Philippines *(1992),* Inside the Cold War: Loy Henderson and the Rise of the American Empire *(1991), and* The Reckless Decade: America in the 1890s *(1995).*

The ambivalence that characterized much American thinking at the end of the Cold War reflected more than the troubled economy. It indicated a sense that Americans were witnessing the end of an era, an era that in many respects had been a golden age for the United States. The country had never experienced such a period of prosperity. With but a few glitches, the years of the Cold War had seen Americans grow wealthier and wealthier. The American standard of living at the Cold War's end was higher than it had ever been, and if pockets of poverty persisted, and if the country's growth rate had tailed off toward the present, nothing in life is perfect. Nor had America ever been more powerful in world affairs than during the Cold War. Indeed, no country in history had ever been more powerful than the United States had been, especially during the Cold War's early phase. It can make a nation giddy to bestride the world, as America had done from the mid-1940s to the 1960s. Heightening the giddiness was a recognition of the apparent irresistibility of American culture, which persisted into the 1990s. On every continent, in nearly every society, wherever one looked, people were emulating American styles of dress, watching American television shows and movies, eating and drinking American foods and beverages. At least outwardly, the world was becoming more like America all the time.

Yet perhaps the most important feature of the Cold War era, and that which would be missed most, was its conceptual simplicity. Charles Krauthammer was probably right when he argued that nations need enemies. During the Cold War, America had an enemy that could hardly have been improved upon. The Soviet Union was officially atheistic, which earned it the hostility of America's semi-official Christian majority. It was dictatorial, which offended American democratic sensibilities. It was socialistic, which threatened the private-property rights most Americans enjoyed or aspired to. It was militarily powerful, which endangered America's physical security. It was ideo-

---

logically universalist, which set it in direct opposition to the United States, which was too. It was obsessively secretive, which precluded knowing just how dangerous it was. Should interest or inclination inspire one to inflate the threat, or simply to err on the side of safety, disproof or convincing correction was almost impossible.

While the Soviet Union remained a credible foe, Americans could congratulate themselves on their own relative goodness. Only the most morally chauvinistic thought America had a corner on the world's supply of *absolute* goodness, but so long as the Kremlin played its malevolent part, Americans merely had to be better than their Soviet rivals to feel virtuous. If America's record on race relations contained flaws, at least those who protested weren't packed off to gulags. If the American political system was sometimes superficial, at least Americans got to vote in genuine elections. If America occasionally settled for less than democratic perfection from its allies and clients, at least it held up a democratic example for them to follow.

Beyond the realm of moral psychology, the Cold War framework simplified the problem of understanding international relations. The bipolar scheme of world affairs reduced the need to delve closely into the motives and objectives of other countries, since a country's position regarding communism served, in the predominant American view, as a litmus test for that country's policies as a whole. To be sure, this test sometimes yielded false results. Neutralists like India often found themselves treated as fellow-travelers, while some right-wing dictators were accorded Free World membership. Moreover, those American officials who made their careers in foreign policy never took the litmus results very seriously. But for Americans who desired a quick and dirty division of the world into friends and foes, the communism-versus-democracy test did the job.

The communist issue served a similar purpose in American domestic politics, although here the problem of spurious results was even worse. Few American voters cared to take the time to educate themselves to the nuances of the possible positions candidates might adopt on issues relating to national security. For that majority who didn't, the question of whether an individual was reassuringly hard or suspiciously soft on communism simplified the sorting process. The trouble was that once candidates caught on to the game, almost everyone passed the test.

The Cold War simplified matters for particular groups in other ways. The forty years of the Cold War were a glorious time for the American defense industry, which might have been accused of colluding with the Soviet defense industry had the latter enjoyed any ability to collude across borders. Collusion or not, the armorers of the two sides shared an interest in heavy defense spending, and they benefited from each other's arms-racing actions. In the absence of such a readily identifiable and consistently threatening enemy as the Soviet Union, American weapons-producers never would have achieved the growth they did during the post-1945 period. Their vested interest in the Cold War appeared in their bottom lines.

Persons and organizations that had hidden behind the Cold War to oppose social reform—regarding race, for example—had a less compelling interest in keeping the chill on East-West relations. For them, the Cold War had been a handy distractive device, but should it be taken away, they would find another—secular humanism, perhaps. All the same, red-baiting would be hard to match for its capacity to change the subject, and to throw advocates of reform on the defensive.

Just as the Cold War had simplified matters for many in the United States, its end promised to complicate things. Psychologically, Americans would have to adjust to a world lacking an agreed-upon focus of evil against which they could favorably contrast themselves. Possible alternative focuses fell short in one respect or another. Saddam Hussein served the purpose for awhile, but he didn't have the staying power required of a real solution to the problem. Japan took some heavy beating on the issue of trade and jobs, but even many Americans thought their country's economic woes were chiefly homegrown. Neither was as soul-satisfying as the Soviets.

Politically, American candidates and public officials would have to come up with a more imaginative national-security agenda than reactive anti-communism. Bush promoted his "new world order" for a time, but acceptance levels were disappointing. Japan-bashers in Congress ran up against the difficulty that Americans liked the goods Nissan and Sony were sending east.

Economically, advocates of high defense spending would have to devise new rationales for keeping the production lines humming. Hussein helped, but not for long. And in the absence of a new threat, the peace-dividenders likely would slash deeply into profits and jobs.

Strategically, American planners would have to figure out how to deal with a world unlike that which they had come to know over forty years. While the demise of the Soviet Union diminished the likelihood of a civilization-shattering thermonuclear war, other sources of tension quickly ruled out a nail-biting moratorium. The Persian Gulf crisis and war demonstrated that troubles would persist into the post-Cold War era. Strikingly, the fact that Washington and Moscow were cooperating in the affair, a fact often cited as evidence of the new possibilities for peace opened up by the Cold War's end, actually deprived Washington of a potentially important diplomatic lever. In previous regional conflicts, when the United States and the Soviet Union had backed opposing parties, American leaders could pressure Moscow to restrain its allies, in the interest of preserving or improving broader superpower relations. The pressure didn't always work as well as Washington hoped, as the Nixon administration's efforts to get Moscow to help stop the Vietnam War short of a North Vietnamese victory demonstrated. Yet even in the Vietnamese case, Hanoi accepted a ceasefire. And, generally, a client's desire for continued Soviet aid acted to moderate its behavior somewhat. In cases where the two superpowers took the same side, the Kremlin card lost its value.

In Europe, the Soviet withdrawal from the center of the continent, accomplished in principle if not in detail during the summer of 1990, rendered the American guarantee of German security almost worthless. The Germans were too business-minded to go on long paying something for nothing. This implied major changes in the structure of European and Atlantic relations. German reunification per se had little to do with the issue, if only because for the near future the annexation of East Germany by West Germany would cost rather than benefit the Germans. Nor did one have to suppose another nasty turn by German nationalism to predict that sooner or later Germany would begin to act more independently. Perhaps the European Community would provide the supra-national framework the Cold War previously had. Perhaps not. The latter possibility was what had Germany-watchers worried. Germany's insistence on swift recognition of the independence of Slovenia and Croatia during Yugoslavia's civil war, while the other European governments and the United States urged caution, didn't lessen the worries.

Future American relations with Japan raised similar concerns. Like the Germans, the Japanese had been persuaded to devote their considerable energies and ingenuity to perfecting the performance of their economy. Matters of defense and foreign affairs they left primarily to the Americans. Although a few nationalist-minded Japanese, and a somewhat larger number of cost-conscious Americans, had complained at the arrangement, it substantially satisfied both parties so long as Cold War Russia presented a plausible danger to Japanese and American interests. As the Soviet threat diminished, however, many Japanese grew less inclined to follow America's lead internationally, and many Americans grew less inclined to pay for Japan's defense. Analogously with the German case, one didn't have to assume a return to the militarism of the 1930s to wonder about the effects of the re-emergence of Japan as an independent East Asian great power. A trade war between the United States and Japan, the first rumblings of which already were echoing through Congress, would be bad enough.

The sudden end of the Cold War, succeeded in short order by the collapse of the Soviet Union, raised some fundamental questions regarding what it had been all about. The most obvious question was whether it had been necessary for Americans to get so worked up over an enemy that proved to be a shell—a large country, to be sure, with formidable-looking weapons, but one with a decrepit economy and a political will insufficient to keep it from breaking apart at the first wind of honest reform. Had the Soviet threat *ever* been very great? How much of the perceived threat had been genuine and how much a figment of American imaginations? Was "cold war" useful, or misleading, as a description of the rivalry between the United States and the Soviet Union?

The "cold war" metaphor had first gained general currency with Walter Lippmann's 1946 book, *The Cold War.* At the time Lippmann wrote, the metaphor was plausible enough. Americans had just fought the biggest war in history, and found themselves confronting circumstances that resembled, in certain respects, those that had preceded the war. Stalin was as much a dictator as Hitler had been, and the Red Army was indisputably powerful. Communist ideology was potentially as expansionistic as that of the Nazis, if less explicitly bellicose. Undeniably, Stalin was a person to keep an eye on.

But the cold-war metaphor worked better as a literary device than as a description of international reality. Wars, at least as Americans historically have understood and fought them, are relatively brief affairs, with readily distinguished enemies and concrete objectives. Sometimes Americans had gained their wartime objectives: independence from Britain, subjugation of the Confederacy, destruction of Hitler. Sometimes they hadn't: acquisition of Canada, preservation of secession and slavery. But in every instance, the enemies and the goals had been clear, and Americans could tell whether they had attained the goals or not.

The objectives of the Cold War were considerably more nebulous, as was the nature of the enemy. Was the enemy communism? Or was it the Soviet Union? Was China an enemy? Then how could it become a friend? Was the United States fighting for territory, or for political and moral principles? Was containment sufficient to America's needs, or must the United States roll back communism?

Had Americans been less beguiled by the Cold War metaphor—had it not served so many purposes beyond the realm of foreign affairs— they might have recognized that the Cold War was no war at all, but simply the management of national interests in a world of competing powers. Because Americans defined their interests globally, and because America's foremost rival possessed mighty military weapons, American interest-management involved incessant effort and careful weighing of the possibility of armed conflict. Yet, though it was new to Americans, this was the sort of thing great powers had done as long as there had been great powers. It wasn't the comparatively placid and uneventful peace Americans had gotten used to in their many years of relative insulation from world affairs, but neither was it war.

Whatever the validity of the Cold War metaphor, Americans during much of the post-1945 period operated according to the premise that the only way to prevent the Cold War from flaring into World War III was to prevent a replay of the events that had led to World War II. This premise rested on a second, more basic premise: that Hitler wasn't an aberration but an archetype, that the model of escalating aggression he had used would be used by other ruthless, ambitious, and powerful national leaders. As it pertained to Stalin and the Soviet Union, this premise was made explicit in the "red fascist" imagery of the early Cold War. But essentially the same idea at various times infused American thinking about such countries as China, North Korea, Vietnam, Cuba, Indonesia, Egypt, and Iraq. The thrust of the argument was that dictators are insatiable, that aggression feeds on weakness, that appeasement merely postpones the day of reckoning.

Without doubt, power creates a certain community among those who wield it. And those who employ force as their primary instrument of policy tend to respond more readily to counterforce than to less direct kinds of appeals. Even so, the Hitler analogy obscured at least as much as it illuminated. Prior to the outbreak of World War II, Stalin showed none of the territorially expansionist compulsions that made Hitler Hitler. If anything, Stalin's reign produced a retreat from the world-revolutionism of Lenin's era, and the Georgian strongman's chief contribution to Marxist-Leninist theory was the notion of "socialism in one country." Neither did Stalin's actions after the war demonstrate much beyond a stubborn desire to prevent a repeat of the recent ruination. The Red Army refused to withdraw from where the war's end found it, but the Kremlin captured no new territory by force. The only significant Soviet military actions after 1945 were the crushings of reform in Hungary in 1956 and Czechoslovakia in 1968, and the Afghanistan war of 1979 and later. The Hungarian and Czech operations, though brutal and morally repugnant, were plainly designed to bolster a tottering status quo, to hold what Moscow had, rather than to extend the Russian writ to fresh territory. The Afghanistan fighting was largely defensive as well, intended to ward off the advance of Islamic fundamentalism toward the Soviet Union's Muslim provinces.

For forty years, the United States and its NATO allies devoted tremendous effort to preparations for the defense of Western Europe against a Soviet attack. During all that time, the attack never came. Why not? Did the Kremlin decide, in the face of the Western preparations, to forget about adding West Germany or France to its European empire? Or had it never intended such additions?

There is no way of knowing. Stalin, like many dictators, took his secrets with him to his tomb. Certainly, the Soviet military had contingency plans for an attack against the West, but planning is what planners get paid to do, and many plans have almost nothing to do with reality. (Until the 1930s, American strategists were drafting contingency plans for a war against Britain). Besides, attacks can be defensive. If you are convinced that the enemy is going to hit you, you'll probably want to hit first. While it is impossible to prove that Stalin did *not* intend to attack the West, neither has it been shown that he *did.*

In the early years of the post-1945 period, when the memories of World War II's horrendousness were still raw, when the Western European countries were in a comparatively exposed position, and when American resources almost overmatched the rest of the world combined, American leaders understandably preferred to err on the side of caution. Less understandably, they continued to err long after circumstances had changed. By the 1960s or 1970s or 1980s, one might have thought, the burden of proof should have been on the alarmists. But by then, of course, the Cold War had been thoroughly domesticated and bureaucratized, providing benefits only barely involving American national security.

If the Hitler analogy obscured what Stalin and the Soviets were up to, it made a mash of what other communists were about. Tito's nose-thumbing at Stalin should have demonstrated that communists could be as fractious among themselves as in relations with capitalists. And anyone with the least sense of Chinese history, or the slightest understanding of the traditional Chinese disdain for most things foreign, could have guessed that the Chinese would follow Moscow's line exactly as long as they discerned advantages to themselves from doing so.

But because it served other purposes—political, economic, psychological—to treat communism as a global conspiracy, and to liken a failure to confront this conspiracy to the failure to halt Hitler, anti-appeasement became the touchstone of American Cold War policy. In anti-appeasement's name, Americans fought a bloody war in Korea, believing they were frustrating the Kremlin's planet-devouring designs. While the Korean War yielded mixed results for South Korea—the fighting devastated the country, but left it beyond Kim Il Sung's obnoxious reach—the cost far exceeded anything Americans would have accepted simply for South Korea's sake. In anti-appeasement's name, the United States fought another bloody war in Vietnam, failing this time to achieve even the preservation of a non-communist government. As if to drive home the lesson that fighting in Vietnam to contain China had been wrongheaded, communist China and communist Vietnam soon fell out, to the point of war in 1979.

Comparisons to Hitler had the perverse effect of overblowing the communist military threat, which was largely nonexistent, and consequently understating the communist political threat, which wasn't. To their credit, some American officials in fact understood that the threat the communists posed was principally political. To their discredit, they did relatively little to share their insight with the wider American public. The Cold War climate in America wasn't conducive to nuance regarding communism. A few brave souls tried to explain such matters as that a communist China needn't be a China unalterably wedded to Moscow and irretrievably antagonistic to the United States, but the personal calumny and professional banishment these few suffered for their efforts alerted their colleagues and successors to the consequences of divergence from the party line. Most American officials chose the safer route of looking on communism as a hungry beast poised to devour the world as soon as America's guard let down. Measures designed to counter the communist political threat—for instance, by improving the economic and political performance, and thereby the attractiveness, of the countries of the "Free World"—were occasionally enacted, with the Marshall Plan being the outstanding example. But for every dollar Washington spent on economic aid, and for every meaningful exhortation American officials made to allies to respect democratic rights, Washington spent a hundred dollars on weapons, and American officials gave a score of speeches calling for staunch resistance to communist aggression.

Most perversely, the call to arms against communism caused American leaders to subvert the principles that constituted their country's best argument against communism. In 1945, the United States stood higher in the estimation of humanity then ever before, arguably higher than any country had ever stood in history. American soldiers and sailors had played a central role in the recent defeat of the almost universally detested fascists. Unlike the British and French, the Americans had no extensive colonial holdings that gave the lie to their professions of support for self-determination—the Philippines were slated for (and received) independence in 1946, and Puerto Rico didn't appear to want it. Unlike the Russians, the Americans treated the peoples of the countries they liberated with respect, and rather than seeming scarcely an improvement over the Wehrmacht, as Red Army troops often did, American GIs brought hope of an end to strife and oppression.

Within a short time, however, world opinion of the United States began to slide. The better to contain communism, Washington aligned itself with colonial and reactionary regimes that flouted the principles Americans had just fought a war to vindicate. Since comparatively few persons outside the North Atlantic region considered communism a greater enemy than colonialism and institutionalized inequality, what appeared a necessary tradeoff to many Americans appeared self-serving and hypocritical to most foreign observers of American actions. People of the Third World—which earned its sobriquet precisely because of its inhabitants' determination to resist the two-worlds framework of the Cold War—often deemed America's alliance-building tantamount to imperialism, of which they had had more than enough. American intervention in the Korean War looked to be misguided meddling in an Asian civil conflict. The war in Vietnam was widely viewed as a case of neo-colonial repression of indigenous nationalism. American backing for rightist regimes elsewhere in Asia, Africa, and Latin America seemed to fit the imperialist pattern.

Self-described "realists" in the United States could ignore the Third World carping—How many divisions did Nehru have?—and contend that any illusions anyone harbored of meaningful American moral superiority were better off debunked. The Cold War, they held, like all great-power conflicts, was essentially amoral. The strong did what they wanted, the weak what they were required, and there was little of right or wrong about the matter. This was the Doolittle philosophy: beat the devil at his own game. And it was the philosophy that, slightly disguised, informed the Kirkpatrick doctrine of support for right-wing dictators and antagonism to left-wing dictators.

The flaw in this philosophy was that it didn't suit the American people. Whatever the objective merits of "realism" as a description of behavior among nations, and whatever its appeal or lack thereof to Germans, Brazilians, Chinese, Nigerians, or anyone else, Americans have from the beginning of their national existence demonstrated an incurable desire to make the world a better place. Sometimes they settled for the stand-offish exemplarism of John Quincy Adams. Sometimes they insisted on the missionary interventionism of Woodrow Wilson. But almost always they believed that America had important lessons to teach their fellow human beings: about democracy, about capitalism, about respect for individual rights and personal opportunity and the rule of law.

This save-the-world inclination was largely responsible for the fervor with which Americans waged the Cold War. It provided much of the impetus behind the Marshall Plan: Americans were going to rescue Western Europe from starvation, disease, and despair. It lay beneath the commitment of American lives to Korea and Vietnam: the United States would preserve those vulnerable countries from the depredations of dictatorship. It motivated the appropriation of billions of dollars in aid to countries of Asia, Africa, and Latin America: American funding would help bring prosperity and dignity to the downtrodden of the planet. To be sure, the rhetoric of American concern for the welfare of other peoples and countries usually involved some hypocrisy, and in back of every important Cold War initiative there lurked careful considerations of self-interest. Yet the very fact that self-interest had to be dressed up in selfless clothing testified to the importance of moral factors in American politics, and consequently in American foreign relations. The staying power of the Cold War paradigm resulted in no small part from its capacity to combine the selfless with the self-interested.

Sometimes the twain parted, though, and when the parting became undeniable, as during the Vietnam-Watergate era, it rent the American Cold War consensus. All but the most hard-bitten Americans found sorely trying the discovery that the United States government had actively sought to assassinate leaders of foreign countries, countries not at war with the United States, whose principal crime consisted of being caught in the crossfire between the White House and the Kremlin. Americans of every political persuasion recoiled from the televised images of South Vietnamese citizens immolating themselves to protest the policies of the government the United States was supporting, from the photographs of naked Vietnamese children running screaming from napalm attacks by American planes, from the descriptions of Vietnamese villages destroyed that they might be "saved." Liberals and conservatives alike resented the corruption of the American political and legal process in the name of national security.

Defenders of American Cold War policies held that compromises were necessary to defend basic American values. Whether they really *were* necessary is impossible to tell. Conceivably, had American agents not conspired in the overthrow of popularly based governments in Iran and Guatemala; had they not tried to assassinate Lumumba and Castro; had they not tampered with elections in the Philippines and Syria and elsewhere; had they not destabilized leftist regimes in Chile and other countries; had they not bombed Indonesian islands and mined Nicaraguan harbors; had the United States not provided arms and money to a score of repressive juntas from Cuba to Pakistan to Zaire; had the FBI not disrupted the lawful activities of legitimate political groups in the United States; had the CIA not violated its own charter and engaged in domestic espionage; had American armed forces not lost 50,000 dead in Korea and nearly 60,000 in Vietnam— conceivably, had the United States not committed these acts, along with other acts presumably more constructive, communism might have conquered the world, or enough of it to render America significantly poorer, unhappier, and less secure.

In the real world, however, what counts isn't the conceivable but the likely. From the vantage point of the 1990s—which, of course, isn't the vantage point of the late 1940s and 1950s—the internal weaknesses of communism seem to have been sufficiently great to have made anything approaching the world-conquest scenarios of NSC 68 and similar manifestoes exceedingly improbable. Although conservatives claimed that American pressure was responsible for finally buckling the Soviet system in the late 1980s, as reasonable a case can be made that American antagonism actually *prolonged* the Cold War. For almost forty years, while Soviet leaders could plausibly cite an American threat to the security of their country—and, considering Washington's success in ringing Russia with American allies, considering the large and ever-growing size of the American nuclear arsenal, and considering the "massive-retaliation" and "evil-empire" language American leaders recurrently resorted to, the threat must have seemed quite plausible—Moscow could put off dealing with the problems inherent in the communist scheme of government. Had the United States not cooperated in playing the villain (just as the Soviet Union played the villain to the United States), the Kremlin might have been forced to confront its true problems sooner.

Similar considerations apply to America's dealing with other communist countries. By backing Chiang in China's civil war, for nearly a generation after that war otherwise would have ended, the United States handed Beijing's new mandarins an issue with which to divert the Chinese masses from their overwhelming domestic difficulties. Washington was consistently Fidel Castro's best friend by being his worst enemy. If Castro had ever had to justify his one-man rule in Cuba on its own merits, rather than on the demerits of the superpower across the Florida Strait, whose leaders still tried to strangle the Cuban economy thirty years after the Cuban revolution, he would have found the going a great deal harder. A principal consequence of American involvement in the Vietnamese war—aside from the millions of deaths, maimings, and displacements the fighting in Indochina produced— would seem to have been the postponement of the day when the Vietnamese communists had to stop fighting, at which they were very good, and start governing, at which they were a disaster.

The fact is that communism—not capitalism or democracy—has been the communists' worst enemy. But nations have had to discover this for themselves. External force has usually succeeded only in delaying the discovery.

Had attempts to force the discovery been costless, the delay might not have meant much. But the cost to America, not to mention to the delayed nations, was very high. More than 100,000 Americans died fighting wars that had almost nothing to do with genuine American security. The American economy, in 1945 the envy of the earth and the engine of global growth unprecedented in history, by the 1990s sputtered and faltered under the weight of four decades of military spending inconceivable before the Cold War. The chronic deficits that were a primary legacy of that military spending prevented the federal government from addressing many of the serious problems that crowded in on the country. Perhaps worst of all, American leaders, sometimes without the knowledge of the American people, sometimes with the people's approval, consistently cut moral corners in the Cold War, contradicting the ideals America was supposed to be defending. In 1945, nearly all Americans and probably a majority of inter-

ested foreigners had looked on the United States as a beacon shining
the way to a better future for humanity, one in which ideals mattered
more than tanks. During the next forty years, American leaders succeeded in convincing many Americans and all but a few foreigners that
the United States could be counted on to act pretty much as great powers always have. If Americans felt ambivalent about their victory over
the Soviet Union, they had reason to.

9

THE CIVIL RIGHTS MOVEMENT

Top-Down or Bottom-Up?

The Civil Rights movement changed the United States forever and mobilized a generation to activism. Images of blacks fighting for equal rights in the segregated South—being attacked by dogs, clubbed, fire hosed, and shot by white policemen—brought racial oppression to the consciousness of white Americans who had mostly been content to ignore it since Reconstruction. Southern white hatred and resistance to change outraged northern public sentiment and embarrassed Washington. The movement overturned Jim Crow laws which had divided the South into white and black, unjustly distributing rewards and services of society, keeping black adults in menial jobs, black children in understaffed and underequipped schools, and both routinely subject to social humiliation and physical brutality. The movement, which had such a massive impact on the study of the history of America, also had its own historians and historiography.

Scrutiny of the movement has moved from studies of its leaders during what biographer Taylor Branch has named the King Years (1954–1963) to studies of the unsung participants and their antecedents in protest going back as far as Reconstruction, but usually focusing on the Depression and World War II. As the movement has receded into the past, questions about strategies and mobilization interest historians eager to understand the huge outpouring of energy and hope which so indelibly marked two decades. King's extraordinary power to bring people together and generate optimism still fascinates scholars, although they are dissatisfied with analyses that exaggerate King's importance. Much of the movement remains only partially explored. Current historians are examining class relations among blacks within the protest tradition and the uneasy relations between liberal protests pursuing civil rights and working class protests pursuing economic justice. Gender relations in the movement remain a contested area, largely unexplored until the 1980s except by the Student Nonviolent Coordinating Committee whose members dealt with gender issues almost from its beginning in 1960. But the progress has been considerable.

Work on the Civil Rights era has led to a much deeper understanding of black protest throughout the century and thus of American and

African American history. The movement itself prompted the new social historians to begin exploring historical phenomena from the "bottom up" so they subjected Civil Rights to the same treatment from the
1970s onward. Instead of studying national leaders, scholars explored
the grassroots sources of protest. At the same time biographers were
writing studies of Martin Luther King, historians were also exploring
communities where King was not influential. They asked, how were
people mobilized? What were the local traditions of activism? Did the
impetus for activity come from leaders or the people themselves? One
of the most important challenges developing in the 1980s was to define the relationship between the struggle for civil rights and for economic justice. And scholars of the 1990s wondered how women, who
had been such a vital part of the movement, were not given a larger
part in its history.

Initially, historians of the movement focused their analyses on its
leaders and its leading organizations because they were the topics easi-
est to research and most familiar. There was an outpouring of work on
Martin Luther King, Jr. as well as the SCLC (Southern Christian Leadership Conference), the NAACP (National Association for the Advancement of Colored People), CORE (Congress of Racial Equality)
and SNCC (Student Nonviolent Coordinating Committee).

The first historians who looked at the movement conceptualized it
as national, headed by King. Its greatest victories were in the Supreme
Court, Congress, and the White House.[1] Their works located the movement's beginning in the *Brown v. Topeka Board of Education* decision
and saw its culmination in the Civil Rights Act of 1964 along with the
famous March on Washington of that year and King's "I Have a Dream"
speech. King's arrival in the national consciousness with the *Brown* decision and his assassination during the period of militant black resistance helped identify King with the years in which the movement,
because of his commitment to nonviolence, attracted its most intense
popular support. Historians such as Harvard Sitkoff believe that King's
death marked the end of the movement's effectiveness. Today there is
general agreement that after the passage of the Civil Rights Act and
King's shift of focus to poverty and its relation to the war in Vietnam the
movement began to fragment.

Taylor Branch's *Parting the Waters* and *Pillar of Fire* are the most
detailed among the many works on King.[2] Biographies of King in-

---

[1]See Steven F. Lawson, "Freedom Then, Freedom Now," for an excellent article reviewing the historiography of the movement: *Journal of American History* 96 (April:
1991): 456–471.

[2]Taylor Branch, *Parting the Waters, America in the King Years, 1954–1963*, (New
York, 1988); Stephen J. Oates, *Let the Trumpet Sound: The Life of Martin Luther King*
(New York, 1982); David L. Lewis, *King, A Critical Biography* (Baltimore, Md., 1970);
David J. Garrow, *Bearing the Cross: Martin Luther King and the Southern Christian
Leadership Conference* (New York, 1986).

evitably present the movement from his perspective, although Taylor Branch's technique of shifting the point of view from King to other significant characters helps "to let the characters define each other."[3] Regarding the movement from King's point of view means seeing its national dimension and impact. This perspective was controversial, even at the time, for ignoring local activists and events that did not make national television. One SNCC worker complained that King had one foot in the cotton field and the other in the White House.[4] And later historians who have presented the movement from many local perspectives have argued that a national view of events was often irrelevant in the field and served to diminish the significance of the countless local initiatives that accounted for the movement's success.

Beginning in the late 1970s, many historians began deemphasizing King and looking at the movement from local and grassroots perspectives. Applying to Civil Rights the tools and concerns of social historians eager to see how uncelebrated people's decisions and acts give shape to larger events, scholars studied both individual southern communities and the South as a whole in the process of movement-building. King was one of many charismatic leaders who developed within the culture of southern black churches. His astonishing oratorical gift and personal intensity made him a natural fit with the particular constellation of common ideas and feelings that characterized the time and place. Scholars have made the point that charisma was a common characteristic of black Baptist ministers in the South and not unique to King or Montgomery. Furthermore, the larger movement needed a figure with King's qualities. Others with similar attributes would have stepped forward if King had not existed.[5]

Between these two extreme visions of King's place in the movement is a newer, compromise view, articulated by Nathan Huggins, who wrote in 1987 that viewing Civil Rights activism through King's eyes was not succumbing to the Great Man fallacy of history, but using a uniquely useful lens on a movement that can be difficult to understand. Huggins stressed the difficulty secular people have understanding the religious beliefs of the movement, particularly the belief that "undeserved suffering is redemptive," without looking closely at what

[3]Branch, *Parting*, Preface, 1.

[4]Adam Fairclough, "The Southern Christian Leadership Conference and the Second Reconstruction, 1957–1973," in David J. Garrow, ed., *We Shall Overcome: Martin Luther King and the Civil Rights Movement* (Brooklyn, N.Y., 1989), p. 186.

[5]See, for example, Clayborn Carson, "Martin Luther King, Jr., Charismatic Leadership in a Mass Struggle," *Journal of American History* 74 (September 1987): 448–454; Manning Marable makes this case very persuasively in *Race, Reform, and Rebellion: The Second Reconstruction in Black America, 1945–1990* (Jackson, Miss., 1990), pp. 77–81; Aldon Morris discusses the availability of charismatic ministers in *The Origins of the Civil Rights Movement: Black Communities Organizing for Change* (New York, 1984) pp. 7–8.

King said that resonated so deeply with southern blacks. He also offers the caution that because of the availability of F.B.I. tapes of King's conversations, much is known about the man's private life. This may perhaps make it easier, but no less misguided, to idealize the movement and belittle the man.[6]

Along with early portraits of King and his indispensability to the movement emerged a fractured before-and-after view of him. Up until the March on Washington in 1963 he was the King of the dream, the nonviolent Christian leader who could unite white and black, rich and poor with his transcendent oratory, which promised to rectify social injustice while turning the other cheek. After 1963, the portrait changed to display another King, a militant opponent of the War in Vietnam, which drained the nation's resources from attacking the poverty rooted in capitalism. Many historians saw King's shifting focus as a philosophically unfounded tactical error.[7]

Scholars of King's theological roots have reconciled this split in King's philosophy and activism. James H. Cone argues that only white audiences, not black, called upon King publicly to explain the influences that shaped his thinking. In these cases, he cited white philosophers. But "The most significant elements that shaped King's theology . . . were the oppression of black people and the liberating message of the black church." Cone argued that King understood that the movement had barely affected the poverty and suffering of the black masses, and he also knew the limits of white commitment to social justice. It was King's faith in the people and the beliefs of the black church that kept him going, not the ideas of Reinhold Neibuhr and other white theologians, whatever he told white audiences.[8]

Many of the newer historiographical questions about the Civil Rights movement came from the perception that it had a successful and an unsuccessful phase—that the economic underpinning of the deprivation of black civil rights was an important force in the struggle which has not been fully integrated into its history. The movement's great successes were in ending most kinds of segregation and gaining blacks political representation. But it has failed to alter in any dramatic way the economic exploitation of the black poor. Initially, historians tended to focus on the first part of the movement, seeing the *Brown* decision as its starting point and the Black Power Movement as the beginning of the end of its successes. In this phase, historians

---

[6]Nathan Irvin Huggins, "Martin Luther King, Jr., Charisma and Leadership," *Journal of American History* 74 (September 1987): 477–481.

[7]Steven Lawson, "Freedom Then, Freedom Now: The Historiography of the Civil Rights Movement," *American Historical Review* 96 (April 1991): 456–471, 460.

[8]James H. Cone, "Black Theology—Black Church" in C. Eric Lincoln, ed., *Martin Luther King, Jr., A Profile* (New York, 1970), p. 252.

tended to focus on leaders, court decisions, and legislation supporting civil rights, as well as the four most important black national organizations: the NAACP, CORE, the SCLC, and SNCC. Only when social historians of the mid- to late-seventies shifted their focus away from King and the national picture did their questions change. They began to ask, Which people participated and in what ways? And later, starting in the mid-eighties, How did activists bring together the civil and economic aspects of deprivation that underlay the movement?

Studies of the composition and dynamics of the movement in particular communities began coming out in 1979 and include accounts of Greensboro, North Carolina, Tuskegee, Alabama, St. Augustine, Florida and Jackson, Mississippi.[9] These studies all take long views of each community's struggle with racial oppression and see the Civil Rights movement as part of a much longer battle, beginning, in some cases, with economic struggles during the Depression, or with the changes in racial relations that World War II brought about. Through their local perspective and corresponding emphasis on the long fight, these studies contradicted a common belief about the movement, cultivated for political reasons by movement participants: that it had sprung up spontaneously because Rosa Parks had tired feet one day. The truth, they argued, was far more complex, and its reasons much deeper.

Robert Norrell's *Reaping the Whirlwind*, for example, located the beginning of the Civil Rights movement in Tuskegee, Alabama in 1941, but traced its roots to as far back as 1870 when white Democrats began their campaign of violence to reverse the gains blacks had achieved in Reconstruction, particularly in holding political office.[10] Norrell began his account in 1941 for two reasons. First, that is when members of the Tuskegee University faculty and Civic Association decided to challenge the procedures by which blacks were prohibited from registering to vote. (Requirements for whites included either $300 worth of property or literacy, but the white election officials demanded of blacks literacy *and* the property requirement, and in addi-

---

[9]William Chafe, *Civilities and Civil Rights: Greensboro, North Carolina and the Black Struggle for Equality* (New York, 1980); David Colburn, *Racial Change and Community Crisis: St. Augustine, Florida* (New York, 1985); Robert J. Norrell, *Reaping the Whirlwind: The Civil Rights Movement in Tuskegee* (New York, 1985); John Salter, *Jackson, Mississippi: An American Chronicle of Struggle and Schism* (Hicksville, N.Y., 1979).

[10]Robert Weisbrot, *Freedom Bound: History of America's Civil Rights Movement* (New York, 1990), begins his account of the movement in Reconstruction as well, but then skips to Montgomery in 1954 (pp. 1–18). Vincent Harding begins with the first slave ships, but then skips to the *Brown* decision, in his introductory section to *A Reader and Guide to Eyes on the Prize*, Clayborne Carson, David J. Garrow, Vincent Harding and Darlene Clark Hine, eds. (New York, 1987).

tion compelled them to have two white people vouch for their character.) Second, with America's entry into World War II, Tuskegee became
the location of a segregated military base to train black pilots. Three
thousand black uniformed men created special tensions in Tuskegee
and brought the town into the national struggle over civil rights. The
newcomers, mostly northern and educated, had difficulty reconciling
themselves to Tuskegee's Jim Crow policies. Moreover, young black
men found it bitterly frustrating to be denied basic freedoms while
preparing to risk their lives for a country that purported to be fighting
for democratic and humanitarian ideals. Tuskegee police made the situation worse because of their hostile mistrust of armed, uniformed
black men.

Norrell's starting point coincides with the beginning of a local
controversy within the black community about whether to accommodate the segregated world or to engage in the politics of integration. A
local black entrepreneur had petitioned for the segregated military fa-
cility to be located at Tuskegee, enraging northern members of the
NAACP who felt that accepting, indeed asking for, a segregated facil-
ity was a retrograde act. From the point of view of the Tuskegee businessman, the military base meant jobs and opportunities for black
people, and he believed he had said nothing about whether or not it
should be integrated. From the standpoint of the NAACP, his act
would perpetuate the oppression of blacks. This debate paralleled the
debate between Booker T. Washington and W.E.B. DuBois over the
best way for blacks to make their way in a hostile white society. It
would also parallel later conflicts between militants and accommodationists in the Civil Rights struggle. Norrell's view describes a building process which began with Washington's emphasis on education,
accommodation, and gradual change. Militants in the late 1960s condemned this approach. But by the 1970s when blacks had replaced
whites in government in Tuskegee, Washington's philosophy had been
rediscovered and revalued.[11]

Scholars concerned with the movement's grassroots nature saw its
potential for the revolutionary transformation of individuals. Whereas
earlier writers had focused on its judicial and legislative agenda, later
students of the movement rediscovered Ella Baker's insistence that
demonstrators were working for more than the right to eat a ham-
burger at an integrated lunch counter.[12] SNCC, Ella Baker's creation,
worked to transform people as well as society; its philosophy held that
each person needed to learn to take responsibility for his or her own
life through participation in the struggle for social justice. SNCC
worked with rural blacks isolated from schools and services for whom

[11]Robert Norrell, *Reaping the Whirlwind*, pp. 35–50; 203–213.
[12]Quoted in Lawson, "Freedom Then," 469.

the possibility of voting was only one of many changes which they would themselves come to demand. SNCC was self-consciously, as Clayborne Carson has written, trying "to create new social identities for participants and for all Afro-Americans."[13] This theme also showed up in the work of King biographers, like Eric Lincoln, who wrote about the black community's exhilaration and sense of empowerment after winning the bus boycott.[14] Scholars not focusing on King saw personal transformation as less the side effect of the struggle' than its point. Historians today continue to stress the transformative element of the movement. Recently, Richard King, a volunteer-turned-political-scientist has argued for the movement's genuine originality in bringing discussion and action together to create a new political environment. For King, its singular contribution was to "create or make evident a new sense of individual and collective identity, even self-respect, among Southern black people through political mobilization."[15]

By the end of the 1980s it was possible for scholars to write that "most historians would agree that the modern civil rights movement did not begin with the Supreme Court's decision in Brown. . . ."[16] The tendency to push back the antecedents of the movement had been developing since the mid-seventies. In 1978, Harvard Sitkoff argued that the New Deal was a crucial time in which progress generated optimism for further change in the black community. He believed that the Depression and the New Deal "constituted a turning point in race relations trends." The most positive results in interracial activity, Sitkoff argued, flowed from the C.I.O.'s (Congress of Industrial Organization's) and, in particular, the United Mine Workers' active promotion of racial equality. These interracial union experiences supported greater black militancy. Although the struggle for civil rights was overshadowed during the Depression by economic issues, interracial labor activism was key in preparing blacks to demand their civil rights in the 1950s.[17]

Robert Korstad and Nelson Lichtenstein, writing in the late 1980s, agreed with Sitkoff that the movement's roots were in the Depression

---

[13]Quoted in Lawson, "Freedom Then," 457.

[14]C. Eric Lincoln, *Martin Luther King, Jr., A Profile* (New York, 1970), p. xii.

[15]Richard King, *Civil Rights and the Idea of Freedom* (Athens, Ga., 1996), p. 4.

[16]Robert Korstad and Nelson Lichtenstein, "Opportunities Found and Lost: Labor, Radicals, and the Early Civil Rights Movement," *Journal of American History*, 75 (1988): 786–811, 810; see also Steven Lawson, *Running for Freedom: Civil Rights and Black Politics in America Since 1941* (Philadelphia, 1991), which dates the origins of the Civil Rights movement to World War II. The exception was Richard King (see footnote 15), who argued for the uniqueness of the movement's transformative goals and feared that studying its historical roots would diminish its real originality.

[17]Harvard Sitkoff, *A New Deal for Blacks: The Emergence of Civil Rights as a National Issue* (New York, 1978), p. ix.

and early 1940s. They emphasized the new, urban working-class character of the black masses. The migration of the 1940s and 1950s transported more than two million southern rural blacks to the urban north and another million to southern urban centers. Black voters registered in northern and southern cities in great numbers; they joined both the NAACP and unions. The C.I.O. was the center of Civil Rights struggle in the Depression and the 1940s. Unionization provided blacks with a link to a government sympathetic to labor, which opened a window for black demands to be heard; church-based demonstrators in the Civil Rights movement had a parallel experience.[18] The expanding economy of the mid-40s produced a period of high employment, high wages, and a supportive and widely felt federal presence, which helped blacks push for a Civil Rights–oriented labor movement. However, the end of the war and the onset of the Cold War radically transformed this environment and temporarily ended the gains blacks were making.

When blacks began organizing through their churches, stressing nonviolence and Christian fellowship, they were able to develop support in much of the nation for increased civil rights. When, however, the movement's focus shifted to poverty and its causes, they were unable to find the same kind of support. They were hampered in this, conclude Korstad and Lichtenstein, because of failures of the integrated labor movement two decades earlier. For example, in Winston-Salem North Carolina at the end of the War, white industrialists had used anti-communism to weaken the integrated labor unions by turning white workers against blacks. With unionized blacks discredited in the McCarthy era atmosphere, the black middle class established the pattern of cooperating with white industrialists to work for reforms, but only by avoiding those of the workplace.[19] This legacy prevented widespread mobilization around the economic issues that King and others came to articulate more frequently after 1964.

Taking a similar long view, Manning Marable argued in *Race, Reform and Rebellion,* that the Cold War and domestic anticommunism retarded the outbreak of the Civil Rights movement. He cited the gains blacks made in the forties in alliance with the left, gains eroded by the middle class's anticommunism in the fifties. Adam Clayton Powell, Jr., congressman from Harlem, was virtually the only legislator to refuse to vote a contempt charge against a Communist who would not give evidence. "Powell recognized that every defender of racial segregation in Congress was also a devout proponent of anticom-

---

[18]Korstad and Lichtenstein, "Opportunities," 787–788.

[19]Korstad and Lichtenstein, "Opportunities," 801–811. See also John Egerton's *Speak Now Against the Day: The Generation before the Civil Rights Movement in the South* (Chapel Hill, N.C., 1994) for an elegiac evocation of the years 1932–1954 in Atlanta and a discussion of anticommunism and its effect on race relations (pp. 553–572).

munist legislation, and that the Negro had no other alternative except to champion the civil liberties of the left in order to protect the black community's own interests." Powell was unique in this understanding and was isolated for years because of his stand. The decline of the Left in the postwar years, and especially the recruitment of the NAACP and the black middle class into the cause of anticommunism, slowed blacks' economic and political progress.[20] Marable's most important contribution was to make clear why the Civil Rights movement should be understood as "the Second Reconstruction."[21] Seeing the movement as part of a long-term historical struggle, Marable showed that economic reform was always closely linked to civil rights. In this way, Marable healed the split that earlier historians had seen between economic and civil rights. King's thinking and the movement's focus did not suddenly change in 1964, but reflected the long-standing historical links in racial politics between economic and political justice.

Sociologist Aldon Morris's 1984 study of the origins of the movement also stressed the convergence of civil and economic motives among activists. In his discussion of the preexisting networks of potential protesters, he pointed out the radical backgrounds of many civil rights demonstrators including Rosa Parks, who had attended a workshop at the radical Highlander Folk School months before she refused to move from her bus seat in Montgomery. Similarly, E. D. Nixon, an important Montgomery boycott activist, had organized the Montgomery chapter of the Brotherhood of Sleeping Car Porters and was a friend of its founder and long-time activist, A. Philip Randolph.[22]

Other scholars who have brought together the economic and political concerns of the black community include Robin D. G. Kelley in *Hammer and Hoe: Alabama Communists During the Great Depression* and Karen Sacks in *Caring By the Hour: Women, Work, and Organizing at Duke Medical Center.* Kelley demonstrated, for example, that Civil Rights activism in Alabama in the 1960s picked up where Communists had left it at the end of the Depression.[23]

Some studies of the long-term movement, understanding Civil Rights as simply a new development in a long process, denied King's

---

[20]Manning Marable, *Race, Reform and Rebellion: The Second Reconstruction in Black America, 1945–1990* (Jackson, Miss., 1991), p. 22.

[21]He was not the first to do this; Adam Fairclough did in 1981: "The Southern Christian Leadership Conference and the Second Reconstruction, 1957–1973," in David J. Garrow, ed., *We Shall Overcome: Martin Luther King and the Civil Rights Movement* (Brooklyn, N.Y., 1989).

[22]Aldon Morris, *The Origins of the Civil Rights Movement: Black Communities Organizing for Change* (New York, 1984), pp. 44, 147–149; Lawson, "Freedom Then," 463.

[23]Lawson, "Freedom Then," 463; Robin D.G. Kelley, *Hammer and Hoe: Alabama Communists During the Great Depression* (Chapel Hill, N.C., 1990); Karen Sacks, *Caring by the Hour: Women, Work, and Organizing at Duke Medical Center* (Urbana, Ill., 1988).

indispensability. Aldon Morris, for example, focused not on King but on the "creativity of the black masses," whom he thought were too often portrayed as unthinkingly responding to influences beyond their control.[24] His book begins, pointedly, not in Montgomery, where King was drafted leader of the bus boycott, but a year before, in Baton Rouge. There a seven-day boycott ended when city officials put almost all seating on Baton Rouge buses on a first-come, first-served basis. Morris shows what Montgomery learned from Baton Rouge. He also demonstrates that some of the reasons for King's assumption of leadership had nothing to do with his talents. Instead, his relative newness to Montgomery meant that he had not accumulated a record of obligations or grievances. He was an innocuous choice.[25]

Like Morris, Douglas McAdam in *Political Process and the Revolution of Black Insurgency* studied the dynamics of the whole movement and thereby overturned older ideas about the allegedly unplanned and spontaneous functioning of grassroots activists. McAdam wrote that theories which "emphasized the irrationality of movement participants and the discontinuity between 'ordinary' political activity and movement behavior, must be seen as ideologically and substantively flawed."[26] Both McAdam and Morris stressed the continuity to be found in the background and beliefs of demonstrators over time and the existence of well-organized lines of communication on which movement activities could rely. They saw integration into black community structures as key in predicting participation in the movement. McAdam looked much farther back than Morris for continuity—to the end of Reconstruction—and traced membership in the NAACP as well as in church organizations. Morris and McAdam understood the political utility of the "spontaneity" argument, that is, its implicit refutation of the accusation of outside agitation igniting the movement, but were distant enough from events to risk challenging it.

In 1984, sociologist Lewis Killian challenged the Morris-McAdam interpretation in a study of one community: Tallahassee, Florida. There Civil Rights demonstrations did not rely on leaders with roots in the ongoing black struggle or on the well-organized community structures that had carried the movement along in Montgomery. Arguing for spontaneity, Killian enriches the complexity of the picture of grassroots activity. In Tallahassee, two female students were arrested for sitting in "white" bus seats, but unlike Rosa Parks, they had no background in protest, and no reason to believe that their actions might have signifi-

---

[24]Morris, *Origins*, pp. v–vi.

[25]Morris, *Origins*, pp. 17–25.

[26]Doug McAdam, *Political Process and the Development of Black Insurgency, 1930–1970* (Chicago, 1982), p. 1.

cant consequences. They were completely surprised when they were arrested, and the ensuing boycott arose too quickly to benefit from leadership of established organizations. While the Tallahassee sit-ins did take some direction from a newly founded CORE chapter and certainly drew on the support of NAACP members, Killian describes a relatively unplanned and unpredictable movement, which threw up a new civic organization and new leaders to shepherd unfolding events. Killian concluded that Morris and McAdam were right to emphasize pre-existing structures, but that spontaneity and emergent leaders and groups were also significant to the Civil Rights story.[27]

Historical acounts of the four major movement organizations, the NAACP, CORE, SCLC, and SNCC, tended to conform to the pattern of studies of the movement as a whole. Initially, historians focused on leaders and the national picture and eventually adopted a perspective that uncovered grassroots activism, including the crucial activism of women.

While there still is no overall history of the NAACP, memoirs, biographies, and monographs have raised important questions about the relation of the black masses to the NAACP's emphasis on litigation and civil rights, its elite leadership, and its goals of integration and equal rights—issues which seem extraneous to the very poor.[28] In 1960, Louis Lomax criticized the NAACP for stodgy tactics, centralized and unresponsive leadership, and elitism. Like Lomax, frustrated activists had respect for the NAACP's work, which culminated in the *Brown* decision ordering the integration of schools, but they had a jaundiced view of its upper class make-up and its on-again-off-again support for direct action.[29]

August Meier, reviewing Lomax's book in 1962, defended the NAACP from some of those charges, although he would later criticize it himself. He argued that it was natural in an organization as old as the NAACP to have a bureaucracy and be less flexible than newer associations like CORE and SNCC but that the NAACP *had* engaged in direct action, sit-ins, and other demonstrations.[30] Nevertheless, when Meier collaborated with Elliot Rudwick in a 1973 work on CORE, he

---

[27]Lewis M. Killian, "Organization, Rationality and Spontaneity in the Civil Rights Movement," Garrow, ed., *We Shall Overcome*, pp. 503–516.

[28]Many books cover NAACP activists and activities, like Jack Greenberg, *Crusaders in the Courts* (New York, 1994); Genna Rae McNeil, *Groundwork: Charles Hamilton Houston and the Struggle for Civil Rights* (Philadelphia, 1983); Charles Flint Kellogg, *NAACP* (Baltimore, 1967); Roy Wilkins with Tom Matthews, *Standing Fast* (New York, 1982); Richard Kluger, *Simple Justice* (New York, 1975).

[29]Louis Lomax, "The Negro Revolt against 'The Negro Leaders,'" in Garrow, ed., *We Shall Overcome*, pp. 603–615.

[30]August Meier, Book Review of Louis Lomax, *The Negro Revolt*, in Garrow, ed., *We Shall Overcome*, pp. 729–735.

suggested that the NAACP's victories were not always meaningful because they could not be enforced. For example, in 1947 CORE activists organized the Journey of Reconciliation in which eight black and eight white men left on a bus tour of the upper south in order to nonviolently protest segregation on public transportation. They found that although a legal challenge to a bus company operating in Virginia had already been successful, the bus company had done nothing to change its practices. This suggested to the founders of CORE the limited nature of the NAACP's single-minded focus on the law, and underscored the need for direct action.[31]

Mark Tushnet's *The NAACP's Legal Strategy against Segregated Education, 1925–1950*, considers the NAACP's effectiveness more broadly. Tushnet, influenced by critical legal theory, sees the law as more than formal decisions and arguments in a social vacuum. He describes all litigation as a "social process" in which enforcement of a decision is as important as the decision itself. Therefore, he argues, the NAACP could not have been very distant from or unresponsive to the communities in which it worked, since it had to rely on local support for its effectiveness.[32] He shows that, though NAACP lawyers did often persuade clients that integrated education was the primary goal they should fight for, not, for example, equalizing racially separate educational facilities, this strategy could not have played out successfully without the support and cooperation of the black community. Where there was not such support, in North Carolina, for example, the NAACP failed to accomplish its objectives.[33]

A recent study has illuminated changing class strategies of the NAACP. Beth Tompkins Bates describes the NAACP uncharacteristically reaching out in 1941 to working-class African Americans at the moment when unionized blacks had achieved some visibility and leverage in the labor movement. Walter White, head of the NAACP, supported a UAW strike against Ford, consciously hoping to attach the new mass of working-class blacks in Detroit to the old elite NAACP. In that instance, White called for collective action and publicly associated the NAACP with the labor movement.[34]

As Kevin Gaines points out in commenting on Bates's article, one of her important contributions is to pinpoint the changing dynamics of interclass relationships among African Americans. The story that emerges

---

[31]August Meier and Elliot Rudwick, *CORE: A Study in the Civil Rights Movement, 1942–1968* (New York, 1973), p. 34.

[32]Mark Tushnet, *The NAACP's Legal Strategy against Segregated Education, 1925–1950* (Chapel Hill, N.C., 1987), pp. 151–153.

[33]Tushnet, *The NAACP's Legal Strategy against Segregated Education*, pp. 138–166.

[34]Beth Tompkins Bates, "The New Crowd Challenges the Agenda of the Old Guard in the NAACP," *The American Historical Review* 102 (April 1997): 340–377.

is of an old elite allying itself with the new northern, urban working class, an interracial and economically radical movement. Simultaneously it abandons the counterproductive strategy of preaching moral uplift to poor blacks.[35] This class analysis of the Civil Rights movement sheds light both on how the black community worked to transcend class differences as well as suggests some of the enduring sources of resentment within the movement. Bates's article exemplifies one promising new direction social-historical studies of the NAACP might take.

Another view of the NAACP highlights its impact on the Civil Rights movement from a negative point of view. In this view, the *Brown* decision provoked such a ferocious backlash that it required intensification of the Civil Rights movement. The most explicit development of this idea is Michael J. Klarman's "How *Brown* Changed Race Relations."[36] Klarman demonstrated that white southerners believed the NAACP to be responsible for the Civil Rights movement, even if historians did not. They initiated a campaign of repression against the NAACP that intensified as the Civil Rights movement gained momentum, displaying their appreciation of its significance and giving the movement an enemy whose opposition was galvanizing. Indeed, the SCLC was organized in response to the massive attacks on the NAACP which were occurring all over the South in response to Civil Rights mobilization.[37]

Some organization historians have downplayed the impact of the NAACP, whatever its composition or the psychological fuel it provided. August Meier and Elliot Rudwick argued in 1973 that CORE, not the NAACP, was the precursor of civil rights methods and concerns. CORE activists were committed to Ghandian nonviolence, dedicating themselves to loving their enemies and refusing violence no matter how provoked, even if it meant dying.[38] This philosophical foundation and CORE's flexible direct action approach provided the basis for Meier's and Rudwick's claim that it pioneered the strategies of the Civil Rights activists, both in tactics and in philosophy, and was essential to the Civil Rights struggle. Committed to integrated action, CORE first came to national attention in 1956 when its Freedom Rides achieved desegregation of interstate bus travel. In summing up

---

[35]Kevin Gaines, "Rethinking Race and Class in African American Struggles for Equality, 1885–1941," *The American Historical Review* 102 (April 1997): 378–387.

[36]For an author who emphasizes this frustration see Robert H. Brisbane, *Black Activism: Radical Revolution in the United States, 1954–1970* (Valley Forge, Pa., 1983); for a very recent, sophisticated treatment of this subject see Michael J. Klarman, "How *Brown* Changed Race Relations: The Backlash Thesis," *Journal of American History* (June 1994): 81–118.

[37]Morris, *Origins*, p. 85.

[38]Meier and Rudwick, *CORE*, p. 12.

CORE's contribution to the Civil Rights movement, Meier and Rudwick cautioned readers not to equate organizational failure, i.e. the subsequent dramatic decline of CORE as an organization, with the failure of its goals, which were achieved in many cases. Ironically, CORE's decline was the result of its success in getting the Civil Rights Bill passed and the resulting challenge of finding a new focus. It also had to cope with the increasing fragmentation of the black movement and with increasing rejection of its integrated structure. As a new mass movement, no longer a small, northern, integrated one, CORE moved toward a black nationalist agenda, eschewed nonviolence, and focused on the battles still unwon: the inequities of capitalism which played particular havoc with the lives of black Americans. As James Farmer, director of CORE, wrote in 1965 of the tension around nonviolence, "It will be difficult to maintain non-violence through the stresses of a mass direct-action movement. And that, precisely, is one of the chief political dilemmas of the Freedom Movement."[39]

Historians today agree that Meier and Rudwick were correct in their high evaluation of CORE's influence, but that writing its history in 1973 limited their ability to gauge its successes. With more distance, historians will be able to provide a better look at CORE's composition, its achievements, and its transition from an integrated, northern, elite organization to a black nationalist one.

The history of the SCLC has been tied much more closely than any other organization to perceptions of King. Initially some scholars like August Meier looked at the SCLC first as organized around King solely to glorify him, raise money, and do his bidding.[40] Later historians have seen it as just one expression of a multifaceted move-ment.The SCLC developed in 1957 in response to the need felt by national figures such as Ella Baker, Stanley Levison, and Bayard Rustin for a coordinating organization to give direction to the many local demonstrations which emerged all over the South. According to Aldon Morris (always deemphasizing King's influence) the SCLC, not King, was the organizational arm of the black church, and it "was the force that developed the infrastructure of the civil rights movement."[41] The SCLC's southern church base was important to its successes and its legitimacy in the South as well as to its failures, for example, when the organization went to Chicago and tried to deal with northern racism and poverty.[42] The

[39]Meier and Rudwick, *CORE*, pp. 409–431; James Farmer, *Freedom—When* (New York, 1965), p. 79.

[40]August Meier, quoted in Fairclough, *SCLC*, p. 232. (See note 42.)

[41]Morris, *Origins*, p. 83.

[42]Adam Fairclough, "The Southern Christian Leadership Conference and the Second Reconstruction, 1957–1973," in Garrow, ed., *We Shall Overcome*, 1: 231–248.

SCLC was a coordinating body of a number of affiliates; in response to early criticisms that it had no structure and its decisions were all made by King, historian Adam Fairclough admitted the truth of these remarks but felt they said little about the organization's utility in raising money, generating optimism, and focusing the movement in the nation's eyes.

The basis for the authority of the SCLC was charisma. It legitimated King's leadership and helped coalesce popular support around it. For those, like Ella Baker, a long-time NAACP worker and the inspiration for SNCC, who disapproved of charismatic leadership as disempowering ordinary people, the SCLC was problematic. Baker thought that King did not understand that the movement made him, and not he the movement.[43] Nevertheless, she was careful in interviews at the time to agree that the charismatic basis of the SCLC was justified in that it provided a reliable focal point.[44] For those who saw King's personality as a movement asset, the fact that the SCLC revolved around him was not a problem.

The SCLC's attention was usually on the national scene and it attempted to coordinate events for maximum national impact. These characteristics could make local organizations feel manipulated. SNCC activists also felt that the SCLC tended to come in and take credit for the long hard work they had been doing.[45] These were immediate sources of friction in the 1960s. Despite this and SNCC's conviction that the SCLC was bourgeois and too religious, Adam Fairclough argued (with twenty years' distance) that the two organizations maintained fairly good relations. For example, unlike the NAACP, both SNCC and the SCLC approved of King's 1965 announcement that he was against the Vietnam War.

Fairclough assessed the SCLC as successful in the South, but not in the North. Seven years later, Thomas R. Peake, in *Keeping the Dream Alive*, assessed the SCLC as having made a creditable start on the enormous problems of the urban north. It had managed to force concessions out of Chicago's wily Mayor Daley, even though he reneged on his promises. Peake's discussion of the SCLC ended when in 1982 it grew a women's caucus, or a "women power network." While this was a gesture of inclusion toward women, Peake does not evaluate the development.[46] Neither Fairclough's nor Peake's work analyzes the

---

[43]Morris, *Origins*, pp. 91–93; Joanne Grant, *Ella Baker, Freedom Bound* (New York, 1998), p. 123.

[44]Morris, *Origins*, p. 92.

[45]Fairclough, *SCLC*, pp. 240–243

[46]Thomas R. Peake, *Keeping the Dream Alive: A History of the Southern Christian Leadership Conference from King to the Nineteen-Eighties* (New York, 1987).

SCLC's membership and inner dynamics. But Joanne Grant's 1998 biography of Ella Baker does offer such an analysis.

Baker was grieved with King and the SCLC because of its male orientation and King's sexist attitudes.[47] Baker had been thinking about leadership for a long time, and the SCLC went against her most cherished egalitarian ideals. Baker believed that change could only come about when people themselves were transformed from passive objects of others' decisions to activists, first and foremost, on behalf of themselves and their communities. It was only with SNCC that Baker found a group interested in trying to live out her ideas. SNCC came into being in 1960 after Baker called the Southwide Student Leadership Conference on Nonviolent Resistance to Segregation, inviting about 600 students, including the four who had initiated the sit-in in Greensboro, North Carolina.

The literature on SNCC includes many memoirs, most notably Anne Moody's poignant and defiant *Coming of Age in Mississippi*,[48] which ended on a note of weariness and of hope that had been all but extinguished. SNCC members' trajectory from nonviolent, loving community to militant, violence-espousing black nationalism was sudden and dramatic. The group's founding statement is so transcendently hopeful that disappointment seems, in hindsight, inevitable.

> We affirm the philosophical or religious ideal of nonviolence as the foundation of our purpose, the presupposition of our faith, and the manner of our action. . . . Through nonviolence, courage displaces fear, love transforms hate. Acceptance dissipates prejudice; hope ends despair . . . mutual regard cancels enmity. Justice for all overthrows injustice. The redemptive community supersedes systems of gross social immorality.[49]

SNCC's youth, the drama of its transformation, and its increasing militancy after 1964 led some historians to see it as a metaphor for the whole movement. In 1981, Harvard Sitkoff published *The Struggle for Black Equality, 1954–1980* in which he depicts SNCC's turn toward black nationalism and Black Power as the end of the Civil Rights movement.[50]

Political scientist Emily Stoper, instead, attributed SNCC's decline

---

[47]Grant, *Freedom*, pp. 105–125.

[48]Anne Moody, *Coming of Age in Mississippi* (New York, 1968).

[49]Quoted in Robert A. Goldberg, *Grassroots Resistance, Social Movements in Twentieth Century America* (Prospect Heights, Ill., 1991), p. 149.

[50]Harvard Sitkoff, *The Struggle for Black Equality, 1954–1992*, rev. ed. (New York, 1993), pp. 199–220.

to internal stresses. She argued that as a "redemptive community" it provided its members with a shared moral vision and a transforming community experience. The influx of outsiders in 1964 and SNCC's own inability to deal with politics as the liberal world practices them, i.e., with compromises and trade-offs, brought the organization to implosion.[51] Most recently, Joanne Grant's biography of Ella Baker traces SNCC's decline to exhaustion and the harassment of the F.B.I. She marks its collapse beginning with what Baker regarded as the rigged election of Stokely Carmichael as chairman. Grant portrays Baker as tolerant of SNCC's turn toward black nationalism and away from nonviolence, understanding of the psychological needs of battle-fatigued activists, and realistic about the organization's decline in efficacy.[52]

Unlike in the other Civil Rights organizations, gender long played an important role in SNCC's history and in its historiography. This is because of the high percentage of female participants, its early ethos of profound egalitarianism, what has been described as a "female style of activism,"[53] and the youth of SNCC participants, some of whom would become active in women's liberation politics. Sara Evans, in *Personal Politics* (1979), argued that SNCC women went on to generate the women's liberation movement after experiencing their own leadership capabilities in a nurturing but still sexist environment.[54] More recently, a number of SNCC women have likewise emphasized their experience of power, but denied the sexism.[55] In 1988, Mary King remembered the paper she co-authored on gender in 1964 as less protest about sexism than a call for SNCC to return to a more "decentralized and democratic" ethos: "We were asking SNCC, will there be room for us as women to act on our beliefs as we had with the early vision of SNCC with the sit-ins?" A related analysis suggests that white and black women experienced the movement differently, particularly during the summer of 1964 when an influx of northern white students resulted in considerable interracial sex and crosscurrents of social tension new to the group.[56]

More broadly, recent memoirs, biographies, and studies of women

---

[51]Emily Stoper, "The Student Nonviolent Coordinating Committee: Rise and Fall of a Redemptive Organization," in Garrow, ed., *We Shall Overcome*, pp. 1041–1062; Lawson, "Freedom Then," 470–471.

[52]Grant, *Freedom*, 125–210.

[53]Lawson, "Freedom Then," 469.

[54]Sara Evans, *Personal Politics: The Roots of Women's Liberation in the Civil Rights Movement and the New Left* (New York, 1979).

[55]Lawson, "Freedom Then," 468–469. Aimee Koch, "The Women of SNCC," unpublished paper, Amherst College, 1999.

[56]Cheryl Lyn Greenberg, ed., *A Circle of Trust: Remembering SNCC* (New Brunswick, N.J., 1998), p. 130; Lawson, "Freedom Then," 469.

have continued to reveal their immense significance to the move-ment.[57] Elaine Brown's description of her years with the Black Pan-thers and her slow awakening to feminism is one of many discussions of the unique difficulties black women have experienced in insisting on women's rights in the context of pervasive racism.[58] Deborah Gray White's *Too Heavy a Load* puts the dilemma of black women in civil rights into a wider perspective while exploring painful class divisions among black women. These divisions, she argues, have inhibited cross-class alliances and repeatedly failed to address the needs of the poor. White reveals the tremendous pressure on women in Civil Rights organizations to shelve their demands for equality with men in the interests of the struggle for racial equality, and particularly singles out the Black Power movement for its misogyny.[59] Her century-long perspective demonstrates that earlier black nationalist movements have also "privileged racial over gender identities."[60]

As the Civil Rights movement recedes in time there remains plenty to discover and much to debate in its history. Restoring women to the movement's history is underway, but unfinished. Understand-ing the role of white sympathizers with Civil Rights remains underex-plored. Articulating a relationship between civil and economic rights becomes more and more crucial at a moment in history where there appear to be no viable alternatives to capitalism. Did the movement destroy itself in a push for economic rights? Or did it abandon larger is-sues on the threshold of progress? Manning Marable has referred to the Civil Rights movement as the Second Reconstruction in order to shine a spotlight on the historical relationship between economic and politi-cal justice. The failure of the federal government to provide economic security by distributing land to newly enfranchised freed people in the South made it possible for elite whites to deprive blacks of the vote for over a century. Black voters in the North and South still do not have the economic power to enforce their political will. Understanding the springs that fed the Civil Rights movement may help to mobilize

---

[57]Martha Prescod Norman, "Shining in the Dark," in *African American Women and the Vote, 1837–1965,* Ann D. Gordon, ed., with Bettye Collier-Thomas, John H. Bracey, Arlene Voski Avakian, and Joyce Avrech Berkman (Amherst, Mass., 1997), pp. 172–199; see especially, Kathryn Nasstrom, "Down to Now: Memory, Narrative, and Women's Leadership in the Civil Rights Movement in Atlanta, Georgia," in *Gender and History* 11 (April 1999): 113–144, and Belinda Robnett, *How Long, How Long: African American Women in the Struggle for Civil Rights* (New York, 1997).

[58]Elaine Brown, *A Taste of Power: A Black Woman's Story* (New York, 1992); see also Paula Giddings, *Where and When I Enter: The Impact of Black Women on Race and Sex in America* (New York, 1984); Pauli Murray, *Pauli Murray: The Autobiography of a Black Activist, Feminist, Lawyer, Priest, and Poet* (Knoxville, Tenn., 1987).

[59]Deborah Gray White, *Too Heavy a Load* (New York, 1999), p. 219.

[60]White, *Too Heavy a Load,* p. 209.

other movements. The historical search for the conditions that produce uncontainable enthusiasm for justice is always vital in an unjust world.

One of the most important questions about the Civil Rights movement is whether Martin Luther King, Jr., was indispensable. Or, as historians arguing the bottom-up viewpoint insist, was he simply one of many possible leaders the movement offered? If he was indispensable, what made him so? If he was not, what is the relationship between grassroots activism, leadership, and organizations such as the NAACP, SCLC, CORE, and SNCC? Can all people, as Ella Baker believed, become their own leaders? What would that kind of transformation mean?

DAVID J. GARROW

DAVID J. GARROW (1953–   ) is professor of political science at the
City College of New York and the City University Graduate Center.
His books include Bearing the Cross: Martin Luther King, Jr. and the
Southern Christian Leadership Conference (1986) and Atlanta, Geor-
gia 1960–1961: Sit-Ins and Student Activism (1989).

Martin Luther King, Jr., began his public career as a reluctant
leader who was drafted, without any foreknowledge on his part, by his
Montgomery colleagues to serve as president of the newly created
Montgomery Improvement Association (MIA). Montgomery's black
civic activists had set up the MIA to pursue the boycott of the city's
segregated buses called by the Women's Political Council (WPC) immediately after the December 1, 1955, arrest of Rosa Parks.

King was only twenty-six years old and had lived in Montgomery
barely fifteen months when he accepted that post on Monday afternoon December 5. Two years later King explained that "I was surprised
to be elected . . . both from the standpoint of my age, but more from
the fact that I was a newcomer to Montgomery." On December 5,
however, King was as much anxious as surprised, for his new post
meant that he would have to deliver the major address at that
evening's community rally, which had been called to decide whether a
fabulously successful one-day boycott would be extended to apply continuing pressure on bus company and city officials to change the bus
seating practices. King later explained that he had found himself "possessed by fear" and "obsessed by a feeling of inadequacy" as he pon-
dered his new challenge, but he turned to prayer and delivered a superb
oration at a jam-packed meeting that unanimously resolved to continue the protest.

Initially King and his MIA colleagues mistakenly presumed that
the boycott would be relatively brief, that white officials would be eager to negotiate a quick solution to the dispute. Indeed, the MIA's
three modest demands asked not for the abolition of segregated seating, but only for the elimination of two troubling practices that the
WPC had been protesting for several years: black riders never could sit
in the ten front "white only" seats on each bus, no matter how
crowded with black riders a bus might be, and black riders seated to
the rear of the reserved section had to surrender their seats to any

David J. Garrow, "Martin Luther King, Jr., and the Spirit of Leadership," Journal of
American History 74 (September 1987). Reprinted with the permission of the Journal of
American History.

newly boarding white riders for whom front seats were not available. Instead, the MIA proposed, blacks would seat themselves from the rear forward, and whites from the front backward, without the two races ever sharing parallel seats. There would be no reserved seats, and no one would have to give up a seat once taken.

Only on Thursday afternoon December 8, after the first negotiating session had ended with the city evincing no willingness to compromise with the MIA's requests, did King and his colleagues begin to realize that the modesty of their demands would not speed white concessions. WPC president Jo Ann Robinson, reflecting back on the white obstinacy, explained that "they feared that anything they gave us would be viewed by us as just a start." The intransigence of the city and bus company officials continued at a second negotiating session and then a third, where King objected strenuously to the addition of a White Citizens Council leader to the city delegation. His objection angered several whites, who accused King himself of acting in bad faith. Still anxious about his leadership role, King was taken aback and left temporarily speechless. "For a moment," he later remembered, "It appeared that I was alone." Then his best friend and MIA partner, Rev. Ralph D. Abernathy, spoke up to rebut the white's claims. Thanks to that crucial assistance, King overcame his first major anxiety crisis since the afternoon of his election.

After that tense session, however, King's doubts about his ability to serve as the boycott's leader increased. He confessed to "a terrible sense of guilt" over the angry exchanges at the meeting, and he became painfully aware that white Montgomery had launched a whispering campaign against him personally. "I almost broke down under the continuing battering," King stated two years later. His MIA colleagues rallied around him, however, and made clear their full support.

By mid-January 1956, as the ongoing boycott received increased press coverage, King became the focal point of substantial public attention. That visibility made King a particular target when Montgomery's city commissioners adopted new, "get tough" tactics against the MIA. On Thursday, January 26, while giving several people a lift as part of the MIA's extremely successful car pool transportation system, King was pulled over by two policemen and carted off to the city jail on the fallacious charge of going thirty miles per hour in a twenty-five-mile-per-hour zone. For the first time since the protest had begun, King feared for his immediate physical safety. Initially, he was uncertain as to where the officers were taking him. "When I was first arrested," he admitted two years later, "I thought I was going to be lynched." Instead, King was fingerprinted and jailed for the first time in his life, thrown into a filthy group cell with a variety of black criminals. In a few moments' time, Abernathy and other MIA colleagues began arriving at the jail, and white officials agreed to King's release. His trial would be Saturday.

That arrest and jailing focused all the personal tensions and anxieties King had been struggling with since the first afternoon of his election. The increased news coverage had brought with it a rising tide of anonymous, threatening phone calls to his home and office, and King had begun to wonder whether his involvement was likely to end up costing him, his wife, Coretta, and their two-month-old daughter, Yolanda, much more than he had initially imagined. The next evening January 27, King's crisis of confidence peaked. He returned home late, received yet another threatening phone call, and went to bed, but he found himself unable to sleep. He went to the kitchen, made some coffee, and sat down at the kitchen table "I started thinking about many things," he later explained. He thought about the obstacles the boycott was confronting, and about the increasing threats of physical harm. "I was ready to give up," he remembered. "With my cup of coffee sitting untouched before me I tried to think of a way to move out of the picture without appearing a coward," a way to hand over the leadership of the MIA to someone else. He thought about his life up until that time. "The first twenty-five years of my life were very comfortable years, very happy years," King later recalled.

> I didn't have to worry about anything. I have a marvelous mother and father. They went out of their way to provide everything for their children . . . I went right on through school; I never had to drop out to work or anything. And you know, I was about to conclude that life had been wrapped up for me in a Christmas package.
>
> Now of course I was religious, I grew up in the church. I'm the son of a preacher . . . my grandfather was a preacher, my great grandfather was a preacher . . . my daddy's brother is a preacher, so I didn't have much choice, I guess. But I had grown up in the church, and the church meant something very real to me, but it was a kind of inherited religion and I had never felt an experience with God in the way that you must . . . if you're going to walk the lonely paths of this life.

That night, for the first time in his life, King felt such an experience as he thought about how his leadership of the MIA was fundamentally altering what had until then been an almost completely trouble-free life.

> If I had a problem, I could always call Daddy—my earthly father. Things were solved. But one day after finishing school, I was called to a little church down in Montgomery, Alabama, and I started preaching there. Things were going well in that church, it was a marvelous experience. But one day a year later, a lady by the name of Rosa Parks decided that she wasn't going to take it any longer. . . . It was the beginning of a movement, . . . and the people of Montgomery asked me

to serve them as a spokesman, and as the president of the new organization . . . that came into being to lead the boycott. I couldn't say no.

And then we started our struggle together. Things were going well for the first few days, but then, . . . after the white people in Montgomery knew that we meant business, they started doing some nasty things. They started making some nasty telephone calls, and it came to the point that some days more than forty telephone calls would come in, threatening my life, the life of my family, the life of my child. I took it for a while, in a strong manner.

That night, however, in the wake of his arrest and jailing and the continuing telephone threats, King's strength was depleted. Then, in what would forever be, in his mind, the most central and formative event in his life, Martin King's understanding of his role underwent a profound spiritual transformation.

"It was around midnight," he explained years later. "You can have some strange experiences at midnight." That last threatening phone call had gotten to him. "Nigger, we are tired of you and your mess now, and if you aren't out of this town in three days, we're going to blow your brains out and blow up your house."

I sat there and thought about a beautiful little daughter who had just been born. . . . She was the darling of my life. I'd come in night after night and see that little gentle smile. And I sat at that table thinking about that little girl and thinking about the fact that she could be taken from me any minute.

And I started thinking about a dedicated, devoted and loyal wife who was over there asleep. And she could be taken from me, or I could be taken from her. And I got to the point that I couldn't take it any longer. I was weak. Something said to me, you can't call on Daddy now, he's up in Atlanta a hundred and seventy-five miles away. You can't even call on Mama now. You've got to call on that something in that person that your Daddy used to tell you about, that power that can make a way out of no way.

And I discovered then that religion had to become real to me, and I had to know God for myself. And I bowed down over that cup of coffee. I never will forget it . . . I prayed a prayer, and I prayed out loud that night. I said, "Lord, I'm down here trying to do what's right. I think I'm right. I think the cause that we represent is right. But Lord, I must confess that I'm weak now. I'm faltering. I'm losing my courage. And I can't let the people see me like this because if they see me weak and losing my courage, they will begin to get weak."

Then it happened.

And it seemed at that moment that I could hear an inner voice saying to me, "Martin Luther, stand up for righteousness. Stand up for

justice. Stand up for truth. And lo I will be with you, even until the
end of the world." . . . I heard the voice of Jesus saying still to fight on.
He promised never to leave me, never to leave me alone. No never
alone, no never alone. He promised never to leave me, never to leave
me alone.

That experience, that encounter in the kitchen, gave King a new
strength and courage to go on. "Almost at once my fears began to go.
My uncertainty disappeared."

The vision in the kitchen allowed King to go forward with feelings
of companionship, of self-assurance, and of mission that were vastly
greater spiritual resources than anything he had been able to draw on
during the boycott's first eight weeks. It also allowed him to begin appreciating that his leadership role was not simply a matter of accident
or chance, but was first and foremost an opportunity for service—not
an opportunity King would have sought, but an opportunity he could
not forsake. His new strength also enabled him to conquer, thoroughly
and permanently, the fear that had so possessed him that Friday night
in his kitchen, while allowing him to appreciate that although his calling might be unique, it was the calling, and not himself, that was the
spiritual centerpiece of his developing role.

That strength and dedication remained with King throughout the
Montgomery protest, which ended in success, with the integration of
the city's buses just prior to Christmas 1956. In the wake of that
achievement, however, some whites directed repeated acts of violence
against the newly desegregated buses, and in mid-January a series of
bombings struck several black churches and the homes of MIA leaders. The violence weighed heavily on a very tired King. Then, on Sunday morning January 27—the first anniversary of King's kitchen
experience—twelve sticks of dynamite, along with a fuse that had
smoldered out, were found on the porch of King's parsonage.

The murder attempt deeply affected King. In his sermon later that
morning to his Dexter Avenue Baptist Church congregation, he explained how his experience one year earlier had allowed him to resolve
his previous fears about the question of his own role and fate. "I realize
that there were moments when I wanted to give up and I was afraid
but You gave me a vision in the kitchen of my house and I am thankful
for it." King told his listeners how, early in the boycott, "I went to bed
many nights scared to death." Then,

early on a sleepless morning in January 1956, rationality left me. . . .
Almost out of nowhere I heard a voice that morning saying to me,
"Preach the gospel, stand up for truth, stand up for righteousness."
Since that morning I can stand up without fear.

So I'm not afraid of anybody this morning. Tell Montgomery they
can keep shooting and I'm going to stand up to them; tell Mont-

gomery they can keep bombing and I'm going to stand up to them. If I had to die tomorrow morning I would die happy because I've been to the mountaintop and I've seen the promised land and it's going to be here in Montgomery.

Those remarks, uttered in January 1957, and so clearly presaging the very similar comments that King made in Memphis, Tennessee, on the evening of April 3, 1968, bring home a simple but crucial point: that Martin Luther King, Jr.'s mountaintop experience did not occur in April 1968, nor even in August 1963, but took place in the kitchen at 309 South Jackson Street in Montgomery on January 27, 1956. King's understanding of his role, his mission, and his fate was *not* something that developed only or largely in the latter stages of his public career. It was present in a rather complete form as early as the second month of the Montgomery boycott.

Appreciating King's own understanding of his role and responsibilities is really *more* crucial than anything else, I would contend, to comprehending the kind of leadership that Martin Luther King, Jr., gave to the American black freedom struggle of the 1950s and 1960s. By 1963–1964, as that role and those responsibilities grew, King thought increasingly about his own destiny and what he termed "this challenge to be loyal to something that transcends our immediate lives." "We have," he explained to one audience, "a responsibility to set out to discover what we are made for, to discover our life's work, to discover what we are called to do. And after we discover that, we should set out to do it with all of the strength and all of the power that we can muster." As his close confidant Andrew Young later expressed it, "I think that Martin always felt that he had a special purpose in life and that that purpose in life was something that was given to him by God, that he was the son and grandson of Baptist preachers, and he understood, I think, the scriptural notion of men of destiny. That came from his family and his church, and basically the Bible."

The revelation in the kitchen gave King not only the ability to understand his role and destiny, but also the spiritual strength necessary to accept and cope with his personal mission and fate. Its effect was more profoundly an ongoing sense of companionship and reassurance than simply a memory of a onetime sensation. "There are certain spiritual experiences that we continue to have," King stated, "that cannot be explained with materialistic notions." One "knows deep down within there is something in the very structure of the cosmos that will ultimately bring about fulfillment and the triumph of that which is right. And this is the only thing that can keep one going in difficult periods."

King's understanding of his life underwent a significant deepening when he was awarded the 1964 Nobel Peace Prize. The prize signaled the beginning of a fundamental growth in King's own sense of mission and in his willingness to accept a prophetic role. "History has thrust me into this position," he told reporters the day the award was announced. "It would both be immoral and a sign of ingratitude if I did not face my moral responsibility to do what I can in this struggle."

More and more in those years King thought of his own life in terms of the cross. It was an image he invoked repeatedly, beginning as early as his 1960 imprisonment in Georgia's Reidsville State Prison. He focused particularly on it, and on the memory of his experience in the kitchen, at times of unusual tension and stress. In mid-September 1966, amid a deteriorating intramovement debate about the "Black Power" slogan, King talked about how his sense of mission was increasingly becoming a sense of burden.

> We are gravely mistaken to think that religion protects us from the pain and agony of mortal existence. Life is not a euphoria of unalloyed comfort and untroubled ease. Christianity has always insisted that the cross we bear precedes the crown we wear. To be a Christian one must take up his cross, with all its difficulties and agonizing and tension-packed content, and carry it until that very cross leaves its mark upon us and redeems us to that more excellent way which comes only through suffering.

More than anything else, the Vietnam War issue brought King face to face with what was becoming a consciously self-sacrificial understanding of his role and fate. He had spoken out publicly against America's conduct of the war as early as March 1965 and had stepped up his comments during July and August 1965, but he had drawn back in the face of harsh criticism of his views stimulated by the Johnson administration. Throughout 1966, King largely had kept his peace, reluctant to reignite a public debate about the propriety of the nation's leading civil rights spokesman becoming a head-on critic of the incumbent administration's uppermost policy. Then, in early 1967, King resolved to take on Lyndon B. Johnson's war publicly as never before.

King knew full well that his new, aggressive stance on the war would harm him politically and might well damage the civil rights movement financially. Those considerations, however, were not enough to shake King from his resolve. "At times you do things to satisfy your conscience and they may be altogether unrealistic or wrong but you feel better," King explained over wiretapped phone lines to his longtime friend and counselor, Stanley Levison. America's involvement in Vietnam was so evil, King explained, that "I can no longer be cautious about this matter. I feel so deep in my heart that we are so wrong in this country and the time has come for a real prophecy and I'm willing to go that road."

King's attacks on the war, and particularly his April 4, 1967, antiwar speech at New York's Riverside Church, brought down a flood of public criticism on his head. Even some of King's most trusted advisers, including Levison, reproached him for the tone of that speech. King, however, rejected the complaints. "I was politically unwise but morally wise. I think I have a role to play which may be unpopular," he told Levison. "I really feel that someone of influence has to say that the United States is wrong, and everybody is afraid to say it."

In late May 1967, King spoke to his aides about how he had come to see the war issue in terms of his understanding of the cross.

> When I took up the cross, I recognized its meaning . . . The cross is something that you bear and ultimately that you die on. The cross may mean the death of your popularity. It may mean the death of a foundation grant. It may cut down your budget a little, but take up your cross, and just bear it. And that's the way I've decided to go.

No longer did he suffer from any indecision on the question of Vietnam.

> I want you to know that my mind is made up. I backed up a little when I came out in 1965. My name then wouldn't have been written in any book called *Profiles in Courage*. But now I have decided that I will not be intimidated. I will not be harassed. I will not be silent, and I will be heard.

King's determination to forge ahead in the face of discouraging political circumstances also manifested itself during the late 1967-early 1968 planning of the Poor People's Campaign, Washington protests intended to be so "dislocative and even disruptive" that the federal government would launch a full-scale program to eliminate poverty in America. On March 28 King's determination to pursue the campaign faltered and turned to despair when a protest march that he had helped lead in Memphis, Tennessee, ended in widespread violence. The next day a deeply depressed King poured out his feelings to Levison in a long phone conversation. Levison refused to accept King's assertions that the Memphis violence was an all-but-fatal blow to King's public status as a nonviolent civil rights leader. King demurred. "All I'm saying is that Roy Wilkins, that Bayard Rustin and that stripe, and there are many of them, and the Negroes who are influenced by what they read in the newspapers, Adam Clayton Powell, for another reason . . . their point is, 'I'm right. Martin Luther King is dead. He's finished. His nonviolence is nothing, no one is listening to it.' Let's face it, we do have a great public relations setback where my image and my leadership are concerned." Levison disagreed, but King insisted that the media reaction would be extremely damaging, and that he would have to help stage a second, completely successful Memphis march to overcome the damage from the first one.

King also told Levison that he was deeply pessimistic about the entire Poor People's Campaign. "I think our Washington campaign is
doomed." Even though he had long been "a symbol of nonviolence" to
millions, in the press coverage of the March 28 violence "everything
will come out weakening the symbol. It will put many Negroes in
doubt. It will put many Negroes in the position of saying, 'Well, that's
true, Martin Luther King is at the end of his rope.'" Levison again responded that King ought to reject the news media's portrayals. "You
can't keep them from imposing it," King answered. "You watch your
newspapers. . . . I think it will be the most negative thing about Martin
Luther King that you have ever seen."

King's expectations proved largely correct. The *New York Times*,
terming the Memphis violence "a powerful embarrassment to Dr.
King," recommended he call off the Poor People's Campaign since it
probably would prove counterproductive to his cause. King, however,
did not give up, and on Wednesday, April 3, he returned to Memphis to
aid in the preparations for a second march. That evening at the cav-
ernous Mason Temple church, before a modest-sized but emotionally
enthusiastic crowd, King vowed that both the Memphis movement
and the Poor People's Campaign would go forward. Then he turned to
an emotional recapitulation of his own involvement in the preceding
thirteen years of the black freedom struggle, expressing how happy and
thankful he was that he had been given the opportunity to contribute
to and to live through its many significant events. Then he closed with
the same ending he had used more than eleven years earlier in Montgomery when he had first explained how the vision in the kitchen had
given him the strength and the courage to keep going forward.

> I don't know what will happen now. We've got some difficult days
> ahead. But it really doesn't matter with me now, because I've been to
> the mountaintop. And I don't mind. Like anybody, I would like to live
> a long life. Longevity has its place. But I'm not concerned with that
> now. I just want to do God's will. And he's allowed me to go up to the
> mountain, and I've looked over, and I've seen the promised land. I
> may not get there with you. But I want you to know tonight that we,
> as a people, will get to the promised land. And so I'm happy tonight.
> I'm not worried about anything. I'm not fearing any men. Mine eyes
> have seen the glory of the coming of the Lord.

In conclusion, then, I want to reiterate that the key to comprehending Martin King's own understanding of his life, his role, his burden, and his mission lies in that spiritual experience that began for
him in his Montgomery kitchen on January 27, 1956. Martin King's
awareness that his calling was to devote and ultimately to sacrifice his
own individual life in the service of a great and just cause ennobled

him as a human being, strengthened him as a leader, and allowed him to accept the symbolic role and accompanying fate that helped propel forward a struggle he rightfully recognized would be never ending.

N A T H A N   I R V I N   H U G G I N S

NATHAN IRVIN HUGGINS (1927–1989) was W.E.B. Du Bois professor of history and Afro-American studies and the director of the W.E.B. Du Bois Institute for Afro-American Research at Harvard University. His works include Black Odyssey: The African American Ordeal in Slavery *(1977) and* Harlem Renaissance *(1971).*

The historical importance of Martin Luther King, Jr., goes beyond his work in the civil rights movement, as important as that was. To begin with, King represents a kind of black leadership generally unknown at earlier periods in United States history. In the past, black leaders, for the most part, whether they were reform minded or accommodationists, had very little tie to a power base. (By and large, black leaders could be characterized as spokesmen and brokers between white power and blacks.) King, however, rested his leadership on a religious establishment that extended beyond his particular church, on a constituency (both white and black) that followed him for reasons of ideology and strategy.

He also differed from conventional black leaders by his seeming independence from party machinery, from institutional constraints. He was free to address himself to issues broader than race and racial justice. Despite objections from conventional leaders in the movement, King spoke out on poverty and economic injustice. He was most daring and independent in his outspoken criticism of the war in Vietnam despite angry opposition from the president and the leadership of the Democratic party. Many liberal leaders, especially blacks in conventional organizations, did not hide their displeasure and their fear that King might help accelerate a shift of national interest from civil rights to peace. Furthermore, the traditional arena for black protest

---

Nathan Irvin Huggins, "Martin Luther King, Jr.: Charisma and Leadership," *Journal of American History* 74 (September 1987). Reprinted with the permission of the *Journal of American History*.

was racial justice and domestic issues akin to race relations. King, however, took his leadership off conventional turf.

The authors of all the papers express some discomfort in singling out Martin Luther King to honor. He was only one man in a movement, although a very prominent one. Focus on him is very likely to cause us to ignore the hundreds of leaders and heroes who were crucial to the movement. Some are troubled by the "great man" implications of such celebrations as this. After all, what happened in the 1960s had more to do with broad social and economic changes and with the wave of young and old people who were willing to put their bodies on the line than with personality and oratory. Others are troubled that such celebrations as this will end in trivializing or co-opting the memory of Martin Luther King. Consider the incongruity of the Marine band concert as a part of the festivities honoring the nonviolent Dr. King. Some are troubled by charismatic leadership itself, wanting to deny the implication that people must await another such individual before the movement can be reborn.

No one is more troubled than I am by Great Man approaches to historical events. We can be sure that some of what occurred in the 1960s would have occurred without any given individual, Martin Luther King included. Yet it is foolish to imagine that the individual actors were interchangeable parts and that, without the particular personality of Martin Luther King, someone else would have served as well. Individuals do make a difference, and when they play such important roles as did Dr. King, we must give them great attention.

Of course it is impossible, counterfactually, to remove Dr. King from those events to see how they would have been different. We know, however, that they would have been very different. And I believe, as I am sure some of you believe, the movement and the rest of us would have been much the losers without him. That means we must study him, and that we are able, by memorializing him, to recapture many of the ideals, aims, and achievements of the movement. Those who were not active in the movement (a number which will grow as years pass) will be unable to rediscover the movement as well by studying any of the other leaders, however heroic and deserving they might be. Because King's role was more central—his vision more inclusive—than those of others, he will offer a better lens through which to see the movement.

Our difficulty with charismatic leadership comes, I believe, from our distrust of the nonrational. We, as scholars, are intellectuals and, for the most part, rationalists. We are also aware that masses who are galvanized by one man for good ends may be subject to capture by another for evil ends. Some of the most fearful and inhuman moments in recent history have been results of some charismatic leader. Furthermore, we would like to think that men and women can organize themselves to act politically without the magnet of someone's intense vision and message.

Yet the nonrational is central to our political and social lives. Lacking strong institutional ties, Americans (white and black) are likely to be organized and moved by individuals with the power to make us believe in their visions. We should not forget that charisma is an *exchange* between the leader and the group. There are values, myths, hopes, fears, anxieties awaiting expression in the crowd to which the charismatic leader gives voice. The exchange is not completely mindless, and charisma touches something genuine, or else it does not exist.

Just as we historians find it difficult to deal with nonrational charisma, we are ill at ease with true religious phenomena. As David J. Garrow has pointed out, Martin Luther King saw the prayerful moment in his kitchen as the turning point in his understanding of his "call." He sat at his table in his Montgomery home, near despair. His earthly father, who had always before been his guide and counselor was in Atlanta. He said that at that juncture he turned to his "heavenly father," and he was told the way to go. From that point on, there would be other moments of dejection and depression, but he never again doubted his purpose, and he would again and again recall that Montgomery moment as the sign, the signal. The moment in the kitchen that King described (although he does not use the words) was the sort of religious experience central to the Christian tradition.

What is the historian to do with that? We mention it of course, but we are poorly equipped to discuss the inner terrain of spirit and mind that was transformed by that event. As social scientists or humanists, our training gives us little to work on. The central point is that Martin Luther King believed in God, in a Christian God, and his life was shaped by that fact, from the inside out. For most of us, that belief remains a mystery. We are products of a secular age in which religion is trivialized or popularized to make it palatable to all. We all will admit to the importance of the black church, but few of us are able to see beyond its institutional character.

Both the religious and spiritual character of Martin Luther King and the charismatic factor challenge us to look deeper into the nonrational and spiritual dimensions of the man and the movement. Sadly, however, we have few scholarly examples to show us the way. Psychology might seem a possible source of guidance, but it is difficult to shake the focus on the pathological in its methodology. I have been drawn again to William James's *Varieties of Religious Experience*. What is remarkable about the lectures contained in that volume is that James takes the religious experience seriously. That is, he does not assume reason to be the norm, and nonrational experience to be in some sense perverse. His lectures in the book—"The Divided Self,"

"Conversion," and "Saintliness"—are much to the point of Martin Luther King's experience.

Dr. King encouraged us to understand his tactics of nonviolent resistance as deriving from Gandhi. While there was no doubt a Gandhian influence, I think it much more important to understand nonviolence in relation to the tradition of the southern black Christian. At least one of King's teachers at Boston University, Howard Thurman, had visited Gandhi and had incorporated some of the Eastern vision into his theology. But the tactic worked in the southern setting because of the deep tradition of Christian stoicism in the black community. Blacks had long appreciated the moral superiority of those who continued to do right despite violence and oppression. When King repeated again and again that "undeserved suffering is redemptive," he was merely iterating a value that his southern black audiences had lived their lives by. Christian stoicism was the traditional base on which southern blacks engrafted King's message of nonviolence.

That it did not work well in the North is not surprising. Northern blacks had lived in a world where institutions like the church were relatively weakened in their influence on individual lives. Theirs was a competitive world in which the "payoff was all that mattered in the end. Pragmatism was the touchstone of northern urban life. Does it pay? Will we win? Does it work? Those were the questions that nonviolent tactics had to answer, and for King's leadership, the answers were too slow in coming. Nonviolence seemed to mean acquiescing in violence against blacks with no real payoff. By 1965–1966, nonviolence had even played out in the South. The message of leaders like Malcolm X had greater power in northern cities and among the young people in the movement.

King and his nonviolence, nevertheless, had a kind of power that alternate strategies lacked. His message was *inclusive*. He spoke always of love, without boundary of race, class, or nation. His audience, from wherever it came, could feel included, invited to join the march to racial and human justice. There was a place for everyone, white and black, Jew and Gentile. That inclusiveness characterized that part of the movement, that phase of the movement, which King dominated. The move away from nonviolence, however understandable, came at the cost of universality. Malcolm X, for example, implied boundaries. Self-defense, after all, *excludes* those other than "self."

Finally, to return to the general concern of many of the papers in this conference the focus on the man rather than the movement. It is my view that we have to focus on the man precisely because he gives us a lens through which to see the larger picture, a picture otherwise lost to those not participants in the movement. It is nevertheless, right to be cautious lest one surrender to hero worship. Fortunately, we know enough of the humanness of King to keep us from that trap.

Robert Moses has spoken of the movement as an ocean, with individuals (Dr. King among them) as waves on that ocean. Without the ocean the individuals would be of little significance. He would have us focus on the movement and not the man. For myself, I am no more comfortable with metaphors of oceans and waves than I am of focus on the central individual. Likening the movement to an ocean implies that it has a constant flood and direction, which frees us from the endless wait for the individual leader. But we have no better understanding of the lunar phases that cause the tides of the movement than we do of the lodestars that come from time to time into our view to give us direction. There is as much danger in romanticizing movements as in romanticizing individual leaders.

C L A Y B O R N E   C A R S O N

CLAYBORNE CARSON (1944–   ) is professor of history at Stanford University and senior editor and director of the Martin Luther King, Jr., Papers Project. His books include In Struggle: SNCC and the Black Awakening of the 1960s *(1981), which won the Frederick Jackson Turner Award,* Eyes on the Prize: America's Civil Rights Years *(1987), and* Malcolm X: The FBI Files *(1991).*

Until recent years, the classical sociological view of social movements prevailed in the study of what is generally called the civil rights movement. Use of the term "civil rights" itself is based on the assumption that the southern black movements of the 1960s remained within the ideological boundaries of previous civil rights activism. . . .

Thus, until recently, the civil rights literature was comprised mainly of studies of the major national civil rights leaders and their organizations. Following the lead of sociologists, most historians assumed that the black insurgences of the decade after the Montgomery bus boycott could best be understood within the context of a national campaign for civil rights reform. They saw mass activism among blacks as an extension of previous institutionalized civil rights reform efforts. To be sure, historians recognized that the new activism went beyond the once dominant NAACP tactics of litigation, lobbying, and propagandizing, but they saw increased black activism as a new tactic within a familiar strategy based on appeals to power. Protest was a product of widespread black dissatisfaction with the pace of racial change rather than with underlying strategies to achieve change. Instead of viewing mass activism as an independent social force, with its own emergent values and ideology, scholars were more likely to see it as an amorphous source of social energy that could be directed by the leaders of national civil rights organizations. . . .

Embedded in this literature is the assumption that the black struggle can best be understood as a protest movement, orchestrated by national leaders in order to achieve national civil rights legislation. As already noted, use of the term civil rights movement, rather than such alternatives as black freedom struggle, reflects the misleading assumption that the black insurgences of the 1950s and 1960s were part of a coordinated national campaign. Viewing the black struggle as a national civil rights reform effort rather than a locally-based social movement has caused scholars to see Birmingham in the spring of 1963 and Selma in the winter and spring of 1965 as the prototypical black protest movements of the decade. In reality, however, hundreds of southern communities were disrupted by sustained protest movements that lasted, in some cases, for years.

These local protest movements involved thousands of protesters, including large numbers of working class blacks, and local organizers who were more concerned with local issues, including employment opportunities and political power, than with achieving national legislation. Rather than remaining within the ideological confines of the integrationism or King's Christian-Gandhianism, the local movements displayed a wide range of ideologies and proto-ideologies, involving militant racial or class consciousness. Self-reliant indigenous leaders who headed autonomous local protest organizations have been incorrectly portrayed as King's lieutenants or followers even when they adopted nonviolence as a political weapon rather than a philosophy of life and were clearly acting independently of King or of the Southern Christian Leadership Conference, which he headed. . . .

Careful examinations of local movements . . . challenge the assumption that national leaders, notably Martin Luther King, orchestrated local protest movements in their efforts to alter national public opinion and national policy. There is much to suggest that national civil rights organizations and their leaders played only minor roles in bringing about most local insurgences. It was more often the case that local black movements produced their own distinctive ideas and indigenous leadership rather than that these movements resulted from initiative of national leaders.

The Montgomery bus boycott, for example, began in 1955 as the result of an unplanned act of defiance by Rosa Parks. Martin Luther

King, Jr., emerged as a spokesman and as a nationally-known proponent of nonviolent resistance only after Montgomery blacks had launched their movement and formed their own local organization—the Montgomery Improvement Association. King's organization, the Southern Christian Leadership Conference, was formed only after the boycott ended. To be sure, the Montgomery struggle was an extension of previous civil rights reform efforts, but it began as an outgrowth of local institutional networks rather than as a project of any national civil rights organization.

Similarly, no national organization or leader initiated the next major stage of the black struggle, the lunch counter sit-ins of 1960. SCLC, CORE, and the NAACP attempted to provide ideological and tactical guidance for student protesters after the initial sit-in in Greensboro, but student activists insisted on forming their own local groups under student leadership. Even the Student Nonviolent Coordinating Committee, which was founded by student protest leaders, was unable to guide the sit-in movement—a fact that contributed to SNCC's subsequent support for the principle of local autonomy.

CORE initiated the Freedom Rides of 1961, but this desegregation effort did not become a major social movement until CORE abandoned the rides after protesters were attacked by whites in Alabama. Student militants formed their own organizations. Hundreds of student freedom riders then brought the movement into Mississippi and later to other parts of the South.

The Freedom Rides provided a stimulus for the massive Albany protests of December 1961, which became a model for mass mobilizations of black communities elsewhere in the South. Each of the national civil rights organizations tried to offer guidance for the mass marches and demonstrations which culminated in the Birmingham protests of spring 1963, but by the summer of that year it had become clear to national black leaders that the black struggle had acquired a momentum over which they had little control. A. Philip Randolph, the black leader who proposed a march on Washington, told President Kennedy, "The Negroes are already in the streets. It is very likely impossible to get them off. If they are bound to be in the streets in any case, is it not better that they be led by organizations dedicated to civil rights and disciplined by struggle rather than to leave them to other leaders who care neither about civil rights nor about nonviolence?" Malcolm X recognized and identified with the local black leadership that mobilized the black insurgences of 1963: "In Cambridge, Maryland, Gloria Richardson; in Danville, Virginia, and other parts of the country, local leaders began to stir up our people at the grass-roots level. This was never done by these Negroes of national stature."

Even this brief discussion of the early history of the southern black struggle should reveal a major weakness of studies that assumed that

King played a dominant initiating role in southern protests. These studies have not determined the extent to which King was actually able to implement his nonviolent strategy in specific places. Studies focused on civil rights leaders and organizations, rather than on local movements, often give the impression that King was not only the major national spokesman for the black struggle but also its prime instigator.

During the period from 1956 to 1961, however, King played only a minor role as a protest mobilizer as opposed to his role as a national symbol of the black struggle. Acknowledgement that King had limited control over the southern struggle should not detract from his historical importance as a heroic and intellectually seminal leader; recognition of King's actual role instead reminds us that his greatness was rooted in a momentous social movement. Numerous black communities organized bus boycotts and, later, sit-in movements with little direct involvement by King, who was seen by many black activists as a source of inspiration rather than of tactical direction. Even in Albany, where he played a major role in the 1961 and 1962 protests, he joined a movement that was already in progress and worked alongside indigenous leaders who often accepted but sometimes rejected his advice. In St. Augustine, Birmingham, and Selma, he also assisted movements that had existed before his arrival. In numerous other communities, movements arose and were sustained over long periods with little or no involvement by King or his organization.

Moreover, these local movements should not be viewed as protest activity designed to persuade and coerce the federal government to act on behalf of black civil rights. There was a constant tension between the national black leaders, who saw mass protest as an instrument for reform, and local leaders and organizers who were often more interested in building enduring local institutions rather than staging marches and rallies for a national audience. Local black leadership sought goals that were quite distinct from the national civil rights agenda. Even in communities where King played a major role, as in Albany, Birmingham, and Selma, he was compelled to work with local leaders who were reluctant, to say the least, to implement strategies developed by outsiders.

Black communities mobilized not merely to prod the federal government into action on behalf of blacks but to create new social identities for participants and for all Afro-Americans. The prevailing scholarly conception of the civil rights movement suggests a movement that ended in 1965, when one of the last major campaigns led by a civil rights organization prompted the passage of the Voting Rights Act. The notion of a black freedom struggle seeking a broad range of goals suggests, in contrast, that there was much continuity between the period before 1965 and the period after. Contrary to the oft-expressed view that the civil rights movement died during the mid-

1960's, we find that many local activists stressed the continuity between the struggles to gain political rights for southern blacks and the
struggles to exercise them in productive ways. Rather than claiming
that a black power movement displaced the civil rights movement,
they would argue that a black freedom movement seeking generalized
racial advancement evolved into a black power movement toward the
unachieved goals of the earlier movement.

In summary, scholars have portrayed the black struggle as an aug-
mentation of traditional civil rights reform strategies directed by national civil rights organizations. They have stressed the extent to
which national civil rights leaders were able to transform otherwise
undirected mass discontent into an effective instrument to speed the
pace of reform.

This conception of the black struggle has encountered a strong
challenge from a new generation of scholars who have closely examined the internal dynamics of the black struggle in order to determine
its sources and emergent norms. . . .

Aldon Morris . . . makes an admirable attempt to do something
that the previous generation of scholars neglected to do—that is, to determine how as well as why movements arise and to do this by actually undertaking serious historical research. His original interviews
with many of the leaders of the black struggle are themselves wonder-
ful contributions to historical scholarship. . . .

On the one hand, Morris seeks to demonstrate that indigenous
black institutional and leadership networks played major roles in sustaining the black struggle; this is a notion I have no difficulty accepting. On the other hand, he also wants to show that preexisting black
institutions invariably initiated and sustained those struggles. His evidence demonstrates that these organizations provided vital resources
for those individuals who initiated the local movements, but far more
careful research into documentary evidence from the period would be
needed to assess the role played by civil rights organizations as opposed to individuals acting independently of those organizations. In
some instances, my own interviews with the same individuals placed
greater emphasis on the restraining influence on black activism of pre-
existing organizations. In numerous instances, isolated individuals engaged in protest-initiating actions that were unauthorized by any
organization, and these voluntary actions served as catalysts for mobilizing existing institutions into action. To conclude, for example, that
spontaneity played little role in the sit-ins of the 1960s because many
individuals involved in initiating the sit-ins were affiliated with organizations is to downplay the disruptive impact of the sit-ins on those
organizations. . . .

It should be possible to direct attention to the fact that preexisting
institutions, leaders, and organizations were critically involved in all

phases of the struggle without losing sight of the numerous ways in which activism served to challenge existing arrangements in black communities. To maintain, for example, that existing black church networks were vital to the struggle should not lead us to ignore the fact that many black churches did little to aid the struggle, did not join the umbrella organizations that came into being to sustain protest activity, and often were unwilling even to allow civil rights meetings to take place inside their buildings. To maintain that pre-existing civil rights groups played crucial roles in the struggle should not lead us to conclude that they always did so without prodding from activists or without considerable internal policy conflicts. To maintain that many black protest leaders were already part of the leadership structure of black communities is to ignore the extent to which the sudden rise to prominence of a leader such as King disrupted existing patterns of leadership. . . .

Careful study of the internal dynamics of the black struggle will make us more aware of the ways in which institutions of various types can sustain movements or can kill them. Studies of the historical black struggles of the 1960's currently being conducted by the many talented scholars entering this exciting field might also suggest how the vastly greater resources of contemporary black communities might be mobilized to renew the struggle.

10

THE WOMEN'S MOVEMENT

Equality or Difference?

American women have been making history and writing history since before the Revolution, but the study of women's history did not become a formal discipline until the 1970s. As with the study of black history, women's history needed a forceful movement and the Civil Rights Act of 1964 to secure its legitimacy in the academic world.

Women's history has always had two faces: one that looks at women's experience as unique and worthy of recounting independently and one that seeks to integrate women into the larger context of U.S. history. In some sense these are complementary goals, and in another, contradictory. Women, like any other group subjected to systematic discrimination,[1] need to have their stories told to present a just picture of events leading to the present. On the other hand, separating women out for their unique history inevitably leads historians to stress their difference from men, which can undermine the political claim for the equality of the sexes. Adding women, blacks, Hispanics, Native Americans, and others to our history broadens the national picture to include the experiences of all Americans, not just the ones who voted and owned property.

The historiography of the field displays the inherent tension between these two goals and its responsiveness to the political aims of feminists. Nineteenth-century women's history emphasized and celebrated women's difference from men.[2] Women influenced by Progressive ideas continued to view the sexes as significantly different. However, they saw economic issues underlying most behavior and studied industrial work and conditions contributing to poverty. Mostly ignored until the 1950s and 1960s, professional women historians following the Progressives documented a variety of women's experiences in the colonial period and nineteenth century, emphasizing what women accomplished despite their limited educational opportu-

---

[1]See William Chafe, *Women and Equality* (New York, 1977), pp. 4–7, for a discussion of the ways in which a majority of people has had minority status.

[2]See General Introduction to *Interpretations*.

nities and the legal and social demands of marriage and motherhood. This history did not stress inherent differences so much as ones growing out of experience and oppression.[3] In the late 1960s and 1970s women activists pointed to ongoing economic and legal inequities. The early historiography that grew out of this Second Wave feminism attempted to retrieve women's experiences, in a search for a past which highlighted the special circumstances under which women labored. The work of this early period focused on white middle-class women and generalized from their experiences, partly because of the backgrounds of the historians and partly because of the relative ease of finding sources.

Historians tended to search for female community distinct from the men's world of politics and business. But in the early 1980s historians began breaking down the idea of "women" into components reflecting race, ethnicity, and class. Emphasizing race and class spotlighted commonalities between men and women which worked against the idea of a shared female experience. At about the same time, gender analysis replaced the retrieval of women's experience as the most important contribution of women's history. Since most gender historians believed that sexual differences stem much less from biology than from widely shared ideas, gender studies required investigating the conditions producing those ideas rather than seeking the development of an intrinsic female culture. Studying gender uncovered *attitudes* about difference, which, in turn, revealed the reasons behind the unequal distribution of power between the sexes. This search included a heightened sensitivity to language as the vehicle for communicating ideas about maleness and femaleness. While gender has become a very productive analytic device, ideas about gender can also be differentiated by race and class; within these categories much distinctive women's experience remains to be recovered. Hence, the need to study difference persists, both to clarify distinctions among women and to distinguish male and female experience.

The 1950s and early 1960s brought many Americans unparalleled prosperity. The postwar years also brought a sharp return to conservative ideas about the family. Men were breadwinners; women were homemakers, despite their widespread and skillful participation in the economy during the war. However, ideology notwithstanding, more and more women were working outside the home, usually at low paying jobs with no future. Thus, both working-class and middle-class women felt discontent. Two immensely important books, Simone de Beauvoir's *The Second Sex* and Betty Friedan's *The Feminine Mys-*

---

[3]See, for example, Julia Cherry Spruill's comprehensive and insightful overview of women in the colonial South, *Women's Life and Work in the Southern Colonies* (New York, 1938), and Elizabeth Dexter, *Colonial Women of Affairs* (New York, 1924).

tique, laid the ideological groundwork for the Women's Movement that came suddenly and unexpectedly alive in the late 1960s.

The Second Sex, published in France in 1949 and translated and published in the United States in 1952, made its way slowly into the intellectual and political imaginations of American women. It was a long, difficult book. De Beauvoir eruditely and agilely combined philosophy, psychoanalysis, biology, and literature with her own acute observations into a narrative that sustained her revolutionary notion: "One is not born, but rather becomes, a woman."[4] Gender, argued de Beauvoir, is a formulation of societal standards, not only a biological fact. Chapter after chapter of *The Second Sex* laid out the argument for the social construction of the sexes, which historians take for granted today.

Another immensely important aspect of de Beauvoir's narrative was the idea that the measures, institutions, and definitions of fitness and rightness in the world were all male. "He thinks of his body as a direct and normal connection with the world, which he believes he apprehends objectively, whereas he regards the body of a woman as a hindrance, a prison—weighted down by everything peculiar to it. . . . Thus humanity is male, and man defines woman not in herself but as relative to him; she is not regarded as an autonomous being. . . . He is the Subject, he is the Absolute—she is the Other." De Beauvoir argued that men have regarded only one another as equals; they exchange women among themselves. "Otherness" and the social construction of gender were only a few of the concepts that de Beauvoir's work made available to readers.[5]

Even if few actually read *The Second Sex* in the 1950s, its intellectual and political half-life was long and intense. It still provides readers with numerous, startling moments of self-recognition.[6] Its most immediate intellectual link to American feminism came through Betty Freidan, for whom it was influential in writing *The Feminine Mystique.*

Published in 1963, Freidan's book found an immediate and large readership which resonated with her argument that postwar consumerism deliberately and cynically sold women on the false fulfillment that could be found in suburban, domestic life, sex, and consumption. Men and the market they controlled were keeping women away from adulthood, intellectual achievement, and creativ-

---

[4]Simone de Beauvoir, *The Second Sex* (New York, 1952), p. 301.

[5]de Beauvoir, *Sex,* xviii–xix; Linda Kerber, "Gender," in Anthony Molho and Gordon Wood, eds., *Imagined Histories: American Historians Interpret the Past* (Princeton, N. J., 1998), p. 43.

[6]Feminists are still in active dialogue with de Beauvoir. Helen Fisher published *The First Sex* (New York, 1999), an account based on anthropology, psychology, and sociobiology, arguing for women's evolutionary primacy.

ity. Friedan's book owed much to current social psychology, especially its emphasis on the relationship between mass culture and conformity. It owed its tremendous popularity to the large number of reasonably affluent women living in discontent in the new postwar suburbs as well as the ever-increasing number of working women in jobs with no futures.[7]

In the same year that Friedan's book came out, the report of President Kennedy's Commission on the Status of Women, which Eleanor Roosevelt had chaired until her death in 1962, documented the many ways in which American women were not full participants in the economy and body politic. The Commission and its report were Kennedy's gesture to women and a way to head off further activism on behalf of an Equal Rights Amendment, which he did not favor. Feminists like Roosevelt and Esther Peterson, assistant secretary of labor and head of the Women's Bureau in the Kennedy administration, were also opposed to an ERA. They believed, as did many women activists, that complete equality with men would destroy much hard-won protective legislation for women workers. Women since the Progressive era had been fighting for laws to protect women from long hours and hazardous work conditions on the basis of their essential difference from men. This had been a strategy that was congenial to voters and productive for women and activists. A constitutional amendment guaranteeing women equal rights threatened decades of legislation and contradicted the philosophy about the sexes popular with the majority of Americans.

Within a few months of Kennedy's assassination, passage of the Civil Rights Act of 1964 seemed to obviate the need for an ERA. At the same time, the women's movement, fueled by years of grievances, many of which Freidan's book articulated, and energized by activists from the Civil Rights and peace movements, was beginning to generate widespread protest.

In the mid-1960s women began to speak up about their second-rate status within the Civil Rights and peace movements. Women were groping toward a full articulation of their own oppression. Many male activists met these early efforts with derision. When women in SDS (Students for a Democratic Society) tried to bring up questions about women's participation, the meeting melted down in ridicule. A subsequent report on the debate in the *New Left Notes* ran a cartoon of a girl with a sign reading "We Want Our Rights and We Want Them Now!" She was depicted in a dress so short her polka dot panties showed.[8]

---

[7]Kerber, "Gender," 44–45.

[8]Sara Evans, *Personal Politics: The Roots of Women's Liberation in the Civil Rights Movement and the New Left* (New York, 1980), p. 192.

Across the country women organized female-only groups in which they could talk with one another without being contradicted or shouted down. In discussing the sex-based inequities in marriage and domestic life, women, many for the first time, saw political patterns where before they had seen only their individual problems. The process women developed for deepening their understanding of their circumstances was called consciousness-raising, and it taught a generation of women that "the personal is the political." This movement, unlike earlier ones, took the struggle not only to the streets but also into kitchens and bedrooms. The bitterness of these personal confrontations gave the movement an inflammatory intensity that polarized many Americans.

The early 1970s saw the beginning of women's search for a relevant and dignified past. The period produced many polemics, but historical work, though born in advocacy, was not so combative. Among the first women's histories in this period were biographies and revaluations of historical women ignored, patronized, or consigned to second-rate status.[9] From the start, the study of women's history has been self-consciously interdisciplinary, borrowing from psychology, anthropology, linguistics, and literary techniques to locate women who were often invisible to traditional methods of research. Movement women provided the first attempts at a theoretical basis for the subjugation of women.

These efforts came from two sources: the socialist Left and the liberal feminists. A student of the movement, Linda Nicholson, identifies two wings of activism: Women's Liberation and Women's Rights. Women's Rights activists were in the majority and worked on the premise that men and women were equal and that what women wanted were only the same opportunities as men within the existing economic and political order. Despite Betty Freidan's radical background,[10] *The Feminine Mystique* appealed to the Women's Rights wing of the movement, making no mention of restructuring society beyond the inclusion of women in present systems. Indeed, the book has been criticized for being blind, not only to structural change to combat injustice, but also to the plight of poor women and women of color for whom life in the suburbs, however unfulfilling for white middle-class women, was unattainable.

---

[9]Jean Strouse and Nancy Milford published influential biographies of Alice James and Zelda Fitzgerald, respectively: *Alice James: A Biography* (Boston, 1980); *Zelda, A Biography* (New York, 1970); Leslie Wheeler edited an edition of the letters of abolitionist feminists Henry Blackwell and Lucy Stone: *Loving Warriors, A Revealing Portrait of an Unprecedented Marriage* (New York, 1981).

[10]For a discussion of her experience before *The Feminine Mystique*, see Daniel Horowitz, *Betty Friedan and the Making of the Feminine Mystique: The American Left, the Cold War, and Modern Feminism* (Amherst, Mass., 1988).

Women's Liberation activists, on the other hand (who were significantly in the minority), came out of Marxist or socialist backgrounds,
often from the civil rights movement. One of their slogans was
"Women who strive to be equal to men lack ambition." They believed
that feminism should lead to structuring a more equitable society or it
would serve no purpose but to let some women into the upper ranks
with men to exploit others.[11] These feminists, as they said at the time,
wanted to be part of the solution, not part of the problem.

Shulamith Firestone in the "Dialectic of Sex" attempted to rewrite
the Marxist analysis of the origins of oppression in relation to sex and
the family rather than to production. Firestone rephrased Engels to
read: "Historical materialism is that view of the course of history
which seeks the ultimate cause and the great moving power of all historic events in the dialectic of sex: the division of society into two distinct biological classes for procreative reproduction, and the struggles
of these classes with one another. . . ."[12] Not all feminists agree that
sexual oppression was the primary kind of oppression, but most scholars influenced by Marx have incorporated gender into their analyses of
social inequality.[13]

Linda Nicholson argued that the Women's Liberation wing was responsible for "difference" feminism, which stressed the ways women
are not like men, while Women's Rights' feminists focused on the
ways women are like men. She is right to point out that these two
wings developed out of the early Second Wave of the 1960s and 1970s,
as the resurgence of feminism came to be called, to distinguish it from
nineteenth century feminists. However, egalitarian feminists—at least
egalitarian feminist historians—are by no means all liberals content
with the structure of the economy and society as it is. Some of the
most insistent egalitarian feminists, Linda Gordon, Alice Kessler-Harris, and Linda Kerber, have also been extremely critical of the existing
economic structure.

The significant early contributions to women's history emphasized
difference at least partly out of necessity. Historians who singled out
women for special treatment *had* to focus on difference. They worked
to recapture the distinctive experiences of women, both imposed and
chosen. Important new books in the late 1970s and early 1980s did not

---

[11]Linda Nicholson, *The Second Wave: A Reader in Feminist Theory* (New York,
1997), pp. 2–4.

[12]Shulamith Firestone, "The Dialectic of Sex," in ibid., pp. 19–26.

[13]For an excellent discussion of class and how its meanings have been clarified since
scholars have added the insights of Foucault and postmodernism to Marx, see Ronald
Schultz, "A Class Society? The Nature of Inequality in Early America," in Carla Gardina Pestana and Sharon V. Salinger, eds., *Inequality in Early America* (Hanover, N.H.,
1999), pp. 203–221.

substantiate the old hopeful view that significant numbers of colonial women had stepped into their husbands' occupations. Mary Beth Norton's *Daughters of Liberty*, Linda Kerber's *Women of the Republic*, Nancy Cott's *The Bonds of Womanhood*, and Laurel Ulrich's *Goodwives*[14] all provided fresh material on women in the colonial and early national periods, looking at women's participation in the household economy and their religious and intellectual lives.

This early work on the Revolution established the notion of the republican mother who was to protect and cherish the young nation's virtue by producing virtuous homes and children. Thus, men's exposure to market forces and the disorder and corruption of politics would not ruin the American republic's innocent young citizens. Republican motherhood also underlined the need for young women to acquire an education to fit them for the demanding task of raising the country's young. Norton particularly saw the ideology of the Revolution benefiting women through emphasizing women's formal relation to the state. While subsequent historians have seen the Revolution more negatively as codifying women's exclusion from citizenship, the emergence of republican motherhood remains central to understanding the early national period.

Nancy Cott's work, published in 1977, looked at white New England women in the late eighteenth and early nineteenth centuries and explored what Barbara Welter had called the "cult of true womanhood" in which these republican mothers surrounded themselves.[15] Nineteenth century domesticity was made up of those ideas and practices which glorified women's childrearing and housekeeping as the apotheosis of virtue. Cott looked at women's private writings to understand how they imagined their own participation in a culture that both imprisoned and idealized them. The "bonds" she wrote about were both affectionate ties to one another and chains attaching them to a repressive world. Her commitment to social history and the women's movement determined her subject, and the work of E. P. Thompson encouraged Cott to look at the way women actively shaped their own culture rather than simply submitting to demands upon them.[16]

Many of the ideas and assumptions upon which Cott based her

---

[14]Mary Beth Norton, *Liberty's Daughters: The Revolutionary Experience of American Women, 1750–1800* (Boston, 1980); Linda Kerber, *Women of the Republic: Intellect and Ideology in Revolutionary America* (Chapel Hill, N.C., 1980); Laurel Thatcher Ulrich, *Goodwives: Image and Reality in the Lives of Women in Northern New England, 1650–1750* (New York, 1980); Nancy Cott, *The Bonds of Womanhood: "Woman's Sphere" in New England, 1780–1835* (New Haven, 1977).

[15]Barbara Welter, "The Cult of True Womanhood, 1820–1860," *American Quarterly* 18 (1966): 151–174.

[16]Cott, *Bonds*, xii–xiii.

book would soon be disputed, which speaks more to the fast-changing field than any weakness in the work. In subtitling her book "Woman's Sphere," she was adopting the then-current notion that male and female spheres were, in the nineteenth century, separate, another idea which scholars would challenge, but which would nevertheless offer a starting point for discussions of nineteenth-century culture. Other historians criticized her focus on women of the northeast as a part of the "New Englandization" of women's history. And, above all, feminists would attack her use of the word "women" until it would be impossible for historians to speak of women without qualifying the term by their race and class. While these critiques testified to the liveliness of women's history and its desire to be inclusive, Cott's work remains of great value in thinking about the nineteenth century.

At the same time that historians were working in the archives to recreate the conditions and contributions of particular women, they were also making theoretical contributions to the practical study of history. Joan Kelly's "The Social Relations of the Sexes" suggested that placing gender at the center of the historical quest called into question three basic historical tenets: periodization, categorization in social analysis, and the reliability of theories of social change.[17] She pointed out, for example, that periods marked by advancement for men, such as the American Revolution, often were marked by losses for women, as in being denied some of the rights of citizenship. Working in a similar vein, Gerda Lerner suggested in "The Challenge of Women's History" that historians must work to insist that women have a history, that they must add gender to considerations of how social change occurs, must develop new sources and techniques to find women apparently lost to history, and must reconceptualize what constitutes history to include women's experience.[18]

Expanding history to include women's experiences, crossing disciplinary boundaries, and refusing to measure female experience by male standards produced many new views of women, some of them stressing women's individual development as markedly different from men's. But focusing on difference could also provoke violent dissension among historians. Carol Gilligan's work attempting to measure women's ethical standards without using male categories received such a response. Lawrence Kohlberg had laid out a six-stage developmental sequence describing how children evolve morally. His male subjects sometimes made it to the sixth or most evolved form, while

---

[17]Joan Kelly, "The Social Relation of the Sexes: Methodological Implications of Women's History," in Joan Kelly, *Women, History, and Theory: The Essays of Joan Kelly* (Chicago, 1984), pp. 1–18.

[18]Gerda Lerner, "The Challenges of Women's History," in Gerda Lerner, *The Majority Finds Its Past: Placing Women in History* (Cambridge, 1979), pp. 168–180.

girls never made it beyond stage three. Carol Gilligan postulated a process specific to girls and set out to investigate. She ended up questioning male-based paradigms and creating new moral categories by which to measure women.

Gilligan's research posited that women had a moral system based on the overriding obligation to sustain relationship, which came from a uniquely female developmental experience. According to Gilligan and the sociologist-psychoanalyst Nancy Chodorow, whose work provided theoretical support for Gilligan's, girls' powerful sense of relatedness stemmed from the ways mothers raise daughters. Girls grow up with identities strongly linked to the welfare of their mothers. This model diverged from the dominant (male) ethical system which developed psychologically from the social imperative boys felt to separate from the mother and things feminine and embrace a system stressing abstract rules and hierarchical values. The difference between Chodorow and Gilligan, however, was that for Chodorow incomplete separation laid the groundwork for male domination, low female self-esteem, and dependence. For Gilligan, it produced sex-linked "goodness."[19]

Many historians and thinkers in other fields rejected Gilligan's work as essentialist, that is, making an argument about woman's basic nature without locating her in time, place, class, and race.[20] There was considerable uneasiness over a system that painted women as better than men. The intensity and the duration of the dispute reflected the unexpected popularity of Gilligan's book and illustrated how close the ties were among the various disciplines studying women and how volatile the issue of difference could become—particularly when it touched on the almost two-hundred-year-old cliché on which Progressives had built their legislative victories: that women were "more moral" than men.

Gilligan's idea of a special female nurturance, based on the study of a relatively small group of white women, seemed to encourage retrograde studies of women as inherently different from men, occupying separate spheres, and the moral high ground. This debate made more urgent the need historians felt to insure that the field would continue

---

[19]Carol Gilligan, *In a Different Voice: Psychological Theory and Women's Development*, (Cambridge, Mass., 1982); Nancy Chodorow, *The Social Reproduction of Mothering: Psychoanalysis and the Sociology of Gender* (Berkeley, 1978); Dorothy Dinnerstein, *The Mermaid and the Minotaur: Sexual Arrangements and Human Malaise* (New York, 1977); see Mary Jo Buhle's excellent discussion of this development in *Feminism and Its Discontents: A Century of Struggle with Psychoanalysis*, (Cambridge, Mass., 1998), pp. 240–279. See also Joan Walach Scott's discussion of Gilligan in "Gender: A Useful Tool of Historical Analysis," in *Gender and the Politics of History* (New York, 1988), pp. 39–41.

[20]Linda Kerber et al. Forum, *Signs* 12 (1986): 304–10; Katha Politt, "Are Women Morally Superior to Men?" *The Nation* (Dec. 28, 1992).

to grow to include the experience of all women, not just middle-class white women.

Historians were simultaneously progressing toward this end. Deborah Gray White published *Ar'n't I A Woman?* in 1985, responding to the new, fast-growing field of studies of the slave community, all of which focused on men.[21] Jacqueline Jones, in *A Labor of Love, A Labor of Sorrow,* provided a thorough history of black women from slavery to the present. Christine Stansell's *City of Women* looked at poor women in colonial and nineteenth-century New York, displaying the tension between them and white middle-class women. And Jeanne Boydston's *Home and Work* argued that a significant amount of the surplus capital on which early entrepreneurs built American industry came from unpaid women's work which society rendered invisible by "pastoralizing" it in the gauzy ideology of the cult of domesticity.[22]

In an influential essay in 1985, called "Beyond the Search for Sisterhood: American Women's History in the 1980s,"[23] Nancy Hewitt pointed out the correspondence between a narrowly conceived women's history and a narrowly conceived women's movement. "For the past decade, the women's movement itself has been accused of forming its own exclusive community, characterized by elitism, ethnocentrism, and disregard for diversity."[24] Hewitt particularly objected to the notion of a community of women which transcended racial and class bounds and which was allegedly created by the common oppression of patriarchy and the forces of modernization. This model, wherein the experience of middle-class community became the paradigm for the experience of all groups of women, Hewitt argued, obscured class conflict.

Hewitt cited slave women and working-class women as nonparticipants in this presumed woman-wide community and proceeded to paint a complex picture of the interworkings among gender, race, and class. Ties between men and women within both the middle and working classes often transcended gender oppression; racial oppression ensured that slave women and slave-owning women shared little community. She challenged the "separate spheres" ideology and recast it as a relic of the sex-segregation of labor in early industrialization,

---

[21]See Volume I, Chapter 9.

[22]Deborah Gray White, *Ar'n't I A Woman: Female Slaves in the Plantation South* (New York, 1985); Jacqueline Jones, *A Labor of Love, A Labor of Sorrow: Black Women, Work and the Family from Slavery to the Present* (New York, 1985); Christine Stansell, *A City of Women: Sex and Class in New York, 1789–1870* (Urbana, Ill., 1987); Jeanne Boydston, *Home and Work: Housework, Wages, and the Ideology of Labor in the Early Republic,* (New York, 1990).

[23]Nancy A. Hewitt, "Beyond the Search for Sisterhood," *Social History* 10 (1985), 299–321.

[24]Hewitt, "Sisterhood," 300.

through which middle-class women were actually not isolated from the outer world but active participants in creating new middle-class values.[25] Middle-class reformers were often blind to the values of working-class communities and attempted to impose their own ideas. At the same time, she admitted, they also inhabited what historian Carroll Smith-Rosenberg called the "female world of love and ritual."[26] As Hewitt summed it up, "In highlighting the importance of collective action for women and the centrality of woman-constructed networks for community-wide campaigns, feminist scholars have demonstrated women's historical agency. Now we must recognize that agency . . . cuts both ways: women influenced and advocated change, but they did so within the context of their particular social and material circumstances."[27] Overextending the middle-class notion of women and women's community misrepresented history and reproduced nineteenth-century myopia.

At the same time that historians and theorists were challenging the notion of any stable idea of "women" as white and middle-class, or, as Gilligan had argued, nurturing or "related," they were also refuting that she was necessarily heterosexual. Gayle Rubin, in her famous 1975 article "The Traffic in Women," argued that compulsory heterosexuality (which occurs as a result of the incest taboo, which Levi-Strauss described, and Freud's oedipal process which differentiates girls from boys) builds in pain and humiliation for females but not for males.[28] And a year later, Blanche Weisen Cooke, biographer of Eleanor Roosevelt, identified the "historical denial of lesbianism."[29]

More recently, Deborah Gray White responded to the call to be attentive to class as well as race and gender. White's *Too Heavy a Load* looked at black women from Reconstruction to the present. She analyzed their class relations and historicized the intricate workings of perceptions of race and gender both within and without the black community, and how these affected women's understandings of themselves, their relationships with one another, and the work they undertook. The complex picture that emerged did much to explain how dominant white gender stereotypes have repeatedly been used against black women and how gender and class both have been significant de-

---

[25]Hewitt's own work, *Women's Activism and Social Change: Rochester, N.Y., 1822–1872* (Ithaca, N.Y., 1984) and Mary Ryan's *The Cradle of the Middle Class: The Family in Oneida County, New York, 1790–1865* (New York, 1984) document this activity.

[26]Carroll Smith-Rosenberg, "The Female World of Love and Ritual: Relations Between Women in Nineteenth Century America," in *Disorderly Conduct: Visions of Gender in Victorian America* (New York, 1986), pp. 53–76.

[27]Hewitt, "Sisterhood," 315.

[28]Gayle Rubin, "The Traffic in Women," in Linda Nicholson, ed., *The Second Wave: A Reader in Feminist Theory* (New York, 1997), pp. 25–62.

[29]Kerber, "Gender," 48.

terminants in the ways in which black women were able to engage in "race work."[30]

Hewitt and many other scholars were afraid that giving sexual difference precedence over class differences would result in a history that overlooked class conflict in favor of general cultural conflicts. To historians who, in the Progressive tradition, saw economic issues underlying historical change, this seemed like a frightening possibility. For them, difference of all kinds had less basis in reality than in social ideas which politicians and businesses eagerly manipulated to their own benefit. Focusing on difference simply gave the ideas credence, when it was their *utility* that needed investigation.

The attacks on essentialism and lack of differentiation among women seemed all the more urgent in the 1980s when two historians of women testified in an EEOC (Equal Employment Opportunity Commission) lawsuit against Sears Roebuck for discriminating against women by not giving them jobs that commanded high commissions. Sears argued (successfully) that women did not want these jobs, and historian Rosalind Rosenberg provided evidence from women's history which supported Sears' case. Alice Kessler-Harris, testifying for the EEOC, argued that the market had historically segregated jobs inequitably according to sex; that women's preferences had not shaped the job market, but the demands of industry and keeping labor costs down had. Whenever women had the opportunity (for example, during both World Wars) they took higher-paying jobs. Both Rosenberg and Kessler-Harris gave accurate if differing versions of aspects of women's history; the case demonstrated very clearly the unfortunate political and economic uses to which divisions among scholars might be put.[31]

At about the same time that the term "woman" was becoming too problematic to be useful, "gender" began to substitute for it, suggesting a wider project for women's history than the recovery of women's history. Analyzing "gender" rather than "women" offered historians a way to integrate women's history into American history as a whole. Historians of women recognized that their subject remained marginal to "American history," and gender studies seemed to promise to make women's history more central. Gender focus stressed the social construction of the sexes, and hence the artificiality and easy manipulation of inequality. This aspect appealed to historians afraid of losing sight of history's aim to reveal the hidden ways power is wielded, not

---

[30]Deborah Gray White, *Too Heavy a Load: Black Women in Defense of Themselves, 1894–1994* (New York, 1999).

[31]*EEOC v. Sears Roebuck & Co.* (628 F. Supp. 1264 [N.D. Ill. 1986]); *EEOC v. Sears Roebuck & Co.* (Appellate Opinion); Alice Kessler-Harris, "A Personal Account," in D. Kelly Weisberg, *Applications of Feminist Legal Theory to Women's Lives: Sex, Violence, Work, and Reproduction* (Philadelphia, 1996), pp. 571–610.

just to chronicle and hence possibly reconfirm stereotypical differences between men and women.

Gender has been used to indicate the social meanings that people in different places and times have attached to biological differences. It has generally replaced "women" as the historical category Lerner and Kelly sought.[32] The growing importance to women's history of postmodernism (which posits the contingent nature of all identities) has underlined the utility of the idea of gender. Joan Scott's essay, "Gender: A Useful Tool of Historical Analysis" (1986), has been a dramatically useful theoretical contribution to women's history.[33] Scott's analysis derived in part from the French historian and philosopher of history, Michel Foucault, who looked for power and domination in all social relations. Power might come from class relations, in the Marxist sense, but it might also emanate from gender, ethnicity, race, or other kinds of historically contingent circumstances. Scott focused on constructions of sexuality as a road to understanding power. Language, as a powerful medium of those constructions, would become the historians' central guide to understanding the power relations of a given society. Scholars began to seek gender meanings in the linguistic baggage of metaphor, simile, and other expressions.[34] Carroll Smith-Rosenberg's article, "Dis-Covering the Subject of the 'Great Constitutional Discussion,' 1786–1789," for example, analyzes magazine rhetoric in that period to show how male identity specifically excluded characteristics of women, blacks, and Indians.[35]

Two years later, in 1988, Scott offered a way of looking at the Sears case by analyzing the differing meanings of gender at different moments in time. The baffling aspect of the case—for the historians involved as well as for feminist observers—was the way equality and difference were ordained as opposites. Scott's technique would rephrase the difference-equality dilemma so that the two were no longer polarized. She argued that groups struggling for equality were always different from the "standard" in some way or there would be no struggle. "Equality, in the political theory of rights that lie behind the claims of excluded groups for justice, means the ignoring of differences between individuals for a particular purpose or in a particular context." Differences, Scott continued, are historically and socially constructed. Just

---

[32]Indeed, Lerner suggested its substitution: Lerner, "Challenges," 172.

[33]Joan W. Scott, "Gender, A Useful Tool of Historical Analysis," *American Historical Review* 91 (December 1986): 1053–75.

[34]See Nancy Fraser, "Structuralism or Pragmatics: Discourse Theory and Feminist Politics" in Nicholson, *Second Wave*, 378–395, for the links between Foucault and Scott.

[35]Caroll Smith-Rosenberg, "Dis-Covering the Subject of the 'Great Constitutional Discussion,' 1786–1789," *Journal of American History* 79 (December 1993): 841–873.

as dominant groups give different races meanings of inferiority that serve their own purposes, so gender differences take on the meanings given them at different times and for different reasons. "There is nothing self-evident or transcendent about difference. . . . The questions always ought to be, What qualities or aspects are being compared? What is the nature of the comparison? How is the meaning of difference being constructed? Yet in the Sears testimony and in some debates among feminists (sexual) difference is assumed to be an immutable fact, its meaning inherent in the categories of male and female."[36]

Some scholars took up Scott's challenge and found many ways gender could be a useful concept. Increasingly, they turned to the state, which had always seemed an unpromising place to find traces of women. Political scientist Carole Pateman's pyrotechnical synthesis of social contract theory and Freudian thought explained how the birth of liberal democracy affected gender and why it has been so hard for women to enter the mainstream of economic and political individualism. In *The Sexual Contract*, Pateman postulated the unspoken agreement made among men at the foundational moment when they joined together to form the social contract. When, as Locke and Hobbes had described, men gave up hierarchical, patriarchal power in return for fraternal power, they agreed to share not only access and control of the political system, but also access to the labor and sexual services of women.[37] Pateman's analysis of the marriage contract, anomalous among formal agreements, and her provocative thesis about women's subordination in the Age of Revolution, ushered in other bold efforts to use gender to understand the creation and functioning of the body politic.

Gender provided Kathryn Kish Sklar with an exciting new approach to women's role in the Progressive era. In Sklar's analysis,[38] women's voluntary associations, ideologically rooted in a widely shared cultural appreciation of women's difference, prepared the way for women to effect the first protective legislation for workers. In her view, popular notions of women's moral sense gave them the power to convince the country at large that the state had responsibilities to care for the health, safety, education, and welfare of its citizens. By focusing first on women and children victimized by industrial capitalism, women Progressives opened the way for the more broad-based welfare state that emerged during the Depression. Ironically, it was only by a concerted insistence on gender *difference* in this period that it became

---

[36]Joan Wallach Scott, "The Sears Case," in *Gender and the Politics of History*.

[37]Carole Pateman, *The Sexual Contract* (Stanford, Calif., 1988).

[38]Kathryn Kish Sklar, *Florence Kelley and the Nation's Work: The Rise of Women's Public Culture, 1830–1900* (New Haven, 1995) and her essay in Chapter 6.

possible to create a nationwide consensus to intervene in what was generally considered the sacrosanct contract between laborer and manufacturer.[39] The net effect, based on ideas of difference, was greater empowerment for women.

Another historian, Glenda Gilmore, looked at another place and time and found another construction of gender that women used to positive advantage. In *Gender and Jim Crow*, published in 1996, she argued that when Reconstruction was overturned and black men disfranchised, black women had to carry on the long-term political work of trying to recover the franchise and the shorter-term political work of trying to procure some part of the state's budget for black communities. In the infamous nadir of black-white relations, only black women could negotiate with local white officials in safety, since, as women, they were not perceived as conducting politics. Southern black women through local organizations and church groups, like Progressive women in the North, managed to improve their communities and educational facilities, letting their gender disguise the political nature of their efforts.[40]

As some historians emphasized the utility of different perceptions of gender to shed light on particular developments, others struggled to use gender as the most significant category in constructing a whole American history. The historian Kathleen Brown published an influential article in 1993 urging the use of comparative "gender frontiers" in studying early America. Influenced by the broadening of early modern history to include the Atlantic World, she argued for a comparative framework for cultural studies to reveal more about all societies. Taking her own advice and building on the work of Edmund Morgan, Brown subsequently recast the first two centuries of life in Virginia using the social construction of gender and race to elucidate Bacon's Rebellion of 1676 and its aftermath. Brown's complex use of constructions of gender to evoke English attitudes toward Native Americans and Africans as well as the way the English *used* those constructions to manipulate the status of both groups further demonstrated what a sophisticated tool gender could be.[41]

A collection entitled *U.S. History as Women's History* bore out the

---

[39]For the elevation of contract to these heights see Morton Horwitz, *The Transformation of American Law, 1780–1860* (Cambridge, Mass., 1977).

[40]Glenda Gilmore, *Gender and Jim Crow; Women and the Politics of White Supremacy in North Carolina, 1896–1920* (Chapel Hill, N.C., 1996); Elsa Barkeley Brown takes exception to Gilmore's argument that black women were substantially safer than black men in "Negotiating and Transforming the Public Sphere: African American Political Life in the Transition from Slavery to Freedom," *Public Culture* 7 (Fall 1994): 107–146.

[41]Kathleen Brown, "Brave New Worlds: Women's and Gender History," *William and Mary Quarterly* Ser. 3, 50 (April 1993): 311–328; *Good Wives, Nasty Wenches, and Anxious Patriarchs: Gender, Race, and Power in Colonial Virginia* (Chapel Hill, N.C., 1996).

promise of its title by using the concerns and categories developed for women's history to expand our ideas about the history of the country. In one essay, Alice Kessler-Harris, for example, displayed the centrality of gender to the way Social Security was conceived and drawn up.[42] And in an essay entitled "Soul Murder and Slavery," Nell Painter evoked the unique familial horrors that slave-owning brought to both blacks and whites. The power of this essay, derived from its cross-disciplinary use of feminist-inspired psychological work on family violence and child abuse, prompted a call for other historians of slavery to resist the temptation to deny its true physical and emotional brutality.[43]

A third essay in the collection, by Jane Sherron de Hart, is one of a number of recent works about women's political activities that re-investigated the Progressive legacy of suffrage and tried to identify women's current political culture and better understand its links to the past. "Rights and Representation: Women, Politics, and Power in the Contemporary United States," revealed two kinds of approaches women have made to recent politics. One, characterizing suffrage workers and pro-ERA activists of the 1970s, centered on a notion of entitlement of all citizens to political rights and responsibilities. The other, more typical of women engaged in electoral politics of the 1980s and 1990s, was based on a notion of representation whereby women's goal was to serve their constituents in office, especially their women constituents, and to change traditional notions of political power in order to rectify age-old gender inequities.

De Hart saw the first group as practicing a kind of educational politics consistent with the Progressive ideas that women were not partisan but above the fray and that their special moral role as women was to selflessly educate the public about issues of concern. Needless to say, this kind of activity has drawbacks when legislation is hammered out through compromise and deal-making. The second group tried to come to terms with the "politics of realism," and learn the rules of the partisan game in order to acquire more leverage for women and their issues. Women were successful at this to the degree that they were able to maneuver without offending public perception about what is appropriate for women to do. In other words, this group had to be extremely knowledgeable about the way in which gender is constructed

[42]Alice Kessler-Harris, "Designing Women and Old Fools: The Construction of the Social Security Amendments of 1939," in Linda Kerber, Alice Kessler-Harris and Kathryn Kish Sklar, eds., *U.S. History as Women's History: New Feminist Essays* (Chapel Hill, N.C., 1995), pp. 87–106.

[43]Peter Wood, "Slave Labor Camps in Early America: Overcoming Denial and Discovering the Gulag," in Carla Gardina Pestana and Sharon V. Salinger, eds., *Inequality in Early America* (Hanover, N.H., 1999), pp. 222–238.

and careful not to violate those constructions more than necessary to achieve goals.

Focusing on constructions of gender differences continues to offer historians very fruitful access to our history. Historians have looked at the years after women's suffrage to understand why the anticipated gender gap in voting did not develop. In Kristi Anderson's study, the central reasons were that women, like all new voting groups, came slowly to use the ballot, and the interests voting women shared with their husbands overruled gender considerations.[44] Recently, Frances Fox Piven has suggested that a noticeable gender gap did come when the family was sufficiently in disarray to mean that a significant number of women were no longer able to depend upon their husbands and looked to the state instead. Their voting patterns reflected their desire to make the state more responsive to the needs of women, mothers, and children.[45] However women's interests have come into being, these studies assume that women voters will have common interests reflecting shared differences from men.

Some historians are working on the assumption that differences among women may be the most important story of all. Elsa Barkley Brown argues that historians should not be afraid of difference; that they are too concerned with isolating a single thematic historical line and too inflexible to see that history is better conceived as countless historical lines crossing and weaving around each other. She used the Creole expression "gumbo ya ya," meaning everybody talking at once, as a metaphor for good history. An historian should be capable of listening, and making sense of everyone talking at once. It would thus be possible to connect, for example, the white middle-class women's increasing employment in the last thirty years with the rising household employment of black, Hispanic, and Asian women supporting white middle-class women's move to professional status. Similarly, to understand the context of the testimony of Anita Hill, one must understand the widely divergent historical constructions of the sexuality of black and white women. Black women, but particularly poor black women who work in white-owned homes and factories, have learned historically to expect and try to ignore sexual harassment, which would only be blamed on their "lascivious" natures.[46] White women's

---

[44]Kristi Anderson, *After Suffrage: Women in Partisan and Electoral Politics before the New Deal* (Chicago, 1996).

[45]Frances Fox Piven, "Women and the State: Ideology, Power and Welfare" in Diane Dujon and Ann Withorn, *For Crying Out Loud: Women's Poverty in the United States* (Boston, 1996).

[46]See also Darlene Clark Hine, "Rape and the Inner Lives of Black Women in the Middle West: Preliminary Thoughts on the Culture of Dissemblance," *Signs* 14 (Summer, 1989): 95.

sexual struggle, conversely, involved throwing off the shackles of what Nancy Cott defined as "passionlessness," an aspect of nineteenth-century female virtue which required respectable women to be ignorant of sexual desire.[47] White feminists who took up Hill's cause, like feminist legal theorist Catharine MacKinnon, Brown argued, mistakenly took Hill's gender as her most significant attribute, neglecting her race and the fact that she was one of eleven children from a family of poor farmers. White women failed to understand her extreme reluctance to testify, a predictable by-product of her race and class. For Brown, a story which does not feature differences prominently will be a white middle-class woman's story.[48]

Theda Perdue's 1998 book on Cherokee women underlined Kathleen Brown's point about the value of comparing gender constructions across cultures.[49] A recent experiment in cross-cultural studies which used gender to illustrate the development of racial ideology throughout the Atlantic world was Jennifer Morgan's "Some Could Suckle over Their Shoulder" in which she showed that travelers' changing images of the reproductive and productive capacities of African and Native American female bodies were central to establishing a racist discourse that encouraged enslaving people of color.[50]

The idea that women do not spring forth naturally but are socially created—as Simone de Beauvoir announced over fifty years ago—and are created differently by circumstance and need—continues to guide historians searching for clues to how women were engaged in the development of the American economy, body politic, and culture. Through the notion of socially constructed gender, historians are arriving at a way to identify differences among women as well as real commonalities that define their differences from men. Laurel Ulrich, for example, an accomplished scholar of early American women, recently published a pair of articles on the prevalence of weaving among late eighteenth-century New England women. Until the last half of the eighteenth century, women spun but did not weave; in Europe, men wove until mechanization displaced them. After the Seven Years' War, the market began to expand, and Ulrich traced women's contribution to that growth. In seeking to explain women's new skill, Ulrich

---

[47]Nancy Cott, "Passionlessness: An Interpretation of Victorian Sexual Ideology, 1790–1850," in Nancy Cott and Elizabeth Pleck, eds., *A Heritage Of Her Own, Toward A New Social History Of Women* (New York, 1979), pp. 162–181.

[48]Elsa Barkley Brown, "What Has Happened Here: The Politics of Difference in Women's History and Feminist Politics," in Nicholson, *Second Wave*, 272–287.

[49]Theda Perdue, *Cherokee Women, Gender and Culture Change, 1700–1835* (Lincoln, Neb., 1998).

[50]Jennifer L. Morgan, "Some Could Suckle over Their Shoulder": Male Travelers, Female Bodies, and the Gendering of Racial Ideology, 1500–1700," *William and Mary Quarterly*, 3rd Ser. (January 1997): 167–192.

discovered that in the late eighteenth century when men were beginning to do wage work, young women were frequently taught weaving. Wage work was considered a social step down for young women, so they learned to make fabrics both to save money on family clothing and linens and to pay for goods from the growing market. They also started subsidizing their own dowries. Ulrich argues that this kind of unpaid labor was a common bond for rich and poor girls, all of whose production "celebrated industry, private property, and a sex/gender system that grounded women's work in the household."[51]

Although the dominant trend in women's history has been to affirm equality with men through the social construction of gender, since the 1980s some theorists and historians have insisted that attention needs to be paid to intrinsic differences between the sexes. Catharine MacKinnon's work to publicize and make illegal sexual harassment and her efforts to ban pornography emphasize an idea of women needing protection from misogynistic attitudes and practices permanently embedded in American culture.[52] Other activists, political scientists, and historians such as Joan Hoff, arguing along the same lines, make the case that the liberalism that emerged from the American Revolution has proved incapable of giving women genuine equality because men and women are situated differently with regard to sex. In *Law, Gender, and Injustice*, Hoff argues that women should be fighting for equity, not egalitarianism, and that women must fight for a feminist jurisprudence based on the idea of women as *women*, not as individuals: "Radical feminism is non-neutral by definition and outside the boundaries of the law because it recognizes without qualification the fearfully harmful results of female oppression, whether in the form of unwanted pregnancies, surrogate motherhood, prostitution, pornography, discrimination in hiring and promotion, or sexual harassment on the job."[53] For Hoff, the liberation of women by male standards is no liberation at all.

Women's history retains its connection to the political movement it grew out of, and contemporary historians continue to struggle with the paradoxes of a political movement that fights for equality for some group called "women" based on their (different) needs, interests, and histories. If they were not different from men's needs, would they need

[51]Laurel Thatcher Ulrich, "Wheels, Looms, and the Gender Division of Labor in Eighteenth Century New England," *William and Mary Quarterly*, 3rd Ser, 60 (Nov. 1998): 3–38; Laurel Thatcher Ulrich, "Sheep in the Parlor, Wheels on the Common: Pastoralism and Poverty in Eighteenth Century Boston," in *Inequality*, Pestana and Salinger, 197.

[52]See Catharine MacKinnon, *Only Words* (Cambridge, Mass., 1993) and *Feminism Unmodified, Discourses on Life and Law* (Cambridge, Mass., 1987).

[53]Joan Hoff, *Law, Gender, and Injustice, A Legal History of U.S. Women* (New York, 1991), p. 372.

fighting for? Would there be a reason to explore women's history and recapture it if it were not importantly different from men's? Can American history be written as women's history? Do women represent an essential historical strand—but nothing more? Over the course of the last thirty years, it has become clear that differences among women require as much attention as similarities and that far too many perceived similarities have been nothing more than misleading attempts to find common threads. Both differences and similarities derive from the perceptions of particular groups possessing differing amounts of power through time—all of which guarantees that women's history will continue to be a lively, contentious, and sometimes confusing field.

WILLIAM H. CHAFE

WILLIAM H. CHAFE (1942–   ) is the Alice Mary Baldwin professor of history at Duke University. He is the author of Women and Equality: Changing Patterns in American Culture *(1977),* Civilities and Civil Rights: Greensboro, North Carolina, and the Black Struggle for Equality *(1980), and* The Paradox of Change: American Women in the Twentieth Century *(1991).*

The resurgence of feminism in the 1960's represented the third incarnation of a dynamic women's rights movement in American history. The first . . . grew out of the abolitionist struggle of the 1830's and featured the legendary leadership of people like Elizabeth Cady Stanton and Susan B. Anthony. The second developed out of the social reform ethos of the early 1900's, and though the lineal descendant of the first movement, exhibited a style of leadership and a tactical approach significantly different from its antecedent. Cresting with the battle over the suffrage amendment, it succumbed to factionalism and public indifference in the 1920's and 1930's. The contemporary movement, like its predecessors, has grown out of a period of generalized social ferment, both drawing upon and reflecting a widespread sensitivity toward discrimination and injustice. The contemporary drive for women's liberation, however, differs from its forerunners in at least three ways: it is grounded in and moving in the same direction as underlying social trends at work in the society; it has developed an organizational base that is diverse and decentralized; and it is pursuing a wide range of social objectives that strike at many of the root causes of sex inequality. Although some of these distinctive characteristics are a source of weakness as well as strength, no previous feminist movement has attempted so much, and none has been better situated to make progress toward the goal of equality.

Probably the chief advantage of contemporary feminism lies in the extent to which its goals and programs have meshed with, or addressed directly, prevailing trends in the society. In the past, the demands of women's rights organizations had often been far removed from the experience and immediate concerns of most women in the population. Although the Seneca Falls Declaration of Sentiments and Resolutions

---

was bold in its vision, it bore little relationship to the world most women found themselves in—a world that was non-urban, populated by large families, and increasingly suffused with the precepts of Victorian morality. The notions of equal access to careers, or being able to preach from the pulpit, appealed to only a select group of women. Indeed, feminist objectives were so far outside the realm of most people's experience that females and males alike tended to dismiss early women's rights advocates as a lunatic fringe.

In a slightly different way, the suffrage movement of the 20th century also displayed misunderstanding of, and lack of contact with, some of the basic realities of the day. In their quest for one of the most fundamental rights of citizenship—the vote—the suffragists overestimated the extent to which a breakthrough in one area would lead to liberation in others as well. By expecting all women to vote together for the same candidates and programs on the basis of loyalty to their sex, the suffragists profoundly misread the degree to which ethnic, class, and family allegiances undermined the prospect of sex-based political behavior. Similarly, in thinking that winning the vote would encourage women to carry the fight for equality into the economic arena as well, the suffragists underestimated significantly the power of traditional forces of socialization. In both cases the fundamental error was to exaggerate the ability of a political reform to transform an entire structure of roles and activities based on gender.

The one area where "emancipation" did take hold—that of sex— also illustrated the extent to which the suffragists were out of touch with some of the trends in society. Throughout the first three decades of the 20th century, a sexual revolution was in progress. For women born after 1900, rates of pre-marital and extra-marital intercourse were approximately double those of women born before 1900. A new awareness of contraceptive devices and an increased recognition of female sexuality signified an important expansion of sexual freedom for middle-class women of the flapper era. Yet many feminists were repelled by the "revolution in manners and morals." To most women's rights advocates, the flapper seemed frivolous and irresponsible. At a time when there were political battles to be fought and careers to be opened up, concern with the libido and sexual freedom appeared counter-productive. Sex was meant for procreation, Charlotte Perkins Gilman remarked, and her views seemed to reflect the generalized dismay of suffrage leaders about the new morality. Improving the status of women in government and the economy required discipline, dedication, and sacrifice—attributes seemingly inconsistent with the concerns dominating the lives of younger women.

In the end, of course, it was the social environment rather than the shortcomings of women activists which prevented the realization of feminist hopes. As long as the day-to-day structure of most women's lives reinforced the existing distribution of sex roles, there was little possibility of developing a feminist constituency committed to far-reaching change. Women in large numbers might support the effort to win the suffrage, but there was no frame of reference in experience, and little support in the culture, for seeking the kind of full-scale equality that would revolutionize the social structure. Although the suffragists participated in the general "progressive" tendency to equate limited reforms with basic change, the real problem was a social milieu which proved inhospitable to more far-reaching change.

In this context, the feminism of the 1960's and 1970's differed from previous women's movements precisely because it grew out of and built upon prevailing social trends. For the first time ideological protest and underlying social and economic changes appeared to be moving in a similar direction. As we have seen already, female work patterns were virtually transformed in the years after 1940. Prior to World War II, female employment was limited primarily to young, single women or poor, married women. Few middle-class wives held jobs. By 1975, in contrast, the two-income family had become the norm; 49 per cent of all wives worked; and the median income of families where wives were employed was nearly $17,000. Although the employment changes did not signify progress toward equality, they ensured that social norms about women's "place" no longer had a base in reality.

As a result, feminist programs spoke more directly than ever before to the daily experience of millions of women. Female workers might not consider themselves feminists; indeed, they might shun any kind of association with the abstract cause of women's rights. But the same workers knew that they did not receive equal pay with men and that most of the higher paying jobs carried a "male only" tag. Similarly, the large number of women workers who had school-age and pre-school children understood the problems caused by inadequate day-care and after-school facilities. Discontented homemakers, who yearned for a more diverse life but saw all the barriers in the way, had a comparable sense of recognition. Thus there developed a common ground on which feminist activists and their potential constituency could stand, and that common ground provided the starting point from which some women moved toward greater collective consciousness of a sense of grievance.

A second social trend which coincided with the revival of feminism was the decline in the birth rate during the 60's and 70's. After World War II a "baby boom" swept the country, peaking in 1957 with a birth rate of 27.2 children per thousand people. There then ensued a prolonged downturn, which in 1967 resulted in a birth rate of 17.9, the lowest since the Great Depression. At the time demographers disagreed about the reasons for the decline, some citing the development of oral contraceptives, others economic and social instability. But all agreed there would be a new baby boom in the early 1970's when the children born twenty years earlier began to reproduce. Instead of rising, though, the birth rate continued to plummet, reaching an all-time low by the mid-70's and achieving the reproduction level required—over time—for Zero Population Growth.

Although many forces contributed to the continuing decline, the interaction of female employment with changing attitudes toward women's roles appears to have been decisive. Throughout the 1960's, women married later, delayed the birth of their first child, and bore their last child at an earlier age. Whether as cause or effect, this trend coincided with many women finding occupations and interests away from the home. The rewards of having a job, as well as the desire for extra money to meet rising living standards, tended to emphasize the advantages of a small family. These values, in turn, were reinforced in the late 60's by the ideology of feminism and the population control movement. Two Gallup polls in 1967 and 1971 highlighted the shift in values. The earlier survey showed that 34 per cent of women in the prime childbearing years anticipated having four or more children. By 1971, in contrast, the figure had dropped to 15 per cent. Two years later 70 per cent of the nation's 18- to 24-year-old women indicated that they expected to have no more than two children. Thus feminist emphasis on personal fulfillment and freedom from immersion in traditional sex roles operated in tandem with long-range social developments which made such goals more objectively feasible.

Finally, changing attitudes and behavior in the realm of human sexuality meshed closely with feminist values concerning personal and bodily liberation. Although suffrage leaders in the early 20th century had exhibited little understanding or tolerance of the sexual revolution, supporters of women's liberation emphasized as one of their strongest themes the importance of women knowing their own bodies and having the freedom to use them as they saw fit. One manifestation of this emphasis was the publication by a woman's health collective of *Our Bodies Our Selves*, a handbook which urged women to understand and appreciate their bodies. (The book had sold 850,000 copies from 1971 through 1976.) Still another manifestation was a generally supportive attitude toward "liberated" personal life-styles, including lesbianism, communal living, and sexual relationships outside of marriage.

Significantly, such attitudes reinforced many of the social trends already developing in the culture, particularly among the young. In the eyes of many observers, a second sexual revolution occurred starting in the mid-60's. One study of women students at a large urban university showed a significant increase after 1965 in the number of women having intercourse while in a "dating" or "going steady" relationship; at the same time guilt feelings about sex sharply declined. Another nation-wide sample of freshmen college women in 1975 disclosed that one-third endorsed casual sex based on a short acquaintance, and over 40 per cent believed a couple should live together before getting married. Most indicative of changing mores, perhaps, was a survey of eight colleges in 1973 which showed not only that 76 per cent of women had engaged in intercourse by their junior year (the male figure was 75 per cent), but that women were appreciably more active sexually than men. Daniel Yankelovich's public opinion polls of college and non-college young people in the 60's and 70's appeared to confirm the major departure in sexual behavior and attitudes. Only a minority of women disapproved morally of pre-marital sex, homosexual relations between consenting adults, or having an abortion. Although women's liberation advocates warned that women could be victimized anew as sex objects under the guise of sexual freedom (just as they had been under a system of more repressive mores), the fact remained that the movement's support for abortion, homosexual rights, and free bodily expression placed it more in harmony with emerging cultural attitudes toward sexuality than in opposition.

In each of these areas, it seemed clear that the women's liberation movement was both drawing upon and reinforcing important changes taking place in the society. Shifts in employment patterns, demography, and sexual mores may have had a momentum of their own, but feminism introduced a powerful ingredient of ideology and activism that sought to transform these impersonal social trends and create new values and attitudes toward sex roles. In that sense, for the first time a dynamic relationship existed between "objective" social changes and feminist efforts to shape those changes in a particular direction. In contrast with each of the previous woman's movements, the women's liberation drive of the 1960's and 1970's operated in a context where the social preconditions for ideological change were present. No longer was feminism irrelevant to most people's daily lives. Instead, its message spoke to many of the realities of the contemporary society. As a result, the possibility of an audience being able to respond was greater than ever before.

The second major distinctive quality of the new feminism is that as a result of a broader social base, the organization and structure of the movement differ significantly from that of the past. When women's rights advocates were on the margin of society and alienated from the world of most women, the organizational basis of the movement was narrow. Supporters of feminism, for the most part, came from the same social class and economic background. To maximize impact, the organizations they formed were national in scope. The women's liberation movement of the 60's and 70's, in contrast, almost defied categorization. Although feminist groups such as NOW and the Women's Equity Action League (WEAL) operated out of national offices in a style similar to that of other reform groups, the grass roots supporters of the movement fit less easily into an organizational niche. Some observers described women's liberation as a "guerilla movement," its headquarters located in every kitchen or bedroom where women developed a more critical and independent sense of self. Whether or not the description was fully accurate, the new feminism appeared both diverse and decentralized, its strength more likely to be found in local communities than in national hierarchies. Since the movement had emerged in response to social conditions affecting a large number of women, it tended to reflect the different backgrounds of its supporters and the special concerns which were of greatest interest to them.

The distinction between the various feminist movements was reflected in their different constituencies. Through most of the 19th century, feminism drew its support primarily from a scattering of upper- and upper-middle-class women who were angered at the growing tendency to deny women the opportunity to use their abilities on the same basis as men. . . .

Suffrage organizations shared the anti-black and anti-immigrant prejudices of their age, passing resolutions that disparaged both groups. Despite achieving a remarkable amount of support from club women and church women, the suffragists, like the Progressives generally, represented a homogeneous middle-class constituency.

With some justification, the same charge of being narrow, elitist, and white middle class has also been leveled at the women's liberation movement. In the late 60's feminism was generally associated with "liberal" university towns, student enclaves, the affluent suburbs, or the cosmopolitan urban centers of the East and West Coasts. . . .

Still, the charge of elitism appeared less applicable to the women's movement of the 60's and 70's than to prior manifestations of feminism. Most supporters of the movement identified with the political left and were highly conscious of the issues of class and race, seeking wherever possible to find ways of transcending those barriers. Rather than criticize or remain aloof from other dissident groups, women liberationists supported organizations like the United Farm Workers and aligned themselves with other groups seeking social change. (The early women's rights movement had done the same, of course, but the concern with racism faded by the late 19th century.) Many of the substantive demands of the movement, in turn, promised to help the poor as well as the rich and middle class. Most well-off women could afford to send their children to nursery school or hire service help. It was working-class women who would benefit most from universal day-care, equal pay, an end to job discrimination, and the availability of inexpensive abortions and birth control assistance. . . .

Perhaps more important, the new social base of feminism produced a thoroughly decentralized structure. When feminism had a narrower constituency, activity tended to focus on a national or state level. Hoping to maximize their influence, women reformers joined together in committees dedicated to securing specific goals such as the suffrage, or a minimum wage bill for women. A few devoted activists would work out of a regional or national headquarters, and in the name of all women, seek to persuade legislators or public opinion leaders of the virtue of their cause. Even when the popular base of the movement broadened in the early 20th century, the structure remained hierarchical, with coordination starting from state and national levels and working down to local branches. Indeed, through most of the 19th and 20th centuries, feminist groups were characterized by a vertical structure in which activity centered in coordinating committees at the top.

The women's liberation movement of the 60's and 70's, in contrast, was almost without any overarching structure. Despite the existence of groups like the National Organization of Women (NOW), the movement functioned primarily through small, informal groups on a local level. Its energy came from the bottom, not the top, and from the immediate ongoing concern of women with the quality of their own lives. Events or issues which were national in scope (such as the Equal Rights Amendment, or the march for equality on the 50th anniversary of the suffrage victory) were certainly not ignored, but the day-to-day direction of the movement grew out of local conditions which were central to the lives of the women most involved. Thus, as long as people in the immediate environment shared a common sense of grievance and a common desire for change, the movement was largely self-sustaining. It did not depend on national leadership. Indeed, many feminists believed deeply that "leaders" were unnecessary, that women could make decisions collectively, and that concepts of hierarchy and command were products of a male culture, hence to be avoided. In this context, the movement was decentralized for two reasons: it was rooted in local communities where women came together to deal with issues in their own lives; and it represented an ideology that viewed large organizations and leadership structures as part of the problem rather than the solution.

Not surprisingly, the absence of conventional leadership structures proved a source of considerable controversy. Some observers criticized the movement for its lack of direction and focus, implying that a disciplined national organization could mobilize a concerted following and secure more immediate results. Women's liberation theorist Jo Freeman warned about a potential "tyranny of structurelessness," arguing that the deliberate rejection of structure by feminists could create situations where a few women with staying power would dominate the movement because of the absence of regularized procedures to guarantee fairness and order. . . .

Reliance on collective good will, without resort to institutionalized checks and balances, tested severely people's ability to withstand the temptation to take advantage of others and impose their own will. Indeed, among some student radical groups, outlasting the opposition during interminable meetings provided a basic technique for controlling—and abusing—the process of participatory democracy.

In addition, the absence of structure helped to narrow the movement's class base, and limit its political effectiveness. . . .

Working-class people in particular favored meetings of limited duration with a specific agenda and a structured format. Moreover, the emphasis of movement supporters on intra-group compatibility unintentionally reinforced a tendency toward middle-class homogeneity. Also, an absence of structure made effective political action less likely. Not only was there no identifiable hierarchy to speak for the movement in developing coalitions or negotiating issues; the emphasis on "personal" issues sometimes diverted attention from public policy.

On balance, though, it seemed that decentralization and the lack of structure were central to the movement's strength as well as its distinctiveness. An ideal social movement might combine the discipline of a national organization with the energy of local grass roots efforts, yet such a combination appeared inconsistent—even contradictory— to the internal dynamics of the women's liberation movement. The vitality of the movement lay precisely in the proliferation of local organizations, each growing out of a particular concern or experience of different groups of women. Because such organizations reflected the immediate priorities of the women who created them, they commanded substantial loyalty and energy. It seemed at least possible, if not likely, that such an investment of local energy and initiative would be difficult to sustain in a hierarchical organization with established policies and strict procedures.

Finally, the pattern of decentralization ensured that the women's liberation movement would not rise or fall on the basis of one organization's activities or decisions. When all attention was riveted on a single national group as the embodiment of a cause, there was always the danger of defeat through internal divisions or the independent action of third parties. Thus some movements have been judged dead or alive on the basis of a single vote in Congress, or a series of public relations maneuvers. A social movement rooted in diverse local situations, however, and organized around a variety of issues, was less vulnerable to symbolic defeats. Thus, just as the movement's relevance to social trends helped to reinforce its ideological vitality, its decentralized structure accentuated its organizational strong point—grass roots support in the local community.

This, in turn, leads to the third distinguishing characteristic of the women's liberation movement, the variety and scope of its objectives. Through most of the 19th and 20th centuries, the women's movement tended to focus on a single issue, showing a tendency characteristic of nearly all American reform efforts. Although the Seneca Falls feminists sought far-reaching change in almost every area relevant to sex discrimination, their approach was too radical, and in a basically uncongenial political atmosphere it made sense to select one issue to effectively symbolize the movement. The problem was that the suffrage gradually became identified *in toto* with the larger issues. In a similar way, the National Women's Party (NWP) became obsessed with the belief that an Equal Rights Amendment (ERA) would prove to be a panacea. . . .

But in the process of seeking the ERA, the NWP, already a small elitist organization, alienated most working women (the ERA prior to 1941 would have brought invalidation of protective legislation for working women such as minimum-wage laws), spent an excessive amount of energy battling other women's organizations, and tended to ignore the extent to which the roots of sex inequality went beyond the reach of even the most powerful constitutional amendment.

The supporters of women's liberation, on the other hand, appeared to recognize the pitfalls of thinking there was any single answer to inequality or sex role stereotyping. The result was a plethora of related but separate activities, giving each individual group maximum leeway to work on the specific aspect of inequality that concerned it most. Although ratification of the proposed Equal Rights Amendment to the Constitution, repeal of abortion laws, or women's political caucuses represented the most visible items on the feminist agenda, most activists understood that success in one venture only meant there would be a new problem to work on. In this sense, feminists seemed to have learned a great deal from the civil rights movement, where the achievement of some goals such as the Voting Rights Act simply disclosed the existence of additional layers of racism to be combated. Implicit in feminist activities was the perception that, as in the Chinese proverb, the problem of inequality was a box within a box within a box, with no single answer. . . .

In the end, therefore, each of the distinctive qualities of feminism in the 60's and 70's was inextricably connected to the next. Because feminist ideas directly addressed contemporary social realities, more people perceived the movement as revelant to their own circumstances. This, in turn, helped to produce involvement in local activities which seemed pertinent to the larger issue. The extent to which the movement grew out of and related back to the immediate experience of large numbers of women made unnecessary the centralized and hierarchical structures of the past, and the absence of such structures encouraged the development of multiple activities, each dealing with a particular aspect of sex inequality. In this sense, the women's liberation movement of the 60's and 70's was more similar to the Southern Farmer's Alliance of the 1880's or the civil rights movement of the 1960's than to earlier manifestations of feminism. It took its direction and vitality from the experience of people in local communities.

As in the history of all social movements, however, contemporary feminism faced serious obstacles. Some reflected internal tensions that emerged from the very diversity and decentralization which distinguished the movement from its predecessors. Others derived from outside sources and mirrored the opposition, tacit as well as organized, which the ideas of women's liberation engendered. Together, they highlighted both the dimensions of the challenge confronting the movement and the scope of its quest for change.

Perhaps the most profound obstacle was the extent to which the movement threatened the sense of identity millions of people had derived from the culture and from the primary transmitter of social values, the family. The words "masculine" and "feminine" were as emotionally powerful in the meanings they conveyed as any other terms, including "white" and "black." People were raised to identify as almost sacred the attributes attached to each phrase, and to view any deviation as a mark of shame. For a boy to be called a "fairy," for example, represented a crushing insult, to be avoided at all costs.

Those who were deeply committed to prevailing values, such as the author George Gilder, believed that such networks of attributes derived from a sexual constitution found in all civilized societies. Within that constitution, women controlled otherwise intemperate male drives by tying men to the family, giving them a bond of fatherhood to their progeny, building up the masculine role of provider, and rewarding the male sex drive through the act of genital intercourse. . . .

In this context, an assault on any components of the sexual constitution—childbirth, the male role as provider, or genital sex—threatened to destroy civilized society itself by unleashing the previously harnessed anti-social drives of males.

Whether or not others would agree with Gilder's description of the sources of civilized society, it seemed clear that feminism was attacking the entire spectrum of traditional male and female roles. . . .

Although such fears were exaggerated, concern about the challenge to traditional "masculine" and "feminine" roles ran deep in the society. The issues raised by feminism went to the root of people's personal as well as social identity. At best such questions had the potential of making people vulnerable and insecure. At worst, they produced bitter hostility. Moreover, there existed a generalized anxiety that the triumph of women's liberation might mean the destruction of human relationships as they had been known, with impersonal competition replacing the warmth associated with woman's traditional role, and a unisex sameness overcoming the rich distinctiveness of previous male-female relationships. Part nostalgia and part legitimate concern about depersonalization, the anxiety provided important kindling for those forces seeking to build a political backfire against women's liberation on such issues as opposition to abortion and the Equal Rights Amendment. Thus the greatest obstacle feminism faced was the commitment of millions of people to the institutions, values, and personal self-images which were associated with traditional sex roles. As conservatives mobilized the political potential implicit in that commitment, feminists found some of their objectives increasingly endangered.

The second major obstacle faced by the movement was that of internal dissension. Though the absence of a centralized structure and focus on a single issue proved to be assets in most respects, the resulting diversity of aims and priorities constituted a seedbed of ideological conflict. Intense factional disputes erupted over both goals and methods. Some feminists believed that only the total abolition of the nuclear family could bring freedom to women. Others accepted the family institution but sought to change its structure to make it more equitable. While some traced discrimination against women to an inherent and irrevocable male malevolence, others saw men as parallel victims of a warped socialization process. . . .

For the most part, supporters of the movement attempted to deal with the danger of dissension in two ways. First, there developed early in the movement a general policy of not excluding groups or points of view for reasons of political unorthodoxy or social unpopularity. The issue surfaced quickly on the question of endorsing the struggle of lesbians; despite deep concern among some that identification with homosexuality would harm the prospect of gaining legislative and political reform, most activists made common cause on the indivisibility of women's rights. In part this reflected the absence of a monolithic organization seeking to impose a party line, and in part an

ideological conviction that disavowing one group of women for reasons of political expediency would lead to the death of the movement.
A second approach—growing out of the first—was a belief that women
could resolve conflict through understanding and conciliation. While
men might go to war rather than admit the possibility of error,
women, it was argued, could work through a problem to a collective
solution. . . .

Not surprisingly, though, the depth of feeling sometimes divided
the movement into warring camps. Gloria Steinem, identified in the
public eye as a major feminist figure because of her writing and the
attention paid her by the media, became a symbol of such divisions
when she was accused by some "radical" feminists of having been a
CIA agent for ten years. Because of her association with the "moderate" *Ms.* magazine and her reluctance to adopt an uncompromisingly
radical stance on some issues, Steinem unwittingly became a scape-
goat in the fight over who would control the movement. Conflicts between lesbians and non-lesbians also frequently reached the stage of
no-holds-barred battle, and some feminists like Betty Friedan viewed
the so-called "lavender menace" as more an enemy to the movement
than male chauvinism. Even more established organizations like
NOW split over the reform/radical issue, and when the 1975 NOW
convention adopted as its slogan "out of the mainstream and into the
revolution," some members withdrew in protest to start their own
organization.

Together with resistance to change within the dominant culture,
then, the constant threat of internecine warfare plagued the movement's efforts to make inroads among its potential constituency. The
questions at issue were neither trivial nor simple, and the distinction
between compromise and surrender was not always clear. Yet there
was a profound difference between viewing the contented homemaker
as a deluded Sambo and reaching out to make contact with her on her
own ground. Similarly, a tremendous chasm separated those who
viewed men as congenitally oppressive and those who saw males as
people in need of support as well as prodding in coming to grips with
their attitudes. In the presence of such conflicts, the potential existed
that the women's movement of the 1960's and 1970's would fall victim
to the same polarization that had torn apart its predecessor in the
1920's, and that energies needed for positive action would be diverted
into sectarian feuding.

Still, what remained impressive was the degree of change that appeared to be taking place notwithstanding the obstacles. Although
most American women might disavow any overt association with the
movement *per se* ("I'm no women's libber," "They're too radical for

my taste"), the same women supported many of the substantive programs of the movement. Day-care centers, availability of abortion services, equal career opportunities, and greater sharing of household tasks all received substantial approval in public opinion surveys of women. As late as 1962 a Gallup poll showed that a majority of female respondents did not believe American women were discriminated against. Eight years later women divided down the middle on the question of whether they supported the movement to secure greater equality. By 1974 those responding to the same question endorsed the efforts toward more equality by two to one.

The greatest impact of the movement appeared among the young and on college campuses. The Yankelovich survey of the early 70's showed a doubling in two years of the number of students viewing women as an oppressed group, with a large majority endorsing concepts of equality in sexual relations, the importance of women's relation to other women, and the notion that men and women were born with the same talents. Two-thirds of college women agreed that "the idea that a woman's place is in the home is nonsense," and only one-third felt that having children was an important personal value. Other polls showed similar results, including a rapid change over time. A 1970 survey of college freshmen indicated that half of the men and more than one-third of the women endorsed the idea that "the activities of married women are best confined to the home and family." Five years later only one-third of the men and less than one-fifth of the women took the same position.

Not surprisingly, changing attitudes toward traditional roles in the home were accompanied by shifting expectations about careers. In the 1970 survey of freshmen, males out-numbered females 8 to 1 in expressing an interest in the traditionally "masculine" fields of business, engineering, medicine, and law. By 1975, in contrast, the ratio was down to 3 to 1. In the same period, moreover, the number of women expecting to enter the "feminine" fields of elementary and secondary school teaching plummeted from 31 per cent to 10 per cent. . . .

The proportion of women in the entering classes of law school skyrocketed by 300 per cent from 1969 to 1974, and many law schools anticipated that women would make up half of each class by 1980. Women doctorates also increased significantly, with the share of Ph.D.'s earned by women growing from 11 per cent in 1970 to 21 per cent in 1975. Although working-class and older women did not share completely all the new ideas, they too seemed to be undergoing change. Non-college young women were less convinced of the value of sisterhood or the reality of discrimination than college women, but the Yankelovich survey showed them endorsing feminist ideas on greater equality in family decision-making, women's right to sexual pleasure, and skepticism toward the traditional homemaker ideal. . . .

There was no way to quantify such consciousness, or to know with certainty what it meant. Yet it seemed to be a palpable reality—taking root, growing, spreading. It appeared in public school brochures where the traditional "he" as the description for everyone was replaced with "he or she." In offices it sometimes blossomed when male bosses, without thinking, automatically assumed that the "girls" would get coffee or buy a Christmas present for a female relative. And in discussions of rape, gynecological practices, who would watch the children, drive the car, or fold the laundry, it could suddenly emerge. Wherever the consciousness appeared, change began to occur because in one way or another, every activity of the day, from interaction with co-workers to reading a night-time story to children, took on a new significance. Social revolutions, to be sure, do not develop full blown from the simple emergence of a new idea. Yet heightened awareness of a set of social conditions is a prerequisite for a change in values, and it seemed likely that as consciousness of sex role stereotyping and discrimination mounted, other social relationships would be cast in a new light also, sparking a rethinking process about one's entire life—work, family, spouse, children, and friends.

Much of the change that had taken place, of course, could be traced to non-ideological forces. Long-term trends in the economy, demographic patterns, and cultural values all contributed substantially. In addition, only a relatively small proportion of the total female population participated, either directly or indirectly, in the women's movement. If a majority identified with some feminist ideas, only a few were activists. Indeed, many of those who were involved in changing their own lives might have done so regardless of the movement, as a natural byproduct of the underlying changes in the society and economy.

Yet the women's movement of the 60's and 70's seems, on balance, to have been decisive to the heightened consciousness of the younger generation. Behavioral change, prompted by impersonal social forces, can go only so far. At some point ideological forces must intervene to spur a transformation of the values which help to shape and define behavioral options. In the late 60's and 70's the woman's movement provided such a spur, criticizing the assumptions, values, and images that had prevailed in the past and offering an alternative vision of what might prevail in the future. Although most men and women did not align themselves vigorously on the side of feminism, political discussions, media coverage, decisions on public school curriculum, employment practices, and the dynamics of family living all reflected the impact of the movement's existence. It had raised questions, presented demands, and introduced ideas which compelled discussion. And even when the discussion was hostile, people were considering issues central to self and society in a way that had not happened before.

L I S E V O G E L

Lise Vogel teaches sociology and women's studies at Rider University, where she is also director of the Multicultural Studies Program. She is the author of Mothers on the Job *(1993),* Marxism and the Oppression of Women: Toward a Unitary Theory *(1987), and* Woman Questions: Essays for a Materialist Feminism *(1995).*

In January 1987, the U.S. Supreme Court ruled on a case that posed the question of whether it is possible to reconcile equality norms with policies treating pregnant workers differently from other workers. The case involved a bank receptionist, Lillian Garland, who sought to return to her job under a California statute requiring employers to provide unpaid job-protected disability leaves to their pregnant employees. When the Supreme Court upheld the legitimacy of the California law, its decision was widely welcomed as a victory for working women.

The meaning of the Lillian Garland case was, however, complex. Feminist attorneys were divided on the case and on the merits and dangers of providing special benefits to pregnant workers. Although the debate at times appeared technical and obscure to nonlawyers, it raised questions analogous to those already emerging in other policy arenas about the limits of equality, the meaning of difference, and the direction of feminist strategy.

Underlying the debate over pregnancy policy was the theoretical question of how to construe sexual difference. For the lawyers, the question initially turned on the nature of pregnancy. Is pregnancy a temporary disability? Is it a unique condition which for the practical purpose of enhancing equal employment opportunity can be analogized to other conditions? Or is pregnancy so special that such analogies demean women and actually impede equal employment opportunity? Implicitly

From "Debating Difference: Feminism, Pregnancy, and the Workplace" in Claire Goldberg and Heidi Hartmann (editors), *U.S. Women in Struggle: A Feminist Studies Anthology.* Copyright © 1995 University of Illinois Press.

or explicitly, the lawyers found themselves confronting basic problems of feminist theory and long-term goals. As feminists, is our objective simply the dismantling of barriers to equal participation in social life? Do we want to push beyond assimilation, which effectively leaves male norms in place, toward a balanced androgyny in a social structure transformed to symmetrically meet women's and men's needs? Or should we frankly recognize woman's special and different nature through the development of woman-centered analysis and a rich women's culture? Is it reasonable to focus just on sexual specificity in a world torn apart by class, race, national, and other differences? What if a person's identity is not fixed but, rather, fluctuates—drawing variously on multiple sources, only one of which is gender? Perhaps we should view feminist goals as more transcendent—pointing beyond equality and difference, and past all dichotomies, to a future community of marvelously diverse persons, simultaneously united and autonomous.

The concerns of the participants in the debate over special treatment of pregnancy in the workplace thus converge with those of recent feminist theory, for pregnancy poses the dilemma of difference in an especially sharp and poignant form. In this essay I outline the controversy over special treatment of pregnancy, briefly explore how feminist legal scholarship conceptualized it, and suggest some broader implications. My purpose is to move beyond the polarization that characterized the debate without losing sight of the larger political context.

Lillian Garland had been employed as a receptionist in a Los Angeles branch of the California Federal Savings and Loan Association (Cal Fed). Her difficult first pregnancy and delivery necessitated several months' disability leave in early 1982, and she expected her position to be protected by a California law mandating that employers grant workers temporarily disabled by pregnancy up to four months of unpaid leave with job security. When she attempted to return to work at the end of the leave, however, Cal Fed claimed no receptionist or similar positions were available. Garland then sought her rights under the state statute. In response, Cal Fed, joined by the California Chamber of Commerce and the Merchants and Manufacturers Association, initiated a suit to invalidate the state law, arguing that it was preempted by the federal Pregnancy Discrimination Act (PDA). At issue was the conflict between the state law's requirement that pregnant employees be treated in a special manner and the federal law's mandate that they be treated the same as other workers. Cal Fed did not provide job-protected leaves to employees temporarily disabled by conditions other than pregnancy, and it wished to treat its pregnant employees in the same niggardly way. The Supreme Court determined, however, that California's disability leave statute was not in conflict with the federal PDA. That is, the Court ruled that special treatment of pregnancy in the workplace does not necessarily contradict the imperatives of equality.

The Supreme Court ruling meant that Garland did indeed have the right to reclaim her job. In this sense, the decision was an unambiguous victory. The question feminist lawyers had been debating was not whether Garland should have her job back but how best to achieve this outcome. To understand the controversy sparked in the feminist legal community by the California case, the litigation must be examined in the context of U.S. maternity and parenting policy.

It is always a shock to find out just how little substantive support for pregnancy and parenting is available in the United States. Despite an entrenched public ideology venerating motherhood and family, the level of tangible benefits and rights supporting parenting in the United States is sharply below world standards. Most industrialized countries, as well as many developing nations, provide comprehensive benefits to eligible workers for childbirth and childrearing. Medical costs are covered, and paid job- and benefit-protected leaves for maternity and parenting are the norm. In Europe, for example, maternity leave ranges from twelve weeks to twelve months and is paid at 80 to 100 percent of the maximum insured wage. Leaves can be extended should pregnancy or delivery prove difficult. Some countries provide additional leave to single mothers, for second and subsequent children, or for multiple births. Many permit mothers (or parents) to take more time, with the additional leave paid at a lower rate or simply job protected. Benefits in Canada, although less generous than those in Europe, are light years ahead of those available on this side of the border—approximately seventeen weeks' leave at 60 percent pay, usually with job, pension, and seniority preserved. The United States is thus unique in the stinginess of its support for maternity and parenting. . . .

Its relatively weak set of substantive maternity supports were mainly instituted through state legislation affecting the employment of women and children but not men. Protective laws limited women's hours of work, regulated their working conditions, and prohibited female labor in certain "dangerous" occupations. Many women workers benefited from such laws, but others were not covered at all, and some found themselves excluded from jobs they wanted.

Over time, special treatment for women through protective legislation not only reinforced sex segregation in the labor market, but it also increasingly became the basis for policies and practices that harmed women workers. In the name of protection, special—but often unfavorable—treatment of pregnant workers thus became a norm that was still in place in the early 1970s. . . .

Feminist legal strategies in the 1960s and 1970s focused on eliminating discrimination against women. Given the ambiguous legacy of protectionist policy in the United States and the burgeoning activity on the civil rights front, it made sense to address the needs of women as a question of rights and equality rather than as protective legislation. Feminist equality strategy sought to make sex-based generalizations generally impermissible and to delegitimate the use of sex as a proxy for specific traits, functions, or behaviors. In the area of employment, the approach was to replace sex-based classifications with distinctions based on function. Instead of designating a job as male, for example, an employer would have to develop job-related criteria, such as strength or height. Characteristics specific to one sex—for example, pregnancy—could, for certain purposes, be viewed as comparable to other characteristics; by establishing comparability in the workplace, unfavorable treatment based on sex-specific characteristics could be identified as discriminatory, hence impermissible.

The campaign to bring pregnancy within the scope of equality norms was thus part of a larger effort, and by the late 1970s it had produced substantial results. Employers and courts began to establish a record of treating pregnant workers as comparable to other workers whose ability to work was similarly affected. Practices that had seemed normal only a decade earlier were redefined as discriminatory and unacceptable. Job security and benefits for pregnant workers, especially in the areas of health, disability, and unemployment insurance, improved. In effect, an implicit national maternity policy was being shaped. Modest and, indeed, peculiar by European standards, it did not center on specific substantive benefits for pregnant workers, nor did it define its goals in terms of social welfare. Instead, its touchstone was an antidiscrimination principle: pregnancy could not be the basis for unequal treatment of a woman worker.

Consistent with this legal framework, Congress enacted the Pregnancy Discrimination Act in 1978. The PDA was designed to nullify several Supreme Court decisions that used pregnancy as a basis to deny women benefits and seemed to be trying to turn back the clock on equality. In these rulings, the Court had insisted that pregnancy is not comparable to other conditions. Rather, said the justices, pregnancy is a unique *"additional risk"*—an extra burden that can properly be treated in a special and unfavorable manner. The Court found that General Electric, for example, was not discriminating against women when it excluded pregnancy from its disability coverage. Outraged, a coalition of feminist, labor, civil rights, church, and even antiabortion groups mobilized to support the passage of the PDA.

The PDA extends the 1964 Civil Rights Act to cover discrimination on the basis of pregnancy and specifically mandates that employers treat pregnant workers the same as other workers who are comparably able or unable to work. To comply with the PDA, employers must generally make decisions about pregnant workers based on their capacity to work, just as such decisions would be made about other employees. If able to work, a pregnant worker cannot be fired or forced to take a leave of absence. If not able to work, she must be treated no differently than other workers similar in their inability to work. An employer who ordinarily permits workers temporarily disabled by illness to return to their old jobs, for instance, must provide the same option to workers temporarily disabled by pregnancy.

The PDA does not shape the substantive content of the pregnant worker's rights and benefits. Rather, the treatment a pregnant worker might receive under the PDA largely depends on her employer's particular policies. Unexpectedly, the federal act seemed to conflict with a handful of recently enacted state laws designed to provide benefits to pregnant women. By attempting to address the substantive needs of pregnant workers directly, these state laws departed from the strategic approach embodied in the PDA. Rather than follow an antidiscrimination principle requiring that pregnant workers be treated in a manner comparable to other workers, pregnancy disability laws provide special benefits for one group of persons with special needs. The contradiction between the two strategies led inevitably to the litigation which culminated in the Supreme Court's Cal Fed decision.

The outcome of the litigation was of great importance to women workers. Employers were attempting to use the PDA to void state laws mandating the provision of benefits on the basis of pregnancy. If successful, their efforts threatened women with the loss of significant benefits. The equality framework that had seemed to be unequivocally on the side of women was revealing hidden ambiguities. At one level, the Cal Fed case pitted mean-spirited employers against pregnant workers needing job-protected disability leave. At another, it posed extremely difficult questions for feminist strategy and theory.

Feminist lawyers across the country discussed the implications of the litigation with more than a little consternation. For over a decade, their attention had been focused on equality. Only a few years earlier, they had mobilized to circumvent backward-looking Supreme Court decisions through the passage of the PDA. The feminist legal community was ill-prepared for an assault on women in the very name of equality.

The issues were intensively debated at numerous meetings and conferences and split the feminist legal community. Participants conceptualized the problem as a choice between two approaches to pregnancy in the workplace: "special treatment" and "equal treatment." Advocates of both positions supported Lillian Garland's right to her leave. Unlike her employer, they agreed that California's disability leave provision is not preempted by the federal PDA and that Cal Fed could and should comply with both statutes. Within this shared framework, they followed differing reasoning and suggested different remedies. Proponents of special treatment argued that the real sexual difference constituted by pregnancy made special treatment necessary to achieve real equality; if Cal Fed complied with California's statute it would automatically meet the requirements of the PDA, because both laws were intended to promote equal employment opportunity. Advocates of equal treatment also argued that Cal Fed could comply with both statutes but only by making unpaid, job-protected leave available on a nondiscriminatory basis to all its temporarily disabled employees. From the special-treatment perspective, then, narrowly drawn laws providing benefits to pregnant workers to accommodate the specific physical burdens of pregnancy were consistent with the equality mandate of the PDA. From the equal-treatment perspective, however, consistency with the PDA required that the benefits provided by such laws be extended equally to all workers. . . .

Feminist legal scholarship articulated the competing positions. Two articles, one by Wendy Williams and the other by Linda J. Krieger and Patricia N. Cooney, were especially critical to the debate. In "The Equality Crisis: Some Reflections on Culture, Courts, and Feminism," published in 1982, Williams pointed to increasing feminist concern about the meaning of equality. Having dealt with the "easy" cases, feminists now confront the "hard" ones, such as rape, military service, pregnancy, and maternity. These cases "touch the hidden nerves of our most profoundly embedded cultural values," causing feminists to question their traditional equality strategy. Williams defended the equality framework as providing, even for the hard cases, both a practical approach and an adequate feminist vision of sexual difference.

In the hard case of pregnancy, for example, Williams maintained that women's special needs can be addressed without creating a classification based on sexual difference, thus removing the pretext for disadvantageous special treatment. The very real physiological uniqueness of pregnancy creates burdens for women workers that can be acknowledged by analogy to other burdensome physiological conditions. Williams cautioned against advocacy of a pregnancy-based classification. New pregnancy laws cannot, she argued, be narrowly drawn to reflect only "real" biological differences; the history of protective legislation shows that an emphasis on the special nature of maternity, however well-intentioned, can provide a basis for unfavorable as well as favorable treatment. Already she observed, there was an ominous convergence between feminist support for special treatment of special needs and the Supreme Court's damaging opinion that pregnancy is an extra burden. Feminists who seek special recognition for pregnancy through maternity legislation cannot guarantee that their interpretation of the special nature of motherhood will be adopted by the state. Only ten years had passed since the Supreme Court first acknowledged sex discrimination could be unconstitutional, she noted, and gains under the emerging norms of gender neutrality were still fragile. In sum, to endorse the doctrine of difference would put women at risk. . . .

Williams also commented on the deeper implications of the special-treatment/equal-treatment dilemma. The special-treatment perspective, she suggested, projects a view of women that is essentially identical to the separate spheres ideology of the past, which assumed women and men to be by nature different and thus provided a basis for discrimination against women. By contrast, the equality approach exemplified by the PDA helps to dismantle the ideology of separate spheres. Feminists need to make a choice, she concluded: "Do we want equality of the sexes—or do we want justice for two kinds of human beings who are fundamentally different?" In a later article, Williams specified that "the equal treatment approach [seeks] to overcome the definition of the prototypical worker as male and to promote an integrated—and androgynous—prototype." In Williams's view, the special-treatment position collapses into endorsement of retrograde separate spheres ideology, but the equal-treatment perspective offers the more feminist vision of androgyny.

In 1983, Krieger and Cooney argued the opposing position, in defense of laws providing special benefits to pregnant workers. They maintained that women's special role as childbearers creates obstacles to equal employment opportunity that men do not face. In the presence of real physiological sex differences, equal treatment can yield unequal results. In particular, an inadequate disability leave policy can amount to a policy of terminating pregnant workers. Given the extra burden of maternity, Krieger and Cooney suggested, women require extra benefits on a permanent basis if they are to achieve real equality. In making special provision for pregnancy, special-treatment legislation "places women on an *equal* footing with men and permits males and females to compete *equally* in the labor market." That is, it enhances equal employment opportunity and is not in conflict with the PDA.

Krieger and Cooney claimed to have a broader and more feminist vision of sexual difference than equal-treatment proponents. They castigated the equal-treatment framework as thoroughly liberal and abstract—focused on form rather than results, denying the reality of difference, and implicitly adopting men as the norm. The relentless individualism of equal treatment may work relatively well for upper-middle-class women, they asserted, but it fails to meet the immediate needs of working-class and single mothers. The masses of women have not made significant progress on the sex-specific issues of pregnancy and abortion, they argued, yet feminist litigators persist in offering the courts only this narrow liberal view of equality. "It is incumbent upon feminists," they concluded, "to provide a new, more humanistic vision for society, a new ideology of equality". . . .

Participants in the debate distinguished the immediate physical needs of childbearing from the demands of childrearing, and they all agreed that the needs of workers as childrearers can best be met through gender-neutral parenting programs and legislation. The dispute centered on childbearing. Although each side recognized that equal employment opportunity requires woman's experience as childbearer to be acknowledged in the workplace, they differed on the means to be used. Those in favor of special treatment supported narrowly drawn pregnancy laws as a way to provide the extra help pregnant women need to achieve equal employment opportunity. Advocates of equal treatment opposed female-specific legislation, cautioning that special treatment in the law has traditionally translated into inferior treatment of the targeted group. They argued that a continued emphasis on equality analysis, which includes sensitivity to adverse impacts of seemingly neutral rules, is consistent with past gains and is the best way to meet the special needs created by pregnancy. Fundamental to the policy dispute, although only partially acknowledged in the debates, were divergent feminist views of sexual difference and women's liberation.

When the Supreme Court ruled on the Cal Fed case in January 1987, its opinion did not settle the special-treatment/equal-treatment controversy. The decision established the legal viability of statutes providing benefits on the basis of pregnancy, but gender-neutral legal norms continue to govern in most other areas affecting women. Efforts to meet women's needs as childbearers can therefore follow either the special-treatment or the equal-treatment strategy. Indeed, the flurry of confused legislative activity following the Cal Fed decision shows that state lawmakers seeking to enact pregnancy or parenting legislation are befuddled; they do not know which approach to adopt. One effect of the Supreme Court decision has been, then, to return the debate to the legislatures. Uncertainty about the relative merits of special and equal treatment of pregnant workers persists. . . .

Participants in the debate over special treatment disagreed about the actual effect of the PDA on women workers. Those favoring special-treatment legislation argued that gender-neutral treatment disproportionately fails to meet the needs of working-class and poor women. Focusing mainly on benefit plans, they implied that the PDA has harmed rather than helped women. Its immediate practical effect has been, they suggested, at best, mixed—benefiting some women but harming many others, especially poor and working-class women, in the name of a purely formal equality. The attempt to deny pregnancy benefits to Lillian Garland, a Black single mother caught in the low-wage ghetto of routine clerical work, seemed to epitomize this interpretation.

Evidence for the critique of the PDA has been largely anecdotal and impressionistic. . . . Although comprehensive studies have not yet been carried out, some data exist. Evidence from the insurance industry, for example, which provides employers with policies to cover employee benefits, can shed light on the PDA's impact on disability and medical coverage. The insurance industry had vigorously opposed the passage of the PDA, arguing that costs would be high. . . . Its fears with respect to costs were confirmed by several studies based on insurance company data that find generally higher short-term disability costs due to payment of benefits mandated by the PDA. . . . A 1984 study of the health plans of twenty-one companies in Iowa, Missouri, and Indiana furnishes additional evidence. Before the PDA's passage, medical benefits for pregnancy in all twenty-one firms were inferior to benefits for other conditions; four of the firms offered no coverage whatsoever for either normal or cesarean delivery. After implementation of the PDA, all the firms covered pregnancy and pregnancy-related conditions on the same basis as other conditions. Improved medical coverage and increased aggregate cash benefits suggest that on average the PDA has aided women monetarily, although no one knows just how many women have benefited nor who they are. The fact that monetary benefits have risen could suggest that the PDA especially benefits working-class women, generally more in need of cash and less able to sustain the unpaid leaves that "middle-class" women can sometimes afford.

Many women work for firms employing fewer than fifteen persons and are therefore not covered by the PDA. With jobs at the bottom of the employment scale and with minimal or no benefits, these are the low-income women for whom special pregnancy legislation at the state level should be especially helpful, according to special-treatment proponents. The actual experience of California is instructive. The guarantee of up to four months of job-protected pregnancy disability leave was one of nine provisions in a package passed by the California legislature in 1978. . . . Of the nine provisions mandating special treatment of pregnant workers, two provide benefits but seven are more ambiguous, permitting employers to treat pregnancy unfavorably. For example, employers . . . are allowed to exclude pregnancy from medical benefit plans. This mixed bag of benefits and exclusions is in effect for California firms with six to fourteen employees. If Lillian Garland had not worked for a big bank, she might have found herself with an unpaid disability leave but without medical coverage for her difficult and expensive pregnancy. All women need both medical coverage and adequate leave provisions, but again, I would argue that for working-class women the medical benefits are especially important. In California, then, the special-treatment approach resulted in statutes that treated pregnancy in contradictory and sometimes unfavorable ways.

More studies are necessary, but available evidence on the PDA's immediate impact suggests that on balance it has resulted in improved pregnancy benefits for large numbers of working women. Any overall evaluation of the PDA's impact must include, furthermore, its protection of all women's access to work. Without the PDA, pregnant women's rights to be hired, to enter training programs, and to continue working while pregnant would be threatened. In an economy in which women increasingly participate in the labor force, the issue of access to work is at least as important to poor and working-class women as it is to "middle-class" women. In terms of practical results, then, the gender-neutral approach to pregnancy cannot be evaluated as negatively as the special-treatment critics would claim.

In addition to practical impact, the choice of a particular strategy carries with it ideological implications. For many of the participants in the special-treatment/equal-treatment debate, these implications have been at the core of the controversy over pregnancy legislation. Special-treatment proponents are repelled by what they see as the equal-treatment approach's representation of pregnancy as a disability and its imposition of male norms on women. At issue in their critique are the meanings attributed to pregnancy and sexual difference. The PDA, in this view, is irreparably tainted by the identification it supposedly makes of pregnancy with disability. By treating pregnancy as a temporary disability, the PDA is said to stigmatize childbearing as a pathological departure from an implicitly male norm. As physician Wendy Chavkin puts it, "pregnancy . . . is not an illness. Rather, it is a unique condition, that may be accompanied by special needs, and sometimes by illness." In sum, according to the critics, the gender-neutral approach to pregnancy devalues its special biological and social nature, attempts inappropriately to standardize women's experience within male-defined medical and work norms, and represents pregnancy as, literally, an abnormal and unhealthy condition.

The image of pregnancy that special-treatment advocates seem to prefer focuses on woman's uniqueness. We should not shrink, they argue, from endorsing difference.

> In observing that [pregnancy and breastfeeding] are the capabilities which *really* differentiate women from men, it is crucial that we overcome any aversion to describing these functions as "unique." Uniqueness is a "trap" only in terms of an analysis . . . which assumes that maleness is the norm. "Unique" does not mean uniquely handicapped.

There is, in this view, a profound and definitional character to the phenomenon of childbearing. It marks all women, constituting a strength and source of unity but also creating specific needs. Policies that positively acknowledge the uniqueness of childbearing, such as those in many European countries, need not be judged by an equality standard. Instead, they show that women's special needs can be accommodated within a framework that emphasizes caring and responsibility.

The special-treatment representation of pregnancy and sexual difference is in many ways compelling. It emphasizes the inadequacy of traditional liberal views that deny sexual difference and seek individualistic assimilation to a single standard. It offers a vision of women and their special needs as not only unique but also profoundly important. It claims to be the best defense of the most needy women, as well as the foundation for the far more adequate maternity policies found in other countries. And it resonates with feminist aspirations to go beyond conventional formulations toward more radical solutions. For many feminists, these characteristics have proven irresistible.

Chief among the ideological accusations made against the gender-neutral framework are that its proponents endorse male norms and that they commit the sin of liberalism. Although the charges can validly be directed at some backers of equal treatment, others seek to transcend the liberalism of which they are accused. Nadine Taub and Wendy Williams, for example, are well aware that the traditional liberal framework tends to override difference and set up a male model as the norm. They point out that "the model is, of course, not only male but also white, able-bodied, English-speaking, and a member of a mainstream religion." And they depict pregnancy as only one of many unique conditions that human beings have or develop—conditions that invariably involve special needs society ought to accommodate. Where special-treatment advocates insist on woman's categorical difference and propose special policies to represent globally special female needs, Taub and Williams move toward an understanding of all persons as differentiated individuals, each with her or his own special needs. To meet these needs, the workplace must be transformed. "The vision is not . . . a workplace based on a male definition of employee, with special accommodation to women's differences from men, but rather a redefinition of what a typical employee is that encompasses both sexes."

Implicit in Taub and Williams's comments is a significantly revised version of the gender-neutral approach to the pregnancy dilemma. Rather than categorize workers into two groups, female and male, this approach acknowledges that all employees have special needs—as expectant mothers; as parents; as aging, handicapped, or temporarily infirm workers; and so forth. It replaces, in other words, the fixed dichotomy of male versus female with attention to individual needs that is simultaneously sensitive to group-based hierarchy. This approach, then, rejects both the formal equality model of traditional liberalism and the special-treatment model proposed by some contemporary feminists. Neither individual assimilation to male norms nor group-based accommodation to categorically defined female needs provides an adequate framework.

In sum, gender neutrality has, like liberalism itself, a radical edge. Disentangled from the abstract individualism of its liberal origins, gender neutrality can support a view of difference that goes beyond the

simplistic oppositions haunting the special-treatment/equal-treat-
ment debate. Within such an expanded gender-neutral perspective,
pregnancy and breastfeeding are no longer seen as abnormal conditions; neither are they viewed as immutably defining characteristics of
sexual difference. Rather, childbearing is represented as one among
many important categorical specificities that must be accommodated
in a society transformed to equally meet the special needs of all.

The debate over special treatment of pregnancy took place in a
charged strategic context. Benefits of immediate usefulness to women
were at risk, as was the categorization of women as a class within the
U.S. legal framework. Questions of immediate impact and short-term
strategy thus converged with problems of long-term feminist vision.
Within the feminist legal community, one either supported the California statute as an adequate implementation of the special-treatment
perspective or opposed it on the basis of some version of the equality
approach. In the heated atmosphere of the developing litigation, too
little attention was paid to evaluating the competing positions as
strategies proposed for a particular time and place and equally fraught
with dangers and contradictions. At most, feminist legal scholars
sought to transcend the dichotomized opposition of difference to
equality in abstract terms.

Some commentators have recently begun to conceptualize dilemmas concerning rights and equality as problems in the use of reforms
to effect social change. Lawyer Elizabeth M. Schneider proposes, for
example, that struggles using the discourse of rights and equality
should be evaluated in terms of multiple criteria. "The assertion or
'experience' of rights can express political vision, affirm a group's humanity, contribute to an individual's development as a whole person,
and assist in the collective political development of a social or political movement." Instead of dismissing rights claims as irredeemably
shaped by their liberal origins, litigators can both acknowledge the
limits of equality discourse and use it to move the struggle forward.
Schneider offers the feminist demands for equality and reproductive
rights as examples of the transformative potential of reform struggles
centered on rights claims. "By concretizing an abstract idea and situating it within women's experience, these rights claims did not simply
'occupy' an existing right, but rather modified and transformed the nature of the right." Legal scholar Patricia J. Williams similarly under-
scores the consciousness-raising and empowering aspects of rights
discourse. Focusing on African Americans, she argues compellingly
that subordinate groups experience the assertion of rights differently
from dominant groups. For Blacks, she shows, rights discourse can be
"deliciously empowering," and the struggle for equal rights is not a
"dry process of reification . . . [but] the resurrection of life from 400-
year-old ashes."

Viewed as alternative reform strategies, variants of both the spe-cial-treatment and equal-treatment approaches to pregnancy ought to be carefully evaluated at several levels. As with any reform, feminists cannot, unfortunately, retain full control over the use and implemen-tation of their conceptualizations—in this case, by legislators, judges, policymakers, and the media. Nor can we fully anticipate the ramifica-tions of the positions we adopt. A number of questions therefore arise. To what extent, for example, will a particular policy approach to preg-nancy in the workplace respond to women's immediate needs? In what ways might it be vulnerable to antiwoman revision in the courts and legislatures? How does a given approach to pregnancy in the work-place contribute to individual empowerment, to political education and organizing, and to the building of the movement? What are the im-plications of the approach for the future, and are they adequate to the feminist vision? Which feminist vision?

I can only sketch answers to these questions. With respect to short-term impact and vulnerability to atavistic revision, I find the practical arguments in favor of the so-called equal-treatment approach hard to counter. Classifications based on difference have always, in the U.S. context, had a sinister capacity to be used against groups so cate-gorized. Nothing occurred during the Reagan years that might suggest a reduced vulnerability to such disadvantageous interpretations, nor is there much basis to predict a major shift in the near future. Although equality strategies are all flawed or incomplete to some extent, they have in fact served U.S. women of diverse class and race origins rela-tively well. It is true that equality is a diffuse and limited notion, but those who on this basis reject the quest for equal rights spin a risky discourse and practice. From the perspective of subordinate groups, de-nial of equality is a burden too heavy to bear, while the assertion of rights can be practically useful and politically empowering.

Still, arguments stressing expediency are not enough to justify a position in favor of equal treatment of pregnancy in the workplace. The theoretical foundations for a radical version of this position must be more completely developed and the linkages to feminist aspirations for the future strengthened. The expanded gender-neutral perspective described here is, in my view, a start. In terms of immediate results and resistance to retrograde misinterpretation, gender neutrality pro-vides minimum standards of equal treatment in the liberal sense. But it need not remain imprisoned in traditional liberal notions of the de-sirable sameness of abstract individuals. An expanded concept of gen-der neutrality can move beyond the imperatives of universal conformity to a single standard.

In short, gender neutrality can underpin policies that treat differ-ence and diversity as entirely normal rather than as phenomena to be ignored or suppressed. The goal, in philosopher Iris M. Young's words, is "to de-normalize the way institutions formulate their rules by re-vealing the plural circumstances that exist, or ought to exist, within them." Rights could thus be extended to all persons in their human va-riety—rather than measured out in contradictorily equal portions to some on the basis of a presumed uniformity. Inclusion rather than ex-clusion would become the standard. Along the way, the meaning of difference could be transformed. As poet Audre Lorde appreciates, di-versity is a boundless resource: "Difference must be not merely toler-ated, but seen as a fund of necessary polarities between which our creativity can spark like a dialectic. . . . Difference is [a] raw and pow-erful connection."

11

THE NEW RIGHT

Populist Revolt or Moral Panic?

The year 1968 appeared to many contemporaries and to some historians as a turning point in the course of left-wing protest politics. The assassinations of Robert F. Kennedy and Martin Luther King, Jr., and the riots that followed the latter, seemed to mark the end of "gradualism" and "liberal reform" and to usher in an era of Weathermen, Black Panthers, bra-burners, and Yippies. In retrospect, however, 1968 seems more the beginning of a rightward turn in American politics. Whatever was happening on the margins of social protest, voter majorities and survey respondents were telling whoever would listen that they were sick of turmoil and wanted law, order, and a reaffirmation of traditional values. They were more likely to congratulate than to condemn the Chicago police for bashing demonstrators at the Democratic National Convention. They were more likely to believe that *Reader's Digest* reflected what was important in America than did *Rolling Stone*. They felt far more threatened by widespread drug use and sexual promiscuity than by bourgeois conformity or suburban tackiness. The fundamental truths of religion seemed to them in need of restating, not debunking. The stars and stripes evoked in them a rush of patriotic reverence, not a shiver of embarrassment or contempt.

Such views were not just passively held; increasingly vocal, angry, and well-financed conservative organizations sprouted in many corners of America. Evangelical churches began organizing congregants to campaign for conservative candidates who supported "family values." The Catholic hierarchy recruited tens of thousands of parishioners to fight the legalization of abortion and, after *Roe v. Wade,* to turn back the tide of abortion rights. Anti-tax groups in many locales canvassed door-to-door, wrote for local weekly newspapers, found statewide business allies, successfully resisted tax increases, and eventually pushed through tax-lowering measures. Parents who had never organized any sort of political campaign—including many who had always loyally pulled the Democratic voting lever and thought of themselves as liberals —threw themselves into efforts to stop school busing.

Such grassroots activism was matched by a massive infusion of big money into conservative causes. Some of America's richest families—with names such as Mellon, Scaife, Coors, and Olin—began to heavily finance (or to create) organizations designed to challenge and over-power what they saw as the cause of America's national decline: lib-eral judicial precedents, liberal special interest groups, liberal academic authority, and the liberal media. Some of these investors un-doubtedly disliked the prospect of higher taxes and expanded govern-ment regulation more than they shared the grassroots activists' sense of families and communities threatened by chaos. Whatever their do-mestic concerns, many of these conservatives brought something else to the new right cause: an intense anticommunism and a sense of mil-lennial danger that transcended ordinary political calculations. Events such as the Cuban missile crisis, the War in Vietnam, and revolution-ary upheavals (accompanied by vocal anti-Americanism) in the Third World, along with ongoing Russian willingness to compete in the arms race and intervene in neighboring countries, provided American con-servatives with evidence enough that a relentless enemy was stalking the "free world." What they now feared was that moral rot in America had suddenly shifted the odds in favor of the stalker. Not unlike the radicals and counter-culturalists who predicted "the dawning of the age of Aquarius" or "the final crisis of capitalism," these conservative millennialists contributed to a general sense of crisis in the United States in the late 1960s.

The combination of grassroots activism and infusions of big money had significant electoral effect. George Wallace, the segregationist for-mer Governor of Alabama, scored surprisingly well in the 1964 Democ-ratic primaries across the country, including in the mid-western states of Wisconsin and Indiana. Running as an independent in 1968, he again ran well in the North, and pulled 13 percent of the national vote. His success rested on his appeal to voters angry about African Americans' attempts to enter into jobs, unions, and neighborhoods that had once been white preserves. He also won the votes of those who resented "pointy-headed liberal" bureaucrats telling them how to run their busi-nesses, dispose of their garbage, educate their children, and generally live their lives. And, in promising to run over any hairy protester who lay down in front of *his* car, he tapped a cultural rage that few other politicians had been willing to exploit so openly.[1] Richard Nixon, who narrowly won the 1968 presidential race, used language that was more veiled, if no less threatening, to communicate to receptive voters a sim-ple message: "those people"—war protesters, Black Panthers, snobs who look down on your middle-class lifestyle, and experts who try to

---

[1] Marshall Frady, *Wallace* (New York, 1986); Dan T. Carter, *The Politics of Rage: George Wallace, the Origins of the New Conservatism, and the Transformation of American Politics* (New York, 1995).

engineer your social behavior—would no longer be tolerated. Couching such messages in moderate language, he managed to seem presidential to many who feared the extremism of Wallace and the Goldwater wing of the Republican party. In 1980 Ronald Reagan even more effectively combined congenial manner and threatening intent to win moderate voters over to his banner. With a smile he reassured voters that he could wage the Cold War more fiercely while magically defending the nation against nuclear attack, cut taxes without exploding the deficit, and clamp down on radicals, pornographers, and welfare cheats without damaging the Bill of Rights or the social fabric.

The Democrats who managed to win the White House after the 1960s—Jimmy Carter and Bill Clinton—were both moderate-to-conservative southern governors who had difficulty holding together the splintering New Deal–Great Society coalition of African Americans, urban liberals, rural southern whites, and foreign policy "internationalists." In the three decades since 1968, historians have seen a process of "disaggregation" of coalitions, and "disalignment" (if not "realignment") of political parties.[2] Southern whites who had once been "yellow dog Democrats" became loyal Republican voters; descendants of immigrants whose political hero was Franklin Delano Roosevelt now cast Republican votes with some frequency; once vibrant Democratic organizations in western states shriveled in the face of a conservative ascendancy that brought Republicans and even Libertarians into state offices. These realignments occurred because the Democratic party came to be associated with the cause of black rights, but also with high taxes and countercultural movements that seemed to threaten the interests and values of white, middle-class Americans. It is within this context that the New Right emerged as a political force and a subject of historical interpretation.

Given the relatively recent vintage of these events, historical views have not quite settled into schools, but certain patterns of interpretation are apparent. One difference among interpreters has to do with whether they see the New Right movements as top-down or bottom-up. A second difference centers on the question of rationality: are right-wing activists pursuing their rational interests, or are they driven by irrational anxieties and fears? A third difference is more overtly political, although it is sometimes intertwined with the others. Those who see the New Right as top-down have tended to be left-leaning; the New Right, in their view, is reactionary and elitist, dedicated to turn-

---

[2]See Walter Dean Burnham, *Critical Elections and the Mainsprings of American Politics* (New York, 1970), especially Chapters 5, 6, and 7; and "The 1980 Earthquake: Realignment, Reaction, or What?" in *The Hidden Election: Politics and Economics in the 1980 Presidential Campaign*, Thomas Ferguson and Joel Rogers, eds. (New York, 1981), pp. 98–140.

ing back progressive social change. The New Right amounts to an engineered backlash against partly successful efforts by minorities, women, and others to make America more just and egalitarian. The engineers of this backlash—corporations and the professional and upper classes— promoted culture wars in order to advance their own interests in scaling back the taxation and regulation of an expanding welfare state. In so doing, some liberals argue, these conservative elites exploited Americans' irrational fears of ethnic and sexual disorder. Conservatives, on the other hand, have always tended to see the New Right movements as insurgencies of the people against faceless bureaucrats and liberal power-brokers in big labor, government, the academy, and the media. In this view, the people whom Richard Nixon called "the silent majority," having been victimized by snobbish, corrupt, and even un-American elites, finally determined to take their country back.[3]

Although political leanings color historians' treatments of the New Right probably less than some conservative critics imagine, it is no doubt true that most historians bend toward the political Left and write critically of the New Right. They tend to interpret the rise of the New Right as a troubling phenomenon, linked to conservative elites' exploitation of grassroots "paranoid" reactions to immigration, urbanization, Civil Rights movements, feminism, and other kinds of social change. However, historians have recently been complicating the story. Increasingly in these movements they have been finding an interweaving of progressive and reactionary, racist and egalitarian, rational and irrational strands. Historians now write more insightfully about the motives of grassroots activists and constituents and more critically about the liberal targets of their rage. Equally important, they have begun to correct a major historiographical oversight: the tendency to ignore or deny the power of conservatism in the American past. Perhaps after twenty years of a conservative tide in American politics, historians and other liberal commentators could no longer explain their society without paying closer attention to the conservative critics of liberalism. Whereas historians until recently had portrayed conservatism as marginal (either elitist or extremist), contemporary historians describe the remarkably mainstream character of its values and political preferences. They have begun to connect conservatism to the republican tradition of virtue and community, showing its influence on phenomena as diverse as women's movements, Progressive reform, the Ku Klux Klan, immigration restriction, anticommunism, the Civil Rights movement, and contemporary communitarianism. Finally, historians are noting the great diversity of conservative types—

---

[3]The classic statement of this view is Kevin P. Phillips, *The Emerging Republican Majority* (New Rochelle, N.Y., 1969).

from patricians to blue-collar ethnics, from Pentecostalists to Catholics, from libertarians to "moral majoritarians," from Yankee tax protesters to Sunbelt immigration restrictionists, from single-issue pragmatists to ideological crusaders. Telling the history of the New Right, therefore, has become part of an important reassessment of politics and group conflict in modern America.[4]

The first historian to take the political Right seriously was Richard Hofstadter. Surprised by the ascendance of Barry Goldwater and his supporters within the Republican party in 1964, liberal politicians and commentators seemed at a loss to explain who these people were and what they wanted. Hofstadter found an answer to these questions in what he called the "pseudo-conservative revolt" and its "paranoid style."[5] Hofstadter's thesis has come under much fruitful criticism and revision in the last three decades, but its power needs to be recognized. An accomplished historian of much of the American past, Hofstadter insisted that the Goldwater phenomenon was not a flash in the pan. Rather, it was connected with both long-term and short-term developments in modern American—and world—history. First, he hypothesized, the two-hundred-year cycle of exploration, conquest, and economic and demographic expansion that shaped American politics and culture had come to a close. The "automatic built-in status elevator" no longer operated so effectively; as a result many frustrated Americans experienced "status resentment" or "status anxiety." Second, the rise of mass media had plunged most Americans into a state of almost continuous excitation; their "private emotions" were now "readily projected" onto a public screen where they were subject to political and commercial manipulation. Third, the intrusion of both the media and the administrative state into once sovereign regions of personal and communal life created a widespread sense of "powerlessness and victimization," which would indefinitely feed strong resentments against politicians, bureaucrats, intellectuals, and other "experts." Fourth, the United States' irreversible plunge into military and diplomatic contestation on the world stage meant that fear of war and even catastrophic destruction would continuously fuel a level of public panic that could only play into conservative politics of loyalty and national security. And, finally, the growth of new wealth in what would later be called the Sunbelt, and the growth of evangelical denominations in the same region, guaran-

---

[4]See Michael Kazin's review essay, "The Grass-Roots Right: New Histories of U.S. Conservatism," *American Historical Review* 97 (February 1992): 136–155; and Alan Brinkley, "The Problem of American Conservatism," Ibid. (April 1994): 409–429, with responses from several historians and a reply by Brinkley on pp. 430–452.

[5]See the essays in Part I of Richard Hofstadter, *The Paranoid Style in American Politics and Other Essays* (New York, 1967); and also his *Anti-Intellectualism in American Life* (New York, 1963).

teed well-financed and organized movements against liberalism for the foreseeable future.

These factors, Hofstadter believed, gave energy to a long-term development in American history, one that accounted for the Klan, Prohibitionism, anti-evolutionism and other forms of anti-intellectualism, anti-immigrant and anti-Catholic movements, and extreme anticommunism. This last phenomenon, in the form of McCarthyism, impressed itself powerfully on Hofstadter's consciousness in the 1950s, seeming to be a version of the same irrationalism that had swept Germans and other Europeans into the fascist maelstrom of the 1930s. As a result, Hofstadter misjudged the extent to which McCarthy had succeeded in seducing former working-class liberals (evidence shows mostly old-line conservative voters rallying to McCarthy's cause), and allowed his fear of such quasi-fascist tendencies in the populace to discredit all "populist" or "mass" political movements. Historians eventually discredited his treatment of the late-nineteenth-century Populist movement, finding not so much paranoia as a rational effort to address class injustice. And they corrected his tendency to see status anxiety in almost every form of protest in American history. Indeed, by the mid-1960s, New Left historians had largely rejected Hofstadter's interpretation and in the process swept off the historical stage almost entirely the conservatives whom Hofstadter had tried, however imperfectly, to understand.

In the 1960s, social conflict became the subject of American history to an extent not seen since Charles Beard and his Progressive school of history had first emerged in the early twentieth century. Where consensus historians saw broad agreement in the mainstream and extremism on the margins of American society, those who came to be called New Left historians saw conflict at the center of American history. But they defined that conflict in altered terms: it was between "market liberal" and "republican" forces, especially in the colonial and early national eras, and between "corporate liberal" and "radical" (or "populist") forces in the industrial era. The idea of republicanism has been discussed at length in Chapters 5 and 6 in this volume. The idea of corporate liberalism reflected the notion current in the 1960s that the "establishment" was itself liberal or that liberalism had become conservative. Whatever radical or progressive tendencies liberalism may have had in the past had been submerged in its marriage to professional, bureaucratic and corporate systems of control. Even worse, liberalism had been transmuted by the marketplace into mindless consumerism. Energies that once fueled abolitionist critiques of slavery and labor's "free speech" campaigns had degenerated into nervous demands for immediate gratification of appetites: the right to be entertained, the need for self-expression. Liberal individualism therefore now played a reactionary role in modern society: distracting people from their true interests, which were bound up with the collective interests of classes and communities; blinding them to the true goods of a good society—not material things but justice, dignity, and human connection.[6]

Animated by such beliefs, New Left historians in the 1960s and 1970s turned the interpretation of numerous groups and events in American history upside down. Thus, the Progressive era became not a chapter in the evolution of democratic reform, but a distinctly anti-democratic moment in the history of modern America.[7] On the one hand, historians such as Gabriel Kolko and Christopher Lasch pictured Progressivism as the installation of top-down control—by corporate managers, technical experts, pragmatic politicians and therapeutic professionals—over a democratic society with radical tendencies. Turn-of-the-century insurgents who once seemed feisty battlers against corporate arrogance now appeared to be business lobbyists (or their dupes) looking to recruit the state into protecting corporate interests. Disinterested crusaders against political corruption, who championed "enlightened" measures such as the referendum and voter registration, now seemed to be ambitious professionals intent on restricting the franchise to the "better classes" and thereby taking over government. On the other hand, historians who did see Progressivism as at least partly a grassroots movement tended to cast the reformers (who once appeared to be benign settlement house workers welcoming immigrants to America) as nativists promoting coercive Americanization, immigration restriction, and Prohibition.

For New Left historians, the true democrats were those radicals who represented the antithesis of the Progressive spirit—the socialist union-

---

[6]The study of "consumer culture" has become a major field in American history. A few landmark works are: David Potter, *People of Plenty: Economic Abundance and the American Character* (Chicago, 1954); Neil Harris, *Humbug: The Art of P.T. Barnum* (Chicago, 1973); Warren Sussman, *Culture as History: The Transformation of American Society in the Twentieth Century* (New York, 1985); Richard Wightman Fox and T. J. Jackson Lears, eds., *The Culture of Consumption: Critical Essays in American History, 1880–1980* (New York, 1983); Roland Marchand, *Advertising the American Dream: Making Way for Modernity, 1920–1940* (Berkeley, 1985); Lawrence W. Levine, *Highbrow/Lowbrow: The Emergence of Cultural Hierarchy in America* (Cambridge, Mass., 1988). A sometimes strained New Left critique of consumerism is found in Christopher Lasch, *The Culture of Narcissism: American Life in an Age of Diminishing Expectations* (New York, 1979), and Stuart Ewen, *Captains of Consciousness: Advertising and the Social Roots of Consumer Culture* (New York, 1976). Other recent approaches incorporate elements of this critique but emphasize the creative engagement of consumers in the making of culture: John F. Kasson, *Amusing the Million: Coney Island at the Turn of the Century* (New York, 1978); Kathy Peiss, *Cheap Amusements: Working Women and Leisure in Turn-of-the-Century New York* (Philadelphia, 1986); David Nasaw, *Going Out: The Rise and Fall of Public Amusements* (New York, 1993); William Leach, *Land of Desire: Merchants, Power, and the Rise of a New American Culture* (New York, 1993).

[7]For more on the Progressive era, see Chapter 6 in this volume.

ist and political candidate, Eugene V. Debs, the anarchist feminist
Emma Goldman, the black activist and scholar W.E.B. Du Bois, and even
the immigrant "bosses" who tried to make life bearable for the "huddled masses." Lawrence Goodwyn persuasively recast the Populists in
light of the Civil Rights movement of the late-twentieth century. Like
the racial egalitarians of the 1950s and 1960s, Goodwyn's Populists were
grassroots democrats bent on saving America from its worst sins: structural inequality and cultural arrogance. A social-justice movement with
its own "movement culture," Populism was anything but the pathetic
lashing-out against modernity that Hofstadter had made it seem. Thus,
as historians focused on Populists and other radicals battling for justice
against an establishment that was labeled "corporate liberal," conservatives seemed to have dropped out of their picture.

Other historians found conservatives but turned them into odd
versions of republican critics of liberal society. Historian Eugene Gen-
ovese, although he never turned slaveholders into heroes, did make
them seem oddly courageous in their refusal to accommodate themselves to market liberalism and industrial capitalism.[8] Ronald P.
Formisano interpreted antimasonic and nativist movements in the
decades before the Civil War as democratic expressions of "antiparty
populism."[9] Whatever their fantastic or irrational elements, these
movements organized thousands of ordinary citizens in well-conceived campaigns against the power of existing and emerging elites;
they fought for the rights of labor and small producers, for fair taxation, and for a political system open to men of small means. To the extent that antimasons and nativists exhibited reactionary or "paranoid"
tendencies, they were not unique to their time and place and, more
importantly, their exceptional commitment to equality far out-
weighed their less admirable qualities.

Similarly, new treatments of the Ku Klux Klan in the 1920s and of
Depression-era right-wingers such as Father Charles Coughlin, while
in no sense complimentary, accentuated the community-centered values of ordinary followers.[10] Religious fundamentalists also underwent
reevaluation. Having once embodied benighted conservatism,[11] they
began to seem defenders of local community and anti-materialist val-

---

[8]See Volume I, chapter 4.

[9]Ronald P. Formisano, *The Transformation of Political Culture: Massachusetts Parties, 1790s–1840s* (New York, 1983).

[10]Alan Brinkley, *Huey Long, Father Coughlin, and the Great Depression* (New York,
1982); recent work on the Klan includes Richard K. Tucker, *The Dragon and the Cross:
The Rise and Fall of the Ku Klux Klan in Middle America* (Hamden, Conn., 1991);
Leonard Joseph Moore, *Citizen Klansmen: The Ku Klux Klan in Indiana, 1921–1928*
(Chapel Hill, N.C., 1991); Nancy MacLean, *Behind the Mask of Chivalry: The Making of
the Second Ku Klux Klan* (New York, 1994).

[11]See, for example, William E. Leuchtenberg, *The Perils of Prosperity, 1914–1932*
(Chicago, 1958), Chapter 11.

ues against the juggernaut of the expansive market, the expansive state, and the ideology of rootless individualism.[12] Garry Wills, among others, saw the anti-evolutionist William Jennings Bryan, and more importantly the local folk for whom he tried to speak, as the unsung heroes of the Scopes trial, while defense attorney Clarence Darrow appeared the corrosive and cynical bearer of the virus of liberal elitism.[13] Other historians showed that the evangelical credentials of nineteenth-century abolitionists and feminists had been impeccable; some found similar credentials among Civil Rights activists in the 1950s and 1960s.[14] A number of cultural historians found in seemingly backward-looking cultural phenomena such as the arts-and-crafts movement and the Gothic revival surprisingly subversive critiques of prevailing values. Promoters of these movements counterpoised traditions of artisan labor and communal piety against the tyranny of a consumerism predicated on the myth of individual "free choice." Abstract expressionism and other forms of modernist art, once lauded as icons of heroic individualism, became expressions of rootless cosmopolitanism, perfectly adapted to the faceless corporate boardrooms and brutal glass-and-concrete museums in which they resided.[15]

In the context of such reevaluations, it was inevitable that some scholars would begin to reassess the meaning and character of conservative political movements of the recent past. A few concentrated on the elite financiers and directors of the New Right phenomenon. Political scientists Thomas Ferguson and Joel Rogers explained the election of Ronald Reagan in 1980 as the result of "extensive elite regrouping triggered by changes in the world economy" and by the weakening of labor and other liberal groups in the United States.[16] Sociologist Jerome Himmelstein and political scientist John Saloma revealed the enormous investments made by America's richest families in conservative think-tanks, foundations, and political action committees.[17]

---

[12]See George M. Marsden, *Fundamentalism and American Culture: The Shaping of Twentieth-Century Evangelicalism, 1870–1925* (New York, 1980), and Martin E. Marty and R. Scott Appleby, *Fundamentalism Observed* (Chicago, 1991).

[13]Garry Wills, *Under God: Religion and American Politics* (New York, 1990). A superb social history of the region within which Scopes and the fundamentalists faced off is Jeanette Keith, *Country People in the New South: Tennessee's Upper Cumberland* (Chapel Hill, N.C., 1995).

[14]Taylor Branch, *Parting the Waters: America in the King Years, 1954–1963* (New York, 1988); on antebellum reformers see Volume I, Chapter 8.

[15]For example, see T. J. Jackson Lears, *No Place of Grace: Antimodernism and the Transformation of American Culture, 1880–1920* (New York, 1981).

[16]Thomas Ferguson and Joel Rogers, "The Reagan Victory: Corporate Coalitions in the 1980 Campaign," in their edited collection, *The Hidden Election: Politics and Economics in the 1980 Presidential Campaign* (New York, 1981), pp. 3–64.

[17]John Saloma, *Ominous Politics: The New Conservative Labyrinth* (New York, 1984); Jerome L. Himmelstein, *To the Right: The Transformation of American Conservatism* (Berkeley, 1990).

There was nothing spontaneous in the surge of neo-conservatism in the 1970s and 1980s, they argued. These new activists were neither Hofstadter's "paranoids" nor his critics' "populists." They were "fat-cats" and their direct-mail functionaries. In the New Right surge, the dominant classes in the United States essentially got what they paid for: congenial kinds of academic expertise and media attention, and increasingly conservative politicians responsive to expensively orchestrated pressure-group campaigns. In injecting such huge quantities of money into politics and opinion-making institutions, both Himmelstein and Saloma seem to say, the New Right financiers altered the political landscape decisively.

Business historian David Vogel narrated the "political resurgence of business" in the late 1970s and 1980s in more cyclical terms. Focusing on the rise of the "public interest" movement, Vogel characterized business as determined to regain the initiative in American politics after having been on the defensive for two decades. As in their reaction to Progressivism and the New Deal earlier in the century, businessmen entered this third cycle of political mobilization in order to forestall new government regulations and taxes and, even more ambitiously, to turn them back.[18]

If some scholars focused on elite patrons of the New Right movements, others took on the task of understanding the interaction of grassroots clients with both liberal and conservative elites. Even in the 1960s and 1970s, some left-leaning commentators had begun to chastise mainstream liberals for ignoring the continuing class grievances of blue-collar Americans. Sociologist Herbert Gans, among others, showed convincingly that white working-class folks felt abandoned by the Democratic party: liberal mayors, governors, and legislators in Boston bulldozed blue-collar neighborhoods to build freeways for middle-class suburbanites.[19] The same politicians supported desegregation plans that subjected lower-class white children to hours of school busing every day, while the children of those very decision-makers attended suburban public and private schools undisturbed by court-imposed desegregation. As Ronald Formisano has argued, echoing his reassessment of nineteenth-century anti-masons and nativists, most of the enraged parents who fought busing in Boston saw themselves as victims of class injustice.[20] Racism undoubtedly played its

---

[18]David Vogel, *Fluctuating Fortunes: The Political Power of Business in America* (New York, 1989).

[19]Herbert J. Gans, *The Urban Villagers: Group and Class in the Life of Italian Americans* (New York, 1965; expanded ed. 1982).

[20]Ronald P. Formisano, *Boston Against Busing: Race, Class, and Ethnicity in the 1960s and 1970s* (Chapel Hill, N.C., 1991). See also J. Anthony Lukas, *Common Ground: A Turbulent Decade in the Lives of Three American Families* (New York, 1986).

part in those mobilizations in Boston, as Thomas Sugrue makes plain it did in Detroit.[21] Still, Formisano leaves little doubt that most of the grassroots opponents of busing in Boston employed with absolute sincerity the language and tactics of the Civil Rights movement. Far earlier than middle-class Americans—and, ironically, with an insight matched only by African Americans and other minority citizens—they felt the decline in real wages and employment opportunities that commentators later called "de-industrialization." They also felt the unfair consequences of transfers of the tax burden from corporations to individuals, and of government resources from cities to suburbs. What added insufferable insult to these injuries was the self-righteous condemnation they felt aimed at them. The weight of America's racial sins, having once been laid at the feet of white southerners, suddenly seemed to have been shifted onto them. Reacting angrily to the charge, these voters—sometimes called "blue-collar ethnics," later "Reagan Democrats"—were spurred on by conservative politicians who quickly sensed the political value of their rage. The movements these disenchanted citizens spawned were a species of "reactionary populism"—to use Formisano's term—and not simply the product of endemic racism or clever, top-down manipulation. The New Right rank-and-file were, however flawed, the inheritors of a venerable republican tradition of communal resistance to political and business elites.

The Edsalls have expanded on this interpretation, interweaving a series of issues—tax revolt, racism, fear of crime, moral revulsion against alternative "lifestyles"—into a general critique of the Democratic Party and the liberal elites who failed to understand the people they claimed to represent. The Edsalls are not neo-conservatives. Liberal journalists both, they condemn the Republican party for inflaming prejudices in order to pry white voters away from the Democratic party. They applaud the Democratic party for championing black equality but excoriate it for refusing to face the costs and traumas that have resulted from its policies. "The Democratic party, once it was committed to the long-range goal of black equality," they argue, "had no alternative but to participate in imposing burdens and costs; the central failure of the party was its refusal to acknowledge those burdens and costs and, consequently, its refusal to make adequate efforts to minimize those costs and to distribute them more equitably."[22] The selection reproduced in this chapter sketches the tactics

---

[21]Thomas J. Sugrue, "Crabgrass-Roots Politics: Race, Rights, and the Reaction against Liberalism in the Urban North, 1940–1964," *Journal of American History* 82 (September 1995): 551–586.

[22]Thomas Byrne Edsall and Mary D. Edsall, *Chain Reaction: The Impact of Race, Rights, and Taxes on American Politics* (New York, 1992), p. 282.

used by conservative Republicans to capitalize on that Democratic failure.

While the Edsalls' analysis of Democratic failure echoes certain conservative criticisms of liberalism, it is also very different from them. Comparing it with the account of the Nixon and Reagan years offered by conservative historian Alonzo L. Hamby makes these differences clear. For Hamby, liberalism is not just errant but "exhausted." Neo-conservatives came to define the American political mainstream not just because they took advantage of Democratic missteps but because they more accurately reflected the interests and values of the American people as a whole. According to Hamby, Nixon and especially Reagan won great victories by promising to rescue Americans from extremists on the Left, not to deliver them to extremists on the Right. Thus, for Hamby, the Republican ascendance was a correction of American politics after an era of liberal excess.[23] In sharp contrast to Hamby, both Formisano and the Edsalls castigate liberal leaders for ignoring and alienating ordinary white folk, but insist that those folk, by virtue of their class interests, should be the liberals' natural constituents.

Other interpreters of the New Right focus even less on elections and tactics and more on endemic patterns of prejudice and principle, of identity and antipathy within the American people. According to James Davison Hunter, contemporary "culture wars" are not the product of clever stage-managers "wagging the dog" of Americans' fears of ethnic difference. Those fears are based in different "living traditions," subcultures with distinctive world views. Conflict among them is normal, not pathological. What can be changed is not the incidence of conflict but the management of it. Here leadership is important, but the heavy lifting, in this view, must be done by ordinary citizens in town meetings, churches, school boards, and the like.[24] Hunter's measured optimism about the possibilities of improved dialogue among culture warriors is not shared by other historians.

Thomas Sugrue has made plain, for example, the deep commitment of blue-collar white voters in Detroit to the practices and policies of racial separation. Before Americans ever heard the words Vietnam or Great Society, and well before either New Left or New Right movements had emerged, post–World War II white homeowners were mobilizing against liberal policies of open housing and school desegregation. Liberal trade union leaders, liberal mayors, and liberal opinion-makers failed (some after battling courageously, others after

---

[23]Alonzo L. Hamby, *Liberalism and its Challengers: From F.D.R. to Bush,* 2/e (New York, 1992).

[24]James Davison Hunter, *Culture Wars: The Struggle to Define America* (New York, 1991).

the briefest moment of resistance) to convince their constituents that racial equality was in their interests. "The local politics of race and housing in the aftermath of World War II fostered a grassroots rebellion against liberalism" that led directly to the New Right surge in the 1970s and 1980s. What is remarkable in this view is that the New Deal coalition hung together for as long as it did. Given the long-term causes of the decline of liberalism, solutions will require more than improved dialogue or clever definitions of "common ground." Facing both their "rational" material interest in, and their "irrational" psychic attachment to whiteness will require from most white American voters more than they have for half a century been willing to give.[25]

If long-term racial politics helps explain the rise of the New Right, so does long-term sexual politics. In the second reading in this unit, John D'Emilio and Estelle Freedman note that fear of pornography, homosexuality, abortion, and sex education have for at least two centuries played a part in generating "moral panics" in America and, more broadly, in the western world.[26] Such fears became inextricably entwined with the New Right cause in the years from the late 1960s through the 1990s, shaping presidential campaigns and school-board elections, injecting contentiousness into public library book selection committees and Congressional debates over foreign aid, United Nations dues, and AIDS research funding. However salient were tax revolts and other disputes over "rational" interests, D'Emilio and Freedman show that fears of sexual chaos played at least as powerful a part as racial antagonisms in shaping the New Right. Disputes over taxes and spending can almost always be negotiated; but compromises are harder to reach when one's campaign slogan reads "Save Our Children" or "Abortion is Murder." Nothing strikes terror into the hearts of parents more than the suggestion that potent forces beyond their personal or local control—e.g., in the media, the educational bureaucracy, the medical establishment—compete with them for control of their children's upbringing. In trying to govern their children's sexuality and sexual expressiveness, parents find themselves subject to deep anxiety even in the best of circumstances. Given the vast expansion of the marketplace of words and images, the continual dissolution of once-sturdy social restraints on sexual expressiveness, the disruption of older kin and communal residential ties, and the emergence of outspoken and feisty representatives of once-marginal practices and identities, parental fears turned into political movements in post-1960s

---

[25]Thomas J. Sugrue, *The Origins of the Urban Crisis: Race and Inequality in Postwar Detroit* (Princeton, 1996).

[26]See, for example, Nicola Beisel, *Imperiled Innocents: Anthony Comstock and Family Reproduction in Victorian America* (Princeton, 1997).

America. Because "sexuality has become central to our economy, our psyches, and our politics," D'Emilio and Freedman conclude, ". . . it is likely to stay vulnerable to manipulation as a symbol of social problems and the subject of efforts to maintain social hierarchies."

While D'Emilio and Freedman do not simply reinstate Hofstadter's theory of the rise of the New Right, they may from one angle be seen as closing the historiographical circle. In their story sexual anxiety does in a sense take the place of status anxiety in explaining the irrational basis of right-wing mobilizations. Those revisionist historians who succeeded Hofstadter almost always insisted that their subjects were rational actors. The Edsalls' tax revolters and Formisano's anti-busing folk were not pathetic or deluded, not nostalgic or reactionary. Though sometimes infected by racism or some other political virus, they embodied the American republican tradition. That tradition offered a rationally coherent and morally profound critique of market values and individualist culture, and a defense of virtue and communal values as the indispensable underpinnings of a good society. Without this populist critique of capitalism, most critics of liberalism imply, liberal politics is capable only of reasserting the individual's right to more goods and services or, worse, to more "self-expression." But historians of sex and sexuality, like historians of race and racial conflict, cannot entirely banish the irrational from their accounts of the rise of the New Right. Our sexual fears, like our tribal fears, are not easily translated into the pursuit of rational interests. Though they are readily manipulated by elites, they originate in regions that are socially and psychically far deeper. Even historians and citizens of a conservative bent cannot fail to take seriously the darker implications of those fears.[27] And those critics (whether Left or Right) who see liberalism as "exhausted" may remind themselves that there is still ample reason to defend individual rights against the possibility not only of state tyranny but of the tyranny that originates within us.

Another important question that remains unanswerable at this time is the effect of the end of the Cold War on American politics, generally, and on the fate of the New Right, in particular. Now that fear of the "Communist Menace" has receded, will big money, along with racial and sexual anxieties and other domestic issues, be sufficient to fuel the New Right in the future? Will a new external threat—China, Islamic fundamentalism, a revived and hostile Russia, perhaps even international drug cartels—take the place of "international Commu-

---

[27]See Kevin P. Phillips, *Boiling Point: Republicans, Democrats, and the Decline of Middle-Class Prosperity* (New York, 1993), and *Arrogant Capital: Washington, Wall Street, and the Frustration of American Politics* (Boston, 1994); and also Andrew Sullivan, *Virtually Normal: An Argument about Homosexuality* (New York, 1995).

nism" in the constellation of conservative issues, or will the New Right rely exclusively on domestic issues to sustain its momentum? Whatever the answer to these questions, the rise of the New Right has taken its place in twentieth-century American historiography alongside the rise of Progressivism, of New Deal liberalism, and of the New Left. Historians will continue to explore the causes of the electoral triumphs of Nixon and Reagan, the decline in Democratic voters and the increase in Republican ones, and the character and trajectory of those movements that promise to keep conservatism at the center of American political life for the foreseeable future.

THOMAS BYRNE EDSALL
AND MARY D. EDSALL

THOMAS BYRNE EDSALL (1941–   ) is a journalist with the Washington Post. *He is also the author of* The New Politics of Inequality
(1984).

MARY D. EDSALL is an independent scholar.

In the aftermath of Richard Nixon's 1972 landslide victory over
George McGovern, the investigation of the Republican break-in at the
Democratic party headquarters—the scandal known as Watergate—
provided the besieged forces of liberalism with an opportunity to stall
the conservative ascendance. Watergate replenished forces on the liberal side of the political spectrum—the Democratic Congress, organized labor, civil rights groups, and the network of public-interest
lobbying and reform organizations—supplying new leverage in what
was otherwise rapidly becoming, in political terms, a losing ideological battle.

The central conflict between liberalism and conservatism since
the late sixties had focused on the aggressive expansion of constitutional rights to previously disfranchised, often controversial groups.
These included not only blacks, but others in relatively unprotected
enclaves (mental hospitals, prisons, ghettos) as well as homosexuals
(who increasingly resented being cast as deviant), ethnic minorities,
and women—who had the strongest base of political support but
whose movement, nonetheless, engendered substantial political reaction. Just as this expansion of rights had run into growing public and
political opposition, the Nixon administration was itself caught flagrantly violating the core constitutional rights of "average" citizens—
rights for which there was, in general, broad consensual support.

The official Republican sanction of the break-in of Democratic
National Committee headquarters, the secret wiretapping of fourteen
government officials and three newsmen, the burglary of anti-war activist Daniel Ellsberg's psychiatrist, and the extensive White House
cover-up, constituted government-authorized violations of fundamental constitutional guarantees: due process, protection from illegal
search and seizure, the separation of powers, and freedom of speech.
The second article of impeachment against Nixon (the article receiv-

ing the greatest number of votes in the House Judiciary Committee, 28–10, in July 1974,) charged that in directing the FBI, CIA, IRS, and Secret Service to attack political adversaries, Nixon "repeatedly engaged in conduct violating the constitutional rights of citizens, impairing the due and proper administration of justice, and the conduct of lawful inquiries, or contravening the laws governing agencies of the executive branch."

The outcry against the actions of the Nixon White House effectively stifled for the moment public expression of the growing resentment toward the liberal revolution. Watergate "is the last gasp of . . . our partisan opponents," Nixon told his aide, John Dean. The Nixon administration had already been damaged by the forced resignation in October 1973 of Spiro Agnew, who, facing the possibility of a substantial jail term, resigned from the vice presidency, pleading *nolo contendere* to charges of accepting illegal payments from Maryland contractors.

For many liberal constituencies, Watergate provided the grounds to attempt to indict and convict the snowballing conservative counteroffensive. For Democratic members of Congress, and for the larger Democratic establishment, the procedural ruthlessness of the Nixon administration—the enemies lists, the attempts to use the IRS and Justice Department to harass political adversaries, the burglaries, and the illegal wiretapping—was part and parcel of a much broader and more threatening administration drive to assault the constitutional underpinnings of the liberal state.

For liberal interest groups, the appeal of Watergate was even more direct: "The election of Richard Nixon as President sent a shiver through the civil rights and anti-war movements—and the ACLU. A symbol of the cold war of the 1950s, Nixon appeared hostile to civil rights and to virtually all the recent gains in civil liberties," wrote Samuel Walker, in his 1990 book, *In Defense of American Liberties: a History of the ACLU*. After the national board of the American Civil Liberties Union (ACLU) voted to endorse impeachment of the president on September 29, 1973, when Congress was still very tentatively exploring the process, membership in the organization shot up. Ads, financed by such liberal bankrollers as General Motors heir Stewart Mott declared that "Richard Nixon has not left us in doubt . . . if he is allowed to continue, then the destruction of the Bill of Rights could follow," and produced a flood of cash and support. "Over 25,000 new members joined in 1973 alone, driving the ACLU's membership to an all-time high of 275,000."

The Watergate-inspired re-invigoration of the left effectively choked off the growth of conservatism from 1973 through 1976, but the suppression meant that instead of finding an outlet within the political system, rightward pressure built throughout the decade to explosive levels. The Democratic party experienced a surge of victory in 1974 and 1976, while developments in the economy, in the court-enforced enlargement of the rights revolution, in the expansion of the regulatory state, in rising middle-class tax burdens, and in the growth of crime and illegitimacy were all in fact working to crush liberalism.

Watergate resulted in a political system out of sync with larger trends. A host of groups on the left of the spectrum—Democratic prosecutors, the media, junior congressional Democrats, new reform organizations, and traditional liberal interest groups—gained control over the political agenda just when a selection of other key indicators suggested that the power of the right should be expanding:

• Family income after 1973 abruptly stopped growing, cutting off what was left of popular support for government-led redistributional economic policies. Inflation (driven in part by the first OPEC oil shock) simultaneously pushed millions of working and middle-class citizens into higher tax brackets, encouraging them to think like Republicans instead of Democrats. As low and middle-income voters began to view the taxes deducted from their weekly paychecks with rising anger, the number of welfare and food stamp clients continued to grow at record rates, forcing a conflict between Democratic constituencies that would lead, by the end of the decade, to a racially-loaded confrontation between taxpayers and tax recipients.

• In courts across the country, the drive by a wide range of civil liberties organizations—from the ACLU to the Mental Health Law Project to the National Gay and Lesbian Task Force—reached its height. These organizations were committed to winning new rights for recreational drug users, the mentally ill, gays, American Indians, illegal aliens and the dependent poor. Their success produced not only benefits for targeted populations, but also conservative reaction in communities in every region of the country.

• Crime rates continued to surge, intensifying public discontent with liberal Democratic support of defendants' and prisoners' rights.

• The movement to liberalize abortion laws, which had been making substantial political progress in state legislatures, succeeded with the Supreme Court's 1973 decision, *Roe v. Wade*; that decision, in turn, produced a political counter-mobilization that rapidly became a mainstay of the conservative movement. Equally important, *Roe* reflected the growing dependence of liberalism on court rulings. The legal arena provided liberal interest groups with a host of victories through the mid-1970s. Court rulings frequently lacked the political legitimacy and support, however, that comes from public debate and legislative deliberation. Liberal court victories reduced incentives for the left to compete in elective politics to win backing for its agenda, while sharply increasing the incentives for the right— both social and economic—to build political muscle.

• The Arab oil embargo of 1973 resulted in gas lines across the country, intensifying in some sectors hostility toward liberal foreign-policy positions seen as supportive of Third World interests. Covert and explicit hostility towards Third World countries intensified and fueled, in some cases, a resurgence of domestic nativism, and even a degree of racism.

• Legislation passed in the civil rights climate of 1965, liberalizing previously restrictive, pro-European immigration policies, produced a surge of Hispanic, Asian, and other non-European immigration; created new competition for employment and housing; increased pressure for public services; and generated a revival of pressures to restore restrictions on immigration.

• The Justice Department, the Equal Employment Opportunity Commission (EEOC), and the Office of Federal Contract Compliance Programs (OFCCP) all capitalized on a sequence of legislative mandates, court rulings, and executive orders to sharply expand enforcement of affirmative action programs in the public and private sectors, increasing the saliency of the issue of quotas, an issue beginning to match busing in terms of the depth of voter reaction.

• Busing, in turn, by the early and mid-1970s, had become a legal remedy frequently imposed to correct school segregation in the North as well as in the South. The 1973 Supreme Court decision in *Keyes v. Denver School District No. 1* significantly increased the likelihood that a northern school system would be found guilty of illegal discrimination, and therefore subject to busing orders.

• In a number of major cities, black political gains were translating into the acquisition of genuine power. An inevitable outcome of the process of enfranchisement, the ascendancy of black politicians meant the loss of power for some white politicians, and in an increasing number of major cities competition for control of City Hall turned into racial confrontation. In 1967, Richard Hatcher and Carl Stokes won the mayor's offices in Gary, Indiana, and Cleveland, Ohio, respectively; in 1970, Kenneth Gibson became mayor of Newark; in 1974 Coleman Young and Maynard Jackson won in Detroit and Atlanta. These contests involved sharply polarized electorates (the only exception being the 1973 election of Tom Bradley, a black, in Los Angeles, where the mayoralty was won with more white than black votes). As Democratic black political power grew in the cities, Republican voting in white suburbs began to intensify, accelerating the creation of what political strategists would term "white nooses" around black cities.

There were forces at work in the 1970s, combining to produce an explosive mix—forces pitting blacks, whites, Hispanics, and other minorities against each other for jobs, security, prestige, living space, and government protection. As weekly pay fell, and as the market for working-class jobs tightened, government intervention in behalf of employment for minorities intensified; the doors opened for a wave of Latinos and Asians legally seeking jobs, at the same time that illegal immigration from across the Mexican border increased. Simultaneously, former civil rights lawyers and activists turned their attention to continuing the extension of rights to the ranks of the once-excluded.

This sequence of developments engendered a form of backlash within key sectors of the majority white electorate, backlash generating conservative pressures on an ambitious and threatening liberalism, conservative pressures which were only temporarily held in check by Watergate. The immediate political consequences of the investigation and prosecution triggered by the Watergate break-in lulled Democratic Party leaders into ignoring the outcome of the 1972 presidential election—into thinking that their majority party status was secure, and that the ability of the Republican Party to dominate presidential elections with a racially and socially conservative message had been washed away in the outcry for official probity and reform.

Politicians, academics, and the media remained largely ignorant of the direction the country would, in fact, take by the end of the decade. Patrick Caddell, who had conducted polls for both McGovern in 1972 and Jimmy Carter in 1976, wrote in a post-1976 election memorandum to President-elect Carter: "When we turn to the Republicans, we find them in deep trouble. Their ideology is restrictive; they have few bright lights to offer the public. Given the antiquated machinery of the Republican Party, the rise of a moderate, attractive Republican in their primary process is hard to imagine. The Republican Party seems bent on self-destruction." Everett Carll Ladd, a political scientist expert in assessing the balance of power between the two parties, wrote in 1977:

> [W]e are dealing with a long-term secular shift, not just an artifact of Watergate. The Republicans have lost their grip on the American establishment, most notably among young men and women of relative privilege. They have lost it, we know, in large part because the issue orientations which they manifest are somewhat more conservative than the stratum favors. . . . The [Republican] party is especially poorly equipped in style and tone to articulate the frustrations of the newer, emergent American *petit bourgeoisie*—southern white Protestant, Catholic, black and the like."

In fact, it was the Democratic party that was continuing to lose its class-based strength. The forces pushing the country to the right exerted the strongest pressures on whites in the working and lower-middle class, and it was among these voters that Democratic loyalty was continuing to erode. Party leaders failed to perceive these trends because losses among low-to-moderate-income whites during the mid-1970s

TABLE 1
Percentage of Vote Received by Democratic Congressional Candidates
from Low, Medium, and High Status Whites

	1964	1974	Gain (+) or Loss (-)
High status whites	48	57	+9
Middle status whites	65	62	-2
Low status whites	74	67	-7

SOURCE: Everett Carll Ladd, Jr., *Transformations of the American Party System* (New York: Norton, 1978), 245.

were compensated for by momentary gains among upper-income, normally Republican white voters who were most insistent on political reform in response to Watergate.

Among middle and low-status whites, voter turnout for Democratic congressional candidates in 1974, and for the Democratic presidential nominee in 1976, was lower than it had been in the 1960s, when the New Deal coalition was stronger. [Table 1] shows the percentage of white support for Democratic congressional candidates in 1964 and 1974, both years producing major gains for Democratic House candidates.

Democrats at the height of Watergate had lost substantial levels of support among low-status whites, and had experienced a modest decline among middle-status whites. Only a surge of support among upscale whites compensated for the difference. A very similar pattern emerges in the comparison of the white Democratic vote for president in two very close elections, both won by Democrats, John Kennedy in 1960 and Jimmy Carter in 1976 [Table 2].

In effect, Democrats were winning in 1974 and 1976, just as the core of their traditional base among whites was crumbling. The party became dependent on upscale, traditionally Republican voters whose new found loyalty would disappear as economic and foreign-policy issues regained their saliency, and as the memory of Watergate faded.

In the buildup of conservative, anti-liberal sentiment in the electorate, the most important development was the fact that 1973, the

TABLE 2
Percentage of Vote Received by Democratic Presidential Nominees from
Low, Medium, and High Status Whites

	1960	1976	Gain (+) or Loss (-)
High status whites	38	41	+3
Middle status whites	53	49	-4
Low status whites	61	53	-8

SOURCE: Ladd, *Transformations of the American Party System*, 289.

year the Senate set up a special committee to investigate Watergate, was also the year that marked the end of a sustained period of post-World War II economic growth. Hourly earnings, which had grown every year since 1951 in real, inflation-adjusted dollars, fell by 0.1 percent in 1973, by 2.8 percent in 1974, and by 0.7 percent in 1975. Weekly earnings fell more sharply, by 4.1 percent in 1974 and by 3.1 percent in 1975. Median family income, which had grown from $20,415 (in 1985 inflation-adjusted dollars) in 1960, to $29,172 in 1973, began to decline in 1974, when family income fell to $28,145, and then to $27,421 in 1975.

Steady economic growth, which had made redistributive government policies tolerable to the majority of the electorate, came to a halt in the mid-1970s, and, with stagnation, the threat to Democratic liberalism intensified. In a whipsaw action, the middle-class tax burden rose with inflation just as the economy and real-income growth slowed. The tax system was losing its progressivity, placing a steadily growing share of the cost of government on middle and lower-middle-class voters, vital constituencies for the Democratic party. In 1953, a family making the median family income was taxed at a rate of 11.8 percent, while a family making four times the median was taxed at 20.2 percent, nearly double. By 1976, these figures had become 22.7 percent for the average family, and 29.5 percent for the affluent family. In other words, for the affluent family, the tax burden increased by 46 percent from 1953 to 1976, while for the average family, the tax burden increased by 92.4 percent. Not only were cumulative tax burdens growing, but they were also shifting from Republican constituencies to Democratic constituencies.

At the same time, one of the most painful elements of the federal income-tax structure, the marginal rate system, had begun to impinge on the vast majority of voters, not just on the affluent. As recently as the early 1960s, 90 percent of the population was effectively exempt from steeply rising marginal tax rates that applied only to those in the top 10 percent of the population. For 90 percent of the population, there were only two marginal rates, 20 percent for nearly half of all taxpayers, and 22 percent for a quarter of the entire population, as the bottom fifth paid no taxes whatsoever. By 1979, however, this same 90 percent of the population faced ten different marginal tax rates. Routine pay hikes regularly pushed taxpayers into higher marginal brackets and, worse, rising inflation meant higher marginal rates without any increase in real income. At the same time, Congress also approved steadily higher Social Security taxes. From 1960 to 1975, the maximum annual Social Security tax liability grew from $144 to $825, a 473 percent increase. During the same period, per capita income grew by only 166 percent, so that the Social Security tax was taking an increasingly large bite out of wage and salary income.

In political terms, the damage was most severe to the Democratic party. Democratic-approved Social Security tax hikes fell much harder on those making less than the median income, voters who had traditionally tended to vote Democratic by higher margins than those above the median. In 1975, for example, a worker with taxable income of $14,100 paid $825, or 5.85 percent of his income, to Social Security, while someone making $75,000 paid the same $825, or just 1.1 percent of income.

These economic developments became one-half of an equation that functioned to intensify racial divisions within the traditional Democratic coalition. The other half of the equation was that taxpayer-financed welfare, food stamps, and other expenditures for the poor were growing exponentially. In the decade from 1965 to 1975, the number of families receiving benefits under Aid to Families with Dependent Children (AFDC), grew by 237 percent. Until that point, the national caseload had been growing at a *relatively* modest pace—from 644,000 households in 1950 to 787,000 in 1960 to 1,039,000 in 1965, an increase over fifteen years of 61 percent.

From 1965 to 1970, the number of households on welfare more than doubled to reach 2,208,000, and then grew again by more than one million, reaching 3,498,000 families in 1975. The Food Stamp program, which was initiated on a small scale in 1961 and then greatly enlarged in 1970, provided benefits to 400,000 people in 1965, 4.3 million in 1970, and increased four-fold, to 17.1 million recipients in 1975. Throughout the 1970s, the illegitimacy rate for both blacks and whites grew significantly, but for blacks, the decade saw illegitimate births begin to outnumber legitimate births. For whites, the illegitimacy rate rose from 5.7 percent of all live births in 1970, to 7.3 in 1975, to 11.0 in 1980; for blacks, the rate went from 37.6, to 48.8, to 55.2 percent in the same period.

The tensions growing out of these economic and social trends were compounded by the substantial conflicts growing directly out of the expansion of the civil rights movement into the broader rights revolution. Lawyers who had been trained in the trenches of the South— often funded by liberal, tax-exempt organizations and foundations, just as civil rights litigation projects had been—moved, in the late 1960s and early 1970s, into the broader rights arena. They developed litigation strategies designed to remedy the longstanding denial of rights to groups in unprotected enclaves (psychiatric hospitals, immigrant detention camps, Indian reservations, jails), and also to social "victims" (homosexuals, the disabled, the indigent). Particularly powerful was the evolving idea that conditions of birth or chance—ranging from gender to race to skin color to sexual orientation to class origin to ethnicity to physical or mental health—should not place any American at a social or economic disadvantage, insofar as it was possible for the state to offer protection and redress. "The rights revolution was the longest-lasting legacy of the 1960s," writes Samuel Walker in his history of the ACLU. "Millions of ordinary people—students, prisoners, women, the poor, gays and lesbians, the handicapped, the mentally retarded and others—discovered their own voices and demanded fair treatment and personal dignity. The empowerment of these previously silent groups was a political development of enormous significance."

The rights movement had already found political expression within the Democratic party, which had not only endorsed a broad spectrum of human rights at its 1972 convention, but which was granting specific recognition to a network of separate caucuses for blacks, women, and homosexuals within the Democratic National Committee. It was not until the mid-1970s, however, that the rights revolution reached its full power, changing some of the most fundamental patterns and practices of society. As these changes began to seep into public consciousness, the political ramifications slowly became felt throughout the majority electorate—an electorate under economic siege and rapidly losing its tolerance for the rapid redistribution of influence, as well for the redistribution of a host of economic and social benefits.

Just as the economy was beginning to stagnate, as oil producing countries were demonstrating their power to hold the energy-hungry United States hostage (with the price of imported oil rising from $1.80 a barrel in 1970 to $14.34 in 1979), and as the shift from manufacturing to services was forcing major dislocations in the job market, the rights revolution assaulted the traditional hierarchical structure of society, and in particular the status of white men.

The strongest of the rights movements was, in fact, the drive for the equality of women, who were included as beneficiaries of the equal employment provisions of the original 1964 Civil Rights Act. Political support for women's rights remained strong, symbolized by the congressional approval in 1972 of the Equal Rights Amendment (ERA) and by a series of legislative victories throughout the 1970s. At the same time, the women's movement—in combination with financial pressures making the one-earner family increasingly untenable—produced a major alteration in family structure, as labor force participation among married women grew steadily, from 35.7 percent in 1965, to 41.4 in 1970, to 45.1 percent in 1975, to 50.7 percent in 1980.

The changes that were taking place in the workplace, in family relationships, and in the balance of power between men and women were not cost-free. The number of divorces, which had remained relatively constant from 1950 through 1967, began to escalate sharply. In 1967, the divorce rate for every 1,000 married women was 11.2; by 1975, the rate had grown to 20.3; and in 1979, the divorce rate reached its height, 22.8—more than double the 1967 level. At the same time, the annual number of children of parents getting divorced grew from 701,000 in 1967, to 1.12 million in 1975, to 1.18 million in 1979.

The more outspoken leaders of the women's rights movement, many of whom cut their teeth in the civil rights and anti-war movements, adopted rhetoric and tactics that exacerbated the anxieties of a host of men already facing diminished job prospects, eroding family incomes, and a loss of traditional status in their homes. "Lesbian sexuality could make an excellent case, based on anatomical data, for the extinction of the male organ," Anne Koedt wrote in "The Myth of the Vaginal Orgasm," an essay subsequently reprinted in an estimated twenty different anthologies of feminist writings.

The women's rights movement was reinforced by the Supreme Court in *Roe v. Wade*, as the Court took the expanded right to privacy established in *Griswold v. Connecticut*, a case involving the sale of contraceptives, and extended the reasoning to establish a woman's right to terminate pregnancy during the first trimester. The sum of these developments—the entry of women into the workforce, the rising divorce rate, and the doubling of the number of reported abortions, from 586,800 in 1972 to 1.2 million in 1976—as well as the halving of the fertility rate between 1960 and 1975—contributed to the building of a conservative response.

The anti-abortion movement and the massive growth of parishioners attending fundamentalist Christian churches during the 1970s were in many ways powerful reactions to the emergence of the women's rights movement. "[T]he danger signs are quite evident: legislation on the national level reflects widespread acceptance of easy divorce, abortion-on-demand, gay rights, militant feminism, unisex facilities, and leniency towards pornography, prostitution and crime. . . . In short, many religious leaders believe that America may soon follow the footsteps of Sodom and Gomorrah," wrote Tim LaHaye, organizer of fundamentalist Christian voters, in his book, *The Battle for the Mind*.

The surge of women newly entering the job market, women now empowered with unprecedented control over their reproductive and sexual lives, coincided with the opening of the nation to another source of competition for employment and, in the Southwest and West, for political power: Hispanic and Asian immigration. Legislation enacted in 1965, growing out of the general climate surrounding the civil rights revolution, ended the racially restrictive immigration policies that had been on the books since the Immigration Act of 1924. The 1965 law opened the door to a wave of new immigration, primarily from Mexico and the Caribbean. The total number of legal immigrants and refugees from Central and South America, rose from 183,717 in the 1950s, to 751,060 in the 1960s, to 1,555,697 in the 1970s. These figures do not include the movement of United States citizens in Puerto Rico to the mainland, nor do they include illegal immigration, nor do they reflect the population growth following immigration—with the total Hispanic population of the United States growing from 9.07 million in 1970 to an estimated 22.4 million in 1990. The rising tide of legal Hispanic immigration was matched by Asian immigration, which grew from 186,671 in the 1950s, to 447,537 in the 1960s, to 1,798,861 in the 1970s. Overall, the Asian population in the United States also grew rapidly—from 1.34 million in 1970 to 7.3 million in 1990.

The drive to achieve equality for women and the abandonment of racially exclusionary immigration policies, in tandem with the civil rights movement, were consistent with the evolution of an egalitarian American political culture. But each evolutionary development contributed in turn to a growing conservative backlash or reaction, which was strengthened in turn by the increasing momentum of the more controversial rights movements. In 1974, the gay rights movement persuaded the American Psychiatric Association to remove homosexuality from its list of mental illnesses; between 1973 and 1975, the movement won approval of gay rights ordinances in eleven cities and counties, barring discrimination on the basis of sexual orientation; by 1989, the drive had produced legal prohibitions against discrimination against gays in housing, employment, and in the provision of other services in sixty-four municipalities, sixteen counties, and thirteen states.

The early 1970s also produced a movement to win legal rights for the mentally ill and for the mentally retarded, accelerating the nationwide process of deinstitutionalization. In 1975, the mental health rights movement won, in *O'Connor v. Donaldson*, a decision by the Supreme Court barring involuntary institutional confinement of nondangerous patients. *Donaldson* was followed by a series of decisions in state and federal courts establishing stringent procedural safeguards for those facing forced commitment, including the right to a formal hearing, the right to appeal, the right to be represented by a lawyer, and proof from committing authorities that confined individuals were dangerous either to themselves or to others. The general public approved these rights in principle, but the practical reality—particularly the lack in every jurisdiction of taxpayer support for costly community-based alternative care—led to the abandonment of large numbers of emotionally fragile men and women to the streets, subways, parks, and storefronts of the nation, where routine commuting, recreational, and shopping experiences became disturbing and often frightening for significant numbers of voters.

Perhaps the most controversial of all the major rights movements identified with liberalism over the past twenty-five years were the initiatives in behalf of criminal defendants and prisoners. In a series of decisions between 1957 and 1966, including *Mallory v. United States, Gideon v. Wainwright, Escobedo v. Illinois, Mapp. v. Ohio,* and *Miranda v. Arizona,* the Supreme Court found criminal defendants, many of them poor and black—and some clearly guilty—entitled to a range of fundamental protections and rights in state as well as federal courts. These included protections against illegally obtained evidence, self-incrimination, deprivation of due process, and cruel and unusual punishment; and called for rights to counsel, to silence, and to a speedy trial. The prisoners' rights movement grew out of both the civil rights struggle and the Supreme Court decisions affirming defendant protections. Proponents of inmate rights took up the issues of prison overcrowding, restrictions within prisons on political activity and free speech, and the authority of prison officials to punish inmates.

The *Miranda, Gideon,* and *Escobedo* rulings, enlarging the rights of defendants and often restricting the activities of police and prosecutors, were issued just as the nation's crime rate began to shoot up. The reaction of much of the public, of the law enforcement community, and of a host of moderate to conservative politicians was intense—and almost invariably hostile. In a 1972 Gallup poll, the percentage of city residents naming crime as the most important issue rose from 4 percent in 1949 to 22 percent; more strikingly, 74 percent said that the courts were not tough enough with defendants.

What was widely seen as a judicial assault on the criminal justice system extended, in addition, to the prison system. In a precedent-setting decision, a federal district court found in *Pugh v. Locke* in 1976 that the entire Alabama prison system was in violation of the eighth amendment prohibition against cruel and unusual punishment. Judge Frank M. Johnson found that "prison conditions are so debilitating that they necessarily deprive inmates of any opportunity to rehabilitate themselves or even maintain skills already possessed." By the late 1980s, thirty-seven states, the District of Columbia, Puerto Rico, and the Virgin Islands were operating prisons under court order, almost all because of overcrowding and inmate violence, lack of medical care, unsanitary conditions, and absence of rehabilitation programs.

Following the reforms of the criminal justice system and at the beginning of the prisoners' rights movement, were a sequence of Supreme Court decisions that rendered the death penalty illegal. In three related 1972 cases, *Furman v. Georgia, Jackson v. Georgia,* and *Branch v. Texas,* the Court overturned all existing death penalty statutes on the grounds that there was a "wanton and freakish" pattern in their application; the decisions effectively took an estimated 600 people across the country off death row. The prohibition against the death penalty stood until 1976, when the court in *Gregg v. Georgia, Profitt v. Florida,* and *Jurek v. Texas,* restored its use.

The expansion of defendants' rights, the prisoner rights movement, and the four-year prohibition on the death penalty coincided with a sharply increasing crime rate and ran headlong into increasingly conservative public opinion on crime—all of which had marked consequences for domestic politics and for race relations. Popular support for liberal policies on crime and rehabilitation had grown steadily from the mid-1930s, when polls were first taken, to the mid-1960s. At that juncture, public opinion shifted in a decisively rightward direction, as crime rates rose sharply. In 1965, a substantial minority of survey respondents, 36 percent, said that the courts treated criminals "about right" or "too harsh[ly]," while 48 percent said the courts were not harsh enough. By 1977, the percentage describing court treatment of criminals as too harsh or about right had fallen to a minimal 11 percent, and those who said the courts were not harsh enough had risen to 83 percent.

For one brief period, 1965–66, a plurality of Americans opposed the death penalty for those convicted of murder (47 percent opposed, 42 percent in favor, 11 percent no opinion in May 1966). Since then, support for the death penalty has steadily grown. By late 1972, the year of the Supreme Court decisions barring capital punishment, 60 percent of those surveyed favored the death penalty, and only 30 percent opposed it; by the end of the 1970s, the ratio stood at 67 percent in favor, 27 percent opposed; and by 1988, 79 percent were in favor, 16 percent opposed.

Increasingly conservative public opinion on the death penalty was a reflection of a much broader and growing base of support for tough sentencing. By 1987, mandatory sentencing laws were adopted in forty-six states, and presumptive sentencing requirements restricting judicial discretion in twelve states. Even more striking evidence of transformed sentencing policy is found in the sharp increase in the nation's prison population, which started to rise sharply in 1974. For the previous fifteen years, the number of people in prisons had held steady at roughly 200,000. From 1974 to 1979, judges began imposing longer sentences, parole releases dropped sharply, crime rates themselves rose, and the prison population shot up to 300,000; it reached 400,000 by 1982 and 755,425 by 1990.

The criminal rights and the prisoner rights movements strengthened the linkage between the rights revolution and one of the most emotionally charged areas of American life: crime. The crime rate, which had surged in the 1960s, continued to grow in the 1970s. [Table 3], compiled from Federal Bureau of Investigation data, traces the pattern.

The sharp rise in reported violent crime had major consequences for both politics and race relations across the country. There are a number of ways to measure differences between crime rates for blacks and whites—the three most common being 1) an annual victimization survey conducted by the Department of Justice from 1973 to the pre-

TABLE 3
The Increase in All Reported Crime and Violent Crime (Murder,
Robbery, Assault, and Rape) from 1960 to 1980
(The figures are in 1,000s so that, for example, in 1960, 3.38 million crimes,
and 288,000 violent crimes, were reported to police, and in 1980, 13.4 million
crimes and 1.3 million violent crimes were reported.)

	1960	1965	1970	1975	1980	% Increase
All Crime	3,384	4,739	8,098	11,292	13,408	296%
Violent Crime	288	387	738	1,040	1,345	367%

SOURCE: Table supplied by the FBI, *Index of Crime, United States, 1960–1988;* and
Crime Index Rate, United States, 1960–1988.

sent; 2) FBI arrest rate statistics from 1965 onward; and, 3) the makeup
of the prison population. All three show a much higher crime rate
among blacks than whites, with the ratio significantly higher for violent crime (murder, robbery, assault, and rape) than for property crimes
(larceny, motor vehicle theft, burglary). From 1960 to 1986, the prison
population shifted from 38 percent to 43.5 percent black. In terms of
the victimization surveys, which suggest lower rates of crime for
blacks than does the FBI compilation of arrest rates, and are thus less
subject to charges of racial bias, the 1974 survey found that while
blacks made up 11 percent of the total U.S. population, victims of ag-
gravated assault said 30 percent of their assailants were black, victims
of robbery said 62 percent of their attackers were black, and victims of
rape said 39 percent of the offenders were black.

The gap between the races has consistently been widest of all for
robbery (muggings, stick-ups, purse-snatches), one of the most threatening and most common of the violent crimes. It is threatening because it is the crime committed most often by strangers; it involves
the use of force or the impending use of force; and it is the crime that
occurs most often where the victim feels most vulnerable, outside of
the home, on the streets and sidewalks. Robbery is the one crime in
which the victim survey and the arrest rates show almost identical ra-
tios between black and white offenders, suggesting that the arrest rates
are a relatively accurate reflection of the rate of commission of robbery. The annual criminal victimization surveys conducted by the Department of Justice consistently show that more robberies are
committed by blacks than whites.

The robbery figures throughout the 1960s, 1970s, and 1980s reflect
at the extreme the challenge posed to Democratic liberalism by rising
rates of social disorder in the wake of civil rights legislation and following upon substantial growth of federal expenditures in behalf of the
poor. This is a dilemma that the Democratic party and liberals have

been reluctant to address, a reluctance motivated by compassion, by fear of provoking backlash, and by the desire to preserve a basis for more effective policy interventions. This reluctance, no matter how understandable, has nonetheless eroded the political credibility of liberalism and of the Democratic party.

For many members of the black leadership class, and for much of the white liberal community, examination of divisive racially freighted issues has been seen as having the potential to produce damaging results. These include the encouragement of a racist and "victim blaming" analysis of black poverty; a disproportionate focusing on black dysfunction, down-playing white criminality and white drug abuse; and failure to recognize the emergence of white underclasses in other highly industrialized and competitive societies, including a largely white underclass in England. A focus on so-called social pathology or on a "culture of poverty" among the most disadvantaged, some liberals argue, can be used to shift the burden of responsibility for institutionalized discrimination from the perpetrators to those who suffer social and economic ostracism at society's hands; to shift to blacks blame for an aberrant culture, rather than holding accountable their historic victimizers. A focus on "social deviance" or on an underclass subculture leaves unaddressed, according to this perspective, the oppressive economic and social structures which make inevitable the set of behavioral responses then labeled pathological. Finally, a number of liberals feel that the public naming of patterns of social disorder, including the use of the word "underclass," draws undue attention to such patterns, attention which can be manipulated by conservative ideological antagonists for political gain. The successful election in 1989 of Republican State Representative David Duke in Louisiana, the president of the National Association for the Advancement of White People, whose campaign stressed with striking success black crime, illegitimacy, and welfare dependency, and Duke's 44 percent vote in the 1990 Louisiana senatorial primary, can be seen as a confirmation of these fears.

Conversely, pointed liberal avoidance of these issues has its own liabilities. First of all, these issues are inescapably in the political arena: voters are seeking a resolution to the violence and social disorder expressed in crime, drug use, and illegitimacy. Secondly, the failure of the left to address such issues has permitted the political right to profit from explicit and covert manipulation of symbols and images relying upon assumptions about black poverty and crime—as in the Republicans' 1988 campaign focus on the death penalty, Willie Horton, and the "revolving prison door" television commercials.

The liberal failure to convincingly address increasingly conservative attitudes in the majority electorate, attitudes spurred in part by crime and welfare rates, has damaged the national Democratic party on a variety of counts. Perhaps most important, it has signaled a failure to live up to one of the chief obligations of a political party: to secure the safety and well-being of its own constituents, black and white. Secondly, self-imposed Democratic myopia has in no way prevented the majority public from forming "hard" opinions on crime, drug use, chronic joblessness, and out-of-wedlock births—nor from judging the national Democratic party as excessively "soft" in its approach to contemporary social issues—nor from voting for politicians whose conservative attitudes on crime and social disorder more completely mirror its own.

JOHN D'EMILIO AND
ESTELLE B. FREEDMAN

ESTELLE FREEDMAN (1947–   ) is professor of history at Stanford University. Her books include Their Sisters' Keepers: Women's Prison Reform in America: 1830–1930 *(1981) and* Maternal Justice: Miriam van Waters and the Female Reform Tradition *(1996).*

JOHN D'EMILIO (1948–   ) is professor of history and women and gender studies at the University of Illinois at Chicago. He has written Making Trouble: Essays on Gay History, Politics, and the University *(1992) and* Sexual Politics, Sexual Communities: The Making of a Homosexual Minority in the U.S., 1940–1970 *(1983).*

For political commentators accustomed to following the byways of post–World War II presidential politics, the 1984 campaign offered an interesting spectacle. Certainly many time-tested issues made their appearance in the course of the year—the strength of the military establishment; the struggle against Communism; taxes and the economy; the continuing fight for racial equality. But there were new dimensions, too. The day before the Democratic convention opened in San Francisco, tens of thousands of homosexuals and lesbians marched

Pages 344–360 from *Intimate Matters: A History of Sexuality in America* by John D'Emilio and Estelle Freedman. Copyright © 1988 by John D'Emilio and Estelle Freedman. Reprinted by permission of HarperCollins Publishers, Inc.

through the city to the convention site, with several dozen openly gay delegates to the convention leading the way. When the party adopted its platform later in the week, it condemned the "violent acts of bigotry, hatred, and extremism" aimed at gay men and lesbians, a phenomenon the platform labeled "alarmingly common." Another plank put the party on record as recognizing "reproductive freedom as a fundamental human right." It opposed "government interference in the reproductive decisions of Americans" and declared that "a woman has a right to choose whether and when to have a child." Though the platform avoided any mention of abortion, Geraldine Ferraro, the Democratic nominee for vice president, spent much of the campaign verbally dueling with the Roman Catholic hierarchy which condemned her defense of women's right to have abortion as an option.

Meanwhile, Ronald Reagan, who was running for reelection, returned to issues of sexuality again and again. During the spring primary season, he told the National Association of Evangelicals that America was losing "her religious and moral bearings." Pornography, once hidden, was now available "in virtually every drugstore in the land." Liberals, he charged, "viewed promiscuity as acceptable, even stylish. Indeed, the word itself was replaced by the term 'sexually active.'" In the liberal-dominated media, sex was everywhere. What was once "a sacred expression of love" had now become "casual and cheap." Reagan and the Republicans returned to these themes again and again. In August, he assured the publisher of the *Presidential Biblical Scorecard* that he would "resist the efforts of some to obtain government endorsement of homosexuality," and identified the sex act as "the means by which husband and wife participate with God in the creation of a new human life." As if to affirm these views, and in order to position itself against the Democratic call for reproductive freedom, the Republican party adopted a platform plank opposing abortion and endorsing legislation to make clear that "the 14th Amendment's protections apply to unborn children."

For any who doubted, the 1984 presidential season made clear that whatever consensus existed in the mid-twentieth century about sexuality had dissolved by the 1980s. The debates about sex, rather than remaining the province of feminists and gay liberationists, were polarizing the nation's politics. . . .

Sexual Politics and the New Right

The rapid pace of change and the dissolution of the liberal consensus about sexuality encouraged a political response from the right. As the 1970s ended, the latest in a long line of purity movements took shape. Reacting to the gains of both feminism and gay liberation, and distressed by the visibility of the erotic in American culture, sexual conservatives sought the restoration of "traditional" values. In its rhetoric, this contemporary breed of purity advocates echoed its predecessors by attributing to sex the power to corrupt, even to weaken fatally, American society. But in other important ways, its efforts departed from the past. It plunged directly into politics, as religious fundamentalists joined forces with political conservatives to make the Republican party the vehicle for a powerful moral crusade. Availing themselves of modern technology, these New Right proponents used computerized mailing lists, direct-mail fundraising, and telephone banks to reach deeply into the population and mobilize a constituency. By the early 1980s, journalists and political analysts were giving them credit for the turn to conservatism in American life.

Although feminism and gay liberation seemed to spark the resurgence of the purity impulse, the conservative sexual politics of the 1950s had never fully died. Placed on the defensive by the decisions of the liberal Warren Court, groups such as Citizens for Decent Literature struggled on. In the 1960s, much of the battle focused on the issue of sex education in the public schools. Distressed by the court-decreed elimination of school prayer, some conservatives banded together in an effort to draw the line at sex instruction. Toward the end of the decade, the John Birch Society began targeting Mary Calderone, the renowned sex educator. In Racine, Wisconsin; Anaheim, California; Minneapolis, and other places, parents fought to keep discussions of sex out of the classroom. Ronald Reagan, then governor of California, pushed legislation prohibiting required attendance in sex education classes. . . .

Since the early 1970s, an important item on the gay movement's agenda had been the extension of civil rights statutes to include provisions prohibiting discrimination on the basis of sexual orientation. Activists devoted much of their energy to securing passage of municipal and county ordinances as a foundation for later efforts at the state and national level. By 1977, they had achieved upward of three dozen victories, of which the law in populous Dade County was one. But, for the first time, they encountered an outspoken opposition, ready to fight back, in Florida. Anita Bryant, who led the campaign to repeal the law, was a foe to reckon with. A former Miss Oklahoma and a popular singer in middle America, she remained in the public eye through her commercials for Minute Maid orange juice, where she projected an attractive, motherly wholesomeness. Bryant was outraged that local legislators had seemed to endorse the lifestyle of homosexuals, whom she described as "human garbage." With the aid of her business-manager husband, she formed Save Our Children, Inc., and succeeded in placing a repeal initiative on the ballot. . . .

In a foreshadowing of the direction the purity movement would take, Protestant fundamentalist ministers assumed a highly visible role. A local evangelist told reporters that "homosexuality is a sin so rotten, so low, so dirty that even cats and dogs don't practice it." Jerry Falwell, a Baptist preacher from Lynchburg, Virginia, and soon to become a national figure, flew in to help the repeal forces. "So-called gay folks," he intoned, would "just as soon kill you as look at you." Backed by the Catholic hierarchy, conservative rabbis, and Miami's daily newspapers, the Bryant campaign won a resounding victory as voters rejected the ordinance by a two-to-one majority.

The media publicity that the Dade County battle received guaranteed that its influence would extend beyond its locale. Over the next year, conservatives mounted similar campaigns in St. Paul, Wichita, and Eugene, Oregon; in each case, citizens defeated gay rights in overwhelming proportions. In California, lesbians and gay men faced an even more serious threat. There, inspired by Bryant's success, an ultraconservative state senator from the Los Angeles suburbs, John Briggs, succeeded in placing an anti-gay measure on the state ballot. The Briggs initiative authorized school systems to fire gay employees, as well as anyone who publicly or privately advocated or encouraged homosexual conduct. Throughout 1978, the gay communities in San Francisco, Los Angeles, and other cities put together a well-organized grass-roots campaign against the measure. Winning the support of labor unions protective of their members' jobs, large-circulation newspapers in the state, and even conservative politicians like Ronald Reagan, who objected to the constraints on free speech, gay activists succeeded in defeating the initiative. . . .

Meanwhile, a movement to curtail the right of women to choose abortion was developing. For Americans who objected to abortion, the Supreme Court's *Roe* decision in 1973 had appeared as a "bolt from the blue," catching them off-guard and unprepared. Though local anti-abortion groups formed almost immediately, the Court's ruling seemed clear and incontrovertible, leaving little room for action. Then, in 1976, Representative Henry Hyde of Illinois succeeded in attaching a rider to an appropriations bill, prohibiting the use of federal dollars to fund abortions. The next year, the Supreme Court ruled that government had the authority to bar the financing of abortion with tax dollars. Congress responded with alacrity, and by 1978, the number of federally funded abortions had fallen from 295,000 to 3,000. States, too, cut back on their coverage; by the summer of 1979, only nine states still paid for abortions. Though the constitutional right to abortion remained intact, anti-abortion forces had succeeded in sharply restricting the access that poor women had to it.

The victory over funding also spurred the movement forward. Local groups became part of national organizations such as March for Life and the National Right-to-Life Committee. They registered voters and made abortion the litmus test of political acceptability, campaigning against candidates based on the single issue of abortion. As Nellie

Grey, of March for Life, explained, "on a fundamental issue, you can't strike a bargain. You are either for killing babies or you're not. You can't be for a little bit of killing babies." . . . By the end of the 1970s, clinics performing abortions were being torched and bombed across the country.

The involvement of purity advocates in politics, whether to defeat gay rights, restrict abortion, or curtail the spread of pornography, held an irresistible allure for traditional conservatives. During the 1970s, a new set of right-wing organizations came into existence, determined to turn back the liberal social-welfare policies of the 1960s and to reverse the retrenchment of America's role in the world. Groups such as the Conservative Caucus, headed by Howard Phillips, the Committee for the Survival of a Free Congress, led by Paul Weyrich, and the National Conservative Political Action Committee, chaired by Terry Dolan, saw the discontent spawned by sexual issues as a force that could propel their politics into power. In commenting on the potential of the alliance, Richard Viguerie, the editor of the *Conservative Digest* and a pioneer in direct-mail fundraising techniques, noted that "if abortion remains an issue, and we keep picking liberals off, this movement could completely change the face of Congress." Paul Weyrich, too, saw issues of sexuality and family life as "the Achilles' heel of the liberal Democrats." In 1979, Phillips and Weyrich helped persuade Jerry Falwell, whose television program *The Old Time Gospel Hour* reached 18 million viewers weekly, to form the Moral Majority as a vehicle to mobilize the fundamentalist population. They also established the Religious Roundtable to bring together conservative politicians and influential television preachers such as Falwell, Pat Robertson, Jim Bakker, James Robison, and others.

This religion-based New Right exploded into the nation's consciousness during the 1980 presidential campaign. While Jimmy Carter, a self-avowed born-again Christian, remained aloof from it, Ronald Reagan actively courted the fundamentalist vote, and appeared openly sympathetic to the New Right's position on abortion, school prayer, and pornography. His fervid Cold War rhetoric also appealed to preachers who feared a "godless" Communism. Reagan addressed a national convention of religious broadcasters. In return, evangelists appealed to their congregations and their television viewers to vote for righteousness. Falwell, whose Moral Majority had already enrolled seventy-two thousand ministers and four million lay members, castigated the "minority of secular humanists and amoralists [who] are running this country and taking it straight to hell." . . . After Reagan won by a landslide and Republicans captured control of the Senate, many political commentators were quick to attribute an almost invincible power to the moralistic politics of the New Right.

When the new Congress reconvened in 1981, the assessment of the media and the worst fears of feminists and gay liberationists seemed ready to be confirmed. Despite their rhetorical opposition to big government, conservatives were prepared to sanction state intervention in issues of sexual morality and family life. In short order, Senator Jesse Helms of North Carolina and Representative Hyde introduced a bill that defined life as beginning at conception, and hence made abortion equivalent to murder. Another anti-abortion politician, Representative Robert Dornan of California, presented to the House a constitutional amendment that identified life as beginning when the sperm fertilizes the ovum, thus including the birth control pill and the IUD as potential abortifacients. Republican conservatives also resurrected the Family Protection Act, which had died an unceremonious death during the Carter presidency. Its thirty-six provisions included one that prohibited federal funds for schools whose curriculum "would tend to denigrate, diminish or deny the role differences between the sexes as they have been historically understood in the United States," and another that denied government benefits, including social security, to anyone who presented homosexuality "as an acceptable alternative life style or suggests that it can be an acceptable life style." Meanwhile, religious leaders kept up the impassioned rhetoric. Falwell aroused his supporters by declaring, "we are fighting a holy war and this time we are going to win." His frequent appeals for funds—by 1981 he was raising over a million dollars a week—enticed contributions with questions such as, "Do you approve of known practicing homosexuals teaching in public schools?" . . .

Despite their apparent power, the purity crusaders of the 1980s made only limited gains at the national level. Although abortion debates proved rancorous, consuming much of the time of Congress, no further restrictions were passed into law. Issues such as abortion or school prayer were too unpredictable, and too threatening to Republican unity, for the Reagan administration to pay much more than lip service to them. Instead, Reagan devoted his energy to expanding the nation's military establishment and dismantling liberal social-welfare programs. Some sops were thrown to the New Right. In 1985, Attorney General Edwin Meese established a commission on pornography that toured the country intent on exposing the social harm allegedly caused by explicit sexual materials. . . . Of greater significance, Reagan also tended to appoint to the federal judiciary men and women sympathetic to the New Right. The five-to-four 1986 Supreme Court decision in *Bowers v. Hardwick* that sustained the constitutionality of sodomy laws directed against homosexuals was, perhaps, a harbinger of things to come.

On a local level, meanwhile, purity crusaders more easily flexed their political muscles. School districts throughout the nation faced increasing surveillance from parents angry over sex education classes or the novels that students were asked to read. In Chicago in 1986, the actions of the Roman Catholic hierarchy succeeded in defeating a gay rights ordinance, the passage of which had seemed certain until church leaders spoke up. An Atlanta campaign against adult theaters and bookstores reduced the numbers of such establishments from forty-four in the late seventies to a mere handful by 1981. North Carolina legislators enacted a new, tougher pornography law that allowed police to seize materials and make arrests without a prior order from the courts. . . .

The effort to contain pornography reveals how complex the alignments over sexual issues had become. A major focus of feminist energy in the 1970s had been efforts to combat sexual violence—rape, harassment, wife battering, and incest. Whether these phenomena had increased in scope, or feminist campaigns had simply brought them to light, is impossible to determine. But, the eruption of pornographic imagery into the public sphere seemed like the last straw for activists who daily encountered the victims of violence. . . . Organizations such as Women Against Pornography put together slide shows aimed at exposing the brutalizing fantasies that some hard-core materials purveyed, and their members conducted tours of the porn districts that had sprung up in the early 1970s. Anti-porn feminists subscribed to the dictum "pornography is the theory, rape is the practice." . . . By the early 1980s Andrea Dworkin and feminist lawyer Catharine MacKinnon were drafting their own model obscenity statutes, which defined pornography as a violation of women's civil rights, and they found themselves in political alliance with the New Right in Indianapolis and Suffolk County, New York, and other places where the anti-pornography impulse was strong. Some anti-porn feminists were also witnesses before the Meese commission, urging it to take a tough stand against sexually explicit materials.

Other feminists, meanwhile, bristled at the potential for censorship contained in the anti-porn movement and at the dangers that this unexpected alliance posed to women's exploration of the erotic. Ellen Willis, who had helped launch women's liberation in New York City, acknowledged that pornography could be a "psychic assault," but that "for women as for men it can also be a source of erotic pleasure." For a woman to enjoy pornography, she wrote, "is less to collaborate in her oppression than to defy it, to insist on an aspect of her sexuality that has been defined as a male preserve. . . . [I]n rejecting sexual repression and hypocrisy—which have inflicted even more damage on women than on men—[pornography] expresses a radical impulse." Willis attacked the "goody-goody" concept of sexuality that anti-porn activists espoused as "not feminist but feminine." It preserved, she argued, the old "good girl—bad girl" dichotomy that denied most women access to erotic pleasure and adventure. . . .

Despite the strange alliance over pornography, most ideologues of the Christian-based purity crusade identified feminism and gay liberation as the evils they were organizing against. Yet the reasons for the New Right's rapid growth was both more and less than the existence of radical movements for sexual liberation. . . . Especially for some women—those for whom mothering was a central task, who did not work for wages, and who remained religiously devout—the values of the post-liberal era seemed to attack the very source of their self-worth. At times, New Right leaders acknowledged that they were attacking not merely a clearly delineated opposition such as gay liberation, but something more amorphous and widespread. Falwell, for instance, in lambasting pornography, called network television "the greatest vehicle being used to indoctrinate us slowly to accept a pornographic view of life. Pornography is more than a nudey magazine," he said. "It is a prevailing atmosphere of sexual license." In an era when much of mainstream culture was promoting the erotic, little wonder that moral conservatives responded with fury.

At the same time, the New Right also had its own well-defined symbolic concern that brought its diffuse anxieties together. Whatever the issue—abortion or the Equal Rights Amendment, gay liberation or pornography, sex education or the lyrics of rock music—the sexuality of youth served as the unifying element in its campaigns. . . . Its attacks on pornography, for instance, first took shape around the issue of "kiddie-porn," which easily became the object of new legislation. In mobilizing their forces, Anita Bryant and other gay rights antagonists repeatedly raised the phantom of child recruitment. Faced with an epidemic of pregnant teenagers, parents targeted the schools, not because of a failure to provide the instruction that might allow the young to have sex safely, but because the schools were allegedly giving adolescents too much information. Even issues such as abortion and the ERA, so central to the feminist agenda for women's equality, resonated with concerns about the young. A right-to-life activist in California, for example, saw abortion as one part of a larger problem of youthful sexual expression:

> I don't think we would have as many sexually active teenagers, first of all, if contraception weren't readily available and acceptable. . . . There's more of a temptation to participate in sex than we had when we were young . . . because you just knew that if you were sexually active you might well get pregnant.

A leader of the anti-ERA forces in New York State also turned to the young in explaining her involvement in politics. "For one thing, it would allow gays to marry and adopt children," she said. "If anything ever happened to me, I don't want to think that gays could adopt my children."

Fears about the sexual behavior of youth give the contemporary purity crusade the historical specificity one would expect to find in a social movement. For of all the changes in sexual mores that occurred in the 1960s and 1970s, the spread of sexual activity among the young marked the sharpest break with the past. . . . Youth engaged not just in occasional experimentation, nor did they have sex only in the context of a marriage-oriented relationship. The erotic became incorporated as a regular, ongoing feature of their maturation. The visibility of sex in American culture gave them a familiarity with sex and an interest in it regardless of their parents' wishes. The lyrics of the songs they listened to and danced to—"Let's spend the night together" or "I want a man with a slow hand," to name just two—incited desire as well as suggested possibilities. That many of them would not marry until well into their twenties, and that cohabitation was an acceptable option, made the marriage-oriented ethic of sexual liberalism increasingly irrelevant to their lives. It was the ability and willingness of youth to explore the erotic that most signaled the passing of sexual liberalism. It also imparted emotional power to a purity crusade that attacked all the manifestations of the post-liberal era and that sought the restoration of a marriage-based sexual system replete with gendered and reproductive meanings.

The AIDS Crisis

While the New Right vigorously pursued political solutions to the new sexual permissiveness, an argument for retrenchment came from another, unexpected quarter. In 1980 and 1981, a few doctors in Los Angeles, San Francisco, and New York began encountering puzzling medical phenomena. Young homosexual men in the prime of life were dying suddenly from a rare pneumonia, pneumocystis carinii, or wasting away from an unusual cancer, Kaposi's sarcoma, that normally attacked older men of Mediterranean ancestry who recovered from the disease. By the summer of 1981 it became clear to these doctors, as well as to the Centers for Disease Control in Atlanta, that a devastating new disease syndrome had entered the annals of medicine. Acquired Immune Deficiency Syndrome (AIDS), as it was labeled, destroyed the body's natural defenses against infection, making the victim susceptible to a host of opportunistic infections which the body seemed incapable of resisting. Unlike other recent new illnesses, such as Legionnaire's Disease or Toxic Shock Syndrome, from which most patients recovered, AIDS had no cure. The immune system did not return to normal, and the mortality rate was frighteningly high. Moreover, the case load grew at an alarming pace: 225 at the end of 1981, 1,400 by the spring of 1983, 15,000 in the summer of 1985, and 40,000 two years later.

AIDS revealed how tenuous the progress of gay liberation had been. Because the initial victims in the United States were gay men, and because a majority of the total cases remained within the male homosexual population, AIDS gave those who were hostile, or even ambivalent, toward homosexuality the opportunity to vent their spleen. The New Right quickly recognized AIDS as a vehicle to whip up hysteria and move its political agenda forward. . . . The military imposed mandatory testing for the presence of antibodies to the virus believed to induce AIDS, while Congress enacted legislation requiring the test for all immigrants. Both measures involved areas where gay activists had sought relief from discriminatory policies, and thus they transformed the disease into a new weapon to preserve inequality. . . .

As the medical establishment searched for explanations, some of the mystery dissolved. In France in 1983, and in the United States soon thereafter, researchers isolated a virus that was apparently the culprit. AIDS was infectious rather than contagious. The virus could not be transmitted casually, but seemed to require the exchange of bodily fluids—blood or semen—between one person and another. Rather than a "homosexual disease," it was apparently a quirk that in the United States AIDS first manifested itself among gay men. But once present in that population, it could be passed from partner to partner through anal or oral sex, with the dense web of sexual relationships in the gay male subculture allowing for its rapid spread. Moreover it soon became clear that gay men were not the only high-risk group. Intravenous drug users, whose sharing of needles allowed blood to pass from one to another, accounted for a significant minority of AIDS cases. The virus could also be transmitted through sexual contact from men to women, and from pregnant mothers infected with the virus to their newborn infants. Indeed, by 1986, much media coverage focused on the alleged dangers of the disease spreading quickly through the heterosexual population.

For the gay male community, AIDS provoked fear, anguish, and soul-searching, as well as an upsurge of organization and political involvement. . . . Gay men woke in the morning to check their bodies for the appearance of lesions that signaled Kaposi's sarcoma. The common cold or flu triggered worries about the onset of pneumonia. For some, the fact of AIDS called into question the viability of a nonmonogamous gay male life. As one person with AIDS ruefully commented, "the belief that was handed to me was that sex was liberating and more sex was more liberating." AIDS seemed to be a cruel outcome of the freedom that gay liberation promised. It also shook the pride and confidence that the 1970s had gradually built. "The psychological impact of AIDS on the gay community is tremendous," said Richard Failla, an openly gay judge in New York City. "It has done more to undermine the feelings of self-esteem that anything Anita Bryant could have ever done. Some people are saying 'Maybe we *are* wrong—maybe this is a punishment.'" . . .

On the other hand, the gay community also responded to the AIDS crisis with an enormous outpouring of energy and determination. In New York City, the Gay Men's Health Crisis formed in 1981, at the very start of the epidemic. It drew in thousands of volunteers to help care for the sick and dying, raised millions of dollars for education and research, and lobbied for state and federal research money to unravel the mystery of the disease and find a cure. In city after city where cases appeared, the gay community mounted similar efforts. . . . AIDS organizations widely publicized "safe-sex" guidelines to cut the risk of transmission. In New York and San Francisco, where AIDS hit first and ravaged the community most severely, the impact of the campaigns in reshaping gay male sexuality could be seen in the large decline in the incidence of other sexually transmitted diseases such as syphilis and gonorrhea. Men used condoms for anal sex, reduced sharply the number of sexual partners they had, and learned to enjoy practices such as mutual masturbation. Business at gay bathhouses that did remain open fell dramatically. Observers within the community pointed to a new emphasis on dating, romance, and monogamous relationships. One study of urban gay males found that between 1984 and 1987 the proportion who were celibate rose from two to twelve percent, while those in a monogamous partnership jumped from twelve to twenty-eight percent. The group in the population that had most symbolized the new sexual contours of the post-liberal era was cutting another path.

By the mid-1980s it was also evident that the fear of AIDS was beginning to reach into the heterosexual population. For a generation raised with penicillin and antibiotics, the long historical association of sexual promiscuity with disease had faded as an inhibitor of behavior. Then, at the start of the 1980s, the media gave play to the prevalence of genital herpes. AIDS added a lethal dimension to the disease problem. Especially as it became clear that AIDS could be transmitted through heterosexual intercourse, and after the death of Rock Hudson made AIDS a household word, many heterosexuals took stock of their own sexual habits. On college campuses, health administrators made AIDS a prime focus of their educational efforts. The director of the health service at the University of Southern California thought that students seemed "less willing to have casual encounters than they were four or five years ago." Many universities reported a sharp decline in the cases of venereal disease on campus. Trust and intimacy loomed larger as factors in a sexual relationship, particularly perhaps for women. As one female graduate student phrased her concerns, "it is no longer a question of just you yourself. It's now a question of the commitment of the person with whom you're involved. If he switch-hits, or if he ever has in the last three or four years, it could be a real problem." . . .

The Reagan administration, led by Secretary of Education William Bennett, latched onto the crisis as an opportunity to promulgate a new chastity message among the nation's youth. One federally financed pamphlet, *Sex Respect,* encouraged teenagers to "just say no." But Reagan's Surgeon General, Everett Koop, who a few years earlier had been a prominent anti-abortion activist, dissented vigorously and urged comprehensive sex education in the schools, including the information that condoms were effective in forestalling the spread of the virus. Organizations working on the issue of teenage pregnancy found that AIDS was opening doors previously closed to them. Marian Wright Edelman, founder and president of the Children's Defense Fund, reported that the new sense of urgency created by the epidemic was accomplishing "what one million teenage pregnancies couldn't do: get us talking about sex. . . . People who were tongue-tied realize that they must address something that is lethal." On some campuses students campaigned to have condom vending machines installed in dormitories. Remaining taboos in the media fell. Some network affiliates began accepting ads for condoms, prime-time series addressed the issues of birth control and "safe sex," and news anchors found themselves speaking of anal intercourse before millions of viewers.

Although the political activity of the New Right and the threat of AIDS seemed to augur a retrenchment in the behavior of many Americans, as the 1980s drew to a close it was not at all clear what the future would bring. Certainly the outcome of current controversies about sex would have to build upon the complicated set of sexual meanings that had evolved over generations. For instance, in seeking a restoration of sexuality to marriage, replete with reproductive consequences, advocates of the new chastity had to contend with the permeation of the erotic throughout American culture, the expansive and varied roles available to American women, and a contraceptive technology that sustained the nonprocreative meanings of sexual behavior. A new sexual system that harkened back to a vanished world could not simply be wished into existence. . . .

For almost two centuries sexuality had been moving into the marketplace. . . . Not only did modern capitalism sell sexual fantasies and pleasures as commodities, but the dynamics of a consumer-oriented economy had also packaged many products in sexual wrappings. The commercialization of sex and the sexualization of commerce placed the weight of capitalist institutions on the side of a visible public presence for the erotic. Political movements based on sexual issues alone, whether of the right or the left, faced huge obstacles in their efforts to alter this trend, unless they tackled other issues as well. Sex was too deeply embedded in the fabric of economic life for a purity movement to reshape its meaning in fundamental ways. Exploitable as it was for profit, sex had become resistant to efforts at containment that failed to address this larger economic matrix. And, for movements such as feminism and gay liberation that attacked the manipulation of sexuality to sustain social inequality, systems of gender relations as well as economic structures required revision if activists were to achieve their goals.

The contemporary debates over sex also highlight the continuing efforts of Americans to define a place for sex in their lives. . . . Spiritual union, emotional satisfaction, individual identity: these and other definitions have competed for hegemony. For much of the nineteenth and twentieth centuries, the values of the white, native-born urban middle class placed a premium on sexual expression within the context of marriage, even as working-class youth, blacks, an emergent gay community, and others pursued alternative sexual ethics. As the dominant middle-class culture has come to attach more value to sexual fulfillment and pleasure, preserving marriage as a privileged site for sexual expression has proven more difficult. Then, too, the easy availability of effective methods of birth control has removed much of the danger that once attached to nonmarital heterosexuality. And, as women have moved out of the home and into the labor market, their interest in keeping sex within a marital context has declined. . . .

Though not free of agencies of regulation, the individual has more autonomy than ever before to make choices about "personal life." And the range of choices is wider than in the past. A permanent monogamous partnership is one, but so is serial monogamy, homosexual identity, singles life, cohabitation, and unmarried motherhood. Were the choices not so varied, the possibility of AIDS spreading through the population would be too remote to evoke such deep concern.

Contemporary events also illustrate the continuing power of sex as a symbol capable of arousing deep, irrational fears. In the nineteenth and early twentieth centuries, female purity most often served as the symbol that mobilized social anxieties, as campaigns against prostitution and the hysteria over white slavery demonstrated. In the South it combined with fears about racial amalgamation to maintain a rigid caste system of race relations. Today, female purity has lost much of its symbolic force. But the response to AIDS certainly proves the ease with which sexual issues can unleash the irrational. . . .

Finally, the AIDS epidemic and the politics it spawned emphasize the persistence of sexuality as a vehicle for social control. The mythology about blacks propagated by slave owners, the nineteenth-century medical campaigns against abortion, the nativist implications of the white slavery scare, the wave of lynchings in the South, the Cold War preoccupation with homosexuality: these and other episodes demonstrate how commonly sexuality has fostered the maintenance of social hierarchies. The response to AIDS continued this long historical tradition. Gay activists attacked the slow response of the Reagan administration as a sign of how little value it placed on gay lives. The reluctance of government agencies to fund safe-sex campaigns and to provide intravenous drug users with sterilized needles as parts of a comprehensive prevention program allowed the disease to keep spreading not only through the gay male community but also among inner-city black and Hispanic populations where drug use is a serious problem. As in the past, state legislatures targeted prostitutes rather than male customers even though female-to-male transmission of AIDS is much less likely than the reverse. The unwillingness of conservative moralists to make birth control and safe-sex information available to sexually active youth not only perpetuated teenage pregnancy but now threatened the lives of some of the young. Power over sex is the power to affect the life and death of Americans. . . .

Women's role in the family and the public realm has altered so profoundly that a gender-based system resting on female purity is not likely to be resurrected. The capitalist seizure of sexuality has destroyed the division between public reticence and private actions that the nineteenth-century middle class sought to maintain. Perhaps what the study of America's history allows us to say with assurance is that sexuality has become central to our economy, our psyches, and our politics. For this reason, it is likely to stay vulnerable to manipulation as a symbol of social problems and the subject of efforts to maintain social hierarchies. As in the past, sex will remain a source of both deep personal meaning and heated political controversy.

INDEX